The Dynamics of Lexical Interfaces

Studies in Constraint-Based Lexicalism

A series edited by
Miriam Butt, *University of Konstanz*
Tracy Holloway King, *Palo Alto Research Center*
Jean-Pierre Koenig, *State University of New York at Buffalo*

The aim of this series is to make work in various nonderivational, lexicalist approaches to grammar available to a wide audience of linguists. In approaches of this kind, grammar is seen as the interaction of constraints from multiple dimensions of linguistic substance, including information about syntactic category, grammatical relations, and semantic and pragmatic interpretation.

Studies in
Constraint-Based Lexicalism

The Dynamics of Lexical Interfaces

edited by
Ruth Kempson
Eleni Gregoromichelaki
Christine Howes

CSLI PUBLICATIONS
Center for the Study of
Language and Information
Stanford, California

Center for the Study of Language and Information
Leland Stanford Junior University
Printed in the United States
15 14 13 12 11   1 2 3 4 5

Library of Congress Cataloging-in-Publication Data

The dynamics of lexical interfaces / edited by Ruth Kempson, Eleni Gregoromichelaki, Christine Howes.
p. cm. – (Studies in constraint-based lexicalism)
ISBN 978-1-57586-615-4 (cloth : alk. paper) –
ISBN 978-1-57586-614-7 (pbk. : alk. paper)
1. Grammar, Comparative and general–Syntax. 2. Linguistic analysis (Linguistics) I. Kempson, Ruth M. II. Gregoromichelaki, Eleni. III. Howes, Christine, 1978-

P291.D96 2011
415–dc22   2011001408
CIP

∞ The acid-free paper used in this book meets the minimum requirements of the American National Standard for Information Sciences—Permanence of Paper for Printed Library Materials, ANSI Z39.48-1984.

CSLI was founded in 1983 by researchers from Stanford University, SRI International, and Xerox PARC to further the research and development of integrated theories of language, information, and computation. CSLI headquarters and CSLI Publications are located on the campus of Stanford University.

CSLI Publications reports new developments in the study of language, information, and computation. Please visit our web site at
http://cslipublications.stanford.edu/
for comments on this and other titles, as well as for changes and corrections by the author and publisher.

Contents

Contributors

Miriam Bouzouita
Universitat de les Illes Balears, Palma, Spain

Ronnie Cann
University of Edinburgh, UK

Stergios Chatzikyriakidis
King's College London, UK

Eleni Gregoromichelaki
King's College London, UK

Christine Howes
Queen Mary University of London, UK

Ruth Kempson
King's College London, UK

Jieun Kiaer
University of Oxford, UK

Nancy C. Kula
University of Essex, Colchester, UK

Lutz Marten
SOAS, London, UK

Yo Sato
Hertfordshire University, Hatfield, UK

Nhlanhla Thwala
University of Witwatersrand, Johannesburg, South Africa

Yicheng Wu
University of Hong Kong, China

The Dynamics of Lexical Interfaces.
Ruth Kempson, Eleni Gregoromichelaki and Christine Howes (eds.).

Preface

The seed that grew into this volume was sown in 2006 at a workshop at the Linguistics Association of Great Britain (LAGB) exploring the possibilities of Dynamic Syntax as a grammar formalism; and the idea for a collection of linguistic and further cognitive/computational applications of the framework grew as a result of conference and workshop contributions during 2007 and 2008. The work reported in this volume extends the formalism through application to novel data and enables its evaluation through discussion of typological, experimental and implementation issues.

One of the pleasures of working in Dynamic Syntax is its cross-disciplinary grounding, which ensures that ideas get enriched by those working in other disciplines. In this connection, we wish to thank in particular Wilfried Meyer-Viol, Graham White, and Pat Healey for their help in articulating the formal underpinnings of the framework and developing methodologies for its experimental evaluation. For ongoing feedback and encouragement, we wish to thank also: Matthew Purver, Andrew Gargett, Gregory J. Mills, Arash Eshghi, Shalom Lappin, Paul Piwek, Holly Branigan, Robyn Carston, Robin Cooper, Hannes Rieser, Nigel Vincent, Mark Steedman, Caroline Heycock, Dan Wedgwood, Nic Gisborne and many others.

The work for this volume was supported by the Leverhulme Foundation (Dialogue Matters F07/054OU), the AHRC (B/RG.AN8675/ APN16312), and the ESRC (Dynamics of Conversational Dialogue (DynDial) RES-062-23-0962), to whom we extend our grateful thanks.

Ruth Kempson
Eleni Gregoromichelaki
Christine Howes

The Dynamics of Lexical Interfaces.
Ruth Kempson, Eleni Gregoromichelaki and Christine Howes (eds.).

1

Introduction: The Dynamics of Lexical Interfaces

RUTH KEMPSON, ELENI GREGOROMICHELAKI AND CHRISTINE HOWES

1.1 Redrawing competence/performance boundaries

Following Chomsky (1965), there has been broad agreement, until recently, that formal linguistic theories must be grounded in the description of (grammatical) sentence-strings without any reflection of the dynamics of language performance. Departures from this anti-functionalist methodology were rejected on the basis that language use is often disfluent and disorderly hence presumed to preclude rigorous systematization, a stance independently propounded by the anti-formalist approach of Ordinary Language philosophy (Austin 1975) followed up by many theoretical approaches to pragmatics. However, amenability to formalization and reflections of performance are far from incompatible (Newmeyer 1998), as seen in the huge growth in context-modelling and information update in formal semantics since the development of DRT and related frameworks. Such developments are now beginning to show that the sentence/proposition-based methodology of standard grammar formalisms is problematic. With no means of reflecting the temporal dynamics of incremental on-line processing and the remit of sentence-level explanation adhered to, all elements displaying context-dependency are definable only by bifurcating them into grammar-internal vs grammar-external processes. But context-dependent phenomena – anaphora, ellipsis, tense-construal, quantification, etc – all allow resolutions of how they are to be understood

The Dynamics of Lexical Interfaces.
Ruth Kempson, Eleni Gregoromichelaki and Christine Howes (eds.).

within AND across sentence boundaries in ways that exploit the gradual accumulation of information in context. Examination of the same phenomena in fundamental domains of language use like dialogue reveals that they are systematically present and explainable under the same assumptions, as well as traditional grammar constraints, provided the unit of explanation is not the sentence/proposition but rather subsentential mechanisms operating on a word-by-word basis (Purver et al. 2009, Gregoromichelaki et al. 2009). So any move to distinguish phenomena with respect to whether they occur sentence-internally or not leads to a mushrooming of unjustifiable ambiguities requiring lexical and syntactic stipulations. As a response to such considerations, grammatical models have recently begun to appear that reflect aspects of performance to varying degrees (Hawkins 2004; Phillips 1996; Lombardo and Sturt 2002; Ginzburg and Cooper 2004; Kempson et al. 2001; Cann et al. 2005).

One of these frameworks, Dynamic Syntax (DS), has the distinctive characteristic of taking a fundamental feature of real-time processing – the concept of underspecification and update – as the basis for grammar formulation. There is underspecification of content, underspecification of structure, and underspecification of structural relations, each of these leading to subsequent update. Under this view, natural language (NL) syntax is given as a constraint-based definition of the process of how representations of content can be built up step-by-step following the order in which words occur in a string. This simple shift of perspective has enabled the modelling of core syntactic phenomena as well as phenomena at the syntax-semantics-pragmatics interface in a unified and hence explanatory way. Amongst these are: anaphora (Kempson et al. 2001), ellipsis (Purver et al. 2006; Cann et al. 2007; Gregoromichelaki et al. 2009; Kempson et al. to appear, Gregoromichelaki et al., submitted), relative clauses (Cann et al. 2005; Cann et al. 2005b; Kempson and Kurosawa 2010), scrambling (Kiaer 2007; Cann et al. 2005; Kempson and Kiaer 2009), left and right periphery effects (Cann et al. 2005; Kempson et al. 2009b), clitic positioning and clustering from both synchronic and diachronic perspectives (Bouzouita 2008a,b; Chatzikyriakidis 2009, 2010). At the heart of this approach is the assumption that grammar constraints, both lexical and general, are all defined in terms of progressive growth of semantic representations, enabling a bidirectional feeding relation between lexical, structural, and semantic specifications. Cross-language variation can thus be explicable in terms of variation in the allocation of resources for updates. Lexically triggered updates provide the potential for stored idiosyncratic specifications; and these can diverge over time, in turn affecting the development of generally available options through their interaction during processing. This volume reports on work extending this program of research, and substantiating its contribution, by discussing a range of phenomena whose explanation remains a challenge for grammars which lack any reflection of the dynamics of on-line update.

1.2 Dynamic Syntax

1.2.1 A constraint-based, lexicalist approach to modelling syntax as the parsing process

The Dynamic Syntax (DS) methodology is explicitly representationalist. It presents two core claims. First, natural-language (NL) content can be represented as structured formulae in a logical language. Second, NL "syntax" is defined exclusively in terms of procedures determining time-linear growth of such semantic representations.

The abstract system underlying DS is based on the type of models defined for Propositional Dynamic Logic (PDL) enriched with a notion of constrained monotonic development through *requirements* that introduce an element of goal-directedness and top-down control. The model specifies a set of structured *parse states* defined in terms of satisfaction of constraints of two types: (a) statements holding at each particular licensed state and basically defining annotated ('decorated') partial binary trees (the *declarative* part); and (b) action definitions which hold at pairs of states and license the transition from one state to a new development (the *procedural* part) (see Kempson et al. 2001: 268-325 for details). These two aspects of the DS model, declarative and procedural, are expressed by means of a formal language, DU_F. Formulae of DU_F express both the general constraints on the well-formed partial objects that can develop to complete fully decorated trees and a set of licensed transitions from parse state to parse state provided by each individual NL. Each such transition must be licensed either by a word of the specified NL (*lexical actions*) or a limited number of general principles (*computational actions*) applicable in variable forms across languages. The parsing process monotonically maps partial incomplete objects to more and more complete ones with the eventual aim of reaching a defined point of termination, a fully decorated tree structure inhabited by a propositional formula.[1]

The data structures of DS are *binary* LINK*ed trees*. The nodes of

[1] For readability, we illustrate the DS apparatus in terms of its models, the licensed tree structures and transitions, rather than the DU_F descriptions. Decorations on the trees are also simplified, e.g., here we delete the *Fo* predicate, standing for 'formula', i.e., the content value on the node, so that See' is to be taken as a simplified notation of $Fo(See')$.

these trees are decorated with the terms of a logical language, namely, *epsilon calculus* expressions (see 1.2.5) built on the basis of the combinatory resources provided by the *lambda calculus*. Decorations consist of formulae of this logical language accompanied by *labels*, i.e. pieces of information facilitating the parsing of the string, e.g. type ($Ty(\ldots)$) information, or adding further content dimensions, e.g. a record of dependencies among variables ($Scope(\ldots)$). The starting point of the parsing task is taken to be the imposition of the goal of building some (e.g. propositional) representation. This is shown as the single root node of some tree accompanied with the requirement to build some formula of propositional type, $?Ty(t)$ (this initial step is called the Axiom). The outcome then of a sequence of licensed parsing steps will be a propositional formula (as the value of the label $Fo(\ldots)$, omitted from the display below for simplicity) with each sub-tree corresponding to a sub-term of that formula. The input and output trees for a parse of (1.1) are given schematically in (1.2).[2]

(1.1) Bob saw someone.

(1.2)

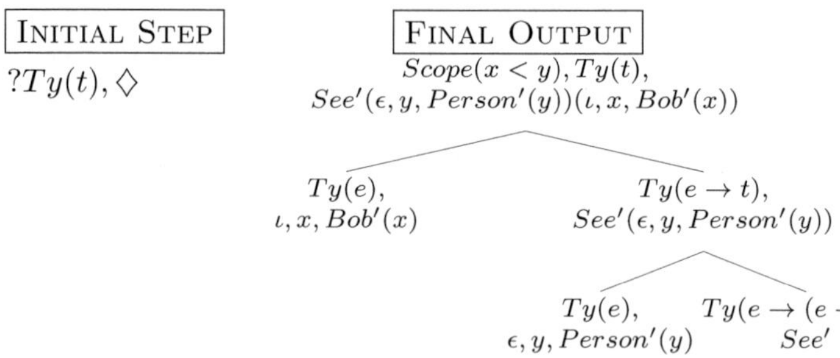

As this display shows, DS trees articulate representations of content, not hierarchical structure over the NL string. Accordingly, *words* themselves are not decorations on the tree; and there is no reflection of string word order in the resulting structure. Word order instead has the effect of inducing (through the lexical specifications) obligatory constraints on how processing of the words in the order given progressively leads to structures like the one shown in (1.2).

1.2.2 Tree structures and tree-growth

By way of setting out DS devices, let us rehearse some formal details in the process of building up the interpretation of (1.1). A DS tree is binary and formally described by means of statements in the logic of finite trees (*LOFT*: Blackburn and Meyer-Viol 1994). *LOFT* is a modal language which provides the potential of describing a tree from the

[2] We omit tense information here but see Cann (this volume).

perspective of any node of that tree: operators such as $\langle\uparrow\rangle, \langle\downarrow\rangle$ define relations of *immediate dominance* (as is standard in formal grammar specifications: Marcus 1980, Rogers and Vijay-Shanker 1994 and others) with subtypes $\langle\downarrow_0\rangle$ indicating presence of an argument daughter, $\langle\downarrow_1\rangle$ for predicate daughter; Kleene star $*$ operations are expressed by modalities such as $\langle\downarrow_*\rangle, \langle\uparrow_*\rangle$ which indicate multiple (yet indeterminate) steps of (plain) dominance. The set of decorations at every node includes semantic formulae with their type information ($Ty(\ldots)$), the treenode address ($Tn(\ldots)$), i.e., the exact location of the node on the tree, and other labels as required. Furthermore, the *pointer*, notated with '$\diamondsuit$' on a single node at each parse state, indicates the 'current' node in processing, namely the one to be processed next, and this plays an important role in governing word order. Via *monotonic updates* of partial trees, complete trees are eventually constructed. Crucial for expressing this goal-directedness are the *requirements*, these being yet unrealized but expected node/tree specifications, indicated by '?' in front of any annotation. For example, the underspecified subject node of a tree may have a requirement expressed in DS with the node annotation $?Ty(e)$, for which the only legitimate updates are logical expressions of type entity ($Ty(e)$). Requirements may also take a modal form, e.g. $?\langle\downarrow\rangle Ty(e \to t)$, a constraint that the daughter node be annotated with a formula of predicate type. All requirements must be satisfied if the construction process is to lead to a successful outcome. But, as illustrated in (1.3) below with the imposition of the outset requirement, $?Ty(t)$, and the second of the two initially imposed subgoals, $?\langle\downarrow_1\rangle Ty(e \to t)$, (see parse state $\boxed{1}$ and $\boxed{2}$), these requirements may not be satisfied until substantially later than the point at which they are imposed:[3]

(1.3)

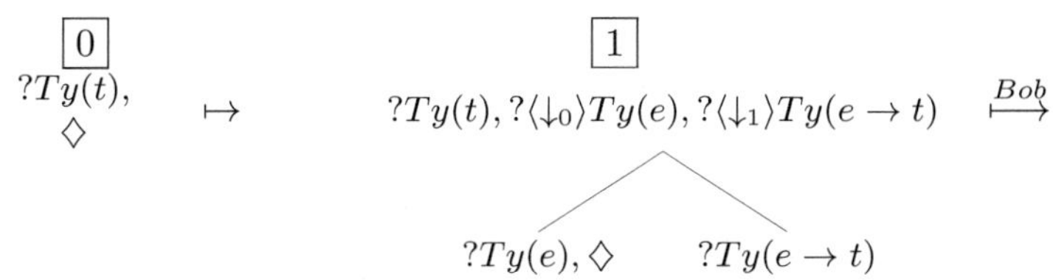

[3]For explanation of the epsilon calculus content values assigned to argument nodes, see section 1.2.5 below. Here suffice is to say that such trees are semantic representations, hence the annotations are not words.

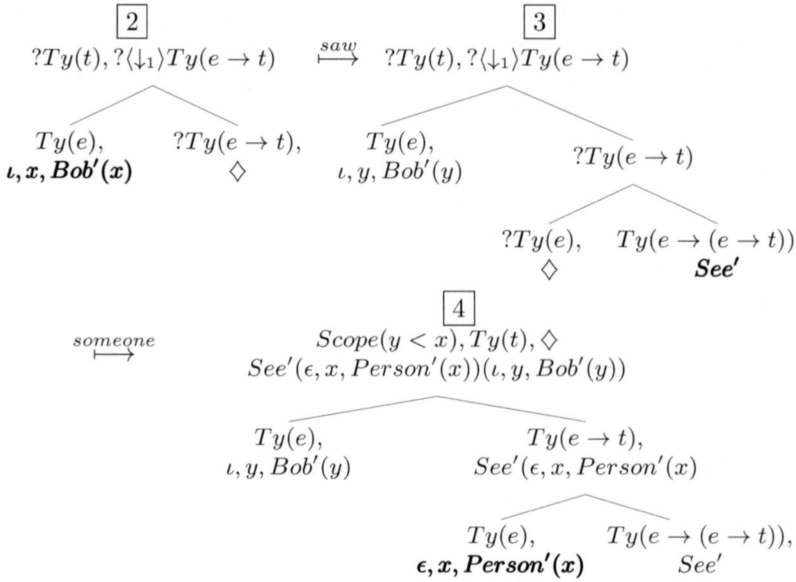

Processing proceeds by the execution of licensed *actions* that map one partial tree to another. Actions are defined in a language involving such commands as $\texttt{make}(\langle\downarrow\rangle)$, $\texttt{go}(\langle\downarrow\rangle)$, $\texttt{put}(\alpha)$, $\texttt{make}(\langle\downarrow_*\rangle)$, ⟨IF..., THEN..., ELSE...⟩ etc. Updates from parse state to parse state are carried out by means of applying sets of such actions incorporated in individual packages of two types: computational and lexical. *Computational actions* govern general tree-constructional processes, such as moving the pointer, introducing and updating nodes, compiling interpretation for all non-terminal nodes. In (1.3), the update of $\boxed{0}$ to $\boxed{1}$ is executed via computational actions expanding the opening AXIOM with the requirements $?\langle\downarrow_0\rangle Ty(e), ?\langle\downarrow_1\rangle Ty(e \rightarrow t)$ (INTRODUCTION), which induces a single-node tree that is then developed by the construction of nodes for accommodating subsequent subject and predicate decorations (by PREDICTION). Not all parsing is top-down, however, since individual lexical items also provide procedures for extending such partial trees in the form of *lexical actions*, inducing both nodes and annotations. In the updates from $\boxed{1}$ to $\boxed{2}$ and $\boxed{2}$ to $\boxed{3}$, for example, as in English, the set of lexical actions for the word *Bob* and then *see* are applied (through the process of SCANNING of the relevant lexical entries), yielding a subject decoration and an emergent incomplete predicate subtree and both annotations and further requirements. Wherever requirements on a pair of daughters are met, pointer movement up the tree takes place accompanied by the introduction of a modal statement stating what holds at the two daughters (COMPLETION).[4] Following this, a process of labelled type-deduction (ELIMINATION) yields decorations at non-terminal nodes, so that in the end result, all nodes have requirements satisfied. Wherever imposed requirements are met, the rule of THINNING removes them from the set of tree decorations, as shown finally at step $\boxed{4}$. A string is *wellformed* just in case there is at least one licensed sequence of steps from some assigned AXIOM statement via system-internal rules, applied strictly following the order of words, leading to a complete tree with all requirements satisfied. Characteristically, there is more than one such sequence of steps without this necessarily giving rise to ambiguity of content, reflecting the wellknown availability of more than one parsing strategy for any given parse process (Ferreira 1996).[5]

1.2.3 The lexicon/syntax interface

Lexical specifications are defined in exactly the same terms as more general tree-growth principles, a mapping from partial tree to partial tree. This allows the relative balance between lexical and computational actions to be subject to language variation. For example, a strict SVO language like English would employ the general rules of INTRODUCTION and PREDICTION to induce anticipation of subject-predicate structure as displayed in step $\boxed{1}$ of (1.3) (Kempson et al. 2001), but subject pro-drop languages would project this structure through the processing of the verb inducing a full skeletal template of predicate plus argument nodes (though see Cann (this volume) for an alternative analysis of English verbs). The lexical actions of *compró/bought* (Spanish/English equivalents) below illustrate the explicit way in which lexical actions induce such tree-structures. In pro-drop cases, *metavariables* (e.g. $Fo(\mathbf{U})$) are inserted in the relevant positions, below that associated with the constructed and decorated subject node in Spanish. Metavariables are devices which induce a content decoration on a node which is essentially

[4]Movement up the tree is not freely available, licensed only after type requirements on the current node are satisfied or through lexical stipulation of pointer movement across some domain. There is however a rule of ANTICIPATION, allowing return of the pointer down the tree to any node which has outstanding requirements (Cann et al. 2005).

[5]*Generation* is defined as following exactly the same mechanisms of incremental tree growth as are adopted in parsing, with the partial trees that are constructed in the tree growth process providing triggers for appropriate lexical selection. The only difference is that there is also a so-called GOAL TREE, available from the outset in the generation process, relative to which each putative update has to be checked for commensurability by a defined *subsumption* relation (see Purver et al. 2006, for details).

identical to that of a pronoun (see 1.2.4):

(1.4)

compró (Spanish 'bought')

IF	$?Ty(t)$	*bought*	
THEN	$\texttt{make}(\langle\downarrow_0\rangle);\texttt{go}(\langle\downarrow_0\rangle);$	IF	$?Ty(e \rightarrow t)$
	$\texttt{put}(Ty(e), Fo(\mathbf{U}), ?\exists\mathbf{x}.Fo(\mathbf{x}));$	THEN	$\texttt{go}(\langle\uparrow_1\rangle);$
	$\texttt{go}(\langle\uparrow_0\rangle);\texttt{put}(+PAST);$		$\texttt{put}(+PAST);$
	$\texttt{make}(\langle\downarrow_1\rangle);\texttt{go}(\langle\downarrow_1\rangle);$		$\texttt{go}(\langle\downarrow_1\rangle);\texttt{make}(\langle\downarrow_1\rangle);$
	$\texttt{put}(?Ty(e \rightarrow t));\texttt{make}(\langle\downarrow_1\rangle);$		$\texttt{go}(\langle\downarrow_1\rangle);$
	$\texttt{go}(\langle\downarrow_1\rangle);$		$\texttt{put}(Fo(\text{Bought'}),$
	$\texttt{put}(Fo(\text{Compró}'),$		$Ty(e \rightarrow (e \rightarrow t)))$
	$Ty(e \rightarrow (e \rightarrow t)))$		$\texttt{go}(\langle\uparrow_1\rangle);\texttt{make}(\langle\downarrow_0\rangle);$
	$\texttt{go}(\langle\uparrow_1\rangle);\texttt{make}(\langle\downarrow_0\rangle);$		$\texttt{go}(\langle\downarrow_0\rangle);\texttt{put}(?Ty(e))$
	$\texttt{go}(\langle\downarrow_0\rangle);\texttt{put}(?Ty(e))$	ELSE	Abort
ELSE	Abort		

With both lexical and general computational actions sharing the very same tree growth procedures, the shift from syntactic to lexical formulation as displayed in syntactic change is naturally expressible (see Bouzouita 2008a,b). Notice that, even in these simple cases, we can see the shift away from a static perspective into a more dynamic one. What the single word *compró* triggers is a procedure which speakers and hearers follow enabling them to establish some (partial) structure as the basis of interpretation. Such encoded instructions provided by a language, lexical or otherwise, constitute a set of mechanisms enabling the processing of expressions of that language to take place.

1.2.4 Generalized underspecification and update

Incorporated into this general tree growth of partial representations are reflections of underspecification both of content formulae, and of tree relations. Underspecification of formulae at intermediate stages are lexically licensed, signalling the need to recover a value from elsewhere. For example, pronouns lexically project a *metavariable* (a variable notated as $\mathbf{U}, \mathbf{V}$ etc) as a place-holder for some value to be assigned (a value which could be an actual variable (x, y, z...) of the language used to express content decorations, as e.g. in cases where pronouns are bound by quantifiers, i.e., bound variables). These metavariables invariably occur with an associated requirement for a fixed formula value (of the form $?\exists\mathbf{x}.Fo(\mathbf{x})$), making such provision of a value essential to a successful outcome. Terms available in the context provide replacements for such metavariables, through the rule of Substitution, as part of the construction process and subject to locality restrictions differentiating e.g. pronouns and reflexives (for details, see Kempson et al. 2001, Cann et al 2005).[6] *Context* in DS involves storage of complete parse states, i.e., the storing of partial tree, word sequence parsed to date, plus the actions used in building up the partial tree. In this respect, whenever a referent is available in the context store, it can be retrieved by use of a pronoun in the linguistic string, as in the processing of the second sentence below in the context of having processed the first one (with indexing here indicating the interpretation being established):[7]

(1.5) John$_i$ came in. He$_i$ smiled.

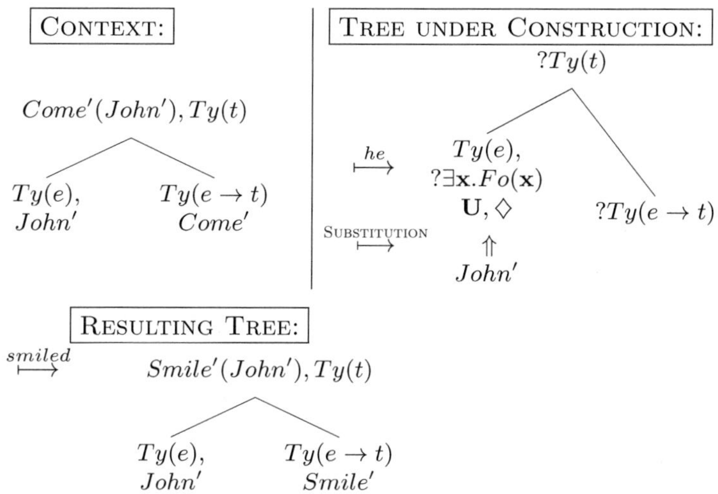

Construction of only weakly specified tree relations (*unfixed nodes*) can also be induced. Such nodes are characterized only as simply dominated by some specific node (allowing an unspecified number of dominance steps), with subsequent update required by the imposition of a requirement ($?\exists\mathbf{x}.Tn(\mathbf{x})$) for a fixed treenode address $Tn()$, specifying the exact immediate dominance relations of that node. The intuition

[6]There are means within DS to differentiate between metavariables as projected by pronouns, and those projected by a non-anaphoric expression such as a verb specifying attributes of their own argument nodes. In particular, it is a property of lexical expressions that their actions decorate a terminal node, characterized by a so-called *bottom restriction*, ($[\downarrow]\bot$), ensuring that the node cannot be further structurally developed, a restriction not holding of a metavariable annotation provided as a subpart of a composite set of actions such as those of a verb (Cann et al. 2005, see also footnote 10). This then provides a basis for diachronic shift from a lexical pronoun into an agreement marker via loss of this bottom restriction (Bouzouita 2002).

[7]Following readability conventions, the trees given here treat names as logically simple, rather than, more accurately, as iota terms.

which this mechanism directly echoes is that, in parsing an initial left-peripheral expression, the particular role of the term constructed from that expression cannot be identified at that point of the interpretation process, hence the node constructed is "unfixed" within that tree. This relation becomes fixed subsequently when further structure is introduced in the tree construction. This process is the basis for the processing of structures characterized as *long-distance movement*, the classic being the left-peripheral *focus* construction. We shall display the process of building such an unfixed node visually as:

(1.6)

$$Tn(a), ?Ty(t)$$

$$\vdots$$

$$\langle\uparrow_*\rangle Tn(a),$$
$$?\exists\mathbf{x}Tn(\mathbf{x})$$
$$?Ty(y), \Diamond$$

The construction process that induces this weak "dominated" relation, lacking any fully determinate specification, is called *Adjunction reflecting the Kleene * operator that is used to define it. This is a familiar way of characterising parsing of long-distance dependencies in psycholinguistic models (Sturt and Crocker 1996, Costa et al. 2002, Miyamoto 2002). However, the construction of weakly specified structural relations is not generally taken to be an inherent component of the syntactic apparatus.[8]

A second more local variant of this rule is defined, introducing an unfixed node whose relation to the overall emergent tree has to be identified within a given local domain (i.e. within a single predicate-argument structure - see Kiaer 2007, this volume). This is expressed as involving the construction of a node that is unfixed along a possibly empty chain of functor relations, involving a Kleene star operation on the modal operator $\langle\uparrow_*^1\rangle$, hence along a functor spine. This process is the basis of what is called in movement paradigms 'local scrambling' (availability of free ordering for argument expressions preceding the verb). The mechanism applies to induce a locally unfixed argument node that can be subsequently enriched as driven by e.g. case specifications to yield the appropriate fixed relation to the locally dominating type-t-requiring node (Cann et al. 2005; Kempson and Kiaer 2010).[9]

[8]Functional uncertainty of LFG is indeed defined for just such structures, but the mapping of such an uncertainty relation at c-structure is projected onto a structure with quite different labellings at f-structure, so the concept of growth as the core notion is not brought out.

[9]Though such a process might seem to be specific to case-rich and free word-order languages, Cann (this volume) argues that it provides a general basis for modelling

In all construction of such weak structural relations, these relations must, like all aspects of underspecification, be structurally resolved within the structure that emerges subsequently. This is achieved via the rule MERGE, which effects a unification of two nodes with compatible annotations. The node with which an unfixed node can merge could be projected by e.g. an accompanying verb, as in the processing of *A María vió* ('Maria he saw', Spanish) below:

(1.7)

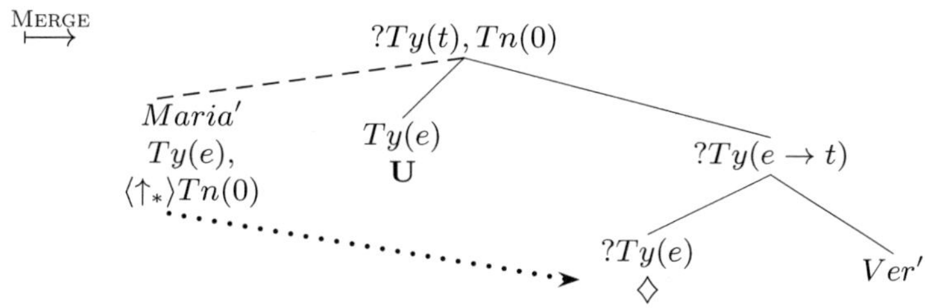

Notice how the output of a process of building one such unfixed node naturally feeds into the lexical actions provided by the verb subsequently, so that in such an NP-V sequence, a complete propositional structure eventually emerges through progressive and interdependently defined processes of tree construction.

The two types of underspecification combine to license complex processing strategies. A pronominal provides an interim value given as a metavariable, e.g., **U**, **V**..., which satisfies a type requirement, allowing the parse to continue, but the update to this formula might be left open to be satisfied later in the derivation. Such a grammaticized delayed resolution occurs with expletive pronouns:

(1.8) *It* emerged *that John was wrong.*

In (1.8), the metavariable projected by *it* in string-initial position licenses the further unfolding of the parse process, allowing the parse of the verb *emerged*.

(1.9)

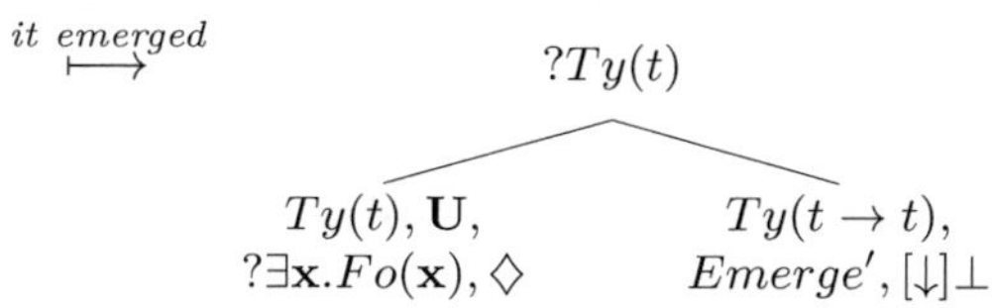

A DS rule called LATE*ADJUNCTION can then apply which builds an

the concept of syntactic subject, and that it is lexical properties of the verb even in a fixed word-order language such as English that determine whether the concepts of syntactic and logical subject coincide (see also Marten and Kempson 2002; Cann et al. 2005 for its applicability in Bantu languages).

unfixed node below a fixed one provided they share type annotations so that they can be eventually unified.[10] This rule will build a node of $?Ty(t)$ below the subject which allows the string *that John is wrong* to be parsed at that point. MERGE of the two nodes can then apply and subsequently the usual computational rules will compile the interpretation on the non-terminal nodes to yield a complete tree and a successful parse:

(1.10)

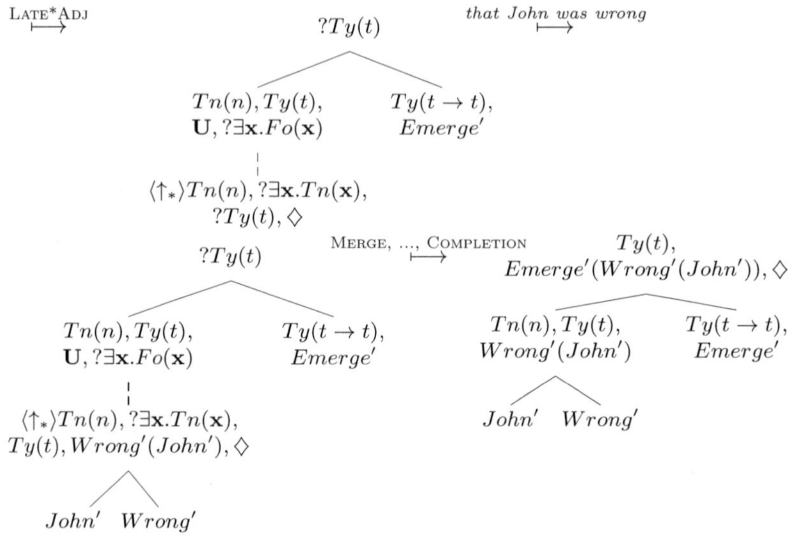

Notice that there is no trace on the eventual tree of the fact that *it*, the expletive pronoun, was involved in the derivation of this particular semantic representation. This is identical to the one derived through the parse of a string like *That John was wrong emerged*, since the truth conditions are identical and the contribution of *it*, like any pronoun, is a temporary place-holder (a metavariable) until a proper value is provided (in this case a proposition).

1.2.5 Quantification

To round out this picture, we sketch the epsilon-calculus account of natural language quantification which DS adopts. The epsilon calculus defines terms, so-called *epsilon terms*, which model the arbitrary names

[10]Notice that it is crucial here that an expletive expression (like *it*) does not contribute the *bottom restriction* ($[\downarrow]\bot$), otherwise LATE*ADJUNCTION and the processing of the upcoming subordinate sentence could not apply. We assume here the type $t \rightarrow t$ is assigned to *Emerge'*, but see Gregoromichelaki (this volume), and Cann (this volume) for discussion of situation/event terms within the DS framework.

used in predicate logic natural-deduction proofs (there are also τ "tau" terms and ι "iota" terms; but each of these is defined on the basis of epsilon terms, e.g. a τ-term is the dual of an ϵ-term and an ι-term is a restricted, uniquely referential variant of an ϵ-term). In DS, such terms are defined to be of type e, and they take the following tripartite form: (a) a quantified binder, e.g. ϵ, (b) an individual variable (e.g. x) and (c) the restrictor ($Candle'(x)$):

$$\epsilon, x, Candle'(x)$$

Semantically, epsilon terms stand for witnesses of existentially quantified formulae – the witness that makes the corresponding existentially quantified formula true. In employing these, the DS account allows a match between the substructure of these terms and the corresponding internal articulation of DPs. More specifically, epsilon terms are eventually derived through progressive construction of type e subtrees, with the top node to be decorated by such a term corresponding to the DP node in standard syntactic frameworks. The quantificational binder is provided by NL determiners, which project the functor type $cn \rightarrow e$, a function from nominal type ($Ty(cn)$) onto a type e term. (This type is equivalent to a function from the NP category onto the DP category.) This NP category provides then another branching to an additional term of type e for the individual variable (which can be further restricted, through e.g. a restrictive relative clause, see section 1.2.6) and a node annotated by nouns, which provide functors from such a variable onto the nominal type, here of type $e \rightarrow cn$:[11]

(1.11)

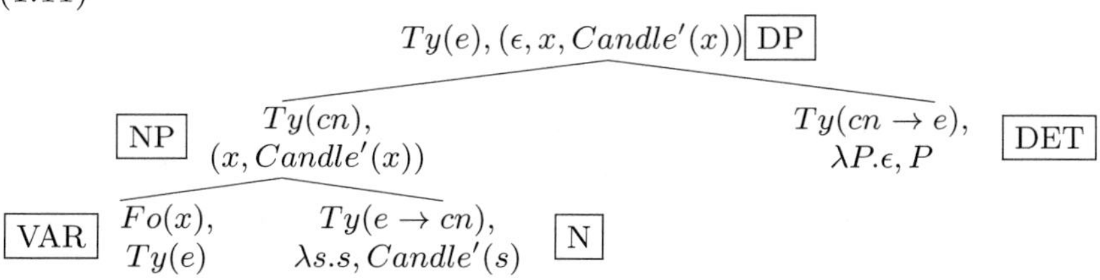

The parallelism between the structure of epsilon terms and NL DPs is what allows DS to incrementally and compositionally derive DP content. Such parallelism is wholly unlike the lack of match between the structuring of NL quantified expressions and the quantifying operators of predicate logic, as the latter are by definition propositional operators occurring exclusively at the left periphery of the domain over which

[11]The labels, DP, D, etc have no independent status within such a semantically grounded tree. Indeed, they are not defined in the theory but seen as epiphenomenal of the semantic structuring.

they bind.

Epsilon terms illustrate the way in which the interpretation of NL expressions in context may reflect not just some encoded word content, but also the content of their containing structural environment.[12] This is the result of the equivalence between epsilon calculus formulae and predicate-logic formulae. The core defining equivalence between predicate logic and the epsilon calculus is:

(1.12) $\exists x.\psi(x) = \psi(\epsilon, x, \psi(x))$

Notice the duplication of the predicate ψ in the epsilon term's restrictor: this is what forces such terms to reflect their containing environment within their own structure, including their dependencies to other terms in the same propositional domain. As implemented in DS, the construction and relative dependencies between such terms is achieved by making them subject to a later, indeed, final set of rules of evaluation (Quantifier-Evaluation rules) which explicitly structure the terms as reflecting their relative scope inter-relations within their restrictor. In order to get this result, firstly, there has to be a derived formula indicating the content of the predicate-argument structure just parsed (as in (1.16)). From this formula, the quantifier-evaluation rules will construct a new compound formula both (a) according to collected scope declarations (stored under the label *Scope*(...) and (b) according to the type of the NL quantificational determiners involved. Thus, for example, in the construal of (1.13), standardly, the predicate-logic formula would be taken to be (1.14):

(1.13) A candle flickers

(1.14) $\exists x.Candle'(x) \wedge Flicker'(x)$

In the equivalent formulation in the epsilon calculus, this same conjunction will be constructed (shown later in (1.18)) but this time the conjunction will also appear inside the term itself (see (1.15)). So, for (1.13), the epsilon term derived must involve the attribution of the two predicates *Candle′* and *Flicker′* internally to its restrictor:

(1.15) $(\epsilon, x, [Candle'(x) \wedge Flicker'(x)])$

To now illustrate the incremental derivation of such terms, in processing a string like (1.13), firstly, consider what functional application will eventually derive as the root node of the propositional tree:

---

[12]For discussion of on-line creation of "ad-hoc" concepts demanding feedback mechanisms from the interpretation process into the construction of novel concepts, see Carston (2002), Wilson and Carston (2006), following Barsalou (1993).

(1.16)

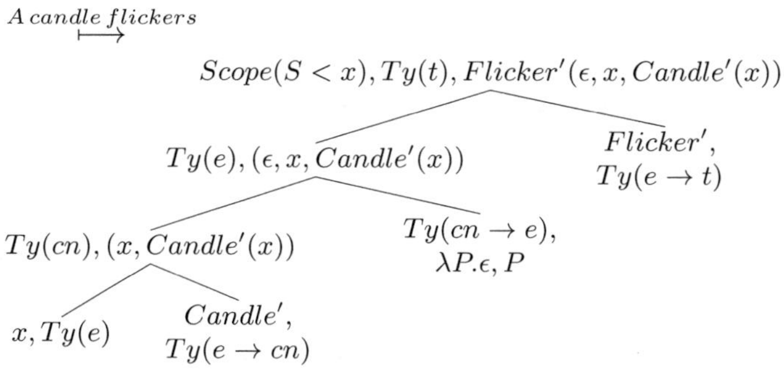

The predicate *Scope* incrementally records scope constraints that result from choices made during the build up of information. Such scope constraints are of the form $x < y$ (to be understood as 'the term with variable y is dependent on the term with variable x'). Though this is a generally defined process, it can also be lexically determined. For example, indefinites project epsilon terms subject to the lexically specified constraint that they are invariably dependent on either another quantifying expression or a term within the temporal specification (here annotated simply as S, the index of evaluation).[13] And names, providing iota terms, are epsilon terms of widest scope.[14]

The tree in (1.16) notably retains the pattern provided by the NL syntax: we have a one-place predicate applied to an argument term, itself of type e. All that is required to express the import of these names following the predicate logic equivalence in (1.12) is the application of the quantifier-evaluation algorithm which transforms the unevaluated terms in order to reflect dependencies as given by the accumulated scope constraints. In the evaluation of (1.16), this will involve constructing a conjunction of a pair of formulae: the first corresponds to the restrictor of the so-far constructed epsilon term, here $Candle'$; the second corresponds to the main predicate $Flicker'$. They are put together with the logical connective $\wedge$ because this reflects the existential force of an epsilon term. (the universal τ-term would involve the connective $\rightarrow$).[15] The argument to which each of these predicates is applied is a name, an epsilon term (abbreviated below as α), which is gradually extended according to its dependencies as recorded in *Scope*(). Here, as the final step of the evaluation process, this name will be extended

[13] See Gregoromichelaki (this volume) and Cann (this volume).

[14] An *iota* term is an existential term expressing the Russellian account of definiteness as existential quantification with a uniqueness predicate.

[15] Square bracketing will be used below to assist in identifying the major connective.

by adding to its restrictor the second conjunct provided by the main predicate, $Flicker'$, to derive the term already shown in (1.15). So the input to the evaluation is (1.17), its output is (1.18):

(1.17) $Scope(S < x), Flicker'(\epsilon, x, Candle'(x))$

(1.18) $\overset{Q-Eval}{\longmapsto}$
$S : [Candle'(\alpha) \wedge Flicker'(\alpha)]$
where $\alpha = (\epsilon, x, [Candle'(x) \wedge Flicker'(x)])$

The effect of the evaluation step is that the resulting term, α, matches, in its restrictor, exactly the content of the environment in which it occurs. This is more explicitly displayed in (1.19) where the abbreviation α has been removed:

(1.19) $S : [\ [Candle'(\ \epsilon, x, Candle'(x) \wedge Flicker'(x)\ )]\ \wedge$
$[Flicker'(\ \epsilon, x, Candle'(x) \wedge Flicker'(x)\ )]\ ]$

In sum, the account of all NL noun phrases is syntactically uniform. The combinatorial process that determines how the meanings of the subparts is built up is a familiar type-deduction process with accompanying beta-reduction. As part of this process, there is an incremental procedure for collecting up scope-related information. It is only at the very last step that the full complexity of quantificational dependencies is made explicit. An algorithm is defined that yields the specification of cross-quantifier dependencies, these all being eventually recorded within the restrictor of the resulting term(s). This achieves the result of the eventually created terms reflecting their containing environment in their own structure: this is a mechanism that can be used to very rich pragmatic effect (Wilson and Carston 2006) and, more directly, in the modelling of *E-type anaphora* (see Kempson et al. 2001, Gregoromichelaki 2006).

1.2.6 Paired structures, sharing of terms

There is one more thing to add to this DS sketch. The trees so far have been simple $Ty(t)$ predicate-argument structures. Some predicates, e.g. *believe*, *doubt*, may be typed to take propositional ($Ty(t)$) arguments, thus introducing recursion. But, in addition, the full complexity of NL structures is largely achieved in DS by defining a general tree-adjunction operation that hooks together independent predicate-argument tree structures through some shared terms, inducing so-called LINKed trees. Such trees involve the construction of a LINK transition from a node conventionally labelled $Tn(\alpha)$ onto a newly constructed node constituting the topnode of a newly initiated tree (the LINKed tree). The LINKed tree is dependent on the main tree in the sense of requiring obligatory copying of some variable or term already introduced in the earlier constructed structure. The canonical case are relative clauses (Kempson et al. 2001; Cann et al. 2005; Cann et al. 2005b). In those, a LINKed structure is introduced, either from the variable associated with the emergent epsilon term (*restrictive* relatives), or from some completed epsilon term (*non-restrictives*), necessitating the sharing of either variable or complete (epsilon) term:

(1.20) A friend who smokes left.

(1.21) John, who smokes, left.

The initiation of the LINKed tree, though itself a freely available adjunct-creating process, may be constrained by associated lexical actions; for example, *relative pronouns* like *who* are defined as decorating an unfixed node built as immediately following the construction of a LINK transition and copying a term from the original tree:[16]

(1.22)

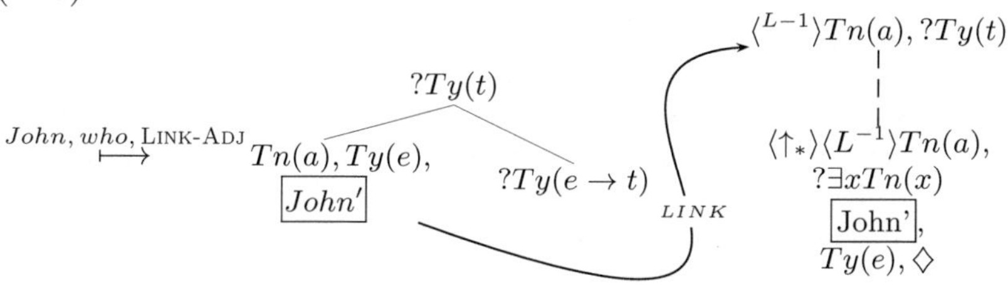

With this partial construction of a LINKed tree, regular tree-internal actions take over; and once both trees are completed, evaluation of the constructed pair can then take place to yield the following:

(1.23)

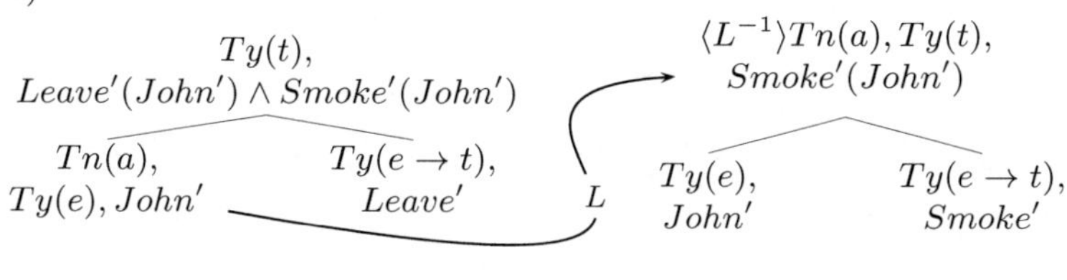

This type of derivation illustrates how, by defining computational and lexical actions in terms of the very same processes, complex interdependencies between specific lexical actions and general computational actions become straightforwardly definable.

---

16 $\langle L \rangle$ and its inverse $\langle L^{-1} \rangle$ are the relevant modalities in LOFT indicating (forward or backward) steps across the LINK relation, see Kempson et al. (2001).

This mechanism for inducing LINKed structures has more general applications. Appositions and *topic structures* are also modelled as LINKed subtrees, with the first tree projected by the initial NP providing the context relative to which the second structure is developed. In topic structures, e.g. *(As for) John, I like him*, this is secured by a constraint to the effect that the term initially provided must also appear somewhere in the newly constructed tree (indicated below as $?\langle\downarrow_*\rangle John'$), matching the quasi- clause-external role that topic NPs may serve in a language. This results in the obligatory substitution of the metavariable provided by the pronoun *him* with a copy of the term provided by *John*. The structure which such a rule (Topic-Adjunction) induces is illustrated below:

(1.24)

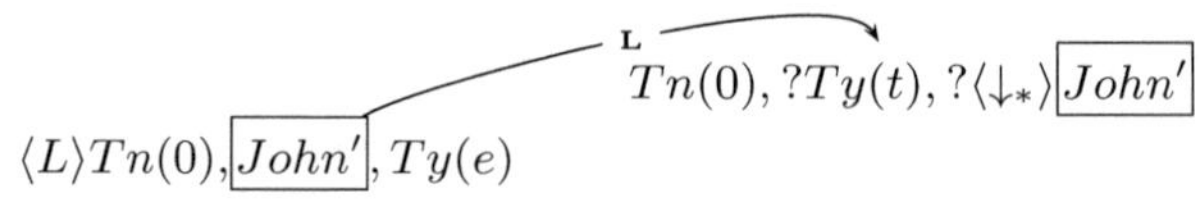

Kempson et al. (this volume) use just such a structure for the modelling of cleft structures in siSwati; and as Gregoromichelaki (this volume) shows, this variant LINK structure rule is also an available option in the processing of clausal adjuncts such as conditionals. Indeed at the outset of any utterance, there will be alternative strategies available for processing: (a) construction of a LINKed structure with some subsequent term identified with the term on the created LINKed node which serves as the context, as outlined here, (b) construction of an unfixed node which unifies with some argument node as independently made available, or, (c) direct local construction of argument nodes. This ensures a flexibility in parsing and production which is independently argued in psycholinguistics to be an advantage (Ferreira 1996). Bouzouita (2008a,b) uses this availability of alternative strategies for a given string-interpretation pairing as a basis for the sequence of syntactic changes in clitic placement in the development from Medieval to Renaissance Spanish. Sato (this volume) explores how efficient use of such processing options can be implemented in parsing and its psycholinguistic correlates.

Like all DS structures, pairs of LINKed trees themselves do not reflect linear order. In consequence, we expect the pairing of such trees to be effected in either order, with first the external term provided as context for the emergent propositional structure, as above, or with the propositional structure being induced first, and some external node to be constructed immediately subsequently. This finds application, not only in phenomena traditionally claimed to involve "rightward movement" (see Gregoromichelaki, to appear) but also in the formulation of head-initial, head-final, and even headless structures (see Kempson and Kurosawa 2010, Kula and Marten, this volume, Gregoromichelaki, this volume). More generally, DS provides a natural framework within which to explain both the generality of structure-building processes across very different languages, and also the asymmetries between left-peripheral and right-peripheral projections of structure, as the incrementally evolving context influences how those processes apply.

1.3 Papers of this volume

The papers of this volume fall into two distinct sections. Section I consists of papers which address the interface between lexicon and syntax from a DS point of view as set out in Cann et al. (2005). Across an array of cross-linguistic puzzles, these argue for the incorporation of incrementality into the grammar formalism itself, with consequent incremental two-way feeding between lexical and syntactic specifications. Kempson et al. provide an account of siSwati cleft structures. Their analysis uses the building of a LINK transition to induce a topic-like structure and combines this with the concept of an expletive pronoun as a place-holder for later development of structure. Kula and Marten develop the account of relatives in Bantu as a means of addressing the phonology-syntax interface within DS, a perspective which imposes a novel phonology-syntax direction of dependency. Their analysis covers head-initial, head-final, and even headless relatives (following an extension of Cann et al. 2005 defined for Japanese head-final relatives by Kempson and Kurosawa 2010). Bouzouita examines the synchronic variation between the analytic and synthetic futures in Medieval Spanish. She shows that this variation interacts directly with clitic placement restrictions. This view is substantiated both at the level of the data and the formal DS analysis: distributional parallels are shown to exist between the various expressions of the future and clitic placement; it is then argued that both these patterns can be captured uniformly by a formal analysis that takes into account the processing environments that are responsible for the variation. Three further papers seek to test the core DS claims with respect to typological generalizations, psycholinguistic experimentation, and computational implementation. Wu uses DS to explore the range of constructions identified as passive (taking English, Chinese, and Navajo as illustrative of three very different types of language). Kiaer argues for the account of scrambling phenomena set out in Kiaer (2007), Kempson and Kiaer (2010) (both local and long-distance), and provides experimental confirmation that on-line prosodic information in Korean is essential to sustaining the DS presumption of incrementality intrinsic to the account of both local and long-distance scrambling. Sato discusses the search-algorithmic issues that arise in the computational implementation of a grammar formalism such as DS, defined to reflect the full set of possible parse moves with ongoing feeding relations between lexical and tree-growth mechanisms. He relates those to the issue of local ambiguity, much debated in psycholinguistics.

The second section of the volume is devoted to papers that address extensions of the framework since Cann et al. (2005). Gregoromichelaki develops the DS framework by incorporating the contribution of situation/event terms as part of the construction and evaluation of trees, using this extension to address the syntactic and semantic issues raised by conditionals. Extension to incorporate event terms is also taken up by Cann in a detailed account of the English auxiliary system, and by Chatzikyriakidis in an account of clitic climbing. Finally, Cann and Wu address in detail the syntactic, semantic and pragmatic properties of the Chinese particle *bei*, extending the framework to allow lexical triggering of optional pragmatic inferences.

References

The following were cited in this chapter: Austin (1975), Barsalou (1993), Blackburn and Meyer-Viol (1994), Bouzouita (2002, 2008a,b), Cann (this volume), Cann et al. (2005), Cann et al. (2005b), Cann et al. (2007), Carston (2002), Chatzikyriakidis (2009, 2010), Chomsky (1965), Costa et al. (2002), Ferreira (1996), Ginzburg and Cooper (2004), Gregoromichelaki (to appear), Gregoromichelaki (this volume) Gregoromichelaki et al. (2009), Gregoromichelaki et al. (submitted), Hawkins (2004), Kempson et al. (2001), Kempson and Kiaer (2009a), Kempson et al. (2009b), Kempson et al. (this volume) Kempson et al. (to appear), Kempson and Kiaer (2010), Kempson and Kurosawa (2010), Kiaer (2007), Kula and Marten (this volume), Lombardo and Sturt (2002) Marcus (1980), Marten and Kempson (2002), Miyamoto (2002), Purver et al. (2006), Purver et al. (2009), Sturt and Crocker (1996), Rogers and Vijay-Shanker (1994), Phillips (1996), Wilson and Carston (2006). See references at the end of the book for full information.

Part I

Applying the framework

2

SiSwati Clefts: The Meeting Ground of Context and Contrast

RUTH KEMPSON, LUTZ MARTEN AND NHLANHLA THWALA

2.1 Introduction: SiSwati clefts

Cleft structures have proved to be a tantalising structure, not easily expressible in current formalisms. Traditionally, they have been taken as a canonical contrastive-focus device, with clearcut presuppositional properties indicating dependence on context of the non-focussed part (Prince 1978), yet, as has emerged from corpus collections and other recent work (see Hedberg 2000, Delin 1990, 1992), there are many divergent uses of clefts, indicating a much more complex relationship between structure and interpretational effect. Despite the subtle variation in the extent and precise nature of the context-dependence implied, structurally the syntactic properties of clefts robustly display a great deal of cross-linguistic uniformity despite minor language-particular idiosyncrasies. And in this uniformity hides another puzzle. Quite generally, clefts display extensive parallelism with relative clauses, even to the extent of using the same morphological indicators as a relative clause sequence; and yet at one and the same time they display properties of left-dislocation.

This paper reports work done during AHRC project B/RG/AN8675/APN16312, whose support made this joint work possible. We are grateful for support and encouragement from Miriam Bouzouita, Cécile de Cat, Stergios Chatzikyriakidis, Eleni Gregoromichelaki, Nancy Kula and Kristina Riedel and from feedback given during the 2006 LAGB workshop.

The Dynamics of Lexical Interfaces.
Ruth Kempson, Eleni Gregoromichelaki and Christine Howes (eds.).

SiSwati clefts display this straddling across relative-clause patterning and dislocation patterning particularly clearly. There are two main types of siSwati clefts; and they all display this split nature – with attributes in common with left-peripheral structures on the one hand, and with relative clause structures on the other. The simple type involve first marking the "clefted" element with a preceding *nge-* marker (for class 2 nouns), and secondly an associated relative clause sequence – relative clauses in siSwati are marked by a *la-* prefix as the first prefix in the verbal complex:[1]

(2.1)

(nge-)ba-fana	*la-*	*ba-*	*to-*	*natsa*	*tjwala*
it-2-boys	REL	2SM	FUT	drink	14.alcohol

'It is the boys who will drink alcohol'

As we shall see in the analysis to be provided, on this account, *nge-* is not analyzed as a copula but as a specialized form of pronominal, as reflected in the literal translations provided.

The ordering of these sub-parts is free, with the relative-clause-like sequence occurring after or before the *nge-* marked noun phrase, in the latter case with a D-linking effect as is common in right-dislocation structures, the relative sequence being in some sense construed relative to context, with the post-posed clefted expression having to reflect whatever assigned interpretation the relative sequence gets:

(2.2)

la-	*ba-*	*to-*	*natsa*	*tjwala*	*nge-ba-fana*
REL	2SM	FUT	drink	14.alcohol	it-2-boys

'They will drink alcohol, the boys'

nge- marking, even where it is possible, is invariably optional, yielding a further sub-type of cleft sentence in which the only feature distinguishing these sequences from left- or right-dislocation structures may be the presence of the relative marker *la-*:

(2.3)

ba-fana	*ba-*	*to-*	*natsa*	*tjwala*
2-boys	2SM	FUT	drink	14.alcohol

'The boys, they will drink alcohol'

(2.4)

ba-	*to-*	*natsa*	*tjwala*	*ba-fana*
2SM	FUT	drink	14.alcohol	2-boys

'They will drink alcohol, the boys'

[1] All examples in this paper were supplied by the third-named author. We will not discuss in detail here morphological variation in nominal or relative marking in clefts (see Ziervogel and Mabuza 1976, Taljaard et al. 1991), nor variation in siSwati relative clause strategies (see Zeller 2004, 2006 for detailed discussion of relative clause formation in different Southern African Bantu languages). SiSwati, like most Bantu languages, has a complex set of noun class markers, amongst which are class 1 markers for singular humans, class 2 for human plurals, and class 17 for locatives.

Indeed in several noun classes, there is no *nge* correlate at all, so the ONLY feature distinguishing these sequences from that of relative clauses is a distinctive tone marking on the "clefted" expression.[2]

(2.5) *(bu-)twjala* *la-* *ba-* *to-* *bu-* *natsa* *ba-fana*
(14-)14.alcohol REL 2SM FUT 14OM drink 2-boys
'The alcohol, the boys will drink it.'

There is then, in addition, a complex form preceding such sequences involving what is diachronically a bleached locative subject marker. This bleached locative *ku-* is followed by a tense marker and then immediately by the expression construed as focussed and the relative-marked sequence, the tense marking in this relative having to agree with the earlier tense marker:[3]

(2.6) *ku-* *to-* *ba* *nge-ba-fana* *la-* *ba-* *to-* *natsa* *tjwala*
DSM FUT COP it-2-boys REL 2SM FUT drink 14.alcohol
'It will be the boys who will drink alcohol'

These more complex forms are NOT associated with any inversion of the clefted expression and the relative-marked sequence. This former locative *ku-* is standardly analyzed as a grammaticalized locative subject marker out of which this expletive marking has evolved (e.g. Marten 2010). As a subject marker, it is used with non-thematic subjects, in subject inversion constructions such as subject questions, presentational constructions and quotative inversion, and for agreement with conjoined NPs. Note that in all these uses, it has lost agreement features, and allows update with a locally introduced post-verbal subject if present. This is interpreted as indefinite, while postverbal subjects following an agreeing verb form are invariably interpreted as definite:[4]

(2.7) *ku-* *fik-* *e* *thishela* *lomusha*
DSM arrive PERF.CONJ teacher new
'A new teacher has arrived'

[2]In fact, nouns of all classes can be marked simply by tonal change. Nouns of class 4 and class 9 (i.e. those whose noun class prefix begins in *i-*) optionally prefix *y-* rather than *nge-* or *ngu-*. In addition, any noun may take a prefix of the same form as the relevant subject marker for the class, such as *bu-* in *bu-tjwala* 'alcohol'. However, the function of these forms is not fully clear, and we will not develop an analysis of them here. See Ziervogel and Mabuza (1976: 32-34) and Taljaard et al. (1991: 89-92) for an overview of the different morphological forms.

[3]We gloss *ku-* here as Default Subject Marker (DSM).

[4]SiSwati has so-called disjunctive and conjunctive markers which signal a structural boundary and lack of one respectively.

(2.8) *ku- ne- kudla edladleni*
DSM COP food kitchen$_{LOC}$
'There is food in the kitchen'

As these examples show, siSwati, like most Bantu languages has a rich verbal complex, in which a verb stem is prefixed with, in order, an obligatory subject marker, a tense marker, one object marker which is optional, and the verb. Independently of these cleft sequences, as long as both subject and object markers are selected, word order is very free. The subject, whose associated subject-marking prefix is obligatory, can occur after the verb, if so, right at the end of any VP sequence. The object expression can occur either before the subject or after the verbal complex, possibly even after some postposed subject, if there is also an associated object-marking prefix; but if there is no such object-marking, which is optional, then the object occurs immediately after the verb, as in (2.3).

Relative clauses in siSwati, whose pattern these cleft sequences follow, are marked with a prefix on the verb which precedes all other prefixes of the verbal complex, and whenever the object position is relativized over, the object marker is obligatory:

(2.9) *twjala la- ba- to- bu- natsa ba-fana*
14.alcohol REL 2SM FUT 14OM drink 2-boys
'The alcohol which the boys will drink....'

This is the regular pattern of languages with obligatory resumptive pronouns, and, following this pattern, locative NPs also require an obligatory resumptive element, but, in this case, there being no preverbal prefix, this takes the form of a demonstrative:

(2.10) *London lapho ngi- hlala khona*
London REL-LOC 1SG.SM live DEM.LOC
'London where I live ...'

(2.11) **London lapho ngi- hlala ...*
London REL-LOC 1SG.SM live
'London where I live ...'

The form *lapho* is a specific locative form of the relative pronoun (in fact a demonstrative); but equally licensed is the same simple form *la-* as is used in the subject and object relatives:

(2.12) *London la- ngi- hlala khona*
London REL 1SG.SM live there
'London, I live there'

Some of the flexibility of independent clauses is retained in relative clauses: in particular there may be a subject preceding that complex, so that the relative clause marker is not necessarily the first element of the relative clause sequence:

(2.13)	*tjwala*	*ba-fana*	*la-*	*ba-*	*to-*	*bu-*	*natsa*
	14.alcohol	2-boys	REL	2SM	FUT	14OM	drink

'Alcohol which the boys will drink ... '

Object and locative forms of cleft structures display equally marked parallelism with this relative-clause pattern: object marking, which is otherwise optional, is obligatory; the subject may follow the verb; equally, the subject may precede the verbal complex:

(2.14)	*tjwala*	*la-*	*ba-*	*to-*	*bu-*	*natsa*	*ba-fana*
	14.alcohol	REL	2SM	FUT	14OM	drink	2-boys

'Alcohol, they will drink it, the boys, that is'

(2.15)	*la-*	*ba-*	*to-*	*bu-*	*natsa*	*ba-fana*	*tjwala*
	REL	2SM	FUT	14OM	drink	2-boys	14.alcohol

'They will drink it, the boys, alcohol, that is'

(2.16)	*tjwala*	*ba-fana*	*la-*	*ba-*	*to-*	*bu-*	*natsa*
	14.alcohol	2-boys	REL	2SM	FUT	14OM	drink

'As for alcohol, the boys, they will drink it'

(2.17)	*?ba-fana*	*la-*	*ba-*	*to-*	*bu-*	*natsa*	*tjwala*
	2-boys	REL	2SM	FUT	14OM	drink	14.alcohol

'The boys, they will drink it, the alcohol, that is'
'It's alcohol which the boys will drink'

(2.18)	*ku-*	*se-*	*London*	*lapho*	*ngi-*	*hlala*	*khona*
	DSM	LOC	London	REL-LOC	1SG.SM	live	DEM.LOC

'It's London where I live'

With both object and locative clefts, as subject clefts, there is a further more complex form, the (*nge-* plus) NP plus relative sequence being paired with an expletive *ku-* plus copula sequence:

(2.19)	*ku-*	*to-*	*ba*	*tjwala*	*la-*	*ba-*	*to-*	*bu-*	*natsa*	*ba-fana*
	DSM	FUT	COP	14.alcohol	REL	2SM	FUT	14OM	drink	2-boys

'It will be alcohol which they will drink it the boys'

Generally, this bleached locative form, *ku-* precedes the copula, but with remote past forms, the auxiliaries precede the subject and in these, the expletive marker may be reduplicated as a form of agreement on the auxiliary:[5]

(2.20)

kw-	*a*	*ku-*	*ngu-*	*se-London*	*lapho*
DSM	REMOTE-PAST	DSM	NGE	LOC-London	where

nga-	*ngi-*	*hlala*	*khona*	*na-*	*make*
1SG-REMOTE-PAST	1SG.SM	live	DEM	with	mother

'It was in London where I lived with my mother'

Overall then, cleft structures in siSwati show the marked parallelism with relative clauses that is characteristic of cleft structures. The question to be asked is: given this striking parallelism, should these structures be analyzed as relatives at some level of abstraction, and so be analyzed as some kind of modifier of the focussed expression? Indeed, given the closeness of the complex and simple forms, should the simple clefts be analyzed as expressing a covert copula, hence be analyzed like the complex form, with the relative sequence taken to be a relative clause modification of the focus head? And, if so, what analysis can be assigned to the double occurrence of the locative expletives, these presumably requiring independent higher projections, but, apparently, without an intervening copula?

The issues raised by these cleft constructions have a significance well beyond explaining the details of an individual language. Across all languages, so-called cleft structures display this mixture of hanging-topic-like structures, so in movement terms base-generated, and yet structures correlative with long-distance dependency, so, in such movement frameworks, requiring characterization through some analogue of movement. This mixture is puzzling because these two analyses, given standard frameworks, have to be seen as incompatible. As a base-generated topic structure, the cleft expressed would be assigned as part of the highest TP projection, reflecting the clause-external status of the clefted expression; as an A' moved expression, it would be analyzed as inhabiting some Spec CP position, hence clause-internal. No single structure can be analyzed so that one and the same expression is analyzed as simultaneously realized within both the highest possible projection and yet at the lower projection. These problems multiply with right-periphery phenomena, where it is much harder to reflect the parallelism with relative clause configurations, and extra VP-internal Focus and Topic projections are very generally assumed (see Maha-

[5]The form of *nge-* is phonologically determined.

jan 1997 for an early instance of this type of analysis). At least, such analyses would have to be extended to the siSwati clefts as, in these, the relative-sequence and the clefted expression occur in either order. On top of this, the fact that the locative-expletive variant does not allow such order variation goes unexplained; as does its potential for duplication.

SiSwati relatives and clefts pose a specific theoretical issue for any account of clefts which is grounded in a Kayne-style analysis of relative clauses involving movement of some NP from the relative clause to become the head: the specifics of that analysis appears to be inapplicable. Given that in object relatives, the subject may precede the whole verbal complex and so also the supposed relativising complementizer, it would seem that not only is the clefted expression external to the clausal sequence, but, more problematically, so is the subject expression preceding that verbal complex. But, given a Kaynian analysis in which the head starts life within the relative sequence and is progressively raised out of that structure to become the head, the presence of that intervening supposedly structure-external subject is awkward at best. The analysis would seem to require copying of the *la-* relative marker at each phase of extraction in order to license the extraction of the head not only out of the verbal projection, but across any such further structure-external projection. Nevertheless what MUST be retained is not the record of that chain with appropriate feature-matching at the head of the chain by some copy of *la-*, but, rather, the copy which is the foot of any such chain, as part of the verbal complex. But this is contrary to other assumptions about movement, and so a stipulation that is problematic for Kayneian assumptions. This problem would then carry over to topic structures, and be replicated there. Another problem arises from the traditional analysis of *nge-* as a copula (see Cheng and Downing 2007 for a formal analysis along these lines), as it is not clear how such an account could be extended to the morphologically complex (double) locative forms as in (2.20) where a double sequence of copulas would appear to be required.The present account to the contrary will involve analyzing *nge-* as a specialized variant of a pronoun, so that the puzzling succession of supposed copulas is removed.

In what follows, we develop this account of siSwati clefts within a Dynamic Syntax perspective, presenting an analysis which reflects directly the dove-tailing of topic and long-distance dependency patterning. More specifically, we shall show that with the dynamic update perspective of Dynamic Syntax, the analogue of long-distance dependency which is the construction of an unfixed node can very simply be fed by a topic-structure building mechanism so that we can construct exactly the mixed effect, part topic-like, part focus-like, which cleft structures require.

2.2 Dynamic Syntax: a characterization of siSwati

Dynamic Syntax is radical in being a grammar formalism that reflects the step-wise way in which interpretation is built up during a parse sequence, with syntax defined as a sequence of parsing actions, inducing a process of tree growth across partial trees. The process of context-dependent growth of semantic representation is the basis of all syntactic explanation: a sentence is defined to be well-formed just in case there is at least one possible route through that process. As we shall see, it is the availability of there characteristically being more than one such route that is diagnostic of the grammar reflecting a set of processing strategies: in particular, such plurality does not correspond to syntactic or semantic ambiguity.

Individual steps, as in all languages, take the parser from a tree with just a single root-node decorated with $?Ty(t)$, indicating the requirement (the assigned goal) of establishing a formula of type t, finally deriving a binary branching tree with all nodes decorated with formula values having used all the words in order (see the TWO trees in (2.22)). So in the parsing of (2.21), we have the initial tree and final tree as in (2.22):

(2.21) *ba-fana ba- to- natsa tjwala*
2-boys 2SM FUT drink 14.alcohol
'The boys will drink alcohol'

(2.22) Parsing *Bafana ba-to-natsa tjwala*

Initial Step — Final step

$?Ty(t), \diamondsuit \quad \rightsquigarrow \quad Fo(Natsa'(\epsilon, x, Tjwala'(x))(\epsilon, y, Bafana')), Ty(t), \diamondsuit$

$Fo(\epsilon, y, Bafana'(y)), Ty(e) \qquad Fo(Natsa'(\epsilon, x, Tjwala'(x))) \; Ty(e \to t)$

$Fo(\epsilon, x, Tjwala'(x)), Ty(e) \qquad Fo(Natsa'), Ty(e \to (e \to t))$

The intermediate steps in deriving such trees are determined either by general computational actions, such as anticipating a subject-predicate structure, or lexical actions triggered by parsing lexical items. All such actions are procedures for making and decorating nodes in a tree, and moving around within a local subtree. Lexical specifications are defined as macros of such actions, hence are essentially procedural:

they do not simply annotate nodes with information about semantic content, but may equally contribute to any aspects of tree building, both to decorating the nodes and to constructing them. Quantification is expressed in terms of variable-binding term operators: quantified NPs like all other NPs are of type e as illustrated in (2.22), with quantifiers analyzed in the manner of arbitrary names posited in predicate-logic natural deduction proof systems. The primary quantifying term is the epsilon term, the internal structure of such terms containing an epsilon binder, ϵ, a variable, and a restrictor: e.g. $\epsilon, x, Bafana'(x)$. Since in most Bantu languages, including siSwati, and indeed in many other languages, nouns are determinerless, they are taken to project full specification of such terms, the structure projected by nouns being a tree of which the quantifying term is the topnode, dominating a subtree decorated with a binder, a variable, and a restrictor specification (see Kempson et al. 2001).[6] Scope constraints are incrementally collected either on a linear order basis or as lexically stipulated, and lead to evaluation rules once the propositional formula is constructed to determine the constructed terms' full restrictor specification.

Languages vary in the balance between lexical and general computational actions. In English, for example (see Cann et al. 2005: chapter 2), verbs project only structure internal to a predicate-requiring node. Verbs in pro-drop languages, on the other hand, project full propositional structure. As Marten and Kempson (2002) have argued (see also Cann et al. 2005), in Bantu languages, it is the tense marker which induces the subject node and predicate, these largely being diachronically bleached auxiliary verbs,[7] the subject and object markers which provide place-holding metavariables internal to the local propositional structure, and the verb, as in English, which induces the predicate-internal structure:

[6]We do not attempt to address in any detail either the concept of plurality or mass. More detailed specification would need to invoke a group-denoting predicate and some specification to determine mass-denoting predicates.

[7]In this paper we retain the simple analysis of tense as an annotation of a propositional-type node, leaving the investigation of a higher event argument as proposed by Cann (this volume) for further research.

(2.23) *to* 'future'

IF	$?Ty(t)$		
THEN	IF	$\langle\downarrow\rangle\top$	Initial Occurrence Constraint
	THEN	Abort	
	ELSE	$\mathtt{put}(FUTURE)$;	Tense Specification
		$\mathtt{make}(\langle\downarrow_0\rangle); \mathtt{go}(\langle\downarrow_0\rangle)$;	Building the Subject Node
		$\mathtt{put}(?Ty(e)); \mathtt{go}(\langle\uparrow_0\rangle)$	
		$\mathtt{make}(\langle\downarrow_1\rangle); \mathtt{go}(\langle\downarrow_1\rangle)$;	Building the Predicate Node
		$\mathtt{put}(?Ty(e \rightarrow t))$	
ELSE	Abort		

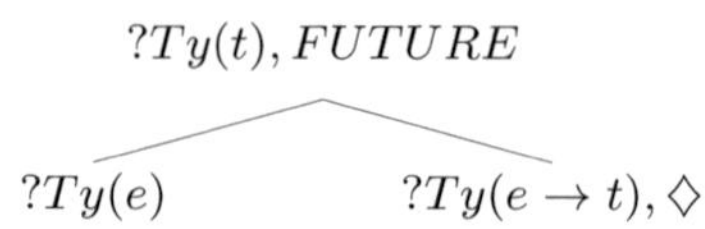

As the actions given in the lexical specification of *to-* indicate, the procedural instructions associated with *to-* induce the building of the sub-tree that hosts the $FUTURE$ specification and also the skeletal structure anticipating a subject and predicate node. The condition on such actions of $\langle\downarrow\rangle\top$ inducing an abort action is the guarantee that, for the update actions induced by *to-* to take place, there must not be any fixed node already present in that structure (if there is any such fixed node, the action sequence will abort). This constraint is satisfied despite the presence of either a lexical subject or a subject-marking prefix. This is because, as we shall see, these do not decorate a fixed node in the tree at this stage in the parsing construction process. Rather, the nodes they decorate are nodes whose position in the tree is not yet fixed (see section 2.2.1). Moreover, this condition on *to-* is critical to determining that the tense specification precedes, in particular, any object-marker, as this occurs only when, contrarily, there is already present a fixed node, namely the subject and predicate-requiring nodes. Hence the accompanying specification of 'initial occurrence constraint'.[8]

(2.24) *natsa* 'drink'

IF	$?Ty(e \rightarrow t)$	
THEN	$\mathtt{make}(\langle\downarrow_1\rangle); \mathtt{go}(\langle\downarrow_1\rangle)$;	
	$\mathtt{put}(Fo(\text{Natsa'}), Ty(e \rightarrow (e \rightarrow t)), [\downarrow]\bot)$	Main Functor
	$\mathtt{go}(\langle\uparrow_1\rangle)$;	
	$\mathtt{make}(\langle\downarrow_0\rangle); \mathtt{go}(\langle\downarrow_0\rangle)$;	
	$\mathtt{put}(?Ty(e))$	Object Requirement
ELSE	Abort	

[8]This specification is somewhat simplified, since to ensure that it occurs only following some subject marker involves making it sensitive to the relatively weak tree-node position which that decorates. See Cann et al. (2001: 302-05) for detailed specification.

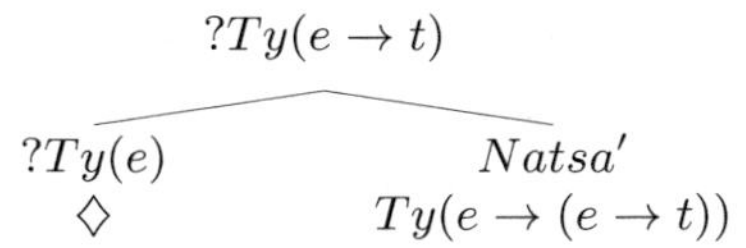

The effect of the verbal complex together is, as in other languages, a projection of full propositional structure (see (2.25)).

(2.25) Result of running lexical actions of *ba-to-bu-natsa*

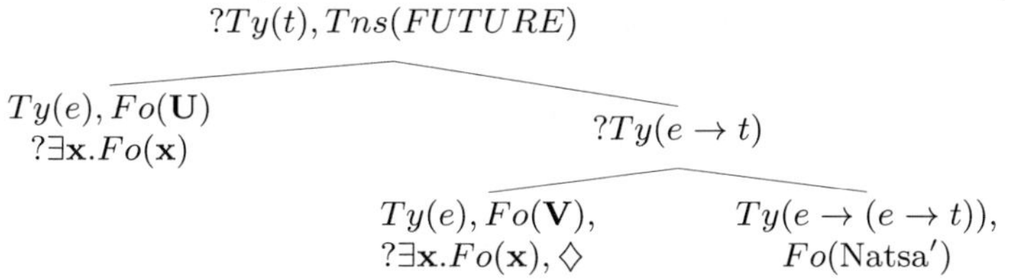

Notice how this tree is the result of composing the two partial trees provided by the tense marker and verb specifications (more strictly extending that provided by the tense marker with that provided by the verb), with the two agreement devices, *ba-* and *bu-* ensuring that there are subject and object argument nodes that are decorated with place-holding metavariables, as anaphoric devices. Thus in parsing a transitive verb complex like *ba-to-bu-natsa* 'they will drink it', a tree structure is projected that expresses the fact that the predicate associated with *natsa* takes two semantic arguments, and these are provided with concept-placeholders, meta-variables **U**, **V**, that stand for some value to be assigned from the context, exactly as though there were separable pronouns in the sequence.[9] This reflects the DS commitment to articulating concepts of underspecification and update for both content and structure. Both pronouns and verb specifications project partial specifications of content through such metavariables, and these have to be replaced as part of the process of constructing an interpretation. This substitution process is directly reflected in the system with a pragmatic process of substitution which enriches some lexically provided metavariable with a term that has already been established in context, which feeds into later structure-building processes.

---

[9] We ignore here the contribution of the class information of the subject and object markers, which can be modelled as presuppositions on their interpretation (see Cann et al. 2005). The difference between the subject and object agreement markers, where the former is more agreement-like than the latter, can be expressed by the distinction between whether or not the decoration of the node in question has an associated terminal-node restriction in the manner of full lexical items. This is the decoration $[\downarrow]\bot$ included in the specification of *natsa*. We ignore these details here though they are critical to determining the supposedly less than full pronominal status of the subject marker: see Cann et al. (2005).

2.2.1 Structural underspecification at the left periphery

This concept of underspecification plus update, being central to the philosophical underpinnings of the Dynamic Syntax framework, extends well beyond the recognition of anaphora as a content-based form of underspecification, in particular to structural forms of underspecification. Discontinuity effects are explained in such terms, with license to construct structural relations that are relatively weak, dominance relations that only subsequently get updated in association with a point at which the initial early partial specification can be fully determined. This includes long-distance dependency effects which are defined as involving the construction of a node in some newly initiated logical structure to be developed downwards from a top type-*t*-requiring node (note that there is no cross-clausal tense matching in these cases – they are fully independent of each other):

(2.26) *babe,* *ema-phoyisa* *a-* *cabanga* *kutsi* *u-* *ta-*
father, 6-police 6SM think that 1SM FUT
tsenga *i-moto.*
buy 9-car
'Father, the police think will buy the car.'

The node decorated by *babe* in (2.26) is, when initially processed, specified only as dominated by the root node, its position within the unfolding tree being otherwise unfixed at this point in the construal process. The point at which this relation is identified comes very considerably later in the interpretation process, in (2.26) when the verb *tsenga* is parsed.[10]

This parallelism with anaphora is further pursued by distinguishing three different forms of structural underspecification in terms of locality restrictions on the domain within which their update must be provided. There is the dominate relation that has to be updated within an individual structure but not necessarily locally (the general case already introduced). There is in addition a more locally restricted dominate relation which has to be updated within an essentially local minimal propositional structure, associated with nodes which are introduced as 'locally unfixed' (see Kiaer 2007, this volume). And, at the other extreme, a weakest form of dominate is defined, which allows update even

[10]There are obvious formal similarities between the DS system and all formal parsing systems which define such underspecified tree relations (Marcus 1980 and many others since, including recently for Japanese, Miyamoto 2002); but all these systems assume any such mechanism constitutes only a parsing mechanism to be defined with reference to some independent core grammar of the language, which has no such device.

across a sequence of trees. In free word order languages with very rich case morphology, such locally unfixed nodes may be introduced as a general tree-growth mechanism;[11] but in siSwati it is only the subject and object markers which induce such locally unfixed nodes, where they play an important role in creating local pairings between full NP expressions and the argument node of the predicate whose thematic role they are construed as satisfying. For example in the parsing of (2.27), the first NP expression *bafana* can be taken to decorate an unfixed node:[12]

(2.27) *Ba-fana ba- to- bu- natsa*
2-boys 2SM FUT 14OM drink
'The boys will drink it.'

(2.28)
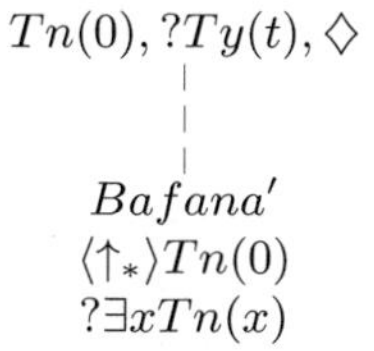

The subject marker *ba-* then both introduces and decorates a locally unfixed node from the local type-t-requiring node with which the first introduced node can merge, thereby providing immediate further restriction on construal of that initial expression:

(2.29)
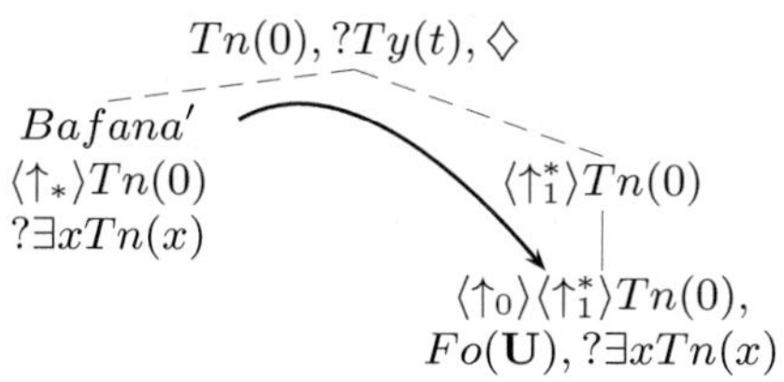

This in its turn can be unified with structure provided by the immediately subsequent tense marker, which induces a binary-branching structure, yielding early identification of the initial expression as subject before the verb is processed:

[11] See Cann et al. (2005) for application of this to the modelling of Japanese.

[12] In siSwati, like in many other languages, noun phrases do not need a determiner, and definiteness is characteristically associated with initial or near-initial position (see Cann and Kempson 2008 for discussion of this with respect to Latin). Since we are not exploring detailed specifications of quantification in this paper, we leave this here, presenting the constructed terms $\epsilon, x, Bafana'(x)$ as though a simple name $Bafana'$. See Bouzouita (2008a, 2008b) for discussion of how the pragmatic restriction of minimising processing costs plays a role in determining this broad association of definite construal with left-edge placement and its significance in diachronic explanations.

(2.30)

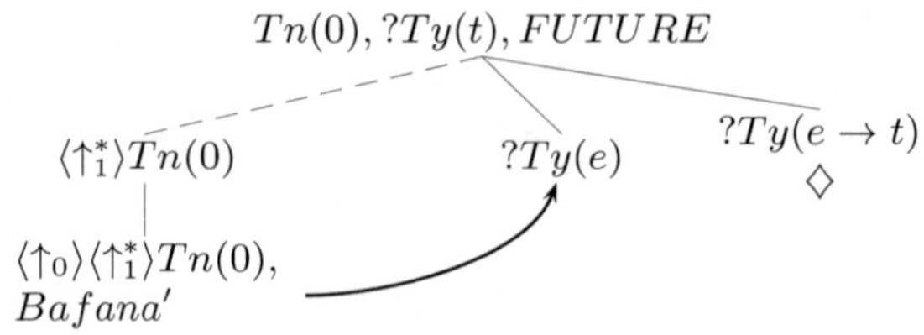

The object marker *bu-* then involves building a node from the predicate-requiring node, and this too is locally unfixed. This imposes the restriction of there being only one object marker, even with ditransitives, a characteristic of many Bantu languages, and the precise argument relation is identifiable only upon parsing the verb.[13] Thus the sequence of actions involved in parsing a basic string involves building up local argument nodes and unifying them with the template provided by tense marker and verb in combination, relative to general constraints on tree growth. So in siSwati, as in other Bantu languages, the projection of a minimal propositional structure involves a complex interplay between the different prefixes and the verb: the overall outcome is, as in all other languages, a fully decorated binary-branching propositional structure.

2.2.2 Building paired trees: topic structures as linked trees

Using solely such structural update mechanisms to provide the basis for subject construal is by no means the only way to construct and decorate a subject node; indeed as we shall see it is arguably a relatively marked strategy. Within the DS framework, paired trees can be built, so-called linked trees, subject to a restriction that they are anaphorically linked but otherwise independent. Cann et al. (2005) argue that both relative clause construal and Hanging Topic Left Dislocation construal make use

[13] The system itself imposes the restriction that there be only one unfixed node of a type at a time, an unfixed node and a locally unfixed node able to co-occur only because these have modally distinct tree-node characterizations. This constraint is a consequence of the tree logic underpinning the system (Blackburn and Meyer-Viol 1994). Formally, nothing prevents the construction of more than one unfixed node, but all nodes in a tree are identified by their relation to other nodes in a tree. If, then, more than one node is constructed from a dominating node characterized only as dominated by that node, these will collapse to a single node yielding inconsistent decorations, and the whole tree will be debarred. Languages which appear not to be sensitive to such a restriction, such as for example the Tanzanian Bantu language Sambaa (Riedel 2009), allowing more than one object-marker, violating Person-Case Constraint restrictions, etc, may be analyzed in terms of one of the relations in question involving a transition to an independent paired tree, hence not violating the restriction (see section 2.3; Riedel 2009; Chatzikyriakidis and Kempson 2010 and Cann, Kempson and Marten, forthcoming for an analysis of both Romance and Bantu patterns in terms of sensitivity to this constraint and possible exceptions to it through emergent homonymy). See also McCormack (2008).

of this device, both involving the construction of a structural context for the processing of the subsequent string. In the case of head-initial relatives, it is the partial structure containing its head which constitutes such a context: in the case of HTLD, the context is induced from the structure constructed solely for decoration by the expression identified as the "topic". In both types of case, the result of creating these contexts is to identify a particular term which is to serve as the constraint on the development of the immediately following emergent linked structure that it contain a second copy of this term.

We now illustrate these two processes in detail as a prelude to addressing the cleft puzzles. Unlike English, where the relative pronoun is an encoded anaphoric device inducing a copy from the head directly within the emergent linked structure, in siSwati the effect of the relative marker is weaker. The relative marker, which occurs as the first element in the verbal complex, *la-*, may induce a LINK transition; indeed it imposes a requirement for there to be an appropriate copy of the formula from the head from which the transition is defined, but it does not itself secure that copy (see Cann et al. 2005: chapter 4). Rather, it is the object and subject markers which play this role, and both subject and object agreement is essential in relative clauses in siSwati, as in many other Bantu languages:

(2.31) *ba-fana* *la-* *be-* *ba-* *natsa* *tjwala* *ba-dzakiwe*
2-boys REL PAST 2SM drink 14.alcohol 2SM-drunk
'The boys who drank alcohol are drunk.'

(2.32) *tjwala* *la-* *ba-* *to-* *bu-* *natsa* *ba-fana* ...
14.alcohol REL- 2SM FUT 14OM drink 2-boys ...
'The alcohol which the boys will drink ...'

All that *la-* provides is information that the structure to which its processing contributes must be such a linked structure. This is a pattern familiar from languages in which resumptive pronouns are obligatory. There is an immediate advantage to this analysis. Precisely because *la* doesn't itself provide either the transition onto an emergent linked tree or the required copy, its very weak specification can be compatible with an occurrence of the subject before it in the relative clause sequence:

(2.33) *tjwala* *ba-fana* *la-* *ba-* *to-* *bu-* *natsa* ...
14.alcohol 2-boys REL 2SM FUT 14OM drink ...
'The alcohol which the boys will drink ...'

(2.34) $?Ty(t)$

$Tjwala', Ty(e)$

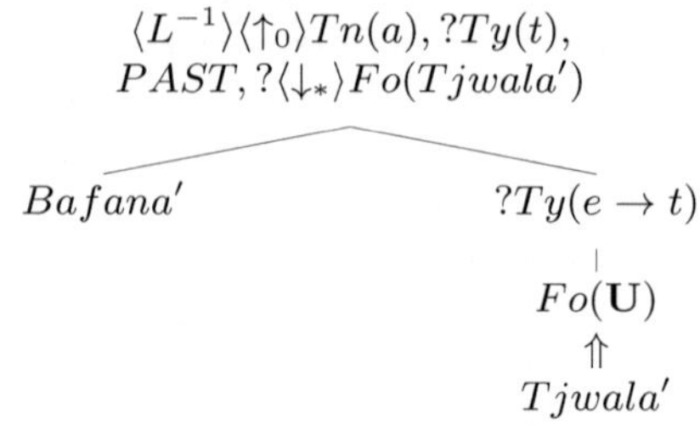

All that *la-* provides is the information that the structure to which its processing contributes MUST be such a linked structure.[14] Notice how in this case, *bafana* must have been taken as decorating an unfixed node following the steps set out above in order to become identified as subject prior to the processing of the object marker. The object marker then, which does not distinguish between indirect and direct object relation projects an underspecified tree relation which is resolved in the presence of the verb

In locative relatives, this pattern of relative-clause marking repeats itself, though with a different form of the resumptive marker (as a demonstrative). We analyse the first demonstrative as imposing a requirement for a copy, and the second, *khona*, as providing the requisite copy, hence its obligatory nature. Furthermore, the subject expression, may, as in object relatives, intervene between the head and the verbal complex which contains the relative marker:

(2.35) *e-ndl-ini* *la(-pho)* *ba-fana* *ba-* *lala*
LOC-house-LOC REL-LOC 2-boys 2SM sleep
khona *ku-* *khiyiwe*
DEM.LOC DSM locked
'The house where the boys sleep there is locked'

Notice that this account is compatible with the analysis of the agreement markers as inducing a locally unfixed node and updating it. In both (2.31) and (2.32) the subject and object agreement markers, despite the unfixed nature of the node they decorate, nevertheless serve to secure the occurrence of the formula in question in the emergent linked tree.

As argued in detail in Cann et al. (2005), this account immediately carries over to simple topic constructions if we assign initial topic constructions the same linked structural configuration, as the obligatory subject, object and locative marking in the main clause sequence will

---

[14]This account will straightforwardly extend to explain the *la-* marking on adjectives.

then be expected:[15]

(2.36)

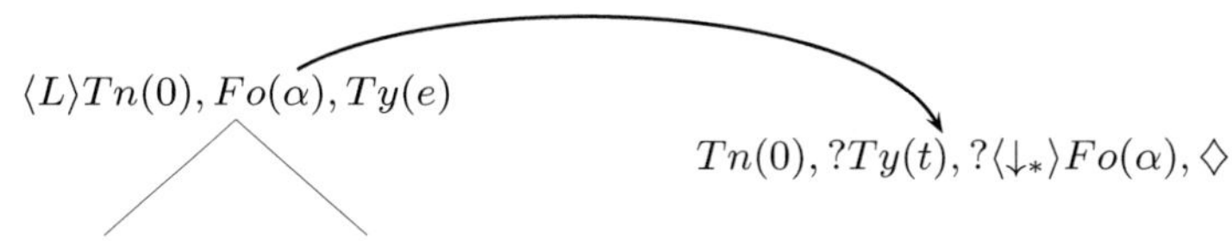

(2.37)	*ba-fana*	*ba-*	*to-*	*natsa*	*tjwala*
	2-boys	2SM	FUT	drink	14.alcohol

'The boys, they will drink alcohol'

(2.38)	*tjwala*	*ba-fana*	*ba-*	*to-*	*bu-*	*natsa*
	14.alcohol	2-boys	2SM	FUT	14OM	drink

'The alcohol the boys will drink it'

(2.39)	*itolo*	*ba-fana*	*ba-*	*nats*	*-e*	*tjwala*	*khona*
	yesterday	2-boys	2SM	drink	PAST	14.alcohol	17.DEM

'Yesterday the boys drank alcohol then'

These strings are the direct analogue of Hanging Topic Left Dislocation postulated for the Romance languages. This transition inducing a linked structure relative to some context constructed as the very first step in the utterance interpretation process, is available for all arguments, so use of this sequence of actions applies equally to subject expressions. Indeed it provides the means of reflecting a canonical aspect of subject construal, that they constitute the point of departure for the assertion that follows. Suppose we take this point-of-departure aspect of subject construal as a reflection of the way in which a structure containing just the node decorated by the subject expression can be secured prior to the introduction of a LINK transition onto a type-t-requiring node, itself to be developed by the processing of the main clause sequence. The result is that we have a direct reflection of the dual role of subject expressions as both an argument in some local structure and as having an identifiable role – that of loosely "topic" – in the dynamics of how information is progressively built up. Following upon the steps of introducing this isolated term as decorating a quasi-independent linked structure, the constraint which that term then imposes on subsequent development will be satisfied as locally as possible by identifying the subject-marker's metavariable with it, hence the unmarked status of such a sequence of actions. In siSwati as a prodrop language, in particular, with its subject agreement marker being an anaphoric device projecting a place-holder sufficient for context-provided identification, we might thus expect this sequence of steps to

[15]We specify here the locality restriction on the new type-t-requiring node as imposing the requirement of a copy within an individual tree for simplicity.

constitute the canonical procedure for construing subject expressions, with the initially constructed tree remaining identifiable as the extraneous node throughout the subsequent tree construction process, hence constituting its structurally identifiable "topic".

2.2.3 Right-periphery effects on construal in siSwati

Given that the availability of building up linked structures and unfixed nodes are tree-growth concepts, they are defined over partial trees rather than strings, and accordingly are not restricted by any string-defined position. We therefore expect similar strategies to be available as construction processes for establishing closing stages of building up propositional structure, where they may give rise to somewhat different communicative effects in virtue of this late positioning. On the one hand, for example, we expect the option of projecting a linked structure in the final stages of the interpretation of some propositional type, giving rise to a backgrounding effect, again without occurrence of *ku-* (see Cann et al. 2005 for detailed arguments):

(2.40)	*ba-*	*to-*	*natsa*	*tjwala*	*ba-fana*
	2SM	FUT	drink	14.alcohol	2-boys

'They drink alcohol, the boys'

(2.41)

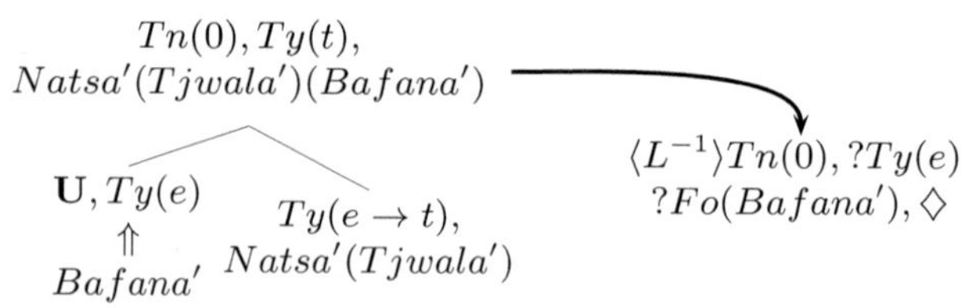

All that this requires is the assumption that the concept of structures with shared terms is not intrinsically directional, so we expect a transition between propositional structure and individual term to be available following the construction of a propositional structure, as well as before. However, there is an asymmetry in the construal of such end-placed NPs: the pronominal marking provided by the subject prefix, given incrementality in the way interpretation is built up has to be identifiable as part of the completion of the first tree, i.e. from the context; and the building of the transition onto the linked structure then imposes a requirement on the construal of the full NP that IT be construed as sharing whatever interpretation is already asssigned to the metavariable projected from the pronominal affix. Hence the backgrounding effect (see Cann et al. 2005, Kempson et al. 2006, for details). We also expect this type of structure to be constructable by carrying over a requirement of identity of any argument term in that first structure, hence licensing the doubling (and backgrounding) effects achieved with object pronominal agreement marking:

(2.42)

ba-	*to-*	*bu-*	*natsa*	*tjwala*
2SM	FUT	14OM	drink	14.alcohol

'They will drink it, the alcohol'

On the other hand, we also expect the building of an unfixed node at the right periphery, that is postverbally, even given that the parsing of the verb plus subject agreement has provided a provisional value for the subject node. As in the building of linked structures, there is asymmetry between early and late application of *Adjunction, but of a rather different sort. At any such late stage in the parsing of a clausal string the process will be used to provide some add-on to what is already a full skeletal propositional structure as induced by the tense-marker verb pair, and accordingly the only possible application will be the direct construction of an unfixed node from a node of the same type already provided in the parse process, such as an argument (see Cann et al. 2005 where this is defined as a discrete process: Late*Adjunction). This local pairing of nodes of the same type is in fact the configuration that arises at the point in processing a left periphery structure at which unification of the unfixed node and its point of update is about to take place, so is a subvariant of *Adjunction. The process is defined to apply to any node decorated with a metavariable, licensing the introduction of an unfixed node of the same type, which with the addition of a formula would then, without any passing down of any unfixed node through the tree, be able to unify directly with the previously formula-incomplete node to provide it with the required value (see the requirement $?\exists x.Fo(x)$ at the fixed subject node in (2.43)). This is characteristic of extraposition structures for the development of expletive forms, but also postposed subject expressions in which *Adjunction applies in the late stages after the predicate has been completed and in preparation for compiling the top propositional node. Indeed, this step is necessary in such derivations as without it, with an outstanding requirement at the subject node, no such propositional formula will be derivable:

(2.40)

ba-	*to-*	*natsa*	*tjwala*	*ba-fana*
2SM	FUT	drink	14.alcohol	2-boys

'They drink alcohol, boys'

(2.43) Parsing *ba-to-natsa tjwala bafana*

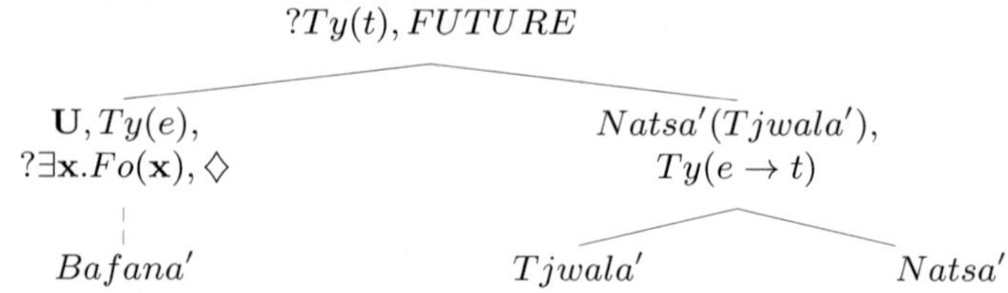

To spell this out more with respect to (2.40), the parsing of the subject marker *ba-*, which induces a metavariable at a locally unfixed node, in conjunction with *to-*, which induces a fixed logical-subject node, duly allows a unification step that yields a fixed logical-subject node decorated with that metavariable prior to the parsing of the verb. And once BOTH the verb and the object are parsed, the construction of a predicate formula can be completed. At this relatively late stage in the derivation, the pointer is then licensed to return to the subject node, allowing that to be further developed by application of LATE*ADJUNCTION, finally yielding a fixed subject value, and from that the value of the propositional formula. There are interpretational effects associated with delaying the parse of the subject in this way; and this order is often preferred to buttress a nonreferential interpretation of an indefinite, for reasons of scope choice (see Kempson and Meyer-Viol 2004 for discussion of scope effects in connection with such delayed subject construal).[16]

There is a consequence to this accumulation of strategies for building both unfixed nodes and introducing independent but anaphorically linked structures, which is that strings may, and characteristically will, be associated with more than one sequence of possible transitions. Thus subject expressions at both left and right peripheries will be able to be analyzed as either decorating a linked structure, or an unfixed node

[16]Such scope inversion effects are achieved because the full presentation of structure from the VP sequence will thus have been made available prior to defining the scope dependency for the the late-placed subject. This provides a possible basis for explaining the restriction on siSwati *wh* expressions, which cannot occur initially at all, with object *wh* terms occurring either in a cleft structure or in situ, and with subject *wh* terms having to occur in cleft structures or post-verbally with expletive (non-agreeing) subject marking. Without providing a full analysis of this, we propose that this is a reflex of strict incrementality, with both anaphoric expressions and scope-dependency effects having to be established incrementally. If, then, we analyse *wh* terms as weak obligatorily locally dependent epsilon terms (see Kempson et al. 2001 for the account of indefinites as invariably obligatorily dependent terms with choice of dependency having to be made in like manner to choices of pronoun construal), their position will have to be that in which the context provides a basis on which to define that dependency, hence after either a verb or in combination with a copula, either of which would provide the tense marking relative to which scope dependency for the *wh* term could be defined.

introduced late on in the derivation. This is the bonus provided by a processing-reflecting architecture, reflecting, as expected, the flexibility in parsing/production judgements that enables successful interaction between participants in real life processing without necessity of absolute success by either in judging the other party's intentions (see Ferreira and Dell 2000).[17] This departure from the more orthodox methodologies in which there is commitment to one-to-one correspondence between string-interpretation pairs will have consequences in our analysis of the range of cleft structures in siSwati.

2.3 SiSwati clefts

All of what has been set out so far is an initial analysis of siSwati based on analyses independently argued for within DS; and we now have everything in place to provide the analysis of siSwati clefts. The intuition we wish to capture is that siSwati clefts display a range of strategies each of which is for the same end result, the building of a pair of linked structures, of which the "clefted" element is taken to decorate a structure of topnode type e, and the relative-clause sequence decorates a propositional structure linked to that node. This structure is built by a range of strategies of varying degrees of explicitness about the structure they induce. At one extreme, a linked structure can be projected with no specific morphological trigger to induce it: these are the regular so-called hanging topic structures (as in (2.44) below). At the other extreme, there may be a complex sequence of expressions whose actions induce a full anticipation of the structure to be built prior to the subsequent fleshing out of that initially ghosted structure by the subsequent processing of the words. In between are a range of intermediate cases in which more encoded indication of the process of building up such paired structures is provided than is available from the minimal specification. The pattern preserved in ALL these available strategies, is the pairing of a structure that is decorated with a type e term and a propositional structure that is linked to it that, by definition, has somewhere within it that very same type e term. There is no invocation of any copula between the clefted expression and the relative-like sequence; there is no reduction of cleft structures to any form of relative: it is simply that there is a mechanism for building paired structures which is put to use in subtly different ways within relative, cleft, and topic structures. What the language displays, rather, is an array of paired structures,

[17] See Bouzouita (2008a, 2008b), who argues that constraints on processing and their routinization into default heuristics provide a natural basis for syntactic change.

with a range of increasingly complex ways of anticipating the structural processes needed to build up the final result, but in which each individual step is independently available in the mechanisms of tree growth which natural language grammars make available.

The most simple of these is not a so-called cleft structure, but the hanging topic left-dislocation structure that we have already sketched (with subject either before or after the verb):

(2.44) *tjwala* *ba-fana* *ba-* *to-* *bu-* *natsa*
14.alcohol 2-boys 2SM FUT 14OM drink
'The alcohol, the boys will drink it'

(2.45) *tjwala* *ba-* *to-* *bu-* *natsa* *ba-fana*
14.alcohol 2SM FUT 14OM drink 2-boys
'The alcohol, they will drink it the boys'

The proposition-inducing sequence and the expression made to be peripheral are predicted to be able to occur in either order, across a pair of linked structures, with a right-placed term providing a backgrounding effect (see Cann et al. 2005: chapter 5):

(2.46) *ba-* *to-* *bu-* *natsa* *ba-fana* *tjwala*
2SM FUT 14OM drink 2-boys 14.alcohol
'They will drink it, the boys, alcohol'

The construction of a linked structure at either left or right periphery can of course combine with other actions. In particular, in a case such as (2.46) the post-posed subject which precedes the final placed object-doubled *tjwala* would be taken to decorate the subject node via a step of Late*Adjunction. The setting up of linked structures as a basis for interpretation can be made more explicit by the use of the *la* particle which explicitly encodes the presence of such a linked structure, again in either order (and again with the subject before or after the verb):[18]

(2.47) *tjwala* *la-* *ba-* *to-* *bu-* *natsa* *ba-fana*
14.alcohol REL 2SM FUT 14OM drink 2-boys
'It is the alcohol, which they will drink it the boys'

(2.48) *la-* *ba-* *to-* *bu-* *natsa* *ba-fana* *tjwala*
REL 2SM FUT 14OM drink 2-boys 14.alcohol
'It is the alcohol that they will drink it the boys'

(2.49) *ba-fana* *la-* *ba-* *to-* *bu-* *natsa* *tjwala*
2-boys REL 2SM FUT 14OM drink 14.alcohol
'It is the alcohol that the boys they will drink it'

[18]The occurrence of the subject before the verb is strongly dispreferred, as in (2.49), since this order fails to provide any means of disambiguation between cleft and relative construal until very late on in the parse.

This strategy may however be dovetailed with an instruction specifically to introduce some new term, by building at that initially introduced type *e* structure, an unfixed node to merge with it – this is the function of *nge-*. *Nge-* is defined, as we shall see, to co-occur with some linked structure, and to introduce into it some term new to the tree under construction (via the construction of an unfixed node). Still with no imposition of specific ordering, the pairing of structures can be in either order:

(2.50)	*nge-*	*ba-fana*	*la-*	*ba-*	*to-*	*natsa*	*tjwala*
	NGE	2-boys	REL	2SM	FUT	drink	14.alcohol

'It is the boys, who they will drink alcohol'

(2.51)	*la-*	*ba-*	*to-*	*natsa*	*tjwala*	*nge-*	*ba-fana*
	REL	2SM	FUT	drink	14.alcohol	NGE	2-boys

Note that here we are not following the English pattern of assuming that anything informally labelled as a "cleft" must have a copula at some overt level even though it is often morphologically null. To the contrary, on this analysis, the *nge-la-* pairing is a codification of the linked structure, without assuming that the *nge*-marked term itself induces a propositional structure – in short, *nge-* is not analyzed as a copula. Furthermore, since the lexical specifications provided by *nge-* are all independently freely available as transitions (the building of a linked structure, the construction of an unfixed node), there is nothing problematic about the morphologically explicit form being restricted to a subset of classes (a generalization notably due to the fact that lexical and general actions in Dynamic Syntax are formally identical). Finally, the entire sequence of actions – the introducing of the independent node across a LINK transition, the introducing of the appropriate tense marking, and the introducing of a subject-predicate structure, may ALL be explicitly set up before any particular conceptual content is introduced; and so we get the complex cleft structures in which the frame to be built up is introduced first, and the particular propositional structure, only subsequently:

(2.20) *ku-* *to-* *ba* *nge-* *ba-fana* *la-* *ba-* *to-* *natsa*
DSM FUT COP NGE 2-boys REL 2SM FUT drink
tjwala
14.alcohol
'It will be the boys who will drink alcohol'

So, even here, we are not assuming in the end result that there is a bi-propositional structure. Rather, the sketch provided by the *ku-to-ba nge-X* sequence provides a single skeletal structure; and the subsequent string develops THAT structure. The end result is a predicate-argument structure as simple as a bare verb plus two argument NPs: but the morphological sequencing makes explicit the intermediate processes that have to be gone through to achieve that result. Furthermore, the asymmetry in these cases with NO inversion potential for the locative-expletive marked sequences is expected (see section (1.1) and the discussion of example (2.6)): the duplication of a bleached locative is by analysis an early setting out of a template of anticipated structure, a multiplication that would be entirely unexpected as a superimposition on an already completed structure.

In essence, the sketch just summarized gives the entire analysis: all types of clefts are seen as a topic plus predication structure, with the contrastiveness taken to be characteristic of clefts being brought out by the construction of a novel term within that structure. So the analysis is neither a reduction of the cleft structure to a relative clause "underlyingly"; nor a reduction to a simple long-distance dependency structure; nor, even, a reduction to a base-generation topic-style analysis. Indeed, these structures do not have to be seen as essentially discrete. The distinguishing property of the DS system which enables it to bring together these various strategies is its dynamic nature, a system for inducing and developing partial structural specifications. Its very design leads one to expect feeding relationships between one form of process and another. Thus, as we shall now see, the process of building a linked topic structure is able to feed into the mechanism for constructing some underspecified node, which in its turn feeds into the mechanism for reflecting the construction of a linked structure (a mechanism which topic and relative clause sequences both make use of). Because the syntactic devices are structure-inducing mechanisms rather than constructions in their own right, no inconsistency results. To the contrary, their interaction provides a natural means of reflecting the fine-grained variation which the language allows.

2.3.1 The simple *la*-marked cleft

The analysis of the simple cleft involving just marking with the relative prefix *la*-, lacking even the particle *nge*- follows directly from the analyses already provided for left and right periphery effects. This cleft is no more than the use of the particle *la*- to make the transition required overt; and accordingly *la*- is defined as providing such a transition. Since, however, the relative sequence may precede the head in such cleft constructions, the definition of actions for *la*- needs to allow for the possibility of a relatively weak update, that is, simply to impose the requirement of such a LINK transition to a type-t-requiring node:[19]

$$?\exists x(\langle L^{-1}\rangle Fo(x) \wedge \downarrow_{*} Fo(x))$$

Such a requirement will have the effect of ensuring that once the processing of *la*- is carried out, at some possibly later stage, a LINK transition must be constructed such that the structure currently under construction is appropriately linked to it (with the two structures suitably sharing a term). This is what structures such as (2.52) provide evidence of:

(2.52)	*la-*	*ba-*	*to-*	*natsa*	*tjwala*	*ba-fana*
	REL	2SM	FUT	drink	14.alcohol	2-boys

‘They will drink alcohol, the boys’

In the use of such postposed topic constructions, despite the fact that this specification is extremely weak, it is not non-trivial, since it ensures that there must be such a transition once *la*- is parsed. But this analysis has the bonus of applying without more ado to cases where the requirement specific to the processing of *la*- is already met. These are the topic-initial cases where, with the building of a LINK transition being a free option, the transition may already have been implemented as in (2.50). However, importantly, the presumption of both the construction of a linked structure decorated by that initial NP, and, back along that LINK relation, the SUBSEQUENT construction of an unfixed node within the newly emergent primary structure also provides a basis for parsing the subject as in (2.16), all of these actions being taken even though there is no morphological confirmation of the need of such actions until the FOLLOWING *la*-:

(2.16)	*tjwala*	*ba-fana*	*la-*	*ba-*	*to-*	*bu-*	*natsa*
	14.alcohol	2-boys	REL	2SM	FUT	14OM-	drink

‘Alcohol, boys they will drink it’

[19]The use of $\downarrow_{*}$ allows the indicated relation to range over both fixed and unfixed nodes on the emergent tree (see Kempson et al. 2001).

As (2.16) illustrates, this sequence of actions must have already been constructed in order to provide the emergent sub-structure within which *bafana* can be identified as the subject of the predicate *-natsa* via taking it to decorate a locally unfixed node provided by the subject marker. So in all such cases, the update which *la-* provides will be no more than confirmation of the type of structure already under development.

Overall, what is needed is a characterization of *la-* which expresses the parallelism between relative structure and topic structure, but which nevertheless allows *la-* to play an extremely weak anticipatory role.[20] This we express as:

(2.53) *la*

IF	$Fo(\alpha), Ty(e)$		
THEN	$\texttt{make}(\langle L \rangle); \texttt{go}(\langle L \rangle);$		
	$\texttt{put}(?Ty(t), ?\langle \downarrow_* \rangle Fo(\alpha))$		
ELSE	IF	$?Ty(t),$	
	THEN	$\texttt{put}(?\exists x \langle \downarrow_* \rangle Fo(x) \wedge \langle L^{-1} \rangle Fo(x))$	
	ELSE	Abort	

The first subsequence of actions introduces the LINK relation as part of the actions associated with *la-*. The second subsequence merely ensures the presence of such a transition at some point in the derivation, equivalently for a relative clause, for a hanging-topic construction, and for cleft-structures in which the clefted expression is postposed, as in all these cases the structural relation will be independently defined. The lexical entry could be simplified to express solely the very weak requirement which the relative marker ensures, but we prefer the greater transparency of specifically defining its constructive role for those relative clauses where, with no intervening subject between head and *la-*, its presence can be taken itself to ensure the transition.

2.3.2 The simple *nge-* clefts

Now we can be more precise about what it is that *nge-* provides, bearing in mind that it is optional. We wish to capture the way in which *nge-* triggers the introduction of a novel item, novel in the sense of being constructed as part of the interpretation process, rather than essentially matching, or being picked out from, the context. What we have also to get right is the obligatoriness of some subsequent item after *nge-*. *Nge-* is not a demonstrative: it cannot occur on its own. Moreover the

[20]It is arguable that the same anticipatory role is the basis of headless relatives, but we leave this on one side here. See Kula and Marten this volume. There is also a quasi-demonstrative prefixed use of *la* which we ignore here.

item that follows it must be a full NP in its own right. We know this because of such as examples as:

(2.54)

ngu-	*lobu*	*tjwala,*	*ba-fana*	*la-*	*ba-*	*to-*	*bu-*
NGE	DEM14	14.alcohol	2-boys	Rel	2SM	FUT	14OM

natsa
drink

'It is this alcohol which the boys will drink'

Assuming an introduction of an unfixed node in exact mimicry of Late*Adjunction but defined as an action triggered lexically by *nge-* will yield exactly the result we need. So we define *nge-* as decorating a linked structure introduced by the general process of Link Adjunction, and then inducing the process which will ensure that a new term is constructed as update:

(2.55) Parsing *nge-*

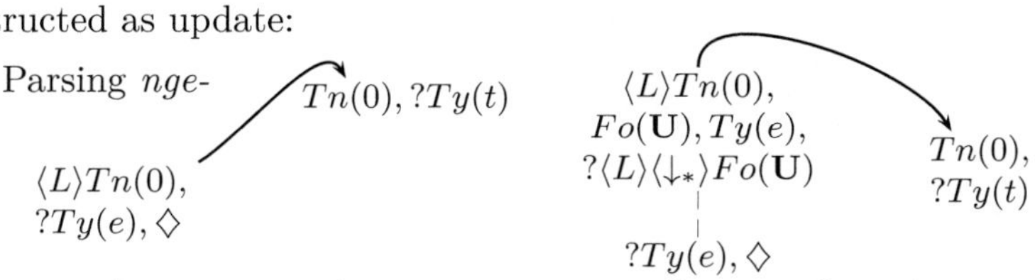

Input to parsing *nge-* Output of parsing *nge-*

(2.56) *nge*

IF	$?Ty(e)$	
THEN	IF	$\langle L\rangle Tn(0)$
	THEN	$\mathtt{put}(Fo(\mathbf{U}), Ty(e), ?\langle L\rangle\langle\downarrow_*\rangle Fo(\mathbf{U}))$
		$\mathtt{make}(\langle\downarrow_*\rangle); \mathtt{go}(\langle\downarrow_*\rangle)$
		$\mathtt{put}(?Ty(e))$
	ELSE	Abort
ELSE	Abort	

Note the $?Ty(e)$ requirement both on the node which *nge-* first decorates, and on the unfixed node which it induces. The first action of decorating the linked node with a metavariable expresses the anaphoric nature of *nge-*. Its expletive effect is then achieved by the building of an unfixed node which is itself decorated with the requirement $?Ty(e)$: it is this that forces the next word to be parsed rather than getting some value from context. This analysis also correctly anticipates that *nge-* does not itself project part of the resulting type e term to be provided: it merely imposes the requirement for actions given by the subsequent word(s) to satisfy it. In (2.54) these are provided by parsing the determiner + noun sequence *lobu tjwala.*[21] The locality restriction

[21]Given that *lobu* is a demonstrative anaphoric device, which in this framework would be analyzed as projecting a metavariable for subsequent update via

on the required second copy correctly restricts this to within the tree from which the linked structure is constructed, as is made clear by the long-distance dependency in the construal of:

(2.57) *nge-* *ba-ntfu* *si-sini* *le-* *si-* *tse* *ti-nja* *ti-*
NGE 2-people 7-friend REL 7SM say 8-dogs 8SM
ba- *coshile*
2OM chased
'It's people who the friend said the dogs chased'

Notice that the decoration of such a linked-structure node is perfectly possible without the presence of *nge-*: it is just that with *nge-* defined as a quasi-pronominal that induces an unfixed node, the presence of a following NP is ensured, thereby creating the same effect as if *nge-* were not present (through unification of the two type *e* nodes so constructed).

We get immediate confirmation of this analysis of *nge-* as inducing a decoration to a linked structure, from the relative ordering at the right periphery of a clefted expression and a postposed subject. In NON-cleft structures, if the subject is to be end-placed, it must be right at the end, and cannot be followed by some temporal adverbial:

(2.58) *tjwala* *la-* *ba-* *to-* *bu-* *natsa* *namuhla*
14.alcohol REL 2SM FUT 14OM drink today
ba-fana
2-boys
'The alcohol, the boys will drink it today'

(2.59) **tjwala* *la-* *ba-* *to-* *bu-* *natsa* *ba-fana*
14.alcohol REL 2SM FUT 14OM drink 2-boys
namuhla
today
'The alcohol, the boys will drink it today'

However in clefted structures in which the clefted expression follows the clausal sequence, the expression in question MUST be absolutely final, as it is the clefted expression which is decorating a quasi-independent linked structure. In such cases, the propositional structure is built first, with *la-* merely inducing the requirement of being a linked

LATE*ADJUNCTION, we would expect that the distinct node constructed in the parsing of *nge-* could itself be decorated with a metavariable and be subject to a similar structural process with later update, i.e. treating *lobu* uniformly as a demonstrative pronoun rather than also a determiner. It is also surely not a coincidence that *la* as a determiner and *la* as a relative pronoun are homophones. We leave all such further variants for future research.

tree, the LINK transition confirming this requirement is then built only once this structure is complete, with the "clefted" element then having to provide a copy of some priorly identified term within that propositional structure. Accordingly, a clefted object expression cannot be followed by the subject:

(2.60)

**la-*	*ba-*	*to-*	*bu-*	*natsa*	*tjwala*	*ba-fana*
REL	2SM	FUT	14OM	drink	14.alcohol	2-boys

'They will drink it the alcohol, the boys'

This distribution enforcing the end-placement of any postposed clefted (and possibly *nge*-marked) expression is however an immediate consequence of the linked-structure analysis, in which the clefted expression is taken to decorate a structurally independent tree, whether at the left or right periphery. Indeed, as we would expect, sequences of arbitrary length and complexity can precede the clefted expression:

(2.61)

le-	*ngi-*	*m-*	*nike*	*kudla*	*nge-*	*phinadzenga-*
REL	1SG.SM	1OM	gave	food	1SG.SM	again

m-	*lelisa*	*ngu-*	*um-fana*
1OM	make-sleep	NGE	1-boy

'It's the boy that I gave him food and again (and) made him sleep'

Nevertheless, we also predict that the *nge*-marked expression might occur apparently on its own, either in answer to a question or, even, in a discourse scenario where the predicate is recoverable directly from the situation:[22]

(2.62)

ngu-	*bani*	*lu-*	*to-*	*natsa*	*emanti?*	*Ngu-*	*Jabulani*
NGE	who	REL	FUT	drink	water?	NGE	Jabulani

'Who is drinking water? Jabulani is'

(2.63)

ngu-	*Jabulani*
NGE	Jabulani

e.g. 'It's Jabulani who is here' (when someone knocks at your door)

At this point, we need to bring into the picture the relativity to context which the DS system allows: indeed Cann et al. (2007) argue that elliptical fragment construal should be explicitly defined as a context-relative mechanism, taking structure which the context provides as

[22]The form *lu-* is due to coalescence of *la-* and *u-*, the relativizer and class 1 subject marker.

the INPUT to the structure-building process.[23] In question-answer exchanges, in particular, the structure is set up by the question, here by analysis a pair of linked structures, the *wh* form indicating a linked structure requiring provision of a substituend. All that this requires by way of an answer is the provision of a substituend, as this is what is required to update that structure which the immediately previous parse has provided. Indeed, this is no more than direct use of context-provided structure, as the DS account would lead one to expect (see Purver et al. 2006 for a detailed account of ellipsis). In the DS perspective, nothing requires that a requirement be met by structure provided solely by linguistic input or within that same sentence. In principle, even if the structure can be provided by induction from the dialogue scenario as in (2.63), it may be so provided.[24]

2.3.3 Complex *ku-* clefts

It might seem that the complex clefts formed using a default subject marker (a bleached form of a locative subject marker), a tense marker, a copula, all in addition to the *nge*-marked sequence would need a much more complex analysis, since, in this more complex form of cleft, it would seem that the relative sequence, in following the *nge*-marked expression itself as complement to a copula, is serving as some kind of modifier of that expression, hence a true relative:

(2.64)	*ku-*	*to-*	*ba*	*nge-ba-fana*	*la-*	*ba-*	*to-*	*natsa*
	DSM	FUT	COP	NGE-2-boys	REL	2SM	FUT	drink
	tjwala							
	14.alcohol							

'It will be the boys who will drink alcohol'

However what is striking is that all the parallelism indicative of the simple clefts carries over in full to the complex clefts. They display

[23] Cann et al. (2007) define a context-relative concept of wellformedness, so that fragments can be defined as well-formed as long as they are construed as providing actions which, relative to some context, can yield a complete tree with no requirement outstanding.

[24] It is notable that this strategy of updating NP fragments from context without any linguistic antecedent from which to construct the appropriate interpretation is only available in highly routinized exchanges, such as request for directions, ordering food, buying tickets, etc. See Stainton (2006) for arguments that this type of case necessitate pragmatic reconstruction as though this was not a structure-building process of the kind syntactically made available. In the DS view, to the contrary, the concept of context is that of some non empty sequence of complete trees plus some partial tree under construction, so the recovery of any such open propositional value from the dialogue context is no less structural than the manipulation of a fragment relative to a previously parsed question (Kempson et al. 2009a).

exactly the same form of patterns as the simpler *nge*-marked clefts, except for one difference: they do not seem to be used in reverse sequence: there is no possibility of the full complex form of opening actions such as *ku-to-ba nge-NP* in (2.64) occurring after the relative sequence that follows. This apart however, the patterns remain identical. So we have object clefts in which the sequences all occur with the preceding complex expletive formula, all requiring object argument marking, and allowing the subject either to precede or follow the verbal complex. This suggests an alternative analysis in terms of that opening sequence of parse actions setting up in outline the very sequence of actions which the simpler cleft form supplies without any such anticipatory opening gestures. And this indeed is our suggestion. We claim that *ku-* is a form of type e expletive, introduced at a linked structure of topnode type e which does nothing more than require that this be a linked structure sharing a term with the propositional node to be subsequently developed, that *to-* as a tense marker induces a subject-predicate structure without any formula decorations (see Marten et al. 2008), and that *-ba* is a form of copula which allows the pointer to move back to the linked node originally introduced, enabling the parsing process to proceed exactly as though that skeletal structure were not there at all. We show the sequence of updates involved in parsing *ku*, *ku-to* and *ku-to-ba* in (2.65)-(2.68) and notice how this skeletal structure will be common to all sequences involving the future tense marker *to-*:

(2.65) *ku-* *to-* *ba* *nge-ba-fana* *la-* *ba-* *to-* *natsa*
DSM FUT COP it-2-boys REL 2SM FUT drink
tjwala
14.alcohol

'It will be the boys who will drink alcohol'

(2.66) Parsing *ku*

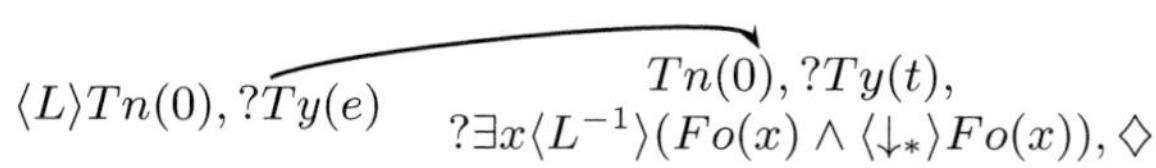

(2.67) Parsing *ku-to*

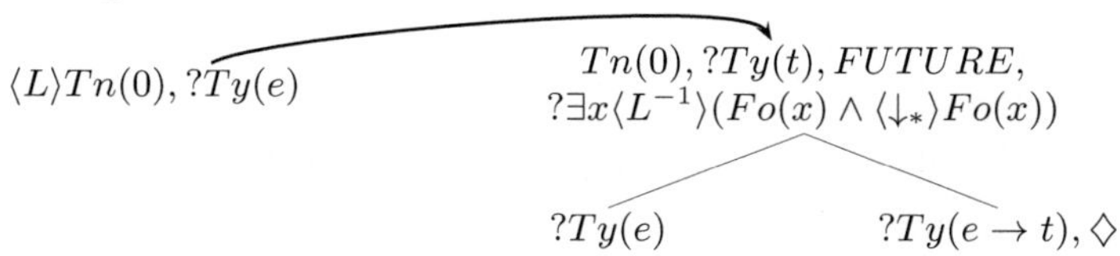

(2.68) Parsing *ku-to-ba*

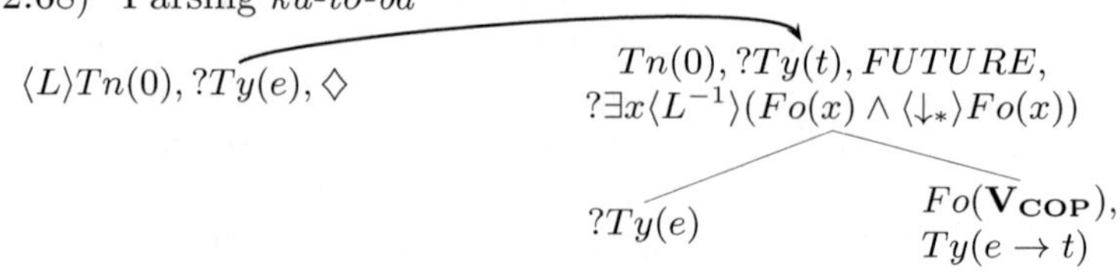

From then on, the update actions will not merely PARALLEL that of the simpler cleft structure, they will be IDENTICAL. So, for example, the parsing of *nge-* will achieve the following transition, still with no formula content specific to the particular proposition under construction:

(2.69) Parsing *ku-to-ba-nge*

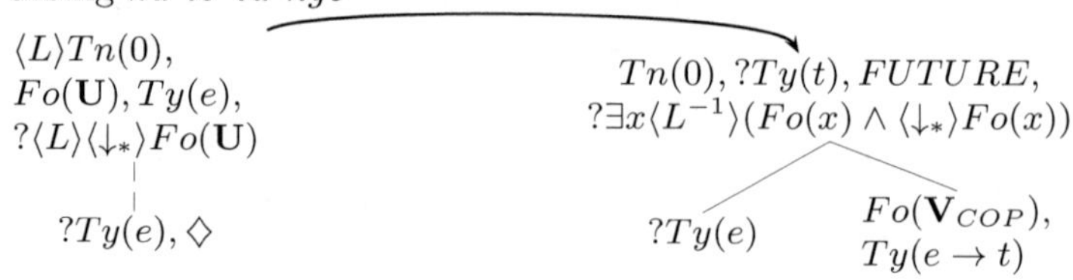

Then, exactly as before, the words will be parsed in sequence, achieving the fleshing out of this structure.

To achieve this, the lexical specification of *ku-* needs to be an action that introduces the requisite independent linked structure, and ensures that the two structures once finally completed have a shared structure. This is ensured by imposing the following requirement on the linked structure node constructed by *ku-*:

$$?\exists x(Fo(x) \wedge \langle L\rangle\langle\downarrow_*\rangle Fo(x))$$

The question, then, is how to flesh out the actions to be incorporated in its lexical specification. One complication needs to be born in mind: this bleached form of the locative marker is not restricted to occurring strictly initially, as it is duplicated as an apparent agreement marker on the remote past:

(2.70)

kw-	*a*	*ku-*	*nge-*	*ba-fana*	*la-*	*be-*
DSM	RemotePast	DSM	NGE	2-boys	REL	PAST

ba-	*natsa*	*tjwala*
2SM	drink	14.alcohol

'It was the boys that drank alcohol'

Furthermore, the past tense form *be-* idiosyncratically occurs before subject marking in the verbal complex, so that with this form of tense marking, *ku-*, as a bleached subject-marking device, occurs second in the string:

(2.71)

be-	*ku-*	*tjwala*	*ba-fana*	*la-*	*be-*	*ba-*
PAST	DSM	14.alcohol	2-boys	REL	PAST	2SM
bu-	*natsa*					
14OM	drink					

'It was alcohol that the boys were drinking'

The definition we propose assumes that *ku-* itself, relative to a context in which no explicit individual term has yet been introduced in the derivation, triggers the construction of an inverse LINK transition (in a duplication of this particle, this occurring trivially but harmlessly):[25]

(2.72) ku_{EXPLET}-

IF	$?Ty(t)$	
THEN	IF	$\langle L^{-1}\rangle\langle\downarrow_*\rangle Ty(e)$
	THEN	Abort
	ELSE	$\mathtt{make}(\langle L^{-1}\rangle); \mathtt{go}(\langle L^{-1}\rangle);$
		$\mathtt{put}(?Ty(e)); \mathtt{go}(\langle L\rangle);$
		$\mathtt{put}(?\exists x(\langle L^{-1}\rangle Fo(x) \wedge \langle\downarrow_*\rangle Fo(x)))$
ELSE	Abort	

Indeed we expect that *ku-* can be duplicated, and it can:[26]

(2.73)

ku-	*to-*	*ba*	*ku-*	*nge-ba-fana*	*la-*	*ba-*	*to-*
DSM	FUT	COP	DSM	NGE-2-boys	REL	2SM	FUT
natsa	*tjwala*						
drink	14.alcohol						

'It will be the boys who will drink alcohol'

Notice that this expresses the restriction of there being a shared term for the two structures being induced on the type-t-requiring node, rather than on the structure to which that node is linked. This is because the pointer has to reside at this node to parse the auxiliary and tense specification, leaving a totally open linked structure to which the pointer will have to return.

With this proposed sequence of actions, there is an immediate prediction, to which the account will commit us. We anticipate, for ex-

[25] *Ku-* can still function as a locative prefix, and has regular subject-marking properties in that core function. However, we assume that, given the development of this particular expletive property, this latter has separated off, and requires discrete lexical specification. Hence the first condition, if not met, will not license the subsequent update which these expletive uses of *ku-* induce.

[26] The specification provided allows iterative applications, but wherever such application yields solely a trivial development, we assume it is precluded by a general tree-growth constraint debarring all such updates. In cases such as (2.73), where repetition is licensed, it involves a nontrivial pointer movement and subsequent monotonic growth of tree decorations.

ample, that there must be identical matching of tense specifications both preceding and following the *nge-* specification, as the specification following the processing of the cleft expression is an overlap of the skeletal template set out before it. This is indeed correct – these temporal specifications invariably match:[27]

(2.6) *ku- to- ba nge-ba-fana la- ba- to- natsa tjwala*
DSM FUT COP NGE-2-boys REL 2SM FUT drink 14.alcohol
'It will be the boys who will drink alcohol'

(2.74) *ku- to- ba tjwala la- ba- to- bu- natsa ba-fana*
DSM FUT COP 14.alcohol REL 2SM FUT 14OM drink 2-boys
'It will be alcohol which they will drink it the boys'

(2.75) *kw- a ku- ngu-se-London lapho ng- a ngi- hlala khona na- make*
DSM- RemotePast DSM NGE-LOC-London where 1SG.SM RemotePast 1SG.SM live DEM.LOC with mother
'It was in London where I lived with my mother'

To complete the details of the DS account, we illustrate the form of update for tense markers by defining the past tense marker so that it obligatorily occurs not merely before the verb, but before any other node in that local domain:

(2.76) *be-* ('past')

$$
\begin{array}{lll}
\text{IF} & ?Ty(t) & \\
\text{THEN} & \text{IF} & \langle\downarrow_1^*\rangle\langle\downarrow_0\rangle\top \\
 & \text{THEN} & \text{Abort} \\
 & \text{ELSE} & \texttt{put}(+PAST);\texttt{make}(\langle\downarrow_0\rangle);\texttt{go}(\langle\downarrow_0\rangle); \\
 & & \texttt{put}(?Ty(e));\texttt{go}(\langle\uparrow_0\rangle); \\
 & & \texttt{make}(\langle\downarrow_1\rangle);\texttt{go}(\langle\downarrow_1\rangle); \\
 & & \texttt{put}(?Ty(e\rightarrow t));\texttt{go}(\langle\uparrow_1\rangle) \\
\text{ELSE} & \text{Abort} &
\end{array}
$$

[27] We take the distinction between remote past and past to be at least in part an anaphoricity effect, noting that the double use of *ku-* creates an interpretation whose identity of tense construal with the following relative sequence is matched by *be-* in (2.70). Further research is needed to confirm this, pending which we omit detailed formulation of remote past tense forms.

The only structural difference between the tense affixes *to-* and *be-* is that while the former can be triggered in the presence of a locally unfixed node (provided by the subject marker), *be-* cannot, hence its rigidly initial position in the affixal template. All such local structural constraints, though requiring specific lexical itemization, are in principle unproblematic given the tree-growth vocabulary defined.

It might seem that there has to be stipulation to force the pointer back to the linked structure that has been introduced in the parsing of *ku-*. However, in fact this is not so. Once having set up a skeletal structure for a shift in context, there must be development of that structure if this strategy is not to be entirely empty. However this restriction is subsumed by the more general restriction on context-relative development (Cann et al. 2007). Context-dependent well-formedness of any sequence of expressions depends on the context in question containing at least one complete sub-tree (with no outstanding requirements). This restriction is precisely what is needed to immediately yield the right result for these structures: any derivation in which the pointer failed to return to any introduced LINK tree would fail, as violating this restriction.

2.4 Theoretical significance

So the overall story is that all types of clefts are seen as a topic plus predication structure, with the contrastiveness taken to be characteristic of clefts being brought out by the construction of a novel term within that structure. Current analyses of cleft structures do not approach the success of this analysis. For example, any approach which analyzes clefts as involving a relative clause would face problems to explain the strict matching of tense construal between the copula associated with the clefted expression and the relative-clause sequence, since, by analysis this sequence is indeed a relative clause, hence with independent tense construal. The particular force of the analysis proposed here is that all details as predicted emerge from the assumption that the underlying syntax is not a set of principles that licenses structures, with each structure being in principle distinct from other structures. More generally, there is no one-to-one correspondence between string and assigned structure. Rather the syntax defines a set of mechanisms that license structure-building processes. These characteristically involve the mapping of one partial structure into another, often providing update to that partial structure that provided the input. So while the processes are defined as distinct from each other, there may nevertheless be feeding relations between them, and updating of a single structure to yield an enriched set of decorations on some already articulated partial tree. It is the interaction between these which gives rise to the overlap effect which is so characteristic of cleft structures, part-relative, part-long-distance-dependency, part-topic-like.

While we have restricted our attention here to siSwati clefts, there is of course the question of the extent to which this form of analysis will be generalisable, as we would surely expect that it would.[28] However, there is a word of caution here: the structures which these processes induce are not structures that are inhabited by words. To the contrary, the DS system is a system of constraints on possible tree growth processes to yield formulae in a conceptual representation system whose formulae include predicates and individual-denoting terms: a "language of thought" (LOT), by definition a universal system of representations.[29] The set of mechanisms for tree-growth, equally, are defined a priori, a fixed system of defining partial conceptual representations and possible forms of transition.[30] This in total constitutes the underlying form of syntax that all natural languages reflect. The sole structural source of variation that they allow is in the balance between what are taken as general forms of tree growth, and what are induced by individual lexical items, individually isolatable triggers for tree growth macros stored in the lexicon. Thus the only concept of syntax specific to natural languages themselves is in the transitions from one partial structure to another, and in this there may be variation according as one language encodes a given transition as an update that is lexically triggered, another leaves the lexicon relatively weakly specified, leaving

---

[28]For English clefts, for example, this would necessitate an account involving compatible forms of enrichment for all cases where the auxiliary in the cleft sequence doesn't match that of the auxiliary in the relative sequence:

(i) It was John that should have been here.

In these past tense cases, given the analysis of auxiliaries as weak place-holding device, nothing would preclude an enrichment provided by the second auxiliary. The only problem concerns the use of the present tense, but there are grounds for analyzing English present tense as essentially a-temporal, picking up on other time specifications as these are made available:

(ii) It is John that saw Mary.

Whether this can be sustained requires detailed DS analysis of auxiliary and modal perspectives (see Cann this volume).

[29]The system presumes on a denotational semantics without this being defined as part of the natural-language system.

[30]Because the particular concepts themselves are acquired through the natural language to which the child is exposed as the means of codifying hence retaining the individuating concepts with which the child can then reason, these are culture-relative, a stock to which the human may add right through life, as exposed to new constructs needing to be individuated.

the transition as a generally available option.[31]

This has consequences for language typologies. The DS system provides a basis for language typologies only via this indirect route of providing mechanisms for building paired structures as induced by words of the language. Thus cleft sequences, relative clause sequences, etc, are simply packages of instructions for building LOT formulae: they are not themselves structures of LOT itself. We would not accordingly expect there to be a fixed single structure associated with a given syntactic pattern, eg clefts, relative clauses and so on. These just constitute different effects which the composite set of options for building linked structures makes available. To ask for a single analysis of the set of strings that are said to constitute cleft structures in any language is thus to ask the wrong question. Languages have different strategies for yielding paired linked structures, and it is the very interweaving of these which may determine informational effects according as this interweaving yields one language ordering or another. Nonetheless, we suggest that what are somewhat loosely called cleft structures involve just this composite combination of a context-creating backgrounding device (via the building of a linked structure) plus a device presenting information updating that incrementally constructed structure. Despite the apparent low-level morphological idiosyncracy, the account is nevertheless definable exclusively in terms of growth of semantic representation.

More generally, what the grammar formalism is providing directly is a universal base-mechanism for parsing structural representations of content. What is then inducible from it is a set of typological expectations of the type of interactions which the associated tree-growth mechanisms would lead one to expect, hence providing part of the stock of data relative to which the grammar can itself be tested. The substance of the grammar itself does not however lie in the typological abstractions themselves: it lies in the claim that syntax is nothing other than the vehicle whereby interpretation for expressions of language is built up.

[31]How strictly this minimal set of assumptions can be sustained depends on the numbers of additional features that need to be posited as part of the DU language as triggers needed to appropriately filter the tree-growth actions. Gender specifications provide one problematic instance; and we note that with every addition that has to be made to any such set of features, the substance of this particularly strong universalist position will be weakened.

References

The following were cited in this chapter: Blackburn and Meyer-Viol (1994), Bouzouita (2008a,b), Cann (this volume), Cann and Kempson (2008), Cann et al. (2005), Cann et al. (2007), Cann, Kempson and Marten (forthcoming), Chatzikyriakidis and Kempson (2010), Cheng and Downing (2007), Delin (1990), Delin (1992), Ferreira and Dell (2000), Hedberg (2000), Kempson and Meyer-Viol (2004), Kempson et al. (2001), Kempson et al. (2006), Kempson et al. (2009a), Kiaer (2007), Kiaer (this volume), Kula and Marten (this volume), Mahajan (1997), Marcus (1980), Marten (2010), Marten and Kempson (2002), Marten et al. (2008), McCormack (2008), Miyamoto (2002), Prince (1978), Purver et al. (2006), Riedel (2009), Stainton (2006), Taljaard et al. (1991), Zeller (2004), Zeller (2006), Ziervogel and Mabuza (1976). See references at the end of the book for full information.

3

The Prosody of Bemba Relative Clauses: A Case Study of the Syntax-Phonology Interface in Dynamic Syntax

NANCY C. KULA & LUTZ MARTEN

3.1 Introduction

The central claim of Dynamic Syntax is that the structure of natural languages reflects the way hearers use natural language to construct representations of content. The DS model aims to show how information provided by words is used incrementally to build increasingly complex semantic representations, a process modelled as tree growth. Due to this incremental perspective, the linear surface order of words plays a much larger role in syntactic analysis in DS than in other models with more emphasis on hierarchical structures or conflicting constraints. Furthermore, the model reflects that on-line choices have to be made about the contribution of a particular piece of information to the overall structure to be developed, and that in some cases, the eventual contribution of some information is not yet known at the time it is encountered. In the formal model, this is reflected by the use of

Earlier versions of this paper were presented at the LAGB Annual Meeting at the University of Newcastle and at the Conference on Interdisciplinary Approaches to Relative Clauses at the University of Cambridge. We are grateful for comments from the audiences at these conferences, as well as from Lisa Cheng, Ruth Kempson and Jochen Zeller. All errors remain ours.

The Dynamics of Lexical Interfaces.
Ruth Kempson, Eleni Gregoromichelaki and Christine Howes (eds.).

different forms of structural underspecification, where the final structure is only determined at a later stage in the derivation. In addition to lexical input, the structure building process is driven by pragmatic information. Contextual, pragmatic information is modelled as interacting with syntax directly, and to contribute to the structure building process in instances where structural or lexically encoded information is underspecified. The interaction between structure and context occurs throughout the derivation, and so from the DS perspective, there is no strict division between grammatical well-formedness, sentence meaning and pragmatic enrichment. Rather, both structural and contextual information together are used in the dynamic establishment of meaning, and so pragmatic information, together with lexical information, feeds into the computational system, whose output is an enriched semantic representation of content (Cann et al. 2005, Marten 2002). In this paper, we are going to propose that similar reasoning applies to the phonology-syntax interface: In contrast to models in which syntax feeds into phonology, from a DS perspective, phonological information feeds into the computational system (Kiaer 2007). We will show this in more detail by providing an analysis of tonal marking of relative clauses in Bemba, where the difference between restrictive and non-restrictive readings is distinguished by different tone marking patterns of the relative clause and of the head noun. The analysis illustrates how prosodic information provides cues for the hearer in establishing appropriate semantic representations, given the lexical input and the context, and how phonological information contributes directly to the incremental building of these structures. As for the syntax-pragmatics interface, the dynamic perspective adopted in DS thus provides a new way of thinking about the phonology-syntax interface.

The paper is organized as follows: Section 3.2 discusses different conceptions of the phonology-syntax interface, while section 3.3 provides a brief introduction to the relevant aspects of DS. In section 3.4, we introduce the data; presenting the prosodic marking of relative clauses in Bemba and differentiating pronominal and tonal strategies of relativization. In section 3.5 we develop a DS analysis for the data presented and finally, in section 3.6 we present some concluding remarks.

3.2 Phonology-syntax interface

The study of linguistic interfaces has attracted increasing attention in formal linguistics over the last few decades. In particular the nature of human syntactic knowledge is often claimed to be related to interface conditions, in that syntactic derivations are constrained by well-formedness conditions at the interface between syntactic computation and phonological and semantic-pragmatic knowledge. Within this perspective, it is furthermore often assumed that linguistic knowledge is modularized, and that syntax and phonology constitute distinct, encapsulated modules with their own vocabularies. Communication between the modules is mediated through interfaces, at which only specific information is visible (cf. Chomsky 1995, Jackendoff 2002, Inkelas and Zec 1990, Selkirk 1984, Szendroi 2001, Truckenbrodt 1999).

(3.1) Chomsky (1995) t-model

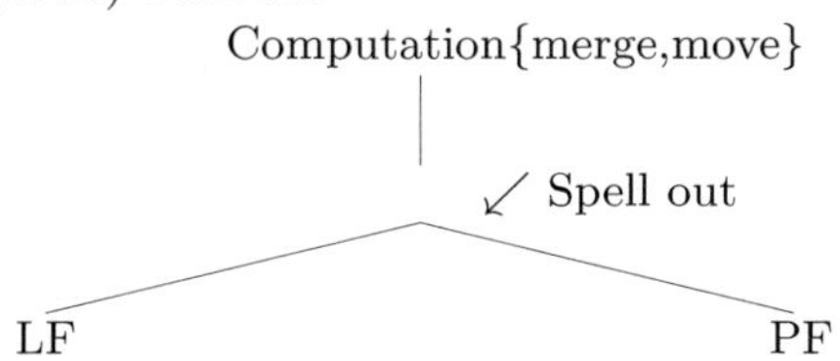

Furthermore, as can be seen in (3.1), syntactic derivation is assumed to proceed without consideration of phonological structure until a complete derivation (or, in other models, a complete cycle, or phase) is merged at the interface. Interface conditions then determine whether the derivation is well-formed, or crashes. Although not intended to be interpreted in that way,[1] the relation between syntax and phonology in the model seems to assume speaking, or language production, as the paradigm case for linguistic knowledge – hence syntactic structure is constructed first, and then sent to the phonological component which among other things translates the syntactic structure into audible sound.

From a DS perspective, in contrast, the interaction between phonology and syntax is characterized by the way in which phonological information feeds into structure building processes, following from the overall parsing-based perspective of the model. As with pragmatic and contextual information, phonological information is assumed to interact directly with syntax, so that phonological information is available at every stage of the derivation. Hence syntactic knowledge and phonological knowledge are not viewed as categorically distinct, represented as encapsulated modules, whose information flow has to be mediated by interfaces. Although both systems operate with distinct vocabulary, they interact freely in that all information available is used to construct an appropriate semantic representation for the utterance at hand. Rather than syntax feeding into phonology, DS postulates a feed-

[1] The model is assumed to be concerned with competence, and is thus meant to be independent of and unrelated to performance factors.

ing relation between phonology and syntax: Phonology provides hearers with parsing cues which are used for lexical access (Kaye 1989), and for building structured semantic representations on a left-to-right basis (Kula 2002, Kiaer 2005, 2007).

(3.2) sound → phonology → lexicon → syntax/pragmatics → interpretation

The role of phonology in this conception is thus two-fold. On the one hand, phonological knowledge of a given language allows the hearer to divide the continuous input stream of sound into discrete units which can be matched against lexical entries, as argued in Kaye (1989). On the other hand, phonological knowledge, in particular suprasegmental phonology, guides the hearer in the parsing process by providing cues indicating how lexical information is to be projected at a given stage in the parse. Kiaer (2007) shows how intonation and phonological phrasing is exploited for the construction of multiple left-dislocation in Korean: Only with the correct intonational pitch are these multiple dislocation sentences acceptable. The choice of the correct structural representation has to be made on-line, and requires appropriate prosodic information. In that sense, as Kiaer argues, phonological information feeds into syntactic structure building. Kiaer's conception of the phonology-syntax interface is confirmed by the analysis to be presented in this paper. We will show that tone plays a central role in structure building in Bemba relative clauses. Tonal information in Bemba can thus be analyzed like intonation in Korean, as feeding into syntactic structure building. However, before we develop our analysis in detail, we will present a brief introduction to the relevant DS background in the next section.

3.3 A Dynamic Syntax perspective on Bemba structure

Before discussing the prosody in Bemba relative clauses, we will provide in this section a brief introduction to assumptions we make about the DS analysis of Bemba morphological and syntactic structure, building on previous DS analyses of related Bantu languages such as Swahili, Otjiherero or siSwati (Cann et al. 2005: Chapter 7, Kempson, Marten and Thwala this volume, Marten 2007, Marten et al. 2008). Bemba has morphologically complex verbs and nouns, and comparatively free word-order with unmarked SVO order. Lexical subjects, and sometimes objects, are co-indexed on the verb by agreement markers, which we analyse as pronominal clitics. In the appropriate context overt NPs can be omitted, and the inflected verb can function as a complete utterance.[2]

(3.3) *bá-ka-fík-a*
SM2-FUT-come-FV
'They will arrive.'

The DS approach to Bemba structure, and Bantu structure more generally, is that individual morphemes of the verbal structure make their own, lexically specified contribution to tree development. For example, the subject marker projects a metavariable which can be resolved from the context, tense markers project partial tree structure in addition to temporal information, and the verb provides conceptual information about the predicate, in addition to, in the case of transitive verbs, licensing the building of an object node. Since basic predicate-argument structure in Bantu can typically be built from morphological information of the inflected verb, overt lexical noun phrases serve in many cases to provide new information, or background information against which the main assertion is to be assessed. In DS terms, overt noun phrases are typically introduced through unfixed nodes or linked structures, and only later associated with a fixed position in the tree, or only related to the main tree through anaphoric linkage. Their function is often related to information structure, and so their contribution to the tree interacts closely with information available (or not available) from the context. In this section, we are concentrating on aspects of Bemba structure relevant to the data and analyses discussed in sections 3.4 and 3.5, and so will focus on core structure building, driven by the inflected verb, as well as on the internal structure of noun phrases, as these provide the structural context in which information from the relative clause is projected.

As already noted, we assume that the subject marker lexically provides a restricted metavariable and, furthermore, that subject markers require the presence of a locally unfixed node, dominated by the local root node.

(3.4) *bá-*

IF	$?Ty(e), \langle\uparrow_0\rangle\langle\uparrow_1^*\rangle?Ty(t)$
THEN	$\mathtt{put}(Fo(U_{CLASS2}), ?\exists x.Fo(x))$
ELSE	abort

[2]We use the following non-standard abbreviations in the glosses: numerals indicate noun class (unless followed by 'sg.' or 'pl.'); Aug = Augment; FV = Final Vowel; OM = object marker; REL = relative marker; SM = subject marker; an acute accent indicates high tone, low tone is unmarked. Note also that there is vowel fusion whenever a low vowel is followed by a high vowel so that a sequence of /a-i/ as in *ka-isa* 'will come', for example, is pronounced as [e:]. We do not represent such fusions in our examples for expository reasons only.

The restriction on the metavariable (U_{CLASS2}) acts as a restriction on substitution, and so we assume that noun classes have semantic content. This is uncontentious for class 1 which denotes humans and class 2 which denotes human plurals or can be used for human singulars to express politeness. For noun classes in Swahili, Contini-Morava (2002) argues that they have a semantic base, and we assume that similar arguments apply to Bemba noun classes. A parse of (3.4) sets out with the information from the subject marker decorating a locally unfixed node, and the metavariable being substituted by an appropriate term from the context, which we here assume is *bamayo* 'mothers'. After parsing the subject marker, lexical information from the future tense marker *-ka-* annotates the root node with appropriate tense information which we represent somewhat simplified as $Tns(FUT)$. However, in addition we assume that the tense marker also contributes to developing the tree by licensing the building of a fixed subject and a fixed predicate node.

(3.5) *bá-ka*
SM2-FUT

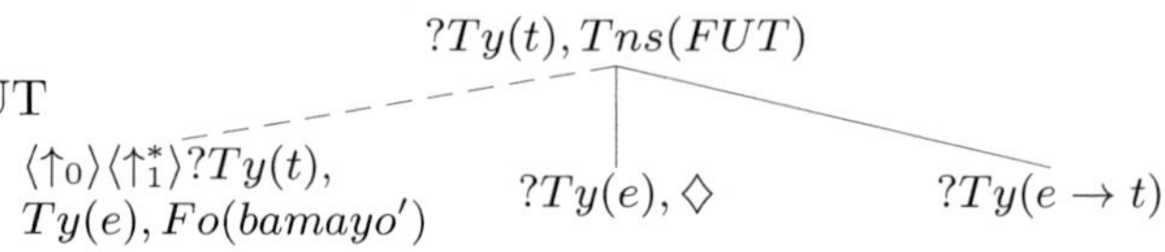

The presence of the fixed subject node allows the unfixed node to merge with the subject node, fulfilling the requirement $?Ty(e)$, and thus to become fixed as the logical subject of the ensuing proposition. The parsing of the subject marker and the tense marker alone is thus sufficient to construct a predicate frame with only information about the predicate outstanding.

(3.6) *bá-ka*
SM2-FUT

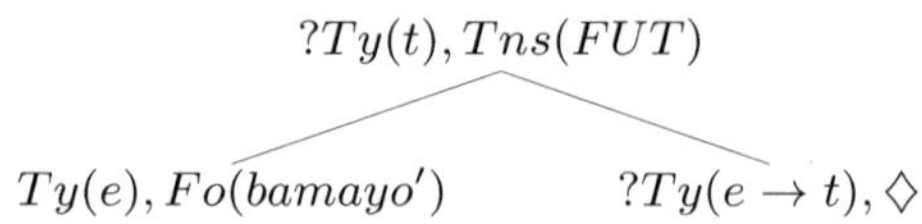

(3.7) *-fík*
IF $?Ty(e \rightarrow t)$
THEN $\texttt{put}(Fo(fík'), Ty(e \rightarrow t))$
ELSE abort

Parsing of the verb *-fík-* 'come' results in the annotation of the predicate node, and the tree can then duly be completed. It is tempting to analyse the final vowel *-a*, which follows the verb root in *bá-ka-fík-a* 'they will arrive', as encoding some restriction on the completion of the tree, similar to the DS analysis of TAM suffixes in head-final languages like Japanese (Cann et al. 2005: 240). However, in transitive clauses, the object normally follows the verb (and hence the final vowel), and so the final vowel cannot be analyzed as requiring the completion of the tree. A more promising line of enquiry might be to relate the final vowel to valency-changing operations, as all verbal derivational suffixes ('extensions' in Bantu terms) precede the final vowel *-a* thus the arity of the predicate has to be fixed before the final vowel is parsed, or in other words, all argument nodes have to be built, although not necessarily be decorated. We will leave the question open for the time being.

A potential problem with the approach taken so far is presented by perfect verbs, as in these TAM markers are not placed between the subject marker and the verb root (as in the future tense example discussed so far), but follow the verb root, replacing the final vowel.

(3.8) *bá-fík-íle* *maílo*
SM2-arrive-PERF yesterday
'They arrived yesterday.'

Since we assume that verbs like *-fík-* 'arrive' have a lexical trigger ?Ty(e → t), as in the lexical entry in (3.7), above, the parse would abort once *-fík-* is encountered, as no fixed predicate node has been built yet. As a solution to this problem, we assume that these cases require the licensing of structure building which anticipates specific tense information. The building of a fixed subject node and a fixed predicate node is licensed after the subject marker has been parsed, but subject to a requirement at the root node that the tense be perfect.

(3.9) *bá-* . . .
SM2

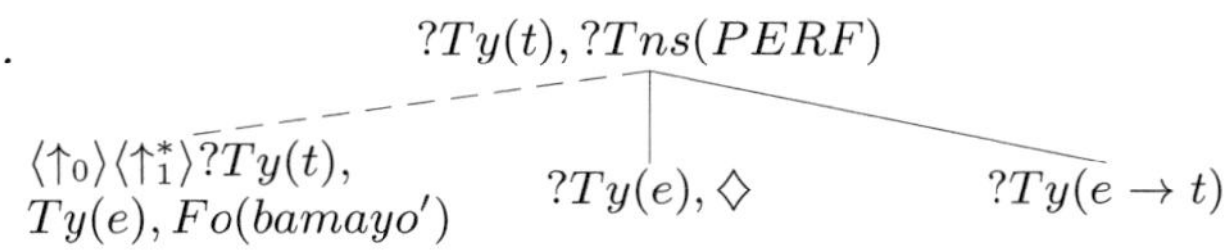

The tense requirement is fulfilled once the perfect suffix *-ile* is parsed, and so the partial tree can be completed (or further developed, for example if an object is following). If, however, the tense requirement is not fulfilled, the derivation fails. The anticipatory building of structure is thus tightly restricted to perfect forms in which tense marking appears after the verb root. For ease of exposition, however, we will restrict the discussion in the following sections to more canonical examples with TAM morphemes before the verb root.

Like verbs, Bemba nouns are morphologically complex, consisting of an augment, or pre-prefix, a noun class prefix, and a nominal stem.

(3.10) *u-mú-ntu*
AUG-1-person
'a/the person'

The augment can be present or absent, depending on the context in which the noun is used. The specific criteria relevant to the presence or absence of the augment provide a heterogeneous set, and are not clearly related to a particular function. Because the augment is absent in word-formation, it is often assumed that it fulfils a syntactic, rather than a morphological function, and in related Bantu languages, the augment has been argued to fulfil semantic or pragmatic functions as well (e.g. in Luganda, Hyman and Katamba 1993, Ferrari-Bridgers 2009). However, the distribution and function of the augment in Bemba is still subject to on-going research (see Givón 1969 for an early account, and Kula 2009 for a recent update), and we will not present a detailed analysis of the morpheme. Similarly, it has been argued that noun class prefixes play a role in syntax as well as in morphology, as exponents of gender or number features (e.g. Carstens 1991), but at least for Bemba, further work is needed to ascertain this. From the DS perspective, we assume that nominals project complex structure, consisting of determiner (in the illustrative example below taken to be existential quantification, with an epsilon (ϵ) term to be created), variable, and restrictor (in the example below *múntu*, 'person').

(3.11) Parse tree for *umúntu*

$?Ty(e)$

$?Ty(cn)$ $\quad$ $Fo(\lambda P.(\epsilon, P)), Ty(cn \rightarrow e)$ [determiner]

$Fo(x), Ty(e)$ [variable] $\quad$ $Fo(\lambda y.(y, \textit{múntu}'(y))), Ty(e \rightarrow cn)$ [restrictor]

This complex structure reflects the compositional semantic structure of noun phrases, in which a nominal variable is restricted by the lexical nominal predicate, and where quantification is modelled with recourse to the epsilon calculus (Blackburn and Meyer-Viol 1994). However, we will not discuss quantification in any detail, other than using epsilon (ϵ) terms for existential, and tau (τ) terms for universal quantification. We assume tentatively that the nominal root and the noun class prefix are part of one lexical representation, which decorates the restrictor node. Consistent with our earlier observation that noun classes have denotational-semantic content, we thus do not assume that noun class prefixes straightforwardly encode number or quantification. On the other hand, we assume that the augment fulfils a functional, rather than a lexical role, even though the exact function still needs to be established, and we will not provide an analysis of this here. Rather, we will assume the representation in (3.11), and that nominals like *umúntu* 'person' project this structure lexically. We also assume for the time being that the pointer is placed lexically at the variable node when the noun is parsed, but we will have reason to revise this when discussing the tone marking of nouns in section 3.5.

We now turn to discussing Bemba relative clauses in the following section, and to a DS analysis of the data in section 3.5, for which the short discussion about Bemba structure provides the background.

3.4 Prosodic marking of relative clauses in Bemba

Like many Bantu languages, Bemba employs different strategies for encoding relative clauses, including the use of relative markers and tone marking of both the relative clause and the head noun (Sharman and Meeussen 1955, Givón 1969, Cheng and Kula 2006, Kula and Cheng 2007, Kula 2007). We first illustrate tone marking of the head noun of relative clauses which distinguishes restrictive and non-restrictive readings of relative clauses, then discuss the use of pronominal relative markers and tone marking of the relative clause and show how the different formal strategies are related to restrictive and non-restrictive readings. Finally we introduce headless relative clauses which are always marked by a pronominal relative marker and show that despite the absence of a head noun carrying tonal marking differentiating restrictive from non-restrictive interpretations, headless relatives have a restrictive-like interpretation.

3.4.1 Tonal marking of the head noun

Nouns functioning as head nouns of relative clauses can be distinguished by their tone marking. A word-final high (H) tone is found with restrictive relatives (3.12), while a final low (L) tone is found with non-restrictives (3.13). In both cases, the predicate of the relative clause is marked as being in a relative clause, as will be discussed in the following section.

(3.12) *abá-ntú* *ábá-ka-ís-a* *bá-ka-fúm-a*
2-people REL.SM2-FUT-come-FV SM2-FUT-come-FV
ku-Lusaka
17-Lusaka

'The people who will come will come from Lusaka.' (restrictive)

(3.13) *abá-ntu* *ábá-ka-ís-a* *bá-ka-fúm-a*
2-people REL.SM2-FUT-come-FV SM2-FUT-come-FV
ku-Lusaka
17-Lusaka

'The people, who will come, will come from Lusaka.' (non-restrictive)

The difference in tone marking of relative clause head nouns in Bemba has first been noted by Sharman (1956), who relates the tone marking to a similar tonal alternation on verb forms, often called a distinction between conjoint and disjoint verb forms (e.g. Meeussen 1959, Creissels 1996). We will return to the relation between nominal and verbal tone marking in section 3.5. In any event, the data so far show that Bemba restrictive and non-restrictive relatives are formally distinguished through tonal marking of the head noun. In the next section we will show that further formal distinctions are found within the relative clause.

3.4.2 Pronominal and tonal marking of the relative clause

In addition to tonal marking of relative clause head nouns, tone marking of the predicate of the relative clause is sensitive to the distinction between restrictive and non-restrictive readings. There are two basic different strategies for relative clause marking in Bemba: a pronominal strategy and a tonal strategy. The pronominal strategy of relativization uses a relative marker in the form of a relative concord in subject relatives and a demonstrative based relative pronoun in non-subject relatives. The two pronominal forms allow for both restrictive and non-restrictive readings as shown in (3.14-3.17) below.

(3.14) *abá-ntú* *ábá-ka-ísa* *bá-ka-fúm-a* *ku-Lusaka*
2-people REL.SM2-FUT-come SM2-FUT-come 17-Lusaka
'The people who will come will come from Lusaka.' (restrictive)

(3.15) *abá-ntu* *ábá-ka-ísa* *bá-ka-fúm-a* *ku-Lusaka*
2-people REL.SM2-FUT-come SM2-FUT-come 17-Lusaka
'The people, who will come, will come from Lusaka.' (non-restrictive)

(3.16) *abá-ntú* *ábo* *Chisanga* *á-mwééne* *maílo* *na-bá-ya*
2-person 2REL Chisanga SM1-see.PERF yesterday TNS-SM2-go
'The people that Chisanga saw yesterday have gone.' (restrictive)

(3.17) *abá-ntu* *ábo* *Chisanga* *á-mwééne* *maílo* *na-bá-ya*
2-person 2REL Chisanga SM1-see.PERF yesterday TNS-SM2-go
'The people, that Chisanga saw yesterday, have gone.' (non-restrictive)

The first two examples show the pronominal strategy in subject relatives expressing restrictive and non-restrictive readings, as can also be seen from the tonal marking of the head nouns. The second pair of examples show object relatives formed with the demonstrative based class 2 relative marker *ábo*, which agrees with the head noun, with both restrictive and non-restrictive readings.

The second relative clause coding strategy is the tonal strategy which is only available to subject relatives.[3] In this strategy no segmental relative marker is used, but the subject concord of the relative predicate is marked with a low (L) tone.[4]

(3.18) (tonal strategy)
abá-Bembá *bà-ikala* *mu-Zambia*
2-Bembas 2REL.SM2-live 18LOC-Zambia
bá-li-shipa
SM2-PROGR-be.brave
'The Bembas who live in Zambia are brave.' (restrictive)

(3.19) (tonal strategy)
**abá-Bemba* *bà-ikala* *mu-Zambia*
2-Bembas 2REL.SM2-live 18LOC-Zambia
bá-li-shipa
SM2-PROGR-be.brave
'The Bembas, who live in Zambia, are brave.' (non-restrictive)

The tonal strategy always gives rise to a restrictive reading. Therefore it cannot be used with non-restrictive marked head nouns as shown in (3.19). Furthermore, the tonal strategy is only available for subject relatives, while non-subject relatives have to be formed with the pronominal strategy. If there is an overt lexical subject in the relative clause it has to be inverted so as to follow the predicate, and cannot intervene between the head noun and the tone-marked predicate.

Thus the two relative strategies shown here differ in that the pronominal strategy can be used for both subject and non-subject relatives, and allows both restrictive and non-restrictive readings, while the tonal

[3]Non-subject relatives can marginally be marked by the tonal strategy but only in cases where the strategy acts to resolve ambiguity resulting from head nouns and subjects of the same class in subject inverted relatives. See Kula & Cheng (2007) for detailed discussion.

[4]To fully show the contrast between the normal subject concord (with H) and the relative subject concord (with L), we mark the L tone here with a grave accent. However, there is no difference between this L tone, and other L tones which by convention we do not mark.

strategy is restricted to subject relatives with restrictive reading. Accordingly, the pronominal strategy can be used with both kinds of head nouns, while the tonal strategy can only be used with the H tone marked, restrictive head noun. Before presenting an analysis of the data, we will briefly discuss headless relatives in the following section.

3.4.3 Headless relatives

Bemba allows relatives to be built without an overt nominal head. Headless relatives can only be formed with the pronominal strategy.

(3.20) *á-bá-ikala* *mu-Zambia* *bá-li-shipa*
2REL-2SM-live 18LOC-Zambia 2SM-PROGR-be.brave
'Those who live in Zambia are brave.'

(3.21) *úo* *á-mwééne* *Chisanga* *maílo,*
1REL 1SM-see.PERF Chisanga yesterday
na-á-fika
TNS-1SM-arrive
'The one who Chisanga saw yesterday has arrived.'

Headless relatives normally require appropriate contextual support and refer (anaphorically) to a given or inferred antecedent, as in (3.22), where the person who opened the door is inferred from the information provided by the preceding sentence:

(3.22) *Ici-ibi* *cá-ali-isuka.* *Á-bá-iswiile* *bééne*
7-door 7SM-PAST-open 2REL-2SM-open.PERF 2owner
ba-nganda.
2GEN-house
'The door opened. (The one) who opened (it) was the owner of the house.'

The tonal strategy cannot be used with headless relatives as the following examples show.

(3.23) (tonal strategy)
**bà-ikala* *mu-Zambia* *bá-li-shipa*
2REL.2SM-live 18LOC-Zambia 2SM-TNS-be.brave
Intd.: 'Those who live in Zambia are brave.'

(3.24) (tonal strategy)
**à-mwééne* *Chisanga* *maílo,* *na-á-fika*
1SM-see.PERF Chisanga yesterday TNS-1SM-arrive
Intd.: '(The person) who Chisanga saw yesterday has arrived.'

The absence of headless relatives with the tonal relative strategy shows a further restriction on the availability of the construction, which is only found with restrictive subject relative clauses with an overt lexical head.

After surveying the relevant examples of relative clause constructions in Bemba, we will show in the following section how the different restrictions and marking patterns can be explained within DS. In doing so, we will show how tone marking of both relative clauses and relative heads interacts with processes of structure building formalized in the DS model.

3.5 Analysis

Our analysis follows the standard analysis of relative clauses in DS (Kempson et al. 2001, Cann et al. 2005), employing a LINK structure to relate the head noun and the relative clause, with a copy of the formula value required to be part of the structure induced by the relative clause. We will propose that the relative pronoun introduces such a copy of the formula value of the head noun in the pronominal strategy. In the tonal strategy, the tonal marking of the relative clause requires not only a copy but more specifically that the copy be a variable, thus interacting with DS noun phrase analyses and ensuring a restrictive reading. Headless relatives are analyzed as building a skeletal antecedent for the pronominal relative marker from the context. Since the constructed head is semantically severely underspecified, its interpretation rests largely on information provided by the relative clause. The effect of this is that, even though headless relatives are technically not restrictive, the interpretation is seemingly restrictive. Since in the tonal strategy, no pronominal element is involved, the tonal strategy cannot be used in headless relatives. Finally, the tone marking on head nouns is analyzed as distinguishing between completed $Ty(e)$ tasks, thus resulting in a non-restrictive reading, and incomplete $Ty(e)$ tasks, which leads to a restrictive interpretation. All in all, we will show that tonal marking in Bemba relatives closely interacts with, and contributes to, structure building. The analysis thus supports the DS conception of the phonology-syntax interface as essentially hearer-based. In the following sections, we will develop our analysis in more detail.

3.5.1 Link and noun phrase structure

Our analysis is based on previous DS analyses of relative clauses and noun phrase structure (e.g. Kempson et al. 2001, Cann et al. 2005). Relative clauses are analyzed in DS as a conjunction of two trees, linked by a shared term. Formally, a LINK structure is built from a $Ty(e)$ node to a new $?Ty(t)$ node, based on the transition rule in (3.25) which results in a schematic partial tree like (3.26).

(3.25) Link Adjunction (for relatives) (Cann et al. 2005: 88)

$$\frac{\{n...Fo(\alpha), Ty(e), ...\Diamond\}}{\{n...Fo(a), Ty(e)...\}, \{nL...?Ty(t), ?\langle\downarrow^*\rangle Fo(\alpha)...\Diamond\}}$$

(3.26)

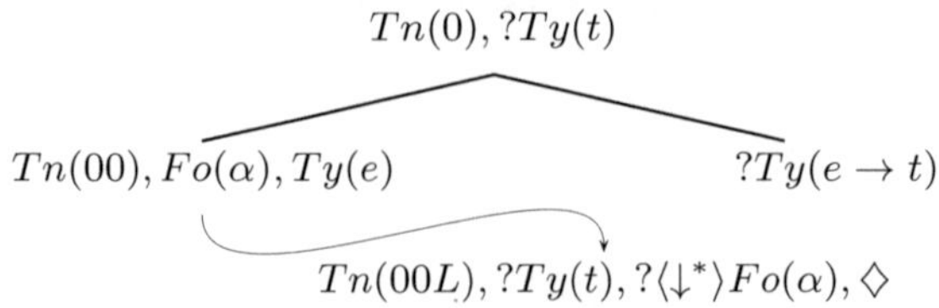

The linked node will be further developed through information from the relative clause, and before it is completed, somewhere in the structure Fo(α) needs to be included so as to fulfill the requirement holding at the root node of the linked tree (displayed in (3.26)). The copy of the formula value of the head noun is often introduced through a pronominal element, either a relative pronoun, or a resumptive pronoun within the relative clause. After completion of the relative clause, the main tree will be developed further with information from the matrix clause.[5]

The LINK rule interacts with the noun phrase structure introduced in section 3.3. Since in (3.27) both the node decorated by the variable, and the top node of the representations of nominals are of $Ty(e)$, a LINK structure can be launched from either - with attendant differences in interpretation.

(3.27) NP representation and possible nodes (in bold) for launching a LINK structure

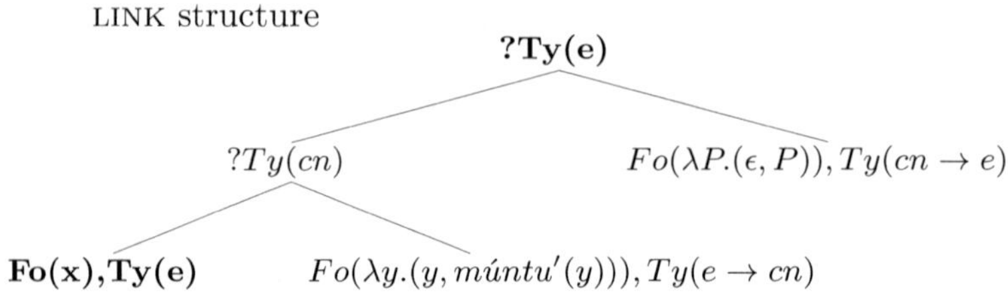

These two alternatives are freely available, and depend on which stage in the derivation the LINK relation is launched, thus giving a formal means to distinguish restrictive and non-restrictive relatives. The LINK relation may be launched at the stage in the derivation at which the nominal variable is introduced, so that the LINK relation modifies/restricts the variable, leading to a restrictive reading. But a LINK relation may also be launched after the semantic representation of the head noun has already been completed, so the LINK relation is launched

[5]The illustration here is of head-initial relatives. Variation in relative clauses is discussed in Cann et al. (2005).

from the $Ty(e)$ node representing the full, completed information from the head noun. This results in a non-restrictive reading.

We will exploit this interaction between LINK structures and noun phrase structure in our analysis of Bemba relatives in the next section.

3.5.2 Pronominal strategy: The pronominal form provides a copy of the head noun

In relative clauses formed with the pronoun strategy, a placeholder is provided by the pronoun which ensures that a copy of the formula value of the head noun is part of the linked tree. The placeholder is provided by the H toned *á-* relative marker which is prefixed to the subject marker of the predicate in subject relatives, and to the independent relative agreement marker in object relatives. The relative marker agrees in class with the head noun, in this case with *bakafúndisha* 'teacher' in (3.28) and with *abántu* 'people' in (3.29).

(3.28) *ba-kafúndisha á-bá-léé-lolesha pansé*
2-teacher 2REL-SM2-TNS-look 16outside
bá-la-péép-a
SM2-PRES-smoke-FV
'The teacher who is looking outside smokes.'

(3.29) *abá-ntu ábo Chisanga á-mwééne maílo*
2-person 2REL Chisanga SM1-see.PERF yesterday
na-bá-ya
TNS-SM2-go
'The people who Chisanga saw yesterday have gone.'

The following snapshots of a derivation of (3.28) show how computational and lexical actions interact in the construction of representations of relative clauses in Bemba. For the moment, we are not concerned with the tone marking on head nouns, to which we will return later. We will start by illustrating the non-restrictive construal, in which the LINK structure is launched from a $Ty(e)$ node decorated with the complete $Ty(e)$ expression, with a requirement for a copy of the formula value at the root node of the linked tree. As the LINK structure is launched from a completed $Ty(e)$, it is the complete, quantified term of which a copy is required to be part of the new linked tree, as in (3.30). We will see below that in restrictive relatives, it is only the variable which is copied, and so any information from the linked tree will be used when the fully quantified term is built.

(3.30) Pronominal strategy: Building of LINK structure with requirement for copy

ba-kafúndisha
2-teacher

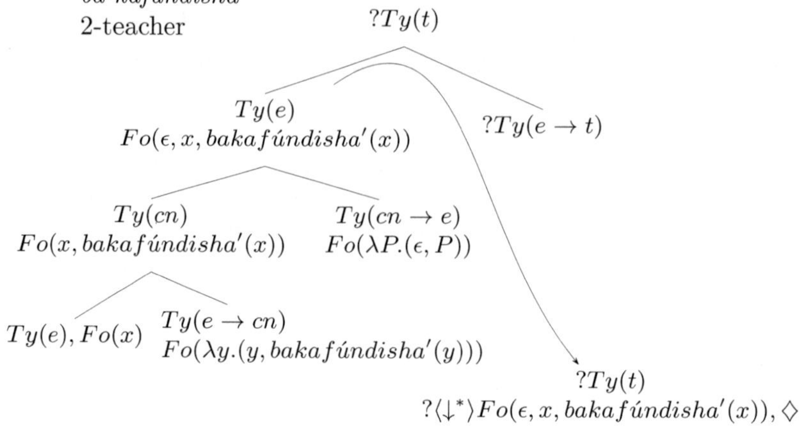

The next steps in the derivation are based on lexical information from the following morpheme *á-* which we analyse as a relative prefix providing a copy of the head noun.

(3.31) Lexical entry for *á*

IF	$?Ty(e), \langle\uparrow^*\rangle(?Ty(t), ?\langle\downarrow^*\rangle Fo(\alpha_{Class2}))$
THEN	$\mathtt{put}(Ty(e), Fo(\alpha_{Class2}))$
ELSE	abort

The lexical entry for *á-* requires a $?Ty(e)$ task at the current node, and furthermore that this node be unfixed with respect to some higher node with the requirement of $\langle\downarrow^*\rangle Fo(\alpha_{Class2})$ that is, a formula value whose referent is of noun class 2. The lexical information of the relative marker thus requires that an unfixed node be built before the information can be used (3.32). This ensures that both subject and object relative clauses can be coded with the pronominal strategy.

Subsequent steps build the linked tree through computational and lexical actions. The subject marker *bá-* decorates a locally unfixed node, which merges with the unfixed node decorated with $Fo(\epsilon, x, bakafúndisha'(x))$. The following tense marker *-léé-* licenses the building of fixed subject and predicate nodes, and the locally unfixed node can merge with the former, thus ensuring that a copy of the formula value of the head noun is in a fixed position within the linked tree. Finally, parsing the verb and the adjunct of the relative clause, *-lolesha pansé* 'look outside' (for which we omit internal representation here) results in decoration of the predicate node as in (3.33).

(3.32) Pronominal strategy: Relative pronoun provides copy

ba-kafúndisha á-
2-teacher 2REL

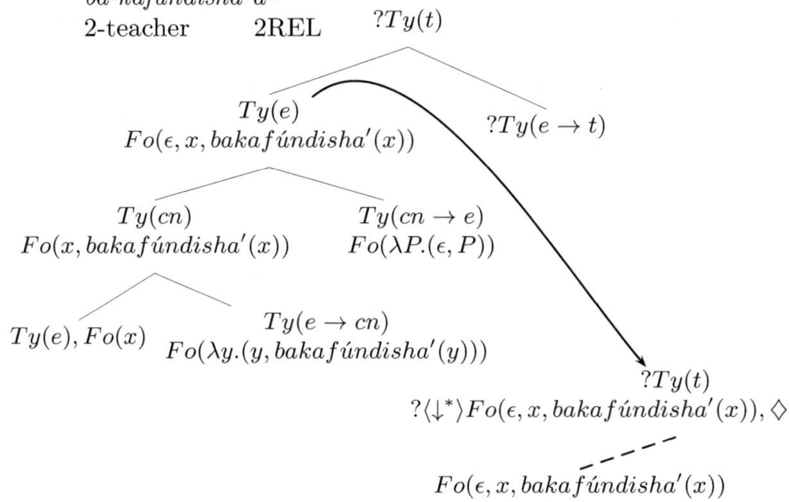

(3.33) Pronominal strategy: Final tree

ba-kafúndisha á-bá-léé-lolesha pansé
2-teacher 2REL-SM2-TNS-look 16.outside
bá-la-péép-a
SM2-PRES-smoke-FV

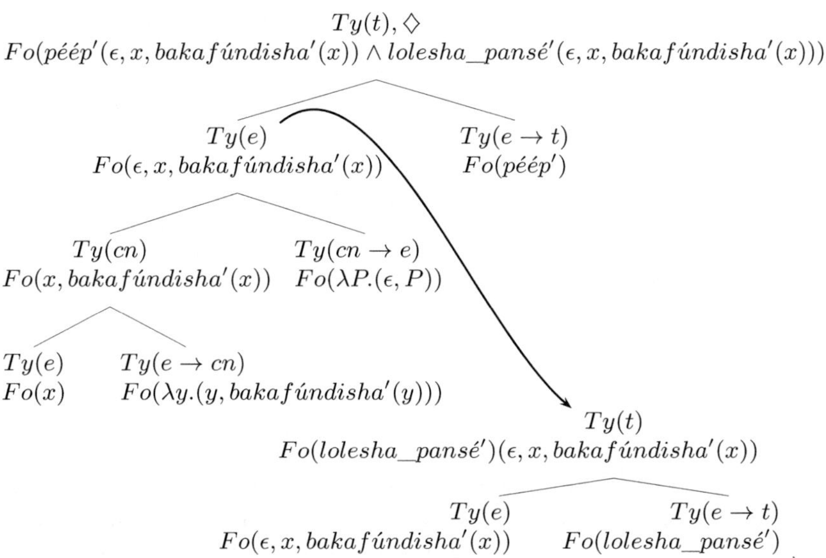

After the relative clause is parsed, information from the linked tree is built into the main tree. Since the subject $Ty(e)$ has already been compiled when the LINK structure was launched, information from the LINK structure has no effect on the interpretation of the subject, as it would have in restrictive relatives. Rather, information from the LINK structure is provided in addition to the information independently established at the subject node.

As noted earlier, the pronoun strategy is also available for restrictive relatives. The difference between non-restrictive and restrictive relatives in DS terms is that in the former, the LINK relation is launched after the $Ty(e)$ expression has been completed, as in the example just discussed. In the latter, the LINK relation is launched from the $Ty(e)$ node decorated by the variable x, that is before all the information of the eventual $Ty(e)$ node has been compiled, as in (3.35).

(3.34) (pronominal)

abá-ntú	*á-bá-ka-ísa*	*bá-ka-fúma*
2-people	2REL-SM2-FUT-come	SM2-FUT-come

ku-Lusaka
17-Lusaka

'The people who will come will come from Lusaka' (restrictive)

(3.35) Pronominal strategy with restrictive reading (a)

abá-ntú *á-*
2-people 2REL

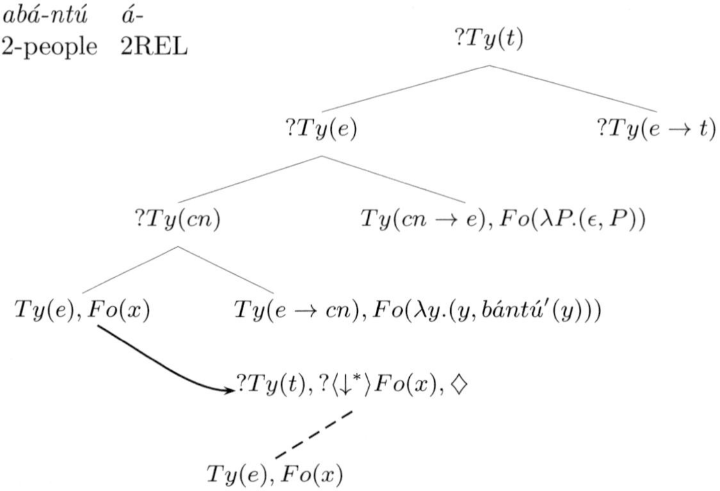

This means that the information from the relative clause restricts the nominal variable in the same way that the information provided by the restrictor node $Ty(e \rightarrow cn)$ restricts it. Information from both sources contributes to the construction of the eventual $Ty(e)$ term, as displayed in (3.36):

(3.36) Pronominal strategy with restrictive reading (b)

abá-ntú *á-bá-ka-ís-a*
2-people 2REL-SM2-FUT-come-FV

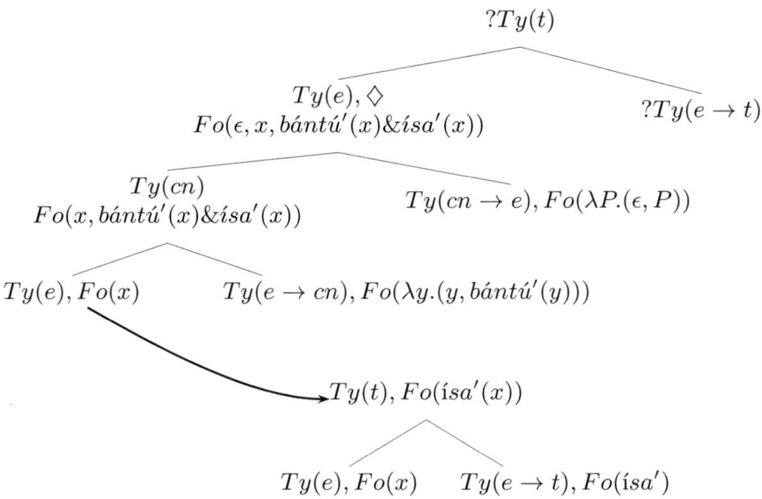

As we will see later, it is only this second tree growth process, leading to a restrictive reading, which is available for the tonal relative strategy.

In the pronoun strategy of Bemba relative clauses a copy of the formula value of the head noun is thus provided by the agreeing relative marker. Since the copying of the formula value of the head noun is achieved through the anaphoric properties of the relative marker, resumptive pronominal object markers in object relatives are not acceptable in Bemba.

(3.37) *icí-puna* *íco* *umu-ánakashi* *á-mweene* ...
7-chair REL7 1-girl SM1-see.PERF
'The chair which the girl saw ...'

(3.38) **ici-puna* *ico* *umu-anakashi* *a-ci-mweene* ...
7-chair REL7 1-girl SM1-OM7-see.PERF
Intd.: 'The chair which the girl saw ...'

The pronoun strategy as discussed so far proceeds like relative clause formation in many other head-initial languages with pronoun-like relative markers. In the following section, we will show how relative clauses marked by the tonal strategy can be analyzed.

3.5.3 Tonal strategy

In contrast to the pronominal relative strategy, in the tonal strategy the relative clause is only marked by an L tone on the subject marker of the verb of the relative clause. The tonal strategy is only possible for subject relatives, and any overt lexical subjects have to follow the relative predicate. The effect of this is that the verb of the relative clause always immediately follows the head of the relative. Furthermore, only restrictive readings are possible with relatives marked with the tonal strategy.

In terms of the DS analysis of noun phrase structure and relative clauses, the fact that only a restrictive reading is available for relatives marked with the tonal strategy can be represented by restricting tonal relatives to a LINK relation build from the embedded $Ty(e)$ node which is decorated with a variable $Fo(x)$. Since the variable and any restrictor associated with it enter the evaluation process of the eventual $Ty(e)$ expression, when information at the terminal nodes is passed up the tree to compute the semantic representation of the mother node, this will lead to a restrictive reading. We propose that this restriction is lexically encoded in the lexical information of the L toned relative subject marker, which can only be used in a tree context where a LINK relation has been built from the internal $Ty(e)$ expression. The restrictive reading is also encoded by the tone marking of the head noun, but we will postpone discussion of this to a later section.

(3.39) (tonal strategy)

abá-Bembá	*bà-lee-ikala*	*mu-Zambia*
2-Bembas	2REL.2SM-TNS-live	18-Zambia

bá-li-shuupa
SM2-TNS-be.difficult

'The Bembas who are living in Zambia nowadays are difficult.' (restrictive only)

The initial steps in the derivation are similar to the preceding example, but in this case as in (3.40), the LINK relation is launched from the $Ty(e)$ node decorated with $Fo(x)$, the nominal variable:

(3.40) Tonal strategy inducing a LINK structure

abá-Bembá
2-Bemba

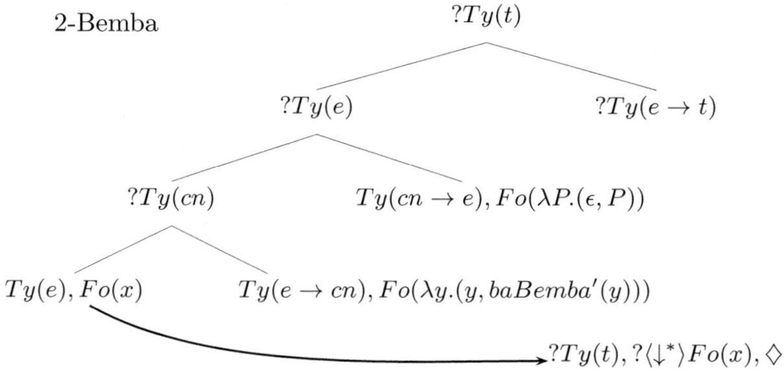

The following relative subject marker provides lexical information similar to the pronominal relative marker. However, there are significant differences. First, the first IF clause of the lexical entry for *bà-* in (3.41) requires the presence of a locally unfixed node, rather than an unfixed node. This reflects the fact that *bà-* is a subject marker, and as such is projected unto a locally unfixed node, as discussed in section 3.3. Secondly, the second IF clause requires that the formula at the node from which the LINK structure is launched should be dominated by $?Ty(cn)$. It is this condition which ensures that the only formula value which can be copied in tonal relatives is the quantificational variable, as this is the only formula value dominated by $?Ty(cn)$. This ensures that only a restrictive reading is possible with tonal relatives. Finally, the third IF clause requires that the restrictor of the linked $Ty(e)$ node be of class 2, thus ensuring agreement between the head and the relative marker. In contrast to the lexical requirements of the pronominal relative marker, in the present case it is not the copied formula itself which is of class 2, this being merely a variable, but class information comes from the restrictor of the variable, hence the need for a more complex restriction here. If all lexical conditions are fulfilled, the lexical entry licences the decoration of the node with an expression of $Ty(e)$ and a copy of the nominal variable as formula value.

(3.41) Lexical entry for *bà-*

IF	$?Ty(e), \langle\uparrow_0\rangle\langle\uparrow^*\rangle(?Ty(t))$		
THEN	IF	$\langle\uparrow_0\rangle\langle\uparrow^*\rangle\langle L^{-1}\rangle(Fo(\alpha)\&\langle\uparrow_0\rangle?Ty(cn))$	
	THEN	IF	$\langle\uparrow_0\rangle\langle\uparrow^*\rangle\langle L^{-1}\rangle\langle\uparrow_0\rangle\langle\downarrow_1\rangle Fo(U_{class2})$
		THEN	$\mathtt{put}(Ty(e), Fo(\alpha))$
	ELSE	abort	
ELSE	abort		

The entry reflects that *bà-* is a class 2 subject marker, while at the same time ensuring that it only occurs in restrictive relative contexts. The lexical actions of *bà-* then result in a locally unfixed subject marker, decorated with $Fo(x)$, and the subsequent information from tense marking provides a fixed subject and predicate node, at which the locally unfixed node can merge. After the verb is parsed and the predicate node annotated, the information from the linked tree can be compiled and serve as an annotation of the root tree as in (3.42):

(3.42) Tonal strategy: Incorporating Information from the LINK structure into the subject node

abá-Bembá *bà-lee-ikala* *mu-Zambia* ...
2-Bembas 2REL.2SM-TNS-live 18-Zambia

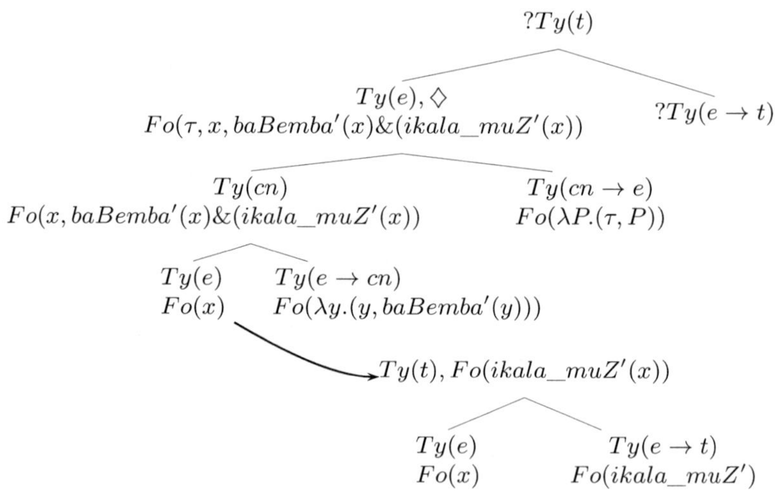

Since the information from the LINK structure is included in the information of the nominal variable, this information constitutes part of the nominal interpretation and is within the scope of nominal quantification, and thus a restrictive reading results.[6]

The difference then between the pronominal and the tonal relative strategies in Bemba is thus that in the pronominal strategy, an overt anaphoric element is introduced into the parse through the pronominal relative marker, and thus the pronominal strategy can be used for both restrictive and non-restrictive readings, while in the tonal strategy, the relative marker requires that the copy be a nominal variable, thus en-

[6]The formal analysis is in some respects similar to the analysis of empty relativizers in English proposed in Cann et al. (2005: 114), and so has applications beyond the specific case discussed here.

suring exclusively restrictive readings. In the following sections, we will extend this analysis to headless relatives, and to the tonal marking of head nouns.

3.5.4 Headless relatives

In this section, we will extend our analysis to headless relatives. Headless relatives are only available with the pronominal strategy, and not with the tonal strategy. Furthermore, headless relatives refer anaphorically to a given or inferred antecedent:

(3.43) *iciibi* *cá-ali-isuka.* *Á-ba-iswiile* *béêne*
7-door SM7-PAST-open 2REL-SM2-open 2owner
ba-nganda.
2GEN-house

'The door opened. (The one) who opened was the owner of the house.'

Headless relatives by themselves cannot be used as fully quantified terms, and in order to express such quantified structures, an overt quantifier such as *bonse* 'all' must be used as overt head:

(3.44) *B-onse* *á-bá-iswiile* *iciibi* *bá-léé-péépa.*
2-all 2REL-SM2-open door SM2-TNS-smoke

'Anyone/everyone who opened the door was smoking.'

This means that clearly restrictive readings as in (3.44) are not possible with headless relatives, even though the reading in (3.43) does not present a typical non-restrictive reading either: the inferred antecedent in (3.43) - glossed as 'the one' - is not unambiguously identifiable from the context, as the following relative provides essential information for the identification of the head. With respect to this blurring of the restrictive/non-restrictive distinction, the fact that only the pronominal strategy is available for headless relatives supports the idea that the construction of headless relatives in Bemba involves the anaphoric interpretation of a maximally weakly specified head provided by the context.

In our analysis of headless relatives, we are building on the DS analysis of head-final relatives in Japanese (Kempson and Kurosawa forthcoming). Kempson and Kurosawa note that in Japanese head-final relatives, similar to Bemba headless relatives, restrictive and non-restrictive readings cannot be clearly distinguished, and that their interpretation blurs this distinction. This results, according to Kempson and Kurosawa, from the fact that Japanese head-final relatives involve the construction of a maximally weak unrestricted epsilon term, of the form

$(\epsilon, x, P(x))$, before the relative clause and the head are parsed. The term serves as structural anticipation for the subsequent provision of the head, so that the relative clause can be projected against some existing structure, however weakly defined. For Bemba headless relatives, we assume, along similar lines, the construction of a weakly specified $Ty(e)$ expression, which serves as antecedent for the subsequent relative clause. Note that, as Kempson and Kurosawa point out, variables as used in restrictive relatives do not have any existence by themselves, without the term which binds them, making it implausible that a variable should be inferred in context. In contrast, $Ty(e)$ expressions as term denoting expressions, can be inferred and constructed in context to enter anaphoric relationships, and we thus assume that headless relatives are constructed against a contextually supplied $Ty(e)$ expression. However, the expression merely provides a skeletal structure without any content, and depends for its interpretation on the information supplied by the subsequent relative clause. While this implies that headless relatives are not restrictive, in the sense of restricting a predicate variable, they nevertheless have a sense of restrictiveness because the constructed $Ty(e)$ expression merely has an underspecified predicate value, and thus the expression depends on further input for its interpretation. The LINK structure for the headless relative can be launched from the anticipatory $Ty(e)$ node, and it is only with the information from the relative, that the predicate variable P is resolved. Our analysis of the relative pronoun used in the pronominal strategy provides a copy of the formula value of the $Ty(e)$ node from which the LINK structure is launched, and this is also true of headless relatives, even though in these cases, the copy does not contain any conceptual information, which is provided only from the information from the relative clause. In contrast, the unavailability of the tonal strategy for headless relatives follows from the fact that a copy of the variable has to be provided through lexical actions for the tonal strategy to be possible, and no such copy of a variable can be provided in headless relatives.

It follows from the analysis that headless relatives, even though not restrictive in the technical sense, still have restrictive appearance, since the information from the relative is essential for identifying the $Ty(e)$ term constructed, as this is constructed just as a skeleton term without conceptual content. However, this effect results from the interaction of the constructed node and subsequent information, and not from the copying of the nominal variable, as can be seen from the absence of truly quantified headless relatives.

3.5.5 Marking on head nouns

In the final part of our analysis, we will turn to the marking of the head noun in headed relatives. The two different marking patterns found with head nouns interact directly with the analysis of restrictive and non-restrictive relatives developed earlier, and in our analysis are sensitive to the presence or absence of a LINK structure at the time the $Ty(e)$ node is compiled. However, we will show at the end of the section that in light of similar data in the verb phrase, ultimately a more general analysis of tonal head marking might be preferable.

Recall that head nouns in relatives are marked with two different tone patterns, which are related to restrictive vs. non-restrictive readings.

(3.45)	*abá-Bembá*	*ábá-shipa*	*bá-ikala*	*mu-Zambia*
	2-Bemba	SM2.REL-be.brave	SM2-live	18-Zambia

'The Bembas who are brave live in Zambia.' (and those who are not live abroad)

(3.46)	*abá-Bemba*	*ábá-shipa*	*bá-ikala*	*mu-Zambia*
	2-Bemba	SM2.REL-be.brave	SM2-live	18-Zambia

'The Bembas, who are brave, live in Zambia.' (i.e. all Bembas are brave and live in Zambia)

In (3.45), the head noun is marked with a final high tone, sometimes called the conjoint tone pattern (Sharman 1956), and the reading of the relative is restrictive. In (3.46) there is a final L tone (the disjoint pattern), and the reading is non-restrictive. Given our discussion of restrictive and non-restrictive relatives above, one analysis is that the conjoint tone pattern (with final H) on the head noun indicates that a LINK relation has to be built immediately, before the value of the $Ty(e)$ expression is computed, while the disjoint tone pattern (with final L) indicates that any LINK relation has to be built after the semantic value of the head noun has been computed.

This idea can be implemented by making use of the complex nominal structure we have argued Bemba nouns project. So far, we have not discussed in detail how the eventual semantic value of the nominal is computed, and it is to this process which we now turn for an analysis of the tone patterns on head nouns. To start with, we assume with Cann et al. (2005: 108) that when the complex nominal structure is built, the pointer is at the variable node. From this node, either the information of this and the sister node can be combined to annotate the mother node and fulfil the requirement $?Ty(cn)$ holding at the node through computational rules (COMPLETION and ELIMINATION), or a LINK relation can be built, as we have seen in the examples of restrictive relatives above.

(3.47) Tonal marking of head nouns

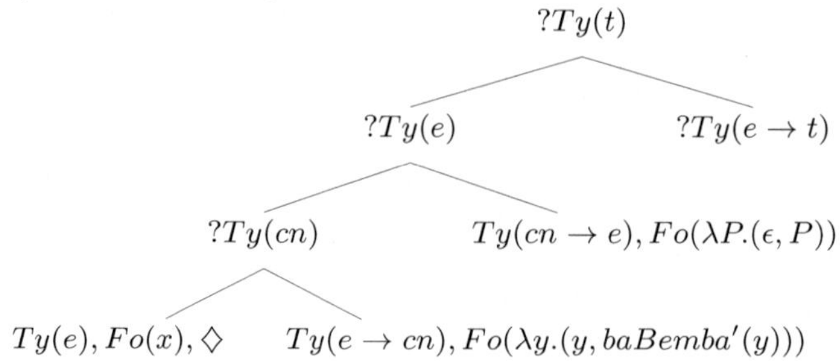

However, in contrast to, for example, English nominals, Bemba nouns include another lexical action. For H toned nouns, inducing a restrictive relative, we assume that they contain the lexical instruction to build a LINK structure. In the schematic lexical entry in (3.48), this is encoded in the last THEN statement, make($\langle L \rangle$).

(3.48) *abá-Bembá*

IF	$?Ty(e)$
THEN	`make`(...), ...`go`(...), `make`($\langle L \rangle$)
ELSE	abort

The entry implies that H toned nouns are always followed by some linked structure, although not necessarily one hosting a relative clause. Although further empirical evidence is needed, Sharman (1956) notes that H toned nouns are found when followed by conjunctions, adjectives or possessives. If our analysis is correct, all these modifiers project a LINK structure. L toned nouns, on the other hand, encode to the contrary that no LINK structure can be built from the variable node. The schematic lexical entry in (3.49) encodes this through the final statement of the THEN clause, $go(\langle \uparrow_0 \rangle), put(Fo(x, baBemba'(x)), Ty(cn))$.

(3.49) *abá-Bemba*

IF	$?Ty(e)$
THEN	`make`(...), ...`go`(...), `go`($\langle \uparrow_0 \rangle$), `put`($Fo(x, baBemba'(x)), Ty(cn)$)
ELSE	abort

The lexical instruction pre-empts the computational actions of COMPLETION and ELIMINATION. The requirement for $?Ty(cn)$ at the mother node is fulfilled through the lexical action encoded in the THEN statement. This means that the pointer moves away from the variable node as part of the lexical actions, and so with L toned nouns, there is never a situation in which a LINK structure could be built from the variable node. Any LINK structure with L toned nouns has to be built from the completed $Ty(e)$ nominal node, and will thus be non-restrictive.

This lexical analysis accounts for the relation between the tonal marking on head nouns and the interpretation of any following relative as restrictive or non-restrictive. However, as briefly mentioned above, there is in fact a more general pattern. Conceptually the distinction between the two noun forms seems to be not so much related to the presence or absence of a restrictive relative, but rather to whether a given nominal form provides enough information to construct a complete $Ty(e)$ term in the context, or whether for doing so, further lexical input is required. Thus, *abá-Bemba* with a final L tone says that all information to construct the $Ty(e)$ term is provided from the lexical information and the context, while *abá-Bembá* with final H says that the construction of the term is not yet complete. From this perspective, the tonal marking acts as an instruction about how the hearer is meant to process a given piece of information (here the noun), whether further relevant information is still to come, or whether the relevant term is meant to be constructed from the information provided by the noun alone. A very similar opposition is also found with verbs - in fact the alternation is probably better known with respect to verbs (e.g. Sharman 1956, Creissels 1996, Buell 2006, van der Wal 2009). Thus in Bemba, the tone marking of a past verb differs according to whether it is followed by a true object as part of the verb phrase (3.50), or by a right-dislocated topic (3.51):

(3.50) *tu-álíí-lóndól-á* *Mutale* (conjoint verb-form)
SM1PL-Past4-find-FV Mutale
'We found Mutale.'

(3.51) *tu-álíí-mú-lóndol-a* *Mutale* (disjoint verb-form)
SM1PL-Past4-OM1-find-FV Mutale
'We found him, Mutale.'

In (3.50) the verb stem is H toned, and the following NP is part of the verb phrase. In contrast, in (3.51) the verb stem is L toned (the H on the first syllable of the verb stem is likely to result from spreading of the H tone from the preceding object marker), and the following NP is a right-dislocated topic, co-referential with an object marker on the verb form. The parallel between the tone marking in the nominal and verbal domain is that in both cases, when the information introduced after the head – the restrictive relative clause or the direct object – makes a central contribution to the establishment of the interpretation of the head, conjoint marking is found on the head. On the other hand, if the following information is non-central – a non-restrictive relative or a dislocated topic – then disjoint marking is found. To bring out this parallelism between tone marking in the nominal and verbal domain, a more abstract analysis is needed, which does not make reference to the specific tree nodes involved. In the schematic rules in (3.52) and (3.53) we propose that the relevant information is about fulfilling the requirement of the mother node.

(3.52) *L TONE*
IF $Ty(X), \langle\uparrow\rangle(?Ty(Y))$
THEN $\texttt{go}(\langle\uparrow\rangle), \texttt{put}(Ty(Y))$

(3.53) *H TONE*
IF $Ty(X), \langle\uparrow\rangle(?Ty(Y))$
THEN $\neg(\texttt{go}(\langle\uparrow\rangle), \texttt{put}(Ty(Y)))$

The rule in (3.52) relates to a L tone in the context of a completed requirement, with an outstanding requirement at the mother node.[7] In this case, the requirement at the mother node can be fulfilled. In the nominal domain, this means, as we have seen above, that from the variable node, the pointer moves upwards and annotates the mother node with $Ty(cn)$. For verbs, this means that the pointer moves from a predicate node of $Ty(e \rightarrow (e \rightarrow t))$ as in (3.51), to the mother node, fulfilling the requirement for $Ty(e \rightarrow t)$, thereby precluding any further development of the verb phrase.[8] In contrast, H tone signals that this move is not allowed, that is, that the pointer should not move to the mother node, as this is not yet completed. The formulation in (3.53) is not entirely satisfactory in modelling this, as the negative lexical instruction does not preclude the application of computational rules to move the pointer to the mother node. However, the formulation does show the generality of tone marking, and we will leave it as it is for the moment. The more important point is that while the tone marking on the relative clause discussed in sections 3.5.2 and 3.5.3 was analyzed lexically, very much like a segmental morpheme, the tone marking on nouns is more akin to prosodic information. Like prosodic information, the H and L tones on nouns, and as we have seen on verbs, are associated with specific lexical items, but make a contribution independently

[7] The exact characterization of the relevant L (and H) tone remains to be refined, as not any L (H) tone triggers these rules, but only those which are found at the right edge of a noun or verb.

[8] This is particularly relevant if verb phrase modifiers are analyzed as $Ty(e)$ expressions (Marten 2002), rather than as functions on expressions of $Ty(e \rightarrow t)$, since under this view, moving the pointer to the $Ty(e \rightarrow t)$ node precludes further modification.

of the particular lexical item they attach to. Hence our eventual analysis does not make reference to the lexical host, but aims at bringing out this contribution irrespective of lexical or indeed categorial context, by relating the tone marking to pointer movement, and thereby to the progression of the process of tree growth. Ultimately the conjoint-disjoint alternation on both nouns and verbs shows that tone marking contributes to structure building at a more abstract level, by providing hearers with information about the time-linear process of constructing semantic representations, independent of the specific representation to be built.

3.6 Conclusions

In this paper we have developed an analysis of Bemba relatives with specific attention to the tonal properties of relative clauses and head nouns. Bemba distinguishes two relative clause strategies, the pronominal and the tonal strategy, the latter of which is only available in restrictive subject relatives. We have proposed an analysis of this difference which turns on the two different $Ty(e)$ positions within the DS representation of nominal structure, and the corresponding formula values copied from the two positions. While in the pronominal strategy, the pronominal element provides a copy of the formula of the head noun and can thus be used to express both restrictive and non-restrictive readings, the tonal strategy requires a lexically provided copy of a nominal variable, and can thus express only restrictive readings. In addition, Bemba has headless relatives which can only be formed with the pronominal strategy. Because headless relatives cannot be formed with the tonal strategy, which is only available to restrictive relatives, and in view of the absence of quantified headless relatives, we have argued that headless relatives are formed in the context of a contextually inferred term which serves as the host of the relative clauses, as in non-restrictive relatives. However, due to the severe underspecification of this term, the information from the relative functions as the only restriction of the head, so that even though technically not a restrictive relative, the interpretation of headless relatives often comes close to a restrictive interpretation, even though due to a different reason. Finally, head nouns are tonally distinguished, differentiating between restrictive and non-restrictive heads, and we have proposed that this reflects a prosodically marked instruction on whether the current task can be completed, or whether further lexical input is required to do so.

The analysis we have proposed is embedded in a wider argument about the relation between syntax and phonology. We have used the

Bemba facts to show how phonological information can be seen as contributing to the establishment of semantic representation in a parsing model like Dynamic Syntax. The analysis shows that tonal marking can be related to the time linearity of natural language parsing, providing hearers with information about anticipated parsing steps. In particular the parallelism in tone marking between head nouns and verbs provides striking confirmation for this view. We were thus concerned in this paper not so much with providing an analysis for Bemba relatives, for which perfectly good analyses exist (Kula and Cheng 2007, Kula 2007), but rather with gauging to what extent the particular interaction between prosody and interpretation found in Bemba relatives is compatible with the DS view of linguistic knowledge as parsing oriented. We have shown that the Bemba data provide evidence for the DS perspective, and that the analyses presented here require no independent syntactic and phonological structures to be assumed. Rather, both syntactic and phonological information contribute to the way semantic representations are built on-line.

References

The following were cited in this chapter: Blackburn and Meyer-Viol (1994), Buell (2006), Cann et al. (2005), Carstens (1991), Cheng and Kula (2006), Chomsky (1995), Contini-Morava (2002), Creissels (1996), Ferrari-Bridgers (2009), Givón (1969), Hyman and Katamba (1993), Inkelas and Zec (1990), Jackendoff (2002), Kaye (1989), Kempson and Kurosawa (forthcoming), Kempson et al. (2001), Kempson, Marten and Thwala (this volume), Kiaer (2005), Kiaer (2007), Kula (2002), Kula (2007), Kula (2009), Kula and Cheng (2007), Marten (2002), Marten (2007), Marten et al. (2008), Meeussen (1959), Selkirk (1984), Sharman (1956), Sharman and Meeussen (1955), Szendroi (2001), Truckenbrodt (1999), van der Wal (2009). See references at the end of the book for full information.

4

Future Constructions in Medieval Spanish: Mesoclisis uncovered

Miriam Bouzouita

This chapter deals with the synchronic variation found in 13th century Medieval Spanish (MedSp) between the analytic future (AF) and the synthetic future (SF).[1] This study aims to demonstrate that the use in future and conditional constructions is directly correlated to general clitic placement principles existing at the time. Despite the interaction of the AF and SF with clitic placement having been pointed out several times in the literature (Castillo Lluch 1996, 2002; Eberenz 1991 inter alia), this correlation has never been worked out in detail and alternative explanations continue to enjoy widespread acceptance (Company Company 1985-6, 2006; Company Company and Medina Urrea 1999 inter alia). By disentangling the various syntactic environments in which each of these future constructions appears and by then comparing them

I would like to thank Ruth Kempson, Stergios Chatzikyriakidis and Andrés Enrique-Arias for helpful input at various stages. Needless to say, any errors that remain are entirely my responsibility. Further, I would like to acknowledge the financial support provided by the Ministerio de Ciencia e Innovación of Spain in the form of a Juan de la Cierva Grant and Grant HUM2007-62259.

[1]This synchronic study of future constructions is limited to 13th century MedSp as substantial changes in clitic placement start taking place at the beginning of the 15th century (Bouzouita 2008a,b, 2009; Castillo Lluch 1996; Granberg 1988 inter alia). Considering this and that I will claim that the variation in futures is directly related to general clitic placement principles, diachronic changes are thus also expected to be found in the use of the various future constructions for those later periods. In this chapter, I leave these diachronic issues aside and refer the reader to Bouzouita (forthcoming a).

The Dynamics of Lexical Interfaces.
Ruth Kempson, Eleni Gregoromichelaki and Christine Howes (eds.).

to those in which clitics have been observed with non-future/conditional tenses, this correlation is made apparent as several distributional parallelisms can be observed (see also Castillo Lluch 1996, 2002). Once this correlation has been brought out, a Dynamic Syntax account (Cann et al. 2005; Kempson et al. 2001) is given both for this variation in future constructions and, more generally, for MedSp clitic placement with finite verbs. As argued elsewhere (Bouzouita 2007, 2008a,b, 2009), preverbal placement seems to be restricted to certain processing environments, whereas postverbal placement occurs in the absence of these environments. These same placement restrictions seem to hold for the future constructions as the SF with anteposition are encountered in the same processing environments as preverbal clitics with non-future tenses, while the AF and the SF constructions with postverbal clitics appear in the absence of these environments. All this suggests that the lexical entry proposed in earlier work for the MedSp clitic can also successfully account for AF cases without the need to posit any changes. In sum, when taking into account the correlation between the choice of future construction and the principles governing clitic placement, the distributional differences between the AF and the SF are fully expected and their variation appears no longer enigmatic.

4.1 Introduction

A striking feature of Medieval (and Renaissance) Spanish, which has received considerable attention from both the functional and the formal schools, is the synchronic variation in the use of different future constructions. This synchronic variation between the so-called analytic futures and conditionals, such as *tornar-m-é* 'I shall return' in example (4.1), and the synthetic ones, such as *daras* 'you will give' in example (4.2), will be the topic of this chapter.[2]

[2]The analytic future construction has been referred to by several terms, each of which reflects to a certain extent the author's way of conceiving the phenomenon in question. Keniston (1937: 72), for instance, dubs them 'split' futures, reflecting as such the idea of tmesis. Within the Chomskyan literature, they have been referred to as 'Long Head Movement' constructions (Lema and Rivero 1990, 1991; Rivero 1993, 1997; Silva Villar 1996) or 'Inverted conjugations' (Lema and Rivero 1992; Rivero 1991; Silva Villar 1996) whereas the synthetic forms as 'Incorporation' cases (Lema and Rivero 1991; Rivero 1991, 1997). In these cases, the terms manifest theory-internal characteristics attributed to these various future forms. In this chapter, I shall use the terms 'analytic' and 'synthetic' as these are the most frequently used ones. Further, the term 'clitic' is used as a pre-theoretical label. For visual reasons, I have decided to put the clitic pronouns in bold regardless of their position with respect to the finite verb. The abbreviations to be used are as follows: AF = analytic future(s)/conditional(s); SF = synthetic future(s)/conditional(s); CL = clitic; SG = singular; PL = plural; ACC = accusative; MedSp = Medieval Spanish.

(4.1) *E* *dixo:* *'Tornar-**m**-é* *a* *Jherusalem'*
and said.3SG return-CL-will.1SG to Jerusalem
'And he said: 'I shall return to Jerusalem [...]" (*Faz*: 194)

(4.2) *E* *dyxo* *ella:* *'Que* ***me*** *daras?'*
and said.3SG she what CL give-will.2SG
'And she said: 'What will you give me?" (*Faz*: 52)

As can be observed from both these examples, the Medieval Spanish (MedSp) future tense consists of an infinitive-like form followed by an auxiliary, which is an indicative present form of the verb *aver* 'to have'.[3] In analytic futures (AF), a clitic pronoun intervenes between these two parts: in example (4.1), for instance, the clitic *m* appears in between the infinitive-like *tornar* and the indicative present *é*. The term *mesoclisis* is generally used to refer to the positioning of clitics in such examples.[4] The synthetic futures (SF), on the contrary, do not contain such mesoclitic pronouns: as exemplified in (4.2), the clitic *me* appears in anteposition.[5] In SF contexts, this preverbal placement is the most frequently encountered positioning. Notwithstanding this, postverbal positioning with SF has also been attested but is quite rare in our corpus (see section 4.3.2).

The aim of this chapter is twofold. Firstly, I shall discuss and bring out the correlation between the different future structures and the general principles underlying clitic placement in 13th century MedSp. Secondly, I shall account for the observed variation in future constructions and, more generally, for MedSp clitic placement with respect to the finite verb.

The correlation between the variation in future constructions and clitic placement principles has been pointed out more than once in the literature, for instance by Eberenz (1991), Enrique Arias (2005: 71-72) and Rossi (1975) among others. Nonetheless, it has never been

[3]Unlike most studies, I do not consider the first part of the MedSp analytic future construction to be an infinitive and shall thus not refer to it as such, opting instead for the term 'infinitive-like' verb form. As we shall see later on, the formal properties of the latter differ from the former (see the lexical entries in (4.58) in section 4.4.2). Conditionals also consist of such an infinitive-like form but are followed by the imperfect past form of the verb *aver*.

[4]In this chapter, the term 'mesoclisis' refers solely to the clitic's syntactic position in AF constructions, without assuming its phonological dependency nor that what follows the clitic, which I dubbed the auxiliary, is a suffix. Since the terms *proclisis* and *enclisis* have been used to indicate not only syntactic positioning but also phonological dependency, I have decided to use the terms *anteposition* and *postposition* whenever referring to preverbal and postverbal placement respectively.

[5]SF can also appear without any clitic pronouns. These cases will not be discussed here.

worked out in detail and alternative explanations which brush this correlation aside, continue to enjoy widespread acceptance (Anipa 2000, 2001; Company Company 1985-6, 2006; Company Company and Medina Urrea 1999; Girón Alconchel 1997, 2002, 2005, 2007 inter alia). By disentangling the various syntactic environments in which each of the future constructions appears, I hope to make apparent the, in my view, undeniable link that exists between the choice of future construction and the principles governing clitic placement in 13th century MedSp. In the following, I shall first give an overview of the different kinds of analyses that have been put forward for the variation under discussion and evaluate them. Subsequently, I shall examine clitic placement with non-future/conditional tenses in 13th century MedSp. Once this has been done, I shall tease out the interaction of the AF and SF with clitic placement: (i) AF will be shown to occur only in those environments in which postverbal clitics are attested with other tenses of the verb, (ii) SF with preverbal clitics appear in the same syntactic contexts as anteposition with other tenses and (iii) SF with postposition, which is relatively rare, has only been observed in those environments which license postverbal clitics with other tenses. In other words, several distributional parallelisms can be observed between the use of the future constructions and the positioning of clitics in non-future contexts.

Once this correlation has been brought out, I shall account within the Dynamic Syntax framework (DS; Cann et al. 2005; Kempson et al. 2001) for MedSp clitics and the variation under discussion. As I argued elsewhere (Bouzouita 2007, 2008a,b, 2009), the pragmatic basis for Latin weak pronoun placement seems to have become routinized as a lexicalized sequence of actions in MedSp. In other words, the original pragmatic mechanism in Latin is being side-stepped in MedSp by the complex lexical entry of the clitic. As we shall see in section 4.4, preverbal placement seems to be restricted to certain processing environments, whereas postverbal placement occurs in the absence of these environments. The same seems to be true for the future constructions as the synthetic forms with anteposition are encountered in the same processing environments as preverbal clitics with non-future tenses, while the analytic and the synthetic constructions with postverbal clitics appear in the absence of these environments. In sum, when taking into account the correlation between the choice of future construction and the principles governing clitic placement, the distributional differences between the AF and the SF are fully expected. To exemplify, since some left-peripheral expressions can be interpreted using different processing environments, synchronic intra-speaker variation between anteposition and postposition is expected within one syntactic environment. This is indeed the case as, for instance, in non-future/conditional contexts both preverbal and postverbal clitics can be found following left-peripheral subjects. The same synchronic variation is then also expected for the future constructions, which is indeed corroborated by the data, as we shall see in section 4.3. If the hypothesis that, in MedSp, the variation between the AF and SF constructions depends directly on the clitic placement principles is correct, the lexical entry of the MedSp clitic, proposed in earlier work (e.g. Bouzouita 2008a), should also be able to account straightforwardly for the future/conditional constructions. As we shall see, this is indeed the case. In conclusion, the interaction between the future/conditional constructions and clitic placement in MedSp can be discerned not only in the data by the distributional parallelisms but also at the level of formal analysis, which is not unexpected.

4.2 Previous analyses

Broadly speaking, there are in the literature two different kinds of analyses that have been put forward to explain the existence of the AF construction.[6] First, there are those studies that consider the AF to be a not fully grammaticalized construction that is 'split' in two by one or more clitics due to restrictions governing MedSp clitic placement (Castillo Lluch 1996, 2002; Eberenz 1991; Meier 1965; Rossi 1975 inter alia). Most of these studies mention explicitly the Tobler-Mussafia Law, i.e. the restriction on sentence-initial clitics, as the raison d'être of the AF construction. In other words, the analytic constructions are considered to be a formal variant of their synthetic counterpart, some sort of a composed future tense. The second view, on the contrary, regards the AF as a marked structure used to indicate 'syntactic emphasis' or topicalization (Anipa 2000, 2001: chapter 6; Company Company 1985-86, 2006; Company Company and Medina Urrea 1999; Girón Alconchel 1997, 2002, 2005, 2007). Consequently, whereas the former view considers the AF and the SF to be equivalent on both the semantic and pragmatic level, this is not the case for the latter perspective as it advances a special discourse function for the AF constructions. In the following, I shall give an overview of these various accounts and the

[6]Company Company (2006: 363-364) distinguishes three kinds of explanations: apart from the two analyses I shall mention here, she also distinguishes those that consider the AF to be an archaic form. Since most of those that hold this view, if not all, also consider the AF to be an equivalent form of the synthetic one but one that is 'split' or a composed tense, I shall not discuss this view separately.

arguments they put forward and critically evaluate their merit.[7]

4.2.1 The analytic future as a product of clitic placement restrictions

It has been observed, more than once, that there exists a correlation between the use of the AF and SF, on the one hand, and MedSp clitic placement principles, on the other. In general, most functional studies that examine MedSp clitic placement, assume that the grammatical nature of the constituent (immediately) preceding the clitic and finite verb determines in some sense the preverbal or postverbal position of the clitic (Ramsden 1963; Elvira 1987; Nieuwenhuijsen 1999, 2002, 2006 inter alia). Because of this, most of these studies tend to give detailed descriptions of the various syntactic environments in which MedSp clitics appear: the descriptions given by Granberg (1988) and Castillo Lluch (1996), for instance, have been carried out with an utmost care for the data and seem to be more or less exhaustive (see also Bouzouita 2008a). I shall argue later on that it is not the grammatical nature of the constituent preceding the clitic that determines clitic placement in 13th (and 14th) century MedSp but the processing strategies used for building up the semantic content of these left-peripheral constituents. In other words, the way in which these left-peripheral constituents are processed (parsed/produced) influences the subsequent positioning of the clitic with respect to the finite verb (for Medieval and Renaissance Spanish see Bouzouita and Kempson 2006; Bouzouita 2007, 2008a,b, 2009; for Cypriot Greek see Chatzikyriakidis 2010: chapter 4). Along the same lines, it has been observed that the synchronic variation observed for the MedSp future constructions is correlated to the syntactic environment in which they appear. For instance, Gessner (1893: 41-42), who was among the first to notice this correlation, noted that AF appear in a matrix clause when in sentence-initial position, following a subordinate clause or the coordination marker *e(t)/y* 'and', or in those syntactic environments in which postposition is found with the other tenses. In subordinate clauses, on the contrary, he states that AF are hardly recorded. Gessner (1893: 41) relates the distribution of futures/conditionals directly to clitic placement restrictions as he claims that analytic constructions surge in those syntactic conditions that would license postposition with other tenses. As we shall see in

[7] I do not aim to give an exhaustive account of all the existing analyses. Furthermore, due to the scope of this chapter, I shall be limiting the analyses to be discussed to those that deal with MedSp and, thus, I shall leave aside those discussing solely Renaissance Spanish or Spanish of later periods (e.g. Anipa 2000, 2001; Eberenz 1991; Girón Alconchel 1997, 2002, 2005, 2007; Keniston 1937).

section 4.3, Gessner's observations seem to be correct as the results from my corpus point in the same direction.

Staaff (1907: 628-629) also considers the MedSp future (and conditional) to be a not fully grammaticalized tense and tries to capture its clitic placement by two rules, the first of which concerns the analytic constructions whereas the second the synthetic ones with anteposition:[8]

> *1. Si le futur (ou le conditionnel) commence la phrase, ce temps est regardé comme composé et le pronom se place entre les deux membres s'appuyant par enclise à l'infinitif.*
>
> *2. Si le futur (ou le conditionnel) est précédé d'un autre mot, le temps est regardé comme simple et le pronom se place avant le verbe s'appuyant par enclise au mot qui precede.*

As regards the first rule, it seems indeed to be the case that, whenever a future construction appears clause-initially, the AF one is by far the most frequently encountered one. However, as Staaff (1907: 628) himself notes, SF cases with postverbal clitics have also been attested. As we shall see later on, my corpus also contains such postverbal synthetic cases but they are very marginal in comparison to the analytic ones. As a result, the first rule given above is not an absolute universal but describes rather a tendency. According to Staaff (1907: 628, footnote 2), this rule also applies to a whole array of other syntactic environments, which he lists separately in a footnote: to wit, when the future form is preceded by (i) a subordinate clause, (ii) an absolute gerund, (iii) a vocative, (iv) the coordination conjunction *e* 'and', (v) the contrastive coordination marker *mas* 'but' or (vi) a nominal complement that is coreferential with the following clitic (the so-called CLLD/HTLD cases). Although he suggests that only AF are expected for the above-mentioned syntactic environments, this is not always case. For instance, in coordination structures introduced by *e* 'and' SF have also been attested, as illustrated by the anteposition example in (4.3) and the postposition one in (4.4).[9]

(4.3)	*Yot*	*acreceré*	*e*	***te***	*muchiguaré*
	I-CL	enlarge-will.1SG	and	CL	multiply-will.1SG

[8]'1. If a future (or a conditional) begins the sentence, this tense is regarded as composed and the pronoun is placed in between the two members while leaning enclitically on the infinitive. 2. If a future (or a conditional) is preceded by another word, this tense is regarded as simple and the pronoun will precede the verb while leaning enclitically on the preceding word' (Staaff 1907: 628, translation is mine).

[9]It should be pointed out that in MedSp SF with postposition is very rare. Moreover, these cases seem to be restricted to certain textual genres, such as poetry (e.g. *Poema de mio Cid*) and biblical translations (e.g. *Fazienda de Ultra Mar*, ms. Escorial I.i.6, ms. Escorial I.i.8). For an in-depth discussion of these SF examples with postposition and an explanation for their occurrence, I refer the reader to Bouzouita (forthcoming b).

'I will enlarge and multiply you.' (*Faz.*: 58)

(4.4)	e	pornedes**las**	sobre	vuestras	fijas	e
	and	put-will.2PL-CL	on	your	daughters	and
	*toldredes**las***	*a*	*los*	*Egiptos*		
	bring-will.2PL-CL	to	the	Egyptians		

'[...] and you will put them on your daughters and bring them to the Egyptians.' (*Faz.*: 63)

As can be seen, in example (4.3) the clitic *te* precedes the SF *muchiguaré* 'I will multiply' following the coordination conjunction *e* 'and' while in example (4.4) the SF *pornedes* 'you will put' and *toldredes* 'you will bring' are both followed by the clitics *las*. Synchronic variation is thus observed within one and the same syntactic environment. This is not only true for the coordination environments with *e* but also for the CLLD/HTLD cases, as we shall see later on (see examples (4.9) and (4.10), and section 4.3). Staaff's first rule is thus not satisfactory as it does not capture all the facts. The same is also true for the second rule. Once again, Staaff (1907: 629) is aware of the shortcomings of his analysis and tries to make up for this by invoking an additional explanation: when faced with cases in which analytic constructions are found after left-peripheral constituents, he attributes the mesoclitic positioning to the presence of a caesura – a phonological pause – after the preposed element. Such a phonological pause is said to prevent the clitic pronoun from occurring preverbally as it needs a phonological host on its left due to its supposedly enclitic nature. The idea that phonological factors are at the basis of MedSp clitic placement has frequently been put forward, not only in the older literature (Menéndez Pidal 1926) but also more recently (Ramsden 1963; Sanchis Calvo 1991: 421; Schmidely 1998: 806; Grecco Ramírez 2001: 23, 82, 94-95). However, this phonological explanation cannot account for all the mesoclitic examples Staaff encountered as some do not have a caesura preceding the AF, a fact he acknowledges but leaves unexplained. The phonological hypothesis Staaff invokes can also be invalidated on the basis of examples in which preverbal placement is attested despite a phonological pause being present after the left-peripheral constituent. Consider for instance the following example from my corpus (see also section 4.4.1):

(4.5)	*Estas*	*bestias*	*grandes*	*que*	*son*	*.iiii.*	*reyes*	***se***
	these	beasts	big	that	are.3PL	four	kings	CL
	levantaran							
	stand-up-will.3PL							

'These big beasts which are four kings will stand up.'

(*Faz.*: 181)

In example (4.5), the clitic *se* precedes the SF *levantaran* 'they will stand up' despite the subject (*estas bestias grandes* 'these big beasts') being followed by a relative clause (*que son .iiii. reyes* 'that are four kings'), a case said to contain a phonological pause after the relative construal. In view of the existence of such counterexamples, the presence of a phonological break can thus not be at the basis of the use of the AF following left-peripheral constituents, as claimed by Staaff, nor, more generally, can it elucidate clitic placement in MedSp (Bouzouita 2008a: 74-80, 250-252; Castillo Lluch 1996: 353-361). In sum, the two rules formulated by Staaff are inadequate and oversimplified as they fail to capture all the facts.

To come back to the distribution of the future constructions, Menéndez Pidal (1926: 399) was among one of the first to note that negation environments invariably contain SF with anteposition, as exemplified below. Moreover, he attributes this to the fact that the negation adverb *non* 'not' invariably triggers preverbal placement of clitics with other tenses, as such acknowledging the link between the use of the future constructions and clitic placement restrictions.

(4.6)	<u>*Non*</u>	***lo***	*podras*	*fer*	*a solas*
	not	CL	can-will.2SG	do	alone

'You won't be able to do it alone.' (*Faz*: 74)

As example (4.6) illustrates, the negation adverb *non* 'not' is followed by a preverbal clitic *lo* 'it' and a SF *podras* 'you will be able'.[10] Although Menéndez Pidal's observation regarding the negation environments seems to be correct, the same cannot be said of his statement that variation is observed whenever another element precedes the future construction (1928: 399). Although it is true that certain syntactic environments in which a constituent, such as a subject for instance, precedes the future form, exhibit synchronic variation, this is certainly not the case for all such environments. Following *wh*-words, for example, only SF with preverbal clitics have been attested (see section 4.3.2). Consequently, Menéndez Pidal's (second) observation draws too general a conclusion.

Rossi's (1975) study, based on a part of the 13th century biblical text ms. Escorial I-i-6 (*E6*), gives a more detailed description of the syntactic distribution of both the AF and SF constructions involving clitic pronouns. For ease of consultation, her findings have been summarized

[10]Note that this example is a clitic climbing case as the clitic belongs logically to the infinitive *fer* 'to do' and not the finite future verb *podras*. For a DS account of clitic climbing, see Chatzikyriakidis (this volume).

in Table 1 (calculations are mine). Based on the data she obtained, Rossi (1975: 393-394) reaches the following conclusions:

(a) Syntactic environments in which a future construction appears following (i) a negation adverb, (ii) a relative pronoun, (iii) an adverb or (iv) a subordinating conjunction, do not license either SF with postposition or AF constructions

(b) Syntactic environments in which a future construction appears (i) sentence-initially following a 'secondary' clause, (ii) following the coordination conjunction *e* 'and', or (iii) in absolute sentence-initial position, do not license SF with anteposition

(c) Syntactic environments in which a future construction appears following (i) an object, (ii) a circumstantial phrase/complement or, (iii) a subject license both SF with anteposition and AF constructions

TABLE 1 Syntactic distribution of future constructions (Rossi 1975)

Syntactic Environment	**SF with Anteposition**	**SF with Postposition**	**AF Mesoclisis**
Negation	100% (10/10)	-	-
Relative pronoun	100% (6/6)	-	-
Adverb	100% (6/6)	-	-
Subord. conj.	100% (3/3)	-	-
Object	66.7% (2/3)		33.3% (1/3)
Circumst. compl.	66.7% (2/3)	-	33.3% (1/3)
Subject	60% (15/25)	-	40% (10/25)
'Secondary' clause	-	7.7% (1/13)	92.3% (12/13)
Coordination conj.	-	8.7% (2/23)	91.3% (21/23)
Sentence-initial	-	-	100% (5/5)
Total	**45.4%** (44/97)	**3.1%** (3/97)	**51.5%** (50/97)

Several remarks and clarifications about Rossi's (1975) observations are in order. To begin with, Rossi's first conclusion seems to be formulated too strongly since both SF with postposition and AF constructions have also been attested in the adverb environments, as exemplified below following the adverb *agora* 'now':[11]

[11] As mentioned earlier, SF with postposition is very rare and seems to be restricted mainly to biblical translations. Example (4.7) proceeds from *E6*, the biblical text on which Rossi's study is based. Note, however, that, whereas this example comes from the prophetic *Book of Isaiah*, Rossi analyzed the *Book of Proverbs*, a sapiential text. See Bouzouita (forthcoming b) for a detailed study of *E6* in which it is shown that SF cases with postposition seem to mimick the syntax of the underlying Latin text. See Matute and Pato (forthcoming) for an alternative explanation.

(4.7) *E* *agora* *mostrare* ***uos*** *que* *fare* *a* *la*
and now show-will.1SG CL what do-will.1SG to the
mi *uinna*
my vineyard

'And now I will tell you what I will do to my vineyard.'
(*E6*: IS 5.5, *Biblia Medieval*)

(4.8) *Agora* *conplir**se*** *an* *tus* *palabras*
now fulfill-CL will.3PL your words

'Now your words will be fulfilled.' (*Faz.*: 208)

As concerns Rossi's second conclusion, she includes in what she dubs 'secondary' clauses both preceding non-root clause environments and CLLD/HTLD cases, such as the one given in example (4.9).

(4.9) *las viandas que comieres,* *camiarás**las***
the food that eat.2SG vomit-will.2SG-CL

'The food that you will have eaten, you will vomit.'
(*E6, Prov.*: 23.8 *apud* Rossi 1975: 393)

Such CLLD/HTLD cases are said to admit either AF or SF with postposition, the latter case being exemplified in example (4.9). However, the situation is more complex than reported by Rossi as SF with anteposition have also been encountered in such syntactic contexts. As can be seen in example (4.10), the coreferential clitic *lo* precedes the synthetic future *quemara* 'he will burn' despite following a left-dislocated object *todo* 'all'. The same remark also applies for the coordination cases with *e* 'and' since anteposition has also been attested, as we saw when discussing Staaff's distribution rules (see example (4.3) and section 4.3.2).

(4.10) *Et* *todo* ***lo*** *quemara* *enell* *altar*
and all CL burn-will.3SG in the altar

'And he will burn it all on the altar.' (*GE1*, CDE s.v. *todo lo* **ara**)

Rossi's third conclusion, which concerns the variation cases, lacks preciseness: a distinction needs to be made between those left-peripheral objects that are coreferential with (one of) the following clitic(s) and those that are not since this difference influences the position of subsequent clitics. To be more specific, non-coreferential complements will always appear with anteposition (see Table 3 section 4.3) whereas variation has been attested for the CLLD/HTLD cases, which contain a coreferential left-peripheral object, as we observed in examples (4.9) and (4.10). In my view, this methodological shortcoming in Rossi's study could have been prevented if she had used a larger corpus (her whole corpus consists only of 97 future cases, of which a mere 50 examples are analytic ones). If she had done so, the differences in clitic placement between these environments would have come out more clearly. Moreover, Rossi's classification of the data is not completely consistent as some CLLD/HTLD cases have been included with the so-called 'secondary' clauses, to wit those which contain a relative clause, whereas those that are not modified have been classified under the object environment.

Notwithstanding the above-mentioned deficiencies, the merit of Rossi's study lies in the fact that it is, as far as I know, the first systematic survey of the syntactic distributions of the different future constructions. Moreover, this investigation also demonstrates, albeit implicitly, that there is a correlation between general clitic placement rules and the use of the future constructions: certain syntactic environments, such as the negation one for instance, exclude the use of analytic constructions and of synthetic ones with postposition as is also the case for postposition cases with other tenses. However, like Staaff (1907), Rossi (1975: 394-397) postulates a rhythmic/phonological explanation for the variation cases mentioned in conclusion (c): the appearance of AF in subject environments, for instance, is attributed to the presence of a pause behind the left-peripheral subject and the following analytic construction. Cases with anteposition, on the contrary, are said not to contain such a pause. As was the case for Staaff's study, this type of explanation leaves unexplained 6 cases out of a total of 97. Rossi (1975: 397) brushes this fact aside by claiming that it is a too small number of counterexamples to invalidate her hypothesis. In my opinion, on the contrary, these cases invalidate the phonological explanation since they constitute 16% of Rossi's corpus, which is not insignificant. Consequently, their distribution remains to be accounted for within this analysis.

Within the generative literature too it has been noticed that there exists in MedSp a correlation between the future constructions and the principles governing clitic placement and this point has been made explicitly. Long Head Movement (LHM), the type of movement proposed to account for the analytic constructions, is considered to be a last resort rule to prevent the violation of the constraint against sentence-initial clitics (Lema 1994; Lema and Rivero 1990, 1991, 1992). As regards the syntactic distributions of the future constructions, LHM patterns are said to be restricted to root contexts where the non-finite V can land in a vacant C. More specifically, Lema and Rivero (1990, 1991, 1992) make the following observations:

(a) Incorporation, i.e. the type of movement licensing SF with anteposition, takes place in (i) negation environments, (ii) *wh*-questions, (iii) fronted NP and PP root contexts with no resumptive clitic, and (iv) in relative and (most) complement clauses

(b) LHM takes place following (i) Left-Dislocations, (ii) adverbs and sentence-initial phrases 'establishing a connection with the previous discourse', and (iii) in complement clauses containing so-called two CP layers

(c) Variation has been attested (i) following subjects, and (ii) in conjunction contexts with *et/y* 'and', *ca* 'because', and *mas/(en)pero* 'but'

Here as well some comments are in order. Firstly, certain PPs, namely those functioning as adverbials, can also appear with AF and not just with SF with anteposition, and this despite there not being a resumptive clitic present. Secondly, Left-Dislocation structures (CLLD/HTLD) do not only exhibit the analytic pattern but also the synthetic one, as illustrated in examples (4.9)-(4.10). Lema and Rivero (1991: 260) also claim that variation is found following the contrastive markers *mas/(en)pero* 'but' without giving any examples. In my corpus, on the contrary, no occurrences of SF with anteposition have been encountered and, as far as I know, this is also the case for all the other studies available on this subject. Since the authors in question do not exemplify their claim, I can only hypothesize that the preverbal cases they encountered do not proceed from 13th (nor 14th) century texts and, thus, that the clitic placement in those cases must be due to a diachronic change. This assumption is not implausible since Lema and Rivero's corpus also includes tokens from the 15th century, a period in which dramatic changes in the clitic placement system start taking place (Arias Alvarez 1995; Bouzouita 2008a,b, 2009; Castillo Lluch 1996; Eberenz 2000; Granberg 1988).[12] In other words, Lema and Rivero might have reached this conclusion for MedSp due to the methodological mistake of having included 15th century data in their corpus. Despite these inaccuracies, Lema and Rivero's work is of great importance as they were, to my knowledge, the first ones to make explicit that in MedSp (i) analytic futures alternate productively with the preverbal synthetic ones 'in almost syntactic complementary distribution' and that (ii) 'the syntax of LHM should be very similar to that of Old Romance enclisis [postposition] with finite Vs', which is indeed the case as we shall see later on (Lema and Rivero 1991: 251-252).

Castillo Lluch (1996: section 3.4), when investigating MedSp clitic

[12]For a detailed account of the different syntactic environments which were affected by this diachronic change, I refer the reader to Bouzouita (2008a,b, 2009).

placement for her (unfortunately unpublished) doctoral dissertation, also comes to the conclusion that there is a correlation between the use of the future forms and the restrictions on clitic placement. In a short article on this subject, she explains that this is evidenced by two facts (Castillo Lluch 2002: 544):

(a) Analytic constructions can only appear in the presence of clitic pronouns

(b) Synthetic forms are used in those phonological-syntactic contexts in which anteposition is found with other tenses, whereas the analytic ones are attested in those contexts licensing postposition (occasionally, synthetic forms with postposition are also encountered in the latter contexts)

The SF with anteposition and AF constructions are argued to be in complementary distribution. SF with postposition is also acknowledged to occur. Moreover, they appear in the same syntactic environments as the AF (Castillo Lluch 1996, 2002; see also Lema and Rivero 1991: 251).

Although Castillo Lluch's description of clitic placement in MedSp is pretty much exhaustive and she correctly notes the correlation under discussion, she concludes, like Staaff (1907) and Rossi (1975), that phonological/rhythmic factors can explain certain clitic placement cases. However, unlike Staaff (1907) and Rossi (1975), she recognizes the existence of examples, such as (4.5), that cannot be explained by these factors alone. She therefore opts to conclude that syntactic-phonological factors govern MedSp clitic placement, without detailing the specifics of the syntactic side (Castillo Lluch 1996: 361). In section 4.4, the phonological factors which seem to regulate MedSp clitic placement will be shown to be an epiphenomenon of the processing strategies used for parsing/producing the left-peripheral constituents preceding the clitics. As such, I do not deny the existence of a correlation between phonology and clitic placement. However, I do not consider there to be a causal relationship between them.

In summary, all these different accounts relate, to a greater or lesser extent, the variation in future constructions to restrictions which constrain the clitic placement system in MedSp, such as, for instance, the Tobler-Mussafia Law. Some of these studies bring out this correlation only implicitly by describing the distributions of the distinct future forms (e.g. Rossi 1975), others, on the contrary, make this link explicit (e.g. Castillo Lluch 1996, 2002; Lema 1994; Lema and Rivero 1990, 1991, 1992). Notwithstanding this, none of the studies describe side by side the clitic placement found for both the future constructions and the other tenses. Furthermore, most of the above-mentioned analyses (e.g.

Castillo Lluch 1996, 2002; Rossi 1975; Staaff 1907) conclude that phonological/rhythmic factors are, to a greater or lesser extent, at the basis of the variation found in the MedSp future/conditional system. I, on the contrary, shall argue in section 4.4 that it is not phonological/rhythmic factors but the processing strategies used for parsing/producing the left-peripheral constituents preceding the clitics that influence MedSp clitic placement and thus also the use of the future forms. In the following, I shall first discuss an alternative view, according to which the use of the AF construction is not related to clitic placement restrictions. Instead, it is posited that analytic structures are marked forms used for topicalization and 'syntactic emphasis'.

4.2.2 The analytic future as a marked form

Analytic futures and clitic placement as uncorrelated phenomena

An alternative theory has first been proposed by Company Company (1985-6) in a seminal article in which she advances that AF constructions, unlike their synthetic counterparts, are marked forms used for topicalization. Topicalization processes are defined in this chapter as involving a change in the regularly encountered word order, whereby a constituent –the topic– is placed sentence-initially. These topicalized constituents are said to bear specific topic features, such as [+definite]. Whole sentences can also be topicalized, in which case the verb tends to be placed initially (Company Company 1985-6: 82). In this paper, the author considers the existence of AF to be completely unrelated to clitic placement (Company Company 1985-6: 95):[13]

> *Considero que la existencia de futuros analíticos en la gramática del español medieval no puede ser analizada en función de restricciones en la distribución de clíticos pronominales dentro de la oración.*

The following four arguments are said to corroborate this view (Company Company 1985-6: 95-96):

(a) Since postposition of the clitic exists also for the SF, the existence of the AF cannot be attributed to the Tobler-Mussafia Law

(b) Considering that both sentence-initial clitics and mesoclisis can be found in 15th century texts, the Tobler-Mussafia Law cannot be the raison d'être for the AF constructions

(c) Since in certain MedSp syntactic environments, such as those with the coordination conjunction *e* 'and', variation between the AF

[13]'I believe that the existence of the analytic futures in the grammar of MedSp cannot be analyzed in function of restrictions on the distribution of pronominal clitics within the sentence' (Company Company 1985-6: 95; translation is mine).

and the SF with anteposition has been observed, restrictions on clitic placement cannot be the basis of this variation

(d) Since AF do not always appear sentence-initially, the clitic has other constituents on which to lean phonologically and, thus, clitic placement restrictions cannot be the reason for the appearance of AF

As regards the first argument, it is indeed correct that SF with postverbal clitics have also been attested. In my view, on the contrary, the existence of this synthetic construction does not undermine the hypothesis that restrictions underlie the appearance of the analytic structure as it has been shown that these SF structures are not only very rare (see section 4.3.2), – something Company Company (1985-6, 2006) does not mention – but also because most cases that appear in MedSp seem to mimick biblical Latin and Hebrew syntax (Bouzouita forthcoming b).[14] In view of the previous, I am inclined to conclude, like some other scholars, such as Castillo Lluch (1996: 385), that there is no real variation between these synthetic forms and the analytic ones.

As shown in Company Company's second argument, she includes, like Lema and Rivero (1990, 1991, 1992), 15th century data in her corpus.[15] As I have explained before, MedSp clitic placement starts undergoing dramatic diachronic changes from the 15th century onwards. One of the changes observed is the loss of the Tobler-Mussafia Law, resulting in the appearance of sentence-initial clitics. However, the fact that this restriction starts eroding in the 15th century does not entail that the principles governing clitic placement were not correlated to the appearance of the AF in MedSp. In view of this, Company Company's second argument is also questionable.

The third argument advanced by Company Company can be refuted on the basis of the fact that variation between anteposition and postposition is also encountered with non-future tenses in certain syntactic environments (see section 4.3). In fact, as we shall see later on, this variation is intrinsic to the clitic placement system and I argue that it is due to different ways of processing the left-peripheral constituents that precede the clitics.

With respect to Company Company's fourth argument, it is indeed correct that not all AF appear sentence-initially. She alludes here to

[14]For an overview of the MedSp SF with postverbal clitics mentioned in the literature, I refer the reader to Bouzouita (forthcoming b).

[15]As pointed out by Eberenz (1991: 501), Company Company's corpus (1985-6) is problematic as it also includes the *Poema de mio Cid*, a text subject to poetic license due to its meter. For more details on how this can influence clitic placement, see Bouzouita (2008a: 35-37, 138-139).

the phonological explanation proposed for MedSp clitic placement, according to which clitics cannot appear sentence-initially as they are said to be phonologically enclitic. As she correctly notes, in the cases in which an AF is preceded by another constituent, the clitic could in theory lean phonologically onto this left-peripheral constituent and thus appear with a synthetic construction. As mentioned earlier when discussing Staaff's analysis, an additional phonological explanation has been invoked for these cases: a phonological pause present before the future/conditional is alleged to prevent the clitic from phonologically leaning on the preceding constituent or word, thereby justifying the use of the analytic construction. Recall, however, that I showed that phonological explanations cannot account for all the clitic placement data as certain examples, such as example (4.5), contain preverbal clitics following such a pause. In view of this, it seems to be correct, as Company Company argues, that the use of the future constructions is not governed by phonological restrictions, which are claimed to govern MedSp clitic placement. What is not taken into account in this argumentation is the possibility that (i) non-phonological factors might be regulating the MedSp distribution of clitics and that (ii) these can also govern the variation seen for the future constructions. In sum, Company Company argumentation which aims to prove that the use of AF constructions is not related to MedSp clitic placement principles is unconvincing.

Analytic futures as reanalyzed marked forms

In later work, the view that AF and clitic placement are uncorrelated phenomena is partially retracted (Company Company 2006; Company Company and Medina Urrea 1999). The following quote from Company Company's latest contribution to the study of futures illustrates this position clearly (Company Company 2006: 384):[16]

> *[...] el origen de los futuros analíticos se debe a restricciones en la colocación de clíticos, pero su funcionamiento en el español medieval, especializado para topicalización y énfasis sintáctico, no se debe ya a la ley de enclisis.*

As can be seen, clitic placement restrictions are said to have been at the origin of the AF constructions. In MedSp, however, these restrictions are claimed to no longer play a role in the variation found between the future forms as the analytic ones have been reanalyzed as a specialized construction for topicalization and syntactic emphasis. Various

[16] '[...] the origin of analytic futures is due to clitic placement restrictions, but its functioning in MedSp, which is specialized for topicalization and syntactic emphasis, is no longer due to the enclisis law (Company Company 2006: 384; translation is mine).

arguments are used to substantiate this claim, two of which will be discussed in the following.[17]

In MedSp, AF never occur in negation contexts, as noted in the earliest studies (e.g. Menéndez Pidal 1926). Although Company Company (2006: 385-387) concedes that originally this might have been due to clitic placement restrictions, she proposes that in MedSp this is due to the AF's purported function of marking topicalization and syntactic emphasis: if these future forms were to co-occur with negation adverbs, these would cancel out the special discourse function for which the AF have been reanalyzed. Additionally, she hypothesizes that, since in many languages negative sentences are marked, the same could be true for MedSp and thus the absence of AF in these contexts might be due to avoiding doubly marked structures. In my view, the reanalysis of the AF which this analysis postulates is unnecessary, since clitic distribution restrictions alone can account for the absence of these futures in negation contexts: postverbal clitics, like AF, are not encountered in negation contexts either (see section 4.3). The reanalysis proposed by Company Company is thus superfluous.

Another argument used by Company Company (2006: 396-402) is that AF have a restricted distribution in comparison to the SF: they often appear in sentence-initial position, and when they do not appear sentence-initially, they can only be preceded by topicalized constituents, which are said to 'bear some sort of syntactic emphasis' (Company Company 2006: 399). She identifies five different topicalized constituents following which AF can appear: (i) direct objects, (ii) subjects, (iii) vocatives, (iv) adverbial modifiers and (v) other constituents which exhibit the topic feature [+definite] (Company Company 2006: 399-401; see section 4.3.1 and 4.3.2 for a discussion of these (and other) environments). This restricted distribution is interpreted by the author as proof for the marked status of the AF. It is indeed correct that AF appear only in certain syntactic environments. However, the same is true for SF appearing with clitics. In view of this, I think Company Company might have come to the conclusion that AF have a more restricted distribution in comparison to the SF as she also seems to include those SF cases which appear without clitic pronouns. In the following section, I shall demonstrate that the distribution of the AF corresponds exactly to the distribution of postverbal clitics with other tenses. In other words, the restricted distribution of the AF is a direct consequence of MedSp clitic placement restrictions. Consequently, the

[17]For a lengthy discussion of the various arguments posited in Company Company (2006), see Bouzouita (forthcoming c).

topicality which Company Company associates with AF can be considered to be an epiphenomenon or a by-product of another phenomenon, to wit the general features of the MedSp clitic placement system.

4.3 Clitic placement in Medieval Spanish

In this section, I shall first discuss clitic placement in non-future or non-conditional root contexts.[18] Subsequently, I shall compare these results with the distribution of clitics found in future and conditional root environments. Through this comparison I shall demonstrate that there exist several distributional parallelisms:

(i) The distribution of the AF patterns exactly with the one for postposition in other tenses
(ii) The distribution of the SF with anteposition patterns with the one for anteposition in other tenses
(iii) The SF with postposition only occur in those syntactic environments for which postposition has been observed with other tenses.

In sum, I shall illustrate in detail that there exists a complementary distribution, as has been observed by others but not worked out in detail. By exposing these distributional parallelisms, I aim to show that the variation in use of the various future forms is not only correlated to the MedSp clitic placement system but also governed by the same underlying principles.

In 13th century MedSp, the predominant clitic position in root clauses which do not contain verbs in the future or conditional tense seems to be the postverbal one: in my corpus, only 19.3% (361/1870) of anteposition is registered (see Table 4 in section 4.3.2).[19] In non-root clauses, on the other hand, the most frequently encountered clitic position is anteposition, with clitics occurring preverbally after relative pronouns, complementizers and subordinating conjunctions.[20] Given

[18] For the study reported here, I analyzed in its totality the *Fazienda de Ultra Mar*, a 13th century biblical text, which is my base corpus. Despite not being unproblematic from a philological perspective, I decided to examine it as it is considered the oldest extended Castilian prose document. Additional corpora have also been consulted, such as the *Corpus del Español* and *Biblia Medieval.*

[19] Other clitic placement studies that examine more texts (but also include the future cases), confirm my results and conclude that postposition is the most encountered position (Bouzouita 2007, 2008a,b; Castillo Lluch 1996, 2002; Granberg 1988).

[20] There are a few exceptions, most explicable as mimicking direct speech or as syntactic calques from Latin. For more details on variation in non-root clauses, see Bouzouita (2008a: chapter 3), Castillo Lluch (1996: 142-196) and Granberg (1988: chapter 2).

this lack of variation, I shall focus in what follows primarily on the clitic distributions in root clauses.

TABLE 2 Clitic placement in root clauses with non-future tenses

Syntactic Environment	**Non-Future/Non-Conditional Root Clauses**	
	Anteposition	**Postposition**
Wh-element or *si/sy*	X	-
Negation	X	-
Non-coreferential object compl.	X	-
Prepositional complement	X	-
Predicative complement	X	-
Verb in 1P	-	X
Paratactic root clause	-	X
Contrastive coord. *pero/mas* 'but'	-	X
Vocative	-	X
Subject	X	X
Adverbial	X	X
Coreferential object (CLLD/HTLD)	X	X
Coordination *e(t)/y* 'and'	X	X
Non-root/absolute clause	X	X

TABLE 3 Clitic placement in root clauses with future/conditional tense

Syntactic Environment	**SF with Antepos.**	**AF Mesoclisis**	**SF with Postpos.**
Wh-element or *si/sy*	X	-	-
Negation	X	-	-
Non-coreferential object compl.	X	-	-
Prepositional complement	X	-	-
Predicative complement	X	-	-
Verb in 1P	-	X	X
Paratactic root clause	-	X	X
Contrastive coord. *pero/mas*	-	X	-
Vocative	-	X	-
Subject	X	X	-
Adverbial	X	X	X
Coreferential object	X	X	X
Coordination *e(t)/y* 'and'	X	X	X
Non-root/absolute clause	X	X	-

The syntactic environments in which clitics occur in root clauses can be classified into three groups on the basis of the syntactic constituent that precedes the clitic (and verb). Whereas the processing of some left-peripheral environments will always induce anteposition, others will always appear with postverbal clitics, yet others exhibit variation between the two clitic orderings within the same syntactic environment (Bouzouita 2007, 2008a,b, 2009; Bouzouita and Kempson 2006; Castillo Lluch 1996; Elvira 1987; Nieuwenhuijsen 1999, 2002, 2006 inter alia). I shall refer to these three groups as the exclusively preverbal, the exclusively postverbal and the variation environments respectively. There is thus a tripartite pattern that emerges for the positioning of clitics which belong logically to verbs that do not appear in the future (nor the conditional) tense, as illustrated in Table 2.

In the following sections, I shall compare and discuss the clitic distribution displayed in Table 2 with the one for the AF and SF with clitics given in Table 3.

4.3.1 Distributional parallelism between analytic futures and postposition

As can be seen when comparing Table 2 and Table 3, there is a striking distributional parallelism: AF appear in exactly the same syntactic environments which license postposition with other tenses. To be more precise, AF can appear in those syntactic contexts which have been identified as allowing only postverbal clitics as well as in those which license variation with other tenses. The following sets of examples illustrate each of these syntactic environments for both the non-future and future tenses respectively.

1. Verb in Sentence-initial Position

(4.11) *Enbio**l*** *Juda un cabrito*
sent.3SG-CL Juda a little goat

'Juda sent her a little goat.' (*Faz.*: 52)

(4.12) *Enprenar**te*** *as e avras fijo*
pregnant-CL will-CL.2SG and have-will.2SG son

'You will get pregnant and have a son.' (*Faz.*: 207)

2. Paratactic Root Clause

(4.13) *Alli [...] fo Sampson luengos tienpos; conta**lo***
there was.3SG Samson long times tell.3SG-CL
Libre Judicum
Book of-Judges

'Samson stayed there for a long time; the Book of Judges states this.' (*Faz.*: 207)

(4.14) *Esta aqui, e yré yo; encontrar**mé** yo*
is.3SG here and go-will.1SG I meet-CL-will.1SG I
con mio Sennor
with my Lord
'He is here and I will go; I will meet with my Lord.'
(*Faz.*: 90)

3. Contrastive Coordination with *pero/mas* 'but'

(4.15) *mas dixo**me***
but told.3SG-CL
'but he told me [...]' (*Faz.*: 207)

(4.16) *mas abatir**las** as*
but knock-down-CL will.2SG
'but you will knock them down.' (*Faz.*: 77)

4. Vocative

(4.17) *Mio pueblo, miembre**t** agora que conseio*
my people remember.3SG-CL now that advice
ovo Balaac
had.3SG Balaac
'My people, remember now the advice that Balaac gave.'
(*Faz.*: 191)

(4.18) *mio pueblo, adozir**vos** hé a tierra de Israel*
my people lead-CL will.1SG to land of Israel
'My people, I will lead you to the land of Israel.' (*Faz.*: 172)

5. Subject

(4.19) *Yo, el Sennor, apparecì**m** a Abraam*
I the Lord appeared.1SG-CL to Abraham
'I, the Lord, appeared to Abraham [...].' (*Faz.*: 65)

(4.20) *e yo, fablar**té** y mis palabras*
and I speak-CL-will.1SG there my words
'and I will speak there to you.' (*Faz.*: 165)

6. Adverbial

(4.21) *e agora dyo**vos** el Criador tierra*
and now gave.3SG-CL the Lord land
'and now the Lord has given you land.' (*Faz.*: 101)

(4.22) *Agora conplir**se** an tus palabras*
now fulfill-CL will.3PL your words
'Now your words will be fulfilled.' (*Faz.*: 208)

7. Coreferential Object (CLLD/HTLD)

(4.23) *e* *al rey de Hay* *preso**lo***
and ACC-the king of Hay imprisoned.3SG-CL
'and the king of Hay, he imprisoned him.' (*Faz.*: 100)

(4.24) *las palabras que avernan* *contar**las*** *edes* *a* *ellos*
the words that have.3PL tell-CL will.2PL to them
'The words that they will have, you will tell them to them.' (*Faz.*: 78)

8. Coordination with *e(t)/y* 'and'

(4.25) *E los mensajeros trobaronse con Elyas, e* *dixo**les***
and the messengers found.3PL-CL with Elias and told.3SG-CL
'And the messengers found themselves with Elias and he told them [...].' (*Faz.*: 123)

(4.26) *Entra a Pharaon e dezir**le** as*
enter.2SG at Pharaoh and tell-CL will.2SG
'Enter at the Pharaoh['s place] and you will tell him [...].' (*Faz.*: 66)

9. Non-root or Absolute Clause

(4.27) *Quando acabo Moysen de fablar,* *abrio**s*** *la tierra de yus delos*
when finished.3SG Moses of speak opened.3SG-CL the earth of under of-them
'When Moses finished speaking, the earth opened itself beneath them.' (*Faz.*: 86)

(4.28) *Quando fueren conplidas tus palabras* *ondrar**te**mos*
when will-be.3PL fulfilled your words honor-CL-will.1PL
'When your words will be fulfilled, we will honor you.' (*Faz.*: 208)

As can be observed, these binary sets clearly show that there is a one-to-one parallelism between the AF, on the one hand, and postposition with other tenses, on the other. Notice that some of these examples contain minimal pairs. Example (4.17) and (4.18), for instance, both contain the left-peripheral vocative *mio pueblo* 'my people', followed by an imperative verb with postposition in the former while by an AF in the latter.[21] Similarly, the subject pronoun *yo* 'I' and the adverb *agora* 'now' are followed by a preterite with postverbal clitic in examples (4.19) and (4.21), and by an AF in examples (4.20) and (4.22). Recall that Company Company (2006: 401) claims that the left-peripheral constituents preceding the AF are always topicalized and thus bear specific topic features such as [+definite]. Applying this claim to the adverbial environment seems, in my view, rather problematic as I cannot see how an adverb such as *quiça* 'maybe', which appears in my corpus more than once with AF, can be attributed this definite feature. Even examples such as (4.22) are debatable as this adverb *agora* 'now' can refer to a specific point in time or an undefined time continuum which starts at the moment of utterance but does not have a clear end point. Notwithstanding this, it is true that in certain syntactic contexts the left-peripheral constituents preceding the AF tend to be definite. This is for instance the case for the CLLD/HTLD examples, as illustrated in (4.24). The definiteness of these left-peripheral constituents is unsurprising as the subsequent clitic is coreferential with them. Notice further that the same observation also applies for CLLD/HTLD cases with postposition, as shown in example (4.23). In other words, the so-called topicality of these left-peripheral constituents seems to be a mere epiphenomenon of the clitic placement restrictions as similar observations can be made for the cases containing postverbal clitics in non-future contexts. Considering this parallel distribution between AF and postposition, one can regard the analytic construction to be the equivalent of the postposition structure.

4.3.2 Other distributional parallelisms

Going back to Table 2 and Table 3, another striking distributional parallelism can be discerned: namely between the distribution of the SF with preverbal clitics and the one of anteposition with other tenses. As in the previous, I shall exemplify below each of these syntactic environments for both the non-future and future tenses.

1. *Wh*-element or Question Particle *sy/si*

(4.29) *Quien* **te** *fyzo* *rey?*
who CL made.3SG king
'Who made you king?' (*Faz.*: 107)

(4.30) *Ay,* *qui* **lo** *vera*
ay who CL see-will.3SG

[21]Unlike Modern Spanish, Medieval and Renaissance Spanish do not have a clitic distribution based on verbal mood. In view of this, imperative, optative and other moods all exhibit the same clitic placement. For a detailed discussion of this, I refer the reader to Bouzouita (2008a: chapter 3; 2008b, 2009).

'Ay, who will see it [...]?' (*Faz.*: 92)

2. Negation

(4.31) *non* ***me*** *oyestes?*
not CL heard.2SG

'Did you not hear me?' (*Faz.*: 55)

(4.32) *Nol* *faran* *mal* *ni* *nol* *afollaran*
not-CL do-will.3PL harm nor not-CL hurt-will.3PL

'They won't harm him nor will they hurt him [...]' (*Faz.*: 164)

3. Non-coreferential Object Complement

(4.33) *Tal gualardon* ***me*** *dyo* *el* *Criador*
such prize CL gave.3SG the Creator

'Such a reward did the Lord give me.' (*Faz.*: 102)

(4.34) *.ij. mios fijos* ***te*** *dexaré*
two my sons CL leave-will.1SG

'Two of my sons I will leave you.' (*Faz.*: 55)

4. Prepositional Complement

(4.35) *Con aquellas* ***se*** *aiunto* *Salomon*
with those CL slept.3SG Salomon

'With those women, Salomon slept.' (*Faz.*: 150)

(4.36) *e* *con las mugieres* ***se*** *iazran*
and with the women CL sleep-will.3PL

'and with the women they will sleep.' (*Faz.*: 196)

5. Predicative Complement

(4.37) *Dia [de] angunstia ed aquexadura* ***nos*** *es* *est*
day of anguish and distress CL is.3SG this

'A day of anguish and distress is this one for us.' (*Faz.*: 155)

(4.38) *huecas* ***las*** *faras*
hollow CL make-will.2SG

'Hollow you will make them.' (*Faz.*: 82)

6. Subject

(4.39) *Yo* ***te*** *do* *una* *tierra*
I CL give.1SG a land

'I give you land [...].' (*Faz.*: 59)

(4.40) *Si* *myo* *padre* *vos* *maio* *con* *verdugos* *yo*
If my father CL crushed.3SG with sticks I
vos *batré* *con* *escorpiones*
CL fight-will.1SG with scorpions

‘If my father crushed you with sticks, I will fight you with scorpions.’ (*Faz.*: 152)

7. Adverbial

(4.41) *e* *agora**l*** *dizen* *Sant* *Georgii* *de* *Ramas*
and now-CL call.3PL Saint George of Ramas

‘and now they call him Saint George of Ramas.’ (*Faz.*: 137)

(4.42) *Agora* ***se*** *tornara* *el* *pueblo*
now CL turn-will.3SG the people

‘Now the people will return [...].’ (*Faz.*: 152)

8. Coreferential Object (CLLD/HTLD)

(4.43) *todos* ***los*** *cativo*
all CL captured.3SG

‘He captured them all [...].’ (*Faz.*: 160)

(4.44) *todo* ***lo*** *contaremos*
all CL tell-will.1PL

‘All we will tell.’ (*GE1*, *CDE*)

9. Coordination with *e(t)/y* ‘and’

(4.45) *todos* *los* *cativo* *e* ***los*** *levo* *a* *Babilonia*
all CL captured.3SG and CL took.3SG to Babylon

‘He captured them all and took them to Babylon.’ (*Faz.*: 160)

(4.46) *Yo**t*** *acreceré* *e* ***te*** *muchiguaré*
I-CL enlarge-will.1SG and CL multiply-will.1SG

‘I will enlarge and multiply you.’ (*Faz.*: 58)

10. Non-root or Absolute Clause

(4.47) *Antes que te formas en el vientre* ***te*** *conoci*
before that CL formed.2SG in the belly CL knew.1SG

‘Before that you were formed in the belly, I knew you.’ (*Faz.*: 165)

(4.48) *Ante que daqui salgades* ***me*** *faredes* *ende*
Before that from-here leave.2PL CL do-will.2PL thus
buen *derecho*
good right

‘Before that you will leave from here, you will do me good.’ (*EE: 420a7*, cited by Granberg 1988: 139)

Notice here as well that several of the given example sets contain minimal pairs, clearly bringing out the distributional parallelism between these constructions: for instance, preverbal clitics are encountered in examples (4.29)-(4.30) following the subject *wh*-element *qui(en)* 'who', in (4.31)-(4.32) following the negation adverb *no(n)* 'no' and in (4.43)-(4.44) following the left-dislocated quantifier *todo(s)* 'all'. Additionally, examples (4.39)-(4.40), which both contain the subject pronoun *yo* 'I', also pattern with the examples (4.19)-(4.20) which display the same subject. The same is true for the minimal pairs in (4.41)-(4.42) and (4.21)-(4.22) which all display the adverb *agora* 'now'. This one-to-one parallelism between the distribution of SF with preverbal clitics and the one for anteposition in non-future or non-conditional contexts also confirms the hypothesis that MedSp clitic placement principles affect the synchronic variation between the various future constructions. Apart from this distributional parallelism and the one discussed in section 4.3.1, there is another argument in favor of this hypothesis: the micro-variation observed in the syntactic environments that license preverbal and postverbal clitics is regulated in the same way in both the non-future and the future constructions. Let us consider the left-peripheral subjects for instance. Company Company (2006: 394, 400) claims that subjects preceding AF are most often contrastive in nature. However, the data in my corpus indicate the opposite: in contrastive cases, only SF with preverbal clitics have been recorded, as exemplified in example (4.40). The subject pronoun *yo* 'I' in this example appears in direct contrast to the subject of the preceding subordinate clause *myo padre* 'my father'. Additional support for this claim comes from similar preverbal configurations found in non-future contexts as it has been noticed by several linguists that subjects preceding anteposition structures seem to be emphatic (e.g. Bouzouita 2008a: 88-99, 2008b, 2009; Castillo Lluch 1996). Granberg (1988: 200), for instance, tried to verify his hypothesis by focusing on 'the semantic role of stress'. By giving contextual analyses for those subject cases he found (i) in notarial prose dating from 1188-1299 and (ii) in prose texts from the period 1200-1250, he convincingly demonstrated that there exists a relationship between the presence/absence of emphasis on the left-peripheral subjects and the placement of the following clitic. As pointed out by Castillo Lluch (1996: 219), contextual analyses are somewhat subjective since stress patterns in old texts are difficult to discern and one can only rely on clues from discourse context. Nonetheless, the fact that other Romance languages, such as Modern Galician and Modern Asturian have a clitic placement system the underlying principles of which are similar, if not identical, to MedSp one seems to indicate that this hypothesis is apposite (Alvarez Blanco et al. 1986: 184; Campos 1989: 22; Saco e Arce 1868: 162; Xove Ferreiro 1986: 522-523; Academia de la Llingua Asturiana 2001: 366-367; D'Andrés Díaz 1993: 36-43; González i Planas 2007;

Sánchez Vicente and Rubiera Tuya 1985: 77). Considering all this, I do not consider subjects preceding AF to be contrastive in nature nor to carry special discourse features (contra Company Company 2006). Rather, subjects preceding preverbal clitics, whether belonging to future or non-future tense verbs, seem to be carrying emphatic stress whereas those that appear with postposition or AF, such as examples (4.19) and (4.20), seem to be lacking such stress. The micro-variation in the CLLD/HTLD context seems to be subject to the same 'rule' as the subject one: whenever the quantifier *todo(s)* 'all', which can be interpreted as carrying emphatic stress, appears left-dislocated, anteposition is observed, as shown in examples (4.43)-(4.44). In the absence of said quantifier at the left periphery, AF or postposition is encountered, as illustrated in example (4.23) and (4.24) respectively. As regards the other variation environments (i.e. coordination structures with *e(t)/y* 'and' and the preceding non-root or absolute clause cases), the micro-variation observed in them also seems to be governed in the same way in the non-future and the future constructions (for more details see Bouzouita 2008a: chapters 2 and 3).

As concerns the SF with postposition, they only seem to occur in those syntactic environments for which postposition has been observed with other tenses. The following sentences, which proceed from a variety of sources, illustrate this: in example (4.49) the SF with postverbal clitic appears sentence-initially while in examples (4.50) to (4.52) the SF with postposition appears following the coordination conjunction *e* 'and', the adverbial *agora* 'now' and the coreferential object *las viandas que comieres* 'the food that you will eat' respectively.[22]

(4.49) *Veras**la*** *con tos oios*
see-will-CL.2SG with your eyes

'You will see her with your own eyes.' (*Faz.*: 95)

(4.50) *Prendra vuestros fijos e porna**los*** *en la batalla*
take-will.3SG your sons and put-will-CL.3SG in the battle

'He will take your sons and make them fight.' (*Faz.*: 104)

(4.51) *E agora mostrare* ***uos*** *que fare a la mi uinna*
and now show-will.1SG CL what do-will.1SG to the my vineyard

[22]See Bouzouita (forthcoming b) for more detailed information on the SF with postposition.

'And now I will tell you what I will do to my vineyard.'
(*E6*: IS 5.5, *Biblia Medieval*)

(4.52) *las viandas que comieres, camiarás**las***
the food that eat.2SG vomit-will.2SG-CL
'The food that you will have eat, you will vomit.'
(*E6, Prov.*: 23.8 *apud* Rossi 1975: 393)

TABLE 4 Clitic placement in root clauses in *Fazienda de Ultra Mar*

Syntactic Environment	**Other**	**Futures & Conditionals**		
	Antepos.	**Antepos.**	**Mesoclis.**	**Postpos.**
Wh-element or *si/sy*	100% (25/25)	100% (15/15)	0% (0/15)	0% (0/15)
Negation	100% (122/122)	100% (46/46)	0% (0/46)	0% (0/46)
Non-corefential obj. compl.	100% (10/10)	100% (8/8)	0% (0/8)	0% (0/8)
Prepositional compl.	100% (2/2)	100% (8/8)	0% (0/8)	0% (0/8)
Predicative compl.	100% (4/4)	100% (2/2)	0% (0/2)	0% (0/2)
Verb in P1	0% (0/334)	0% (0/22)	95.5% (21/22)	4.5% (1/22)
Paratactic root clause	0% (0/31)	0% (0/21)	95% (19/20)	5% (1/20)
Contrastive coord.	0% (0/3)	0% (0/1)	100% (1/1)	0% (0/1)
Vocative	0% (0/14)	0% (0/3)	100% (3/3)	0% (0/3)
Subject	61% (80/131)	81% (34/42)	19% (8/42)	0% (0/42)
Adverbial	64.6% (93/144)	63.4% (26/41)	36.6% (15/41)	0% (0/41)
Coreferential object	19% (5/27)	0% (0/8)	100% (8/8)	0% (0/8)
Coordination *e(t)/y* 'and'	1.7% (17/983)	2.6% (5/194)	93.3% (181/194)	4.1% (8/194)
Non-root/ absolute cl.	8% (3/39)	0% (0/12)	100% (12/12)	0% (0/12)
Total	**19.3%** (361/1870)	**34.3%** (145/423)	**63.4%** (268/423)	**2.4%** (10/423)

As mentioned previously, SF with postposition is quite rare in MedSp and seems restricted to certain textual genres (poetry, biblical translations). To illustrate this, whereas 10 cases of SF with postposition have been registered for the biblical text *Fazienda de Ultra Mar* (1.4 occurrences per 10.000 words), not a single example has been found for the (non-biblical) *Libro de los ejemplos del conde Lucanor y de Patronio.*[23] Notwithstanding this difference, both texts have very similar percentages for the other future structures in root clauses: while the former text records 63.4% (268/423) of AF and 34.3% (145/423) of SF with anteposition (see Table 4), the latter contains 63% (46/73) and 37% (27/73) respectively.[24] As can be seen, in both texts AF appear more frequently than SF in the root clause environments. Company Company (2006: 369-370) claims that these analytic structures are numerically marked as they occur less frequently compared to the SF cases. Although this observation seems to be correct for the author's corpus, this conclusion cannot be extrapolated to all other corpora as the frequency of AF and SF depends on the ratio of root and non-root clauses present in the corpus, which in turn depends on register and discourse style (Kabatek 2008). More specifically, since AF (and postposition with other tenses) are by and large restricted to appearing in root clauses, these structures may appear less frequently if the corpus contains a large amount of non-root clauses.[25] In view of this, the frequency difference between AF and SF cannot be used as an valid argument for the purported marked status of AF.

4.3.3 Summary of the data

In conclusion, we saw that (i) the distribution of AF patterns exactly with the one for postposition in other tenses, that (ii) the distribution of SF with anteposition patterns with the one for anteposition in other tenses and that (iii) the SF with postposition only occur in those syntactic environments for which postposition has been observed with other tenses. These distributional parallelisms corroborate the hypothesis that the MedSp clitic placement principles also regulate the synchronic variation observed in the use of the future constructions. In view of the previous, Company Company's claim (2006) that, although clitic placement restrictions were originally at the basis of the existence of AF, these analytic constructions have been reanalyzed as a

[23]Note that, despite being preserved in a 15th century manuscript, this 14th century text does not present novel anteposition cases (see Bouzouita 2008a).

[24]For this study, the first 46 *ejemplos* have been analyzed, which roughly corresponds to 57.000 words.

[25]Note that this is not always necessarily the case. In the *Fazienda de Ultra Mar*, for instance, mesoclisis remains the most encountered position even when the non-root clauses, in which preverbal placement is by far the most predominant positioning, are taken into account: 55% (292/526).

marked structure to signal topicalization and syntactic emphasis seems unlikely and unfounded. This seems even more so as clitic placement restrictions alone can account for the distributions of the various future constructions. The so-called topicality for which they are claimed to be reanalyzed seems to be an epiphenomenon of the clitic placement restrictions as these topicality features can also be attributed to the postposition examples in non-future contexts (e.g. for the CLLD/HTLD cases, cf. examples (4.23), (4.24) and (4.52)). As regards the frequencies, we saw that AF are not uncommon, unlike SF with postposition, which seem to appear only in certain textual genres. Consequently, I do not consider there to be real variation between these two structures (contra Company Company 1985-6, 2006 inter alia).

Now that correlation between clitic placement and the variation in the future constructions has been brought out, I shall account for both MedSp clitics and the variation under discussion within the DS framework (Cann et al. 2005; Kempson et al. 2001).

4.4 Processing environments, clitics and futures

4.4.1 Modeling Medieval Spanish clitics

As described in the introduction to this volume, DS is a grammar formalism that reflects the dynamics of the parsing/production process, with syntax defined as the incremental growth of semantic trees following the time-linearity of utterance production. These semantic trees represent a possible interpretation of the natural language string. Once the processing process is completed successfully, the top node of the tree will be decorated with some propositional formula and each daughter node with some sub-term of that formula, representing a predicate-argument structure. Various processing strategies i.e. different ways of building up semantic content for a natural language string, are made available. DS licenses the construction of (i) fixed nodes, (ii) unfixed nodes, which represent structural underspecification and which can be constructed locally or non-locally (Cann et al. 2005; Kempson and Kiaer 2010), and (iii) LINKed structures, i.e. trees that are hooked together and often share semantic content (Cann et al. 2005; Kempson et al. 2001). Moreover, a natural language string can quite often be parsed/produced in more than one way with little or no difference in content (see Bouzouita and Chatzikyriakidis 2009 for the different processing possibilities of Latin subject expressions). Processing variability is thus an inherent characteristic of the DS framework, which makes it a good candidate for explaining language variation and change.

Recall that we saw that MedSp clitic placement with non-futures and non-conditionals presents a tripartite system: there are the exclusively preverbal, exclusively postverbal and variation environments (see Table 2). We also saw that the use of anteposition and postposition is correlated to the syntactic environments on the left periphery. Within the DS framework, this can be interpreted as follows: the variation in MedSp clitic placement seems to be linked to the processing strategies used for the left-peripheral constituents which precede the clitics (for Medieval and Renaissance Spanish see also Bouzouita 2007, 2008a,b, 2009; Bouzouita and Chatzikyriakidis 2009; Bouzouita and Kempson 2006; for Cypriot Greek see Chatzikyriakidis 2010: chapter 4). Put differently, the way of constructing the semantic interpretation of the constituents that appear early on in the parsing/production process, determines where the subsequent clitic(s) can appear. The dynamics of the interpretation process is thus quintessential for understanding MedSp clitic placement as the use of a clitic depends on earlier used processing mechanisms. Concretely, this translates into a complex lexical entry for the MedSp clitic, as in (4.53), which contains two parts – one characterizing anteposition and the other postposition –, each of which comprises different triggers referring to the processing environments used for the constituents parsed/produced earlier in the interpretation process. As can be seen in this lexical entry, preverbal placement is restricted to appear only after the following processing environments: negation ($[NEG+]$), the unfixed node strategy ($\langle\downarrow_*\rangle Fo(\alpha), ?\exists x.Tn(x)$), or the requirement for a tense marker ($?\exists x.Tns(x)$) on the $?Ty(t)$-node. This cluster of anteposition triggers is said to be stored as part of the clitic's lexical specification due to a routinization process (Pickering and Garrod 2004) and is in this sense a historical reflex of earlier freely available processing strategies (see Bouzouita 2008a,b and Cann and Kempson 2008 for more details).

Recall that the exclusively preverbal environments are those in which the preverbal clitic is preceded by (i) a *wh*-element or interrogative particle *si/sy*, (ii) a negation adverb, (iii) a non-coreferential object complement, (iv)-(v) a prepositional or predicative complement at the left periphery. By claim, these all reflect the introduction of a novel propositional domain. The processing of most of these syntactic environments involves in DS terms the use of the unfixed node strategy, i.e. the computation rule of (LOCAL) *ADJUNCTION will introduce an unfixed node which is then decorated with the expression of the syntactic environment under discussion. The interrogative particle *si/sy* environment does not make use of this processing strategy: instead the lexical entry of this particle will introduce on the top node a requirement for a tense specification. The introduction of this requirement is a historical vestige of an earlier lexical specification: the particle *si/sy* is etymologically derived from the Latin subordinating conjunction *si* introducing indirect questions whose lexical entry also introduces a tense requirement (for the lexical entry of *si/sy* see Bouzouita 2008a: 225-227). The introduction of this tense requirement by the particle *si/sy* is thus a mere historical artifact.[26] The negation environment remains without formal characterization: to signal the presence of an negation adverb, I therefore opted for the use of the feature $[NEG+]$.

In the modeling of the exclusively postverbal environments, on the other hand, only fixed nodes are needed and in some cases also the LINKed structure strategy (e.g. for the vocative or contrastive coordination *mas/pero* environments; see Bouzouita 2007: 62, 2008a: chapter 5, 2008b: 250 for more details and illustrative examples). Postverbal clitics seem thus to appear in the absence of the three triggers previously discussed. As shown in (4.53), when attempting to process a postverbal clitic, the presence of one of these triggers will result in the parsing/production process being aborted (by the first Abort function in the second part of the lexical entry). Note that the triggers for postposition are more complex in comparison to the ones for anteposition: to be more specific, the former all have the following format: $\langle\uparrow_0\uparrow_1^*\rangle^+(?Ty(t),[...])$. This is due to the different points in the interpretation process at which the preverbal and postverbal clitics are parsed/produced: in the latter case but not the former, the lexical specifications of the finite verb will have built the type-t-requiring predicate-argument structure.[27] As can be seen in (4.53), there are thus two complementary clusters of triggers which restrict MedSp clitic positioning by spelling out the processing environments which license each positioning. Despite this binary character of the lexical entry of the MedSp accusative clitic, the variation cases are not problematic since in DS certain expressions can, as mentioned before, receive more than one analysis. More concretely, the variation in such environments, as found for instance following subjects or coreferential objects, is licensed

[26]Other syntactic environments that make use of this requirement and which trigger anteposition (but I do not discuss in this chapter) are the MedSp complement clauses whose complementizers are responsible for introducing it. Here the presence of the requirement can be justified on the basis that the verbs that precede these complementizers can also appear with infinitival complements, as is the case for instance for *querer* 'to want'. The tense requirement will ensure that no such infinitival complements can follow after the use of the complementizers. For more details on clitic placement in non-root clauses and their analyses in DS, I refer the reader to Bouzouita (2008a: 273-286).

[27]Note the use of the + operator, which ensures, unlike the Kleene star *, that there must be at least one instance of the relation to which it applies.

as the left-peripheral constituent preceding the clitic can be analyzed (i) as involving one the processing environments listed as an anteposition trigger in which case preverbal clitic placement is obtained, or (ii) as involving some other processing strategy that does not trigger anteposition (e.g. fixed nodes, LINKed structures). The variation environments, which can appear both with anteposition and postposition, are thus not enigmatic and can be accounted for with the proposed lexical entry given above (see Bouzouita 2008a: 246-272 for an extended discussion for each of these syntactic environments).

(4.53) Lexical entry of Medieval Spanish accusative clitic *lo(s)/la(s)*

IF $?Ty(t)$
THEN IF $[NEG+] \lor$ } Negation marker
$(\langle\downarrow_*\rangle Fo(\alpha), ?\exists x.Tn(x)) \lor$ } Unfixed node
$?\exists x.Tns(x)$ } Tense requirement
THEN $\texttt{make}(\langle\downarrow_1\rangle); \texttt{go}(\langle\downarrow_1\rangle);$
$\texttt{make}(\langle\downarrow_0\rangle); \texttt{go}(\langle\downarrow_0\rangle);$
$\texttt{put}(\mathbf{U}, Ty(e), ?\exists x.Fo(x),$
$[\downarrow]\bot, ?\langle\uparrow_0\rangle Ty(e \rightarrow t))$
ELSE Abort
ELSE IF $?Ty(e),$
$\langle\uparrow\rangle\top$
THEN IF $\langle\uparrow_0\uparrow_1^*\rangle^+(?Ty(t), [NEG+], \exists x.Tns(x)) \lor$
$\langle\uparrow_0\uparrow_1^*\rangle^+(?Ty(t), \langle\downarrow_*\rangle(Fo(\alpha), ?\exists x.Tn(x)),$
$\exists x.Tns(x)) \lor$
$\langle\uparrow_0\uparrow_1^*\rangle^+(?Ty(t), ?\exists x.Tns(x))$
THEN Abort
ELSE $\texttt{put}(\mathbf{U}, Ty(e), ?\exists x.Fo(x),$
$[\downarrow]\bot, ?\langle\uparrow_0\rangle Ty(e \rightarrow t))$
ELSE Abort

In section 4.2.1, we saw that some studies, such as Staaff (1907), Menéndez Pidal (1926) and Rossi (1975), refer to the presence of a caesura or a phonological pause to explain the appearance of AF (and postposition with the non-future tenses) following left-peripheral constituents. Although it seems to be the case that there is indeed often a pause present in mesoclitic and postverbal cases, we saw that there exist cases which occur with preverbal placement, despite containing a pause, as illustrated in example (4.5), repeated below as (4.54), and in example (4.55). Both contain left-peripheral subjects, modified by a relative clause and followed by an apposition respectively:

(4.54)

Estas	*bestias*	*grandes*	*que*	*son*	*.iiii.*	*reyes*	***se***
these	beasts	big	that	are.3PL	four	kings	CL

levantaran
stand-up-will.3PL

'These big beasts which are four kings will stand up.' (*Faz.*: 181)

(4.55) *Dios, el Vuestro Sennor* ***vos*** *dio esta tierra*
God the Your Lord CL gave.3SG this land

'God, your Lord, gave you this land.' (*Faz.*: 96)

In the following, I shall explain why the presence of a pause is not the governing principle of MedSp clitic placement, although there seems to be a correlation between the presence/absence of a pause and subsequent clitic placement. According to my claim, postverbal placement will appear following preverbal subjects that are parsed/produced as annotating a LINKed tree. Since this subject is processed as a separate structure and not as part of the same tree in which the clitic pronoun occurs, positing a phonological pause in between seems not unreasonable. When processing an unfixed node, on the contrary, such a pause is not expected, as this node, despite being structurally underspecified, belongs to the same tree as the remainder of the parse. This seems to be true as long as the term annotating the unfixed node is not modified by expressions annotating a LINKed structure, as is the case for examples (4.54) and (4.55). To be more precise, if there appears at the left periphery an unfixed node, it is possible to construct from this node a LINKed tree either with a requirement for a type t ($?Ty(t)$) or a type e ($?Ty(e)$), as shown in (4.56). If such a LINKed tree is built from an unfixed node, there will be a phonological pause once completed as another tree has just been constructed, albeit embedded within the global tree. Cases whose subject is processed as just described can then exhibit preverbal placement as the unfixed node strategy is used at the left periphery, despite a phonological pause preceding the clitic in question.

The processing of examples (4.54) and (4.55) is a case in point: both these examples involve, under the analysis proposed here, the construction of a LINKed tree subsequent to the parse/production of the subject as annotating an unfixed node. The processing of the former example will involve the application of the LINK ADJUNCTION rule, as the left-hand side tree in (4.56), due to the presence of a relative clause, while the parse of the latter will involve a LINKed type-e tree for the apposition, introduced by the LINK APPOSITION rule, as on the right-hand side of the following figure. The preverbal clitic positioning in these cases is expected as one of the three anteposition-triggering processing environments is present: namely, the unfixed node strategy has been used for processing the preverbal subject. The presence of a pause, following the complete construction of the LINKed tree, is equally expected as this unfixed node is linked to another tree structure, which will then be decorated by the terms projected by the apposition or relative clause. In sum, cases that contain a pause but which nevertheless exhibit anteposition are by no means enigmatic and can be accounted for, unlike in some other accounts (e.g. Staaff 1907, Rossi 1975 inter alia).

(4.56) Parsing subjects with relative clauses or appositions

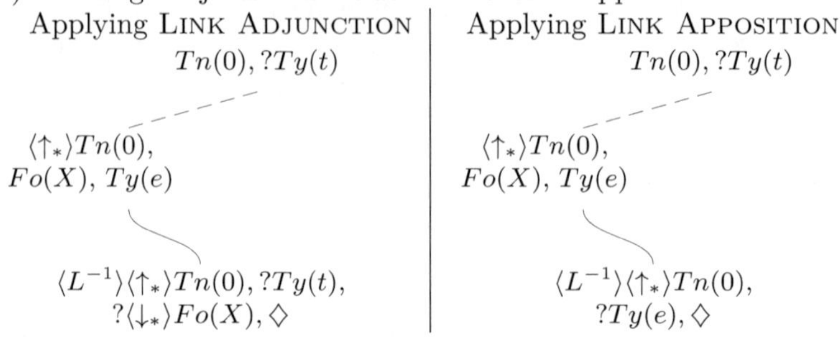

To summarize, the preverbal or postverbal positioning of clitics in MedSp finite verb contexts appears to be influenced by the processing strategies used for the constituents at the left periphery. Preverbal placement only appears in certain processing environments, whereas postposition is precluded in them. This is directly reflected in the lexical entry for the MedSp accusative clitic, which is complex and disjunctive. We also saw that, although there appears to be a correlation between phonology and clitic placement, this effect is only epiphenomenal: the occurrence of a pause seems to be a side-effect of the use of LINKed structures, which tend to be used in contexts appearing with postposition or mesoclisis but which can also be used following the unfixed node strategy, in which case anteposition is possible.

Now that the lexical entry for the MedSp (accusative) clitic has been introduced and discussed, I shall show in the following that this lexical entry can also be used to account for the variation encountered between the SF and AF.[28]

4.4.2 Modeling Medieval Spanish analytic futures

We shall see that the MedSp future constructions do not pose a problem for DS: AF can be modeled as constructions consisting of three lexical

[28]In the following, I shall only discuss the AF constructions and leave the SF ones aside due to space limitations. However, this account assumes that SF use exactly the same lexical entries as AF.

parts, i.e. an infinitive-like verb, a clitic and an auxiliary.[29] The view that MedSp AF are constructions is not controversial and has been proposed by others (Company Company 2006; Girón Alconchel 2007 inter alia). I shall also show that the lexical entry given for the MedSp accusative clitic *lo* occurring in non-future/conditional contexts can be used for those clitics appearing in future/conditional environments too.

For ease of understanding, I shall tease out the parsing process of an AF construction. Consider the example given in (4.57). As can be seen, there is an AF following the conjunction *e* 'and'. The lexical entry of this conjunction will introduce a type-t-requiring LINKed tree, on which there is no requirement for shared information.[30]

(4.57) *Guardaredes* *las* *palabras* *del* *firmament* *e*
guard-will.2PL the words of the firmament and
*fer**las** edes*
do-CL-will.2PL
'You will guard the words of the firmament and you will carry them out.' (*Faz.*: 93)

(4.58) Lexical entries for *fer/fazer* 'do'

$Fer/Fazer_{Infinitive-like}$		$Fer/Fazer_{Infinitive}$	
IF	$?Ty(t)$	IF	$?Ty(t)$
THEN	$\texttt{put}(Tns(\text{FUT}))$; $\texttt{make}(\langle\downarrow_0\rangle)$; $\texttt{go}(\langle\downarrow_0\rangle)$; $\texttt{put}(?Ty(e))$; $\texttt{go}(\langle\uparrow_0\rangle)$; $\texttt{make}(\langle\downarrow_1\rangle)$; $\texttt{go}(\langle\downarrow_1\rangle)$; $\texttt{put}(?Ty(e \rightarrow t))$; $\texttt{make}(\langle\downarrow_1\rangle)$; $\texttt{go}(\langle\downarrow_1\rangle)$; $\texttt{put}(Fer', [\downarrow]\bot, Ty(e \rightarrow (e \rightarrow t)))$; $\texttt{go}(\langle\uparrow_1\rangle)$; $\texttt{make}(\langle\downarrow_0\rangle)$; $\texttt{go}(\langle\downarrow_0\rangle)$; $(\texttt{put}(?Ty(e)) \vee (\texttt{put}(?Ty(e))$; $\texttt{gofirst}(?Ty(t))))$	THEN	$\texttt{make}(\langle\downarrow_0\rangle)$; $\texttt{go}(\langle\downarrow_0\rangle)$; $\texttt{put}(?Ty(e))$; $\texttt{go}(\langle\uparrow_0\rangle)$; $\texttt{make}(\langle\downarrow_1\rangle)$; $\texttt{go}(\langle\downarrow_1\rangle)$; $\texttt{put}(?Ty(e \rightarrow t))$; $\texttt{make}(\langle\downarrow_1\rangle)$; $\texttt{go}(\langle\downarrow_1\rangle)$; $\texttt{put}(Fer', [\downarrow]\bot, Ty(e \rightarrow (e \rightarrow t)))$; $\texttt{go}(\langle\uparrow_1\rangle)$; $\texttt{make}(\langle\downarrow_0\rangle)$; $\texttt{go}(\langle\downarrow_0\rangle)$; $(\texttt{put}(?Ty(e)) \vee (\texttt{put}(?Ty(e))$; $\texttt{gofirst}(?Ty(t))))$
ELSE	Abort	ELSE	Abort

[29] At least one other way of modeling the AF constructions is possible: one could, for instance, model them as one complex lexical entry. This lexicalist-heavy approach presents two major disadvantages. Firstly, such an approach leads to a huge increase in the lexicon as each AF construction will need its own lexical entry. Secondly, it fails to capture the parallelism between AF and postposition with non-future tenses.

[30] Arguably, what is shared is the event term, but I ignore this here.

Once the LINKed tree with a $?Ty(t)$-node has been introduced, the AF construction *ferlas edes* 'you will carry them out' can be parsed. The first part to be processed will be the infinitive-like verb, which is in this case *fer* 'carry out/do'. The uttering of this infinitive-like verb will trigger the activation of its lexical specifications, given on the left-hand side in (4.58). As can be seen, the lexical entry of the infinitive-like verb *fer* used in AF constructions resembles the lexical entry of the infinitive *fer/fazer*, given on the right-hand side, but at the same time also differs from it.[31] Notice that the lexical entry of the infinitive-like *fer* introduces at the top node, like the lexical actions of finite verbs but unlike those of infinitives, a tense value which is in this case the future tense value ($Tns(\textsc{fut})$).[32] One could postulate an additional difference by annotating the type-*e*-requiring object node with the requirement $?(?\exists x.Fo(x))$ in order to restrict the range of possible $Ty(e)$-expressions that can decorate this node. This restriction is basically a requirement for a requirement for a full formula and prevents full NPs from decorating this $?Ty(e)$-node as their lexical specifications will not introduce a requirement for a full formula. The lexical actions of a clitic (but also those of a strong pronoun), on the contrary, do introduce this requirement as the metavariable they introduce needs to be eventually substituted by a full formula value. However, I do not deem this restriction as necessary as this account assumes this lexical entry to be part of a construction in which the clitic will follow the infinitive-like form.[33] The infinitive-like verbal form also exhibits formal similarities with the infinitive: the lexical entry of the former does not annotate the subject node with a type nor formula value, but merely decorates it with a requirement for a type *e* ($?Ty(e)$), as is also the case for infinitives but not for finite verbs. The decoration of the subject node with type and formula values will be carried out by the following auxiliary, as we shall see shortly.

Going back to the parse of example (4.57), the scanning of the lexical

[31]Due to space limitations, I shall not go into the justification for distinguishing the so-called infinitive-like verbs from 'real' infinitives. Instead, I refer the reader to Lema and Rivero (1990, 1991) where a detailed account of the differences in behavior can be found.

[32]At first sight, the tense value $Tns(\textsc{fut})$ might seem incompatible with the $\langle\uparrow_0\uparrow_1^*\rangle^+(?Ty(t), ?\exists x.Tns(x))$ trigger of the lexical entry of the MedSp clitic given in (4.53). This trigger makes the parse of an utterance crash whenever a requirement for a tense specification is decorating the $?Ty(t)$-node while trying to parse a postverbal clitic. Note, however, that what is needed for this to happen is a requirement for a tense specification and not a tense specification itself.

[33]For the moment, I assume that constructions form part of the lexicon. The formal details of this remain to be worked out as DS does not have a theory of the lexicon yet.

entry of the infinitive-like *fer* can then give rise to the parse display on the left in (4.59). As can be seen, the pointer $\diamondsuit$ is left at the object $?Ty(e)$-node.[34] The uttering of the accusative clitic *las* will then cause its lexical actions to get activated (see (4.53) for the lexical entry). Since no [NEG+] feature, unfixed node or tense requirement is present, the parse will proceed with annotating duly this type-*e*-requiring node. The result of the lexical specifications of the clitic *las* annotating this object node is shown in the parse step given on the right in (4.59):

(4.59) Parsing *e ferlas-* in example (4.57)

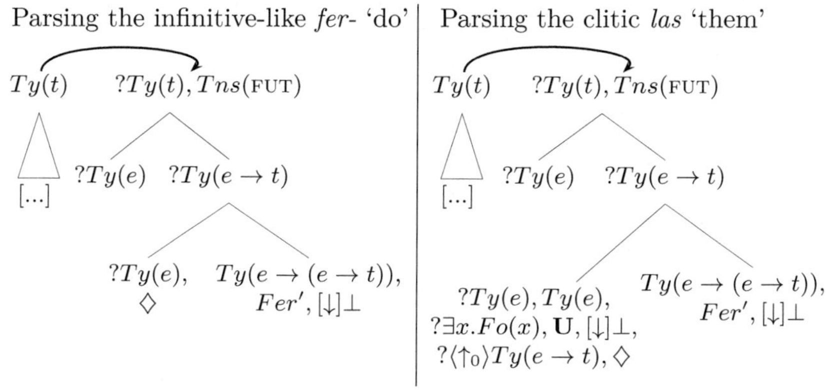

(4.60) Parsing *-edes* in example (4.57)

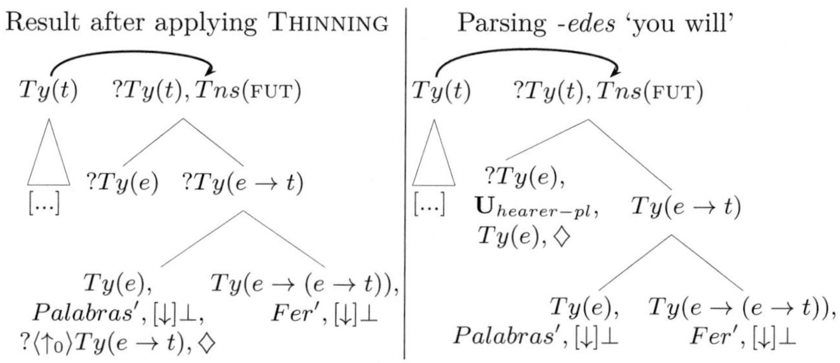

(4.61) Lexical entry of auxiliary *-edes* 'you will'

IF	$?Ty(t), Tns(\text{FUT}), \langle\downarrow_1\rangle\top$
THEN	$\texttt{go}(\langle\downarrow_0\rangle)$; $\texttt{put}(\mathbf{U}_{hearer-pl}, Ty(e))$
ELSE	Abort

[34]Note that the lexical entries in (4.58) can also leave the pointer at the type-*t*-requiring node. The SF will make use of this option in order to parse the following auxiliary.

The computational rule of Thinning will then eliminate the satisfied requirement on the object node ($?Ty(e)$). Subsequently, the pragmatic rule of Substitution will replace the metavariable **U** introduced by the lexical entry of the clitic with the full formula value $Palabras'$, at which point Thinning can apply again to eliminate the requirement for a full formula ($?\exists x.Fo(x)$), resulting in the tree given on the left in (4.60).

Notice that the subject node still has a requirement outstanding, namely one for a type e value. As mentioned, the scanning of the auxiliary, in the case of example (4.57) this is *-edes* 'you will', will decorate this subject node later on in the parse once the pointer is left at the top node. In order to annotate this subject node, the pointer will first need to move to the $?Ty(t)$-node: the computational rule of Completion is responsible for moving the pointer upwards. After several computational rules have taken place (e.g. Completion, Elimination) and the pointer is back at the top node, the uttering of the auxiliary *-edes* will then activate its lexical entry, given in (4.61). As can be seen in this figure, this auxiliary does not, unlike full verbs, annotate the predicate structure: it merely introduces a type specification ($Ty(e)$) and a metavariable ($\mathbf{U}_{hearer-pl}$) for the subject node. This lexical entry of the auxiliary can only be parsed successfully if (i) a future tense specification ($Tns(\text{FUT})$) introduced by a previously parsed infinitive-like verb decorates the $?Ty(t)$-node and (ii) there is a functor daughter below the top node ($\langle\downarrow_1\rangle\top$). The parsing step that shows the result of having scanned the lexical specifications of this auxiliary is given on the right in (4.60). Following the parse of this auxiliary *-edes*, various computational and pragmatic rules (e.g. Thinning, Completion and Elimination) can apply, resulting eventually in a completed $Ty(t)$-tree with a full formula value and no outstanding requirements.

In conclusion, the parse of example (4.57) shows that the lexical entry posited for the accusative MedSp clitic can also account for the AF constructions, without having to alter its lexical specifications. This corroborates that the variation in future constructions directly depends on MedSp clitic principles since the same processing triggers operate in both future and non-future contexts.

4.5 Conclusions

To recapitulate, the claim that the synchronic variation between AF and SF construction interacts directly with clitic placement in 13th century MedSp can be substantiated both on the basis of the data and on the level of formal DS analysis. With respect to the data, we saw that there are various distribution parallelisms: (i) the syntactic distribution of AF structures patterns exactly with the one for postposition in other tenses, (ii) the distribution of SF with anteposition coincides with the one for anteposition in other tenses and (iii) the SF with postposition only occur in those syntactic environments for which postposition has been observed with other tenses. As concerns the DS analysis, the lexical entry posited for MedSp accusative clitics can also account for AF (and SF) structures as AF appear in the same processing environments as postverbal clitics. In view of this, the claim that the AF construction is a marked structure, reanalyzed to indicate topicalization and syntactic emphasis, seems implausible (contra Company Company 2006 inter alia), even more so as clitic placement restrictions alone can account for the distributions of the different future constructions. In sum, when taking into account the correlation between the choice of future construction and clitic placement, the distributional differences between the AF and the SF are fully expected.

Sources

Biblia Medieval = http://www.bibliamedieval.es

CDE = *Corpus del Español*, http://www.corpusdelespanol.org

E6 (book, chapter, verse) = *Biblia romanceada.* Escorial ms. I.i.6.

Faz. (page) = *La Fazienda de Ultra Mar.* Edition of M. Lazar, Salamanca: Universidad de Salamanca, 1963.

GE1 = *General estoria I.* Electronic Texts and Concordances of the Madison Corpus of Early Spanish Manuscripts and Printings. Prepared by John O'Neill, Madison/New York, 1999. Madrid Nacional ms. 816.

References

The following were cited in this chapter: Academia de la Llingua Asturiana (2001), Alvarez Blanco et al. (1986), Anipa (2000, 2001), Arias Alvarez (1995), Bouzouita (2007, 2008a,b, 2009, forthcoming a,b,c), Bouzouita and Chatzikyriakidis (2009), Bouzouita and Kempson (2006), Campos (1989), Cann and Kempson (2008), Cann et al. (2005), Castillo Lluch (1996, 2002), Chatzikyriakidis (2010, this volume), Company Company (1985-6, 2006), Company Company and Medina Urrea (1999), D'Andrés Díaz (1993), Eberenz (1991, 2000), Elvira (1987), Enrique Arias (2005), Gessner (1893), Girón Alconchel (1997, 2002, 2005, 2007), González i Planas (2007), Granberg (1988), Grecco Ramírez (2001), Kabatek (2008), Kempson and Kiaer (2010), Kempson et al. (2001), Keniston (1937), Lema (1994), Lema and Rivero

(1990, 1991, 1992), Matute and Pato (forthcoming), Meier (1965), Menéndez Pidal (1926), Nieuwenhuijsen (1999, 2002, 2006), Pickering and Garrod (2004), Ramsden (1963), Rivero (1991, 1997), Rossi (1975), Saco e Arce (1868), Sánchez and Rubiera Tuya (1985), Sanchis Calvo (1991), Schmidely (1998), Silva-Villar (1996), Staaff (1907), Xove Ferreiro (1986). See references at end of book for full information.

5

Towards A Dynamic Typology of Passives

YICHENG WU

5.1 Introduction

In this paper we attempt to provide a preliminary typology of passive constructions within the Dynamic Syntax framework (henceforth DS, Kempson et al. 2001, Cann et al. 2005). Due to space considerations, we will focus on three typologically different languages, English, Chinese and Navajo, for they display distinct characteristics in terms of voice behaviours. In English, the voice change from active to passive involves regular alternations in verbal morphology, signaling alternate allocations of nominals among positions in structural configurations; in Chinese, voice change from active to passive entails no alternation in morphosyntactic relations between the verb and its nominals, but the assignment to some sentential arguments of informational salience; in Navajo, voice change is manifested in the verbal complex which indicates alternations in the ontological statuses of its core nominals, with the object nominal assigned the ontological salience that the subject nominal usually has. The examples below illustrate the point (Navajo data from Hale 1964: 300-301).

(5.1) The teacher saw Tina. [English]

(5.2) Tina was seen by the teacher.

(5.3) The workers have built the bridge.

The author is grateful to Ronnie Cann and Ruth Kempson for inspiring him to pursue the topic and for providing invaluable input into the paper.

The Dynamics of Lexical Interfaces.
Ruth Kempson, Eleni Gregoromichelaki and Christine Howes (eds.).

(5.4) The bridge has been built.

(5.5) *laoshi kanjian le Tina*
teacher see ASP Tina
'The teacher saw Tina.' [Chinese]

(5.6) *Tina bei laoshi kanjian le*
Tina BEI teacher see ASP
'Tina was seen by the teacher.'

(5.7) *gongrenmen chaichu le na-zuo qiao*
workers demolish ASP that-CL bridge
'The workers have demolished the bridge.'

(5.8) *na-zuo qiao bei chaichu le*
that-CL bridge BEI demolish ASP
'The bridge has been demolished.'

(5.9) *łįį' dzaanééz yi-ztał.*
horse mule kicked
'The horse kicked the mule.' [Navajo]

(5.10) *dzaanééz łįį' bi-ztał.*
mule horse kicked
'The mule was kicked by the horse.'

(5.11) *łééchąą'í mósí yi-shxash*
dog cat bit
'The dog bit the cat.'

(5.12) *mósí łééchąą'í bi-shxash*
cat dog bit
'The cat was bitten by the dog.'

In each of the pairs above in the three languages, the second of the pair, which may be said to be 'derived' from the first, is called a passive construction because the alternations in the configurations of nominal statuses with which verbs are in particular relationships, as driven by morphological and ordering differences, result in the foregrounding of the patient object and possibly the highlighting of its affectedness. As can be seen in (5.1)-(5.12), passives in these languages are manifested in a similar fashion in that they all have a patient argument in sentence-initial position, the most prominent syntactic position in a sentence, and, in each case, the agent argument is omissible. Additionally, the fronting of the patient or undergoer argument is always local, unlike standard types of left periphery phenomena such as those exhibiting topic and focus effects (see below).

However, there are some notable differences in both syntax and semantics between them. Syntactically, the passive in English is marked by the inflectional morphology of the verb plus a copular auxiliary which entails linear rearrangement of its core arguments — the patient argument occurs in initial (subject) position, and the agent argument is either expressed in marked position as in (5.2), or suppressed as in (5.4). The passive in Chinese, on the other hand, is marked by an independent morpheme *bei*. This invariably signals that the preceding argument is the patient being acted upon and the following argument the agent if there is one, with the verb being completely unaffected morphologically. Finally, the passive in the SOV language, Navajo, is marked by the bound element, *bi-*, an apparent pronominal prefix (Hale 1973), in the verbal complex. It is this which signals the changed statuses of its core arguments, namely the logical object becoming the syntactic subject, again in initial position, and the logical subject becoming the syntactic object which is placed adjacent to the verbal complex.

There are semantic differences, too. In English, active and passive counterparts mean much the same (modulo possible scope effects), whereas in Chinese passives generally express a sense of adversity and highlight the affectedness of the dislocated patients (see Wang 1959, Li and Thompson 1981, Chappell 1986). The active sentence (5.5), for instance, simply describes a seeing event in which the affectedness of the patient is not salient at all, but with the occurrence of *bei*, the patient has to be fronted to sentence-initial position which marks the entity as the most prominent argument of the verb. In other words, the syntactic prominence resulting from displacement makes the argument the focus of attention. The affectedness of the fronted argument is highlighted by the use of the particle *bei*, which was originally a verb meaning 'receive' and which, by emphasizing the passivity of the recipient of the action, encourages a pejorative meaning.[1] Thus (5.6) implies the adverse situation *Tina* faced subsequent to the seeing event, i.e. consequently she might be scolded or disciplined. Because of the adverse implication encoded by *bei*, English passive sentences such as (5.4) cannot be translated directly into a Chinese passive, which is why a sentence like (5.8) is employed.

[1]It is worthwhile mentioning that although traditionally Chinese passive constructions generally have a pejorative implication that the pre-*bei* argument is negatively affected by the action designated by the predicate, a very small number of *bei* sentences in Modern Chinese, as discussed in C. Li & Thompson (1981: 496-497), are more or less free of such pragmatic commitments due to the influence of translation from Indo-European languages.

As regards passives in Navajo, they are said to be subject to the restriction that both arguments of the predicate must be animate, a constraint which is a precondition for voice alternations, a constraint not found in either English or Chinese. Restrictions of this sort are closely related to the fact that speakers tend to assign salience to nominal referents based on their real-world capacities to control situations (see Dixon 1979, Comrie 1980, Klaiman 1991). The verbal prefixes, *yi-* and *bi-*, are analyzable as bound pronominals in the verbal complex which always index the core arguments of the predicate. The choice between them depends on the logical status of the indexed argument: *yi-* is selected when the syntactic object coincides with logical object, whereas *bi-* is selected when the syntactic object coincides with logical subject (cf. Klaiman 1991). For this reason, the Navajo passive is considered a case of subject-object inversion (see Hale 1973). Although it has been argued that animacy is key to the differences between *yi-* and *bi-* constructions (e.g. by Hale 1973), more accurately these involve relative animacy, with *bi-* being used to express a situation in which a less animate noun phrase has more syntactic prominence. It is, rather, the possibility of control that is the guiding property in the use of this form, marking a surprising or unusual reversal of the expected controller in some situation. So, for example, the *yi-* form is not possible in (5.13) because it would be more normal for a man to control his kicking of some baby (sic) and so be normally the subject, while in (5.14) the situation is reversed and the *bi-* form is acceptable (example quoted in Klaiman 1991:176 from Creamer 1974: 34):

(5.13) *awéé'chí'í diné yi-tzał*
baby man kicked
'The man kicked the baby'

(5.14) *diné awéé'chí'í bi-tzał*
man baby kicked
'The man was kicked by the baby'

Typologically, the English passive encompasses behaviours usually treated under the rubric of passivization and hence is often termed *derived type*. The Chinese passive may be ascribed to *syntactic/semantic type*, since it is associated with expressing a sense of adversity by highlighting the affectedness of the pre-*bei* patient. The Navajo passive might be more appropriately be said to be of *pragmatic* type, as voice alternations marked by the verbal complex reflect the relative ontological salience of nominal referents, a reflection of the viewpoint of the participants in the discourse. Navajo passives can also be classified as an instance of an *inverse type*, in that the logical relation between the core nominals is expressed in an inverse fashion.[2]

In this paper we show that under the DS approach that reflects the dynamics of left to right processing, passive constructions of different types can be characterized in a consistent way. The paper is structured in the following manner. In section 5.2, we generally delineate the passive phenomena from a crosslinguistic perspective. In section 5.3, we introduce the part of the DS mechanism relevant to the present study. In section 5.4, we present a DS analysis of passives exemplified in the given three languages, which can be extendable to passives in other languages. Some concluding remarks are given in the final section.

5.2 The properties of passives

Before presenting an analysis of passives within DS, some discussion is in order concerning the syntactic and semantic properties of such constructions in general. In mainstream generative linguistics, familiar syntactic mechanisms that have been developed to account for passive constructions include NP movement (e.g. Chomsky 1981), case absorption (e.g. Jaeggli 1986) or argument suppression (e.g. Grimshaw 1990), which apply mostly to passives of derived type such as those in the familiar European languages. English passives, for instance, virtually always involve valence reduction or detransitivization: they either suppress or downgrade the argument assigned as subject by the active verb, namely eliminating it from the valence or reassigning it as an adjunct. However, this is not exactly the case in passives of other types such as Chinese and Navajo. In the Navajo passives (5.10)-(5.12), for example, there is no suppression of logical subjects nor detransitivization of transitive verbs specific to this construction, as verbs in the inverse form are still transitive. Detransitivization does not occur in Chinese passives either.

Based on a crosslinguistic perspective, passive constructions are often considered as involving operations which give rise to both foregrounding and backgrounding effects which share points of similarities with topicalizations and left dislocations (see Keenan 1985, Shibatani 1985). More needs to be said, however, as the terms *topicalization* and *left dislocation* are used in conflicting ways in the literature. In this paper, *left dislocation* will be used for left peripheral placement

[2]It should be pointed out that here we borrow the terminologies from Klaiman (1991) but use them differently. Although he admits that there does exist some parallelism between the inverse form and the passive voice, Klaiman (Chapter 4) disagrees with several authors (e.g. Hale 1973) who characterize the Navajo examples cited here as passives. In this paper we follow many authors and treat the Navajo examples as passives, based on syntactic and semantic/pragmatic grounds.

associated with contrastive interpretations as in (5.16), whereas the term *topic structures* and *topicalization* will be used to reflect strings where their pragmatic construal is that of backgrounding, as in (5.19).[3] The similarities of passive constructions with topicalizations have been well noticed and discussed. Givón (1979:186), for example, defines 'passivization' as 'the process by which a non-agent is promoted into the role of a main topic of the sentence'. Roberts (1998:112) claims that 'passivization can be regarded as one way of making a functional topic more prominent syntactically.' As for the three types of passives exemplified in section 1, their formations appear to operate in a similar fashion, in the sense that an object or patient expression is promoted into sentence-initial position and is thus foregrounded to the extent that this left-dislocated patient object will certainly attract our attention and yet it is naturally also the topic for the subsequently presented discourse context. In this respect, the passive construction simultaneously displays a foregrounding operation like left dislocation as in (5.16) and yet equally a backgrounding topic effect as in (5.19).

(5.15) The policeman beat Paul.

(5.16) Paul the policeman beat.

(5.17) Paul was beaten by the policeman.

(5.18) People make fun of the President.

(5.19) As for the President, people make fun of him.

(5.20) The President is made fun of by people.

Commensurate with the usage of topicalization (or topic structure) adopted here, the concept of topic is often used as a general label for some aspect of information being conveyed which is taken as background and to which other expressions may be anaphorically linked. The concept of focus, on the other hand is construed as involving an isolated term which provides some given propositional form (see Erteschik-Shir 1997) - hence the appropriateness of the term *left dislocation*. This also holds for passives of inverse type such as Navajo, which as a case of subject-object inversion promote the object to a position prior to

[3]Keenan (1985:243-244) and many others following him, for example, refer to sentences like sentences like (5.19) as left dislocations, referring to (5.16) as topicalization, a term indeed regularly used for at least a sub-class of long-distance dependency effects. One of the reasons for the different usages may be attributed to the fact that both constructions share one notable property, that is, they both have an element placed in a left-peripheral position standardly not adjacent to the verb of which they are to be construed as either argument or adjunct. In virtue of this position, they may be construed both as in contrast to what precedes, hence contrastive and so focussed, but nevertheless the point of departure for what follows, hence the topic.

the subject, as well as passives of semantic type such as Chinese. The Chinese equivalents to the English passives (5.17) and (5.20) are (5.21) and (5.23), which are marked by the passive morpheme *bei.* Omission of this passive marker would result in topic sentences (5.22) and (5.24), which are truth-conditionally the same as their passive counterparts apart from the affectedness reading associated with the logical object.

(5.21) *Paul bei jingcha da le.*
Paul BEI policeman beat ASP
'Paul was beaten by the policeman.'

(5.22) *Paul jingcha da le.*
Paul policeman beat ASP
'Paul, the policeman beat.'

(5.23) *zongtong bei renmen quxiao.*
President BEI people make fun of
'The President is made fun of by people.'

(5.24) *zongtong renmen quxiao (ta).*
President people make fun of him
'(As for) the President, people make fun of him.'

The parallelism between passive constructions and topic constructions and left dislocations nevertheless allows there to be differences between them. One difference lies in that in most languages what is 'passivized' is usually the object, whereas what is topicalized is not subject to this constraint. Another significant difference is that apart from the foregrounding operation which is also found in topic constructions and left dislocations, passives tend to background the subject in the active, an operation which is not found in the related two constructions. Furthermore, passive constructions differ in semantics and pragmatics from topic constructions and from left dislocations. Strikingly, the difference lies in the lexical grounding of passive constructions, and the lack of any such grounding in topic constructions and left dislocations. Semantically, what is distinct about passives from the two related structures is that they usually highlight the semantic aspect of the affectedness inherent in the patient relation (cf. Shibatani 1985). In other words, the 'derived' subject or the dislocated patient in a passive is often understood to be more affected by the action than when it is presented in the object position of an active, although the degree of affectedness may vary in different languages. In English, the derived subject in the passive is often not considered to be more affected than the corresponding object of the active. This is, however, not always the case. In some environments, as Keenan (1985) points out, passive sentences do give rise to a somewhat strong sense of affectedness. Consider the following examples (from Keenan 1985:269).

(5.25) John is watching Mary.

(5.26) Mary is being watched.

(5.27) John saw Mary entering the building at 6 o'clock.

(5.28) Mary was seen entering the building at 6 o'clock.

Keenan suggests that in each of the pairs (5.25)-(5.26) and (5.27)-(5.28), only the latter allows any implication that Mary's action could possibly have some negative consequences for her. While this might be contentious for English, the pragmatic salience of such an interpretation is one of the major characteristics of Chinese and Navajo passives. In Chinese, the passive construction marked by the morpheme *bei* is often understood as negatively affecting the pre-*bei* patient argument, since it generally expresses a sense of adversity with emphasis on the passivity of the recipient of the action. The passive particle signals assignment to the dislocated patient some informational salience relative to the situation of discourse or the intention of speakers.

Similarly in Navajo, the passive is also a strategy for highlighting the patientness of the argument, indicating a lack of control over some action. The salience of the object is achieved not simply by inverting subject and object, but by the use of a different pronominal prefix *bi-* which signals that the agent argument or logical subject occurs in a position usually occupied by the object. Exactly what the effect of this prefix is is open to some debate, but Willie (2000) argues that its function is to topicalize the patient argument, thus foregrounding it. The agent argument may then be in focus (although as Navajo is a pro-drop language like Chinese, the Agent may be omitted altogether). It is then the process of topicalizing the patient that gives rise to the pragmatic effect of the event being described as having unusual properties, such as that the agent is lower in animacy or lacks some proto-agent property such as control (Dowty 1991).

To summarize, formation of passives is simultaneously both a foregrounding and backgrounding operation relative to their active counterparts. As a consequence, passives have their own syntactic and semantic attributes. Syntactically, they usually involve the dislocation of a patient argument to sentence-initial position, which creates focus as well as topic effects. Semantically, the dislocated or foregrounded patient is likely to be interpreted as being affected by the action designated by the predicate, albeit the degree of affectedness may vary in different languages and different situations. As will be shown later in section 5.4, these attributes can be captured under the DS approach, without any postulation of topic or focus as primitives.

5.3 The DS framework

Before we present a DS account of passive constructions, we provide a brief introduction to the relevant parts of the framework needed for handling the passive phenomena. The DS paradigm seeks to develop a grammar formalism for characterizing the structural properties of language by modelling the dynamic process of semantic interpretation. According to this theory, natural language understanding is a process of monotonic tree growth which is defined over the left-right sequence of words uttered in context. Like Minimalism (Chomsky 1995), there is only one significant syntactic level, namely Logical Form. Unlike Minimalism, logical forms are representations of real semantic content, i.e., pure representations of argument structure and other meaningful content.

The design of the DS model reflects a number of significant observations. First, natural language understanding is highly dependent on context and the change of context is not merely sentence by sentence, but also word by word. Second, processing, like other cognitive activities, involves manipulation of partial information. This model extends incomplete specifications from semantics and pragmatics to the domain of syntax, and thus allows the interaction between three types of actions, computational, lexical and pragmatic, in the parsing process. Intrinsic to this process is the concept of underspecification, both syntactic and semantic, which is manifested in a number of different ways and whose resolution is driven by the notion of requirements (i.e. goals and subgoals) which determine the process of tree growth and must be satisfied for a parse to be successful. The critical aspect for our account will be the interaction between these three types of actions, all of which are expressed in the same terms of tree growth, hence freely allowing interaction between them. Since this interaction is important to the case to be made, I briefly introduce the vocabulary of tree growth decorations and the way it captures the concept of progressive tree growth.

5.3.1 Requirements and tree growth

The starting point is to build a tree the root node of which is the goal of interpretation formalized as a universal requirement $?Ty(t)$, where ? indicates the requirement, the label Ty the type and its value t the type of a proposition. To satisfy such a requirement, a parse relies on information from three sources. First, there are computational rules which give templates for the building of trees. A pair of general computational rules called INTRODUCTION and PREDICTION allow a tree rooted in $?Ty(Y)$ to be expanded to one with an argument daughter $?Ty(X)$ and a predicate daughter $?Ty(X \rightarrow Y)$, reflecting the functor/argument status of the typed, lambda logic employed. By this rule, the minimal tree with the initial requirement $?Ty(t)$ can be expanded to a partial tree as in (5.29), where the diamond is the 'pointer' which is used to identify the particular node under construction, here the external argument or subject node.

(5.29) An initial expansion

$?Ty(t), \Diamond \quad \Rightarrow$ $?Ty(t)$ [daughters: $?Ty(e), \Diamond$ and $?Ty(e \rightarrow t)$]

Second, information about tree building may come from actions encoded in lexical entries, which are accessed as words are parsed. Take the utterance *George likes Gillian* as an example. A lexical entry for the word *George* contains conditional information initiated by a trigger (the condition providing the context under which subsequent development takes place), a set of actions (here involving the annotation of a node with type and formula information) and a failure statement (an instruction to abort the parsing process if the conditional action fails). The lexical specification further determines, through the annotation $[\downarrow]\bot$, that the node in question is a terminal node, a general property of contentive lexical items.

(5.30) Lexical entry for *George*:

IF	$?Ty(e)$	trigger
THEN	$\texttt{put}(Ty(e), Fo(George'), [\downarrow]\bot)$	actions
ELSE	abort	failure

The information derived from parsing *George* provides an annotation for the external argument node and thus satisfies the requirement on that node for an expression of type *e*. Then the pointer moves on to the predicate node as shown in (5.31).

It should be pointed out that in the DS literature (see Cann et al. 2005) the external argument node is usually taken as the subject node, since the subject expression in many languages and in many constructions is the agent or the external argument of the predicate. It is however not applicable to all sentence patterns, especially the passive pattern in which the subject expression has a 'derived' nature and is usually the patient or the internal argument of the predicate. Rather, the DS concept of subject within a tree is that of the unique Ty(e) node immediately dominated by the topnode, hence strictly speaking the external argument or logical subject node, the DS tree being essentially a semantic tree representing the predicate-argument structure. But of course this immediately opens up the challenge of providing a universal definition of subjecthood which appears to be a multi-factor concept (see Keenan 1976, Comrie 1981), to which this paper is in part a response (see also Cann this volume).

(5.31) Parsing *George*

$$?Ty(t)$$

$$Fo(George'), Ty(e), \qquad ?Ty(e \rightarrow t), \Diamond$$

Lexical entries may make reference to nodes in the tree other than the trigger node, either building them or annotating them, by employing a few instructions such as 'make', 'put', 'go', which have obvious interpretations. To formulate both computational and lexical actions in these terms, DS adopts The Logic of Finite Trees (LOFT), a modal logic for describing finite trees. This logic is central to the DS framework and utilizes a number of operators of which the following are used in this chapter:

$$\langle\downarrow\rangle, \langle\downarrow_0\rangle, \langle\downarrow_1\rangle, \langle\uparrow\rangle, \langle\uparrow_0\rangle, \langle\uparrow_1\rangle, \langle\downarrow^*\rangle, \langle\uparrow^*\rangle, \langle L\rangle$$

These modalities are interpreted by a discrete relation between the nodes in a tree: $\langle\downarrow\rangle$ is evaluated over the daughter relation, so $\langle\downarrow_0\rangle$ and $\langle\downarrow_1\rangle$ mean an argument daughter and a functor daughter below a certain mother node respectively; conversely $\langle\uparrow\rangle$ over the mother relation, thus $\langle\uparrow_0\rangle$ and $\langle\uparrow_1\rangle$ mean an argument daughter and a functor daughter of a certain mother node respectively; $\langle\downarrow^*\rangle$ is interpreted over the dominance relation and $\langle\uparrow^*\rangle$ over the inverse of dominance; $\langle L\rangle$ is evaluation over a relation of "LINK" pairing two trees. The way LOFT operators are used can be demonstrated in the lexical entry for *likes* in the above utterance.

(5.32) Lexical entry for *likes*:

IF	$?Ty(e \rightarrow t)$
THEN	$\texttt{go}(\langle\uparrow_1\rangle), \texttt{put}(Tns(PRES)), \texttt{go}(\langle\downarrow_1\rangle);$
	$\texttt{make}(\langle\downarrow_1\rangle), \texttt{go}(\langle\downarrow_1\rangle)$
	$\texttt{put}(Ty(e \rightarrow (e \rightarrow t)), Fo(Like'), [\downarrow]\bot);$
	$\texttt{go}(\langle\uparrow_1\rangle), \texttt{make}(\langle\downarrow_0\rangle), \texttt{go}(\langle\downarrow_0\rangle), \texttt{put}(?Ty(e)))$
ELSE	abort

The pointer is manipulated by the lexical actions to annotate different nodes. Firstly, it moves from the predicate node of $?Ty(e \rightarrow t)$ to the top node $?Ty(t)$ where the present tense information is annotated[4], then returns to the open predicate node. Then the lexical semantics of

[4]See Cann (this volume) for a more detailed account of tense in English.

the transitive verb *like* takes action: it not only licenses the building of a two-place predicate node, but also that of an internal argument daughter with a requirement to construct a formula of type *e*. After the parse of the verb, the pointer moves to the $?Ty(e)$ node, indicating that this is to be developed next. The tree in (5.33) represents the parse state where both the subject and the verb have been parsed.[5]

(5.33) Parsing *George likes*

$$?Ty(t), Tns(PRES)$$

- $Fo(George'), Ty(e)$
- $?Ty(e \rightarrow t)$
  - $?Ty(e), \Diamond$
  - $Ty(e \rightarrow (e \rightarrow t)), Fo(Like')$

Finally the object NP *Gillian* is parsed to satisfy the open term requirement in the internal argument position, the processing of which is the same as that of the subject NP *George*.

(5.34) Parsing *George likes Gillian*

$$Ty(t), Fo(Like'(Gillian')(George')), Tns(PRES)$$

- $Fo(George'), Ty(e)$
- $Ty(e \rightarrow t), Fo(Like'(Gillian'))$
  - $Ty(e), Fo(Gillian')$
  - $Ty(e \rightarrow (e \rightarrow t)), Fo(Like')$

The parsing process is not yet complete, however, as some requirements on the tree remain to be satisfied. Completion of the tree involves functional application of functors over arguments, driven by modus ponens over types, yielding expressions which satisfy the type requirements associated with intermediate nodes (the rules in question are called COMPLETION and ELIMINATION, the former noting modal statements of type decorations, these then triggering the construction of the appropriate lambda term at the mother). 5.34 shows the completed tree the root node of which is decorated with a propositional formula value representing the final result of interpreting the utterance.

5.3.2 Anaphoric expressions

As mentioned above, DS also allows pragmatic actions in the parsing process, which can be illustrated by the processing of anaphoric

[5]For convenience, all argument nodes are put on the left-hand side and functor nodes on the right-hand side in the tree displays. Also, the internal structure of the terms is ignored in the tree displays, as they play no role in the argument in this paper.

expressions. Assuming the general stance that words provide lexical actions in building up representations of content in context, we can say that anaphoric expressions such as pronouns may pick out some logical term if that term is provided in the discourse context. This sort of semantic underspecification is treated in the DS model as involving the articulation of anaphoric expressions as projecting a metavariable to be replaced by some proper representation. Put in another way, anaphoric expressions can be construed as a bound variable or a placeholder which can be replaced by some selected term from the context. Such a replacement is established through a pragmatically driven process of SUBSTITUTION which applies as part of the parsing process.

Considering the processing of pronouns such as *she* and *him* in the utterance *George likes Gillian, but she doesn't like him.* In parsing the first pronoun *she*, the external argument node of the conjunct clause is first decorated with a metavariable $\mathbf{U}_{female}$, with an associated requirement $?\exists\mathbf{x}.Fo(\mathbf{x})$, to find a contentful value for the formula label, as shown in (5.35).

(5.35) Lexical entry for *she:*

IF	$?Ty(e)$
THEN	$\mathtt{put}(Ty(e), Fo(\mathbf{U}_{female}, ?\exists\mathbf{x}.Fo(\mathbf{x}), ?\langle\uparrow_0\rangle Ty(t), [\downarrow]\bot)$
ELSE	abort

Construed in the given context, SUBSTITUTION will determine that the metavariable $\mathbf{U}_{female}$ can only pick out the logical term *Fo*(*Gillian'*) established in the first clause, since she requires to be identified with a referent that is female or that can be attributed with female properties.

5.3.3 Left periphery effects

Apart from the two sorts of underspecification which are encoded by requirements to construct nodes of certain types and to identify the formula value of a node respectively, a third sort of underspecification is that of a tree relation, associated with a requirement to identify where in a tree a node should be fixed. Such positional underspecification is often used to account for long-distance dependency effects which are analyzed in terms of a tree growth process involving an initially unfixed node whose position in the emergent tree structure is fixed at some later state in the parsing process. There is a computational rule called *ADJUNCTION that achieves this effect, defining a transition from an initial tree of $?Ty(t)$ (with treenode address $Tn(a)$, where a is some string of 0s and 1s, see Kempson et al. 2001) with only a single node to a tree that contains in addition a node carrying a treenode address, $?\exists\mathbf{x}.Tn(\mathbf{x})$, a requirement to identify a fixed address within the unfolding tree. The effect of this construction rule is illustrated in (5.36).

(5.36) *ADJUNCTION

$$Tn(a), ?Ty(t), \Diamond \quad \mapsto \quad Tn(a), ?Ty(t)$$

$$\langle\uparrow^*\rangle Tn(a), ?Ty(e), ?\exists\mathbf{x}.Tn(\mathbf{x}), \Diamond$$

The rule of *ADJUNCTION finds its best application in the characterization of left dislocation structures,[6] since it captures the intuition that the left-peripheral expression requires a fixed position for the overall structure to be interpreted. The parse of a string such as *Gillian, George likes* is shown in (5.37).

(5.37) Parsing *Gillian, George likes.*

$$Tn(a), ?Ty(t)$$

$$\langle\uparrow^*\rangle Tn(a), Ty(e), Fo(Gillian'), ?\exists\mathbf{x}.Tn(\mathbf{x}) \qquad Ty(e), Fo(George') \qquad ?Ty(e \to t)$$

$$?Ty(e), \Diamond \qquad Ty(e \to (e \to t)), Fo(Like')$$

At the point when the verb has been processed, there remains outstanding an unfixed node and a requirement to construct a node of type e, as indicated by the pointer. In such an environment, a process of MERGE can take place, which unifies the information on the unfixed node with that on the internal argument node. Although the output tree for the left dislocation structure is identical to that for the canonical structure *George likes Gillian*, the informational differences between them are captured in the parsing process: the left-dislocated object projects a term that provides an update to a propositional structure, thus creating a type of focus effect in virtue of providing a derivation which involves both the construction of an unfixed node within the incremental process of building up structure from the words in order and its later update (see Kempson et al. 2009a).

Each of these trees has been simple. There is, in addition, a general process for building pairs of such structures, called *linked* trees; and such trees are constructed through the imposition of a shared term. This was defined in Kempson et al. 2001, Cann et al. 2005 for the modelling of relative clause construal (see Kula and Marten this volume); but it is also used to model topic structures, such as (5.19) where one term is in some sense construed as external to the primary structure and provides

[6]There is also a localized variant in which the unfixed node is along an underspecified functor relation. See Kempson and Kiaer 2010, Kiaer this volume.

the point of departure for building up that structure (see Cann et al 2005, Kempson, Marten and Thwala this volume). The LINK mechanism is a general computational action which projects, from a node decorated by some term, α, a linked tree which is required to contain a copy of α and permits a characterization of topic structures as involving an initially constructed tree of type e, decorated by some term, LINKed to a propositional tree required to contain somewhere within it a copy of that term. This schematic structure is shown in (5.38).

(5.38) Building a LINK Transition for topic structures.

$$\langle L\rangle Tn(0), Fo(\alpha), Ty(e) \qquad Tn(0), ?Ty(t), ?\langle\downarrow^*\rangle Fo(\alpha)$$

Note here the tree decoration, $?\langle\downarrow^*\rangle Fo(\alpha)$ which is a requirement that somewhere in the tree as it develops there must be a node decorated with $Fo(\alpha)$, whatever α might be.In English, this can be lexically induced through explicit encoding of the composite preposition *as for* as in (5.19) (notice its obligatory left-peripheral positioning), but this structure is also available through a general process of constructing such linked structures:

(5.39) Our new representative, he's a Norwegian.

(5.40) Our new representative, have you met him yet?

The overall framework thus makes available not only construction plus update of structural relations within a single tree, but also the construction of paired trees.

5.3.4 Right periphery effects

These processes are available in modified form in the closing stages of constructing propositional representations. The construction of linked structures for example is available as modelling a backgrounding effect at the right periphery, where the identification of a pronoun from some independently available context then imposes on the interpretation of the late-introduced expression a coreferential interpretation (Cann et al. 2005):

(5.41) He's a Norwegian, our new representative

Late application of *ADJUNCTION can also be invoked, for example, in a situation in which there is some node in the tree whose development has been incomplete, leaving some unfulfilled requirement, under a variant called LATE*ADJUNCTION. This would be the case, for instance, if a metavariable or placeholder should fail to get a fixed formula value through SUBSTITUTION from the context. In such circumstances, the node decorated by the metavariable, albeit type complete, is still formula incomplete. Application of *ADJUNCTION can allow the parse of a right-dislocated expression by creating an unfixed node whose formula value will satisfy the outstanding requirement through the process of MERGE, leading to a successful update of the unfolded tree. In English, such a sequence of actions is associated with expletives (see also Kempson, Marten and Thwala this volume), the decoration of the subject pronoun being provided with a metavariable, and only subsequent return to that node and its development by LATE*ADJUNCTION yielding the requisite output representation:

(5.42) It is likely that Mary will succeed

By way of illustration, I take up the case of subject inversion in Chinese. Since Chinese as an SVO language does not show VSO ordering, subject inversion with transitive verbs has the object preceding the subject, which gives rise to the VOS order, as in (5.43).

(5.43) *wan* *youxi* *ne* *haizimen.*
play game PARTICLE children
'The children are playing games.'

Given that Chinese is a pro-drop language where the subject expression is optional in context, the subject node is constructed by general transition rules and is initially decorated with a metavariable and completed type.[7] As for the parsing of the verb phrase sequence, it is just like that of a canonical sentence. The effect is illustrated in (5.44), where the pointer returns to the external argument node after the entire verb phrase has been processed.

(5.44) Parsing *Wan youxi ne.*

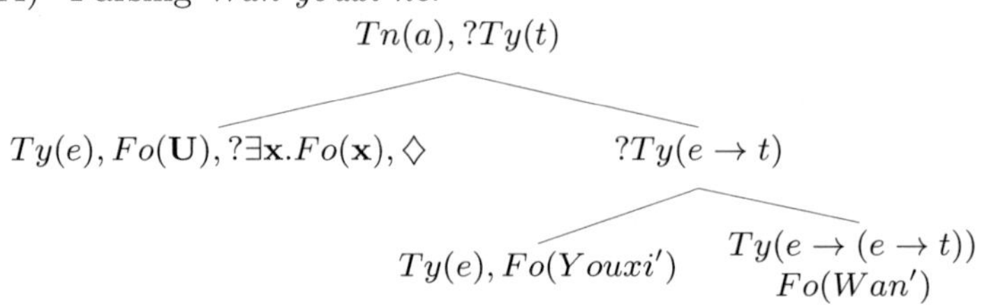

Following such a sequence of steps, there are several alternatives. At this point, SUBSTITUTION of the metavariable could occur from the context. But LATE*ADJUNCTION can also be applied to the external

[7]Since Chinese freely omits arguments (e.g. subject or object) when it is clear what those arguments should be from context, the parsing of subjectless sentences in this language is different from other pro-drop languages such as Italian where the parsing of verbs results in the projection of a full propositional template, decorating the subject node with a metavariable (see Cann et al. 2005 for discussion).

argument node. In the latter case, it projects an unfixed node with a requirement of the same type as the subject node from which it is projected. This permits the parse of the postposed subject expression. (5.45) shows the effect of applying MERGE as normal,[8] which leads to the final output *Fo*(*Wan'*(*Youxi'*)(*Haizimen'*)) as desired.

(5.45) Parsing *wan youxi ne, haizimen*

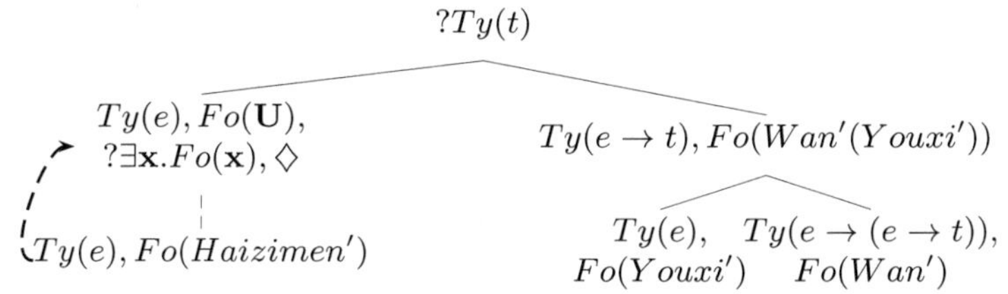

This sequence can also be modelled as involving the final construction of a linked structure following the pattern of (5.40), if in actual speech there is a clear intonation break between the verb phrase and the postponed noun phrase. The very range of alternatives thus provides a basis for capturing the way in which such inverse orderings provide the potential for both emphasis and backgrounding effects.

5.4 A dynamic analysis

In this section, we provide a dynamic analysis of the three different types of passives in section 5.2. Given the cross-linguistic evidence that passive in general involves the highlighting of a patient argument, usually by means of linear re-assignment of the object, we have good reason to treat them as a species of left dislocations, though they differ in nature from canonical left dislocation structure. We show that a parsing-oriented DS analysis can capture not only the functional similarities between passive constructions and left dislocations and topic constructions but also, through a combination of lexical and general tree-growth actions, the syntactic differences between them.

5.4.1 English passives

We first deal with passive constructions of derived type as manifested in the English language. As already discussed in section 5.2, passivization is a syntactic means of foregrounding the active object, which is an operation also found in left dislocations and topic constructions, and backgrounding the active subject, which is an operation not found in

[8]Note that MERGE is licit here because the external argument node is not decorated with the bottom restriction, $[\downarrow]\perp$. The node may therefore accommodate an unfixed subtree.

left dislocations and topic constructions. The foregrounding and backgrounding mechanisms should be reflected in the DS analysis. Consider (5.2), repeated below, a so-called long passive with an agent phrase.

(5.2) Tina was seen by the teacher.

Compared with its active counterpart *The teacher saw Tina*, the passive draws our attention to the patient argument *Tina*, as it appears in a prominent syntactic position where an agent argument is usually presented. Under an interpretive approach such as DS, therefore, it is natural to analyze this foregrounded patient or derived subject in terms of an initially unfixed node (as in (5.46)), with an entirely open dominance relation to the topnode as with ordinary left dislocations.

(5.46) Parsing *Tina*

$Tn(a), ?Ty(t), \Diamond \quad \mapsto \quad Tn(a), ?Ty(t) \quad \mapsto \quad Tn(a), ?Ty(t), \Diamond$

$\langle\uparrow^*\rangle Tn(a), ?Ty(e), ?\exists\mathbf{x}.Tn(\mathbf{x}), \Diamond \qquad \langle\uparrow^*\rangle Tn(a), Ty(e), ?\exists\mathbf{x}.Tn(\mathbf{x}), Fo(Tina')$

After the patient element is processed and the pointer moves back to the topnode, a full propositional template is constructed through a parse of the the passive form of the verb. I assume that passive verb forms in English are triggered by an open propositional node, unlike their active counterparts which are triggered by on open predicate node, because the general rules, Introduction and Prediction, introduce an open term node in logical subject position. This requires immediate scanning of some noun phrase in English, as the language lacks the pro-drop property, but the passive requires the logical subject to be provided later in the parse (if at all). Hence, the lexical actions associated with the passive verb form must provide a placeholder metavariable in this position and then the appropriate propositional template of the main verb. (5.47) provides the requisite lexical actions.[9] The actions are complex as they not only build a complete propositional template,

[9]This lexical specification of *was seen* treats the passive form as though a single lexical entry along the lines of the active English verb forms, eg *upset*, where the tense marking is intrinsic to the verbal form itself. In doing so, it glosses over the distinct function of auxiliaries, for simplicity, as not essential to the characterization of a passive typology. The sub-part of this lexical specification which constitutes the actions of the passive form of the verb essentially maintains the spirit of DS in defining distinct verbal forms for a single stem as projecting onto a single predicate-argument structure, irrespective of what form a verb takes. Given the availability of lexical specifications of verbs taking the top $?Ty(t)$ node as a trigger for some verb forms, it remains an open question whether English, hence the rule of Prediction quite generally, should be seen as a lexically induced action, rather than a discrete computationally defined process (see Cann this volume, where this is proposed).

but decorate the logical subject node with a metavariable and impose a locality condition on the unfixed node ($\langle\uparrow_0\rangle\langle\uparrow_1\rangle$) which requires the node to be fixed in a strictly local position, i.e. as the internal argument within the current propositional array. The result of running this set of actions from the final tree is given in (5.48).[10]

(5.47) The lexical entry for *was seen*:

IF $?Ty(t) \wedge \langle\downarrow^*\rangle\top \wedge Tn(a)$
THEN IF $\downarrow\top$
THEN Abort
ELSE $\texttt{go}(\langle\downarrow^*\rangle), \texttt{put}(?\langle\uparrow_0\rangle\langle\uparrow_1\rangle Tn(a)),$
$\texttt{go}(\langle\uparrow^*\rangle), \texttt{put}(Tns(PAST)),$
$\texttt{make}(\langle\downarrow_0\rangle), \texttt{go}(\langle\downarrow_0\rangle),$
$\texttt{put}(Ty(e), Fo(\mathbf{U}), ?\exists\mathbf{x}.Fo(\mathbf{x})),$
$\texttt{go}(\langle\uparrow_0\rangle), \texttt{make}(\langle\downarrow_1\rangle), \texttt{go}(\langle\downarrow_1\rangle),$
$\texttt{put}(?Ty(e \to t)), \texttt{make}(\langle\downarrow_1\rangle), \texttt{go}(\langle\downarrow_1\rangle),$
$\texttt{put}(Ty(e \to (e \to t)), Fo(See'), [\downarrow]\bot)$
$\texttt{go}(\langle\uparrow_1\rangle), \texttt{make}(\langle\downarrow_0\rangle), \texttt{go}(\langle\downarrow_0\rangle), \texttt{put}(?Ty(e))$

(5.48) Parsing *Tina was seen*

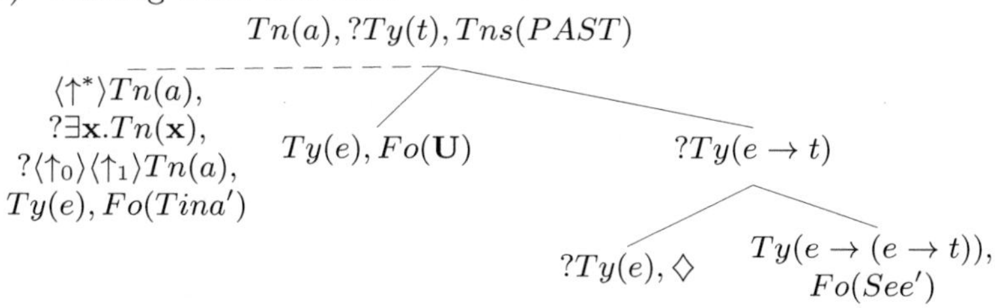

As can be seen in (5.48), the pointer sits at the open argument node, which provides the context in which the merge of the unfixed node projected by the derived subject NP takes place to satisfy its locality requirement. After the merge of the unfixed node with that of the internal argument node, the pointer moves up to the topnode via COMPLETION and ELIMINATION from the predicate node. Because the external argument node still carries a formula requirement, the pointer must move back down to the argument daughter in order to complete the requirement on this node (ELIMINATION requires that all requirements at the two daughters be met, this a reflection of strict compositionality on the emergent tree: Cann et al. 2005). At this point, the rule of LATE*ADJUNCTION can apply to permit the parse of the the adjunct *by*-phrase following the passive verb, as in (5.49).

[10]The symbol $\top$ is the symbol indicating that there is some formula true at that node, hence indicating that there is at least one decoration holding there.

(5.49) Parsing *Tina was seen by the teacher*

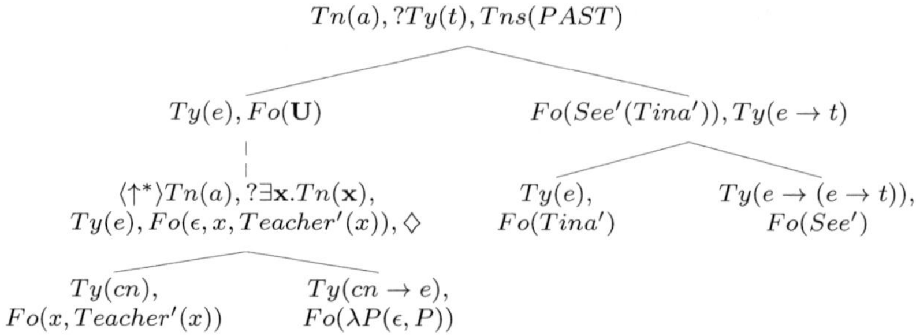

The processing of the adjunct expression proceeds in exactly the same way as that of a right-dislocated phrase. Completion of the unfixed node invokes Merge, providing the satisfaction of the formula requirement on the external argument node by replacing the metavariable with a value $Fo(\varepsilon, x, Teacher'(x))$. Notice how analysis of this sort captures our intuition: prior to the processing of the adjunct *by*-phrase, we already know that there is someone who saw Tina; it is only after the occurrence of the agent expression that we know that someone is the teacher. The analysis also captures the fact that the adjunct phrase *by the teacher* is the agent expression which serves as the logical or semantic subject of the transitive verb *see*, from which the passive verbal phrase is derived. Completion of the propositional tree leads to a final propositional formula $Fo(See'(Tina')(\varepsilon, x, Teacher'(x)))$, which is exactly the same as the output of parsing a left dislocation structure *Tina, the teacher saw.* This analysis has the bonus of reflecting the similarities and differences between passive constructions and left dislocations. Under the DS approach, both constructions are shown to be foregrounding constructions in which the leftmost expressions create some focus effects, in that they both project unfixed nodes which provide update terms for a main propositional tree representing the argument structure of relevant sentences. Apart from reflecting the operation of foregrounding inherent in passives (see Keenan 1985), the DS analysis also reflects the operation of backgrounding the active subject, as shown in the late completion of the external argument node.[11] Notice as well how the differences between passivization and left dislo-

[11]We do not specify quantifier dependencies in this paper, hence not the quantifier-tense dependency in an example such as this; but it is notable that the analysis of syntactic subjects in passive constructions as initially decorating an unfixed node and completion of the processing of the logical subject by the *by* phrase despite its end-placement in the clausal sequence allows a natural characterization of narrow scope construction of indefinite subjects of passive constructions:
(i) A number of mistakes were made by each candidate.

cations are captured under the DS approach. As is well known, what is distinctive about passivization is that the restrictions it imposes are essentially local, hence a property induced by the particular verb form. This is straightforwardly achievable in DS, despite the interaction with the left dislocation process, which is essentially general. Given that the passive verb indicates that the preverbal NP is the patient argument appearing in a position where it usually does not appear, and that the logical subject is optional, the DS analysis reflects this in the parsing process in which parsing of the passive verb imposes a locality restriction $?\langle\uparrow_0\rangle\langle\uparrow_1\rangle Tn(a)$ on the unfixed node so that this node has a specific target position. By contrast, since the unfixed node in left dislocation structure does not inhabit any determinate position in the tree, the information associated with this node has to be checked against each partial tree as successive pairs of daughter nodes are introduced, until a fixed position for the node can be established.

With the successful characterization of long passives, we now turn to short passives in English, namely passives without agent phrases. Presumably, the parse of agentless passives such as (5.4) *The bridge has been built* proceeds in the same fashion as that of agentive passives having just been discussed: the preverbal patient NP is analyzed as initially projecting an unfixed node on which a locality constraint is subsequently imposed through parsing of the passive verb which identifies the dislocated NP as its internal argument and annotates the external argument with a metavariable. (5.50) represents the stage when, after all lexical items are processed, the pointer sits at the external argument or logical subject node, requiring it to find some substituend.

(5.50) Parsing *The bridge has been built*

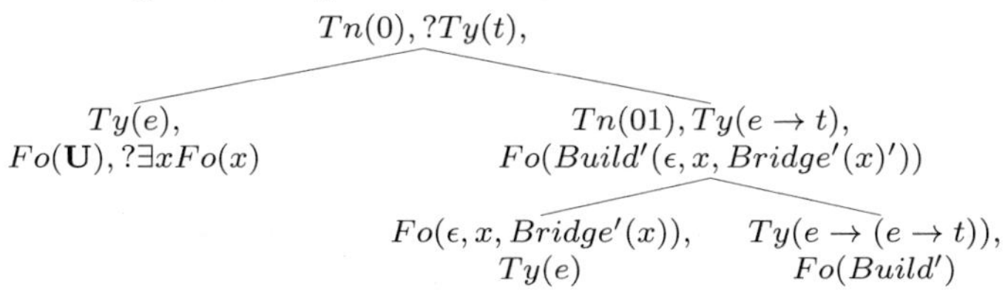

Substitution for this metavariable, as discussed above, is essentially a pragmatic matter. The substitution rule allows flexibility in the way the substituend or the agent is found: (i) it can be identified as part of the construction process as we have already seen; (ii) it can be identified from the previous context relative to the passive sentence; (iii) it can be specified by the speaker in a response to an agent-oriented question (e.g. *by whom?*) raised by the hearer if the latter is keen to know the doer or performer of the action designated by the verb; (iv) it can be figured out by the hearer with the help of his or her common-sense knowledge, which is often the case if they consider it unnecessary to specify the agent; the substituend for the metavariable **U** in (5.50), for instance, could be of some general term such as 'workers'. It is reasonable to assume that people very often rely on their world knowledge to find a substituend for the metavariable if there is no explicit agent expression from the context and also if there is no necessity of asking the speaker to specify it. With regard to the events described by the sentences below, for example, we are easily capable of determining what the implicit agent expressions are: in (5.51), we know that the booing action was done by racists; in (5.52) it was the referee who showed Rooney the red card and then sent him off; in (5.53) the murderer was caught by the police; in (5.54), it is the government of the relevant country that bans smoking in public places.

(5.51) Black players got booed in the friendly match against Spain.
(5.52) Rooney was shown the red card and was sent off immediately.
(5.53) The series murderer has finally been caught in West London.
(5.54) Smoking in public places has been banned in many countries.

Here we are not claiming that all agentless passives contain implicit agent expressions that can be easily determined by hearers without recourse to context or further clarification from speakers. However, the fact that hearers usually have no trouble understanding short passives suggests that they have the adequate pragmatic knowledge to figure out the doer of the action involved.

5.4.2 Chinese passives

Turning to passive constructions of syntactic/semantic type, as in Chinese, we need to spell out their grammatical characteristics before providing a DS analysis. Since Chinese passives are marked by the morpheme *bei*, previous analyses have naturally focused on the status of this particular word. There have been three influential analyses in the literature, the Preposition, the Dual Function, and the Verb Analyses. The preposition analysis (e.g. J. Li 1955, L. Li 1980, C. Li & Thompson 1981) treats the morpheme *bei* as a preposition on a par with the preposition *by* in English. The advantage with this analysis is that the presence of the agent NP in sentences like (5.6), repeated below, might receive a natural explanation if the predicate could be interpreted as passive.

(5.6)	*Tina*	*bei*	*laoshi*	*kanjian*	*le*
	Tina	BEI	teacher	see	ASP

'Tina was seen by the teacher.'

However, verbs in Modern Chinese, as pointed out in Chao (1968) and Lü (1982), do not show voice distinctions and thus do not exhibit passive meanings directly. Moreover, there is a further disadvantage with this analysis in that the omission of the agent NP would result in the stranding of a preposition, as in (5.8), repeated below.

(5.8) *na-zuo* *qiao* *bei* *chaichu* *le*
that-CL bridge BEI demolish ASP
'The bridge has been demolished.'

As is well-known, however, prepositions of any type in Chinese may not be stranded in any type of construction (see C. Li & Thompson 1981). In view of the 'distributional' problem of *bei*, a few researchers like Lü et al. (1980) and Shi (1997) postulate that the word *bei* has a double function: it is a preposition with the presence of the agent NP, but a helping particle or a passive marker with the absence of the agent NP. Analysis of this kind, which clearly has an *ad hoc* flavour, is against native speakers' intuition that the morpheme in question has only a single function, i.e. marking sentences with a passive flavour by giving the information that the pre-*bei* NP is acted upon in some manner specified by the verb. This can be confirmed by the fact that if speakers deliberately pause after *bei* is uttered in the course of conversation, hearers would consistently raise an event-oriented question about what happens to the preceding argument, and the response to the question could either be an agentive or agentless sentence, as in (5.55).

(5.55) **A:** *Tina* *bei* ...
Tina BEI
B: *Tina* *bei* *zenme* *le?*
Tina BEI how ASP
A: *bei* *(laoshi)* *ma* *le.*
BEI teacher scold ASP
'(She) was scolded (by the teacher).'

Zenme in the above question can be construed as 'What happened (to Tina)?' with a strong disposal sense (see L. Wang 1959, C. Li & Thompson 1981). This is convincing proof that *bei*'s grammatical function is not associated with the presence or absence of the agent argument and hence there are not two instantiations of *bei*, as preposition and helping particle.

In view of the inadequacy of the previous two analyses, a number of authors (e.g. Hashimoto 1968, 1987; Tan 1987, Ting 1998, J. Huang 1999) propose that the puzzling morpheme should be analyzed as a verb, which historically it was, meaning 'suffer' in Classical Chinese.

For example, Hashimoyo's analysis is based on the assumption that *bei* as a special verb can take a predicate or clause as its complement. Accordingly, a passive sentence like (5.56) has the underlying representation in (5.57).

(5.56) *Tina bei laoshi kanjian le.*
Tina BEI teacher see ASP
'Tina was seen by the teacher.'

(5.57) $[_S\ [_{NP}$ Tina$][_{VP}$ bei $[_S$ [laoshi $[_{VP}$ [kanjian-le $[_{NP}$ Tina]]]]]

Under the verb analysis, Chinese passive construction, unlike its English counterpart, involves a complex sentence: what follows *bei* is a nominalized clause with the object omitted. The omission of the object is attributable to the fact that it is identical to the subject and thus undergoes deletion. As for the absence of the agent NP, it should be treated as a special case of null subject. Thus all the problems with the previous analyses could be given a satisfactory solution.

It should be pointed out that although all the authors listed above treat *bei* as a verb, they take different approaches. Hashimoto takes the non-movement approach as presented here, while Tan adopts Lexical-Functional Grammar, and Ting and J. Huang the Government-Binding framework. Also it should be noted that some authors' analyses have changed over time. For instance, J. Huang (1988) argues for the dual function analysis; J. Huang (1993) among other papers treats *bei* as a preposition on a par with the English preposition *by*; J. Huang (1999) is against the prepositional analysis and opts instead for the verb analysis.

The treatment of *bei* as a special verb, however, faces a number of serious problems. All full verbs, for example, can take an aspect marker as in (5.58) and can also be employed in the V-not-V question form as in (5.59), but *bei* cannot (see also Y. Li 1990 among others), which suggests that the morpheme in question is not in fact a verb.

(5.58) *Tina ai/****bei le*** *laoshi ma.*
Tina get/BEI ASP teacher scold
'Tina got a scolding from her teacher.'

(5.59) *Tina ai-mei-ai/****bei-mei-bei*** *laoshi ma?*
Tina get-not-get/BEI-not-BEI teacher scold
'Did Tina get a scolding from her teacher?'

Based on the above discussion, we analyze *bei* as neither a preposition nor a verb, but a grammatical word or particle which consistently assigns an object role to the argument preceding it and invariably signals that this term is the passive recipient of the action. In other words, *bei* is responsible for the fronting of the object, as in passivization in

Indo-European languages like English. Our claim is therefore that passive in Chinese involves the promotion of object to sentence-initial position and that *bei* induces the dislocation of the object to (unique) topic position. As has been noted in Hashimoto (1968), Lapolla (1989), Y. Huang (2000) and others, passive constructions in Chinese share some points of similarity with topic constructions, which is consistent with the crosslinguistic observations (e.g. Givón 1979, Shibatani 1985, 1988).[12]

Having spelled out the grammatical characteristics of passive constructions in Chinese, we now turn to its analysis within the the DS framework.[13] Given that the pre-*bei* NP is a left-dislocated constituent, it is appealing to analyze it in terms of an initially unfixed node, as the derived subject NP in English passives is construed. The parse of *bei* then identifies this unfixed node as the internal argument of the main verb. In other words, the passive particle restricts the locality of the node associated with the dislocated expression precisely, even though it remains strictly unfixed at this point of the parse. This exactly parallels the effect of parsing the passive verb complex in English as defined in (5.47) above.

To illustrate the proposed analysis of the passive construction in Chinese, we first tackle long passives with (5.6) *Tina bei laoshi kanjian-le* (Tina was seen by the teacher) as an example. The fact that not only is the pre-*bei* expression interpreted as the internal argument of the main predicate, but also as being strongly affected by the action denoted by the verb, as discussed in section 5.1, indicates that the affectedness reading as the remnant of the verbal interpretation of *bei* should be encoded in the content of the relevant proposition. We can provide this information in the form of a 'presupposition' attached to the term constrained by the passive particle *bei*. This is shown as α_{AFF} where α is the term and AFF is intended as a constraint on interpretation such that whatever the thematic role of the main predicate the term is identified with it must also involve strengthening to an affected role.[14]

[12]See also Cann and Wu (this volume) for further discussion of this point.

[13]Note that this analysis differs markedly from that in Cann and Wu (this volume) which makes certain different assumptions about the interaction of *bei* and the rest of the clause. Nevertheless, the current analysis, based on Wu (2005), is in essence consistent with the more complex approach of that paper.

[14]As argued in Yamanaki (2009), all such semantic restrictions are straightforwardly in the manner of a meaning postulate, and these can be straightforwardly expressed using the concept of linked structures, viz. paired structures, one of which is propositional and making use of the term from which the LINK transition is built. But see Cann and Wu (this volume) for an alternative and more detailed means of capturing this effect.

The derivation proceeds as follows. The first step is to utilize the general rule for introducing an unfixed node which allows the parse of the pre-*bei* expression *Tina*. Then the voice particle is scanned, the lexical actions of which, given in (5.60), impose both a semantic constraint on the interpretation of the term in relation to some larger proposition, and also a strict locality constraint on the position of the unfixed node, as discussed above. The former is imposed by building a linked structure and defining a decoration on the top propositional node of this newly introduced tree which enforces the affectedness constraint on the individual denoted by the term just constructed, while leaving open what is the source of this affectedness. The latter is defined by simply imposing a requirement on the update of the unfixed node that it must meet the condition that it be the internal argument of a predicate node dominated by the already introduced proposition-requiring node. The effect of parsing the passive marker *bei*, given an unfixed node decorated with $Fo(Tina')$ is shown in (5.61).

(5.60) The lexical entry for *bei*

IF	$?Ty(t) \wedge Tn(n)$		
THEN	IF	$\langle\downarrow^*\rangle(Ty(e) \wedge Fo(\alpha)$	
	THEN	$\texttt{go}(\langle\downarrow^*\rangle); \texttt{put}(?\langle\uparrow_0\rangle\langle\uparrow^1\rangle Tn(n));$	
		$\texttt{make}(\langle L^{-1}\rangle); \texttt{go}(\langle L\rangle); \texttt{put}(?Ty(t));$	
		$\texttt{make}(\langle\downarrow_0\rangle); \texttt{go}(\langle\downarrow_0\rangle); \texttt{put}(Ty(e), Fo(\alpha));$	
		$\texttt{go}(\langle\uparrow_0\rangle); \texttt{make}(\langle\downarrow_1\rangle); \texttt{go}(\langle\downarrow_1\rangle);$	
		$\texttt{put}(Ty(e \rightarrow t), Fo(Affected'));$	
		$\texttt{go}(\langle\uparrow_1\rangle\langle L^{-1}\rangle\langle\uparrow^*\rangle?Ty(t))$	
	ELSE	abort	
ELSE	Abort		

(5.61) Parsing *Tina bei*

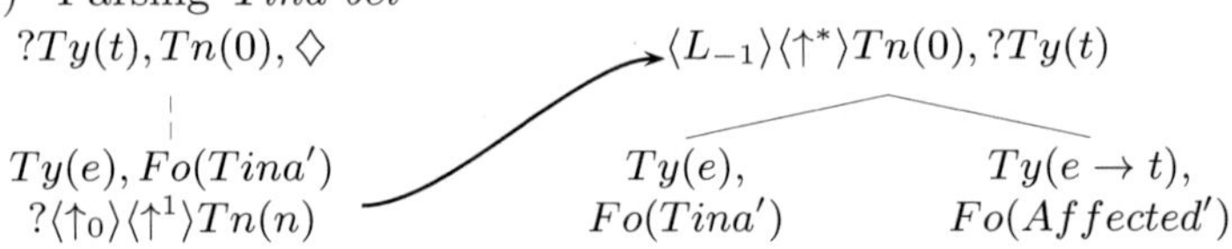

The parse then proceeds as before with nodes for external argument and predicate being introduced by INTRODUCTION and PREDICTION, allowing the parse of the agent argument *laoshi* 'teacher' and the verb *kanjian* 'see'. The lexical actions from the verb result in the building of a two-place predicate node and an internal argument node. The pointer then moves to the internal argument node, providing the context in which the merge of the pre-*bei* constituent must take place (ignoring the LINK structure which provides the affectedness reading). After the merge of the unfixed node with the internal argument node, the whole tree can be completed, which would yield a final output $Fo(Kanjian'(Tina'_{AFF})(Laoshi'))$ (5.62).

(5.62) Parsing *Tina bei laoshi kanjian-le*

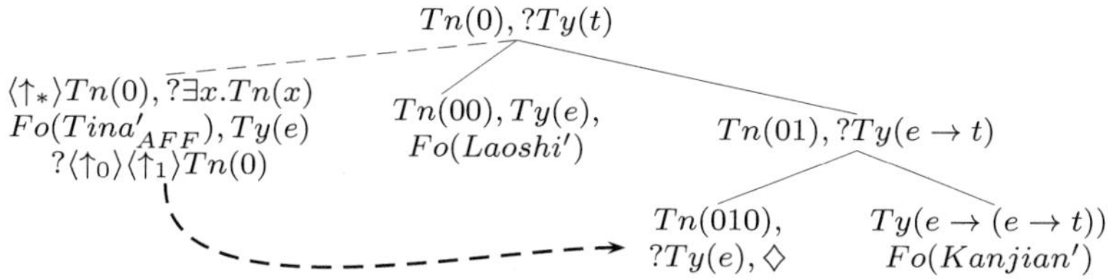

The propositional formula is interpreted in such a way that the experiencer role assigned by the verb *kanjian* 'see' to its internal argument is strengthened to give the added information that *Tina* was affected directly by the seeing event. More precisely, the formula must be interpreted as something like 'there is an event of seeing with *laoshi* 'the teacher' as agent and *Tina* as the experiencer and this event affected *Tina*' (see Cann and Wu this volume).

The analysis of the agentive pattern provides a template for analyzing short passives, i.e. the agentless pattern: a left-peripheral argument projects an unfixed node which through the parse of the passive marker *bei* merges with the internal argument node of the one-place predicate to derive a well-formed proposition. Thus in (5.8) *Na-zuo qiao bei chaichu-le* (The bridge has been demolished), the initial two words have been parsed as above. Application of the general transition rules, INTRODUCTION and PREDICTION, introduce the external argument node and predicate node, with the former being decorated with a metavariable to satisfy the type-requirement. After all the words in the string have been processed, as in the parse of an English passive, the pointer moves down to the agent argument node, requiring the metavariable to find some contentive value. Substitution for the metavariable could be of some salient substituend from the context or some arbitrary term standing for 'some people or someone'. In spoken discourse, however, native speakers prefer to use a generic NP like *ren* 'people' in the post-*bei* position instead of a null agent if the agent is unknown to them or unnecessary to specify, as (5.63)-(5.64) illustrate. This implies that the agentless pattern has obligatory pragmatic effects in the sense that the agent, albeit absent in the syntax, is pragmatically 'present' in the mind of speakers and hearers.

(5.63) *na-zuo* *qiao* *bei* *(ren)* *chaichu* *le.*
that-CL bridge BEI people demolish ASP
'The bridge has been demolished (by some people).'

(5.64) *zhe-sou chuan bei (ren) shaohui guo.*
this-CL boat BEI people burn ASP

'This ship has been burned (by someone).'

Notice how the similarities and differences between passives in English and Chinese are captured within this account: passives in both languages are characterized as a strategy of foregrounding the patient and backgrounding the agent, as the initial NPs in both languages are shown to project an unfixed node which updates a propositional structure and hence creates some (topicalized) focus effects; in the English passive, the unfixed node is assigned a fixed tree address by parsing the passive verb, which captures the fact that passivization takes place at the level of verb-phrase syntax, whereas in the Chinese passive, the unfixed node is assigned additional semantic information as well as a fixed address by parsing a grammatical particle, which captures the fact that Chinese passives usually display informational salience.

5.4.3 Navajo passives

With the successful characterization of both the English and the Chinese type of passive constructions, we now turn to the inverse type of passive constructions as manifested in Navajo Consider the examples (5.9, 5.10), repeated below.

(5.9) *łį́į́' dzaanééz yi-ztał.*
horse mule kicked

'The horse kicked the mule.'

(5.10) *dzaanééz łį́į́' bi-ztał.*
mule horse kicked

'The mule was kicked by the horse.'

The prefixes on the verb appear to identify the preceding NP as logical subject or logical object – *bi* as subject, *yi* as object. However, as noted above, the *bi-* prefix appears to be associated with a topicalizing function of the patient argument (Willie 2000) and so we may then interpret this construction as involving a topic structure where the topic sits 'outside' the main propositional frame and *bi-* provides a copy of that topic in the logical object position. This can be modelled in DS by the use of the LINK operator $\langle L \rangle$ and its inverse $\langle L^{-1} \rangle$ which connects two independent propositional trees that share some term. This same structure can be used to analyse the Navajo inverse construction. Taking (5.10) as the example, the first nominal can be parsed using the rule that derives the structure in (5.38) to provide a formula $Fo(Mule')$ on the LINK node with a requirement on the main propositional node that a copy is to be found within that tree. The second noun phrase is parsed using the rule of *ADJUNCTION, as we have seen above and then the pronominal prefix *bi-* is parsed. We take this to construct an internal argument node and put a copy of the formula decorating the LINKed tree as specified in (5.65):[15]

(5.65) Lexical actions for *bi-*

IF	$?Ty(t)$	
THEN	IF	$\langle L^{-1}\rangle Fo(\alpha)$
	THEN	$\mathtt{make}(\langle\downarrow_1\rangle), \mathtt{go}(\langle\downarrow_1\rangle), \mathtt{make}(\langle\downarrow_0\rangle), \mathtt{go}(\langle\downarrow_0\rangle)$ $\mathtt{put}(Ty(e), Fo(\alpha)), \mathtt{go}(\langle\uparrow_0\rangle\langle\uparrow_1\rangle)$
	ELSE	Abort
ELSE	Abort	

Parsing the verb then constructs a propositional template to give the tree in (5.66) (some details omitted). Note that the internal argument node created by the pronominal prefix necessarily collapses with that projected by the verb[16], leaving the only open argument node as the agent/external argument position with which the unfixed node must merge.

(5.66) Parsing (5.10)

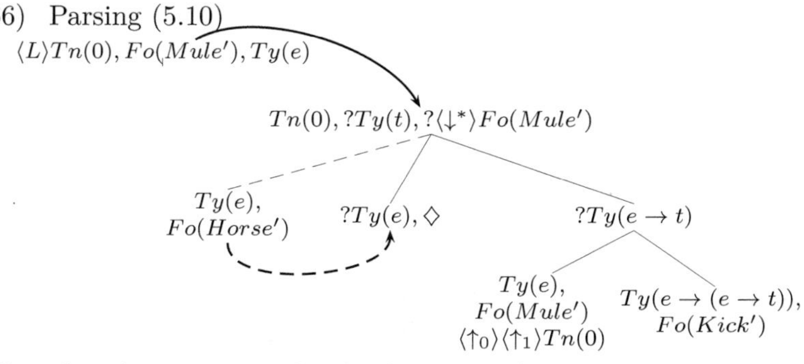

How then do we account for the direct, *yi-*, form? There are a number of ways this could be done, depending on more data being available, but taking the lead from Willie (2000), we will assume here that the direct form either involves a LINK topic structure where appropriate or an application of INTRODUCTION and PREDICTION where the subject is not a topic. Taking the latter option and illustrating the construction using example (5.9) will allow the initial NP to be parsed as the logical subject after which an application of the local variant of *ADJUNCTION

[15] Note that these actions will need to be revised to account for possessive and postpositional uses of the pronominal prefix.

[16] This is a general property of the LOFT logic used to describe trees: nodes with the same modality are necessarily identical.

may apply to yield a node that allows the parse of the second NP. The pronominal prefix *yi-* then yields actions that fix the latter node as the internal argument, as defined in (5.67) and illustrated in the first tree in (5.68). This figure is then completed through a parse of the verb to give that in the second tree.

(5.67) Lexical actions for *yi-*

IF	$?Ty(t)$	
THEN	IF	$\langle\downarrow_1^*\downarrow_0\rangle Fo(\alpha) \wedge ?\exists \mathbf{x}.Tn(\mathbf{x})$
	THEN	$\texttt{make}(\langle\downarrow_1\rangle), \texttt{go}(\langle\downarrow_1\rangle), \texttt{make}(\langle\downarrow_0\rangle), \texttt{go}(\langle\downarrow_0\rangle)$ $\texttt{put}(Ty(e), Fo(\alpha)), \texttt{go}(\langle\uparrow_0\rangle\langle\uparrow_1\rangle)$
	ELSE	Abort
ELSE	Abort	

(5.68) Parsing (5.9)

Tree 1 Tree 2

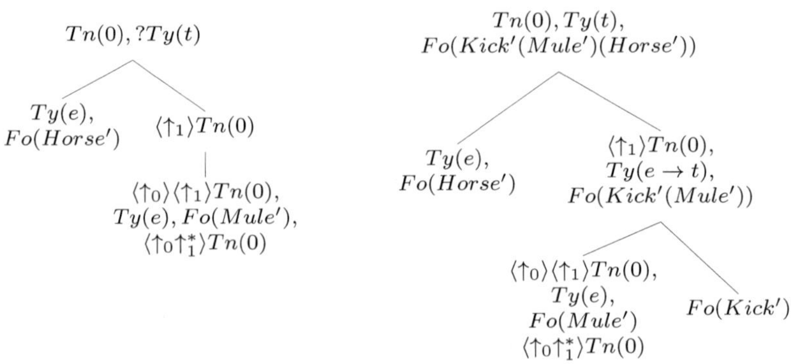

The question then remains as to what should be presented to express the relative animacy restriction.[17] Given the gradient effect of these data, we take this to be a purely pragmatic effect, a preference for isolating one argument in a predicate-argument structure as the primary term to be individuated, with this being taken to be some term that is independently itemized in the discourse context, and hence identified relative to which additional pragmatic inferences will be drawn. At this juncture, the Dynamic Syntax formalism remains neutral, being a framework for modelling the interaction of encoded grammar-internal specifications and enrichment devices that lead to interpretation in context. Should these restrictions turn out to be fully encoded, then the vocabulary defined for articulating the growth of semantic represen-

[17]Rather similar constraints apply in the Bantu languages, where proper names are very commonly associated with obligatory agreement marking, these being essentially pronominal reflexes (see Marten and Kempson 2005, Cann et al. 2005).

tations is surely rich enough to express the restriction, but without further data, any such modelling would be premature. Nonetheless, the concept of building linked structures as applied to the modelling of topic structures in which one term is identified as independent of the primary tree, linked to it only through the sharing of one isolated term, provides a structural basis from which the structural patterns displayed by the associated prefixes can be modelled.

5.5 Summary

In this paper we have sketched a preliminary analysis of passive constructions of distinct types within the DS framework, which models the process of how information is built up through a left-to-right dynamics, with emphasis on what information is available at every step of the process. Reflecting the different morpho-syntactic devices used in the three languages – 'promotion to subject' and complex verb structure, 'passive' morpheme and patient fronting and pronominial prefix plus topicalization, our account also involves different grammatical means for essentially solving a functional need: to foreground the patient and background the agent. In all cases, the former is pushed towards the left periphery and the various means of achieving this in DS are used: unfixed nodes and LINK structures. Differences come from the interaction of these basic operations and the effects of parsing particular words and morphemes. So in English, the identification of the initial noun phrase as patient is induced through lexical actions associated with a verbal complex involving a copula and a past participle. In Chinese, that identification is done by the specific particle *bei* which also induces an affectedness reading which in turn disallows some verbs or sentences from appearing in this construction through semantic selection, rather than a more restricted form of lexical selection. Finally, in Navajo, the inverse, *bi-*, pronominal prefix identifies an initial topic noun phrase as the patient of the verb and pragmatically induces interpretations that suppress one of the proto-agent properties of the agent itself, in this case a lack of control.

The interest of this work is that it shows once again that it is not taxonomic linguistic labels such as 'passive' that are of significance, but the various means by which some functional or communicative need is achieved in different languages. The outputs are similar, but not identical, and may nevertheless achieve the same ends.

As a grammar formalism that allows the interaction between syntactic, semantic and pragmatic information, DS also allows us to characterize the different semantic properties of passives of distinct types in terms of how the strategy of building a propositional structure, building unfixed nodes and decorating nodes with underspecified metavariables can interact in different ways to yield a unifying typology of passives. The successful characterization of three exemplified passive constructions, albeit possibly incomplete in many respects, leads us to conclude that syntactic generalizations can be grounded in the time-linear projection of the requisite predicate-argument structure, and thus the core syntax can be claimed to lie in the metalevel task of constructing a semantic representation of the propositional content.

References

The following were cited in this chapter: Chao (1968), Chappell (1986), Chomsky (1981), Chomksy (1995), Comrie (1980), Dixon (1979), Dowty (1979), Erteschik-Shir (1997), Givón (1979), Grimshaw (1991), Hale (1964, 1973), Hashimoto (1968, 1987), C. T.-J. Huang (1988, 1993, 1999), Y. Huang (2000), Jaeggli (1986), Keenan (1985), Klaiman (1991), Lapolla (1989), J. X. Li (1955), L. Li (1980), Y. Li (1990), C. N. Li and Thompson (1981), Lü (1980, 1982), Marten and Kempson (2005), Roberts (1998), Shi (1997), Shibatani (1985), Tan (1987), Ting (1998), Wang (1959), Willie (2000), Wu (2005), Yamanaki (1999). See references at end of book for full information.

6

Word-Order Variation in Korean and the Architecture of Grammar

JIEUN KIAER

Word-order variation (i.e. scrambling) in Korean (and Japanese) remains puzzling in the theory of syntax due to its lack of morphosyntactic trigger, non-obligatoriness and semantic vacuity. Independently, in the psycholinguistics literature, it is argued that building structure in a verb-final language like Japanese/Korean is also incremental just as in languages like English. Here a puzzle arises. Given that the argument structure is unfolded by a predicate only, in both derivational and non-derivational frameworks, no structure should be built in principle before the end of a sentence, since the verb comes only at the end. This paper focuses on how native speakers of Korean, despite freedom in word order licensed by the language other than its rigid verb-finality, can indeed parse/produce structure step-by-step.

In this paper, I presume on the parsing-based syntactic framework Dynamic Syntax (Cann et al 2005). I aim to show that solving puzzles of scrambling brings new insight into the study of verb-final languages and also into the architecture of grammar, including the competence-performance relation. I argue that the strong locality effects found in structure building implies the necessity of grammar-formalisms which adopt a parsing perspective.

6.1 Introduction

Korean is a verb-final language with flexible ordering. Noun phrases can occur in any order at a remove from the verb with which they are

The Dynamics of Lexical Interfaces.
Ruth Kempson, Eleni Gregoromichelaki and Christine Howes (eds.).

associated as is shown in (6.1)-(6.2), known as *short-distance scrambling*. Moreover, they can occur across a clause boundary as in (6.3), known as *long-distance scrambling*). Unlike Japanese, subjects can also occur across a clause boundary as in (6.4).

(6.1) *Jina-ka* *sakwa-lul* *mekesseyo.*
Jina-NOM apple-ACC ate
'Jina ate an apple.'

(6.2) *Sakwa-lul* *Jina-ka* *mekesseyo.*
apple-ACC Jina-NOM ate
'Jina ate an apple.'

(6.3) *Sakwa-lul* *Yuna-nun* *Jina-ka* *mekessta-ko*
apple-ACC Yuna-TOP Jina-NOM ate-COMP
saynggakhaysseyo.
thought
'Yuna thought that it was Jina who ate the apple.'

(6.4) *Halmeni-kkese* *Yuna-nun* *sakwa-lul*
grandmother-NOM(HON) Yuna-TOP apple-ACC
coaha-si-n-ta-ko *saynggakhaysseyo.*
like-HON-PRES-DECL-COMP thought
'Yuna thought that her grandmother liked an apple.'

Even though the ordering of NPs is very flexible, the ordering within a verbal cluster is rigid: (6.5) is ungrammatical, because the ordering between an embedded verb and a matrix verb is changed.

(6.5) **Yuna-nun* *Jina-ka* *sakwa-lul* *saynggakhaysseyo*
Yuna-TOP Jina-NOM apple-ACC thought
coahanta-ko.
like-COMP
'Intended reading: Yuna thought that Jina liked an apple.'

In addition, locating expressions at the right periphery of a clausal sequence is much more restricted than order variability at the left periphery. (6.6) and (6.7) are ungrammatical because, given the matrix verb *saynggakhaysseyo* ('thought'), *Yuna-hanthey* can be only interpreted within the embedded clause, not in the matrix clause, that is construed as dislocated but only immediately outside its local domain. That is, in (6.6), if the dative NP *Yuna-hanthey* could be interpreted as part of the embedded clause, the sentence should be grammatical. Yet it isn't. Hence the fact that it is ungrammatical shows that the dative NP can't be incorporated into the embedded clause, even though it immediately follows it.

(6.6) **Jina-ka* *sakwa-lul* *cwuessta-ko* *Yuna-hanthey*
Jina-NOM apple-ACC gave-COMP Yuna-DAT
Mina-ka *saynggakhaysseyo.*
Mina-NOM thought

'Intended reading: Mina thought that Jina gave an apple to Yuna.'

In (6.7), also, if the dative NP *Yuna-hanthey* were able to be interpreted within the embedded clause, in a manner analogous to left-peripheral dislocation as in (6.4), the sentence should be grammatical. The fact that it is ungrammatical shows that the dative NP can't be incorporated from the right periphery into that embedded clause, but only into the closest clause, which is the matrix clause. Notice that (6.8) is grammatical because *Yuna-hanthey* can be incorporated into the matrix clause verb, which can take a dative NP as its argument.

(6.7) **Jina-ka* *sakwa-lul* *cwuessta-ko* *Mina-ka*
Jina-NOM apple-ACC gave-COMP Mina-NOM
saynggakhaysseyo *Yuna-hanthey.*
thought Yuna-DAT

'Intended reading: Mina thought that Jina gave an apple to Yuna.'

(6.8) *Jina-ka* *sakwa-lul* *cwuessta-ko* *Mina-ka*
Jina-NOM apple-ACC gave-COMP Mina-NOM
malhaysseyo *Yuna-hanthey.*
said Yuna-DAT

'Mina said to Yuna that Jina gave an apple.'

There are thus absolute restrictions on left- and right- periphery effects. However the puzzle is broader than this.

A further puzzle which I want to focus on in this paper is that even though there is massive freedom in structure building, native speakers of Korean do not arbitrarily produce any grammatical form, but show a strong preference within these observable limits for specific grammatical forms. Such a preference is observed both in perception and production. Native speakers understand a certain form of grammatical sequence with much more efficiency, and produce that form with much more frequency. For instance, (6.9) is a possible form, but it is very hard to understand and hardly, if ever, produced. However, (6.10) is very easily understood and frequently produced by native speakers. In the Sejong corpus of ten million words,[1] double-embedding as in (6.10) occurred

[1]The ten million word Sejong corpus was developed by the National Academy of the Korean Language.

4,447 times, yet the corresponding structure with three consecutive nominative/topic-marked NPs didn't occur at all.[2]

(6.9) *???Yuna-nun Jina-ka Mina-ka sakwa-lul*
Yuna-TOP Jina-NOM Mina-NOM apple-ACC
coahanta-ko malhayssta-ko saynggakhaysseyo.
like-COMP said-COMP thought
'Yuna thought that Mina said that Jina liked an apple.'

(6.10) *Mina-ka sakwa-lul coahanta-ko Jina-ka*
Mina-NOM apple-ACC like-COMP Jina-NOM
malhayssta-ko Yuna-nun saynggakhaysseyo.
said-COMP Yuna-TOP thought
'Yuna thought that Mina said that Jina liked an apple.'

It seems that the complexity of a structure (eg. the depth of embedding) does not matter too much to native speakers as long as the building blocks of propositional structure are locally located (i.e. subject and verb appear locally) in a systematic way: the most embedded clause comes first, being object of the clause one level up, this being locally positioned with respect to subject of that clause, and so on, with the matrix clause coming last. The order between embedded clauses is crucial. Hence, (6.11) is ungrammatical, since the leftmost clause is not the most embedded clause.

(6.11) **Jina-ka malhayssta-ko Mina-ka sakwa-lul*
Jina-NOM said-COMP Mina-NOM apple-ACC
coahanta-ko Yuna-nun saynggakhaysseyo.
like-COMP Yuna-TOP thought
'Intended reading: Yuna thought that Mina said that Jina liked an apple.'

As we have seen above, though syntactic-structure building is very flexible in Korean, there are some noticeable restrictions. In this paper, I argue that native speakers can understand/produce somewhat complex sentences with great efficiency because they don't build a syntactic structure at once at the end of a sentence, but rather do so in an incremental way, even when all structural relations are not yet fully decided. As we shall see in more detail, explaining such syntactic behaviour in Korean involves a new way of searching for linguistic universals, somehow narrowing the unnecessary gap between competence and performance (see Hawkins 2004). In the following section, I will show a number of syntactic puzzles of Korean word-order variation

[2]This result excluded that of multiple nominative constructions which have multiple nominative NPs sharing one core predicate.

and will show how those puzzles can be explained within a processing perspective.

6.1.1 Syntactic puzzle of flexible constituency

Lack of scope asymmetry between different word-orders

In this section, I will briefly discuss some syntactic puzzles/issues of Korean word-order variation. I will start with the major issues discussed mainly in transformational/derivational frameworks and provide the overall approaches in lexicalist frameworks. Scrambling in Korean (and Japanese) is known to be (i) non-feature driven; (ii) non-obligatory; and (iii) semantically vacuous. In short, there is no clear morpho-syntactic trigger for a certain word-order.

In the literature, there are two major views in approaching scrambling: (i) the configurational approach; (ii) the non-configurational approach. In a configurational approach, a basic order is assumed and the rest of the orders are all assumed to be derived via movement. In a non-configurational approach, there is no one basic order. All orders are regarded to be base generated.

Saito (1985) took a configurational approach. He argued that Japanese-like languages fit well in a configurational, binary syntactic architecture. Crucial evidence for the configurational approach come from structural asymmetry between subject and argument. Kuroda (1971) first observed that scrambling leads to a new scope relation, hence scopal asymmetry between S O V and O S V structures. Consider (6.12)-(6.13).[3]

(6.12) *Dareka-ka* *daremo-o* *aisiteiru.* [Japanese]
someone-NOM everyone-ACC love

'someone loves everyone.': some > every, *every > some

(6.13) *Daremo-o* *dareka-ka* *aisiteiru.* [Japanese]
everyone-ACC someone-NOM love

'someone loves everyone.': some > every, every > some

The above asymmetry was used as crucial evidence for the movement framework. The apparently newly created scope in (6.13) was regarded as the consequence of moving *daremo-o* to the front, on the presumption that S O V is the underlying basic order. On this view (6.13) involves dislocation of the object over the subject, this being taken to be the basis of the additional scopal reading on (6.13). However, such scope asymmetry seems to be very weak in Korean. In understanding (6.14)-(6.15), most native Korean speakers strongly prefer to choose 'some >

[3] All the examples in this paper are Korean, unless otherwise stated.

every' scope reading in an S O V order as well as in an O S V order even though the non-indefinite object precedes the subject in (6.15):

(6.14) *Nwukwunka-ka motun pyo-lul saperiessta.*
someone-NOM every ticket-ACC bought
'Somebody bought all the tickets.'

(6.15) *Motun pyo-lul nwukwunka-ka saperiessta.*
every ticket-ACC someone-NOM bought
'Somebody bought all the tickets.'

It is argued that such short-distance scrambling involves movement to the argument (A) position, whereas long-distance scrambling involves movement to the non-argument ($\overline{A}$) position. Though debates continue, the difference between the two types of scrambling is generally assumed. However, the scopal preference for wide-scope construal of the indefinite irrespective of ordering as observed in short-distance scrambling is applicable to long-distance scrambling as in (6.16). In (6.16), the strongly preferred reading is that there is one person who bought all the tickets, despite the positioning of the pertinent indefinite *nwukwunka-ka* at the right periphery of the sequence of NPs.

(6.16) Single long-distance scrambling
Onul kongyen-uy motun pyo-lul Jina-nun
today performance-GEN every ticket-ACC Jina-TOP
nwukwunka-ka saperiessta-ko tulesseyo.
someone-NOM bought-COMP heard
'Jina heard that somebody bought all the tickets for today's performance.'

This pattern persists even when a sequence of NP is long-distance scrambled as in (6.17): the dominant scope reading is still 'some > every'.

(6.17) Multiple long-distance scrambling: [O S] scrambled
Onul kongyen-uy motun pyo-lul
today performance-GEN every ticket-ACC
nwukwunka-ka Jina-nun i maypyoso-ese
someone-NOM Jina-TOP this ticket.office-at
saperiessta-ko tulesseyo.
bought-COMP heard
'Jina heard that somebody bought all the tickets for today's performance at this ticket office.'

Thus in Korean, word-order doesn't seem to contribute that much to the so-called asymmetric scope reading (i.e. not matching linear order).

Consider one more example, which, again, shows lack of asymmetry between short and long-distance scrambling. Tests for anaphoric binding used by Chomsky (1981), Phillips (1996) and others, as in (6.18), may be taken to indicate the subject NP asymmetrically c-commands the object NP and hence support the assumption of VP constituency. Yet, in Korean, (6.19b-c) are perfectly grammatical unlike (6.18b).

(6.18) a. Wallace and Gromit really hate each other.
b. *Each other really hated Wallace and Gromit.

(6.19) a. *Walace-wa* *Gromit-i* *selo-lul* *cengmallo* *miwehayyo.*
Wallace-CONJ Gromit-NOM each.other-ACC really hate
'Wallace and Gromit really hate each other .'

b. *Selo-lul* *Walace-wa* *Gromit-i* *cengmallo* *miwehayyo.*
each.other-ACC Wallace-CONJ Gromit-NOM really hate
'Wallace and Gromit really hate each other .'

c. *Selo-lul* *Jina-nun* *Walace-wa* *Gromit-i* *cenmallo* *miwehanta-ko* *malhaysseyo.*
each.other-ACC Jina-TOP Wallace-CONJ Gromit-NOM really hate-COMP said
'Jina said that Wallace and Gromit really hate each other.'

Scopal asymmetry between NPs (eg. subject and object) has been regarded as crucial in proving the configurationality of free word-order languages like Korean and Japanese (See Miyagawa 2003 and Saito 2003 among others). The heart of their claim is that if, as in Kuroda's original example, a new scope is created when the word order is switched from [S O V] into [O S V], it provides unambiguous evidence that the [O S V] ordering of expressions is derived from the [S O V] ordering, with the latter taken as basic. If both word-orders are basic orders, scopal relations should be the same in each. Notwithstanding the weakness of any empirical evidence for scopal asymmetry in Korean, grammatical theories of Japanese/Korean have been based on the assumption that such asymmetry is fully confirmed. Japanese/Korean syntacticians' major concern therefore was to reveal the details of the architecture within that belief. Now, let's turn to the second syntactic puzzle.

Non-order preserving nature of surprising constituents

In Korean/Japanese, there is an interesting-looking syntactic constituent as shown in (6.20) and (6.21). In both examples, the fronted

DO-IO/IO-DO pair plays a role as one syntactic constituent, occurring in either order. I will skip the actual constituency tests, merely noting that the fronted pair of NPs passes most of the criteria used in constituency tests (eg. coordination, ellipsis, reciprocal binding).

(6.20) DO2 IO2 [S1 [S2 V2] V1]

password-lul	*spai-hanthey*	*Kim-kemsa-nun*	
password-ACC	spy-DAT	Kim-prosecutor-TOP	
park-kica-ka	*mollay*	*malhayssta-ko*	*mitesseyo.*
Park-reporter-NOM	secretly	said-COMP	believed

'Prosecutor Kim believed that reporter Park told the password to the spy secretly.'

(6.21) IO2 DO2 [S1 [S2 V2] V1]

spai-hanthey	*password-lul*	*Kim-kemsa-nun*	
spy-DAT	password-ACC	Kim-prosecutor-TOP	
park-kica-ka	*mollay*	*malhayssta-ko*	*mitesseyo.*
Park-reporter-NOM	secretly	said-COMP	believed

'Prosecutor Kim believed that reporter Park told the password to the spy secretly.'

In generative grammar, the constituency of this pair of NPs is regarded as peculiar, hence surprising[4], since the basic architecture assumes that an object forms a VP constituent with a verb and that this constituent forms a bigger constituent S. The verb is thus the head of the sentence and essential to the projection of its structure. Though the details of the proposal have been updated, this idea has been maintained throughout the development of generative grammar. There are two major approaches to such peculiar/surprising constituents in generative grammar. The first is to assume that this peculiar constituent is not generated as a unit (moved as a pair), but moved one by one separately from the basic structure. This was the approach used by Koizumi (2000). He assumed that the surprising constituent is formed by overt verb raising. This is the so-called remnant movement analysis (i.e. verb raising and subsequent constituent formation with the remnant NPs and verbal trace) and it fits well into the X-bar schema, as it preserves VP constituency. In this remnant movement analysis, a string of multiple lexical items in a 'scrambled order' is regarded as a result of multiple applications of remnant movement. On the other hand, a string of multiple lexical items in a 'canonical order' is regarded as a result of a single application of remnant movement. Consider Koizumi's crucial examples (6.22)-(6.23) (Koizumi 2000:239-240).

[4]This term is from Takano (2002).

(6.22) *[$_{VP}$Hawai-de Masami-ni prezento-o t_v]*
Hawai-at Masami-DAT present-ACC trace
[John-ga [Kiyomi-ga katta$_v$-to] omotteiru]
John-NOM Kiyomo-NOM bought-COMP believed
[Japanese]

(6.23) *[???Prezento-o$_3$ Masami-ni$_2$ Hawai-de$_1$] [John-ga*
present-ACC Masami-DAT Hawai-at John-NOM
[Kiyomi-ga t1 t2 t3 katta-to] omotteiru]
Kiyomo-NOM t1 t2 t3 bought-COMP believed
[Japanese]

Koizumi reported that (6.22) is grammatical, contrary to (6.23), which is highly unacceptable. This is due to a Subjacency violation.[5] If two or more lexical items are scrambled out of an embedded clause, without keeping the order of the original constituency, as in (6.23), the resulting sentence will be degraded. However, if the multiple lexical items are scrambled together across the clause boundary as in (6.22), keeping the order of the original constituency, the grammaticality of the resulting sentence will be much improved. Yet, contrary to his judgement, ordering variation internally to a short or multiple long-distance scrambled sequence does not increase ungrammaticality in Korean, as we have seen already: both (6.20) and (6.21) are perfectly grammatical.

Another approach to such structures was suggested by Takano (2002). Takano adopted an adjunction-like oblique movement to analyze a surprising constituent found in Japanese cleft constructions as in (6.24). Takano claimed that in (6.24), *Mary-ni* goes through an oblique movement to the sister position of *hon-o* and forms a surprising constituent with it, as illustrated in (6.25).

(6.24) *John-ga agata-no wa hon-o Mary-ni da*
J-NOM gave-NM TOP book-ACC M-DAT BE
'It is a book to Mary that John gave.'

(6.25) *Hon-o Mary-ni* as a Constituent via Oblique Movement

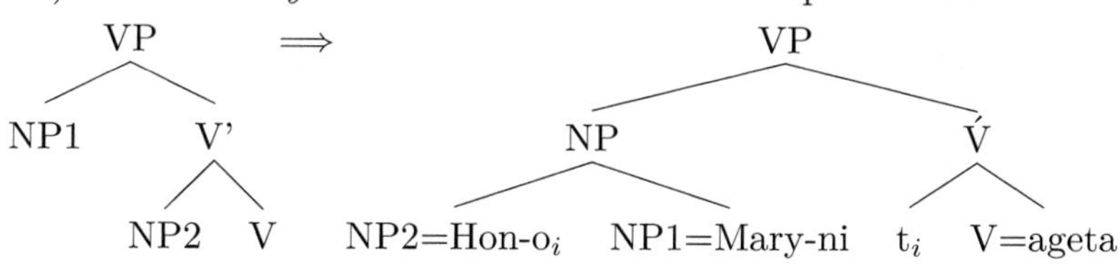

The crucial question for this analysis is whether the invention of a new movement as such is reasonable, because this type of movement

[5]Chomsky (1986) and Lasnik and Saito (1992) argued that application of more than one long-distance movement from within the same clause necessarily yields a Subjacency violation.

is not ordinary. The following *naze* 'why' example in (6.26) remains a puzzle for this account. Consider (6.26). (6.26) is originally from Sohn (1994). Sohn claimed that the ungrammaticality of (6.26a) is slightly improved in (6.26b) when *naze* forms a surprising constituent with the following NP *hon-o* and they move together to the front.

(6.26) a. **John-wa [Mary-ga sono hito-o naze uttaeta*
J-TOP M-NOM that person-ACC why sued
toyoo uwass]-o kiita no
that rumour-ACC heard Q
'Why did John hear the rumour that Mary sued that person?'

b. *??Naze*$_i$ *sono hito-o*$_j$ *John-wa [Mary-ga* t_i
Why that person-ACC John-TOP M-NOM trace
t_j *uttaeta toyoo uwass]-o kiita no.*
trace sued that rumour-ACC heard Q
'Why did John hear the rumour that Mary sued that person?'

(6.26a) is ungrammatical because given that *naze* is an adjunct, if it overtly moves out of a complex NP, it causes a violation of the Empty Category Principle (i.e. empty categories must be properly governed: Chomsky 1981). Takano also assumes that adverbial adjuncts in Japanese cannot move long-distance. However, regardless of this hindrance, if *naze* moves together with *sono hito-o* as in (6.26b), the sentence becomes less ungrammatical. Takano explains this 'saving effect' as a result of oblique movement as shown in (6.25). Yet the rationale behind this is that once moved together long-distance, the constituency between *naze* and *sono hito-o* can nevertheless be broken. So, in (6.26b), *naze* alone will be interpreted within the matrix clause, whereas *sono hito-o* is to be interpreted within the embedded clause. Therefore, the evidence of (surprising) constituency between *naze* and *sono hito-o* is not observed on the surface level. A similar problem occurs in (6.27).

(6.27) *Ringo-o*$_j$ *kinoo Bill-ni*$_i$ *John-ga [Mary-ga*
Apple-ACC yesterday Bill-DAT John-NOM Mary-NOM
t_i t_j *ageta-to] kitta.*
t_i t_j gave-COMP heard

a. 'John heard that Mary gave apples to Bill yesterday.': Embedded reading of *kinoo*

b. ?? John heard yesterday that Mary gave apples to Bill. : Matrix reading of *kinoo* - Not available.

According to Takano, this example can be derived as follows: First the dative object of the embedded clause *Bill-ni* scrambles to the matrix TP, then the adjunct *kinoo* is adjoined to the matrix TP by Merge (assuming that it can be base-generated there) and finally the accusative object of the embedded clause scrambles to the matrix TP. This derivation should yield an interpretation in which *kinoo* is construed as a matrix clause modifier. Yet, in fact, *kinoo* is interpreted only within an embedded clause as in (6.27a). Takano himself notes (2002:265) that the lack of relevant reading in (6.27) is not excluded by syntactic reasons, but perhaps by a processing reason as processing three pre-subject elements together seems to be much easier. At this juncture, we can ask whether (6.27) is just an exceptional example or whether it shows some fundamental problem in the theory and the necessity of looking at syntax from a processing perspective. Takano doesn't have any similar examples with multiple argument long-distance scrambling. However, we can infer from (6.27) that once a cluster of NPs are scrambled together across a clause boundary, their constituency should, according to the analysis, also be broken as in the case of (6.26b). Yet, this is not true. In multiple long-distance scrambling, the constituency between NPs is still kept and they must be interpreted in the same local domain, as we've seen. If we assume the constituency of NPs is to be destroyed after going through long-distance scrambling, we face a great many puzzling sentences as in (6.27), which go directly counter to the expectation Takano's theory generates. No expressions which are stuck in the middle of a long-distance expression can be interpreted in a different propositional structure from that of their preceding and following long-distance scrambled expression. If the theory can't predict this right, its validity must be reconsidered. As in Koizumi's analysis, the 'non-order preserving' surprising constituent is not assumed to form a surprising constituent in Takano (2002) either. Instead, it is understood as multiple occasions of oblique movement. Hence, as in Koizumi (2000), it is difficult to capture the structural parallelism between surprising constituents, displayed in different orders. As Takano noted for the case of (6.27), within the pure syntactic analysis, set up in the Minimalist Program, it may be hard to capture the 'flexible' nature of the surprising constituent, since the basic core configuration assumed in the framework is not 'flexibly-built.'

Even though morpho-syntactic motivations for the scrambling type of movement were regarded as weak, within the Minimalist Program, it has been assumed that scrambling is an instance of feature-driven movement. Based on this assumption, further theoretical assumptions and analysis were proposed. A notable case is the distinct treatment of multiple *wh*-fronting and multiple NP fronting (i.e. multiple long-distance scrambling). In GB/minimalism, multiple *wh*-fronting and multiple NP fronting have been treated as different grammatical processes, because the former is feature-driven but the latter is not. Multiple NP fronting (i.e. multiple long-distance scrambling) is considered to be a result of remnant movement across a clause boundary (Koizumi 2000) or an adjunction-like oblique movement (Takano 2002). Grewendorf (2001:89) argued that languages like Japanese have the a 'covert' cluster- forming operation. He noted that the crucial difference between overt *wh*-fronting languages such as Bulgarian and Romanian[6] and covert *wh*-fronting languages such as Japanese, lies in the difference of feature strength. In the latter group of languages, the D-feature of *wh*-phrases is said to be relatively weak. Yet, as he noticed, it is not clear how minimalism can express different feature strength (See also Chomsky 2000 and Newmeyer 2005). According to Grewendorf, the crucial difference between multiple *wh*-fronting and multiple NP fronting (i.e. multiple long-distance scrambling) in Japanese-like languages is that the latter is non-feature-driven, whereas the former is very weakly feature-driven. Nevertheless, even though empirically the feature strength is not so strong, categorial distinctions between the two have been assumed in feature-driven syntactic frameworks.[7]

6.1.2 Locality restrictions at the right periphery

Takano hinted that some syntactic puzzles can be solved via considering processing. In this paper, extending this view, I argue that most syntactic puzzles can be intuitively accounted for once syntax is viewed as step-wise, dynamic structure-building 'processes'. By comparison, however, constraints in generative grammar are no more than stipulations that are not further reducible to core properties of syntactic structure. Consider the following two examples. In generative grammar, (6.28) is regarded as ungrammatical because of the Proper Binding Condition violation (Lasnik and Saito 1992) and (6.29) is regarded as ungrammatical because of the Right Roof Constraint (Ross 1967): both are separate and independent constraints.

[6]There is growing evidence that the ordering of multiple wh-phrases within a sentence is conditioned by non-syntactic factors (Hofmeister et al 2006).

[7]Despite the power of *wh*-feature apparently not being strong in Japanese-like languages, Aoshima et al (2005) argued that parsers of Japanese can detect long-distance dependency when the fronted NP is a *wh*-NP contrary to the case of a referential NP. Given that the strength of *wh*-feature in Japanese/Korean is very weak, it is surprising that parsers of Japanese pro-actively use *wh*-feature as a cue for long-distance dependency. I will come back to this issue later.

(6.28) **Mina-ka* *Jina-ka* *sakwa-lul* *cwuessta-ko*
Mina-NOM Jina-NOM apple-ACC gave-COMP
Yuna-hanthey *saynggakhaysseyo.*
Yuna-DAT thought

'Intended reading: Mina thought that Jina gave an apple to Yuna.'

(6.29) **Mina-ka* *Jina-ka* *sakwa-lul* *cwuessta-ko*
Mina-NOM Jina-NOM apple-ACC gave-COMP
saynggakhaysseyo *Yuna-hanthey.*
thought Yuna-DAT

'Intended reading: Mina thought that Jina gave an apple to Yuna.'

By way of a preliminary, let's take the Proper Binding Condition as displayed in (6.30) more in detail.

(6.30) **[$_{TP}$[Hanako-ga* t_i *iru* *to]$_j$* *[Sooru-ni$_i$* *[Taroo-ga* t_j
Hanako-NOM t_i be that Seoul-at Taroo-NOM t_j
omotteiru]]] *(koto).*
think fact

'[That Hanako is t_i]$_j$ in Seoul Taroo thinks.'

The Proper Binding Condition is the restriction that all traces must be properly bound by a c-commanding antecedent within a suitable local domain. This restriction is not met in (6.30) because with *sooru-ni* having first been moved out of the clause and subsequently the constituent containing its trace having been moved above it, that trace is not properly governed. Hence, although Korean and Japanese allow relatively flexible NP ordering and various scrambling phenomena, (6.30) is ungrammatical. Lasnik and Saito (1992) proposed this Proper Binding Condition to capture the ungrammaticality of (6.30). According to this analysis, (6.30) is derived from two-step movements: the first step is (6.31a) to (6.31b) and the second step is (6.31b) to (6.31c).

(6.31) a. *[$_{TP}$ Taroo-ga* *[Hanako-ga* *Sooru-ni* *iru-to]* *omotteiru]*
Taroo-NOM Hanako-NOM Seoul-in be-that think
(koto)
fact

'Taroo thinks that Hanako lives in Seoul.'

b. *[$_{TP}$ Sooru-ni$_i$* *[Taroo-ga* *[Hanako-ga* t_i *iru*
Seoul-DAT Taroo-NOM Hanako-NOM t_i live
to] *omotteiru]]* *(koto)*
COMP think fact

'In Seoul, Taroo thinks that Hanako lives t_i.'

c. *[$_{TP}$[*Hanako-ga* **t_i** *iru to*]$_j$ [*Sooru-ni*$_i$ [*Taroo-ga*
Hanako-NOM t_i be that Seoul-at Taroo-NOM
t_j *omotteiru*]]] (*koto*).
t_j think fact

'[That Hanako is t_i]$_j$ in Seoul Taroo thinks.'

In (6.31a), the PP Sooru-ni 'in Seoul' is first scrambled from the embedded clause to the matrix initial position as in (6.31b). And then, the embedded CP [$_{TP}$[*Hanako-ga* t_i *iru to*] is scrambled to the position preceding the PP *Sooru-ni* in (6.31c). The resulting sentence (6.31c) is totally ungrammatical. According to Saito, the ungrammaticality is caused by the unbound trace t_i in (6.31c). The problem however is that the level of S-structure no longer plays any role in movement frameworks. Saito (2003) explained the ungrammaticality of (6.31c) by reformulating the Proper Binding Condition as a constraint on the application of Merge. Merge combines two linguistic objects to form a constituent. The two objects to be combined by Merge must be a 'complete' constituents. A constituent which has only a part of a chain, e.g. a trace but not its antecedent, does not qualify as a constituent. In (6.31c), [$_{TP}$[*Hanako-ga* t_i *iru to*] is disqualified as it is not a complete constituent. Hence, this sequence cannot be subject to Merge (See Saito (2003) for a detailed discussion). However, given the pro-drop property of Korean and Japanese, it is not clear how to decide whether a constituent is complete or not.

Consider also (6.28)-(6.29) again. Any reading of (6.29) is precluded, as this would have to involve movement of *Yuna-hanthey* rightward, and only then the leftward movement of the remainder VP (*Jina-ka sakwa-lul* e_i *cwuessta-ko*) with its containing trace of that earlier moved dative.

These analyses are missing a more fundamental property of structure-building in Korean, which is that though word-order is flexible, lexical items cannot be incorporated when a complementizer closes-off its local structure building. This is a direct piece of evidence which shows that structure is built from left-to-right. So, to put it differently, the ungrammaticality of (6.31) is not because of some not-properly bound trace, but because simply the complementizer has already closed off the embedded-clause structure. I assume that undoing this already-closed structure to incorporate any additional constituent is very costly and the ungrammaticality is due to such cost. Notice however, in a colloquial form, such incorporation is also possible. In that case, the post-complementizer item (*cip-e* 'at home' in (6.32) forms one intonational unit with the verb-COMP phrase. In this case, I presume that intonation overrides the closing-off function of the complementizer *-ko/mye*.

I will return to the role of intonation, in terms of defining a syntactic domain, later. Note, however, that examples like (6.32), which are easy to produce and frequently observed will make the Proper Binding Condition more puzzling.

(6.32) *Jina {assta-ku/mye cip-e}% emma-hantheyse tulesse.*
Jina came-COMP house-at mum-from heard
'I heard from mum that Jina came at home, right?'

Now, let's consider (6.33) again. The ungrammaticality of this example is supposedly due to the violation of the Right-Roof Constraint (Ross 1967), a separate and independent constraint from the Proper Binding Condition.

(6.33) **Mina-ka Jina-ka sakwa-lul cwuessta-ko*
Mina-NOM Jina-NOM apple-ACC gave-COMP
saynggakhaysseyo Yuna-hanthey.
thought Yuna-DAT
'Intended reading: Mina thought that Jina gave an apple to Yuna.'

The core idea of that restriction is that unlike left-dislocation, right-dislocation is restricted, hence, the expression should be interpreted within the root clause only. Such left-right asymmetry is regarded as the consequence of movement rather than being viewed as some 'side-effect' of left-to-right, step-wise structure building. I propose that the oddity of (6.33) simply reflects that structure is built/composed/wrapped in an incremental way. Hence, given that structure-building is almost finished at the stage of hearing the final verb, asserting any expression which requires undoing any arbitrary level of structure seems to be very costly indeed. The fact though that (6.32) sounds acceptable as compared to (6.33) means that, just as in the case of (6.32), intonation can override the close-off function of sentence-ending suffix *-yo*, even though Korean is a verb-final language. If we think that a structure is built incrementally from left-to-right, freedom at the beginning of a sentence and restriction towards the end of a sentence - or gradual restriction as the sentence progresses - is naturally expected without evoking any constraint.

More than 50% of the world languages are verb-final languages and most of them show free/flexible word-orders. Though details may differ and the amount of linguistic investigation differs from language to language, what I assume is that regardless of verb-finality, native speakers of those languages can understand their linguistic structure step-by-step incrementally. The more the structure is specified, the more its interpretational open-endedness decreases. However, if we assume that structure is projected purely via top-down manner, core properties such as left-right asymmetry of structure-building across languages will simply remain puzzling or will have to be stipulated rather than explained. In his pioneering work, Phillips (1996, 2003) showed that even the very basic unit of syntactic structure building, the *constituent* cannot be defined properly without considering time-sensitive growth of a structure. If it is true as Phillips argued that the notion of incrementality or growth should be considered in defining the basic block of syntactic structure building, we need to re-consider the set of tools in the grammar formalism and seriously think about what kinds of formal devices are required to capture such dynamics in the grammar.

6.1.3 Syntax-phonology interface

A first such step is to reconsider the role of prosody. In generative grammar, grammaticality judgements have been regarded as the most useful tool in shaping grammar-formalisms, since it is shared by all ideal, individual native speakers. However, as Kitagawa and Hirose (2006) among many others showed, grammaticality judgments are not purely syntactic. Consider. (6.34) (% refers to an Intonational Phrase boundary following the convention used in Intonational Phonology):.

(6.34)	*{Nwuka*	*ece*	*way}%*	*Jina-nun*	*Kiho-hanthey*
	who	yesterday	why	Jina-TOP	Kiho-DAT
	satang-ul	*cwuessnun-ci*	*alkosipta.*		
	candy-ACC	gave-Q	would.like.to.know		

'Jina would like to know who gave Kiho a box of candy yesterday and why they did so.'

In (6.34), the sequence of NPs *nwuka ece way*, which is to be interpreted within the embedded clause is to be pronounced together. Otherwise, as in (6.35), it will be judged to be ungrammatical.

(6.35)	**{Nwuka*	*ece}%*	*way*	*Jina-nun*	*Kiho-hanthey*
	who	yesterday	why	Jina-TOP	Kiho-DAT
	satang-ul	*cwuessnun-ci*	*alkosipta.*		
	candy-ACC	gave-Q	would.like.to.know		

Binding principles also interact with prosody. *Cakicasin* 'self' is known as a local anaphor: in (6.36)-(6.37), there are two possible antecedents for *cakicasin* ('self'), but as in the referential dative NP cases, the interpretation of *cakicasin* ('self') is sensitive to the location of a prosodic boundary.[8]

[8]See Kim and Yoon (2006) for the result of some empirical tests regarding the resolution of *cakicasin* 'self'.

(6.36) *Jina-nun%* *cakicasin-hanthey* *Mina-ka* *nemwu*
Jina-TOP self-DAT Mina-NOM very
strict-hayssta-ko *saynggakhay.*
strict-did-COMP think

a. Jina thinks that to herself (=Mina), Mina is very strict. (IP boundary after *Jina-nun*)
b. ??Jina thinks that to herself (=Jina), Mina is very strict. (IP boundary after *Jina-nun*)

(6.37) *Jina-ka* *cakicasin-hanthey%* *Mina-nun* *nemwu*
Jina-NOM self-DAT Mina-TOP very
strict-hayssta-ko *saynggakhay.*
strict-did-COMP think

a. Mina thinks that to herself (=Jina), Jina is very strict. (IP boundary after *caki-casin-hanthey*)
b. ??Mina thinks that to herself (=Mina), Jina is very strict. (IP boundary after *caki-casin-hanthey*)

Syntax interacts with phonology "during" the structure-building processes. As we shall see increasingly, structure-building strategies along with appropriate structural assignment can be signalled in Korean by early prosody as well as by context: indeed without such prosodic indication, the strings in question are judged to be ungrammatical. Such a situation is hard to predict for many frameworks. In the literature of the syntax-phonology interface, particularly according to the tenets of generative grammar, phonological structure is projected from syntactic structure, rather than the reverse order of dependency. This is the wellknown view of Prosodic Phonology (See Selkirk 1984 among others), adopted by most syntacticians. Yet the evidence of both grammaticality judgments and incrementality shows how it is prosody that affects syntactic structure formation rather than syntax projecting how prosody should be structured (e.g. its phrasing pattern). As Jun (1993) pointed out, if the latter view is correct, countless mismatches between syntax and phonology are expected as a result. For one thing, the original X-bar theory has changed over the period, giving rise to proposals for DP as a constituent, and the need to make allowances for surprising constituents. Its prediction for a prosodic phrasing might be expected to have changed to reflect such shifting analyses. However, the phrasing native speakers might assign to such sentences will not have changed in like manner. Consider (6.38)-(6.39). No matter what syntactic analysis is given, native speakers of Korean invariably phrase the fronted NP-DAT NP-ACC or NP-ACC NP-DAT sequence as one prosodic unit.

(6.38) *{Pooh-hanthey ice-cream-ul}% mengmengi-nun nwuka*
Pooh-DAT ice-cream-ACC puppy-TOP who
cwuessta-ko saynggakhayyo?
gave-COMP think

'Puppy thinks who gave an ice-cream to Pooh?'

(6.39) *{Ice-cream-ul Pooh-hanthey}% mengmengi-nun nwuka*
ice-cream-ACC Pooh-DAT puppy-TOP who
cwuessta-ko saynggakhayyo?
gave-COMP think

'Puppy thinks who gave an ice-cream to Pooh?'

In this paper, I will not go through in detail how lexicalist frameworks such as LFG, HPSG and CCG can deal with these puzzles (see Kiaer 2007). However, I point out two major challenges which Korean creates for these frameworks. First, lexicalist approaches may specify left-to-right asymmetry within the lexicon as proposed by Karamanis (2001). He adopted features such as *[+Front]* and *[-Front]* to capture left/right periphery effects in Greek. Yet, such approaches are neither appropriate nor explanatory. Given that leftward freedom and rightward gradual restriction are applicable to all lexical items, the effect is to end up expanding the lexicon immensely, without capturing core principles in the grammar that might yield a more explanatory account. Second, the derivations within lexicalist grammar frameworks show step-wise combination, yet they are not necessarily left-to-right – indeed such frameworks are in general studiously neutral with respect to linearity considerations – making it hard to predict time-sensitive, incremental, structure building particularly in verb-final languages. For instance, to explain a verb-less 'surprising constituent' as discussed earlier, the grammar must assume the applicability of complex processes such as the type-raising operations of CCG before the full structure is available which might trigger the building of such a constituent. The need for such a procedure would however only be predictable given a global perspective that includes the argument structure projected by the predicate. Hence, it could not be time-sensitive: at the point of having the fronted surprising constituent, native speakers can have no anticipation of the specifics of the upcoming structure, and the processes to induce such structure must be applicable in all possible derivations. But with this move, a lexically based solution is not appropriate. Therefore lexicalist approaches cannot capture time-sensitive incremental structure building in verb-final, scrambling languages such as Korean. McConville (2001) showed how incrementality can be captured in CCG, yet he had to assume a final 'ruthless reduce-first parser' to avoid such problems. As in the generative grammar, in lexicalist approaches of grammar, deterministic views on structures have been prevalent. In other words, linguists try to figure out what is the basis of grammatical/ungrammatical sentences by looking at the complete sentence. Incomplete sentences were outside their remit. They aim to show how to explain a certain set of well-formedness/ill-formedness judgements by reference to either configurational hierarchy or lexical specifications alone. These approaches are static on the whole, hence risk being insufficient for capturing the dynamics and growth of linguistic structures. In the following section, I will discuss the extent to which incrementality has been expressed in the grammar.

6.1.4 Incorporating incrementality in the grammar

Recently, a vast amount of evidence has been collected which establishes the incrementality displayed in pre-verbal structure building in Japanese/Korean (see Mazuka and Itoh 1995 and Aoshima et al. 2004 among others). Yet, crucially the notion of incrementality has been seen as nothing to do with the architecture of grammar. This is because current grammar formalisms are not built with any reflection of time-linearity, which is closely linked to incrementality. To the contrary, transformational grammar formalisms build structures based on configurational hierarchy. On the other hand, lexicalist grammar formalisms combine lexical items based on constraints articulated largely in lexical entries, though there may be additional general constraints; and these too reflect hierarchical considerations only. It is, rather, independent parsing theories which carry the burden of defining left-to-right parsing strategies to be commensurate with these constraints, but these are not reflected in the architecture of the grammar (Miyamoto 2002).

Most researchers in Japanese parsing have viewed delay in real-time processing as evidence of complexity encoded in grammar. Hence, it is often argued that scrambled word-order, which is derived from a canonical word-order, should cause difficulty in processing. Mazuka, Itoh and Kondo (2002) and Miyamoto and Takahashi (2002) claimed that scrambling causes processing inefficiency. Mazuka and her colleagues observed longer reading times at *Mariko-ga* in the scrambled position (6.40a) when compared to *ototto-o* in the canonical position as in (6.40b).

(6.40) Scrambled order: Longer reading time at *Mariko-ka*

a. *Ototto-o* *Mariko-ga* gap_i *mita.*
brother-ACC Mariko-NOM gap saw
'Mariko saw her brother.'

Canonical order: Shorter reading time at *ototto-o*

b. *Mariko-ga* *ototto-o* *mita.*
Mariko-NOM brother-ACC saw
'Mariko saw her brother.'

However, this processing result remains controversial (see Yamashita 1997, and Nakayama 1995 among others). It is easy enough to say that an [S O V] ordering is a more efficient structure to parse than an [O S V] ordering because it is by assumption the canonical word-order, hence no movement cost (e.g. gap postulation) is involved. Yet I will show that this line of thinking is misleading. If movement is the real cause of delay, complicated movements should cause more inefficiency in parsing. Yet, this is not the case as we see below.[9]

(6.41) Embedded clause dislocation, yet efficient in parsing, frequently found in the corpus [[S3 O3 V3]$_{O2}$ [S2 V2]$_{O1}$ [S1 V1]] :

a. *Yuna-ka* *sakwa-lul* *mekessta-ko* *Kiho-ka*
Yuna-NOM apple-ACC ate-COMP Kiho-NOM
malha-n-kess-ul *Jina-ka* *tulesse.*
say-REL-thing-ACC Jina-NOM heard
'Jina heard the thing Kiho said that Yuna ate an apple.'

No movement involved, yet very inefficient in parsing, hardly found in corpus [S1 [S2 [S3 O3 V3]V2 REL] O1 V1]:

b. *Jina-ka* *Kiho-ka* *Yuna-ka* *sakwa-lul*
Jina-NOM Kiho-NOM Yuna-NOM apple-ACC
mekessta-ko *malha-n-kess-ul* *tulesse.*
ate-COMP say-REL-thing-ACC heard
'Jina heard the thing Kiho said that Yuna ate an apple.'

(6.41a) yields much more efficient processing than (6.41b)(See Mazuka, Itoh and Kondo 2002 for similar results in Japanese). Processing inefficiency significantly increases from (6.41a)-(6.41b), though no movement process is involved in (6.41b). In addition, as we've discussed briefly, in the Sejong corpus study, no structures such as (6.41b) were found, whereas structures like (6.41a) were very frequently observed. I will come back to this issue later.

The rationale behind many recent psycholinguistic studies on Japanese/Korean is that parsers and producers alike have some sort of

[9]Detecting movement in on-line processing is also not easy in Korean, since scrambling is a form of movement which is not lexically triggered. The long-lasting puzzle of scrambling in Japanese/Korean is its lack of morpho-syntactic motivation to move, compared to other sorts of movement such as *wh*-movement in English. In short, the semantic vacuity (Saito 1992) of this sort of movement remains problematic.

configurational hierarchy in their mind, presuming a concept of canonical underlying constituent order. Hence, it is expected that any sort of scrambled order, which is derived from some such initial configuration as dictated by the grammar, should cause a subsequent surprising "delay" effect. However, the surprising effect caused by word-order variation within a "local" structure (i.e. short scrambling) is very marginal, and is not sufficient to confirm the type of GB configurational hierarchy proposed in Japanese/Korean. In fact, it seems that processing is efficient as long as the arguments are all localized in the same domain regardless of a certain word-order variation.

Generative grammar-formalisms are clearly limited in their ability to explain the source of efficiency/incrementality displayed in Korean/Japanese parsing, because the logic of the formalism is not sensitive to the left-to-right linear order of the word sequence. Phillips (1996, 2003) argued that even the basic task of defining constituenthood may be difficult unless linear order is taken into consideration, for one and the same string of words can be diagnosed as a constituent by one constituency test, but to be not a constituent by another constituency test. (6.42) shows a case of constituency conflict. (6.42) is from Phillips (2003). When co-ordination is taken as a test for constituency, in (6.42a), *Gromit a biscuit* passes the co-ordination test and thus, is regarded as a constituent. Yet, in (6.42b), taking permutability as a criterion, *Gromit a biscuit* cannot pass the movement test and thus, is not regarded as a constituent.

(6.42) Constituency Conflict

[Gromit a biscuit] is a constituent by co-ordination test:

a. Wallace gave [Gromit a biscuit] and [Shawn some cheese] for breakfast.

[Gromit a biscuit] is NOT a constituent by movement test:

b. $*[VP$ Gromit a biscuit] Wallace gave VP_t for breakfast.

Based on constituency shift and constituency conflict phenomena, Phillips argued for the Incrementality Hypothesis as in (6.43).

(6.43) Sentence structures are built incrementally from left-to-right.

As shown in (6.44), Phillips assumed that syntactic relation must respect constituency at the point in the derivation when the relation is established. Yet, once this relation is licensed, constituency (between A and B) may change subsequently (i.e. be destroyed); and this he argued was the basis for such conflict.

(6.44) Incremental constituency via a build-and-destroy process

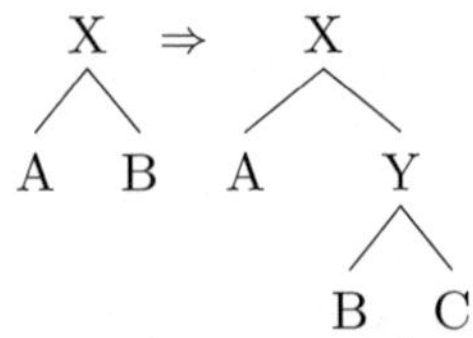

Given that defining constituency is a crucial matter in syntax, it is striking that such a core notion should be so difficult to sustain while also reflecting incrementality. In fact, when it comes to head-final languages like Korean or Japanese, threading incrementality into grammar formalisms becomes highly problematic, since the architecture of most grammar formalisms was established based on European languages, mostly on English. To explain incrementality within such frameworks, one has to start with many *ad-hoc* assumptions about structure building, with additional movement processes set up specific to individual derivations. Aoshima and colleagues (Aoshima et al 2003, 2004) have argued that, in Japanese, the sentence-initial *wh*-dative NP undergoes *unforced revision* during online structure building to allow its interpretation within the 'most' embedded clause. Consider their examples:

(6.45) Scrambled, Declarative complementizer: Typing Mismatch Slow Down Effect

Dono-seito-ni	*tannin-wa*	*koocyoo-ga*
which-student-DAT	class-teacher-TOP	principal-NOM

hon-o	*yonda-to*	*tosyositu-de*	*sisyo-ni*
book-ACC	read-DECL	library-at	librarian-DAT

iimasita-ka?
said-Q

'Which student did the class teacher tell the librarian at the library that the principal read a book for?'

(6.46) In-situ, Declarative Complementizer: Typing Mismatch Effect

tannin-wa	*koocyoo-ga*	*dono-seito-ni*
class-teacher-TOP	principal-NOM	which-student-DAT

hon-o	*yonda-to*	*tosyositu-de*	*sisyo-ni*
book-ACC	read-DECL	library-at	librarian-DAT

iimasita-ka?
said-Q

'Which student did the class teacher tell the librarian at the library that the principal read a book for?'

(6.47) SCRAMBLED, QUESTION PARTICLE: No Typing Mismatch Effect

Dono-seito-ni	*tannin-wa*	*koocyoo-ga*
which-student-DAT	class-teacher-TOP	principal-NOM

hon-o	*yonda-ka*	*tosyositu-de*	*sisyo-ni*	*iimasita*
book-ACC	read-Q	library-at	librarian-DAT	said

'The class teacher told the librarian at the library which student the principal read a book for?'

(6.48) IN-SITU, QUESTION PARTICLE: No Typing Mismatch Effect

tannin-wa	*koocyoo-ga*	*dono-seito-ni*
class-teacher-TOP	principal-NOM	which-student-DAT

hon-o	*yonda-ka*	*tosyositu-de*	*sisyo-ni*	*iimasita*
book-ACC	read-Q	library-at	librarian-DAT	said

'The class teacher told the librarian at the library which student the principal read a book for?'

Aoshima et al found that both when the *wh*-phrase was in situ as in (6.46) or in (6.48) or when they are scrambled long-distance as in (6.45) or in (6.47), Japanese speakers were surprised to encounter a declarative complementizer *-to* in the embedded clause. Based on this result, they argued that Japanese speakers at first posit a gap in the matrix clause as in (6.50) but revise it into being in the most embedded clause as shown in (6.49).

According to Aoshima et al, the shift from (6.50) to (6.49) is "unforced". Nevertheless,[10] they still assumed that the motivation of such revision is feature-checking.[11]

[10] Aoshima et al(2004:42) noted, "*By unforced reanalysis, we mean a revision that is not licensed by any incompatibility of the initial analysis of the parse with subsequent material.*" Simply, there is no morpho-syntactic motivation to revise a structure and thus, structural revision as such is not compulsory.

[11] Aoshima et al (2003a) assumed that the *Wh-* phrase has two features, namely a *wh*-feature and θ-feature. Yet, at the point of the first gap, neither of these features are satisfied, because no verb has yet been seen. Furthermore, since the gap is not pronounced, positing a new gap doesn't entail any phonological commitment. When readers encounter the Q-particle on the embedded verb as in (6.47), both the *wh*-feature and the θ-feature will be checked. The wh-feature is checked because the Q-particle is a scope marker and the θ-feature is also to be checked because it can be recognized as an argument of the verb. On the other hand, in (6.45), when readers encounter the first verb without a Q-particle, the θ-feature can be checked, but the *wh*-feature cannot be checked.

(6.49) Gap in the Matrix Clause

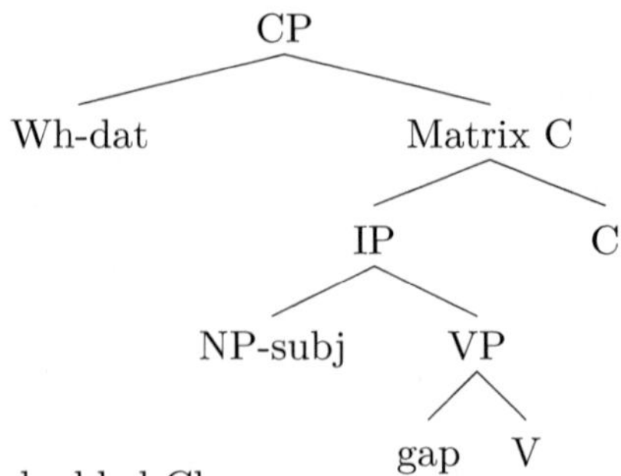

(6.50) Gap in the Embedded Clause

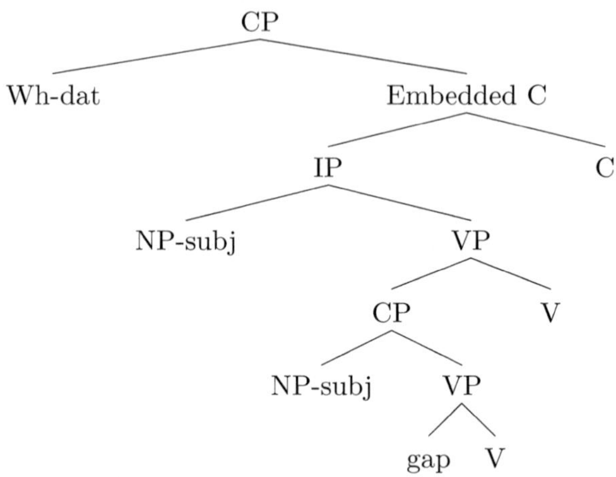

In other words, Aoshima and her colleagues have argued that the slow-down in the embedded clause with a declarative marker is caused because of the failure in feature-checking, in particular, failure to check the *wh*-feature. Aoshima et al (2005) argued that this is why referential NPs in a sentence initial position do not undergo unforced revision. However, given that the strength of *wh*-feature in Japanese/Korean is supposedly very weak (Grewendorf 2001), it is hard to see why native speakers can and do make distinctions needed for the future structure building from the two types of NPs at such an early stage. In addition, given that local word-order variation (=short-distance scrambling) is predominant compared to non-local word-order variation (=long-distance scrambling), it is also surprising that in particular the *wh*-dative NP is preferably understood as being long-distance scrambled rather than as short-distance scrambled.

Aoshima et al (2004) also argued that the parser prefers to satisfy requirements imposed by the initial dative NP as soon as possible, hence, within the most embedded clause, since in Japanese/Korean the most embedded verb comes earliest and the matrix verb comes last. However, without getting the full picture of a structure, it is impossible to know how many embedded structures are used in the given sentence. Hence, we can't see from which source structure such revision should take place until the end of the processing of the structure is reached. In general, both in Korean and Japanese, syntactic information such as the number of embeddings or the type of embedded structure (e.g. relative clause) can only be specified/revealed by parsing the verb near the end of parsing. Yet, crucially, this doesn't mean that structure-building decisions have to be delayed until the verb is reached. The heart of my claim shares a great deal with Aoshima et al. in that structure-building in head-final languages such as Korean/Japanese is incremental regardless of its head-finality and flexible word-order. The difference lies in the source of incrementality, which we will turn to soon, and the way of enabling incrementality to be defined as intrinsic to the architecture of the grammar. Aoshima et al. used a GB framework as the platform from which to explain incrementality, whereas I adopt Dynamic Syntax as providing such an explanation. The problems in Aoshima et al.'s account regarding *unforced revision* are resolved within the DS framework. This is because incrementality is related to structural growth along the time-line from the initial introduction of some underspecified structure to its subsequent enrichment yielding a more specified structure. To the contrary, in GB, structure building is not sensitive to linear order. And accordingly, any notion related to growth such as underspecification and partial structure building is not applicable in that system.

Indeed, within the GB framework, uncertainty is not tolerated at any stage of structure-building. Hence, in the system, parsers are expected to make fundamental structure building decisions as early as possible. These decisions include (i) mono-/multi-clausal decisions (i.e. how many layers will this structure have?) and (ii) filler-gap dependency postulation (e.g. is the sentence-initial left-peripheral lexical item to be locally interpreted? If not, in which level of embedding should it be interpreted?). In terms of hierarchical distance assumed in GB/MP, the matrix clause will always be the first option for the initial NP, since it is the structure unfolded first from a strictly top-down view. Yet, in terms of processing the string, the matrix verb is the most nonlocal option for the hearer to choose in terms of string length, given that it will be the last constituent of all. Given this conflict, unforced revision analysis might seem a possible solution but, as we have discussed, the unforced revision analysis is independently unsatisfactory. Hence, the conflict between strict top-down structure building and left-to-right structure building remains unresolved.[12]

As we've seen so far, threading incrementality into current grammar-formalisms is hard in the given configurational template (see Miyamoto 2002:312 for similar discussion). This is because incrementality inevitably involves the notion of underspecification or earlier structural uncertainty (i.e. an underspecified head in Miyamoto's terms) and time-linearity in the course of derivation. Yet, utilizing undeterministic, in other words, partial information to predict further structure was criticized in the GB framework, given that it is at best tentative but lacks full determinism. These are the reasons why indeed much sentence processing evidence seeks an independently-motivated parsing strategy rather than incorporating any such notion into the grammar.

In the following section, I will introduce Dynamic Syntax briefly and discuss the necessity of adopting the notion of underspecification and incremental growth in the architecture of grammar.

6.2 Dynamic Syntax: Grammar formalism with parsing dynamics

Dynamic Syntax assumes that a structure is built incrementally from left to right, following the linear order of a linguistic sequence. Following Sperber and Wilson (1995), DS takes as the starting point in any parsing effort the goal to establish some propositional formula as interpretation, and this overall goal may lead to other subgoals as more information comes in. In DS, there are three sources of structure-building driven by: (i) computational actions, (ii) lexical actions and (iii) pragmatic actions. And what is being built in DS is a representation of semantic content. The tree gives no indication of word order, as this is a representation of content, inhabited by concepts, not by the words of the string.

A structural skeleton is progressively induced as the structure grows. Its core claims are close to that of Phillips (1996) and Combinatory Categorial Grammar (see Steedman 2000), the former in virtue of the objective of reflecting incrementality within the grammar formalism, the latter in virtue of making use of operations of type deduction.

As we've seen in the previous section, Phillips argued that even defining a constituent may be difficult without taking linear order into consideration. Yet a Phillips style of explanation has limitations in

[12] If unforced revision is the correct analysis, it should also be observed more universally in other constructions as well as in other languages.

capturing the 'full' nature of incrementality since it is based on the assumptions of mainstream generative grammars. So when it comes to head-final languages like Korean and Japanese, many *ad-hoc* assumptions (e.g. unforced revision) are required. Most of all, in the Phillips-style approach, structure building is invariably deterministic. Nevertheless, the Phillips-style build-and-destroy approach is the best that a generative grammar framework can offer in capturing the incremental structure building of Korean and Japanese. Given that there are still major debates regarding the necessity of incorporating processing evidence in the grammar-formalism, due to the rigid barrier between competence/grammar and performance/parser, Phillips' work in reflecting real-time processes within the heart of grammar formalism is highly significant.

Unlike Phillips' build-and-destroy approach, the Dynamic Syntax approach can be summed up as a 'sketch-and-specify' approach. For instance, when the sentence-initial dative NP is heard, the parser/native speakers do not need to have the whole picture of a structure (eg, level of embedding). They do not have to fix it into a default argument of a matrix clause or the most embedded clause. That kind of syntactic shape will only be available at the later stage of structure-building when more information is incorporated. In Dynamic Syntax, it is possible not to make any structural commitment at the first specification of structure unlike in other grammar formalisms. This is because the notion of underspecification, that is, both content and *structural nondeterminism*, constitutes a key notion of this grammar formalism. In principle, any structural relation can remain underspecified during the course of structure building. Nonetheless, as we shall discuss in the next section, individual speakers have a strong tendency to resolve any such underspecified structural relation as soon as possible, hence at the first available structure. This structure is not necessarily that of the matrix clause. In fact, 'defining' the concept of first available structure, in other words, the first upcoming structure in the string is not easy within either transformational or non-transformational frameworks, since the term can be defined only in linear order terms not in those of configurational hierarchy. In this paper, based on evidence gathered from psycholinguistic tests and corpus extraction, I will argue for resource-sensitivity of syntactic-structure building. That is, I claim that syntactic structure is constructed with an aim to minimize production costs rather than allowing arbitrary delay. That is why some syntactic forms are much more straightforward to understand than others, and more frequently observed and highly preferred that their counterparts, despite the grammaticality of both. That is also why native speakers strongly prefer to resolve any grammatical dependency as soon as possible, rather than arbitrarily - at any level at any time.

Combinatory Categorial Grammar (CCG, Steedman 2000) is close to Dynamic Syntax in terms of its stepwise syntactic derivation, with adjacent expressions being assigned types that allow their pairwise combination through type lifting. However CCG lacks the structural unmderspecification which gives DS its flexibility. CCG has to capture flexibility of syntactic structure building in verb-final, scrambling languages like Korean and Japanese by using type-raising mechanisms or by putting modal control in the lexicon. However, as McConville (2001) pointed out, in CCG it is hard to thread the time-sensitiveness of real-time structure-building into the structural derivation, since though it is step-by-step, derivational procedures in CCG are not sensitive to linear order at all. Just as in the tradition of transformational grammar, to yield a well-formed derivation in CCG, human parsers/native speakers must know the whole structure at hand. Structural determinism is assumed: indeed, as in other categorial grammar formalisms, there is no concept of underspecification, either of structure or of content.

Contrary to CCG, Dynamic Syntax assumes left-to-right directional derivation and underspecification plus update. This assumption makes it possible to thread real-time understanding into the heart of the grammar, even though interpretation projection may be discontinuous. In principle, there is no fundamental difference between processing and grammar in DS: the grammar provides mechanisms for use in processing. To the contrary, DS adopts a parsing dynamics as a basic syntactic concept. In the following, I will introduce its basic characteristics.

6.2.1 Underspecification and incrementality

The use of underspecification is not a brand-new idea in linguistic theory, though it has not been actively adopted in syntactic frameworks (See Hausser 1984, 1994, Kaplan and Zaenan 1989 for exceptions). In particular, what has not been thoroughly investigated is HOW underspecified structures might get systematically and dynamically specified/resolved in the grammar to reflect a concept of information growth. I will argue in this paper, by exploring the notion of underspecification and its incremental resolution, that we should bridge the unnecessary gap between linguistic theory and real-time use of language and so provide a more explanatory account of verb-final, scrambling languages such as Korean.

Dynamic Syntax assumes that a structural relation is specified/updated as the structure grows in real-time from left-to-right. Rather than assuming a fully-fledged complete structure at the very initial step of structure building, DS assumes that, at each stage, some more specific structural skeleton may remain yet to be specified. Consider (6.51).

(6.51) *Jina-hanthey* ⋯
Jina-DAT

At the stage of hearing/reaching the sentence-initial expression, native speakers can't have any idea of the overall, fully-fledged structure. The only thing they will know at this stage is that the host verb is going to be a di-transitive verb (e.g. corresponding to give', inform', introduce') rather than a transitive verb(e.g. like', eat'). And the information as follows may not be available: (i) how many levels of embedding exist in the current structure; (ii) where the current expression is to be interpreted - i.e. at which level of embedding; (iii) will the current expression be interpreted together with the following expression or not? Nevertheless, this doesn't hinder native speakers' left-to-right, step-by-step structure-building procedures. On the contrary, they can uniformly build a partial structure with the information given. In verb-initial languages, this may be possible through processing a *verb*. In verb-final languages, however, this is made possible through other functional properties of those languages such as case morphology. I will turn to this issue in the next section.

6.2.2 The logic of finite trees and constructive case

The core architectural properties of DS are grounded in the modal logic of finite trees (LOFT: Blackburn and Meyer-Viol 1994). For our purposes here, its properties can be introduced by way of illustration, using the tree given in (6.52). The trees are binary branching with decorations at each node of some predicative formula Fo for formula, e.g. the predicate $Manna'$ represented as $Fo(Manna')$ (='met'), the type-decoration for a formula at a node, e.g. propositional type $Ty(t)$ (Ty for type), plus a predicate Tn indicating tree-node identifier, e.g. the decoration $Tn(0)$ is assigned to the rootnode. Complete trees provide a tree representation of a propositional formula, with predicate-argument internal structure, each node decorated by a partial development for a sub-term of such a formula. All partial trees are trees under development, with a pointer, $\Diamond$, which indicates the node currently being developed. The concept of requirement,?X for any X ranging over all such categories of decoration, is the central concept of the framework: all requirements, whether of content, structure, or type, have to be met by the end of a sequence of parse actions. $?Ty(t)$ indicates the overall goal of establishing a proposition of $Ty(t)$ with the sub-goal of a predicate, $?Ty(e \rightarrow t)$; and the requirement for update of content $?\exists x Fo(x)$

is a constraint that a fixed formula value be assigned as decoration to the node in question. The particular tree specification given here as illustration is the lexical characterization for the stem form of the verb *manna* ('met'):

(6.52) Propositional structure projected by *manna*'('met')

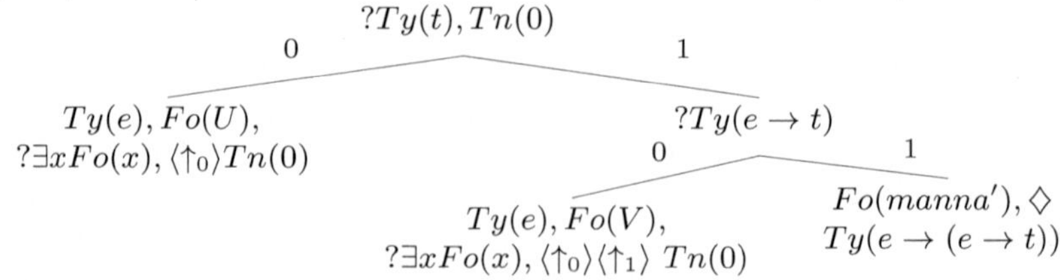

First, there is the top node, labelled as $?Ty(t), Tn(0)$, indicating that a proposition is required: this is the overall goal of structure building. In fully pro-drop languages like Korean/Japanese, a verb on its own can project a propositional structure: indeed this tree constitutes the information projected by the verb *manna*, a full predicate-argument structure with arguments nodes as well as a predicate node, with place-holding devices for the arguments licensing the update of such intermediate specifications from the context. $Tn(0)$ is associated with the label of TREE NODE($=Tn$), which has the information on the address of each node in the overall structure, $Tn(0)$ indicating that this node is the top node.

Then, moving from the top node to the next node along with an argument (0) relation (the 0 relation indicates an argument relation and 1 relation a functor relation). The subject argument node of this skeletal propositional structure is labelled as $\{Fo(\mathbf{U}), Ty(e), ?\exists x Fo(x), \langle\uparrow_0\rangle Tn(0)\}$. **U** is a place-holding metavariable: its content is to be updated by the context. $?\exists x Fo(x)$ is the requirement for a formula/content value for the current node, forcing an update substituting for that metavariable at some point in its parse process. In *LOFT*, two basic relations are defined: $\langle\uparrow\rangle$ and $\langle\downarrow\rangle$. In the DS application two subrelations are defined, for argument, and for functor relations. $\langle\uparrow_0\rangle Tn(0)$ refers to the modal relation of immediate dominance stating that from the current node, if the parser goes up $\langle\uparrow_0\rangle$ along an 0 (=argument) relation, there is a top node ($=Tn(0)$). The other daughter node under $?Ty(t), Tn(0)$ is the predicate node. This node is the functor argument. $?Ty(e \rightarrow t)$ is the TYPE label, which indicates that a predicate is required. This node can be addressed as $\langle\uparrow_1\rangle Tn(0)$.

From this node, two sub-nodes are further developed. Moving to the node along the argument (0) relation from the $?Ty(e \rightarrow t)$ node.

This node is to be an object node. This node is labelled as $\{Fo(\mathbf{V}), ?Ty(e), ?\exists x Fo(x), \langle\uparrow_0\rangle\langle\uparrow_1\rangle Tn(0)\}$. $Fo(\mathbf{V})$ is another place-holding metavariable, projected by the verb, $\langle\uparrow_0\rangle\langle\uparrow_1\rangle Tn(0)$ uniquely describes the relation of this treenode within this tree, hence constituting its tree node address, which states that if the parser goes up along the argument(=0) node relation and then the functor node (=1) relation, there is a top node. The other (functor) node branched from $?Ty(e \rightarrow t)$ is the verb node. This node can be addressed as $\langle\uparrow_1\rangle\langle\uparrow_1\rangle Tn(0)$.

Abstracting away from all these individual tree relations, a concept of *dominate* and *be dominated by* is defined. A node α is dominated by a node n at which some decoration X holds if $\langle\uparrow_*\rangle X$ holds at α, that is X holds along either at that node itself or at its immediately dominating node, or at a node immediately dominating that. And so on. In DS, the Kleene star (*) operator is used to characterize an underspecified tree relation. This is the Kleene* star closure relation defined over $\langle\uparrow\rangle$, standardly used in tree logics to provide a characterization of dominance:[13]

(6.53) $\langle\uparrow_*\rangle X \equiv \mathrm{X} \vee \langle\uparrow_1\rangle\ \mathrm{X} \vee \langle\uparrow_1\rangle\langle\uparrow_1\rangle\ \mathrm{X} \cdots$

From this core concept of dominate, more local relations can be defined over $\langle\uparrow_1^*\rangle$. Taking, for example, the two arguments of the verb *manna*, they can be defined as local because both meet the characterization of being locally dominated by the same node:

(6.54) $\langle\uparrow_0\rangle\langle\uparrow_1^*\rangle X \equiv \langle\uparrow_0\rangle\ \mathrm{X} \vee \langle\uparrow_0\rangle\langle\uparrow_1\rangle\ \mathrm{X} \vee \langle\uparrow_0\rangle\langle\uparrow_1\rangle\langle\uparrow_1\rangle\ \mathrm{X} \cdots$

With a characterization of all nodes in terms of their relation to other nodes in the tree (here the root node), we can now characterize case in such tree-relational terms, combining the concept of relations with that of requirement. Subject case can be defined as the requirement $?\langle\uparrow_0\rangle Ty(t)$, meaning that at some future development of the tree the node so decorated must turn out to have a mother node that is decorated with a formula of propositional type; accusative case as the requirement $?\langle\uparrow_0\rangle Ty(e \rightarrow t)$, i.e. that its mother must be developed so as to be decorated with a formula of predicate type. In a verb-final language such as Korean, case morphology can then be used to induce the local update of argument nodes decorated by NPs from such unfixed relation to a fixed relation before the structural array is unfolded by a predicate via LOCAL*ADJUNCTION (see Cann et al 2005 for a formal definition of this operation). Yet not all structural relations are to be fixed immediately from such an unfixed relation to a fixed relation within its local structure. Some structural relations may be fixed later

[13] It is formally identical to the concept of functional uncertainty adopted in LFG: Kaplan and Zaenen 1989.

during the course of structure building even across clause boundaries, reflecting the more general concept of dominance, this being the basis of long-distance dependency, to which I return later.

The concept of tree growth can then be defined to induce tree structures displaying these underspecified relations. The core concept is that of *ADJUNCTION which introduces an unfixed node reflecting the general concept of domination, with a requirement for update at some later point in the tree development process; the more localized variant is that of LOCAL*ADJUNCTION. In local scrambling effects, the effect is both to introduce a locally unfixed node and, via the case specifications to induce local structure for the argument nodes prior to the projection of full propositional structure by the verb. This licenses the construction of a node that is constrained to be local to the node from which it is constructed, i.e. if applied from the root at the outset of a parse derivation, along a relation $\langle\uparrow_0\rangle\langle\uparrow_1^*\rangle Tn(0)$.

Such general procedures are then taken to interact with lexically provided information. In particular, the concept of case in DS interacts with the structural growth process, constraining updates of underspecified structure projected by NPs. For instance, in a local scrambling sequence as in (6.55), when the parser processes *Mina*, with no other specification, *Mina* may turn out to decorate a subject, an object or a dative. In DS terms, if such a NP is to decorate a locally unfixed node, it will be decorating a structure whose relative position is merely $\langle\uparrow_0\rangle\langle\uparrow_1^*\rangle Tn(0)$ ('the root node locally dominates this node'). However, given that *Mina* is nominative case-marked, this characterization can be made considerably more precise, since this marking imposes a requirement that the node is immediate daughter of a $Ty(t)$ requiring node: $?\langle\uparrow_0\rangle Ty(t)$ ('There must in the outcome be a formula of type t at my mother node'). Following a step of LOCAL*ADJUNCTION, such a requirement can be taken to determine a fixed tree relation as a next step. If accusative case-marked, the requirement is that the node be immediate daughter of a predicate-requiring node: $?\langle\uparrow_0\rangle Ty(e \rightarrow t)$, again used immediately to determine a fixed tree relation. And so on. Derivations involving LOCAL*ADJUNCTION plus enrichment to reflect such given case specifications follow the pattern in (6.56).

(6.55) *Jina-lul* *Mina-ka* *manna-ss-e* *[O S V]*
Jina$_{ACC}$ Mina$_{NOM}$ meet$_{PAST,DECL}$
'Mina met Jina'

As (6.56) displays, each NP can be parsed by presuming on a step of LOCAL*ADJUNCTION inducing a weakly specified tree relation, which is enriched into the particular argument relation given by the particular case specification. The effect is that argument nodes can be introduced into a structure independent of the projection of the predicate itself, allowing incremental projection of structure from the words, despite the verb not occurring until the end of the string.

(6.56) LOCAL*ADJUNCTION and parsing the NP sequences in (6.55)

(i) Parsing *Jina-lul* :-*lul* updates $\langle\uparrow_0\rangle\langle\uparrow_1^*\rangle Tn(0)$ into $\langle\uparrow_0\rangle\langle\uparrow_1\rangle\ Tn(0)$ to reflect the case filter $?\langle\uparrow_0\rangle Ty(e \rightarrow t)$

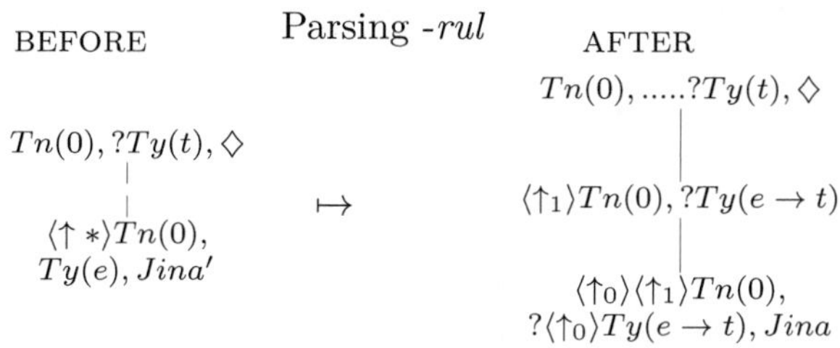

(ii) Parsing *Mina-ka*:-*ka* updates $\langle\uparrow *\rangle Tn(0)$ into $\langle\uparrow_0\rangle\ Tn(0)$ to reflect the case filter $?\langle\uparrow_0\rangle Ty(t)$

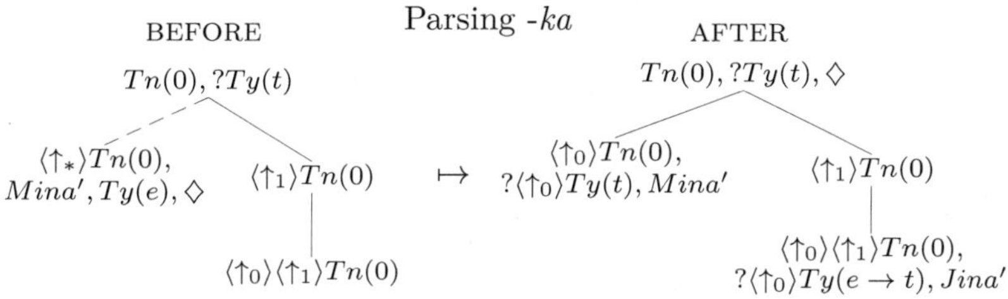

6.2.3 Long-distance dependency in DS

Nevertheless, some underspecifications projected from lexical items may fail to be updated immediately, their update occurring at some later stage of the structure-building process. Kiaer (forthcoming) reports that among fifty-one native speakers, on average, 63% of the time, they preferred to choose an object long-distance scrambled option like A1 relative to the canonical order option as in A2. In the question/answer set-up, an object expression in the answer was previously given in the question, whereas the embedded subject comprised the answer for the wh-question, which therefore became new information. The results of this forced-choice test show that native speakers of Korean tend to dislocate the given information in the left periphery, even across a clause boundary (i.e. long-distance scrambling).

(6.57) Q: *Yumi-ya, Jina-nun nwuka ku sakwa-lul*
Yumi-VOC Jina-TOP who the apple-ACC
mekessta-ko saynggakhaysse?
ate-COMP thought?

'Yumi, who did your sister think ate the apple?'

A1: *Ah, siktak-uye sakwa-lul Jina-nun Mina-ka*
Ah, table-on apple-ACC Jina-TOP Mina-NOM
mekessta-ko saynggakhaysse.
ate-COMP thought

'Ah, that apple on the table - Jina thought that Mina ate.

A2: *Jina-nun Mina-ka siktak-uye sakwa-lul*
Jina-TOP Mina-NOM table-on apple-ACC
mekessta-ko saynggakhaysse.
ate-COMP thought

'Jina thought that Mina ate the apple on the table.

When an expression occurs across a clause boundary from its site of construal (i.e. long-distance scrambling as in (6.57), the fronted item is accompanied by an intonational phrase boundary, which is indicated by the last syllable of the lexical item being lengthened.

It is this intonational marking which cues that the utterance is to be understood as involving manipulation of *ADJUNCTION rather than LOCAL*ADJUNCTION. In tandem with case morphology, prosody or context plays an indispensable role in incremental structure building, helping parsers to decide whether to build the currently-parsed lexical item locally to the previous structure or not (see Kiaer 2007 for more detail). The role of prosody has been discussed intensively in the parsing literature, but rarely with recourse to any grammar formalism. Kiaer (2007) argued that the role of intonation is crucial for indicating non-immediate structural growth. Based on DS, I tentatively assumed that the lexical action of IP boundary (BREAK) is as follows. Informally, it states that if the pointer is at the $?Ty(t)$ node at the current point and if there is any underspecified argument already constructed then the action simply waits for further processing, but if there is no such node, then some such weak dominance relation (D) is to be constructed with the pointer shifting to that newly constructed node:

(6.58) Lexical action of IP boundary (BREAK)

IF	$?Ty(t), Tn(a)$	
THEN	IF	$\langle\downarrow_*\rangle(Ty(x), ?\exists x Tn(x))$
	THEN	1
	ELSE	$\mathtt{make}(\langle D\rangle); \mathtt{go}(\langle D\rangle); \mathtt{put}(\langle U\rangle Tn(a))$
ELSE	Abort	

This lexical action is thus associated with non-local structure building, either because already constructed, or by the construction of such a boundary.

Nevertheless, as we shall see in the next section, native speakers of Korean (and Japanese) strongly prefer to build a localized structure in an incremental manner, unless overt prosody or context intervenes. Such a tendency is hard to explain in static grammar formalisms. In the next section, I will show how the DS grammar formalism with its reflection of parsing dynamics can explain this phenomenon.

6.3 DS analysis of "localized" structure building

6.3.1 Ordering fragments: Korean/Japanese

Here I will specifically discuss the results of a task involving the ordering of expressions in Korean and Japanese. The purpose of this task is to investigate native speakers' preferences for localized structures, in particular, in producing embedded clauses. Word sets which could be ordered into wellformed strings were presented to students as a randomized list of words, and subjects were asked to order them as naturally as possible. In the first of these fragment-ordering tasks, twenty-nine native speakers of Korean from Kwanak High School took part: they were instructed to list the given fragments as naturally as possible.[14] Thirty items with six fragments as in (6.59) are given.

(6.59) {Malhaysse(said),}{yenpil-ul(pencil-ACC),}{Mina-hanthey(Mina-DAT),}{Kiho-ka(Kiho-NOM),}{Yuna-ka(Yuna-NOM),}{pilliecwuessta-ko(lent-COMP)}

Though there is great freedom of ordering, no native speaker produced even a single sentence which had two consecutive nominative NPs. In the second fragment-ordering task, twenty eight native speakers were asked to list the given fragments as naturally as possible. Twenty items as in (6.60) were given.

(6.60) {Malhaysse(said),}{yenpil-ul(pencil-ACC),}{Mina-hanthey(Mina-DAT),}{Kiho-nun(Kiho-TOP),}{Yuna-ka(Yuna-NOM),}{pilliecwuessta-ko(lent-COMP)}

---

[14] I am very grateful to Hyunjoo Kang and pupils for helping in this experiment.

Fourteen out of twenty eight speakers strongly preferred to start a sentence with NP-TOP NP-NOM sequence (92% of the time). Three out of twenty eight speakers chose 50% of the time NP-TOP NP-NOM sequence. The rest of the eleven speakers strongly preferred to start a sentence with either NP-TOP or NP-NOM only (83% of the time). Similar results are observed in Japanese too. Kiaer (forthcoming) reports the results of thirty four native Japanese speakers participating in the fragment ordering experiment close to (6.60). The results show that among thirty four speakers, thirty one speakers strongly prefer NP-TOP NP-NOM ordering 83% of the time (average 25 items among 30).

6.3.2 Why localized structure?: Structural optimization

In this section, we will discuss how locality effects, namely strong preference towards structures like (6.62) over structures as in (6.61), can be explained within DS.

(6.61) [S1 [S2 O2 Verb2-COMP Verb1]]: Centre-embedded structure

Jina-ka	*Mina-ka*	*sakwa-lul*	*mekessta-ko*	*malhaysseyo.*
J-NOM	M-NOM	apple-ACC	ate-COMP	said

'Jina said that Mina ate an apple.'

(6.62) [S2 O2 Verb2-COMP]$_{O1}$ S1 Verb1]]: Pre-posed alternate

Mina-ka	*sakwa-lul*	*mekessta-ko*	*Jina-ka*	*malhaysseyo.*
M-NOM	apple-ACC	ate-COMP	J-NOM	said

'Jina said that Mina ate an apple.'

So far, most analyses of "preference" puzzles as above have been given presuming on a clear distinction between competence and performance (Miyamoto 2002, Gibson 1998 among others). Yet, recently, Hawkins (2004) and Wasow (2002) among others have argued that what is regarded as performance data are indeed the reflection of linguistic competence. My current claim is in line with theirs. I argue that efficient and incremental structure building which takes the most accessible structural platform as the first basis of structural template is a direct piece of evidence for the necessity of incorporating processing considerations into the grammar formalism even though not the actual basis for such a choice.

In DS, to successfully build a structure as in (6.61), it is necessary to have cues such as intonation or contextual information. This is because without any use of such devices, native speakers may build two nodes decorated by nominative NPs within the same local structure. As it stands, nothing in the system of growth precludes this except the overall global constraint that nodes in a tree must be able to lead to a successful derivation to establish a propositional predicate-argument structure; and this is not possible if any one of those nodes bears inconsistent decorations, unless some additional computational action can be made available.[15] To avoid any derivation which would yield such possibly late termination of the derivation, for which a sizeable amount of parsing effort would turn out to have been in vain, a non-canonical, non-default structure-building option will have to have been used, as in (6.61), and furthermore indicated as needed to prevent the otherwise automatic use of default, i.e. routinized, preferences. In contrast, structure building to establish a construal for (6.62) doesn't require any such indicators to induce successful pairing of string and interpretation. All case-marked NPs will have been used to decorate nodes introduced by LOCAL*ADJUNCTION and then, after parsing the complementizer *-ko*, the local structure building will be finished off, and duly taken to constitute an argument in the emergent tree, whose major predicate will be given by the verb, of which that composite propositional structure will be its complement argument. That is, instead of assuming that the complement clause is moved out from the matrix clause, DS is able to reflect ordering variation between complement clause (ie. direct object) and subject NP within a matrix clause as different choices in how the requisite output structure is built up. In short, structure building as in (6.62) only involves default operations, which optimizes native structure building by minimizing native speaker's structure building effort. That is why strings such as (6.62) are preferred to strings such as (6.61). We have thus shown how, as a grammar formalism which has parsing dynamics and which is able to reflect locality-preserving options very directly, Dynamic Syntax can capture why human parsers strongly prefer the optimized/most economic option for structure building to its counterpart, presuming only that performance itself involves manipulating the processes which the grammar formalism makes available in conjunction with the assumption that choices are made relative to a least effort constraint (as presumed by Sperber and Wilson 1995 among others). This itself guarantees that local operations are to be preferred over non-local ones. We argue that regardless of the word-order, building all arguments within the same local structure is invariably the most economic option, because it only involves default, canonical operation; and with this grounded in a completely general cognitive constraint of minimizing cognitive effort for any given effect, the explanation has

[15]Korean, for example, allows double object marking, which we assume allows the building of an extension of the term in question. We ignore this complication here.

strong independent motivation. Experimental investigation of the most appropriate way to measure the mental cost of utilizing different structure building operations is of course the next step of the research. But we hope this small application of DS assumptions illustrates how initial corpus analysis of culled data can provide a valuable first step in establishing grammar formalisms for natural language.

6.4 Towards competence grammars for verb-final languages

The challenge of Korean/Japanese syntax is more than just confirming or disconfirming the claims made in the literature mainly based on European languages. Indeed, they provide the testing ground for grammar, parser and their relationship.

The broader methodology on which this argument has depended is that evaluation of competence grammars should not lie solely in the detailed mechanism itself, but in the elegance of the generalization which captures the data of language use. I propose as one criterion for such a formalism that simplicity and complexity of grammar should be evaluated for how well it comports with the efficiency or conversely complexity of real language use. This is in conflict with generative linguistics methodologies, where it has been implicitly assumed that complex structures are usually associated with complex grammatical operations and simple structures are close to some original structure which constitutes the starting point for all derivations. Nevertheless, how to give substance to the correspondence between simplicity/complexity of the abstract syntax and efficiency/complexity of real language use is not an easy task. Though the general idea as above is agreed across formalisms, linguists have until very recently not considered, as an alternative, that the methodologies of competence study and performance study, far from being disjoint, are interwoven with simplicity and complexity of the competence system being reflected in either parsing or production systems. In generative linguistics, syntactic architecture is proposed as corresponding to some ideal speaker's knowledge of language without any reference to context. Hence, resource- or context-sensitive aspects of natural language syntax (e.g. incremental structure building, use of context/prosody) have been regarded as nothing to do with the native speaker's innate linguistic ability, often referred to as competence or I-language. In this paper, by looking at some empirical test results in Korean, I have argued for the need to consider 'procedural aspects' of linguistic competence, which can be captured by shifting away from orthodox views on competence grammar to those of procedural and dynamic grammar. If we assume that the purpose of any grammatical theory is to retain explanatory adequacy, we certainly need a way of evaluating the elegance of such a theory, within an overall cognitive perspective.

References

The following were cited in this chapter: Aoshima et al (2005), Cann et al (2005), Chomsky (1981), Chomsky (2000), Grewendorf (2001), Hawkins (2004), Hofmeister et al (2006), Jun (1993), Karamanis (2001), Kiaer (2007), Kim and Yoon (2006), Kitagawa and Hirose (2006), Koizumi (2000), Kuroda (1971), Lasnik and Saito (1992), McConville (2001), Miyagawa (2003), Newmeyer (2005), Phillips (1996), Phillips (2003), Ross (1967), Saito (1985), Saito (2003), Selkirk (1984), Takano (2002). See references at the end of the book for full details.

7

Local Ambiguity, Search Strategies and Parsing in Dynamic Syntax

YO SATO

7.1 Introduction

Dynamic Syntax (DS: Kempson et al. 2001; Cann et al. 2005) is a parsing-based, or process-oriented framework modelling incrementality. In this respect, this framework could be invoked as a plausible model providing accounts for human sentence processing. It is, however, not immediately clear exactly in what sense, and to what extent, this is so. I will indeed argue generally for the suitability of DS to this purpose, but hasten to add that DS only restricts parsing strategies in very broad terms and does not impose/favor any of the specific strategies argued by psycholinguists for human online processing. The task of the present article is, therefore, firstly to identify what 'broad restrictions' DS does impose, and secondly (and more importantly) to indicate in what way it can underpin studies of sentence processing. For this purpose, I take up the issue of *local ambiguity*, one of the most crucial issues for the sentence processing research, be it psychological or computational.

Local ambiguity concerns the multiplicity, at a mid-point in online parsing, of applicable syntactic rules that can lead to an eventual construal of a sentence. For example, a sentence beginning with *Cotton clothing*, which would most likely induce the human parser to postulate that it constitutes a single NP (modified nominal), may end up split with a topicalized NP plus subject: *Cotton clothing is mostly woven from in this region*, or, even, *Cotton clothing is made of grows in*

The Dynamics of Lexical Interfaces.
Ruth Kempson, Eleni Gregoromichelaki and Christine Howes (eds.).

Mississippi, a celebrated 'garden path' example.[1] These distinct eventualities represent mutually incompatible structural options all but one of which will ultimately be chosen. Hence they constitute *local* ambiguity in the sense that the ambiguity is temporary and will be resolved in the course of parsing.

Examples such as the above have attracted attention from psycholinguists in the context of the debate on what extent the human sentence processing is *serial* (see Frazier (1987) for the classical serial model) or *parallel* (see Hickok (1993); Gibson (1998) *inter alia* for models that incorporate parallel processing). In these debates, the focus is set on the contrast between the cases where it is difficult to recover from an unsuccessful reading ('garden path' examples, taken to indicate a 'serial' mode of parsing) and those in which it is less so (an indication of a 'parallel' mode), hence ending up with a few, in most cases two, contrasting local readings. From a broader perspective, however, local ambiguity can be taken to be a general phenomenon that occurs at *every* input word in a parse. The first input alone, say the word *That...*, is locally ambiguous in the sense that it could be developed into a variety of eventual structures e.g. NP→ Det N (*That book...*), NP→ Det Adj N (*That red book...*), S→ NP VP (*That is...*), CP→ Comp S (*That he is a student is...*), and so on. The same is the case for a string that appears to be nearly or fully completed as a sentence, for example *The boy saw the girl*, which could be part of the eventual *The boy saw the girl enter the room.* In a sense, multiple choice always confronts the parser. It is local ambiguity in this generalized sense that is of relevance to DS as a general parsing mechanism and will be discussed, from one point of view, in this article. This notion of local ambiguity is useful as it connects parsing strategies with the general notion of *search strategies* familiar in artificial intelligence (AI). Traditionally represented in a state transition graph that describes the traversal(s) for a solution, a search strategy makes every step that reaches a certain goal explicit, including the 'unsuccessful' steps (see e.g. Russell and Norvig 2003). In this representation, not only do parsing strategies involved in local ambiguity phenomena find natural translations, but also can be made more precise and explicit. Various forms of search strategies are also increasingly employed in the recent natural language processing (NLP) algorithms (see Manning and Schütze (1999) for an introduction and Huang (2008) for a survey on the recent proposals).

We will see in what follows that in DS, various search strategies can

[1] The example comes from Marcus (1980), although his example is with the determiner '*the*'.

be straightforwardly superimposed, because all the steps that could be taken in parsing are explicitly represented therein. The framework's strength lies, it will be argued, in the fact that it provides representations upon which detailed processing strategies *could* be precisely elaborated. The rest of this chapter is organized as follows. After illustrating the relevance of local ambiguity to parsing in general (Section 7.2.1) and to the DS style parsing in particular (Section 7.2.2), I will illustrate how the DS model can be usefully represented as a *graph*, so that its exact 'procedural' character and computational properties are highlighted, and more detailed characterizations of parsing strategies may be modelled over it (Section 7.3). Examples of applying this representation of DS to the domains of NLP and psycholinguistics follow in Section 7.4, namely the probabilistic parsing models and Gibson's (1998) complexity metric, respectively. Overall, it is hoped that the procedural characteristics of DS, illuminated in this work, provide a representational basis for sentence processing research in general.

7.2 Local ambiguity and Dynamic Syntax

7.2.1 Local ambiguity, top-down control and search strategies

We start, as a preliminary, with the illustration on the implications of local ambiguity for parsing and search strategies in general. Consider the example quoted in the Introduction:

(7.1) *Cotton clothing...*

Our two word sequence may be followed by a matrix verb, being a compound NP subject, as in:

(7.2) *Cotton clothing is comfortable to wear.*

or, still being a compound NP, it can be a topicalized object:

(7.3) *Cotton clothing I usually wear.*

It may also be followed by another nominal as two adjacent modifiers as in:

(7.4) *Cotton clothing shops are...*

Further, it may be two separate NPs, the first constituting a topicalized object e.g.

(7.5) *Cotton clothing is mostly woven from in this region*

or finally, still two NPs, but the first being the antecedent of a relative clause, ending up in the garden path sentence quoted above.

(7.6) *Cotton clothing is made of grows in Mississippi.*

Local ambiguity is of interest in the present context because it highlights the familiar trade-off between completeness and efficiency. If we were to be cautious and guard against any failure, we would opt for the 'fail-safe' route with a *bottom-up method*, by postponing the upper node processing until all the lower sub-constituents have been instantiated. Typically, in this strategy, one would first assign all the lexical categories to words, and then move on to higher categories as these have been instantiated. Even for the hard-to-process (7.6), no confusion would then be incurred. One would gather all lexical category information (i.e. N→ cotton, N→ clothing, Aux→ is, Vpp→ made, P→ of, V→ grows, P→ in and N→ Mississippi) and only then start processing phrases. One way of doing this is to be led by the applicable rules: find the rules that have all their sub-constituents instantiated, then the higher rules that have all theirs instantiated as a result, and continue this process until all the words in the string have been processed. With our garden path sentence, the first round will be to apply NP→ N for *cotton*, *clothing* and *Mississippi* and VP→ V for *grows*, as well as PP→ P ϵ and PP→ P N for *of* and *in Mississippi* respectively; the second round comprises the applications of VP→ Aux Vpp for *is made* and VP→ VP PP for *grows in Mississippi*; thirdly again VP→ VP PP for *is made of*; fourthly S→ NP VP for *clothing is made of*; fifthly NP→ NP S for *cotton clothing is made of*, before reaching the grand finale, with S→ NP VP. What has just been demonstrated is a *depth-first* variety of search, as you go 'deeper' for each rule before another is tried. Notice that, as a result, parsing goes 'back and forth' on a string. This bottom-up/depth-first combination is normally called the *shift-reduce* strategy. Shortly we will see an alternative – bottom-up/breadth-first combination – but the point here is that a bottom-up strategy is generally *complete*: as long as there is a solution, you will eventually get there.

This fail-safe method suffers from two major drawbacks. One is lack of efficiency. Although I showed in the last paragraph only a 'selection' of rules – ones leading to a successful parse for that particular string – there are of course other local parses that will be unsuccessful, the string being locally ambiguous. A purely bottom-up strategy is not equipped with any mechanism that lets you know if you are in the right track half-way down: all the applicable rules are checked exhaustively. For example, there are only two rule applications shown above in the 'second round' of phrasal processing, but there really are a lot more: at least five, including the nominal modifier, topicalization and '*is* as the main verb' possibilities. Each rule application might trigger a chain of further rule applications, from which, if unsuccessful, the parser needs to *backtrack* to where it was and start again. Notice that the number of rule applications could grow exponentially – each option might lead to a further multiple choice – and it may take a long time until you reach a dead end and come back. Of course you may be lucky – the rule you first try may lead to a success – but the more options you have the less likely such luck becomes. The second drawback is that the shift-reduce strategy is not incremental. As we have seen, the parsing goes back and forth on the string, not left-to-right, word-by-word. The issue of local ambiguity surrounding *online* parsing is simply not addressed, as it gathers all the words first, and the situation where you have only encountered part of a string, say only *Cotton clothing* and not the rest in our example, simply does not arise.

It might be thought that what is at fault is the depth-first search rather than the bottom-up approach. Indeed, one could parse somewhat incrementally with the *breadth-first* counterpart, though still within the bottom-up strategy. You would then be led by the string, word-by-word, and try to find the rules that are applicable to that string. At the point where you have two words, *cotton* and *clothing*, you will have assigned N to both, and activate the rules N→ NP and NP→ N NP in that order to get a modified NP. However this is the farthest you can get. Being bottom-up, no further rule is triggered without instantiation. One would only get the 'more difficult' readings when you get those words that can constitute them. In our example, you will in fact only get the opportunity to apply NP→ NP S at the end of the string, after a chain of relevant lower rule applications. Whether this can be rightfully called incremental is doubtful, as it does not respect *monotonicity*: a new phrasal rule can crop up with a chain of rule applications in a batch. Furthermore, the breadth-first approach does not help on the efficiency count either. It doesn't backtrack, but sidetrack instead. As it searches for possible expansions at each and every input, it simply takes more time at each word while dispensing with backtrack. Worse, you cannot get lucky, because you will not get to the end of the string until every applicable rule has been tried.

Thus, while being complete, purely bottom-up approaches can be inefficient and non-incremental in general. What about the top-down alternative? In a *top-down* method one would start with the top node and 'decompose' it into lower subconstituents successively, without instantiation, until you reach lexical categories that match the input words. Thus you start with S, which is then decomposed into its subconstituents, say NP VP. Each will be further decomposed, say N and V, which might then be matched to, say, *John snores*. This 'naive' version of top-down strategy, however, is nearly totally unusable. First it is not complete, with its vulnerability to *left recursive* rules such as VP→ VP PP. For if VP is expanded to VP PP, the same rule can then again be applied, expanding to VP PP PP, and again, falling into an infinite loop. Further, as it is, it is even less efficient than bottom-up methods, as all the chains of expansions of S are tried, including entirely irrelevant ones. However, these problems can be rectified straightforwardly with a minimum bottom-up support, with the method of *left-corner parsing*, according to which only those rules are invoked whose first (leftmost) constituent is confirmed to be instantiated (e.g. if the sentence starts with *the*, only those rules starting with Det will be tried). With such support, a top-down method can be rendered much more efficient than the pure bottom-up methods. Its greatest asset is that it can *look ahead*, and this *predictive* capacity makes it possible to invoke all sorts of 'educated guesses' rather than relying on luck. Depending on the extent and accuracy of these guesses, the subsequent parsing will be greatly constrained.

Importantly, with top-down methods, the depth-first/breadth-first opposition in search strategy, which is almost inconsequential in the bottom-up approach, has great bearing both on completeness and efficiency of online parsing. In fact, the psycholinguists' notion of serial/parallel online parsing, though sometimes used rather vaguely, appears to correspond to the top-down depth-first/breadth-first contrast. Contrasting consequences arise precisely because of the predictions top-down parsing can make. Let us suppose that some parser employs the left-corner strategy of top-down parsing and has just encountered a single word, *cotton*. As this word could either be a noun or an NP in itself, the left-corner parser would 'predict' a number possible structures starting with either an NP or N, including the matrix subject reading and the modifier.

If you further opt for a depth-first search, you will get what psycholinguists commonly call serial, or what is better known in the NLP community as *deterministic*, parsing (Aho et al. 1975). Faced with a multiple choice as predicted above, a deterministic parser commits itself to one choice and pursues it until it either reaches a successful final result, or else fails, in which case it backtracks. If, on the other hand, you opt for a breadth-first search, you first check whether the first subconstituent of each rule applies, and then the second one of each, and so on. This contrast may appear entirely analogous to the depth-first and breadth-first comparison for the bottom-up approach: depth-first is a risky, hit-and-miss business, while breadth-first is a slow, but surer, way. However a crucial difference lies in the fact that one can choose which one of the predicted structures to check first, without its subconstituents instantiated. If you predict accurately, you could make the risky method less risky, and the slow method less slow. Thus depending on parsing order, the efficiency of the whole parsing changes quite dramatically, particularly for deterministic parsing, as the 'saving' of steps can be large between the case in which an unsuccessful choice is made first and that in which one hits the successful option first. The cost saving would still be significant for the breadth-first method too, as an option that can be known to be unsuccessful early can be killed off early. This search method, whether depth-first or breadth-first, of choosing what is considered to be the best prediction and processing it first, has its name: the *best-first* search.

It must be noted here, however, that the best-first method, unlike the depth-first and breadth-first strategies, does not refer to a particular parsing strategy, but really is a group of strategies that can come in many forms. Various strategies can be mixed in various ways to make for more efficient or complete implementations. Present-day parser implementers primarily compete on this ground, namely what best-search strategy really is the best. Most use some probabilistic approach (Charniak 1997; Collins 1999; Roark 2001), owing its origin to the Probabilistic Context Free Grammar (PCFG) (Booth 1969), a natural basis for best-first parsing, as we shall see in a later section. Also from a psycholinguistic point of view, a best-first method appears to be a possible model, and we will see a theory essentially based on this method, namely Gibson's SPLT, although given the complexity and possible individual idiosyncracies of human parsing, various other accounts are possible (see e.g. Vasishth and Lewis 2006 for an alternative view).

Somewhat surprisingly, however, local ambiguity, as well as its closely related issue of search strategies, have drawn little attention from formal grammarians, who, in contrast, are more interested in the recognition of complete sentences, often along with the issue of their favoured framework's 'generative capacity' (i.e. what class of language it can maximally recognize) and its worst-case time complexity (e.g. Joshi 1985; Barton et al. 1988; Steedman 2000). These issues are naturally central to any parsing-based grammar building, including DS, and need to be tackled, but are *not* the concern addressed in this chapter. Instead, along with the AI and psycholinguistic research, I will focus on the more search-algorithmic issue of how multiple paths are traversed when faced with multiple local readings, which formal grammarians have conventionally been silent about. To put it simply, my claim here is that DS is well suited for the analysis of search strategies, particularly best-first ones. In this sense, therefore, it is also uniquely well placed to make a significant contribution to the issue of local ambiguity.

7.2.2 Predictivity of Dynamic Syntax and best-first search

We start our characterization of DS by making clearer what 'broad strategies' DS assumes for parsing. As most parsers in practical use, DS is equipped with both bottom-up support and top-down control. Amongst the 'actions' that comprise its tree-building inventory (see this volume's Introduction for an overview of available actions), bottom-up elements come from lexical actions while the top-down control stems from some of the computational actions. A lexical 'macro' (applied in a batch without intervention) for a lexical item instantiates a node with a particular content ($Fo(\ldots)$) as well as type ($Ty(\ldots)$) and as parsing proceeds on a word-by-word basis in DS, no non-instantiated tree can be built. What provides the top-down control in DS is, on the other hand, the actions that *create new nodes*, including those that initialize a tree (as a node would be part of the tree), such as INTRODUCTION (see Introduction 1.2.1), *ADJUNCTION (Introduction 1.2.2) and LINK-ADJUNCTION (Introduction 1.2.5). Some lexical actions also create a new node, as in (di)transitive verbs for example. We focus on the top-down aspect of the framework in the discussion that follows, as it is more pertinent to the immediate issue at hand, i.e. search strategies.

(7.7) DS trees for initiating parsing

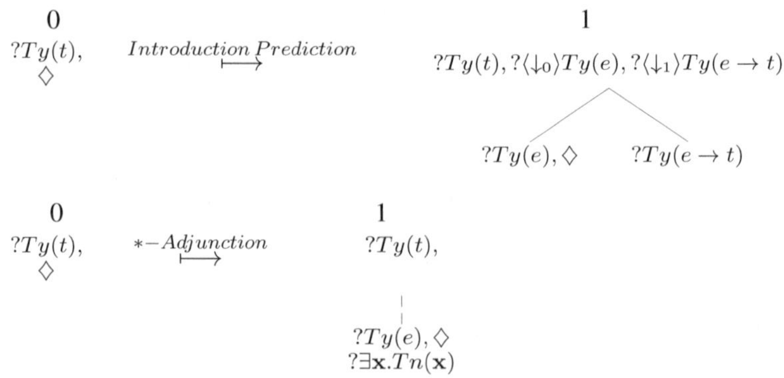

Let us concentrate on the standard case where parsing in DS originates from the actions that require a type t (propositional) node ($?Ty(t)$), depicted in (7.7). Immediately before parsing a sentence, that is, before encountering any words, there already are two computational actions applicable to the AXIOM requiring a $Ty(t)$ node, INTRODUCTION and *ADJUNCTION, corresponding to the possibilities without and with an extracted constituent.[2] In English, the former option is followed by PREDICTION, creating required $Ty(e)$ and $Ty(e \to t)$ nodes, with the pointer placed at the former (see the first tree growth step in (7.7)).

Furthermore, with a type $Ty(e)$ node then instantiated, LINK ADJUNCTION is applicable requiring a further $Ty(t)$ node, and hence the same set of actions can then be triggered. Consider (7.8) where the relative clause for the string *Cotton (that) clothing is made of is ...* has been initiated.[3]

(7.8) LINK ADJUNCTION and initiating parsing of relative clause

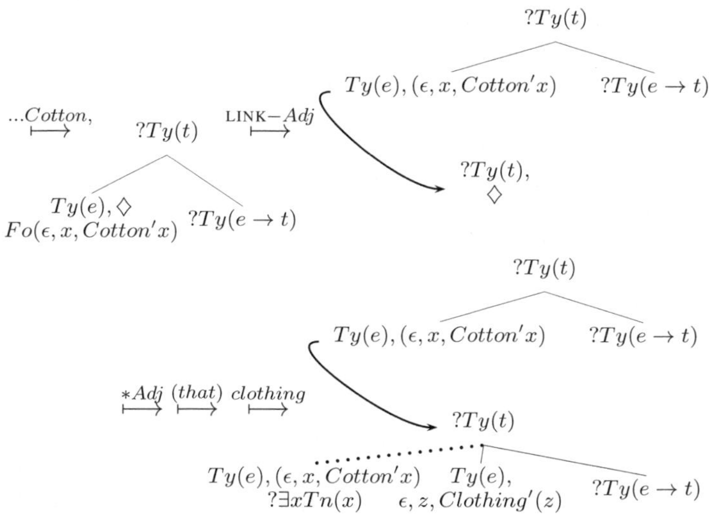

From then on, various subgoals are created depending on the input. Details apart, the point here is that the processing of *requirements* leads to a host of *structural predictions* as to what types of nodes can be expected. This multiplicity of possible forthcoming structures corresponds to local ambiguity.

One noticeable characteristic of the predictivity in DS is that some structures are predicted without *any* of their nodes having been instantiated, as exemplified in the above cases. We call this characteristic *strong predictivity* in DS, in contrast to *weak predictivity*, in which a structural prediction is only made with part of the structure instantiated, in other words, it is partially input-driven (as in the left-corner

[2]Another option is TOPIC-ADJUNCTION, see Introduction 1.2.5 but we leave this aside here.

[3]For simplicity of the graphs we illustrate with a non-restrictive reading here.

parsing). The 'pure' version of top-down parsing will thus be strongly predictive. However, most modern-day parsers, even if they adopt a mainly top-down method, rely on some input for every rule expansion and hence do not predict strongly (e.g. Roark 2001). Thus strong predictivity may be said to be a feature of DS parsing that is characteristic, if not unique.[4]

In DS, the most crucial environment in which strong predictivity applies is that in which a propositional type, the type t, is required. This strong predictivity in terms of propositions leads to various important computational properties, the most relevant to our present discussion being the fact that a number of search paths are created whenever a type t requirement has been registered. As a device for the computation of sentence structures, this can cut both ways. The main disadvantage is that the number of possible paths could easily multiply exponentially. Consider again the locally ambiguous *Cotton clothing....* In DS, two strong predictions are made at the very beginning i.e. when no word has yet been parsed, one for the eventuality with extraction and the other for that without. When the first NP, *Cotton*, is encountered, a further possibility of Link Adjunction, and hence a further type t node, is added, multiplying the possibilities. Moreover, there is also a nominal modifier reading, which predicts a further nominal to follow. Thus at this stage, at which a mere single word has been encountered, there are 2×3 possibilities. With the second word *clothing*, the permutations become $2 \times 3 \times 3$, and given the recursive nature of such NPs, the complexity of a compound of NPs become $O(3^n)$, given n NPs. Although a nominal compound with many nominal modifier iterations may be rare, the same order of complexity ensues with any t-requirement embedding, e.g. a clause complement which is more likely to be recursively embedded, so the issue cannot simply be dismissed on frequency grounds.

This potential intractability, however, should not necessarily cause concern for two reasons. First remember that DS parsing proceeds word-by-word, each input providing bottom-up support. Thus one does not have to follow through the whole string even for deterministic parsing since, as will be made clear in the next section, it will be split into word segments, in each of which the search paths that turn out to be inapplicable are killed off before proceeding to the next segment.[5]

[4]A notable exception is the classical Earley parser (Earley 1970) as well as its modern-day variants (Hale 2001), where the start symbol (typically S) is strongly predicted initially.

[5]It is this combination of the word-by-word processing *and* the top-down predictions, not the former alone (as we have seen in Section 7.2.1), that provides

Secondly, this is the worst case complexity, and although word-by-word parsing would not help, as it would not treat 'unlikelier' or garden path structures any differently, some best-first method can be introduced to reduce the search space. On this count, the strong predictivity can be turned into an advantage, as such predictivity means that various structural options are brought forward where t nodes are anticipated, without any daughter instantiated, making it possible to choose from them. For example, after *Cotton*, one can handle not just the structures weakly predicted from this input (i.e. this word as a matrix subject via PREDICTION and as an extracted NP for *ADJUNCTION), but also those that are strongly predicted (LINK ADJUNCTION for relative clause or nominal modifier) in some preferred order. In short, the strong predictivity of DS lends itself to modelling best-first search strategies when faced with local ambiguity. We will illustrate this point with a concrete comparison with a weakly predictive search in a later section (7.4.2).

I have been characterising, as a strength of DS as a procedural and incremental framework, its amenability to top-down search strategies. In the next section I proceed to represent DS parsing as a state search graph just as in the standard AI research, so as to make the relationship between the framework and search strategies explicit.

7.3 DS parsing as a cumulative directed graph

DS parsing may be illustrated in terms of sequential tree-growth via actions, where the focus is usually on an ultimately successful parse. This mode of presentation may well give the impression that the procedure is somewhat deterministic, one action necessarily followed by another single particular action all the way through. However, as has been illustrated in the preceding section, the predictive nature of DS means that an action may be immediately followed by a number of actions, forming multiple paths, each constituting a local, and potentially global, interpretation for the string. Therefore, to capture the DS parsing of a sentence as a whole, some other representation that encompasses all the local interpretations, whether plausible or not, seems desirable, so that at any point in parse, all the allowable paths from which the parser could choose are explicitly displayed.

I propose that a suitable representation for illustrating how this choice mechanism may work is a state search graph with a transition function/relation, as traditionally employed for artificial intelligence in general. In AI, state search graphs are invoked to model search for *so-*

---

monotonicity in DS tree growth and hence deserves to be called *incrementality*. See Kempson et al. (2009a) for details.

lutions, or *goals*, where all that matters in most cases is how to traverse these states to reach a solution, unlike formal grammars and automata theories, where transition functions that enable a move from the current state to another state are as important. Along with AI research, this chapter abstracts out our concern – local ambiguity – and concentrates on the issue of how the actual search paths can be chosen, assuming the mechanisms of tree updates. The only, albeit major, difference is that a search graph is *segmented* into words, to reflect the incremental nature of DS. Figure 7.1 shows a sample graph for a *single word.*

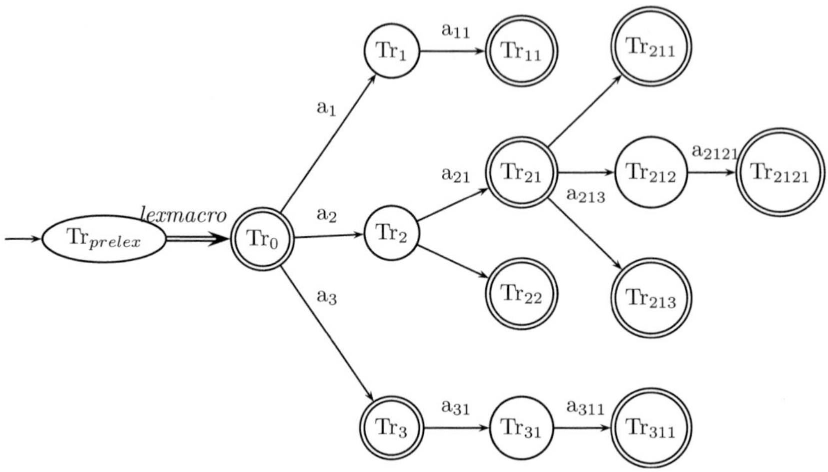

FIGURE 7.1 A state search graph for a single word

The 'start' state, on the far left, is marked with an 'incoming' arrow on its left side, following the notational convention in automata theory, named 'Tr$_{prelex}$', as it is the state before processing a word. The 'parse' starts with the input of a word (SCANNING), which triggers the set of lexical actions (lexical macro), here represented with a double-line arrow, registered in the lexicon for the input word. A lexical macro is scanned and processed *serially*, i.e. one action after another without intervention as specified in the macro, updating a single tree into another single tree, namely without ramification. After the macro, the tree (Tr$_0$) is further updated (or 'grows'), but this time via potentially multiple applicable computational actions, represented here as labels on the edges as 'a$_n$', into several trees (Tr$_1$-Tr$_3$ in our figure). Each of the resultant states goes through the same process, with the results of each state again, and so on. Computational actions are then repeatedly applied until there are no further applicable actions, reaching the *tail* states of the paths (Tr_{11}, Tr_{211}, Tr_{2121}, Tr_{213}, Tr_{22}, and Tr_{311} in the figure), marking the end of the parse of a word.

The states notated with double-line circles represent goal states, though we call them *subgoals* instead, as they are 'provisional' ones in the sense that they can be further updated with subsequent inputs. The conditions for a state to be a subgoal need to be independently defined. Intuitively, a subgoal is a 'viable' state, which represents a distinct interpretation and can be followed up by the next input word, though I refrain here from fleshing this out in a formal definition, which would be theory-dependent. Thus the subgoals reached by parsing a word may now become the start states in the next input. Although we assume here all the tail states are subgoals,[6] it is important to note that not all subgoals are tail states, as exemplified in our figure by Tr_{21} and Tr_3. The computational action of MERGE is a case in point. For example, in the parsing of the string *Rain, Tom expects*, at the end of this three-word sequence, merging of the unfixed node annotated by *Rain* with the object node of *expect* might occur. But at this stage there is uncertainty. The string maybe *Rain Tom expects she hates*, and then merge should take place later for this path. The sentence might even go further on, ending up *Rain Tom expects she hates the consequences of*, and so on. In short, MERGE appears to be an "optional" action, which the parser may decide either to take or not to take. For the case in which it is not taken (yet), as in *Rain Tom expects she hates...*, it is necessary to mark a state before MERGE as a subgoal despite the fact that it is not a tail state, as it can be continued by the following word, or put another way, be a start state in the parse of the following word.

Crucially, each diversion (branching out) with different computational actions is a source of (structural) local ambiguity, as computational actions, which 'update' trees, are to DS what "syntax" is to the standard linguistic theories and have a direct bearing on the resultant structures. Thus each branching-out adds to the number of readings by the number of branches, each of which will reach at least one subgoal (a local interpretation). Thus there are at least as many (local) readings as the number of paths, and potentially more, since an intermediate state may be a subgoal.

When a further word is scanned, essentially the same process is repeated, with every subgoal in the parsing of the preceding word being potentially a start state for this incoming word. Only potentially, as

[6]This represents the assumption that no computational action would produce a wasteful path, though there is no a priori reason why this should be the case.

some subgoals may not be continued by the next word input: only those that are applicable for the lexical actions of that word (i.e. those that satisfy the IF condition of the lexical macro) are followed by a further set of paths. Thus a graph is cumulatively expanded at each word input, comprising a large single graph as a whole and propelling the parse forward. The parse then ends when any of the subgoals for the last input satisfies the condition of being a *complete* tree, i.e. one where all the requirements have been satisfied.[7] Such a subset of subgoals are solutions, or we may call them *final goals*, of the parse. There may be more than one final goal in a parse, which represents the case of global ambiguity.

Consider Figure 7.2 on page 219, for how the parse paths of an actual sentence pan out, with the example of *Rain Tom expects.* To avoid clutter, we pretend in this graph that there was no lexical ambiguity and assume *rain* to be exclusively a noun and *expects* to subcategorise only for an object NP (not a CP). As we do not consider lexical idiosyncrasies here, the graph would therefore generalize to any string sequence of mass noun – proper noun – transitive verb. First, notice that DS may require a rather large search space during a parse, as is the case with the parse up to *Rain Tom*, due to its strongly predictive nature. All the subgoals nevertheless represent viable local readings, as the indicated 'possible' eventual sentences on the graph show. The degree of a search space expansion, however, very much depends on the input word. If the second input was a finite verb, say *came* instead, only one subgoal (i.e. the top one) would be continued with further paths. Thus, at any word transition point, the number of paths can either be radically expanded or reduced. A radical reduction of paths is in fact observed at the third and last word input ('*expect*') in our example. The graph representation makes clear the property of DS that there are a potentially large number of paths (local interpretations) during the parse, most of which do not lead to a solution (global interpretation).

The parse segment for the last word '*expects*' in the figure shows an example of subgoals not being tail states and further continued, with slightly different graphic effects from the preceding general case figure, aligning all the subgoals on the right end, to make it clear that they can all be continued with some following word (if any). The top path in this segment represents the local relative clause reading that corresponds to '*Rain which Tom expects...*'. Its top subgoal, where the Merge

[7] And also, the last input word must be the last word of a sentence.

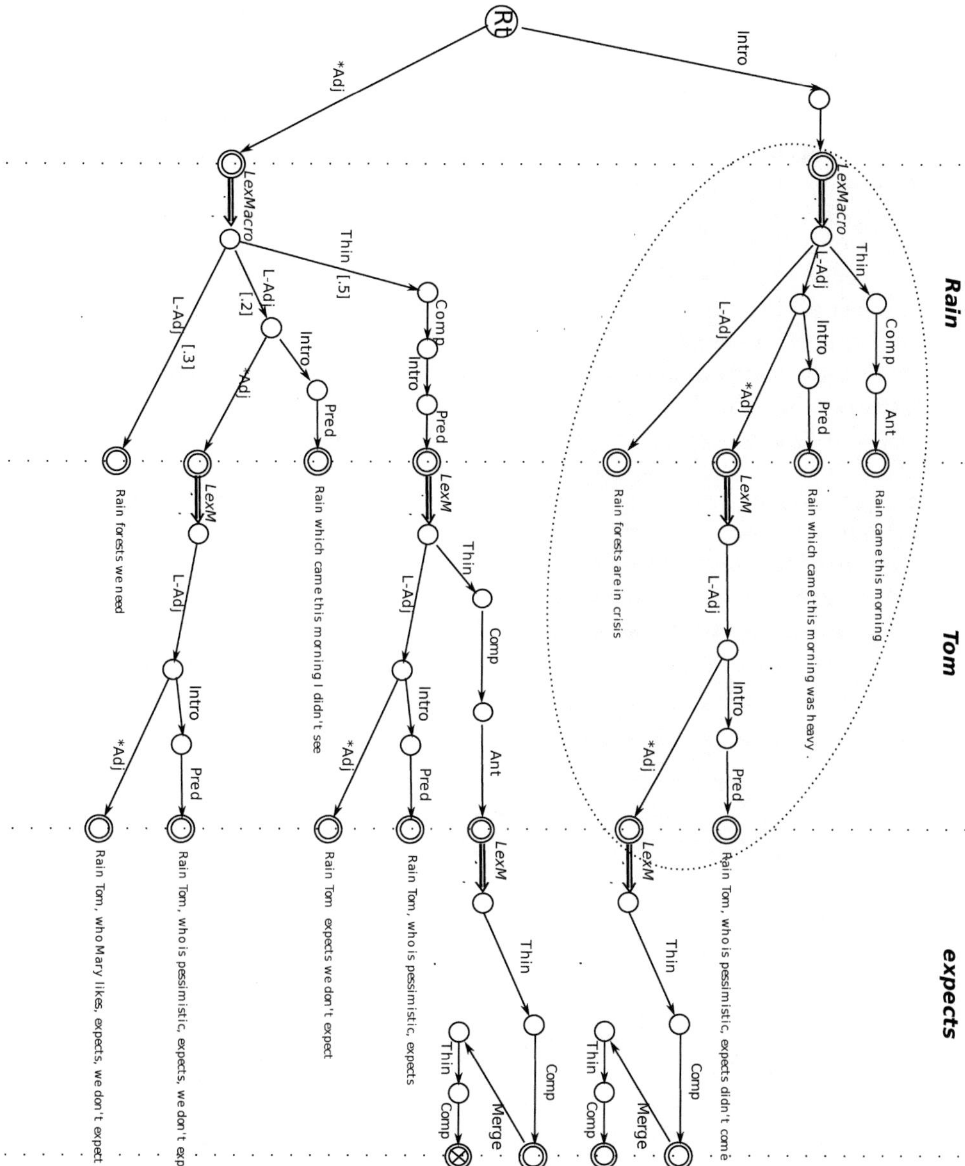

FIGURE 7.2 An example cumulative graph for '*Rain Tom expects*'

action has not been taken, may be continued with (*Rain Tom expects*) *the consequence of...*(still continues), for example, while the second, post-Merge subgoal would be continued with the matrix verb, as in (*Rain Tom expects*) *will not come.* As it turns out, however, this is not a relative clause but topicalization, therefore the path below is the successful one. Among the subgoals for that path, one corresponds to the case where the Merge operation is skipped and there is further input e.g. *Rain Tom expects the consequence of* (full stop). The other one is for the case where the Merge action is taken and parsing is completed there and then. This state is also marked with X, to indicate that it is a final goal.

The main advantage of such a representation is that it connects parsing models with the rich resources of search strategies developed in AI, whose computational properties such as completeness and efficiency are also well established.[8] Further, a major added bonus will be that the psycholinguistic findings in terms of parsing strategies can now find procedural representation as a search. Take for example the circled two-word portion of the parse in Fig 7.2, reproduced below with an enumerator for each state with some simplification (no action labels, etc., also without subgoal alignment). We take the state 22112, with the short arrow on the right hand side, to be the goal, as it is the one that is eventually followed up:

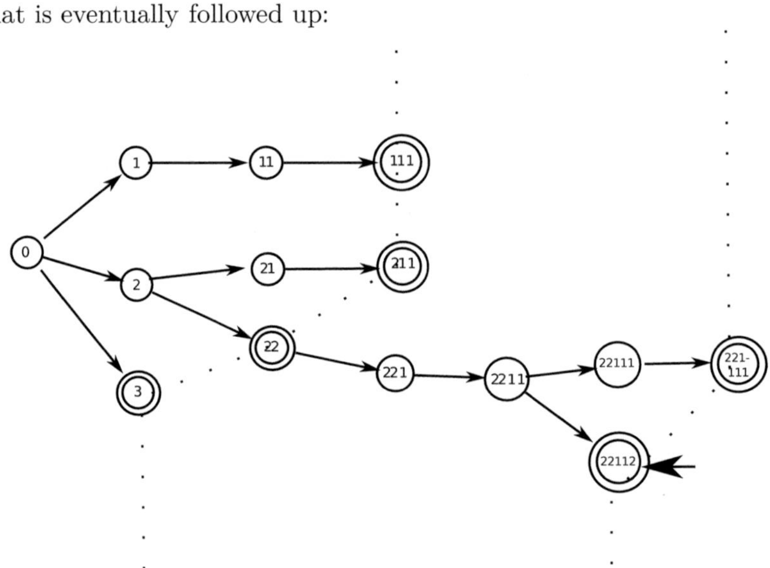

[8]See an AI textbook, e.g. Russell and Norvig (2003), for such established results.

For example, the simple (uninformed) depth-first search with backtracking would trace the following traversal, where only a single path is pursued at a time:

0→ 1→ 11→ 111→ 0(backtrack)→2 →21 → 211→ 2(backtrack) →22 →221→ 2211→22111 →221111 →2211(backtrack) →22112(Goal) (→0 (backtrack) →3)

and this corresponds to the deterministic parsing which psycholinguists generally invoke in some form to account for the garden path phenomena. When a graph diverges in local ambiguity and the chosen path reaches a dead end, e.g. at the state 111, the parser will have to backtrack and continue. Thus it may take a large number of steps (time complexity) in the worst case, if you are not lucky, but the advantage of this search is that it requires relatively little memory (space complexity) as in backtracking the memory can be emptied, and it does reach the goal quickly if you are lucky.

Alternatively, one certainly could implement the simple breadth-first search instead, which would proceed, for the same example, in the following order:

0→ 1→ 2→ 3→ 11→21 →22 → 111→ 211 →221 →2211→22111 →22112(Goal)

An implication of such a search will be that the parser would be free from garden paths altogether, while being imposed a relatively large memory load, as all the visited states for a path need to kept in memory until it reaches its tail state. Thus this is not quite the way online processing appears to work (particularly in terms of DS actions, as it seems very implausible that actions for different paths are taken in parallel on the sublexical level), but implementations in memory-rich computers do employ bread-first approaches in *chart parsing*, which records all the intermediate results during parsing.

A more important point here is that the strategy modeler is allowed to 'pick and mix' any strategies between these two extremes. A more sensible model that mixes both strategies, for example, is an *iterative deepening* strategy, where the frontier is always expanded by one depth (to what is generally called 'fringe' in AI literature, the set of immediately following states) before deepening. Taking the same example, the start state (0) is first expanded to its fringe, 1, 2 and 3 in a breadth-first manner, but except the first depth each path is serially searched in a depth-first manner:

0→ 1→2 →3 →11 →111 →21 →22 →211 →221 →2211 →22111 →221111 →221112(Goal).

Now in the above simulation, we just apply each strategy from top to bottom when there is a path diversion, but, being an uninformed search, this order is entirely coincidental. Consider the following 'mirror image' graph, which is equivalent to the original one, the lowest branch becoming the highest, and so on.

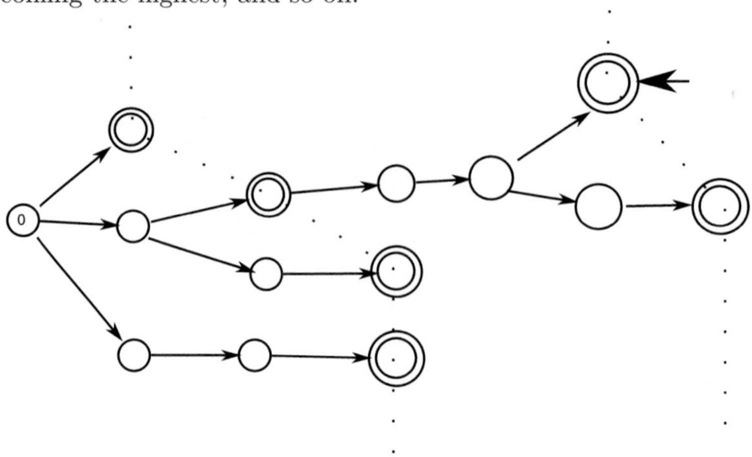

While in the original graph the breadth-first search happens to reach the goal more quickly than the depth-first counterpart, the depth-first wins over in this graph.

The best-first approach, which we saw in section 7.2.1, is introduced primarily to overcome the limitation of this accidental nature of uninformed search, by selecting the order of paths to pursue, or kill some unlikely paths off ('pruning', as in *beam search* to be briefly described in 7.4.2). A best-first search usually relies on some heuristic function when faced with branching to determine the order of preference amongst the fringe (following) states. Best-first strategies can be straightforwardly incorporated by annotating edges in a graph, as we will see in the next section.

Furthermore, a strength specific to DS, also made clear in this representation, is that a search strategy can be modelled for the processing of any portion of a sentence, as the graph will be segmented into each input word. Therefore, it is also made possible to dynamically implement different strategies, switching from one to another even mid-sentence for example. One can even focus on a sub-part of the processing of a single word (say, the phase in the parsing of a word after its lexical macro). Thus numerous possible combinations of different parameters open up, not just depth/breadth-first, deterministic/non-deterministic or uninformed/heuristic oppositions, since each pair can be mixed in various ways. Thus the graph representation, which makes explicit the fact that DS predictively indicates the possible paths early on, provides the parsing strategist with many possible choice points to implement flexibly various strategies. Given the likelihood that humans resort to more than one type of strategy, this is also of general benefit to psycholinguists.

7.4 DS graph and best-first search models

7.4.1 NLP: PCFG and its descendants

One of the possible applications of the graph representation of DS parsing is to Probabilistic Context Free Grammar (PCFG), widely adopted as the basis for parsing engines in NLP applications. The two formalisms, DS and PCFG, though very different in generative capacity and motivation, share an important feature: a mechanism that can be used for dynamic path selection for parsing. For this purpose, PCFG introduces probability weights for the production rules that share the LHS symbol. Suppose for example that there were three (and only three) production rules for NP, the figures in each square bracket indicating their probabilities:[9]

(7.9) An example of PCFG fragment
NP→ (Det,) Noun [.5]
NP→ (Det,) Noun, S [.2]
NP→ (Det,) Noun, Noun [.3]

This set roughly corresponds to the structural predictions triggered at the input of a word contributing content of type *e* in DS (with the proviso that, in DS, characterizations such as NP, Det, Noun etc. correspond to semantic types). All one needs to do to make DS parsing, presented as a graph, function like a PCFG is to weight the relevant edges with applicable probabilities (see the '*Rain*' portion in the second major branch in figure 7.2 for example probability annotations). In DS terms, multiple structural predictions from a given type form edges that can be weighted. Although PCFG itself does not dictate any search strategy, the implication – and the practical usage – is that the weights are to be used to prioritize the paths, e.g. the parse proceeds according to the weights' (descending) order. Whenever some local ambiguity (branching-out in the graph) arises, one could be led to the branch with the highest probability first, the second highest second, and so on,

[9]This is certainly a linguistically inadequate oversimplification, and at the very least a recursive intermediate category ('nominal') should be invoked, e.g. Nom→ Noun; Nom→ Noun Nom. This correctness is glossed over for simplicity of presentation (in light of the following discussion of lexicalization in particular).

in a best-first manner.

PCFG in this simplest of versions has been further developed by NLP practitioners into more sophisticated sub-varieties, in response to its inadequacy due to not being sensitive to the context in which the RHS constituents occur. The probability of a particular noun, for example *rain* as in figure 7.2, appearing in the third rule above (i.e. followed by another noun), may be discovered to be less frequent than, say, the noun *evening*, with its capability to modify anything that could take place in the evening (evening class, evening meal, evening party etc.). Thus the probabilities could be adjusted as below, given some corpus that substantiates the adjustments:

(7.10) An example of LPCFG fragment

NP→ (Det,) rain [.7]	NP→ (Det,) evening [.45]
NP→ (Det,) rain, S [.1]	NP→ (Det,) evening, S [.1]
NP→ (Det,) rain, Noun [.2]	NP→ (Det,) evening, Noun [.45]

This exemplifies the technique of *lexicalization* in the probabilistic parsing, and a *lexicalized PCFG* (LPCFG) has become the de facto standard for probabilistic parsing (Black et al. 1993).

It is straightforward to model a PCFG or an LPCFG over a DS graph. For our PCFG fragment, one can simply annotate the edges from any type e tree with the corresponding probabilities, while for our LPCFG fragment one would annotate the edges from a particular lexical item, *rain* or *evening*, with their corresponding probabilities (figure 7.2 is annotated for PCFG).

Lastly, but potentially most importantly, although PCFG was not originally conceived for incremental parsing, there have been attempts to render probabilistic parsing more amenable to incrementality, precisely by using the standard graph search techniques. These attempts generally invoke a *dynamic programming* approach (Bellman 1957) in which to 'guess' the most probable parse. They range from the use of classical algorithms such as Dijkstra (Dijkstra 1959) and Viterbi (Viterbi 1967) search, through variants of forward-backward algorithms which indeed use predicted paths (known as *inside-outside* algorithms, proposed in Baker 1979 and extensively used by Charniak 1997), to more elaborate A* variants (Klein and Manning 2003). These proposals essentially rely on some reasonable decision mechanisms at choice points where there are multiple predictions, and are capable of being incorporated into the graph representation of DS.

7.4.2 Psycholinguistics: Gibson's complexity metric

Memory cost of SPLT

As an example of a 'heuristic' best-first search strategy that is proposed for human online parsing and can be suitably modelled on the graph representation of DS, we take up Gibson's *Syntactic Prediction Locality Theory* (SPLT), an influential psycholinguistic theory of sentence processing that provides a *complexity metric* based on syntactic predictions (Gibson et al. 1994; Gibson 1998). Gibson's fundamental assumption is that the strategy taken by humans for parsing is one of *ranked parallel processing*. Roughly speaking, this amounts to the claim that the possible readings in the face of local ambiguity are retained in parallel in memory, but are ranked with their respective levels of activation.

What determines this ranking is the *complexity metric*, an indicator of processing difficulty, calculated with two measures in SPLT, viz., *memory cost* and *integration cost*. We focus on memory cost in this chapter, as it relates to structural predictions and constitutes a connection to DS. Memory cost is essentially determined by the number of 'unresolved nodes', i.e. the ones that dominate uninstantiated nodes, of the predicted structures, although the nodes of the matrix clause – always predicted – do not count towards the total unit (assumed to be zero). Consider again our first example of sentence-initial *Cotton clothing*, partially reproduced below, one also quoted by Gibson et al. (1994):

(7.11) *Cotton clothing is comfortable to wear.*

(7.12) *Cotton clothing is mostly woven from in this region.*

(7.13) *Cotton clothing is made of grows in Mississippi.*

The memory units (the basis for memory cost) for example (7.11) amount to zero, as the only unresolved node is the matrix VP node, while example (7.12) amounts to 1 and example (7.13) to 2, because discounting the matrix nodes, the VP node of the lower S is the only unresolved node for Example (7.12), and the lower S as well as the lower VP nodes are unresolved for (7.13). The number of unresolved nodes for each reading can be clearly seen in the standard tree representation, as shown in (7.14), where (a), (b) and (c) correspond to (7.11), (7.12) and (7.13) respectively, and the unresolved nodes are marked with '?'. 2 units is regarded as a threshold beyond which a structure would no longer be kept in the working memory, accounting for the garden path effect of (7.13).[10]

---

[10]Integration cost, on the other hand, concerns incorporation of a later input to

(7.14) Unresolved nodes in three local readings of *Cotton clothing*

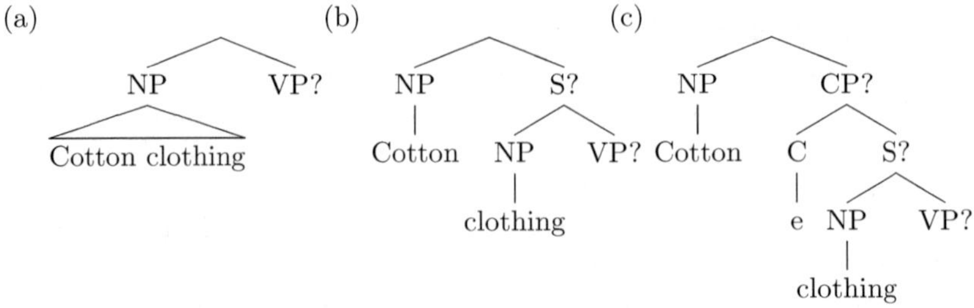

However, while Gibson elaborates on how the metric is computed (i.e. how the preference is determined) for local readings in detail, the discussion of *how* each reading is searched, particularly how deep a pursuit of one reading will go (deterministic or breadth-first) is largely absent, except the statement that it is conducted in the manner of ranked parallel processing. Here the graph notation can help to illustrate various possible strategies, and we will see in the next section one possibility that Gibson may have in mind, the *beam search*, with his emphasis on 'parallel' and 'activation level threshold' (ibid:p.10). This roughly corresponds to the breadth-first search, but with pruning. In the beam search, the parser first 'probes the fringe' as we saw in 7.2.1 for the iterative deepening strategy, and then eliminates the unlikelier states below a certain threshold. Beam search is favoured also by other psycholinguists, as it does not require much memory, while remaining essentially breadth-first (parallel).[11] We will see in the next section that SPLT's memory cost metric, as well as its related search strategy, can be explicitly represented on the DS graph.

---

some previously predicted but unresolved node, and is mainly determined by the 'distance' – i.e. the number of intevening 'discourse referents' – between the points where a structure is predicted and where that prediction is borne out with an input. This metric may thus account for the processing difficulty contrast in cases where the memory costs are the same, e.g. adverbial attachment ambiguity (as in '*Jim said Tom would come today*'). Although this metric could certainly be incorporated into the graph representation, this will require a bookkeeping of the number of (some of the) states on a single path.

[11] Jurafsky (1996) explicitly argues for this strategy as a better account of garden path phenomena than the traditional backtracking-based account (Frazier 1987).

Connecting DS with SPLT via search strategy

(7.15) DS trees for local readings of *Cotton clothing*

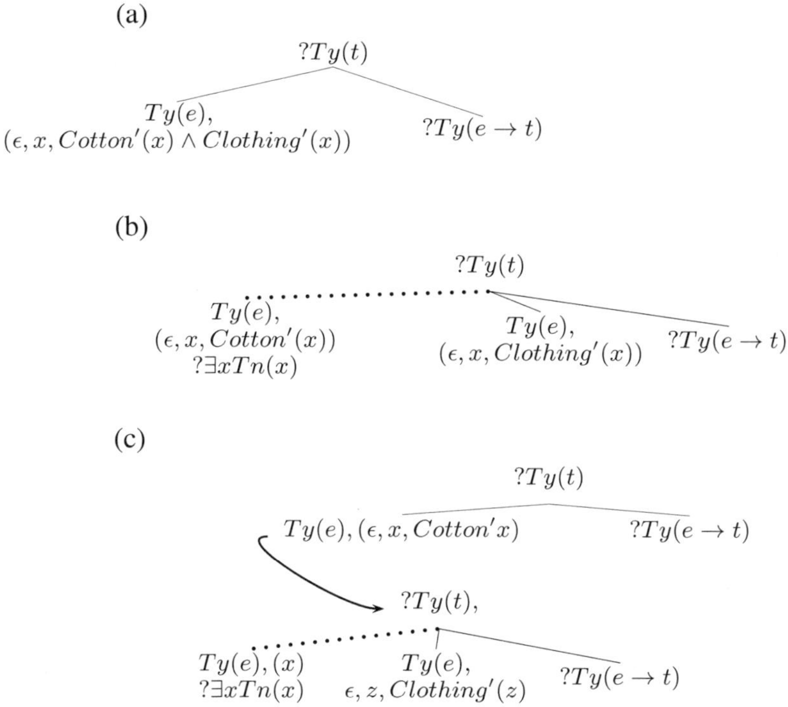

Now, DS has a natural correlate to the unresolved nodes that count towards SPLT's memory cost: outstanding *requirements*. Consider the local readings of *Cotton clothing* again, the DS tree representation of which is shown in (7.15), where the requirements are represented, as standard, with '?'. The requirements that would count towards the cost are underlined in this figure. Compare these with those in (7.14). The 'unresolved' VP node found in all the trees in this figure corresponds to the $?Ty(e \rightarrow t)$ node in the DS trees, while the unresolved CP node in (c) to the lower (LINKed) $?Ty(t)$ node (shown via an arrow link) in the same-numbered DS tree. The remaining 'S' node in (7.14b) – one with a trace or gap – receives a different treatment in DS. Since DS does not represent long-distance dependencies through distinct structural options but through the option of introducing *unfixed nodes* (displayed with a dotted line) the equivalent memory unit for S? in (7.14b) is the requirement for a fixed tree-position $?\exists x Tn(x)$, i.e. that the node should be 'merged' eventually in some lower node of the local tree.

Also notice that there are requirements that are not part of SPLT, and these are the strongly predicted ones. The top $Ty(t)$ node of each tree is not registered as an unresolved node as in SPLT. Neither is the lower type $Ty(e \rightarrow t)$ node in (c), which is strongly predicted to come as a result of the series of actions triggered by LINK ADJUNCTION, namely INTRODUCTION and PREDICTION. In fact, this is not the only prediction DS makes after LINK ADJUNCTION, since *ADJUNCTION is also applicable for the eventuality of another extraction which would constitute an even harder centre-embedding case than the ones being considered, as in *Cotton clothing shops buy is made of grows in Mississippi.* Another set of strongly predicted readings that starts with *ADJUNCTION, which would correspond to the cases where the compound NP as a whole is extracted, have also been left out, as in, for example, *Cotton clothing is made of the farmer grows in Mississippi.* The predictive power of DS is stronger than SPLT, whose 'unresolved nodes' are only a subset of DS predictions. We will include these readings in the next figure, which is the DS graph of *Cotton clothing.*

Let us now see the DS predictions on a graph. Figure 7.3 on page 229 shows the possible state transitions on a DS graph (where we omit the actions irrelevant to the metric in discussion). We identify a state in a grid style, using a combination of a numeral (corresponding to the word count so far in a string, indicated at the top) and a lowercase roman letter (indicated beside the state), i.e. *0a* and *0b* for the two states immediately after the root, *1a*, *1b*, ... *1h*, and so on. As has just been stated, one will first notice that there are significantly more local readings predicted than the ones in SPLT. The number of unresolved nodes for each local reading is represented by the number at its state (inside the circle). The eventual memory cost metric value will be obtained by deducting one (for the matrix $?Ty(e \rightarrow t)$, only one instance of which exists for each path after it is predicted). Generally speaking, *ADJUNCTION and LINK ADJUNCTION that require a new $Ty(t)$ node increase the number by one. Two comments are in order. First, in this representation it is clear at which point one would add such a metric value and hence which operation is exactly responsible for such an increase. Second, it should also be clear – see the broad array of possible structures at the end of *cotton clothing* – that there are more options available of state transitions (edges) one can assign such a value to. This is because (a) there are more paths predicted due to the strong predictivity of DS, and (b) there can be multiple transitions inside the stretch of processing a single word, with intra-lexical non-tail states.

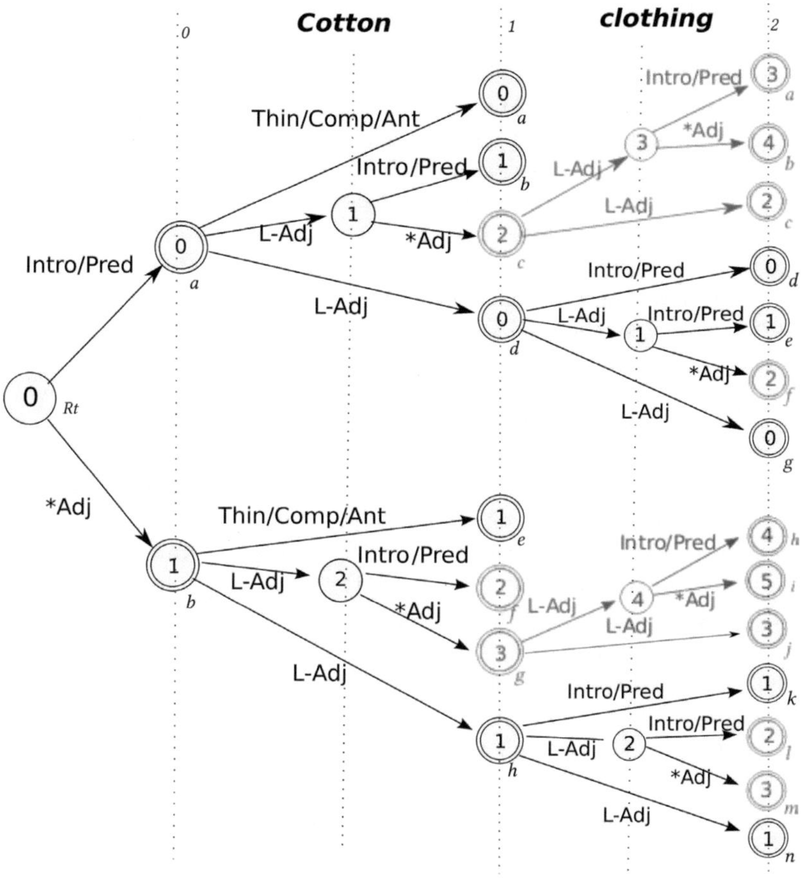

Examples:

2a.	Cotton clothing is made of grows in Mississippi.	*2h.*	Cotton clothing is made of the farmer grows in Mississipi.
2b.	Cotton clothing shops buy is made of grows in Mississippi.	*2i.*	Cotton clothing shops buy is made of grows in Mississippi.
2c.	Cotton clothing shops buy grows in Mississippi.	*2j.*	Cotton clothing wholesalers buy shops then buy.
2d.	Cotton clothing is comfortable to wear.	*2k.*	Cotton clothing is woven from in this region.
2e.	Cotton clothing which is comfortable grows in Mississippi.	*2l.*	Cotton clothing which is comfortable the farmer grows in Mississippi.
2f.	Cotton clothing Tom likes grows in Mississippi.	*2m.*	Cotton clothing Tom likes Jim likes too.
2g.	Cotton clothing shops are in the street.	*2n.*	Cotton clothing shops Tom likes.

FIGURE 7.3 Beam search of SPLT on DS graph

The second point illuminates the difference between DS's strong predictivity and the only weakly predictive theories like SPLT. Many tail states after *cotton clothing* are strongly predicted structures, with various memory cost units. Half ot these tail states are in fact strongly and not weakly predicted (i.e. *2b, 2c, 2e, 2f, 2i, 2j, 2l* and *2m*) at this point, as well as half of the tail states after *cotton* at this point (*1b, 1c, 1f* and *1g*), offering the opportunity to deal with them at each point. To predict a structure of which you have not even seen any part of may sound rather too strong, but at least predicting strongly a relative clause to come as opposed to a modified nominal or matrix verb could be perfectly feasible in actual spoken utterances, since there can be a prosodic difference (see e.g. Kiaer, this volume).

Turning our attention to the search strategy, let us now describe the state traversal of the beam search. To avoid complication we will not consider the non-tail states. One will start from the root, and next probe the fringe, that is, going to *0a* and *0b*. We calculate their metric values, found to be 0 and 1. Let us here set the threshold for pruning to 2. Neither state reaches this threshold, so we keep both. Then we repeat the procedure for each state, and find, for the fringe (omitting the intra-lexical state) of *0a*, *1c* to reach the threshold. The paths from this state onward therefore are pruned and not pursued. The pruned paths, including the states from which they are to be pruned, are greyed out in the figure. Below we display a transition, where the stage at which paths are eliminated is marked with '*'.

0a→ *0b*→ *1a*→ *1b*→ *1c**→ *1d*→ *1e*→ *1f**→ *1g**→ *1h*→ *2d*→ *2e*→ *2f**→ *2g*→ *2k*→ *2l** → *2m** → *2n*

Note that this is only an example, on the assumption that the parallel ranked processing goes in the beam search manner, but it should be clear that any search strategy could be superimposed and any heuristic function could be implemented on a DS graph, as long as the former is within DS's broad restrictions and one can find the correlate in the DS actions. Thus, DS, represented in a graph, can clarify what exact strategy is meant by a psycholinguistic processing theory. In some cases it may be trickier to find correlate DS actions that correspond to heuristic functions since, as we have just seen, it would not be generally likely to find a one-to-one mapping. Nevertheless, even if there is a discrepancy between DS and the target theory, the endeavour to find the meeting point could be mutually beneficial, in the sense that they could be reshaping each other's formulations.

Relationship of DS with processing theories

Before reaching a conclusion, I would like to mention one caveat, by dispelling one possible misunderstanding about DS's relationships with processing-oriented algorithmic theories such as the ones we have just seen. That is, I have not been arguing for some 'equivalence' in any sense between DS and processing algorithms, but only for the applicability of combining DS with most of such algorithms. DS is not tied to any specific processing algorithm but generally is *inclusive* of many particular algorithms, containing all the paths over which they can be deployed.

For example, the strong predictivity of DS is in contrast with, but entails (though is not entailed by), the 'weak' predictivity of SPLT. It was noted that with our *Cotton clothing* example, it is only when both words have been encountered that various predictions are triggered in SPLT, while these predictions have already been in place in DS only with the first word processed. But this fact does not prevent DS from being applied to SPLT, since the latter can be characterized *inside* the former. At the second word instantiation stage, the applicable paths are already there anyhow. DS is a general formalism that shows the class of all the possible parsing paths, and SPLT, or any other processing theory, concerns a subclass, the actual parsing paths usually strategically selected. This contrast – the inclusive nature of DS as a general theory and the particularity of processing algorithms modelled over it – cannot be emphasized enough to avoid confusion.

Looking from the reverse angle, another accompanying caveat would be that the computational properties of DS in the general (i.e. worst) case and those of an algorithm implementable on DS are two entirely different issues. I have generally confined myself to the latter algorithmic issue, though the former general issue is equally important not only in its own right but also in relation to the latter issue, for if, for example, the complexity of a general recognition problem is identified, this determines the upper bound of algorithmic complexities.[12] Given the strong interest in processing issues, I see no reason why they should not be pursued independently of the general recognition problem, but at the same time, we should not be misled to think that the results in processing algorithms have a direct bearing on the DS formalism in general.

---

[12]See Talman (2005) for formal grammar theoretic results for a subset of DS. For general discussion on the relationship between algorithmic and general complexities, see Barton et al. (1988).

7.5 Conclusion

In this chapter we have seen the DS formulation from a perspective different from the standard one in order to draw out its potential use as a formalism for actual search strategies in parsing, particularly when faced with local ambiguity. While the usual tree-update illustration only focuses on a single, ultimately successful path, we have seen here how the actual description can be presented in such a way as to also cover the eventually unsuccessful paths in a graph representation capturing the 'whole picture' of DS parsing. From this perspective several features of DS have become obvious. Even though DS is a *bona fide* grammar, it both predicts and facilitates specific parsing strategies and methods. Thus, parsing compatible with DS has been characterized as 'strongly' predictive given the top-down control included in the DS architecture. With bottom-up support also in place, given in the formulation of lexical actions, it has been argued, DS provides for various search strategies, particularly best-first strategies based on predictions, as its expanding paths provide many choice points where the parsing modeler can intervene. To make this characteristic explicit, the state graph representation has been proposed, where one could demonstrate how parsing proceeds in various search strategies in an intuitive manner.

Further research is required to illuminate the proposed interaction of DS and processing-oriented methods. For example, although we have been emphasizing as a benefit for DS the fact that the state search paths are made explicit, the question still remains as to whether there is a firm consensus in what constitutes a state. We have been assuming that any update in a tree would form a new state, but this is not necessarily a widely accepted assumption in computer science and psycholinguistics. In automata theory, for example, the serial operations that are always executed in sequence tend to be merged into a single function while the DS notion of computational actions operating under the trigger of a single word would be unfamiliar in psycholinguistics. However, such a consensus about statehood is an empirical issue and DS provides the ground for deciding among the alternatives. Given that DS is a grammar in which the procedural steps proposed by sentence processing theories can be modeled precisely, it is hoped that it can provide an apparatus that potentially offers a bridge between formal grammatical work, psycholinguistic theories and empirical and computational sciences.

References

The following were cited in this chapter: Aho et al. (1975), Baker (1979), Barton et al.(1988), Bellman (1957), Black et al. (1993), Booth (1969), Cann et al. (2005), Charniak (1997), Collins (1999), Dijkstra (1959), Earley (1970), Frazier (1987), Gibson (1998), Gibson et al. (1994), Hale (2001), Hickok (1993), Huang (2008), Jurafsky (1996), Kempson et al. (2001), Kempson et al. (2009a), Klein and Manning (2003), Manning and Schütze (1999), Marcus (1980), Roark (2001), Russell and Norvig (2003), Talman (2005), Vasishth and Lewis (2006), Viterbi (1967). See references at end of book for full information.

Part II

New departures

8

Conditionals in Dynamic Syntax

ELENI GREGOROMICHELAKI

8.1 Introduction

The purpose of this chapter* is to propose a general framework for the processing of expressions whose interpretation involves quantification over entities commonly referred to as *situations* or *eventualities* through an account based on the formal apparatus defined in the framework of *Dynamic Syntax* (DS; Kempson et al. 2001; Cann et al. 2005). As a case study we examine *conditionals*, a construction whose semantics involves a concept central to cognition and action but whose linguistic expression has baffled researchers for long time:

> "Conditionals involve virtually every problem - logical or linguistic, descriptive or theoretical - that has ever been raised"
> (Smith and Smith 1988: 350).

Given this widely noted complexity (see also von Fintel, to appear) it seems worthwhile to examine conditionals from the innovative analytic perspective suggested by DS, a formalism which approaches linguistic phenomena from the point of view of the processing mechanisms.

According to DS, since parsing (and production) are arguably conducted incrementally in successive stages, their modelling necessitates the characterization of the partiality of information available at each stage and the formulation of time-linear constraints that define the alternatives open for further processing. These features of DS are taken to provide explanations of the syntactic properties of natural language

*I am very grateful to Ruth Kempson for invaluable comments and suggestions. Many thanks also to Ronnie Cann, Gregory Mills, Gunnar Björnsson and Lutz Marten. The work was supported by ESRC RES-062-23-0962 (DynDial).

The Dynamics of Lexical Interfaces.
Ruth Kempson, Eleni Gregoromichelaki and Christine Howes (eds.).

(NL) expressions. In addition, the radical context dependence of NL processing suggests that the linguistic/grammatical specification of words or structures, which significantly under-specify their eventual interpretation, must include specified parameters that are resolved by reference to the general context. In the domain of conditionals where inherent vagueness and context dependence of interpretation has been noted by various researchers, the methodology then suggested by the DS perspective is to attempt to resolve the puzzles by defining unitary lexical/structural specifications which in combination with available processing strategies integrate both the contribution of the context of processing and the time-linearity of the available information at each stage. Therefore, our challenge here is to identify a suitably underspecified encoded content for *if*-clauses which can then be enriched either by input from its context of occurrence or in accordance with its time-linear presentation in order to provide the requisite interpretations, as well as, in parallel, explanations of the syntactic properties of such structures.

8.2 Dynamic Syntax

DS is a model of how interpretation is built up incrementally. Crucially, the output of any processing task is a representation of the content of a discourse uttered in a particular context (not a representation of some hierarchical structure defined over a string, i.e., not a *sentence type* abstracted out of various contexts). On this view, NL "syntax" is conceived of as the *process* by which semantic representations are dynamically constructed. Since pragmatics may interact at any point with the online interpretation process, output semantic representations (formulae) for the same string may differ as it is uttered in different contexts. Formally, DS is a lexicalized grammar using labeled word sequences and trees: the sequences are time-linearly presented strings of words with accompanying phonological, morphological and word-boundary specification; the trees formalize the semantic, functor-argument structure induced from utterances of such sequences in the form of (unordered) trees labeled by terms of a typed lambda calculus and other process-control labels. The basis of the formal characterization is the (modal) logic of finite trees (LOFT: Blackburn and Meyer-Viol 1994) which permits addressing any node in the tree from the perspective of any other node using the *immediate-dominance* modalities $\langle\downarrow\rangle$ and $\langle\uparrow\rangle$ and variations over these. Such operators can be used to indicate nodes that exist already in the tree (e.g. $\langle\downarrow\rangle\alpha$ indicates that there is a daughter of the current node annotated with label α), with variants distinguishing

$\downarrow_0/\downarrow_1$ as argument/functor daughter respectively, and Kleene * operations over these to define general, less specified, *dominance* relations. The parsing process is driven relative to the imposition and subsequent satisfaction of requirements: $?X$ for any annotation X on a node constitutes a constraint on how the subsequent parsing steps must progress, i.e. X must be derived (eventually). Terms of only a small, fixed set of semantic types are used (defined as the domain D_{Ty}), so no new types (functions) can be constructed. The main requirement is $?Ty(t)$, the type requirement to produce a formula of proposition type (t) from the word string; imposition of such requirements for other types, e.g., $?Ty(e)$, $?Ty(e \rightarrow t)$ impose constraints on tree development that formulae of the relevant types must be provided by the end of the parsing process. Such requirements may also be modal, e.g. while a decoration $?Ty(e)$ requires a term to be constructed at the current node, $?\langle\downarrow\rangle Ty(e)$ requires a daughter node to be so decorated. Consider in (8.1) a sketch of the general process of parsing as the induction of a sequence of partial trees, whose input is a one-node tree annotated with only the requirement $?Ty(t)$ and a pointer, $\diamondsuit$, indicating the node under development (the *Axiom*). The output is a binary branching tree whose nodes reflect the content of some propositional formula:[1]

(8.1) John upset Mary:

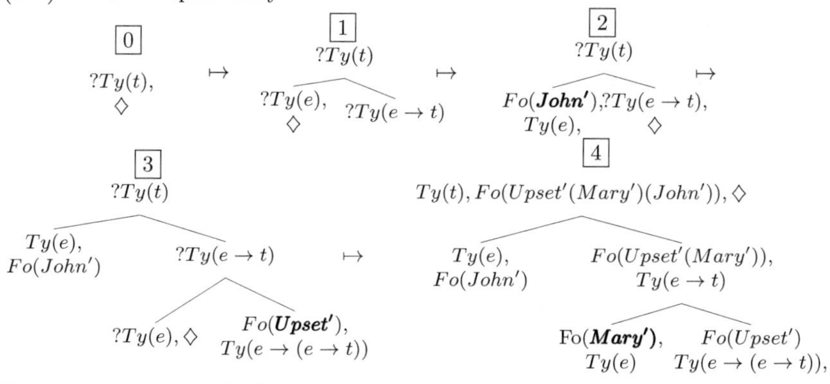

Processing proceeds by the execution of licensed *actions* that map one partial tree to another. These are defined in a language involving such commands as $\texttt{make}(\langle\downarrow\rangle)$, $\texttt{go}(\langle\downarrow\rangle)$, $\texttt{put}(\alpha)$, $\texttt{make}(\langle\downarrow_*\rangle)$, $\langle$IF ..., THEN ..., ELSE ...$\rangle$ etc. Sets of such actions incorporated in individual packages can be either general *computational rules* or *lexical*

[1] For purposes of illustration here we show the formulae specifications of nodes as simplified semantic terms/concepts (e.g. *John'* derived from the word *John*), i.e. we omit the details of the contribution of names and the lambda terms indicating predicates.

actions associated with words contributing content-formulae and other aspects of structure. *Computational rules* divide into two broad types: those for developing a tree-structure for which a number of strategies may be available (e.g. INTRODUCTION/PREDICTION); those annotating non-terminal nodes through algorithmic application of β-reduction and its associated type-deduction (COMPLETION, ELIMINATION). These in combination yield a resulting structure, with all nodes properly annotated and no requirements outstanding if a grammatical string has been processed.

Words are interpreted as instruction packages, including actions to construct parts of a lambda term (as values of the label Fo which takes values from a defined domain D_{Fo}) in a labeled tree representation. The packages are executed word-by-word from-left-to-right. The terminal nodes of the lambda term produced by a grammatical sentence do not necessarily stand in one-to-one correspondence with the words of the sentence as an individual word may induce sub-structure containing more than one labeled node; and there is no direct relation between the yield of the eventual tree and the sequential order of the string. For example, verbs in English are parsed when the pointer resides at a node decorated with $?Ty(e \rightarrow t)$ induced by a computational rule. The verb itself contributes not only a logical formula (e.g. $Fo(Upset'))$ but also creates a new object node and moves the pointer to this node (the transition induced is that of transition 2-3 in Figure 8.1).[2] Parsing of an NP next will then provide the appropriate formula value for this node and rules like ANTICIPATION, COMPLETION and ELIMINATION can then compositionally determine the combination of those formulae to satisfy the requirements remaining in a strictly bottom-up fashion.

The tree is incrementally constructed, but there are two ways to escape the strict linear processing order: by *structural underdetermination* and by *underdetermination of labels*; both may lead to delay in choices to be made. Structural underdetermination involves the addition of a sub-structure to the tree, an *unfixed node*, whose location in that tree is characterised as merely dominated by a previously constructed node ($\langle\uparrow_*\rangle Tn(\alpha)$) without, as yet, a fully specified hierarchical position. So, for example, in the processing of a string like *Mary, John likes* the *ADJUNCTION rule licenses the introduction of a node into the tree to accommodate the content specified by the word *Mary* that cannot yet be given a fixed location in the tree skeleton under construction. Underspecification in the labels dimension is implemented

[2]Formally: IF $?Ty(e \rightarrow t)$, THEN$\texttt{make}(\langle\downarrow_1\rangle), \texttt{go}(\langle\downarrow_1\rangle), \texttt{put}(Fo(Upset'), Ty(e \rightarrow (e \rightarrow t))), go\langle\uparrow_1\rangle, \texttt{make}(\langle\downarrow_0\rangle), \texttt{go}(\langle\downarrow_0\rangle), \texttt{put}(?Ty(e))$, ELSE ABORT.

by means of employing *meta-variables*, indicated as $Fo(\mathbf{U})$, $Fo(\mathbf{V})$, etc., as temporary labels requiring their substitution by terms from context (given constraints such as gender, person, and so on). Thus pronouns and other anaphoric elements (e.g. ellipsis sites) provide such metavariables as initial formula values which are required (through the injunction $?\exists\mathbf{x}.Fo(\mathbf{x})$) to be instantiated (through the rule of SUBSTITUTION) at some point during the parsing process.

8.2.1 Quantification and anaphora

All noun phrases, even quantified ones, project terms of type e. Quantifying expressions are analyzed in the manner of arbitrary names of predicate-logic natural deduction, as formulated in the *epsilon calculus* of Hilbert and Bernays (1939), a conservative, but more expressive, extension of predicate logic. Introduction of such terms in the language is based on the following equivalence:

$$\exists x.F(x) \equiv F(\epsilon, x.F(x))$$

This indicates that an existential statement is equivalent to one in the epsilon calculus in which a *witness* of the truth of the statement can appear as an argument of the statement's predicate. Such a witness appears as an *epsilon term* containing as its *restrictor* the predicate itself and denotes some arbitrary entity satisfying the predicate (if such an entity exists, if it doesn't, any arbitrary entity). The dual of an epsilon term is a tau-term ($\tau - term$) which is equivalent to universal quantification.

Exploiting these equivalences, in DS, such terms are compositionally constructed through the time-linear processing of determiners, which introduce the binders (below $Ty(cn \rightarrow e), \lambda P.\epsilon, P$) and common nouns which contribute the restrictor (below $Ty(cn), (x, Man'(x))$). Both combine to produce complex subtrees of $Ty(e)$ annotated with an epsilon calculus term becoming eventually the argument of the predicates contributed by verbs and VPs:

(8.2)

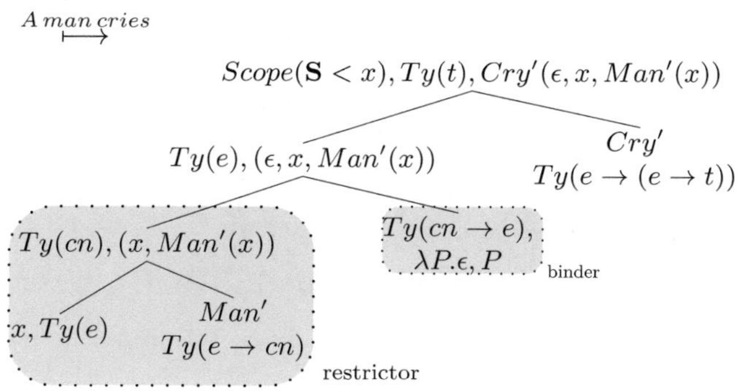

Quantifier scope is not expressed as part of the tree architecture but through scope constraints collected incrementally during the parse process. Scope dependencies (<) are declared as collected statements stored in the label *Scope*(...).[3] Epsilon calculus terms are employed by DS because they may carry a record of the context within which they occur inside their restrictor. According to defined computational rules of QUANTIFIER EVALUATION (see Kempson et al. 2001), an intermediate interpretation of a sentence such as *A man cries* will take the form $Fo(Cry'(\epsilon, x, Man'(x)))$ derived by simple functional application as shown in (8.3). But this will be eventually algorithmically transformed to a formula where an appropriate epsilon term, abbreviated as a below, appears as the argument of the conjunction of the predicates contributed by the common noun and verb:

(8.3) $\overset{A\,man\,cries}{\longmapsto} Cry'(\epsilon, x, Man'(x)) \overset{\text{Q-EVALUATION}}{\longmapsto}$
$Man'(\alpha) \wedge Cry'(\alpha)$ where $\alpha = (\epsilon, x, Man'(x) \wedge Cry'(x))$

On the other hand, a $tau - term$ will induce universal quantification:

(8.4) $\overset{Every\,man\,cries}{\longmapsto} Cry'(\tau, x, Man'(x)) \overset{\text{Q-EVALUATION}}{\longmapsto}$
$Man'(a) \rightarrow Cry'(\alpha)$ where $\alpha = (\tau, x, Man'(x) \rightarrow Cry'(x))$

Multiple quantification of course yields more complex restrictor specifications, but the evaluation algorithm applies to arbitrarily complex combinations of terms and with variation in the connective depending on the type of quantifier involved. The restrictor of all such terms contains a record of the propositional structure that gave rise to it so that it provides a suitable antecedent for subsequent cases of *E-type anaphora* (see Kempson et al. 2001).The effect of the interpretation of pronouns as bound variables is achieved via the independent assumptions of the content of pronouns as providing invariably metavariables and the QUANTIFIER EVALUATION rules. For example, processing the string in (8.5) below will initially produce a representation where a metavariable **U** will temporarily occupy the argument position (see (8.6)). Subsequent substitution of this metavariable with the unevaluated tau-term in subject position (see (8.7)) will eventually lead to a logical form where both subject positions of the two propositions involved are occupied by variables bound by the tau binder:

(8.5) Every student$_i$ believes he$_i$ is clever.

(8.6) $Believe'(\tau, x, Student'x)(Clever'(\mathbf{U}))$

(8.7) $\overset{\text{SUBSTITUTION}}{\longmapsto} Believe'(\tau, x, Student'x)(Clever'(\tau, x, Student'x))$

---

[3] **S** in (8.2) above is a metavariable that can be substituted by the index of evaluation for the proposition.

(8.8) $\overset{\text{Q-EVAL}}{\longmapsto}$ $Student(\alpha) \rightarrow [Believe'(\alpha)(Clever'(\alpha))]$ where $\alpha = \tau, x, [Student'(x) \rightarrow Believe'(x, (Clever'(x)))]$

The effect that results from these various forms of underspecification and update is a process of dynamic transitions through partial trees and annotations that leads to a licensed eventual logical form representing the proposition expressed in a particular context. In DS, all syntactic phenomena are reformulated in these terms, leading to the comprehensive claim that NL syntax does not involve a separate level of representation besides what is needed for semantics (Cann et al. 2005, and elsewhere).

8.2.2 Subordination in DS

Conditionals present one of a number of cases where there is tension between analyses in terms of the traditional notions of *coordination* and *subordination*. As regards our purposes, DS distinguishes only two ways of combining the input provided by the processing of distinct clauses in order to produce a complex proposition as their content:
(a) a clause can contribute the argument of a predicate as in, e.g., the propositional object of a verb, see e.g. (8.6) earlier; in this case the *local tree* will consist of two predicate-argument structures one embedded into the other, or,
(b) two clauses can introduce two separate trees connected by a LINK relation between their nodes. This mode of processing results in an overall structure called the *global tree* which can encompass any number of LINKed trees and is a representation equivalent to an inferential/cognitive unit (cf. Blakemore 1987; Carston 2002). LINKed trees are associated through the LINK modality, $\langle L \rangle$. Adjuncts, coordinations and other structures are processed by employing this device which allows incorporation within a tree of information that is to be structurally developed externally to it. Relative clauses, being one core case of adjunction, are processed through the construction of a LINKed tree bearing a requirement that it contains as a sub-term the formula on the source-node from which the LINK relation is defined ($John'$ below):

(8.9)
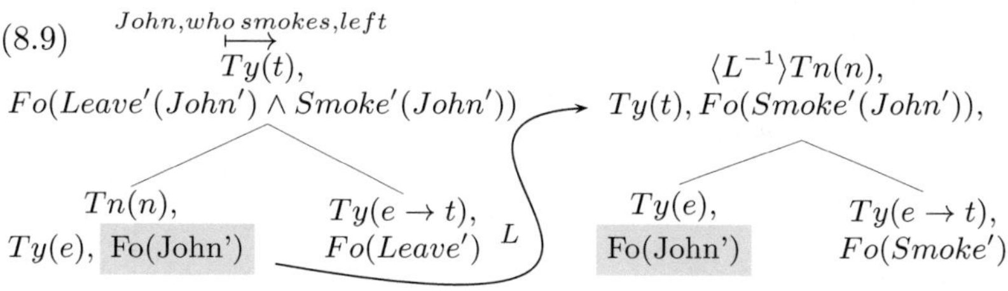

In the building up of such paired LINKed trees for relative clauses, the requirement imposed for a common term is satisfied by the processing of the relative pronoun which induces the copying of that term. As this copy is initially introduced on an unfixed node, it is then necessarily constrained to appear within the newly emergent propositional structure (reflecting the *island constraints* associated with such structures).

8.3 Conditionals: Structure and processing

8.3.1 Syntactic properties: The tension between coordination and subordination

The analysis of an NL conditional structure under the truth-functional material implication interpretation and a compositional view of the syntax-semantics interface implies a logical form where the two clauses are conjoined by a two place connective and are equivalent in status. Under one such possible account, NL *if ... then* can be viewed as a discontinuous connective relating two sentences of equal status (see e.g. Chomsky 1957: 22, Strawson 1986). However, even disregarding the fact that the appearance of *then* is not necessary in conditionals, the relation between antecedent and consequent is unlike that of two conjuncts related by *and/or/but* (see e.g. Geis 1985). So, even though coordinate structures are taken to induce LINKed trees in DS, this does not seem to be an adequately restrictive approach to the syntactic properties of conditionals. Instead, *if*-clauses seem to pattern more with another type of structure, also analyzed in terms of the LINK relation, namely, *relative clauses*. First of all, *Right Node Raising* is precluded between antecedent and consequent as is also the case with relative clauses:

(8.10) John will support and Mary will try to promote the manager of their department

(8.11) *If John supports ___ Mary will try to promote the manager of their department

(8.12) *[Mary will support ___] [if John tries to promote ___] the manager of their department

(8.13) Mary will support John Petropapadopoulos, who Bill met yesterday ⇒

(8.14) *[Mary will support ___] [who Bill saw ___] John Petropapadopoulos.

Two clauses related by a conjunction can be made to share a common subject (*Conjunction Reduction*). This structure is not allowed for *if*-clauses (and relatives alike):

(8.15) John [bought the newspaper] and [sold the milk]

(8.16) *John [bought the newspaper] if [sold the milk]

(8.17) *If John [sold the milk] [bought the newspaper]

(8.18) *Mary [will support John], who [met yesterday]

Another difference that points to distinct analyses for conjunctions on the one hand and *if*-clauses (and relatives) on the other is the phenomenon of *Gapping*:

(8.19) John will buy the newspaper and [Mary ___ the milk]

There is no corresponding construction for *if*-clauses (neither with relatives):

(8.20) *John will buy the newspaper if Mary ___ the milk

(8.21) *John saw Bill who ___ Mary

Coordinated clauses allow for the phenomenon of *Across-the-Board extraction*:

(8.22) The man who [John dislikes ___] and [Mary loves ___] came to see me yesterday

(8.23) Who [did John dislike ___] and [Mary love ___]?

If-clauses do not generally permit extraction:

(8.24) Who did John dislike ___ if Mary saw ___ ?

The fact that a conditional consists of two asymmetrically related clauses is also supported by the fact that the *if*-clause cannot bear independent speech act indicators, that is, the verb form inside the *if*-clause cannot be in Imperative or Interrogative mood:

(8.25) *If come to the partly it will be fun

(8.26) *It will be fun if come to the party

(8.27) *If are you busy you will come to the party?

In this respect *if*-clauses resemble subordinated clauses and relatives which are also unable to have independent speech act indicators:

(8.28) *John asked that did Mary come home?

(8.29) *John said that come home

(8.30) *John, who did you like, came home

As, in fact, there are conditional assertions, questions and commands, these are indicated by the grammatical form of the consequent which is what has motivated the traditional claim that the consequent provides the primary structure and the *if*-clause is an adjunct:

(8.31) If you are not busy come to the party.

(8.32) If you are not busy are you coming to the party?

(8.33) Will you come to the party if you are busy?

The *if*-clause, like other adjuncts, can appear in different positions without obvious truth-conditional effects:

(8.34) If John shouts, Mary gets upset.

(8.35) Mary gets upset if John shouts.

A syntactic account of *if*-clauses then needs to provide the resources for processing them at different positions. Moreover, there is no strict adjacency requirement between antecedent and consequent. The consequent corresponding to a clause-initial antecedent might be embedded as can be seen in the cases below:

(8.36) [If John leaves] Mary believes that Bill will stay =
a. Mary believes that if John leaves Bill will stay
or
b. If John leaves then Mary believes that Bill will stay.

(8.37) If the dinner had been ready Mary believes that John would not have complained
a. [If the dinner had been ready] (then/in that case) Mary believes that John wouldn't have complained
or
b. Mary believes that [if the dinner had been ready] (then/in that case) John would not have complained

However, the distance between antecedent and consequent is not arbitrary. Their separation respects what in the linguistic literature are sometimes called *island restrictions*, e.g., the *Complex NP-constraint*, Ross 1967):

(8.38) Mary called the man [who will be hired if John leaves]. ⇒
*If John leaves Mary called the man [who will be hired].[4]

This seems to imply that antecedent and consequent stand in some kind of local relation that has to be expressed. Moreover, extraction is not allowed from inside an *if*-clause, i.e., *if*-clauses, like relative clauses, are themselves islands:

(8.39) John saw the man [who shot Mary] ⇒

(8.40) *Who did John see the man [who shot ___]?

(8.41) John will fire Mary [if she calls Bill]. ⇒

(8.42) *Who will John fire Mary [if she calls ___]?

(8.43) If John sees Mary he will kiss her. ⇒

(8.44) *Who [if John sees ___] will he kiss her?

[4]Ungrammatical under the intended interpretation.

These syntactic facts point then to the conclusion that *if*-clauses behave as some kind of relative clause. However, in the present context, given that DS takes a processing perspective, such syntactic evidence can be taken in two ways: either as indications of the structural properties of the eventual representation derived or as properties of the processing apparatus utilized to derive this final representation. Unlike other frameworks where syntactic issues are very generally taken as independent of and prior to semantics, in DS, NL "syntax" is taken to be nothing more than the progressive compositional construction of some logical representation. This logical representation has its own syntax as a domain of LINKed trees. But, as we said earlier, such trees neither reflect word order nor can be associated one-to-one with single strings since there can be various parsing routes deriving the same tree structure, a structure which directly reflects the interpretation assigned to the NL input processed. So now we need to examine what kind of interpretational facts we need to take into account in the processing of conditionals and how these relate to the syntactic restrictions mentioned above.

8.3.2 Interpretational effects in conditionals

Haegeman (2001, 2003) claims that, syntactically, there appear to be two entirely different types of conditionals:[5]
(a) *event conditionals* in which the *if*-clause modifies the event denoted by the main clause:

(8.45) If it rains we will all get terribly wet and miserable

(b) *premise conditionals* in which the *if*-clause contributes a proposition which has to be taken as "the privileged context" for the processing of the consequent:

(8.46) If (as you say) it is going to rain, why don't we just stay at home and watch a video?

In terms of semantics, Haegeman argues that the antecedent in an event conditional provides a "cause" leading to the "effect" denoted by the content of the main clause. Premise conditionals, on the other hand, are usually "echoic" and have their own illocutionary force. So, in terms of structure, event conditionals are fully integrated in the (syntactically encoded) speech act of the main clause so that the semantic differences between the two types of conditional have a transparent syntactic ba-

[5]Iatridou (1991) distinguishes three types of conditionals: *hypothetical*, *factual* and *relevance* conditionals. For factual conditionals, we assume that an analysis as in Noh (1998) will assimilate them, under a unified type, with the hypothetical ones.

sis. *If*-clauses in event conditionals are merged inside the VP/IP domain whereas antecedents of premise conditionals are located in the CP domain (therefore the two types exhibit distinct *external syntax*). Haegeman also assigns distinct internal syntactic articulation to each type of *if*-clause (their *internal syntax*). Event conditionals, according to Haegeman, are reduced clauses in that they lack the full CP articulation, e.g. (illocutionary) force (and other) heads are missing, while premise conditionals are intact in that they include the same CP structure as main clauses. Shaer (2003) and Gregoromichelaki (2006) provide data showing that there are no definitive criteria that distinguish the two types of conditional that Haegeman postulates, for example, "temporal subordination" and "root transformations" are equally possible in both types (and, in any case, the existence of a strict two-way ambiguity in terms of semantics is also in doubt as Edgington 2003 argues). Hence, since both types of conditionals seem to be uniform in terms of syntactic properties a unified account should be pursued.

However, a widely adopted unified account of conditionals also faces problems: examining cross-linguistic distributional evidence Haiman (1978, 1993) has claimed that *if*-clauses are generally *topics*. From the present perspective, this claim is contradicted by the fact that *if*-clauses can occur post-verbally (and this without any necessary indication of a revision or afterthought construal). Notice especially that such postverbal *if*-clauses can accommodate bound anaphoric elements which depend for their content on the previous clause and contribute to the complex predicate attributed to the subject:

(8.47) Every student$_i$ will succeed if he$_i$ is not lazy.

If *if*-clauses were consistently analyzed as "topics", i.e. introducing background or given information, external to the main assertion, such dependencies are not easily explained. Moreover, although it has been claimed (Rooth 1985) that *if*-clauses, unlike *when*-clauses, cannot be focussed, von Fintel (1994) and Bhatt (1996) show that they can both be the new information conveyed by an answer to a question and bear nuclear accent:

(8.48) A: What would motivate John to shave?
B: John always shaves, [if his MOTHER is coming to visit]$_F$

So an analysis that takes *if*-clauses to uniformly introduce "topics", somehow loosely associated with the main clause, can reflect neither their intepretational nor their informational structure and syntactic properties. On the other hand, a syntactic ambiguity account, as in Haegemann (2003), is also undesirable since, at least in English, there is no justification for positing two distinct underlying structures.

8.4 A DS view of conditionals

The present account is an attempt to make sense of these very mixed data while adopting what is a broadly agreed set of semantic assumptions about conditionals. The parallel properties of *if*-clauses and nominal relatives, which contrast with the properties of coordinate structures, have led several researchers to the assumption, which will be adopted here, that, in some sense to be made precise, *if*-clauses fall within the same class of structures as relative clauses in the same way that *when*-clauses and *where*-clauses can be taken as relatives over implicit time or location specifications (see e.g. Geis 1985; Bhatt and Pancheva 2006). What is then crucial for us here is to determine what kind of element an *if*-clause attaches to as a relative which brings us to the issue of what type of semantic representation we should assume to be constructed out of the processing of a conditional sentence. Since, in DS, syntactic and semantic issues are fundamentally inter-dependent this means that the semantic representation and its derivation as the outcome of parsing a conditional should crucially be compatible with the syntactic facts mentioned above.

From a structural point of view, in DS terms, the parallels in the behaviour of *if*-clauses and relatives point to the conclusion that an analysis in terms of LINKed structures should be assigned to both. This, under standard DS assumptions, will explain the data in (8.40)-(8.44) regarding their status as islands with respect to extraction. However, the kinds of movement allowed for the *if*-clause shown above in (8.34)-(8.37) indicate that there is a difference: relative clauses cannot appear freely in any position unless they follow a dislocated argument to which they attach (besides cases of extraposition). This shows that *if*-clauses behave more like arguments in terms of their positioning within the sentence. In addition, in the same way that arguments cannot be dislocated out of "islands", the same restriction holds for *if*-clauses as shown in (8.38). This means that in order to capture the parallels between *if*-clauses, arguments and relatives there has to be an argument node inside the tree representation constructed from the consequent to which the content of the *if*-clause attaches via the LINK relation. The licensed variability in the positioning of arguments would then allow us to account for the freedom of movement of the *if*-clause.

In terms of semantics, along with other researchers, we will assume here that *if*-clauses are relatives that introduce the restrictor of a term inducing universal quantification over a domain of contextually specified events or situations (see e.g. Lycan 2001). This term is a $Ty(e)$ argument of the main clause, the consequent. Even though the data shown in (8.47)-(8.48) are problematic for the *conditionals-as-topics* thesis they are not problematic for the analysis of *if*-clauses as contributing restrictors to quantificational terms. As von Fintel (1994) shows, restrictors in nominal terms can also be focused:

(8.49) A: Who here is clever enough to solve this problem?
B: Well, most of the $[\text{GRAD STUDENTS}]_F$ should be able to help you.

For the present analysis of *if*-clauses as relatives we can observe that elements in a relative clause can also be focused:

(8.50) A: Did you see the man that John dislikes?
B: No, but I saw the woman that John $[\text{ADORES}]_F$

(8.51) A: Who did John hit?
B: John hit whoever $[\text{APPROACHED}]_F$

We take these as evidence that *if*-clauses provide a consistent input as far as their contribution to the semantic representation is concerned, i.e. they provide specifications of the $Ty(e)$ situation argument of the representation. Under the DS assumptions made here, an appropriate pragmatic theory should be more suitable to derive the exact interpretation associated with the processing of conditional structures in context without the semantic representation explicitly encoding every type of effect (which might very well be an open-ended number cf. Declerck and Reed 2001). But, in general, it is widely accepted that a sentence-initial *if*-clause somehow provides the context for the processing of the consequent. We can give formal substance to this intuition in an illuminative way within DS. Without attributing any ambiguity to the encoded content of the *if*-clause itself (unlike Haegeman 2003), exploiting the same mechanisms available in the processing of NPs, we can assume that *if*-clauses too can be processed either as LINKed structures occupying independent subtrees or as providing content occupying structurally underspecified (unfixed) nodes. We should then expect that, as is the case with free word order languages and NP-dislocation phenomena, distinct parsing routes will be exploited for contextual effects facilitating one type of interpretation over another (see, e.g. the distinction between "focus" and "topic" NP-interpretations, Cann et al. 2005).[6]

[6] Although evidence for such distinct parsing strategies for *if*-clauses is not readily available in English (apart from intonation), in languages with V2 we find two syntactically distinguished ways of associating the *if*-clause with the consequent, see Koenig and van der Auwera (1988), Gregoromichelaki (2006).

So, in some cases, *if*-clauses can convey new/non-backgrounded information and we assume that the analysis as annotating unfixed nodes is more appropriate:

(8.52) A: Under what conditions are you prepared to surrender?
B: [(Only) If JOHN surrenders]$_F$ I might do.

(8.53) A: Are you going to play soccer on Sunday?
B: We'll play [if the SUN shines]$_F$ (von Fintel 1994: 82)

On the other hand, we assume that the specific interpretation usually characterised in the literature as *topic*, i.e. "given" or "background" information, is only available at the left-periphery under a construal in which a left-peripheral *if*-clause is processed as the *head*, the point from which the LINK relation originates. The situation argument that is introduced in this preliminary way will be then necessarily unified with the situation argument of the main clause. This is a natural characterisation since only in this structure can we assume that what is provided initially is introduced explicitly as the background for processing the following assertion. For cases of LINKed subtrees contributed by right-peripheral *if*-clauses we will see that they provide confirmation for the choice of an already contextually given element. As these effects are exactly parallel to those widely observed in the processing of nominal phrases the approach taken here is in line with Schlenker's (2006) view regarding the fundamental symmetry that underlies linguistic reference in ontological domains like individuals, times and worlds despite the apparently variable syntactic means employed in individual languages.

We will now proceed to show how these assumptions can be implemented with minimal extensions to the standard DS apparatus. First we will show how to incorporate the situation argument as occupying its own node in the standard DS tree representations (8.4.1) and then how the processing of *if*-clauses targets this particular node (8.4.2). We will then see two additional ways of processing *if*-clauses, as unfixed nodes (8.4.4) or LINKed -trees (8.4.4), exactly as any other argument and with similar interpretational effects.

8.4.1 Introduction of the situation argument

Following much current work in the formal semantics literature, we will employ an additional argument for propositional representations standing for the situation of evaluation (see Heim 1990; von Fintel 1994; Chierchia 1995 a.o.). Farkas (1997) proposes that for each world w we define an extensional model $\mathcal{M}_w =< S_w, U_w, V_w >$ where S_w is a set of situations in w, U_w is the set of individuals in w and V_w assigns values to the constants of the language with respect to the situations in S_w. As suggested in Kratzer (1986), we assume that situations are parts of worlds, each situation part of a unique world. Worlds are then defined as maximal situations. Truth of a logical form (*lf*) in a world w is determined with respect to truth in a situation in w:

(8.54) An *lf* is true in w with respect to $\mathcal{M}$ iff there is a situation s in S_w such that the *lf* is true in s with respect to $\mathcal{M}_w$.

Adapting this assumption to DS terms, the situation argument of a predicate will be explicitly represented on the tree and will combine with it by the usual means of function application. So we will add a new type in D_{Ty} in order to allow the situation argument to be processed. We will call this new type $Ty(e_s)$. We assume then that the values in D_{Ty} are sorted with $Ty(e)$ as a general type with subtypes of $Ty(e_s)$ for situations and $Ty(e_i)$ for individuals, $Ty(e_w)$ for worlds etc. However, for simplicity of illustration we will continue to notate the type of individuals as $Ty(e)$, i.e. we will omit the subscript when no ambiguity arises. Metavariables can be specified to take values either of the most general type ($Ty(e)$) or the more specific types ($Ty(e_i)$, $Ty(e_s)$ etc.). The content assigned to verbs (and predicates in general but we omit discussion of this issue here) comes from the lexicon with an additional situation argument slot which combines with a situation term available from the (linguistic or extra-linguistic) context.

In order for the situation argument to be introduced through the usual DS processing apparatus,[7] the rules of INTRODUCTION and PREDICTION will be employed to provide for a further $?Ty(e)$ position. INTRODUCTION and PREDICTION starting from the $?Ty(t)$ axiom:

(8.55) $?Ty(t), World(w_0), Scope(w_0), \diamondsuit$

induce two additional nodes: a node with a requirement for $Ty(e_s)$ and its sister $?Ty(e_s \rightarrow t)$. The scope statement ($Scope(...)$) includes the world of evaluation which we have assumed to be w_0, the actual world as a default (see Papafragou 1996: 186-187, 2000 for justification in the context of a pragmatic theory). The situation argument can be initially introduced as a metavariable, $\mathbf{S_i}$, $\mathbf{S_j}$, $\mathbf{S_k}$ etc., since it is possible to supply a value for it from the context (as an instance of *saturation*, see e.g. Recanati 1999). In the tree below, with the pointer at the type e_s node the metavariable will be inserted by a computational

[7] Gregoromichelaki (2006) presents an alternative way of introducing the situation argument as an optional addition to the representation in case it is needed (as e.g. in the case of a conditional structure). This option follows Recanati (1999) and is the one compatible with the Cann (this volume) account of tense. As we are not dealing with tense and modality here we follow the simpler route.

rule.[8] A requirement for the term substituting for the metavariable to participate in some scope statement is also inserted:[9]

(8.56) $\overset{\text{INTRODUCTION}}{\longmapsto}\overset{\text{PREDICTION}}{}$ $\overset{\textit{Situation Metavariable Introduction}}{\longmapsto}$

$$?Ty(t), Scope(w_0 < \mathbf{S}),\ ?\exists\mathbf{x}.Scope(w_0 < \mathbf{x})$$

$$Ty(e_s), Fo(\mathbf{S}), \diamondsuit \qquad ?Ty(e_s \rightarrow t)$$

If there is no appropriate value available for the metavariable the underspecified value and requirements can be left to await resolution until the latter stages of the parse. Any quantificational terms introduced subsequently will also be able to depend on this metavariable. Crucially for the present analysis, the situation argument can be a variable, an epsilon term or a tau term. These terms will contribute to the scope statement as any other regular argument. This is motivated by the interaction between quantification over individuals and situations. Simplifying somewhat, the sentence below can be taken as ambiguous between the two logical forms displayed below it:

(8.57) Henry gracefully ate all the crisps

(8.58) ∀y. Crisp'(y) → ∃e. Eat'(Henry', y, e) ∧ Graceful'(e)

(8.59) ∃e. ∀y. Crisp'(y) → Eat'(Henry', y, e) ∧ Graceful'(e)
(from Taylor 1985)

In addition, Farkas (1997) argues that the situation argument must scopally interact with individual quantificational terms in order to derive the range of interpretations possible for the following:

(8.60) If *a boy he likes* comes over, Johnny shows *him* his turtle.

The indefinite in the above can be interpreted as having either wide scope with respect to the situations of evaluation, in which case there is a particular boy being mentioned, or it can have narrow scope in which case for each situation considered there is potentially a different boy involved. The obvious way to deal with these cases in DS is to allow terms representing situations to appear in the scope statement and interact freely with the variables contributed by the nominal terms. As is standard in DS, we assume that indefinites contribute epsilon terms which must necessarily depend on some other term in the current tree. In the case above in order to derive the wide scope of the epsilon term derived from the indefinite, we need a DS representation in which this term outscopes another term representing the range of situations

[8]Note that ANTICIPATION can move the pointer downwards if the situation argument is to be developed immediately afterwards.

[9]For exact specification of the rules see Gregoromichelaki (2006, Ch 4).

introduced by the conditional. The term derived from the indefinite will in turn be outscoped by the world of evaluation which must be taken as necessarily the first element in the scope statement.[10]

The rest of the parsing rules remain as usual. As regards the tree in (8.56), the $?Ty(e_s \to t)$ node (which is equivalent to the $?Ty(t)$ node in the standard presentations of DS) can now be expanded with INTRODUCTION and PREDICTION to accommodate the subject and the predicate. We can now process the lexical input provided by the subject, e.g. *John*, and this will decorate the type e node. Pointer movement will proceed to the predicate node where the verb can be parsed. The modified lexical entry for an intransitive verb like *run* is shown below (tense and mood specifications are omitted):

(8.61) *run*

IF	$?Ty(e \to (e_s \to t)), \Diamond$
THEN	$\mathtt{put}((Fo(\lambda x.\lambda s.Run'(x)(s)), Ty(e \to (e_s \to t))))$
ELSE	$\mathtt{abort}$

An epsilon term available from the context can now be provided to resolve the metavariable at the $Ty(e_s)$ node, we annotate this in schematic form as $\epsilon, s, p(s)$. By means of the QUANTIFIER-EVALUATION Rule the formula on the root node will be converted to a quantificational structure where it is declared that there is a situation that satisfies the descriptions p and $Run'(John')$:

(8.62) $\overset{\ldots\text{COMPLETION}\ldots\ \text{Q-EVALUATION}}{\longmapsto}$

$$Ty(t), \Diamond, Scope(w_0 < s), Fo(Run'(John')(\epsilon, s, p(s))) \overset{Q-Eval}{\longmapsto}$$
$$Fo(w_0 : p(\alpha) \wedge Run'(John')(\alpha) \text{ where } \alpha = \epsilon, s, [p(s) \wedge Run'(John')(s)])$$

$Ty(e_s)$, $Fo(\epsilon, s, p(s))$ | $Ty(e_s \to t)$ $Fo(\lambda s.Run'(John')(s))$

$Ty(e), Fo(John')$ | $Ty(e \to (e_s \to t))$ $Fo(\lambda x.\lambda s.Run'(x)(s))$

[10] Although we will not deal with modality and tense issues in the present work we will assume that the world of evaluation w_0 will also eventually appear as a label on the formula decorating the root node of a propositional tree as is standard in DS. This is because we do not expect that there are any scope ambiguities regarding terms and the world of evaluation for each proposition. Being the label, the world of evaluation has necessarily widest scope and acts as a point of reference for the evaluation of all other terms. The actual world w_0 is the default world of evaluation. Modals and other intensional operators can be seen to optionally introduce new worlds of evaluation by existentially or universally quantifying over worlds accessible from w_0, see Chatzikyriakidis (this volume).

According to the semantics presented in (8.54) above, the *lf* that is the *Fo* value at the root node of the tree in (8.62):

(8.63) $Fo(w_0 : p(\alpha) \wedge Run'(John')(\alpha)$ where
$\alpha = \epsilon, s, [p(s) \wedge Run'(John')(s)])$

is true in world w_0 iff there is a situation s satisfying the restrictor p in w_0 that also satisfies the nuclear scope, $Run'(John')$, in w_0. We now have most of what is needed to allow the processing of conditional sentences. Let's see what more needs to be added.

8.4.2 Conditionals: Logical form

Under the present analysis, sentences containing *if*-clauses will be assumed to give rise to two LINKed trees: processing of the main clause, the *consequent*, results in one tree, the *main tree* from now on, while processing of the *antecedent* results in another, the LINKed tree. The latter appears connected to the situation node of the main tree through the LINK relation. The establishment of this relation will also effect a unification of values between two nodes of the joined trees in the following way: the final result of processing the antecedent of a conditional will produce a tau term ($\tau - term$) as the root of the LINKed tree (highlighted in (8.64)):[11]

(8.64) The tree derived by processing *if p* from the string *if p, q:*

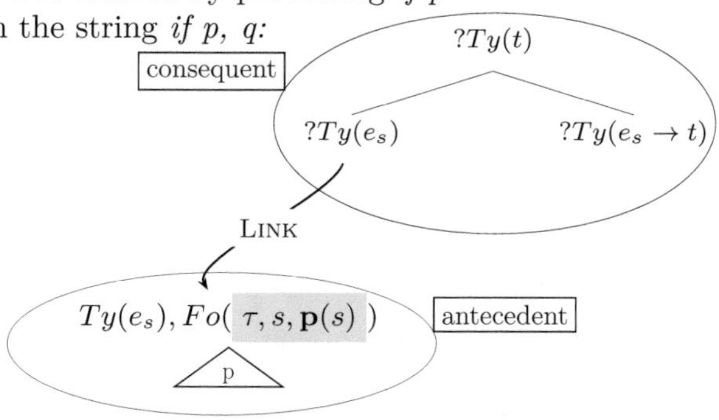

This term once derived will be copied in the main tree in order to serve as the Formula value of its situation node. The newly introduced τ-term in the main tree, being an ordinary argument of the predicate, will be incorporated in the proposition derived at the root through the usual function-application process:

[11] We omit reference to the world of evaluation from now on. We also omit scope statements and any other irrelevant detail.

(8.65) The *global tree* derived from *if p, q:*

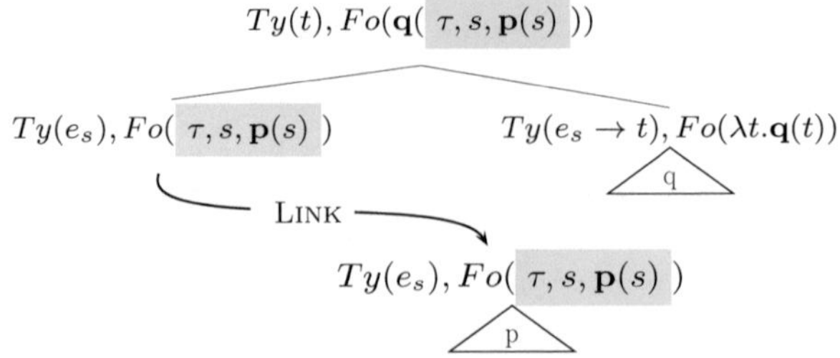

Since the shared term is a quantificational τ-term, it will contribute to the Scope Statement of the main tree. The DS rules for processing quantification structures (Q-Evaluation) will apply at the end of the parse and yield a propositional structure at the root node:[12]

(8.66) Initial formula value derived by parsing *if p, q*:
$q(\tau, s, ps)$
Formula that results after application of Q-Eval Rule:
$p(\alpha) \rightarrow q(\alpha)$
where $\alpha = \tau, s, (ps \rightarrow qs)$

We thus derive a proposition where the content of the consequent (q, above) is construed as a property of situations. What is asserted is that this property q is true of all the situations that satisfy the description p provided by the content of the *if*-clause: $q(\tau, s, ps)$. That is, the content of the *if*-clause, p, becomes the Restrictor in a universal quantification over situations (τ, s, ps) whereas q becomes the Nuclear Scope. According to the semantics proposed in (8.54) above, the *lf* in (8.66) is true in a world w iff all the values of s that satisfy the restrictor, p, in w also satisfy the nuclear scope, q, in w. By the Q-Evaluation rules we also derive a term (α in (8.66) above) which can serve as the situation argument for another proposition or as the replacement for the metavariable contributed by a pronominal.

Since we want to capture the contextual dependency of situational quantification[13] as an instance of *saturation* (see Recanati 1999) we will assume that the Restrictor itself includes a metavariable that has to be substituted by appealing to the context of utterance. This means that only situations that are considered "relevant" will be included in the set of situations quantified over according to the Restrictor. Although we will not include it in the tree representations for simplicity, we assume therefore that the Restrictor includes a metavariable that

[12]We omit brackets freely for readability.

[13]This is a standard assumption, see e.g. Lycan's (2001) "envisaged" and "real" possibilities.

has to be substituted by the context of utterance: $\tau, s, (ps \wedge \mathbf{R}s)$. $\mathbf{R}$ is a metavariable that has to be substituted by a predicate of situations (a complex proposition) expressing "what is expected" or "envisaged" given the propositions in the *Discourse Context* (see also von Fintel 1994).[14] This will allow us to derive the distinct flavours associated with the meaning of types of conditionals that have been discussed in the literature without having to make syntactic distinctions encoding those differentiations. Notice also that, according to DS, given that the grammar interfaces with context incrementally at each point, propositions derived by processing NL sentences can also incorporate inferentially derived content, for example, not just the bare proposition expressed but also any higher level explicatures as argued in Purver et al. (2010). This allows us to address some problematic aspects of conditionals. For example, Noh (1998) analyses "metarepresentational" conditionals which show a pattern problematic for standard truth-functional accounts:

(8.67) A: Two and eleven makes thirty
B: If two and eleven makes thirty, you need more work on maths. (from Noh, ibid)

As Noh argues, such cases (and many others) can be accommodated if we assume that the content assigned to the antecedent is (meta)-representing not simply the proposition expressed by the previous utterance but rather the higher-level explicature associated with it. So the proposition expressed by the antecedent is not simply "two and eleven makes thirty" but rather "if *you say/believe that* two and eleven makes thirty". As in DS no representation over strings is defined, the (optional) derivation of speech act information will naturally license this interpretation that accommodates the content of this higher level explicature plus any other contextually relevant assumptions. Under this view, the final propositional content expressed by B's utterance in (8.67) above will be: "All situations in which you believe/say that two and eleven makes thirty ... are situations in which you need more work on maths".

In more concrete terms, let's look at the completed tree derived for a sentence like *if John cries, Mary laughs*. The diagram is shown below:

[14] Note that the *Discourse Context* is not assumed to contain only information that has been made available by processing linguistic input; it can also be extended by means of inference and perception.

(8.68)

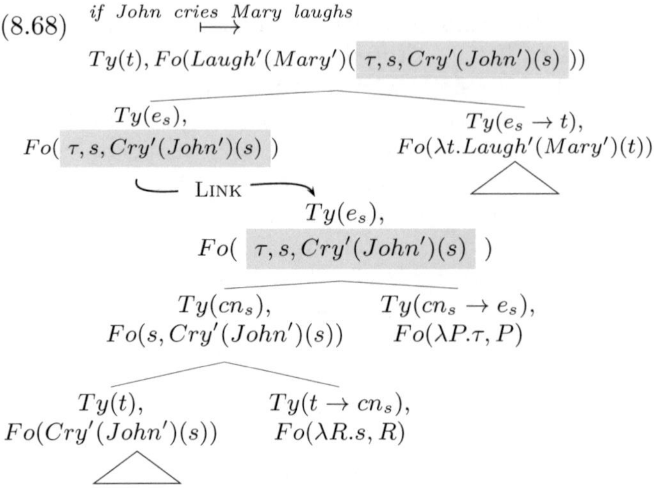

The $Ty(t)$ proposition derived by the processing of the antecedent, $Cry'(John')(s)$, becomes the argument of a function that copies its situation argument (which must be a free variable, s in (8.68) above) and creates a Restrictor in the appropriate format required for the construction of a τ-term: $s, Cry'(John')(s)$. The τ-binder is then applied to the Restrictor by means of function application and the τ-term is eventually derived: $\tau, s, Cry'(John')(s)$. This term is subsequently copied at the situation node of the main tree and serves as the situation argument there. The proposition decorating the root node of the global tree, $Laugh'(Mary', (\tau, s, Cry'(John')(s)))$, can be interpreted as:

"Mary laughs in all situations that John cries"

or

"All situations in which John cries are situations in which Mary laughs".

Hence, the role of the content of the *if*-clause here is simply to provide the restrictor of the τ-term that ensues by processing the lexical item *if* and the antecedent. In that respect, there is no independent assertion of the proposition *John cries* which is as it should be according to the desired truth conditions. The formula $Laugh'(Mary')(\tau, s, Cry'(John')(s))$ will be transformed by the Q-EVALUATION rule to:

(8.69) $Cry'(John')(\alpha) \rightarrow Laugh'(Mary')(\alpha)$
where $\alpha = \tau, s, [Cry'(John')(s) \rightarrow Laugh'(Mary')(s)]$

According to the semantics proposed in (8.54) above, the *lf* in (8.69) is true in a world w iff all the values of s that satisfy the restrictor, $Cry'(John')$, in w also satisfy the nuclear scope, $Laugh'(Mary')$, in w.

In this configuration a semantic representation containing the connective $\rightarrow$ is derived compositionally at the root node of the main tree without any explicit encoding of it by any NL lexical item.[15] This connective is the same as the one derived by the processing of universally quantifying expressions like *every man* and appears in the logical form by similar means. That is, we assume that material implication is only *part of* the encoded meaning of *if*, the residue being the quantification over situations, so the analysis is richer but not incompatible with the standard material implication interpretations.[16]

This result is achieved in DS in the same way that conjoined propositions are derived from linguistic input containing relative clauses: it is the combination of the lexical and computational actions associated with the parsing of a conditional that derive such universally quantified implicational structures. Indeed, under this analysis, conditional sentences are assumed to derive representations of a similar form as nominal relative clauses, in that a term is shared between the two trees. However, although the main tree in nominal relative constructions provides itself the term to be copied and the LINKed tree provides additional predicative content on that term, here the "relative", the *if*-clause, leads to the construction of a term newly introduced to the main structure. In this respect, the processing of *if*-clauses resembles, in the nominal domain, *headless relatives* in English and other languages like the following:

(8.70) John eats [what(ever) he likes]

(8.71) John will arrest [whoever called]

(8.72)	o Giannis	xeretise	[opion irthe]	*Modern Greek*
	the John	greeted	[who came]	
	John greeted [whoever came]			

In both cases, a term is derived from a secondary tree that is being developed in parallel to the main one. This term is copied to the main tree in order to serve the role of an argument of the predicate in that proposition. As we will see later, the presence of this secondary tree, its attachment to the main structure by the LINK relation and the incorporation of its informational content to the main tree is what explains the subordination features exhibited by *if*-clauses. It is also the reason

[15] However, this is not an analysis where *if* is assigned no contribution and the *if*-clause just provides a restrictor of some other operator cf. Kratzer (1986). Hence scopal dependencies with other operators are expected to occur, see e.g. Geurts (2004).

[16] Alternatively, the connective can be interpreted as in Belnap (1970) as argued in Huitink (2008).

that explains the free appearance of *if*-clauses at different positions in the clause as well as their differential contributions to interpretation. We now turn to see the dynamic process that puts all the information together so as to derive the above structure.

8.4.3 The lexical entry for *if*

We will now illustrate the precise route followed by the parser in order to accomplish the construction of a structure such as in (8.68) above from an input string in the form of a conditional sentence. We will start with the instructions stored into the lexical entry for *if*. These are responsible for initiating the building of a new LINKed tree which is going to accommodate the content of the antecedent. Because the result of this process must be a τ-term of type e_s the rules in the lexical entry for *if* initiate structure that is going to derive the required term through the usual structure-building means of DS, i.e., type deduction in parallel with function application. The following is the lexical entry triggered by the parsing of the particle *if*:

(8.73) ***if***

$$
\begin{array}{lll}
\text{IF} & ?Ty(e_s) & (1)\\
\text{THEN} & \texttt{put}(?[\exists \mathbf{x}.Fo(\mathbf{x}) \wedge \langle L\rangle Fo(\mathbf{x})]); & (2)\\
 & \texttt{make}(\langle L\rangle);\ \texttt{go}(\langle L\rangle);\ \texttt{put}(\ ?Ty(e_s)); & (3)\\
 & \texttt{make}(\langle\downarrow_1\rangle);\ \texttt{go}(\langle\downarrow_1\rangle); & (4)\\
 & \texttt{put}(Ty(cn_s \rightarrow e_s)), Fo(\lambda P.\tau, P);\ \texttt{go}(\langle\uparrow_1\rangle); & (5)\\
 & \texttt{make}(\langle\downarrow_0\rangle);\ \texttt{go}(\langle\downarrow_0\rangle);\ \texttt{put}(?Ty(cn_s)); & (6)\\
 & \texttt{make}((\langle\downarrow_1\rangle)); & (7)\\
 & \texttt{put}(Ty(t \rightarrow cn_s)),\ \texttt{freshput}(\mathrm{s}, Fo(\lambda R.\mathrm{s}, R));\ \texttt{go}(\langle\uparrow_1\rangle); & (8)\\
 & \texttt{make}(\langle\downarrow_0\rangle);\ \texttt{go}(\langle\downarrow_0\rangle);\ \texttt{put}(?Ty(t)); & (9)\\
 & \texttt{make}(\langle\downarrow_0\rangle);\ \texttt{go}(\langle\downarrow_0\rangle);\ \texttt{put}(Ty(e_s); Fo(\mathrm{s}));\ \texttt{go}(\langle\uparrow_0\rangle) & (10)\\
\text{ELSE} & \texttt{abort} & (11)
\end{array}
$$

We will illustrate the effect this lexical entry induces by sketching the parsing steps required in processing the string *If John cries Mary laughs.* We start assuming, as above in (8.56), that INTRODUCTION and PREDICTION have created the two nodes lying under the $?Ty(t)$ root node and the pointer now appears at the left argument daughter where there is a requirement for a node of type e_s to be derived ($?Ty(e_s)$):

(8.74) $?Ty(t), \Diamond \overset{\text{INTRODUCTION PREDICTION}}{\longmapsto}$ $?Ty(t)$

$?Ty(e_s), \Diamond$ $\qquad$ $?Ty(e_s \rightarrow t)$

With this being the case, the IF-condition at the lexical entry of *if* is satisfied and the actions specified in the following lines can take place. By line (2) the requirement for a shared formula with a LINKed node is inserted: $?\exists\mathbf{x}.(Fo(\mathbf{x}) \wedge \langle L\rangle Fo(\mathbf{x}))$. The first conjunct of this requirement can only be satisfied by a proper Formula value from the domain D_{Fo}, appearing on the node, i.e., not a metavariable but a proper term. The second conjunct will be satisfied only when the same Formula value appears at a node LINKed to the present one. In combination with the rest of the processing rules, this second part of the requirement will narrow down the choice for a Formula value to just a quantificational term newly derived in the LINKed structure. By the instructions in line (3), $\texttt{make}(\langle L\rangle);\texttt{go}(\langle L\rangle);\texttt{put}(?Ty(e_s))$, a new node connected with the LINK relation to the current one is built and a requirement to derive a term of type e_s is introduced there. This is the node where the derived τ-term of type e_s will eventually appear. Lines (4)-(5) instruct the parser to construct the functor daughter of this node. This is the node where the functor that introduces the τ-binder appears. The sister of this node will provide an argument of $Ty(cn_s)$, the restrictor for the $\tau - term$. This is built by line (6) and a requirement for the appropriate type, a set of situations, is inserted. The structure that is being created here is completely equivalent to a nominal quantificational term restrictor even though the type is sorted to range over situations. At lines (7)-(8) the parser is instructed to introduce another functor daughter which takes as its argument a proposition of type t with a free variable situation argument. The formula value on this node is introduced as follows: $\texttt{freshput}\ (\mathbf{s}, Fo(\lambda R.\mathbf{s}, R))$. The action `freshput` selects and inserts as (part of) a Formula value for a node the first available variable that has not appeared earlier in the tree being constructed. This ensures that a fresh variable is always introduced. The variable introduced here by the action `freshput` will be identical to the one introduced as the situation argument of the propositional tree built out of processing the antecedent (this is ensured by the employment of rule-level variables annotated as bold and lower case). The Formula value on this node will bind that variable in order to create a Restrictor of the appropriate shape for the τ-binder at the next level up. By line (9) the propositional tree for the content derived from the antecedent is initiated; this node will eventually be decorated by a formula of type t and will provide the set of situations quantified over. In all respects the tree derived by the antecedent will be a simple predicate-argument structure of type t with the only distinctness being that its situation argument will be necessarily a free variable. This will allow the structure derived to be interpreted as the (description of) a set of situations and thus to serve as the restrictor for a quantificational term:

(8.75) $\overset{if}{\longmapsto}$

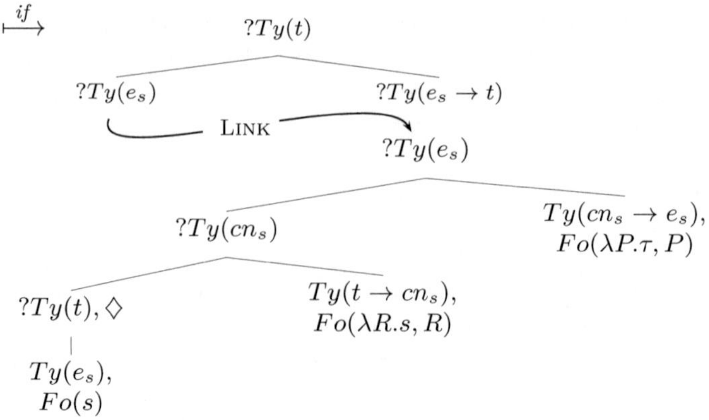

Now the regular parsing processes can take over and continue the processing of the antecedent (the fact that the situation accommodating daughter has already been introduced does not affect the operation of INTRODUCTION and PREDICTION). At the parsing stage shown below, the antecedent, *if John cries*, has been successfully completed although in terms of interpretation the representation at the type t node is that of a set of situations, not truth-evaluable as a proposition without further ado. The usual rules of function application and type deduction can apply to complete the nodes up to the level at which the LINK relation terminates:

(8.76) $\overset{if\ John\ cries}{\longmapsto}$

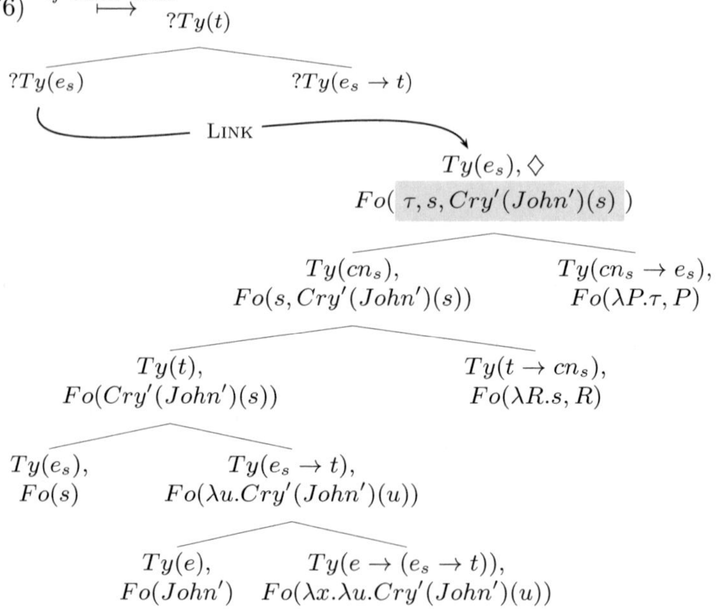

The newly introduced τ-term has as its restrictor the propositional content derived by parsing the string *John cries* under the assumption that a free variable was selected as its situation argument. We now need to copy this term to the main tree. At this point, the pointer appears at the top node of the τ-term's subtree. In order to be able to move the pointer back to the main tree and copy the term to its situation node a rule of EVALUATION is required. The rule belongs to the family of rules characterised as LINK EVALUATION rules. It very simply copies the formula from one node to another one which is related to it by means of the LINK relation and simultaneously moves the pointer there. Application of this rule to the tree in (8.76) above will result in the appropriate copying and the requirement at the situation node can now be satisfied:[17]

(8.77) *if John cries*

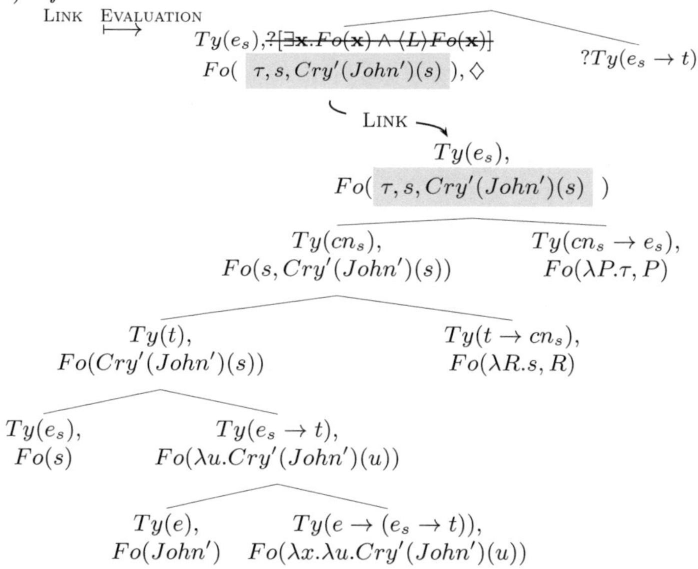

The parsing of the consequent can now go on as usual deriving the tree shown already in (8.68). The final formula derived at the top node of the global tree will be a universal quantification ranging over (contextually restricted) situations at which John cried and predicating of those that they satisfy the description of Mary's laughing. The QUANTIFIER EVALUATION rules will then derive the appropriate representation

[17] The LINK EVALUATION rule will also introduce a requirement for scope resolution concerning the τ-term (?Sc($\mathbf{x}$)) and an underspecified scope statement at the root node (Scope($\mathbf{U} < \mathbf{x}$)).

in terms of scope and the situation $\tau - term$:

(8.78) $Ty(t), Fo(\ Laugh'(Mary')\ (\tau, s, Cry'(John')(s))\ )\ \overset{Q-Eval}{\longmapsto}$
$Fo(\ [Cry'(John')(\alpha) \rightarrow Laugh'(Mary')(\alpha)]$
$\quad \text{where } \alpha = \tau, s, [Cry'(John')(s) \rightarrow Laugh'(Mary')(s)]\ )$

Let's see now how the syntactic properties of *if*-clauses are accounted for according to this analysis.

The absence of low construals The parallel properties of *if*-clauses and nominal relatives have led several researchers to the assumption, which is also adopted here, that *if*-clauses are a type of relative clause in the same way that *when*-clauses and *where*-clauses can be taken as relatives over implicit time or location specifications (see e.g. Geis 1985; Bhatt and Pancheva 2006). Nevertheless, there is one difference between these clauses and *if*-clauses. Consider the following:

(8.79) John left when Mary claimed that Bill left

The above is ambiguous between the following two interpretations:

(8.80) John left at the time at which, according to Mary, Bill left

(8.81) John left at the time at which Mary made the following claim: "Bill left"

Unlike *when*-clauses, *if*-clauses are not ambiguous in that respect:

(8.82) John left if Mary claimed that Bill left.

(8.83) In any case that is such that Mary made the claim: "Bill left", John left (in that case)

(8.84) # John left in any one of the circumstances that Bill left according to Mary's claims

When *if*-clauses are analyzed as the same type of construction as nominal relatives and *when*-clauses this pattern of idiosyncratic behaviour regarding the strict locality requirement internal to the antecedent is awkward for frameworks that employ uniform processes of movement, or movement-like operations as ad hoc restrictions of the general mechanisms is required in explaining this difference in extractability. In contrast, DS (as well as other lexicalist frameworks) can deal comfortably with idiosyncrasies of this type since, by definition, each word is individually associated with a particular set of procedural actions which, it is plausible, may deviate from their common historical patterns under functional or pragmatic pressures. Hence, in the present analysis, the locality is captured naturally because the initiation of the LINKed tree has been assigned to the actions associated with the word *if* where the situation argument is created immediately as a fixed node on the new tree. In contrast, for *when*-clauses/*where*-clauses, as in nominal relatives, we can assume that the situation argument is constructed by general rules as initially unfixed, hence the possibility of low construal readings.

8.4.4 Conditionals: Processing strategies

As we said, terms denoting individuals ($Ty(e_i)$) in DS can be processed by utilising two additional strategies besides their processing in the usual argument positions: either as unfixed nodes initially or finally in the parse or on their own individual subtrees which must be LINKed to another tree of type t. Given that we assume here that *if*-clauses behave as relatives introducing predications on $Ty(e_s)$ arguments we would expect the same strategies to be available to them. First we will examine parsing of *if*-clauses when associated with unfixed nodes and then their contribution to LINKed structures.

8.4.4.1 *If*-clauses as unfixed nodes

A. Sentence-initial *if*-clause For sentence-initial *if*-clauses we can assume that parsing starts as usual with the $?Ty(t)$ node introduced through the AXIOM and bearing the pointer. As standardly, the rule of *ADJUNCTION, can apply and introduce an unfixed node of type e_s.[18] Diagrammatically we can see the creation of the unfixed node in the following tree which is the initial point of parsing without yet any lexical input:

(8.85) $Tn(a), ?Ty(t), \diamond \quad \overset{*\text{ADJUNCTION}}{\longmapsto} \quad Tn(a), ?Ty(t)$

$\qquad\qquad\qquad\qquad\qquad\qquad\qquad\qquad\qquad\qquad |$

$\langle\uparrow_*\rangle Tn(a), ?Ty(e_s), ?\exists\mathbf{x}.Tn(\mathbf{x}), \diamond$

As soon as this happens, we are ready to process lexical input since the pointer is in an environment matching what is required for application of the instructions in the *if* lexical entry (see line (1) in (8.73)). According to the instructions given there, a requirement will be then inserted at the unfixed node that a formula value for it must be found at the root of a LINKed tree. The construction of the new LINKed tree will also be initiated and the fresh variable ranging over situations that has been introduced will eventually end up bound by the τ-binder. The rest of the antecedent can then be processed and the LINKed tree will be completed. The LINK EVALUATION rule will copy the term constructed on the unfixed node, as already shown earlier:

[18] Remember that we have defined type e as being the more general category covering both individual entities and situations.

(8.86)

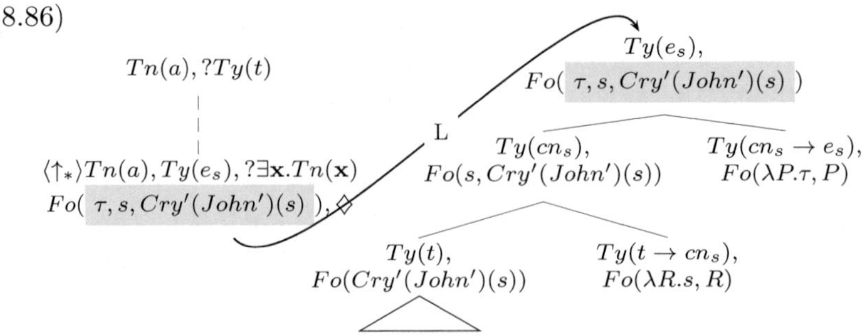

At this point the rule of COMPLETION will move the pointer to the $?Ty(t)$ node and INTRODUCTION and PREDICTION will construct a situation node and its sister. With the pointer at the situation node, MERGE can apply to unify it with the unfixed node. Alternatively, MERGE, which is an optional operation, will not apply and the parsing will go on constructing more structure with the unfixed node pending. The tree shown below displays a stage of the parsing of a string like *If John cries Mary believes that Bill will be upset*:

(8.87)

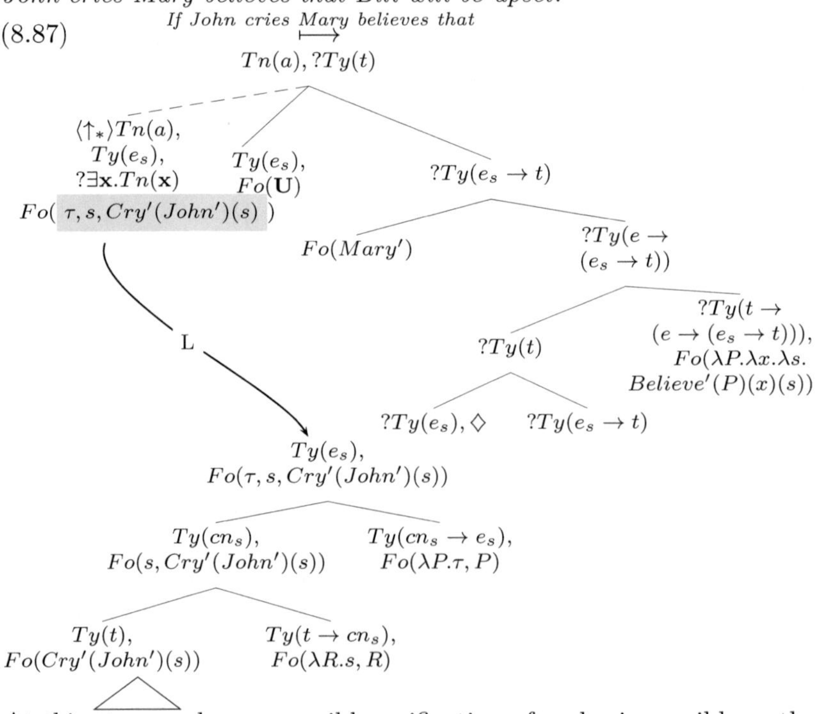

At this stage, only one possible unification of nodes is possible so that the pending requirement ($?\exists\mathbf{x}.Tn(\mathbf{x})$) will be satisfied: the unfixed node must merge with the embedded situation node, which will provide a fixed position for it and an appropriate argument for the propositional object of *believe*:

(8.88) $\overset{Merge}{\longmapsto}$

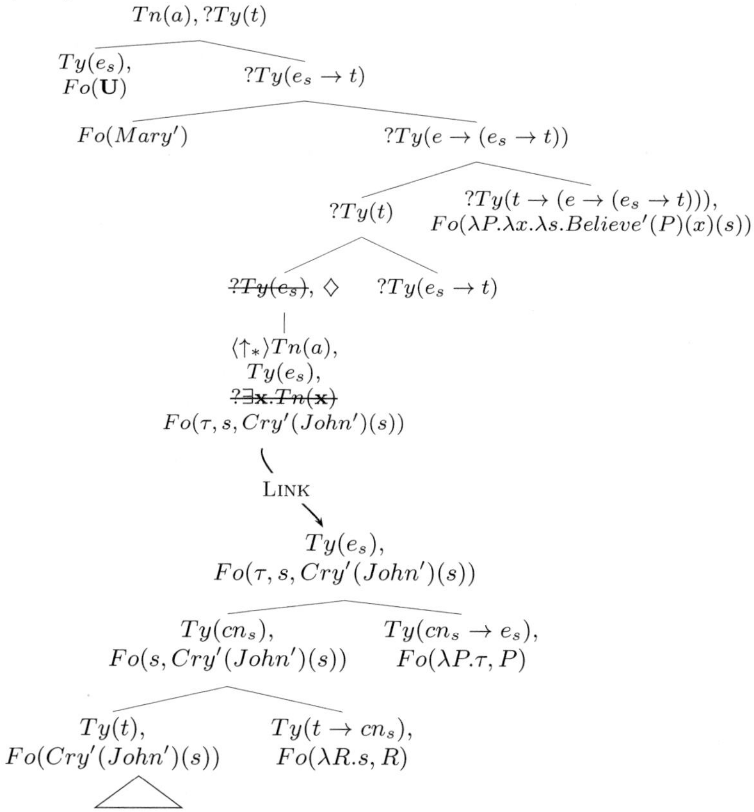

The procedures defined here explain why the processing of such strings might result in two distinct readings, represented by distinct trees according to where Merge has applied:

(8.89) If John cries Sue believes that he just pretends.

(8.89) a. Sue has the following belief: all situations where John cries are situations where he just pretends, or

(8.89) b. all situations where John cries are situations where Sue has the belief that he just pretends.

The two readings are derived in our analysis by assigning to the processing of the sentence two distinct structures. The first reading results when the unfixed situation node that has been created initially and which carries the LINK structure along with it merges with the situation node of the tree created by the processing of the clause which is the object of the verb *believe*, as shown above in (8.88). The second reading is derived if the unfixed situation node is merged with the situation node of the tree derived by the processing of the matrix clause.

B. Post-verbal *if*-clause If the antecedent appears post-verbally as in (8.90) below

(8.90) John cries if he is upset

then the main tree will have been completed up to the node $Ty(e_s \to t)$ before processing of the *if*-clause starts:

(8.91)

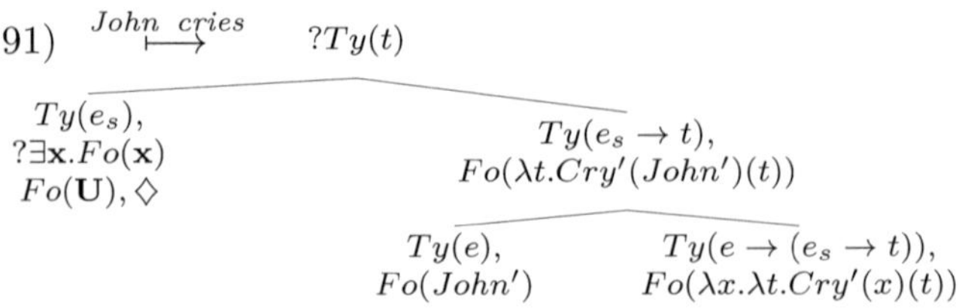

At this stage, the rule of LATE-*ADJUNCTION can apply to create a locally unfixed copy of the $Ty(e_s)$ node:

(8.92)

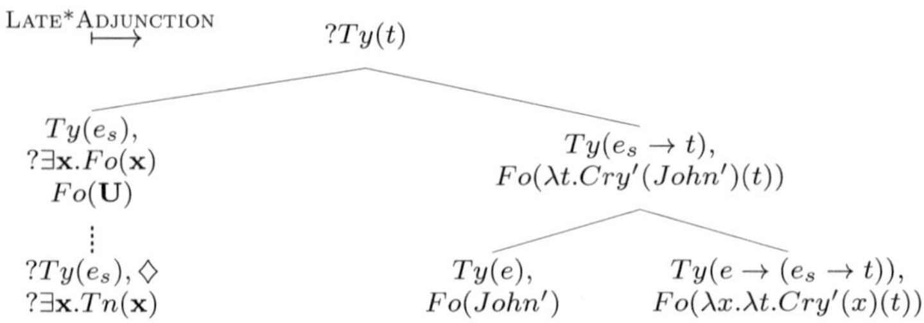

This rule has now created an appropriate context matching what is required for the processing of the word *if* in (8.73). As above, a LINKed tree is constructed from this node and the process and outcome are exactly the same as in the previous cases. The only difference will be that the unfixed node is constructed locally, so that it becomes completed and merges with its mother before any processing of the main tree resumes. Below is the state of the tree after processing of the *if*-clause but just before MERGE has occurred:

(8.93)

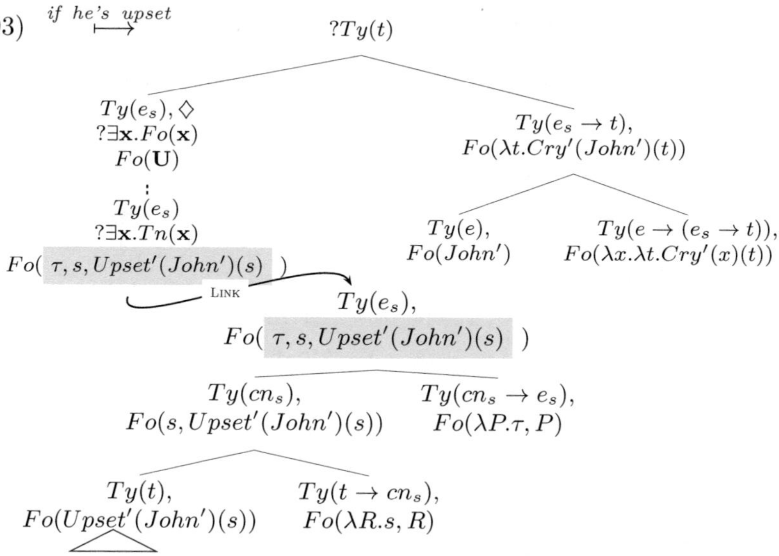

MERGE can now occur so that both the requirements at the unfixed and fixed nodes can be satisfied. After MERGE, the usual rules will finish the main tree and the result will be indistinguishable from the tree derived by processing a preverbal *if*-clause like *If John is upset he cries*:

(8.94)

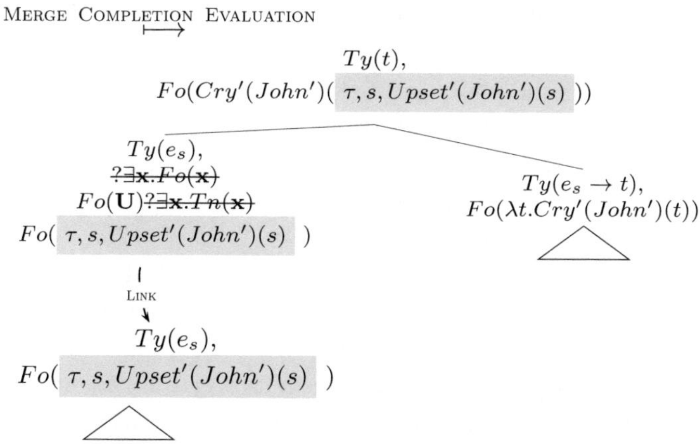

Thus, even with post-verbal *if*-clauses, the processing and completion of the tree derived from the antecedent will have been finished before completion of the tree derived from the consequent. This is as it should be since we assume that the antecedent provides a restrictor for the situation argument of the main proposition, a proposition therefore that cannot be completed until that argument is provided. The lexical entry for *if* derives this outcome by allowing the *if*-clause to be processed, if not sentence-initially, only when the pointer is located at the situation argument node of the main tree just before its completion.

The fact that even sentence-initial *if*-clauses need to be able to be processed at unfixed nodes is not required just for the processing of structures like the one in (8.89). As an added advantage, this parsing strategy also allows us to explain the apparent cataphoric effects observed in cases of *reconstruction*:

(8.95) [Which of the pictures he_i dislikes] did every $professor_i$ try to hide?

(8.96) If she_i's late again $Mary_i$ will be punished

(8.97) [If pictures of $himself_i$ are on sale], $John_i$ will be happy

As shown in Gregoromichelaki (2006), (8.96)-(8.97) above can be licensed in the same way as (8.95) if the antecedent can be maintained as initially unfixed, which allows delay in the resolution of the pronominals until some appropriate value for them has been introduced through the processing of the consequent. In addition, this strategy allows *quantificational subordination* phenomena that occur with conditionals to be accounted for in the same way as the bound variable interpretations we saw in (8.5)-(8.8) earlier:

(8.98) [If her_i child is late from school], every $mother_i$ is upset.

Despite contrary claims in the literature, Gregoromichelaki (2006) has shown that such bindings are possible in either direction, both from the antecedent and from the consequent:[19]

(8.99) If every $choice_i$ is an opportunity, it_i's also a sacrifice

(8.100) ...even if every $spaceship_i$ were made of diamonds, it_i would be cheaper in comparison with its_i virtual price.

(8.101) ..., because if every $player_i$ knew he would be going on the block at the end of every season, he_i would hustle his tail off and make it to every practice,...

The option of parsing *if*-clauses as annotating unfixed nodes allows the modelling of such bindings as naturally following from the parsing strategy selected, even when linearity, quantificational binding and syntactic subordination present conflicting requirements as in (8.98)-(8.101): whether in sentence-initial position or sentence-finally, as we saw, the *if*-clause always provides content that is subordinated to the consequent since it provides a restrictor for one of its arguments that

[19]For more data and sources see Gregoromichelaki (2006).

has to be completed first; however, the fact that the node bearing this content can be processed as unfixed, i.e., as pending until the consequent has been partially completed, allows quantificational elements to be introduced in either of the two LINKed trees with licensed dependencies extending to elements of the other tree (and since scope is dissociated from tree-architecture extra-wide scope is also independent from these requirements).

8.4.4.2 *If*-clauses as LINKed nodes

We have now provided ways of processing preverbal and postverbal antecedents by utilising a single lexical entry for *if* and without introducing any new processing methods to the DS toolbox except the assumption that the situation of evaluation can be processed as a regular (potentially optional) $Ty(e)$ argument. There remains the final challenge of making sense of the heterogeneity apparently indicated by the Haegeman suggestion that there are two wholly different types of *if*-clauses (part of how to resolve this issue has already been discussed above in 8.4.2 with respect to (8.67)). We will now turn to examine whether the rest of the apparatus utilised in DS for the processing of arguments contributed by nominals can be also employed for the processing of conditionals so as to establish an exact parallel between the two types of $Ty(e)$ terms, situations ($Ty(e_s)$) and individuals ($Ty(e_i)$).

A. *If*-clauses in the left periphery *Topicalization* is the phenomenon of a left-peripheral DP associated with some position more deeply embedded in the following structure:

(8.102) John, Mary said Bill dislikes ___.

In DS the rule of *ADJUNCTION allows for the initial processing of such left-dislocated DPs as unfixed nodes and the rule of MERGE takes care of their eventual incorporation in the tree. Such constructions contrast with ones that involve anaphoric-like dependencies between left-dislocated phrases and an argument position inside the following structure:

(8.103) (As for) That woman you dislike$_i$, I saw her$_i$ leaving

DS licenses such structures by means of the construction of two independent subtrees, nodes of which are connected with the LINK relation. Here there is only an obligatory copying relation between the two trees and no merging of nodes. Processing of the left-dislocated phrase is achieved by the TOPIC ADJUNCTION rule (Cann et al. 2005). From the AXIOM, the rule allows for the building of a new node required to be of type e. This node is LINKed to the main tree in a sense analogous to it providing the head of a relative clause. Processing of the left-peripheral element can then proceed as usual. After its processing has been completed a LINK EVALUATION rule is employed to move the pointer to the $?Ty(t)$ node and simultaneously introduce a requirement for a copy of the Formula value appearing at the linked $Ty(e)$ node to appear in some embedded position ($\langle D\rangle$) of the main tree. For illustration consider the tree derived by the processing of such a string:

(8.104) $\overset{(As\ for)\ John\ Mary\ dislikes\ him}{\longmapsto}$

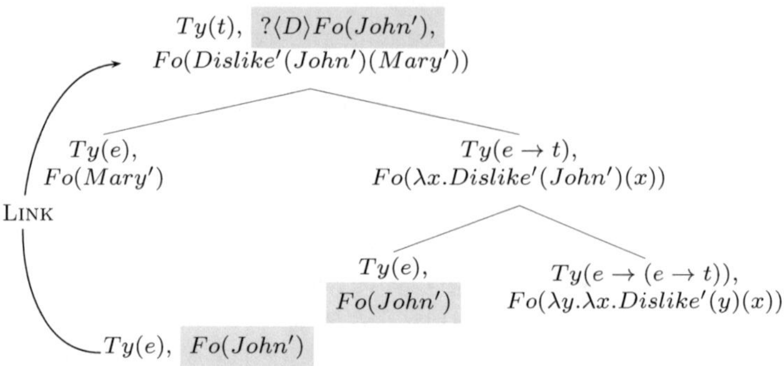

Since the present analysis assumes that processing of *if*-clauses results in the construction of a term of type e it is natural to assume that the same TOPIC ADJUNCTION RULE should be applicable here too. Under this assumption, a situation argument might be constructed independently, externally to the main structure, and a requirement for its Formula value to appear inside the tree representing the consequent can be imposed. The instructions included in the lexical entry for *if* in (8.73) above will be employed unchanged here too to derive a structure similar to that appearing during the processing of nominal topics (see Gregoromichelaki 2006 for full demonstration):

(8.105) $\overset{\text{...TOPIC-ADJUCTION ...}if\ John\ cries...}{\longmapsto}$

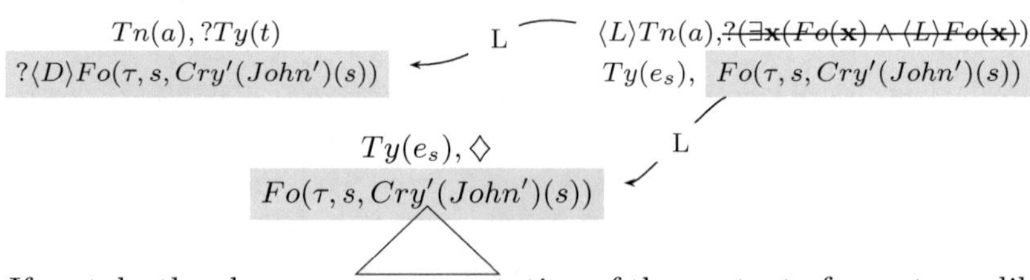

If we take the above as a representation of the content of a sentence like *if John cries, Mary laughs* then the situation metavariable of the main propositional tree must be replaced with the $\tau - term$ derived on the LINKed node otherwise the requirement $?\langle D\rangle Fo(\tau, s, Cry'(John')(s))$

will not be satisfied. By this imposed copying the situation argument of the tree representing the content of the consequent will be unified with the formula value at the top node of the LINKed subtree:

(8.106)

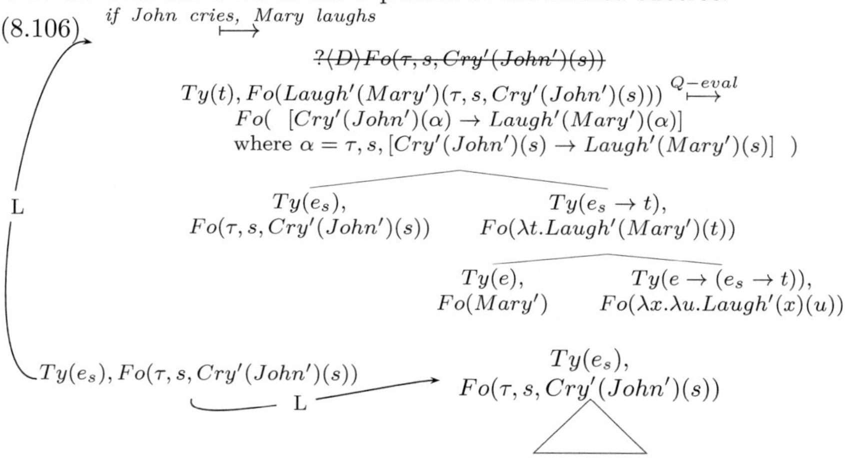

While it seems that there are no evident syntactic differences that distinguish this type of processing conditionals in English[20] it is true that different types of interpretations and inferential effects can be associated with them. The most convincing case for a distinct type of conditional is the *relevance* or *speech act* type, illustrated below:

(8.107) If you are thirsty, there is beer in the fridge.

According to Iatridou (1991), here the antecedent is not used to single out the cases in which the proposition in the consequent is claimed to hold because that proposition is asserted to be true unconditionally. Instead, the antecedent here is taken to specify the circumstances in which it is *relevant*/appropriate to perform the speech act of informing the addressee of the truth of the proposition expressed by the consequent. It has been argued that in such structures there is an implicit performative verb in the main clause which explains the truth conditions. For the example in (8.107) above the underlying structure is claimed to be:

(8.108) If you are thirsty, then [*it is relevant for me to tell you that*] there is beer in the fridge.

One should note that this distinction between *relevance* and other conditionals, in contrast to other distinctions that can be accounted for by purely pragmatic means, has some syntactic basis in V2 languages like

[20] Apart from intonational clues which, we assume, are not discreetly encoded in the signal.

German (see e.g. Ebert et al. 2008; Koenig and van der Auwera 1988) and Afrikaans. Native speakers' judgements[21] indicate that it is impossible to sustain the same interpretation between the two conditionals below:

(8.109) *As jy my nodig het, ek is by die kantoor* [Afrikaans]
if you me need has, I am at the office
'If you need me, I am at the office'

(8.110) *#As jy my nodig het, is ek by die kantoor*
if you me need has, am I at the office
not: If you need me, I am at the office
but: # If you need me, THEN I am at the office

If the antecedent appears as the first element before the verb as in (8.110) then it cannot be assigned a "relevance" interpretation (although it can be assigned a "factual", metarepresentational or echoic interpretation, see (8.67) above). A general account for conditionals needs then to be able to account for why such distinct interpretations are freely available according to context in languages like English while in other languages they seem to have been grammaticised in that they feed or bleed other derivational options. As in V2 languages the *if*-clause can, sometimes, count as the first constituent for V2 (see (8.110)) this necessitates a DS modelling in terms of the unfixed node strategy as this is what underlies the DS characterisation of the V2 phenomenon. We take cases where *if*-clauses appear initially but do not count as the V2 first element as explicit grammaticised indications that they are more "peripheral" to the main structure. This intuition can be given a formal characterisation by taking the *if*-clause as providing content which appears on a node LINKed to the main tree. In such cases, "relevance" interpretations will be preferable (but not obligatory) while with the unfixed node strategy they would be excluded given the information structure requirements associated with this strategy as discussed above in section 8.4 with respect to (8.52)-(8.53).

B. *If*-clauses in the right periphery Dancygier and Sweetser (2005: 174) observe that *if*-clauses (P-clauses in their terminology) appear in the following formal patterns which they assume contrast in terms of interpretations:

(8.111) if P, Q: If the home computer breaks down, I'll work in my office.

(8.112) If P Q: If the home computer breaks down I'll work in my office.

[21] Data from Gregoromichelaki (2006).

(8.113) Q if P: I'll work in my office if the home computer breaks down.

(8.114) Q, if P: I'll work in my office, if the home computer breaks down.

We have now provided an analysis that explains the intuitions discriminating the first three patterns (i.e. LINKed situation node vs. argument situation node). We can now provide a formal basis for the intuition underlying the fourth pattern, i.e. the claim that that the construction indicates that the P-clause relies on prior contextual justification of its content:

> "The Q-clause is then followed (after a comma/pause) by P, which either further restricts the context in which the assertion of Q is valid, or justifies the communication of Q as appropriate (this may involve conditions on speech acts and metalinguistic conditions)"
> (Dancygier and Sweetser ibid: 175).

In DS a similar pattern as regards nominals has been identified (Cann et al. 2005, Ch. 5):

(8.115) He cries, Bill

A right-peripheral nominal expression can be presented with an anaphoric expression inside the main clause necessarily identified as coreferential with it. The DS parsing strategy that handles this pattern employs the rule of RECAPITULATION (Cann et al. 2005). According to this, following the completion of a propositional type t structure, the rule initiates a LINKed tree which bears the requirement to include a formula value identical to one appearing inside the tree from which the LINK relation originates. Since the latter has necessarily been completed prior to the application of the rule, the formula value that needs to be copied must have already been provided contextually. As an illustration, consider the (schematic) tree that will be derived for the string in (8.115) (where the double arrow indicates SUBSTITUTION of a metavariable formula value on a treenode by a contextually provided value):

(8.116)

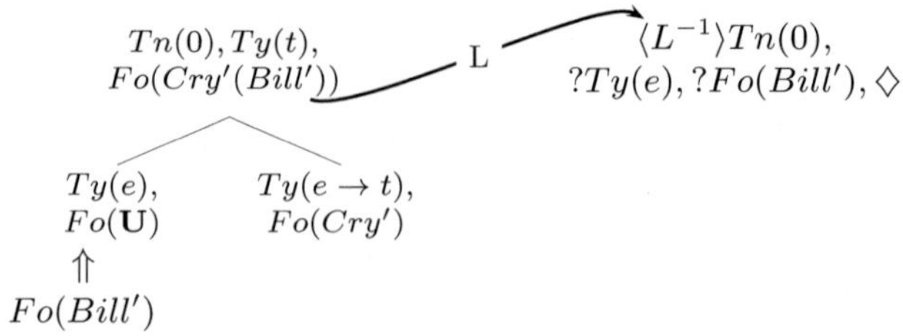

We can give a parallel analysis for the pattern in (8.114). The right peripheral *if*-clause can provide justification for the selection of the contextually derived situation term or further restrict it by means of providing additional clues for the value of the metavariable $\boldsymbol{R}$, the contextual restriction always included in such terms (see section 8.4.2). As an illustration, consider the tree derived from the Q-clause in (8.114) after application of the RECAPITULATION rule (now taking the type e mentioned in this rule as the general supertype). The contextual provision of a value for the metavariable at the situation argument node and the requirement for it to appear again in the new $?Ty(e_s)$ tree initiated are shown. Parsing of the *if*-clause provides the required value. After processing of the P-clause has been finalised the (schematic) structure that ensues for (8.114) above is as follows:

(8.117)

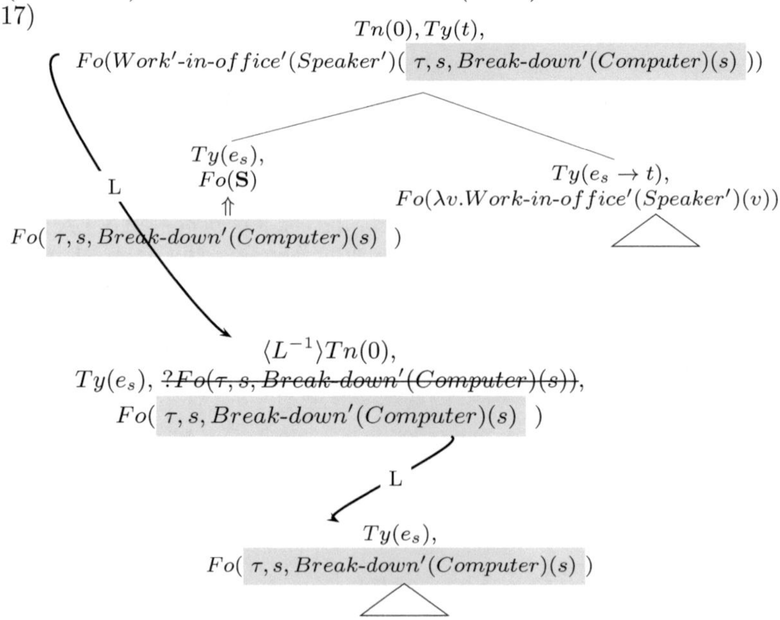

8.5 Conclusion

There are multiple analyses of conditionals which attempt to classify their disparate interpretations (see e.g. Declerck and Reed 2001 who identify a multitude of semantics) and ground those on the basis of underlying structural ambiguities. In contrast, an account in the spirit of DS ought to allow such a multiplicity of interpretations not as directly encoded in the linguistic system but as the effect of the inherent context dependence of the lexical/structural resources and the processing strategies available. In accordance to this, the aim of the present account was to provide the minimal skeletal form of the truth conditions of conditionals which (a) further processes of reasoning and pragmatic inferencing will take as input in order to derive the requisite interpretations (see Björnsson and Gregoromichelaki, in prep) and (b) provide the source for providing answers to puzzles in the syntax/semantics interface. Given that DS is more parsimonious in terms of representational levels, eschewing the postulation of a level of hierarchical organisation over strings, while at the same time allowing the compositional derivation of the requisite semantic representation, this account is preferable as it covers all the syntactic facts (see, e.g. section 8.3.1) via independently motivated processing considerations. In terms of interpretational effects, the review of the data leads to the conclusion that there is a distinction between peripheral and more integrated *if*-clauses, a fact reflected here in their processing, via identical lexical/syntactic resources, as either annotating a LINKed subtree or an unfixed node. Unlike a structural ambiguity account, this is a natural explanation of the distinctions observed as variation in the time-linear presentation of truth-conditionally equivalent forms reflects differences in information status, a well-known factor that underlies the existence of variable processing methods in general. Moreover, both from a functional and a psycholinguistic point of view, the availability of alternative strategies is an essential component of NL processing as it both facilitates incremental processing (Ferreira 1996) and allows the structuring of expressions according to the gradual contextual availability of information.

References

The following were cited in this chapter: Belnap (1970), Bhatt (1996), Bhatt and Pancheva (2006), Björnsson and Gregoromichelaki (in preparation), Blackburn and Meyer-Viol (1994), Blakemore (1987), Cann et al. (2005), Carston (2002), Chierchia (1995), Chomsky (1957), Dancygier and Sweetser (2005) Declerck and Reed (2001), Ebert et al. (2008),

Edgington (2003), Farkas (1997), Ferreira (1996), von Fintel (1994), von Fintel (to appear), Geis (1985), Geurts (2004), Gregoromichelaki (2006), Haegeman (2001, 2003), Haiman (1978, 1993), Heim (1990), Hilbert and Bernays (1939), Huitink (2008), Iatridou (1991), Koenig and van der Auwera (1988), Kratzer (1986), Kempson et al. (2001), Lycan (2001), Noh (1998), Papafragou (1996, 2000), Purver et al. (2010), Recanati (1999), Rooth (1985), Ross (1967), Shaer (2003), Schlenker (2006) Smith and Smith (1988), Strawson (1986), Taylor (1985). See references at end of book for full information.

9

Towards an Account of the English Auxiliary System

Ronnie Cann

9.1 Introduction

The latter half of the twentieth century spawned numerable accounts of the verbal auxiliary system in English, following on from the elegant transformational account put forward in Chomsky (1957). The system is complex with a number of interlocking morphological dependencies and ordering constraints between verbal elements, as partially illustrated in the data in (9.1,9.2).

(9.1) a. Mary dances/danced/*dance/*dancing.
b. Mary will dance/*dances/*danced/*dancing.
c. Mary has danced/*dances/*dance/*dancing).
d. Mary is dancing/*dances/*danced/*dance).
e. Mary was praised/*praises/*praise/♮praising.[1]

(9.2) a. Mary will be dancing.
b. Mary will have been dancing.
c. Mary will have been being praised.

This paper was a long time gestating and is based on a series of talks I gave in the mid-1990s on the passive and perfect in English. I am grateful for comments at various stages of the composition to Ruth Kempson, Eleni Gregoromichelaki, Shalom Lappin, Mary E. Tait, Nik Gisborne, and Dan Wedgwood. I am grateful to the Leverhulme trust for support during the final stages of the paper (Major Research Fellow, F00158BF).

[1] I use the symbol ♮ before a string to indicate that the string itself is grammatical but has an interpretation that significantly differs from some intended one (such as that here Mary should be the 'praisee' not the 'praiser').

The Dynamics of Lexical Interfaces.
Ruth Kempson, Eleni Gregoromichelaki and Christine Howes (eds.).

d. *Mary is will dance.
e. *Mary will be having danced.
f. *Mary is been praised.
g. *Mary is had praised

The other topic of primary interest is that auxiliary verbs in English engage in syntactic constructions that main verbs do not:[2]:

A the sentential negation marker, *not*, follows auxiliary verbs but precedes main verbs and auxiliary forms may host a cliticized negation marker, or have negated forms:

a. Mary will not go to the ball.
b. Mary (*not) goes (*not) to the ball.
c. Mary didn't go to the ball.

B auxiliary verbs may precede a subject but not main verbs:

a. Will Mary go?
b. Has Mary gone?
c. *Went Mary?

C auxiliary verbs may mark ellipsis sites whereas main verbs do not:

a. Mary won't go, but Bill will.
b. Mary wants to go, and Bill does, too.
c. *Mary wants to go, and Bill wants, too.

D main verbs permit 'do support' but auxiliary verbs do not:

a. Mary does/doesn't want to go.
b. *Mary does have gone.
c. *Mary does will go.

Characterizations of these constructions and their interactions are legion in the theoretical literature within different frameworks. In the earliest example which set the scene for most later characterizations, Chomsky proposed an extremely elegant and simple analysis of the complex data in (9.1) that has had a remarkably long period of popularity. The analysis solved the problem of the apparently discontinuous dependencies between the auxiliary verbs *have* and *be* and the appropriate suffixes on the following verb forms by concatenating them at deep structure using the phrase structure rule in (9.3a). A transformational rule of Affix Hopping, (9.3b), was then responsible for moving the affixal morpheme rightward over an adjacent verbal element to attach it as a suffix at surface structure. Thus, the deep structure string in (9.3c) is transformed into the surface string, underlying *Mary had been dancing* as in (9.3d).

[2]A - C are often referred to as the 'NICE' properties.

(9.3) a. Aux $\rightarrow$ Tns - (M) - (have+en) - (be+ing) - (be+en)
b. Affix-hopping: X Af Vb Y $\Rightarrow$ X Vb+Af Y.
c. Mary Past have+en be+ing dance.
d. Mary have+Past be+en dance+ing.
e. Mary had been dancing.

Later developments within the transformational literature, led to concepts of verb raising and Affix lowering (Chomsky 1981, etc.), but the problems posed by the data in (9.1,9.2) have not really found a more comprehensive coverage in such frameworks than that given in Chomsky (1957).

However, in non-transformational frameworks, there have been a number of interesting accounts of the phenomena beginning with the GPSG analysis of Gazdar et al. (1982) to the formally more elegant characterizations found in Warner (1993, 2000), amongst others. In these, auxiliary verbs typically function as heads of their verb phrases with verb phrase complements that require heads with particular forms, with such forms defined in terms of features. So, for example, in Warner (1993) modals are defined to take [+BSE;-FIN] (i.e. base form) complements, while *be* takes complements that are marked as [-BSE;+PRD]. Constraints on collocation are also specified in terms of subcategorization. The form *being*, for example, is defined to take a [-ING] complement (to exclude **being singing*) and modals are confined to [-TO,-PRD] base forms (**Mary will to sing/*Mary will singing*).

It is not my intention here to review the published accounts of the (morpho-) syntax of the English auxiliary system, but to highlight the obvious omission of such accounts: their failures to account for the *interpretation* of auxiliary strings in any compositional or dynamic way. In general, if the semantics of the various combinations of auxiliaries are discussed, it is in terms of more general syntactico-semantic categories such as tense and aspect. Such broad views of the subject do not lend themselves to discussions of how or why the various combinations of modals, *have*, *be* and the different participial forms, give rise to such specific semantic constructs as progressive aspect, perfect, pluperfect, etc. Only the passive gets any serious attention as a non-TMA (Tense-Mood-Aspect) construction whose interpretation is assumed to be straightforwardly derived from the active paraphrase.

I cannot, in the space of a short paper, hope to account for all of these issues nor to provide a full detailed syntax and semantics of the English auxiliary system. My aims here are more modest. I try to show how an incremental approach to the system can be constructed that induces a gradual build up of semantic structure, not in terms of complex and undefined predicates that take other predicates as arguments (as would be the case for a semantics of the GPSG/HPSG frameworks), but in terms of the progressive elaboration of an event term that is the argument of the contentive predicate expressed by the main verb, as in neo-Davidsonian theories of verb semantics such as Parsons (1990). This event term underspecifies the meaning of particular collocations but provides just enough temporal structure to induce enrichment through the lexical semantics of the main verb. In this way, the model I sketch is an attempt to implement the view of grammar motivated from psycholinguistics and historical linguistics in Cann (2000). In addition, I try to show how a Dynamic Syntax approach to the auxiliary constructions can capture the combinatorial properties illustrated in (9.1) through manipulation of the lexical actions associated with different verbs and verb forms, thus providing the syntactic process on which the interpretation of auxiliary clusters depends. Less centrally, I will sketch how some of the syntactic properties listed above can be captured in the framework, such as Subject-Auxiliary Inversion and Ellipsis, although this is a only a secondary thread of the argument.

9.2 Foundations: Syntactic subjects and tensed verbs

Unlike structuralist-based theories of grammar, whether transformational or monostratal/lexical, DS assigns no *grammatical* significance to combinations of strings of words, phrases and clauses, or to types of dependency that are often said to hold between them, such as headedness, complementation, modification, etc. Although such concepts may be derivable from the strings of words licensed by the grammar, they do not provide the basis of analysis nor the vocabulary in which relevant syntactic processes are expressed. Instead, DS treats words and morphemes, not as static objects that enter into some computation of licensed structures over strings of words, but as triggers for performing packages of actions that indicate how semantic content is to be integrated into whatever content has already been constructed. The means of representing such content is the use of binary trees decorated with formulae in some typed lambda calculus, the trees representing a proof path that guarantees a propositional output for any well-formed string of words. Syntax is thus construed as the process by which such semantic trees are constructed. Critically also, DS is strictly incremental: strings are processed on a word-by-word basis with the string of words already processed providing the context in which the next word is parsed. The process is goal-driven, determined by requirements of various sorts: to derive some formula of a specified type from the parse of a string; to identify the exact semantic function of bit of semantic content; or to identify the content of some node from some contextually given value.

The first type of requirement provides the driving force behind the parsing process. A requirement $?Ty(t)$ (or $?t$) is the basic goal to derive some propositional content from some string of words (called the axiom). In Kempson et al. (2001), two general computational rules INTRODUCTION and PREDICTION are defined to break down one type requirement into two subgoals $?Ty(X \rightarrow Y)$ and $?Ty(X)$ which, when satisfied, can be combined to satisfy an original goal $?Ty(Y)$, via modus ponens over the types and functional application of the two derived formulae. Thus, the initial propositional requirement $?Ty(t)$ can be broken down into two subgoals, $?Ty(e \rightarrow t)$, requiring a one place predicate, and $?Ty(e)$, requiring some term. The use of these two rules is used extensively in Marten (2000), Kempson et al. (2001) and Cann et al., (2005), and elsewhere, to account for a range of linguistic phenomena, including parametric variation. Thus, it is hypothesized that in some languages like Irish and Japanese the propositional structure (predicate-argument array) is provided directly by the parse of a verb while in languages like English and Chinese, INTRODUCTION and PREDICTION first derive more structure and the parse of verbs provide any remaining necessary structure, internal argument structure for English and just decoration of the main functor node in Chinese (see Wu 2005). Although a reasonable basis for exploring cross-linguistic variation (e.g. in word order), it does so at the expense of any unitary characterization of the notion of syntactic subject or the projection of argument structure by verbs. In this paper, I eschew the use of the two computational rules, INTRODUCTION and PREDICTION in favour of an analysis in which lexical semantic structure only results from the parse of appropriate word-forms and so verbs build all the core argument structure determined by their lexical semantic properties. Hence, the parsing of verbs in English I assume is triggered by a propositional requirement and induces the construction of all relevant semantic argument nodes.

In English, of course, subjects precede main verbs and the question then arises as to how such pre-verbal expressions can be parsed in the absence of structure, including an appropriate type requirement, having been provided by the parse of a predicate-projecting expression and in the absence of computational rules such as INTRODUCTION and PREDICTION. This can be done using a type of underspecification involving another sort of requirement: that of a requirement to find a semantic function within the emerging propositional tree for some word-string already parsed. Such positional underspecification is used in DS to model left dislocation using a general computational rule called *ADJUNCTION (pronounced 'star-adjunction') which introduces a node which does not have a fixed position in a tree, merely being marked as dominated by the topnode through the underspecified modal relation, $\langle\uparrow_*\rangle Tn(0)$, where $Tn(0)$ is the treenode address of the topnode.[3] This unfixed relation needs, at some point in the construction process, to be fully specified, thus fixing the node in the structure. Since only fixed nodes in a tree have a treenode address, unfixed nodes are associated with the requirement $?\exists\mathbf{x}.Tn(\mathbf{x})$.

However, as it stands, this particular rule is not appropriate for the parse of subjects in English (and pre-verbal, scrambled constituents in other languages). As defined in Kempson et al. (2001), the rule can only operate in a context in which no dominated node is already constructed in order to ensure only one 'true' left dislocated constituent per clause. Because subjects are not always string initial in sentences in English (and, of course, most other languages), being preceded by WH-expressions and other focused elements, the use of such a rule is precluded. Instead we may take up a variant of *ADJUNCTION that is introduced in Cann et al. (2005) to account for scrambling phenomena in languages like Japanese. This is a localized variant that may apply even if other dominated nodes have been constructed, but requires the projected unfixed node to be fixed locally within the current propositional domain. This is defined in Cann et al. (2005) using an operator $\langle\uparrow_0\uparrow_1^*\rangle$ which is defined over paths in the tree from one argument node up through any number of functor nodes (including none) to the dominating node. A variant of this rule, called LOCAL*ADJUNCTION may be used to introduce syntactic subjects in English without the use of INTRODUCTION and PREDICTION.

If one assumes that LOCAL*ADJUNCTION operates in English, there are two obvious ways of incorporating this: to assume that locally unfixed nodes are required to be fixed as logical subjects by imposing a requirement $?\langle\uparrow\rangle Ty(t)$ (above the current node must at some point be a completed propositional node); or to assume free fixing within a local propositional domain with the parse of particular verb forms fixing a locally unfixed node to a particular local position. In order to incorporate the passive construction in which, by hypothesis, the syntactic

[3]Treenode addresses are defined by the predicate Tn which takes values from strings of binary numbers (i.e. the language $0\{0,1\}^*$). These binary numbers indicate the relationship of a node with respect to the topnode, 0 indicating an argument node and 1, a functor node. In other words, a node is introduced that is related through an unspecified sequence (possibly null) of mother relations ($\uparrow$) to the topnode.

subject is realized as some logical object, only the latter will in fact do. The variability in interpretation of syntactic subjects as logical subjects or objects (or even subjects of embedded propositional structures in raising constructions) is determined in all cases by the properties of the main verb and the form it takes. Thus, bare infinitive and present and perfect participial forms of non-raising main verbs will, in English, fix the syntactic subject as the logical subject while passive participles will fix it as a logical object and raising verbs will (somehow) push the fixing of logical position onto some other embedded main verb.[4] The precise location of a locally unfixed node is thus lexically determined and is not part of the definition of the rule that introduces it.

The computational rule of LOCAL*ADJUNCTION that I adopt is essentially that given in Cann et al. (2005: ch. 6), with the additional restriction that its procedures abort if there is any fixed node below the current one. This guarantees that the rule can only fire once in any local propositional domain, accounting for the lack of full local scrambling in English. The rule given in (9.4) allows at least terms and propositions to be locally unfixed.[5] In the rule, I represent the locality operator as $\langle\uparrow_\Lambda\rangle$ (and its inverse $\langle\downarrow_\Lambda\rangle$ instead of $\langle\uparrow_0\uparrow_*^1\rangle$ of Cann et al. (2005). This is because, when raising is taken into account, the simplicity of the latter can't be maintained. For the purposes of this paper, however, they can be taken as equivalent. Furthermore, I use the $< IF \ldots THEN \ldots ELSE \cdots >$ format of lexical entries instead of the axiom format of Kempson et al. (2001). The reason for the change has to do with issues of diachrony and the fact that conditions do have to be imposed on the operation of computational rules (such as ELIMINATION) which is more perspicuously shown in the procedural format than the axiom format.

(9.4) LOCAL*ADJUNCTION

IF	$?Ty(t)$	
THEN	IF	$\downarrow_* \top$
	THEN	Abort
	ELSE	$\texttt{make}(\langle\downarrow_\Lambda\rangle), \texttt{go}(\langle\downarrow_\Lambda\rangle)$,
		$\texttt{put}(?Ty(\alpha), ?\exists\mathbf{x}.Tn(\mathbf{x}))$ $[\alpha \in \{e, t, \ldots\}]$
ELSE	Abort	

Parsing a simple clause such as *Mary sang* thus induces the three steps shown in (9.5) for the parse of *Mary*.[6]

[4] I leave on one side here any discussion of raising and control verbs, despite the fact that certain modals show properties of both types of construction.

[5] Depending on how gerunds and infinitival *to* phrases are handled this may need to be expanded.

[6] Note that on trees I omit label predicates such as Fo, Ty, Tn in tree displays

(9.5) Parsing *Mary*

AXIOM		LOCAL*ADJUNCTION		*Mary*
$?t, a, \diamondsuit$	$\mapsto$	$?t, n$	$\mapsto$	$?t, n$
		¦		¦
		$?e, \langle\uparrow_{\Lambda}\rangle n,$ $?\exists\mathbf{x}.Tn(\mathbf{x}), \diamondsuit$		$e : Mary',$ $\langle\uparrow_{\Lambda}\rangle n, ?\exists\mathbf{x}.Tn(\mathbf{x}), \diamondsuit$

As noted above, I assume here that tensed verbs (and modals) are parsed in a propositional context ($?t$) and construct a full set of argument nodes. Of course, finite verbs construct more than the basic argument structure of their associated predicates. In particular, they need to specify tense information. Following Gregoromichelaki (2006), therefore, I assume that verbs also project an event argument of type e_{sit} which, according to Gregoromichelaki (2006), is the type of a term sorted over situations and which here I assume to cover at least eventualities, times and worlds (but other parameters may be relevant). This argument, I will further assume, has the structure of an epsilon term rather than an event variable or metavariable[7] whose content comes variously from the verb stem, any tense or aspect inflection and collocated auxiliary verbs. In DS, all terms are of type e but quantified terms have internal structure derived from the epsilon calculus of Hilbert and Bernays (1939). Such terms, the formal equivalent of arbitrary names in natural deduction, consist of an operator, ϵ (or ι for definite terms), a bound variable and a restrictor over that variable. The epsilon term associated with an indefinite noun phrase *a table* is thus:

$$(\epsilon, x, Table'(x))$$

Following Gregoromichelaki's lead I extend the use of such terms to situation or event terms where tense, aspect and types of aktionsart information provide appropriate restrictors on some situation or event variable.

For simple tenses, the situation epsilon term will consist of a restrictor on the temporal relation of an event with respect to the utterance time ($\mathbf{s}_{\text{NOW}}$) and a reference time ($\mathbf{R}$), on which more below. I assume here a very simple, pseudo-Reichenbachian, account of the tenses, following Reichenbach (1947) and variations such as those postulated in Kamp and Reyle (1993), etc., but ignoring the complexities postulated, for example, in van Lambalgen and Hamm (2005), Fernando (2006) and

for ease of reading.

[7]Although there may be reasons for taking a more flexible approach when dealing with the full range of non-finite constructions.

others. In particular, I take past tense in English to involve a simple restrictor to the time of events occurring before now by relating a reference time, **R**, to be prior to the utterance time: $\mathbf{R} < \mathbf{s}_{\text{now}}$. Individual predicates, however, specify whether the event they describe overlaps with **R** ($e \bigcirc \mathbf{R}$) for states or is contained within (or 'holds at') **R** ($e \subseteq \mathbf{R}$) for events proper (see Kamp and Reyle 1993: 504 ff.).[8]

Lexical actions for tensed verbs will thus be complex, but have at their core the basic semantic content of the verb stem. For (intransitive) *sing* this core content is as in (9.6) which will be a part of the lexical entries of all forms of the verb.[9] Note that there is no trigger here. The entry is thus a 'macro-entry' for the **lexeme** SING providing its aktionsart, semantics and argument structure, nothing more. As will be seen below, it is called by other lexical actions which specify within them $\text{SING}_{content}$.

(9.6) $\text{SING}_{content}$
$\texttt{make}(\langle\downarrow_1\rangle), \texttt{go}(\langle\downarrow_1\rangle)$
$\texttt{put}(Ty(?e_{sit} \rightarrow t))$
$\texttt{make}(\langle\downarrow_1\rangle), \texttt{go}(\langle\downarrow_1\rangle),$
$\texttt{put}(Ty(e \rightarrow (e_{sit} \rightarrow t)), Fo(\lambda x \lambda e[Sing'(e, x)]))$
$\texttt{go}(\langle\uparrow_1\rangle), \texttt{make}(\langle\downarrow_0\rangle), \texttt{go}(\langle\downarrow_0\rangle), \texttt{put}(?Ty(e))$

Tensed verbs will thus, in addition to projecting argument structure, construct an event term decorated with tense information derived from the morphological form and aktionsart information derived from the lexical stem. Main verbs also need to ensure that unfixed syntactic subjects are fixed to a particular argument position. Typically, this will be logical subject for active verbs and some logical object for passive ones, but may, with raising verbs, involve 'pushing down' the unfixed node to be fixed as an argument of some embedded verb or even, for

[8]Present tense I take to involve a restrictor $\lambda E[E \bigcirc \mathbf{R}]$ (with $\mathbf{R} = \mathbf{s}_{\text{now}}$) where $\bigcirc$ is the temporal overlap relation and E may be instantiated as some state or some plural event, all of whose subevents are of the sort described by the main verb. The latter is to account for the typical habitual, generic or quantified interpretation of the simple present tense in English. Thus, *Mary sings* is typically interpreted as singing being an habitual property of Mary so *sings* might be given the interpretation $\lambda E \forall e[E \bigcirc \mathbf{s}_{\text{now}} \wedge (e \in E \rightarrow Sing'(e, Mary'))]$. I will not go further into the complexities of the English present tense here. See also Michaelis (2006) who explicitly treats the English present as stative, a move reflected here in the state-like property of overlap with the relevant time.

[9]Such a move assumes a typed lexicon which is likely to reconstruct many of the notions usually associated with structuralist syntax, such as word class, construction, etc. If this turns out to be feasible it will strengthen the argument that only semantic representations are built by syntactic rules, since typical syntactic representations will be epiphenomenal and parasitic on (meta-)lexical properties that link clusters of lexical actions.

(subject) control verbs, fixing the current unfixed node and copying the formula on that node onto some new node locally unfixed with respect to an embedded propositional node. For a simple verb like *sang*, the subject is fixed as logical subject and this is achieved by imposing a modal requirement, $?\langle\uparrow_0\rangle\langle\uparrow_1\rangle Tn(n)$, on the locally unfixed subject node which requires it to be fixed as the first argument daughter ($\langle\uparrow_0\rangle$ of the event predicate node which is the first functor node ($\langle\uparrow_1\rangle$) of the root node ($Tn(n)$). The verb form *sang* is thus associated with the lexical entry in (9.7), the initial condition of which prevents clause initial main verbs by aborting the action if there is no locally unfixed node below the root (and notice the embedded instruction to run the actions specified in (9.6)). The result of running these actions from the partial tree in (9.5) is that in (9.8).

(9.7) *sang*[10]

IF	$?Ty(t) \wedge Tn(n)$	
THEN	IF	$\langle\downarrow_\Lambda\rangle\bot$
	THEN	Abort
	ELSE	$\texttt{go}(\langle\downarrow_\Lambda\rangle), \texttt{put}(?\langle\uparrow_0\rangle\langle\uparrow_1\rangle Tn(n)),$
		$\texttt{go}(\langle\uparrow_\Lambda\rangle), \texttt{make}(\langle\downarrow_0\rangle), \texttt{go}(\langle\downarrow_0\rangle),$
		$\texttt{put}(?Ty(e_{sit})), \texttt{make}(\langle\downarrow_1\rangle), \texttt{go}(\langle\downarrow_1\rangle),$
		$\texttt{put}(Ty(cn \rightarrow e_{sit}), Fo(\lambda P.(\epsilon, P)),$
		$\texttt{go}(\langle\uparrow_1\rangle), \texttt{make}(\langle\downarrow_0\rangle),$
		$\texttt{go}(\langle\downarrow_0\rangle), \texttt{put}(?Ty(cn_{sit})),$
		$\texttt{make}(\langle\downarrow_0\rangle), \texttt{go}(\langle\downarrow_0\rangle),$
		$\texttt{freshput}(\mathbf{s_i}),$
		$\texttt{go}(\langle\uparrow_0\rangle), \texttt{make}(\langle\downarrow_1\rangle), \texttt{go}(\langle\downarrow_1\rangle),$
		$\texttt{put}(?Ty(e_{sit} \rightarrow cn))$
		$\texttt{make}(\langle\downarrow_0\rangle), \texttt{go}(\langle\downarrow_0\rangle),$
		$\texttt{put}(Ty(e_{sit}), Fo(\mathbf{R})), \texttt{go}(\langle\uparrow_0\rangle)$
		$\texttt{make}(\langle\downarrow_1\rangle), \texttt{go}(\langle\downarrow_1\rangle),$
		$\texttt{put}(Ty(e_{sit} \rightarrow (e_{sit} \rightarrow cn_{sit})$
		$Fo(\lambda e\lambda e'[(e', e < \mathbf{s}_{\text{now}})))$
		$\texttt{go}(\langle\uparrow_1\rangle\langle\uparrow_0\rangle\langle\uparrow_0\rangle\langle\uparrow_0\rangle)$
		SING$_{content}$
	ELSE	Abort
ELSE	Abort	

[10]In lexical entries, head items in small capitals are lexemes and in small case italics word forms.

(9.8) Parsing *Mary sang*

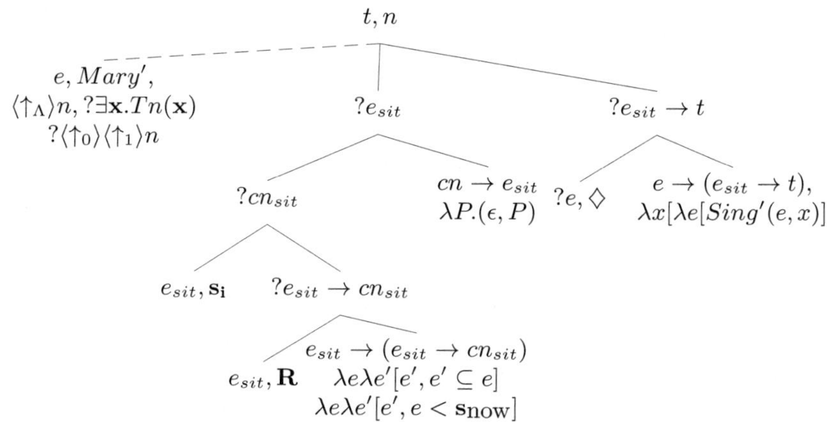

At this point the locally unfixed node necessarily merges with the logical subject node (because of the requirement, $?\langle\uparrow_0\rangle\langle\uparrow_1\rangle Tn(0)$) imposed by the verb) and COMPLETION and ELIMINATION can start to operate over the propositional template to provide as output of the event predicate (type $e_{sit\to t}$) the formula $\lambda e[Sing'(Mary')]$. The pointer then moves to the event term. Note, however, that the event restrictor node has two formula values, one from the aktionsart of the stem ($\lambda e\lambda e'[(e', e' \subseteq e)]$) and one from the tense of the morphological form ($\lambda e\lambda e'[(e', e < \mathbf{s}_{\text{now}})]$). Normally more than one label value decorating a node yields inconsistency. However, Cann et al. (2005), Cann (2006, 2007) adopt a formula resolution rule that combines two formulae of the same type via some form of generalized conjunction that ultimately reduces down to conjoined propositional formulae with appropriate lambda abstraction.[11] Thus from the two values a conjoined formula value is constructed

$$\lambda e\lambda e'[(e', e' \subseteq e \ \wedge \ e < \mathbf{s}_{\text{now}})]$$

The tree can now be fully compiled to give an output formula

$$Sing'((\epsilon, \mathbf{s_i}, \mathbf{s_i} \subseteq \mathbf{R} \wedge \mathbf{R} < \mathbf{s}_{\text{now}}), Mary')$$

Scope evaluation then applies (see Introduction, this volume, Kempson et al. 2001; Cann et al. 2005) to give:

$$Sing'(a, Mary') \wedge a \subseteq \mathbf{R} \wedge \mathbf{R} < \mathbf{s}_{\text{now}}), Mary')$$
$$a = (\epsilon, \mathbf{s_i}, \mathbf{s_i} \subseteq \mathbf{R} \wedge \mathbf{R} < \mathbf{s}_{\text{now}} \wedge Sing'(\mathbf{s_i}, Mary'))$$

[11] Technically, this may be achieved by treating additional formula values as decorating nodes LINKed to the event restrictor node, but this adds a great deal of technical complexity to the exposition, obscuring the main points. So, I will present the build up of information on this node in the current informal way.

This complex expression is, by the epsilon calculus equivalence $\exists x[F(x)] \equiv F(\epsilon, x, F(x))$, equivalent to a predicate logic formula that, as required, asserts the existence of an event of Mary's singing that occurred before the time of utterance:

$$\exists \mathbf{s_i}[Sing'(\mathbf{s_i}, Mary') \wedge \mathbf{s_i} \subseteq \mathbf{R} \wedge \mathbf{R} < \mathbf{s_{now}}]$$

Of course, this representation is not complete as it contains an uninstantiated metavariable, **R**, which requires properly to have some specific formula value, just like metavariables projected by pronouns. I have referred to this term as a reference time, but in fact unlike Reichenbach and other systems I do not specify that this is necessarily a temporal interval nor exactly what sort of value it should have. Instead, I take the position that this reference point may be a time, an event or even a world, and that its value is contextually determined. It may, as the *r* discourse referents in Kamp and Reyle (1993) take the value of some preceding event or time, or may simply by realized as some contextually given, relevant situation. In the example here, given a preceding context like *I went to a concert last night*, **R** may be instantiated as a time interval *last night* or more specifically as a durational adjunct *during the concert* and so on. As will become apparent below, this openness with respect to the exact identification of the reference point is what allows us to incrementally build up semantic representations of the semantic contributions of the various elements that make up auxiliary sequences in English.

9.3 Modals and non-finite main verbs

As noted above, one property that differentiates auxiliary from main verbs is that the former may appear string initially, most notably in questions, but also in other inversion constructions such as temporal adverbial fronting (*Never will I do that again*), conditionals (*Were she there, she would have done the same*) and wishes (*Would it were so!*). I assume, therefore, that in the absence of a locally unfixed node, the parse of a modal will induce some label (such as the interrogative speech act label $+Q$ of Kempson et al. 2001) and construct an event term, a locally unfixed node with an underspecified type (to account for propositional, term and other types of subject (*that I am right will become obvious to all, To eat five portions of vegetables a day will become our goal, Ronnie will become thinner*) and an event predicate node. To account for this, I propose a general rule in (9.9) into which actions of specific auxiliaries may be embedded at the point at which the action (meta-)variable AUX_*content* appears:

(9.9)	SAI			
	IF	$?Ty(t)$		
	THEN	IF	$\downarrow\top$	
		THEN	Abort	
		ELSE	IF	$\langle\downarrow_{\Lambda}\rangle\bot$
			THEN	$\mathtt{put}(+Q)$,
				AUX_*content*
				$\mathtt{go}(\langle\uparrow_1\rangle), \mathtt{make}(\langle\downarrow_{\Lambda}\rangle), \mathtt{go}(\langle\downarrow_{\Lambda}\rangle)$,
				$\mathtt{put}(?Ty(\alpha), ?\exists\mathbf{x}.Tn(\mathbf{x}))$
				$[\alpha \in \{e, t, \dots\}]$
			ELSE	AUX_*content*
	ELSE	Abort		

Specific modals then induce different lexical actions, one of which is to construct an event predicate and decorate it with some metavariable. This generalizes Cann (2006, 2007)'s account of the copula *be* to all proper auxiliaries[12], although with modals being differentiated from the others in decorating the event predicate node rather than the main predicate (see below for further discussion). The reason for adopting this general view is to account for the elliptical properties of auxiliaries as illustrated in section 1. As discussed in detail in Purver et al. (2006) and Cann et al. (2007), the effect of the metavariable is to allow for pragmatic substitution of some antecedently given event predicate[13], just like substitution of a metavariable projected by some pronoun.

I take, for the purposes of this paper, the modal *will* as an example, in its use as a future marker which I assume imposes the restrictor $\lambda e \lambda e'[(e', \mathbf{s}_{\text{now}} < e \wedge e = e')]$ in the event term, requiring the reference and event times to be identical.[14] The reason for this is that it does seem that this is precisely what futurate *will* entails: the event expressed by the main verb is in the future with respect to the time of utterance, whether or not it is a state or event. For example, all the short texts in (9.10) seems to be pragmatically odd in their future reading. (9.10b)

---

[12]I leave aside the quasi-auxiliaries like *need, use* and *dare* which might require a different sort of analysis.

[13]Or for the re-run of some antecedently given set of actions to account for sloppy ellipsis readings. See works cited for discussion.

[14]There is an additional constraint to be added here. No modal can be followed by non-verbal predicates in non-elliptical contexts (**Mary will happy/in the garden*). To account for this, we can add an additional restriction on the event term that the event itself (not the reference point) denotes an eventuality (i.e. a state, activity, accomplishment or achievement). This will prevent what Maienborn (2003, 2007) calls K-states (see below), the types of state that copular predicates denote, from acting as predicates of such verbs. As this is not germane to the current discussion, I leave this refinement to one side.

is fine with the second clause being a correction, but not otherwise and (9.10c) is reasonable only with the 'higher order' interpretation which is something like 'If we ask James, he will be able to tell us the answer'. Thus, future seems to mean future event irrespective of the lexical semantic properties of the main verb.

(9.10) a. ??Mary will sing. In fact she's singing now.
b. ??John will succeed. In fact he's already done so.
c. ??James will know the answer. In fact he already does.
d. ??Louisa will be tall. In fact she already is.

Given the actions specified in (9.11), a parse of the first word in *Will Mary sing?* will yield the tree in (9.12) from the Axiom, $\{?Ty(t), \Diamond\}$.

(9.11) $\text{WILL}_{aux\_content}$

$\texttt{make}(\langle\downarrow_0\rangle), \texttt{go}(\langle\downarrow_0\rangle), \texttt{put}(?Ty(e_{sit}))$
$\texttt{make}(\langle\downarrow_1\rangle), \texttt{go}(\langle\downarrow_1\rangle), \texttt{put}(Ty(cn_{sit} \rightarrow e_{sit}), Fo(\lambda P.(\epsilon, P)))$
$\texttt{go}(\langle\uparrow_1\rangle), \texttt{make}(\langle\downarrow_0\rangle), \texttt{go}(\langle\downarrow_0\rangle), \texttt{put}(?Ty(cn_{sit})),$
$\texttt{make}(\langle\downarrow_0\rangle), \texttt{go}(\langle\downarrow_0\rangle), \texttt{put}(Ty(e_{sit})), \texttt{freshput}(s), \texttt{go}(\langle\uparrow_0\rangle),$
$\texttt{make}(\langle\downarrow_1\rangle), \texttt{go}(\langle\downarrow_1\rangle), \texttt{put}(?Ty(e_{sit} \rightarrow cn_{sit})),$
$\texttt{make}(\langle\downarrow_0\rangle), \texttt{go}(\langle\downarrow_0\rangle), \texttt{put}(Ty(e_{sit}), Fo(\mathbf{R})), \texttt{go}(\langle\uparrow_0\rangle),$
$\texttt{make}(\langle\downarrow_1\rangle), \texttt{go}(\langle\downarrow_1\rangle), \texttt{put}(Ty(e_{sit} \rightarrow (e_{sit} \rightarrow cn_{sit})),$
$Fo(\lambda e \lambda e'.(e', \mathbf{s}_{\text{now}} < e \wedge e' = e))), \texttt{go}(\langle\uparrow_1\rangle\langle\uparrow_1\rangle\langle\uparrow_0\rangle\langle\uparrow_0\rangle),$
$\texttt{make}(\langle\downarrow_1\rangle), \texttt{go}(\langle\downarrow_1\rangle), \texttt{put}(Ty(e_{sit} \rightarrow t), Fo(\mathbf{U}))$

(9.12) Parsing *will*

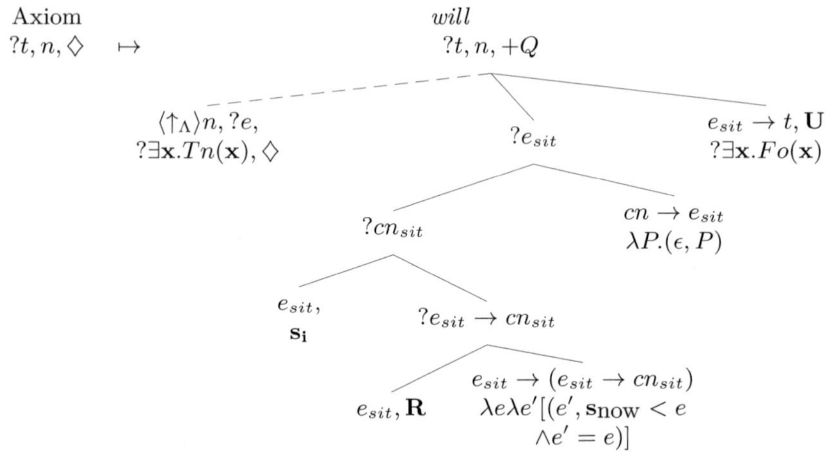

At this point, the pointer is at the locally unfixed node and the syntactic subject *Mary* can be parsed. The pointer now moves to the topnode after completion and to the type-complete, but formula-open event predicate node by anticipation. By hypothesis, the parse of non-finite verb forms in English is triggered by such a node, not by an open propositional node. (9.13) is the lexical entry for the base verb *sing*, whose only differences from the content of the verb stem are to fix the locally unfixed node as logical subject and to impose its lexical aspectual properties on the incomplete event term. This it does by adding the formula value $\lambda e \lambda e'[(e', e' \subseteq e)]$ to the event restrictor node, giving the temporal structure of an event. The lexical actions are, however, constrained to fire only in a context in which no node lower than the event predicate node has been constructed. As we shall see in later sections this has the effect of excluding base forms after *be*, correctly excluding strings like **Mary was sing.*

(9.13) $sing_{bse}$

IF	$(Ty(e_{sit} \rightarrow t) \wedge ?\exists \mathbf{x}.Fo(\mathbf{x}) \wedge \langle\uparrow_1\rangle Tn(n))$	
THEN IF	$\downarrow \top$	
	THEN	Abort
	ELSE	$\mathtt{go}(\langle\uparrow_1\rangle, \langle\downarrow_\wedge\rangle), \mathtt{put}(?\langle\uparrow_0\rangle\langle\uparrow_1\rangle Tn(n)),$ $\mathtt{go}(\langle\uparrow_\wedge\rangle\langle\downarrow_0\rangle\langle\downarrow_0\rangle\langle\downarrow_1\rangle\langle\downarrow_1\rangle),$ $\mathtt{put}(Fo(\lambda e \lambda e'[(e', e' \subseteq e)])),$ $\mathtt{go}(\langle\uparrow_1\rangle\langle\uparrow_1\rangle\langle\uparrow_0\rangle\langle\uparrow_0\rangle\langle\uparrow_0\rangle\langle\downarrow_1\rangle),$ $\text{SING}_{content}$
ELSE	Abort	

Parsing *Will Mary sing?* thus yields the tree in (9.14) and the two formula values on the event restrictor node may be resolved as discussed in the previous section to

$$\lambda e \lambda e'[(e', e' \subseteq e \wedge \mathbf{s}_{\text{now}} < e \wedge e = e')]$$

from which (ignoring the effects of $+Q$) the tree compiles to give an output formula

$$Sing'((\epsilon, \mathbf{s}, \mathbf{s} \subseteq \mathbf{R} \wedge \mathbf{s}_{\text{now}} < \mathbf{R} \wedge \mathbf{s} = \mathbf{R}), Mary')$$

which, since $\mathbf{s} \subseteq \mathbf{R} \wedge \mathbf{s} = \mathbf{R}$ is only true if $\mathbf{s} = \mathbf{R}$ is equivalent (after scope evaluation) to the required formula, for some pragmatically determined value of $\mathbf{R}$, effectively giving Reichenbach's definition of future tense:

$$\exists \mathbf{s}[\mathbf{s} = \mathbf{R} \wedge \mathbf{s}_{\text{now}} < \mathbf{R} \wedge Sing'(\mathbf{s}, Mary')]$$

(9.14) Parsing *will Mary sing?*

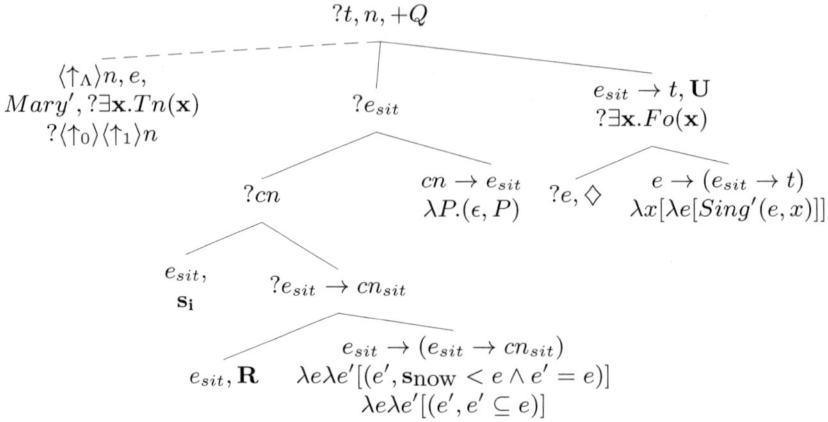

Notice that the tree in (9.14) does not have a node decorated by the modal that takes the one decorated by the main verb as an argument. The only node that the modal decorates with semantic information is the restrictor of the event term and this is the pattern that I adopt for all auxiliary verbs considered here. Such expressions are thus not treated as functors over verbal content, main or auxiliary, and are thus not in any normal sense 'heads' of their constructions. In Falk (2003)'s terms the analysis is not an *aux-predicate* one. But, equally, it is not an exponent of the type of analysis that he sets against it, the *aux-feature* analysis: there are no features. Falk argues that different auxiliaries require different types of analysis. However, as will become clearer below, in the current account whereby it is the accumulation of semantic information in the restrictor of the event term that is important, we can break out of the straightjacket of the concepts that the notion of purely syntactic structure imposes and provide a more unitary account of the auxiliary verbs in English.

Although not normally considered a modal verb as such, the 'support verb' *do* shares many of the syntactic properties of the modals. Like the modals, *do* as an auxiliary appears only initially in a verbal complex (**Mary will do sing, *Mary has done sing, *Mary is doing sing*) and takes a base form of a verb after it (**Mary does sung*).[15] Unlike the modals, however, it is finite in form and, more importantly, cannot appear with any following auxiliaries, at least in standard British

[15]Note that *Mary does singing* is grammatical, but in this instance *do* appears not to be an auxiliary (*?*Does Mary singing, *Mary doesn't singing*) and the *ing* form is a gerund not a participle (*Mary does weird singing, Mary does John's singing for him*).

and American dialects: **Mary does have sung, *Mary does be singing, *Mary does be drunk*. Part of this distribution can be accounted for by treating *do* exactly as if it were a modal like *will* with an identical constraint on the context in which it can be parsed, i.e. no fixed node may be constructed below it. Excluding other auxiliaries from following the verb is not so straightforward and I will return to this matter below.

The lexical actions associated with forms of *do* are straightforward. They mimic the actions associated with modals but only add tense information to the event term. Running the lexical actions in (9.15) yields the tree in (9.16) in a parse of *Mary did sing*, from the AXIOM via LOCAL*ADJUNCTION to parsing the individual words in the string, all steps that have been rehearsed above. Notice the double formulae on the event restrictor as discussed above in relation to the modals, as well as the metavariable **V** projected by *do* whose value is directly provided by the content of predicate plus its non-event arguments. Note that this partial tree compiles to give the same output as for a parse of *Mary sang* with no further information being added by the auxiliary verb, since the conjunction induced by the double marking reduces to $\lambda e \lambda e'.(e', e < \mathbf{s}_{\text{now}} \wedge e' \subseteq e)$, which is exactly what the finite form of *sing* imposes as the restrictor for the event term (see (9.7)).[16]

(9.15) $did_{aux\_content}$

$\texttt{make}(\langle\downarrow_0\rangle), \texttt{go}(\langle\downarrow_0\rangle), \texttt{put}(?Ty(e_{sit})),$
$\texttt{make}(\langle\downarrow_1\rangle), \texttt{go}(\langle\downarrow_1\rangle), \texttt{put}(Ty(cn_{sit} \rightarrow e_{sit}), Fo(\lambda P.(\epsilon, P))),$
$\texttt{go}(\langle\uparrow_1\rangle), \texttt{make}(\langle\downarrow_0\rangle), \texttt{go}(\langle\downarrow_0\rangle), \texttt{put}(?Ty(cn_{sit})),$
$\texttt{make}(\langle\downarrow_0\rangle), \texttt{go}(\langle\downarrow_0\rangle), \texttt{put}(Ty(e_{sit})), \texttt{freshput}(\mathbf{s}), \texttt{go}(\langle\uparrow_0\rangle),$
$\texttt{make}(\langle\downarrow_1\rangle), \texttt{go}(\langle\downarrow_1\rangle), \texttt{put}(?Ty(e_{sit} \rightarrow cn_{sit})),$
$\texttt{make}(\langle\downarrow_0\rangle), \texttt{go}(\langle\downarrow_0\rangle), \texttt{put}(Ty(e_{sit}), Fo(\mathbf{R})), \texttt{go}(\langle\uparrow_0\rangle),$
$\texttt{make}(\langle\downarrow_1\rangle), \texttt{go}(\langle\downarrow_1\rangle),$
$\texttt{put}(Ty(e_{sit} \rightarrow (e_{sit} \rightarrow cn_{sit})), Fo(\lambda e \lambda e'.(e', e < \mathbf{s}_{\text{now}})))$
$\texttt{go}(\langle\uparrow_1\rangle\langle\uparrow_1\rangle\langle\uparrow_0\rangle\langle\uparrow_0\rangle), \texttt{make}(\langle\downarrow_1\rangle), \texttt{go}(\langle\downarrow_1\rangle),$
$\texttt{put}(Ty(e_{sit} \rightarrow t), \mathbf{U})$

[16]I have omitted from this discussion any account of the fact that supportive *do* is always phonologically stressed. I consider this to be a lexical property connected to the general process of stress focus in English and resulting from the emphatic properties of the use of this verb. As far as I am concerned, there is nothing mysterious about this fact that needs explaining, given a Relevance Theoretic view in which the use of 'unnecessary' material should give rise to pragmatic effects. Phonological stress helps to induce a reading that puts emphasis on the polarity of the proposition expressed, a verum focus effect.

(9.16) Parsing *Mary did sing*

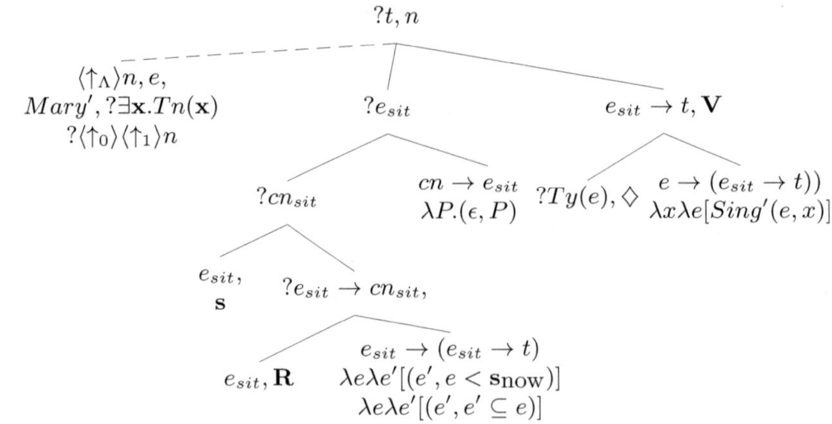

9.4 Be

The previous section provides the basis on which the rest of the auxiliary system is built that accounts for how interpretations of auxiliary strings are constructed, the differences between the main auxiliaries and their similar syntactic behaviour with respect to subject auxiliary inversion and ellipsis.[17]

In Cann et al. (2005), Cann (2006, 2007) the copula is treated as uniformly projecting an underspecified predicate metavariable, **BE**) of type $e \to t$ that is restricted to substitutions by predicates denoting Kimian or K-states (Maienborn 2005, 2007). Maienborn (2007:112) describes K-states as ontologically poorer than Davidsonian (D-)states and conceives of them as a combining the notions of Kim (1969, 1976)'s "temporally bound property exemplifications" and Asher (1993)'s abstract objects as mentally constructed concepts. She defines them tentatively as: "abstract objects for the exemplification of a property P at a holder x and a time t" (Maienborn 2007:113). From this she derives the consequences that K-states are not accessible to direct perception, being facts, propositions, infons or the like, and have no location in space but do in time. Expressions that are argued in Maienborn (2007) to denote such objects are verbs such as *know, resemble, own* and, particularly, the complements of copulas such as *happy, tired, in the garden*, etc. Extending this analysis to the current theory incorporating event terms, I take the restriction to K-states as being imposed within the restrictor of the unfolding event term.

[17] I do not here provide an account of negation or the other so-called NICE properties.

Like the modals, *be* allows ellipsis (*John isn't happy, but Mary is*) and so, by hypothesis, parsing forms of the copula will induce a decoration of a metavariable on some functor node. Unlike the modals and *do*, however, I adopt the position that the node so decorated by *be* is not an event predicate node, but a predicate node that takes some term as argument, i.e. a node of type $e \rightarrow (e_{sit} \rightarrow t)$.[18], which is referred to henceforth as the main predicate. So progressive and passive participles I assume are triggered by a type complete, but formula incomplete main predicate node. In a sense, this follows Warner (1993)'s analysis of the English auxiliary system in which both progressive *ing* and passive *en* forms are characterized as [+PRD] (differentiating them from gerunds and past participles, respectively, which are characterized as [-PRD]). We may thus further assume that the semantic counterpart of [+PRD] is a K-state, or at least compatibility with a K-state, so that the morphemes *ing* and *en* must induce or combine with some K-state derived from the eventuality denoted by the verb stem. In fact, I take the position that the finite tensed copula projects an event term with restrictor that carries tense information, past or present, and a predicate over the **reference point** that it is a K-state. Taking the reference and not the event point to be a K-state allows us to maintain that the participial morphemes do not fundamentally affect the lexical semantics of the verb stem. Thus, *singing* still denotes a set of singing activities, but those singing activities are related to some K-state that expresses some abstract object relating to the content of a lexical verb stem and its arguments.

For the past tense of the copula, *was, were*, therefore, the restrictor on the event term relates the event point to being anterior to now and requires the reference point to be some K-state that overlaps with the time of utterance:

$$\lambda e \lambda e'[(e', e < \mathbf{s}_{\text{NOW}} \ \wedge \ State'_K(e)]$$

Parsing a string initial occurrence of *was* given the lexical actions in (9.17) thus yields the partial tree in (9.18).[19]

[18]Or more strictly speaking some argument of unspecified type, term, proposition, etc: $\mathbf{U} \rightarrow (e_{sit} \rightarrow t)$ to allow for collocation with verbs that take sentential or other forms of subject. I leave this refinement to one side.

[19]I put on one side here all considerations of person/number agreement.

(9.17) $was_{aux\_content}$

$$\begin{array}{l}
\texttt{make}(\langle\downarrow_0\rangle), \texttt{go}(\langle\downarrow_0\rangle), \texttt{put}(?Ty(e_{sit}))\\
\texttt{make}(\langle\downarrow_1\rangle), \texttt{go}(\langle\downarrow_1\rangle), \texttt{put}(Ty(cn_{sit} \rightarrow e_{sit}), Fo(\lambda P.(\epsilon, P)))\\
\texttt{go}(\langle\uparrow_1\rangle), \texttt{make}(\langle\downarrow_0\rangle), \texttt{go}(\langle\downarrow_0\rangle), \texttt{put}(?Ty(cn_{sit})),\\
\texttt{make}(\langle\downarrow_0\rangle), \texttt{go}(\langle\downarrow_0\rangle), \texttt{put}(Ty(e_{sit})), \texttt{freshput}(\mathbf{s}), \texttt{go}(\langle\uparrow_0\rangle),\\
\texttt{make}(\langle\downarrow_1\rangle), \texttt{go}(\langle\downarrow_1\rangle), \texttt{put}(?Ty(e_{sit} \rightarrow cn_{sit}))\\
\texttt{make}(\langle\downarrow_0\rangle), \texttt{go}(\langle\downarrow_0\rangle), \texttt{put}(Ty(e_{sit}), Fo(\mathbf{R})), \texttt{go}(\langle\uparrow_0\rangle),\\
\texttt{make}(\langle\downarrow_1\rangle), \texttt{go}(\langle\downarrow_1\rangle), \texttt{put}(Ty(e_{sit} \rightarrow (e_{sit} \rightarrow cn_{sit})),\\
Fo(\lambda e\lambda e'.(e', e < \mathbf{s}_{\mathrm{now}} \wedge\ State'_K(e)))))\\
\texttt{go}(\langle\uparrow_1\rangle\langle\uparrow_1\rangle\langle\uparrow_0\rangle\langle\uparrow_0\rangle), \texttt{make}(\langle\downarrow_1\rangle), \texttt{go}(\langle\downarrow_1\rangle), \texttt{put}(Ty(?e_{sit} \rightarrow t))\\
\texttt{make}(\langle\downarrow_0\rangle), \texttt{go}(\langle\downarrow_0\rangle), \texttt{put}(?Ty(e)), \texttt{go}(\langle\uparrow_0\rangle)\\
\texttt{make}(\langle\downarrow_1\rangle), \texttt{go}(\langle\downarrow_1\rangle), \texttt{put}(Ty(e \rightarrow (e_{sit} \rightarrow t)), Fo(\mathbf{U}))
\end{array}$$

(9.18)

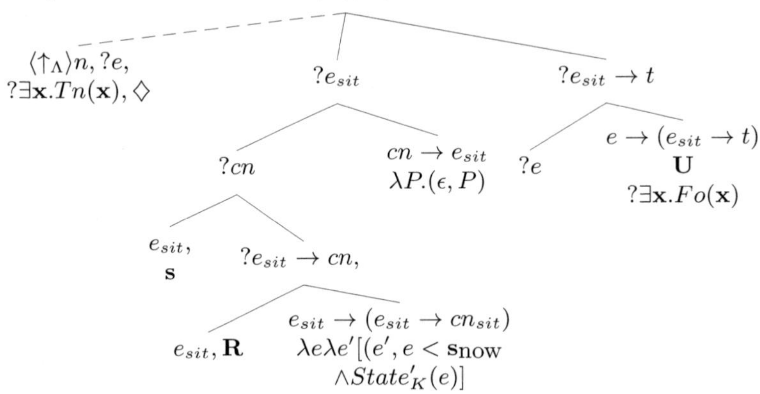

In 'ordinary' copula clauses, such as *John was happy*, predicates like *happy* are, I assume, triggered in a context in which the main predicate node is decorated with a metavariable. They provide the content of the predicate metavariable ($\lambda e\lambda x[Happy'(e, x)]$), fix the subject as the logical subject, just like non-passive verbs, and annotate the restrictor of the event term with the aspectual information that the event variable is itself a K-state and that it overlaps with the reference point ($\lambda e\lambda e'[e' \bigcirc e \wedge State'_K(e')]$). The latter allows us to account for examples like: *John was happy. In fact he still is.* Here, John's having been happy in the past is not denied, as the relation $\bigcirc$ between the event and reference points does not exclude the possibility that the same relation holds between the event point and the utterance time. The reference point, **R**, thus just gives some arbitrary slice of the (K-)state of being happy that is in the past.

9.4.1 Progressive

Returning to auxiliary uses of *be*, I follow a number of writers (e.g. Huddleston and Pullum 2002), and make the assumption that the progressive interpretation comes from the participial ending *ing* rather than the copula, or indeed the combination of both, taking it to project a predicate that provides an event which is an activity which is contained within a K-state reference point. The restriction of the progressive to activities, or activity subparts of an event is well documented and reflected in the grammaticality pattern in (9.19), where the coerced interpretations of the sentences marked by a question mark are acceptable but literal ones are not:

(9.19)
a. Mary was singing well. (Activity)
b. Felicity was drawing a circle. (Accomplishment)
c. ?The dog was recognising its owner. (Achievement)
d. ?John was knowing the answer. (State)
e. ?Lou was being tall. (K-state)

As noted above, I want to keep the notion that present participles still denote events of the appropriate sort as expressed by the verb stem. In the case of *ing*, activities. However, the effect of the ending is to provide a K-state, compatible with the appearance with a copula verb, which acts as the reference point for the activity expressed by the verb stem. Following Reichenbach and others, I also assume that the reference time is located in the event time, $\mathbf{R} \subseteq \mathbf{s}$ to capture the intuition that progressive forms indicate a viewpoint from within the event described. We will see in due course that this is not entirely unproblematic, but it captures the essence of continuative/progressive aspect. I therefore assume that *-ing* forms add the following restrictor to the unfolding event term:[20]

$$\lambda e \lambda e'[(e', Activity'(e') \wedge e \subseteq e' \wedge State'_K(e))]$$

Consider, then, the parse of *A woman was singing.* After LOCAL*ADJUNCTION provides the context in which the subject can be parsed, the auxiliary is parsed to yield a partial tree like that in (9.18) but with the pointer at the main predicate node. This triggers the parse of the progressive participle which fixes the locally unfixed subject, annotates the event predicate node with information from the participial ending, and constructs the argument structure of the main predicate as provided by the lexical actions in (9.20) to yield the tree in (9.21), after MERGE of the unfixed node.

[20] We see below that the actual decoration of the event restrictor node may be lexically determined by the main verb, e.g. for accomplishments.

(9.20) *singing*

IF $Ty(e \rightarrow (e_{sit} \rightarrow t)) \wedge ?\exists \mathbf{x}.Fo(\mathbf{x})$
$\wedge \langle\uparrow_1\rangle\langle\uparrow_1\rangle\{Tn(n), ?Ty(t)\}$

THEN $\mathtt{go}(\langle\uparrow_1\rangle\langle\uparrow_1\rangle\langle\downarrow_\Lambda\rangle), \mathtt{put}(?\langle\uparrow_0\rangle\langle\uparrow_1\rangle Tn(n)),$
$\mathtt{go}(\langle\uparrow_\Lambda\rangle\langle\downarrow_0\rangle\langle\downarrow_0\rangle\langle\downarrow_1\rangle\langle\downarrow_1\rangle)$
$\mathtt{put}(Fo(\lambda e\lambda e'[(e', \mathit{Activity}'(e') \wedge e \subseteq e' \wedge \mathit{State}'_K(e))]))$
$\mathtt{go}(\langle\uparrow_1\rangle\langle\uparrow_1\rangle\langle\uparrow_0\rangle\langle\uparrow_0\rangle\langle\downarrow_1\rangle)$
$\mathrm{SING}_{content}$

ELSE Abort

(9.21) Parsing *a woman was singing*

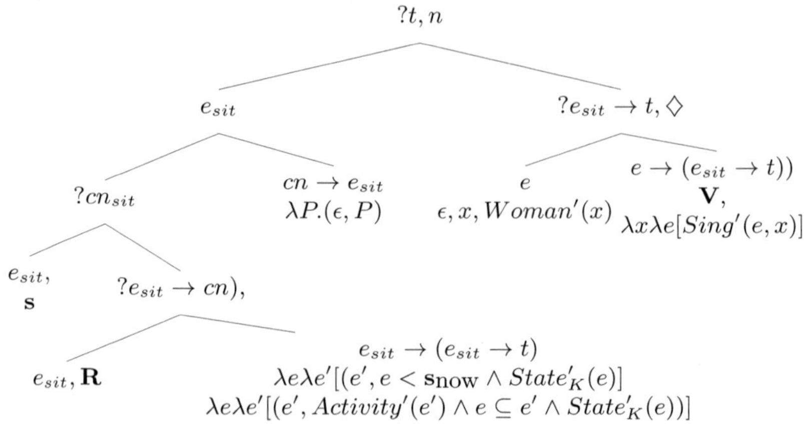

After reconciling the double marking on the event restrictor, the resulting event term compiles to give:

$$(\epsilon, \mathbf{s}, \mathbf{R} < \mathbf{s}_{\text{now}} \wedge \mathit{State}'_K(\mathbf{R}) \wedge \mathit{Activity}'(\mathbf{s}) \wedge \mathbf{R} \subseteq \mathbf{s})$$

where $\mathbf{R}$ may be substituted by some contextually given K-state that can indicate some aspect of the situation under discussion, whether a time (*yesterday evening*), a duration (*three minutes*), and so on, any of which may be explicitly given within a sentence. The characterization given to the progressive is thus traditional in that it focuses on a point within some larger eventuality (Comrie 1977) and theoretical accounts (Dowty 1979; Moens and Steedman 1988; Kamp and Reyle 1993 etc.) but differs in that the reference point is some abstract (K-)state. Thus, *Mary was singing* is interpreted as there being some activity of Mary's singing that contains a K-state, possible a temporal interval, that is before the time of utterance. It makes no claim that the activity has ceased at the time of utterance and so predicts the lack of oddity with regard to sentences like *Mary was singing five minutes ago and hasn't stopped yet.*

An immediate objection to the above characterization, one that has received much attention in the literature, is that it implies that the activity denoted by the verb must exist. Yet progressives may appear with accomplishment verbs as in *Mary was singing my favourite song*, but without implying that the bounded event is completed. Kamp and Reyle (1993:576) suggests that the progressive operator in such cases applies to the verb, creating a distinction between $PROG$(Vb) and Vb. Here, I take a similar stance in the sense that I assume that the activity structure defined by *ing* applies to some eventive predicate that is related somehow to the event denoted by the specified predicate. This, for transitive *sing*, is whatever is denoted by intransitive *sing*, while in *bake a cake* it is some activity or set of activities that may, if all goes according to plan, give rise to some cake having been baked. This is in the spirit of Moens and Steedman's (1988) notion of 'preparatory stage' of some event that may culminate with some result stage. It is not, however, the duty of the participial formative *ing* to specify this (which only makes essential reference to activities), but part of the lexical semantics of some verb. Hence, I take it that the activity expressed by the present participle is specified lexically for each individual verb. While it may be that generalizations may be made over classes of particular verbs (Levin 1993; Levin and Rappaport-Hovav 2005), these are meta-lexical generalizations and not part of the grammar as such. To characterize this approach and to try and exclude unwanted existential commitments, I assume that the lexical semantics of a verb interacts with the basic progressive participial meaning to provide an appropriate activity that is the focus of the progressive but with a modal statement that says that there *may* exist an event of which that activity is part that culminates in an accomplishment. Transitive, accomplishment *singing* will thus be associated with the predicate formula:

$$\lambda y \lambda x \lambda e[Sing'(e, x) \wedge Possible'(\exists e'[e \subseteq e' \wedge Sing'(e', x, y)])]$$

I do not detail the parse of *Mary is singing my favourite song*, as it follows the general pattern we have already seen and the tree displays are already becoming complex, but its output formula, after formula resolution and compilation is:[21]

$$Sing'(a, Mary') \wedge$$
$$\lambda y \lambda x \lambda e[Possible'(\exists e'[e \subseteq e' \ \wedge Sing'(e', x, y)])](song'_{21})(Mary')(a))$$
$$a = (\epsilon, \mathbf{s}, \mathbf{s} < \mathbf{s}_{\text{NOW}} \ \wedge State'_K(\mathbf{R}) \ \wedge Activity'(\mathbf{s}) \ \wedge \ \mathbf{R} \subseteq \mathbf{s})$$

[21] The term $song'_{21}$ is intended as the name of whatever song is my favourite at the time of utterance.

Note that the two individual arguments and the event argument cannot substitute into the intensional context invoked by the modal operator *Possible′* and so are assessed as having some non-null denotation (see any introduction to Montague semantics, e.g. Cann 1993 ch. 10). This means that all three arguments must denote something that exists. This is no problem for the event argument: for *John is (now) writing a letter* there must be some act of writing. The existence of the letter, however, is more controversial: is a letter a letter, if only one word has been written? Our view is that these questions are metaphysical ones and not linguistic issues (see Parsons 1989), and so will leave discussion to one side. The sketch given here, however, has the advantage of not entailing that there need be any completed letter writing event and has the advantage that, unlike any other theory of the English progressive, the interpretation is compositionally constructed from the tense of *be*, the event composition of *ing* and the lexical semantics of the main verb.

9.4.2 Passive

Alone of all the auxiliary combinations *be* plus the *en* participle involves the manipulation of the argument structure of the main verb. However, this does not mean that there is no effect on the event structure of the predicate. In unpublished talks given in the mid-1990s, I argued that that the passive and perfect participles in (standard) English are the same and that the passive and perfect readings result from the interaction of the very underspecified semantic properties of the morpheme -*en* and the semantic structures induced by the verbs *be* and *have*. That the perfect and passive participles are the same in English is hypothesized in Huddleston and Pullum (2005) and is taken to be the case in this paper, except that the passive is taken to involve an additional 'binding' of some argument of the predicate (at least in 'normal' cases, putting on one side peculiar passives such as *this plate was eaten meat off*, Davison (1980)). The basic meaning of the participle is nevertheless treated as the same in both perfect and passive uses, only giving rise to differences in the actions they induce on being parsed (i.e. their syntactic behaviour).

Of course, it is possible that, although diachronically descended from the same participial (passive) form in Old English, in contemporary English the grammaticalization of the participles yields homonymy with no contentful overlap between perfect and passive participles. However, there are striking similarities in the semantic behaviour of both the participles that would be inexplicable if they share no synchronic properties In the first place, the *en* participle appears to denote a (bounded) state:

(9.22) a. *What Kim did was have kicked the cat.
b. *What the cat did was be kicked.
c. *Deliberately kicked by Kim, the cat became very upset. (= the cat determined the kicking)
d. *Lou forced Kim to have kicked the cat.
e. *Lou forced the cat to be kicked.

Furthermore, the state that the participle denotes immediately follows the culmination of the event denoted by the main verb, or if this is a state, some non-initial portion of this event.

(9.23) a. Although known by all the students, the answer continued to elude the lecturer.
b. Harassed by the students, the lecturer decided to quit.

Putting these together, I conclude that *en*-forms denote bounded states which are 'consequent' on some prior event, where consequence is to be interpreted in a weak or underspecified sense which requires some form of enrichment from linguistic or other form of context. For example, it is possible that someone could assert *I have sung Der Winterreise today but was interrupted partway through by a complaining neighbor* without contradiction I will return to this briefly below.[22]

Given the approach presented in this paper, the information that the *-en* participle denotes a bounded state consequent on some other eventuality can be represented in terms of an additional restrictor in the event term

$$\lambda e \lambda e'[e' \propto e \ \wedge \ State'(e)]$$

where $\propto$ is an underspecified relation that may be instantiated as 'consequent on' ($\bowtie$) (Kamp and Reyle 1993;[23], Mollá Aliod 1996) or overlap ($\bigcirc$), the latter only for states (Portner 2003). This is to allow for interpretations of stative passives that may overlap the utterance time such as *The proof was understood by all the students (and still is).* The predicate, $State'$, is intended to cover both Kimian and Davidsonian states. The participle *sung* thus is taken to express a relation between a state consequent on some singing event involving two individuals while *understood* expresses between a relation between two states one of which is consequent on, or overlaps with, the other.

In addition, as noted above, the passive construction that has the base meaning of the passive/perfect participle but the external argument of the verb is 'absorbed'. I interpret this concept as involving the

[22]I am grateful to Ruth Kempson for discussion of this point.

[23]Where the symbol $\supset\!\subset$ is used.

projection of an impoverished epsilon term as logical subject, essentially only having content from the lexical semantics of the verb, i.e. the participant role it associates with its logical argument. This term can be left impoverished giving rise to an arbitrary 'whoever' reading or enriched in context to some more contentful term.[24] In the actions below I do not specify the construction of this epsilon term or show it in tree displays and just return the epsilon term as $(\epsilon, x, Singer'(x))$. This yields the following set of actions for passive uses of *sung*:[25]

(9.24) $sung_{pas}$

IF	$Ty(e \rightarrow (e_{sit} \rightarrow t)) \wedge ?\exists\mathbf{x}.Fo(\mathbf{x}) \;\wedge\; \langle\uparrow_1\rangle\langle\uparrow_1\rangle Tn(n)$
THEN	$\mathtt{go}(\langle\uparrow_1\rangle\langle\uparrow_1\rangle\langle\downarrow_\Lambda\rangle), \mathtt{put}(?\langle\uparrow_0\rangle\langle\uparrow_1\rangle\langle\uparrow_1\rangle Tn(n)),$
	$\mathtt{go}(\langle\uparrow_\Lambda\rangle\langle\downarrow_0\rangle\langle\downarrow_0\rangle\langle\downarrow_1\rangle\langle\downarrow_0\rangle)$
	$\mathtt{put}(\lambda e\lambda e'[e' \bowtie e \;\wedge\; State'(e)]),$
	$\mathtt{go}(\langle\uparrow_0\rangle\langle\uparrow_1\rangle\langle\uparrow_0\rangle\langle\uparrow_0\rangle\langle\downarrow_1\rangle\langle\downarrow_0\rangle)$
	$\mathtt{put}(Ty(e), Fo(\epsilon, x, Singer'(x)), [\downarrow]\bot), \mathtt{go}(\langle\uparrow_0\rangle\langle\downarrow_1\rangle)$
	$\mathtt{make}(\langle\downarrow_1\rangle), \mathtt{go}(\langle\downarrow_1\rangle), \mathtt{put}(Ty(e \rightarrow (e \rightarrow (e_{sit})),$
	$Fo(\lambda y\lambda x\lambda e[Sing'(e, x, y)]))$
	$\mathtt{go}(\langle\uparrow_1\rangle), \mathtt{make}(\langle\downarrow_0\rangle), \mathtt{go}(\langle\downarrow_0\rangle), \mathtt{put}(?Ty(e))$
ELSE	Abort

So the complete effect of parsing a passive participle is to: project an additional formula value for the event restrictor; project two arguments, one of which is decorated by a lexically determined epsilon term; and to fix the locally unfixed subject node, not as logical subject but logical object. A parse of *A song was sung* thus gives the partial tree in (9.25).

The partially evaluated output formula of this tree is:

$$Sing'(a, (\epsilon, y, Singer'(y)), (\epsilon, x, Song'(x)))$$
$$a = (\epsilon, \mathbf{s}, \mathbf{R} < \mathbf{s}_{\text{now}} \;\wedge\; State_K(\mathbf{R}) \;\wedge\; \mathbf{s} \bowtie (\mathbf{R})$$
$$\wedge\; Sing'((\mathbf{s}), (\epsilon, y, Singer'(y)), (\epsilon, x, Song'(x))))$$

The fully evaluated meaning of this sentence is that there was an event of Mary's being seen (by someone unspecified) that occurred before the time of utterance such that a K-state that overlaps with the time of utterance is consequent on the seeing event. As before, the value of the consequent K-state is to be pragmatically inferred.

---

[24] I leave to one side the vagaries of anaphoric reference to this unexpressed term, noting merely in passing that anaphora is not impossible:
i. John was attacked. There were three of *them*.

[25] Notice that I do not use $\text{SING}_{content}$ here as that is for intransitive uses of *sing*. If the actions for transitive *sing* had been defined, this would have appeared in (9.24).

(9.25) Parsing *A song was sung*

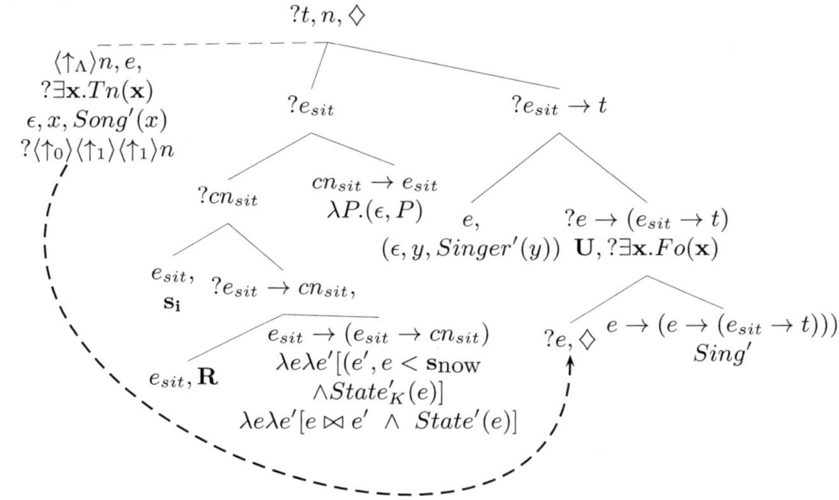

9.4.3 Have

So now I come to the final auxiliary, *have* which collocates with the past/passive participle to give a perfect reading. I have already indicated that the *semantic* contribution of the participle remains constant between the two uses of passive and perfect, so that some of the structure associated with the English perfect is already given: an eventuality that has a consequent state or overlaps with a state, the latter overlapping with the utterance time or preceding it depending on present or past tense marking. Overlap between the eventuality denoted by the main verb stem is, as mentioned above, only permissible with stative verbs and yields continuative perfect readings such as *Mary has lived in Leith for three years (and still does)* (see Portner 2003). Other readings of the perfect include resultative (*Mary has sung a song*), experiential (*It's the worst thing that has ever happened to me*) and perfect of the recent past (*The dog has (just) caught a pheasant*) (see Huddleston and Pullum 2002: 141 ff.). Portner (2003:459) also talks of an existential perfect (*The earth has been hit by giant asteroids (and it probably will be again)*) and a "hot news" perfect (*The Orioles have won!*)[26], although the latter can be categorized in terms of the recent past. I take the position here, following Portner to some extent, that these various readings, except the continuative, are pragmatically determined and effectively reduce to the temporal or consequential relationship between

[26]Portner 2003 examples (3) and (6), respectively.

the eventuality, reference and utterance points.

Like the other auxiliaries, *have* allows SAI and does not fix the position of its syntactic subject, since the subject may ultimately be the internal argument of a passive participle (*A song has been sung*). Unlike *be*, however, but like the modals and *do*, it does not build a main predicate, but decorates the event predicate node with a metavariable. These actions are shown in (9.26) for the present third singular form *has* (triggered as before by being embedded in (9.9)).

(9.26) $has_{aux\_content}$

$$\begin{array}{l}
\texttt{make}(\langle\downarrow_0\rangle), \texttt{go}(\langle\downarrow_0\rangle), \texttt{put}(?Ty(e_{sit})),\\
\texttt{make}(\langle\downarrow_1\rangle), \texttt{go}(\langle\downarrow_1\rangle), \texttt{put}(Ty(cn_{sit} \rightarrow e_{sit}), Fo(\lambda P.(\epsilon, P)))\\
\texttt{go}(\langle\uparrow_1\rangle), \texttt{make}(\langle\downarrow_0\rangle), \texttt{go}(\langle\downarrow_0\rangle), \texttt{put}(?Ty(cn_{sit})),\\
\texttt{make}(\langle\downarrow_0\rangle), \texttt{go}(\langle\downarrow_0\rangle), \texttt{put}(Ty(e_{sit})), \texttt{freshput}(\mathrm{s}), \texttt{go}(\langle\uparrow_0\rangle),\\
\texttt{make}(\langle\downarrow_1\rangle), \texttt{go}(\langle\downarrow_1\rangle), \texttt{put}(?Ty(e_{sit} \rightarrow cn_{sit}))\\
\texttt{make}(\langle\downarrow_0\rangle), \texttt{go}(\langle\downarrow_0\rangle), \texttt{put}(Ty(e_{sit}), Fo(\mathbf{R})), \texttt{go}(\langle\uparrow_0\rangle),\\
\texttt{make}(\langle\downarrow_1\rangle), \texttt{go}(\langle\downarrow_1\rangle), \texttt{put}(Ty(e_{sit} \rightarrow (e_{sit} \rightarrow cn_{sit})),\\
\lambda e \lambda e'.(e', e \bigcirc \mathrm{s_{now}} \wedge State'(e)))\\
\texttt{go}(\langle\uparrow_1\rangle\langle\uparrow_1\rangle\langle\uparrow_0\rangle\langle\uparrow_0\rangle), \texttt{make}(\langle\downarrow_1\rangle), \texttt{go}(\langle\downarrow_1\rangle),\\
\texttt{put}(Ty(e_{sit} \rightarrow t), \mathbf{U}, ?\exists \mathbf{x}.Fo(\mathbf{x}))
\end{array}$$

Note that there is no mention in the lexical entry for (perfective) *have* directly of consequence between eventuality and reference points, only that the reference point is a state. That information derives from the past participle which adds the information that there is a state that is consequent on $\bowtie$ or overlaps with $\bigcirc$ some other eventuality, the reference point.

Although the passive and perfect participles are assumed here to provide the same semantic input, their behaviour is different and they are triggered in different contexts. As we have seen, the passive use of the participle is triggered by a type complete but formula incomplete main predicate and yields a set of actions that provides a non-referential logical subject and fixes the syntactic subject as some internal argument. The perfect participle, on the other hand, is triggered by a type complete but formula incomplete event predicate node, fixes the syntactic subject as logical subject and constructs all the rest of its argument structure. The pointer ends up on the lowest open node, allowing the parse of the object for transitive verbs and permitting merge with the subject position for intransitives. The actions associated with the perfect use of the transitive participle *sung* are given in (9.27).[27]

[27]Note that I don't here try to explain *why* the collocation of *have* plus past/passive participle gives rise to different actions from collocations with *be*. Such an explanation is most likely to be a historical one concerned with the development

(9.27) $sung_{prf}$

$$
\begin{array}{lll}
\text{IF} & Ty(e_{sit} \rightarrow t) \wedge \langle\uparrow_1\rangle Tn(n) & \\
\text{THEN} & \text{IF} & \downarrow\top \\
 & \text{THEN} & \text{Abort} \\
 & \text{ELSE} & \texttt{go}(\langle\uparrow_1\rangle\langle\downarrow_\Lambda\rangle), \texttt{put}(?\langle\uparrow_0\rangle\langle\uparrow_1\rangle Tn(n)), \\
 & & \texttt{go}(\langle\uparrow_\Lambda\rangle\langle\downarrow_0\rangle\langle\downarrow_0\rangle\langle\downarrow_1\rangle\langle\downarrow_1\rangle) \\
 & & \texttt{put}(\lambda e\lambda e'.(e', e' \bowtie e \wedge State'(e)) \\
 & & \texttt{go}(\langle\uparrow_1\rangle\langle\uparrow_1\rangle\langle\uparrow_0\rangle\langle\uparrow_0\rangle\langle\downarrow_1\rangle); \\
 & & \texttt{make}(\langle\downarrow_0\rangle); \texttt{go}(\langle\downarrow_0\rangle); \\
 & & \texttt{put}(?Ty(e)), \texttt{go}(\langle\uparrow_0\rangle), \texttt{make}(\langle\downarrow_1\rangle), \\
 & & \texttt{go}(\langle\downarrow_1\rangle), \texttt{put}(?Ty(e \rightarrow (e_{sit} \rightarrow t))) \\
 & & \texttt{make}(\langle\downarrow_1\rangle), \texttt{go}(\langle\downarrow_1\rangle), \\
 & & \texttt{put}(Ty(e \rightarrow (e \rightarrow (e_{sit} \rightarrow t))), \\
 & & Fo(\lambda y\lambda x\lambda e[Sing'(e, x, y)]), [\downarrow]\bot); \\
 & & \texttt{go}(\langle\uparrow_1\rangle); \texttt{make}(\langle\downarrow_0\rangle); \texttt{go}(\langle\downarrow_0\rangle); \\
 & & \texttt{put}(?Ty(e)) \\
\text{ELSE} & \text{Abort} &
\end{array}
$$

The parse of *Mary has sung a song* proceeds in a predictable manner in the way that we have already seen with other constructions with the only real difference being the annotations on the event restrictor node. No tree is thus displayed, but the partially evaluated output yields:

$$
\begin{array}{l}
Sing'(a, Mary', (\epsilon, x, Song'(x))) \\
a = (\epsilon, \mathbf{s}, \mathbf{R} \bigcirc \mathbf{s}_{\text{now}} \ \wedge \ State'(\mathbf{R}) \ \wedge \ \mathbf{s} \bowtie \mathbf{R} \\
\wedge \ Sing'(\mathbf{s}, Mary', (\epsilon, x, Song'(x)))
\end{array}
$$

which is equivalent after full evaluation to the first order predicate logic formula:

$$
\begin{array}{l}
\exists \mathbf{s} \exists x[Sing'(\mathbf{s}, Mary', x) \ \wedge \ Song'(x)) \ \wedge \ \mathbf{R} \bigcirc \mathbf{s}_{\text{now}} \ \wedge \ State'(\mathbf{R}) \\
\wedge \ \mathbf{s} \bowtie \mathbf{R}]
\end{array}
$$

Of course, the metavariable **R** has to be instantiated. In the case of the latter this will be some predicate like ‘result from’ and may indicate the immediate past between event and reference points (as in a situation in which Mary has been struggling to regain her voice and is finally heard to complete some song) or further separated in time as in reportative perfects. The reference point itself is most transparently interpreted as some state that has ‘present relevance’. Other contexts and other expressions will give rise to different interpretations constrained by tense relations and whatever it is that the consequence relation is.

---

of the participle from its earliest appearances with interpretation as ‘passive’ (i.e. as a modifier of a noun interpreted as its object) to spreading collocation with *have* and subsequent change to the fully grammaticalized collocations in modern English. I do not consider a synchronic explanation to be necessary or even possible.

9.5 Auxiliary Clusters

The analysis of all the individual auxiliary constructions has now been set out: modal, do-support, progressive, passive and perfect. In this section, I explore how certain collocational restrictions can be captured in the system and how interpretations of complex auxiliary clusters are built up as restrictors in event terms are incrementally updated. The significance of these projected analyses is how the incorporation of event terms within the representation system and the incremental growth of the information provided by such terms have an important role to play in enabling restrictions of apparently wholly language-particular kind to be expressible in general terms.

9.5.1 Collocational Restrictions

Much of the interest in the English auxiliary system concerns the complex collocational restrictions between the various auxiliaries and verb forms as exemplified in (9.2) and neatly summarized in Chomsky (1957)'s original formulation given in (9.3.a) and repeated below:

(1) Aux $\rightarrow$ Tns - (M) - (have+en) - (be+ing) - (be+en)

In other words, modals and auxiliary *do* must appear first in any auxiliary cluster, followed by a base form of *have, be* or a main verb. Forms of *have* must be followed by a (perfect) *-en* participial form of *be* or a main verb and forms of *be* must be followed by an *ing* form of *be* or a main verb, or of a (passive) *-en* form of a main verb. In what follows, I provide means of accounting for these restrictions in DS using the basic mechanisms established above, giving an different and original perspective on such matters from other published analyses. In particular, we can rely on constraints on tree-growth in the form of the context in which some expression is parsed to do the work that in other frameworks must be established through restrictions in feature collocations.

As is standard in DS, syntactic collocation is handled through constraints on lexical actions. In the first place, I adopt the general consensus (as in all theoretical models) that modals and auxiliary *do* only have finite forms. In the current analysis this means that their forms are only triggered by a propositional type requirement, $?Ty(t)$, and must therefore only appear as an initial auxiliary in any complex collocation and cannot appear in non-finite embedded contexts:[28]

[28]This is slightly simplistic for auxiliary *do* as the status of the form in strings like those below is not clear. The fact that it cannot appear with a following base form (b) indicates that it is not an auxiliary here, but the fact that it licenses ellipsis (c,d) goes against a main verb analysis. I leave the issue open.

(9.28) a. *John has done sing a song.
b. *Joan wanted to will go.
c. *Mary persuaded John to do sing.

Secondly, passive and progressive verb forms can only be parsed in a context constructed by *be* in virtue of the trigger for such forms being a type complete main predicate rather than an event predicate. Thus, the strings in (9.29) are directly excluded:

(9.29) a. *Mary will/does/has singing.
b. *Mary will/does/has shot (by John).

The base infinitival forms appear after the modals and *do*, but not after *have* or *be*. With respect to the copula, strings like **Mary is sing* are already excluded on the assumption that base forms are triggered by a type complete event predicate ($\{Ty(e_{sit} \rightarrow t), Fo(\mathbf{U})\}$) which is not provided by finite forms of the copula. A collocation *will be* does, however, provide such a node and, if the pointer can move from the type-complete main predicate node ($\{Ty(e \rightarrow (e_{sit} \rightarrow t)), Fo(\mathbf{U})\}$) constructed by parsing the copula to the type-complete event predicate node, the strings like **Mary will be sing* are derivable. This problem can, in fact, be straightforwardly solved by assuming an additional constraint on parsing any base form (including *have*) that no node lower than the event predicate node has been constructed, using the condition plus action $\langle IF \langle\downarrow\rangle \top, THEN Abort, \ldots\rangle$. This simple constraint will exclude all base forms from appearing after the copula.

This does not completely solve the problem of the base forms, however, as there is no obviously simple context that includes both *will* and *do*, but excludes *have*. Given that in English there are two infinitives, base form verbs and the same preceded by *to*, one could again take a hint from Warner (1993) and suggest the introduction of a new label $To(\alpha)$ where α ranges over $+$ and $-$ and then adopt the position that the lexical entries for modals and *do* include an action that puts a requirement, $?To(-)$ on the event predicate ($?Ty(e_{sit} \rightarrow t)$) node. Base forms then may be treated as being sensitive to this requirement, adding the required annotation, $To(-)$. However, such a move goes against the commitment of DS that its representations are of semantic content. Instead, I will, without argument, take up a suggestion put

a. I do sing.
b. *I will do sing.
c. I will do.
d. I will do so.
e. I will do the dishes.

forward in Mittwoch (1990) and, within a functionalist perspective, in Duffley (1992), that *to* infinitivals differ from bare infinitives in that, in causative constructons, the latter express events that are coincident with that expressed by the causative while the former express non-coincident events.[29] In terms of the theory put forward here, we may construe any such difference in terms of whether or not the infinitive introduces an event term independently of any antecedently introduced event term: *to* infinitives introduce a new event term, but bare ones do not. Modals and *do* then may impose a constraint that no daughter of the trigger node be an event term, a constraint captured by the imposed requirement: $?\neg\langle\downarrow\rangle Ty(e_{sit})$. No tree growth operation that introduces such a node, as hypothesized for infinitive *to*, will lead to a coherent tree structure since the requirement could never be met.

This same constraint may also be used to determine that base form verbs do not occur after *have* and *be* by making their parse be sensitive to the appearance of this condition. The revised entry for (intransitive) base form *sing* in (9.30) shows this revision in the highlighted condition.

(9.30) $sing_{bse}$

IF	$?Ty(e_{sit} \rightarrow t) \wedge \langle\uparrow_1\rangle Tn(n)$		
THEN	IF	$\langle\downarrow\rangle\top$	
	THEN	Abort	
	ELSE	IF	$?\neg\langle\downarrow\rangle \mathbf{Ty(e_{sit})}$
		THEN	$\mathtt{go}(\langle\uparrow_1\rangle\langle\downarrow_L\rangle)$, $\mathtt{put}(?\langle\uparrow_0\rangle\langle\uparrow_1\rangle Tn(n))$, $\mathtt{go}(\langle\uparrow_L\rangle\langle\downarrow_1\rangle)$, $\text{SING}_{content}$
		ELSE	Abort
ELSE	Abort		

Non-finite *have* can appear only after modals (9.31) and in base form only: the auxiliary form of the verb has no progressive, past or passive participial forms (9.32):

(9.31) a. Mary will have sung.
b. *Mary does have sung.
c. *Mary does be singing.
d. *Mary is have sung.
e. *Mary is having sung.

(9.32) a. *Mary is having sung. (Mary is having dinner.)
b. *Mary has had sung. (Mary has had dinner.)
c. *Mary was had shot. (Mary was had (by John))

[29] This is an oversimplistic presentation of the views expressed in these two papers, but is sufficient for my purposes here.

The exclusion of the strings in (9.31d,e) is already determined by the general base form constraint, discussed above, to abort if any node below the event predicate node has been constructed also. Assuming with others that *had* is not an *en* form of auxiliary *have* excludes (9.32.b,c) automatically, since there would be no relevant lexical entry. Unfortunately, it is not possible merely to assume the non-existence of *having* since participial adjuncts are fully acceptable:

(9.33) Having left the room, John burst out crying.

I cannot give an account of such adjuncts here, but merely note that again a suitable constraint can be defined that requires the parse of *having* not to occur in the local context of a type-complete main predicate node $(e \rightarrow (e_{sit} \rightarrow t))$, ie. as part of a local predicate-argument array. Whatever condition triggers the parse of a participial adjunct, it can be safely assumed that it will not be in such a context which, by hypothesis, is only constructed by a parse of the copula.

There remains the problem of how to exclude base form *have* or indeed *be* after *do*. Warner (1993) achieves this by requiring the verb to subcategorize for only [-AUX] (non-auxiliary) complements. We have already seen that modals are already excluded from following *do* (since they are necessarily triggered by a propositional type requirement), but the exclusion of both *have* and *be* from this position is not straightforward. One could try some form of semantic filtering of *be* by having auxiliary *do* impose a negative condition on the event restrictor node that it not be decorated by a K-state formula: $\lambda e \lambda e'[\neg State_K(e)]$. The status of such constraints is problematic, however, as such semantic filtering may have consequences beyond the immediate desire to exclude certain collocational restrictions and is certainly methodologically suspect. There is, furthermore, also no obvious way of excluding *have* by such filtering as it the auxiliary seems to add nothing uniquely identifiable to the event restrictor. It is possible that the exclusion in British and American standard dialects of English may be to do with the verum focus effect of auxiliary *do* and that it somehow requires some immediate content to be provided for the main predicate. A possibility is to have *do* project a *modal* formula requirement for the functor daughter node $?\langle\downarrow_1\rangle\exists\mathbf{x}[Fo(\mathbf{x})]$ and have parses of all auxiliaries abort in the immediate context of such a requirement. I do not spell out this refinement here as it is straightforward and follows other abort conditions given above, reflecting the sensitivity of the parsing process to the partial structure as so far induced, all parsing/content construction being inherently sensitive to context.

There are now only the relative order of the non-finite forms of *be* to account for and this is relatively straightforward. The ordering constraints are that *been* must precede *being* and *be* must be first:

(9.34) a. A song will be being sung.
b. *A song will being be sung.
c. A song has been being sung.
d. *A song has being been sung.

That the base form comes first follows from the general restriction on such forms that they are triggered by a type complete event predicate node and the parse aborts if there is a lower constructed node (see the entry for *sing* in (9.30)). This disallows any form of *be*, finite or non-finite, from preceding the base form. Secondly, *been* is clearly a perfective form and so, by hypothesis, has the same triggering context and condition on parsing as the base forms. Under the assumption that parsing *been* constructs a lower main predicate node decorated by a metavariable, this will ensure that only *being* or some progressive or passive participle follows and since *being* is a progressive participle it is triggered by a type complete main predicate and so can never precede *been*. For the sake of completeness, (9.35) and (9.36) give the lexical actions associated with parsing *been* and *being*, respectively.[30]

(9.35) *been*

IF $Ty(e_{sit} \rightarrow t)$
THEN IF $\langle\downarrow\rangle\top$
  THEN Abort
  ELSE $\texttt{go}(\langle\uparrow_1\rangle\langle\downarrow_0\rangle\langle\downarrow_0\rangle\langle\downarrow_1\rangle\langle\downarrow_1\rangle)$,
  $\texttt{put}(Fo(\lambda e\lambda e'[(e', State_K(e) \wedge e' \propto e)]))$
  $\texttt{go}(\langle\uparrow_1\rangle\langle\uparrow_1\rangle\langle\uparrow_0\rangle\langle\uparrow_0\rangle\langle\downarrow_1\rangle), \texttt{make}(\langle\downarrow_0\rangle)$,
  $\texttt{go}(\langle\downarrow_0\rangle), \texttt{put}(?Ty(e))$
  $\texttt{go}(\langle\uparrow_0\rangle), \texttt{make}(\langle\downarrow_1\rangle), \texttt{go}(\langle\downarrow_1\rangle)$,
  $\texttt{put}(Ty(e \rightarrow (e_{sit} \rightarrow t)), Fo(\mathbf{U}))$
  ELSE Abort
ELSE Abort

(9.36) *being*

IF $Ty(e \rightarrow (e_{sit}) \rightarrow t) \wedge ?\exists \mathbf{x}.Fo(\mathbf{x})$
THEN $\texttt{go}(\langle\uparrow_1\rangle\langle\uparrow_1\rangle\langle\downarrow_0\rangle\langle\downarrow_0\rangle\langle\downarrow_1\rangle\langle\downarrow_1\rangle)$,
$\texttt{put}(Fo(\lambda e\lambda e'[(e', Activity'(e') \wedge State'_K(e) \wedge e \subseteq e')]))$
$\texttt{go}(\langle\uparrow_1\rangle\langle\uparrow_1\rangle\langle\uparrow_0\rangle\langle\uparrow_0\rangle\langle\downarrow_1\rangle\langle\downarrow_1\rangle)$
ELSE Abort

[30]I do not give an entry for base form *be* as this just constructs main predicate and logical argument nodes and does not annotate the event restrictor node.

9.5.2 Interpretation

Having accounted for the syntactic collocations of the auxiliaries, I now turn my attention to the semantic formulae that are constructed in complex examples and see how the accumulation of restrictions on the event variable give rise to semantic objects that reflect the various interpretations of auxiliary clusters. Such objects will underspecify the very specific interpretations of particular aspectual types given in the literature (see, for example, Comrie 1977), but provide a sufficient basis for enrichment to such interpretations. The discussion here is necessarily brief and does not explore all pragmatic and semantic ramifications of the current analysis, but it does provide the background for such an exploration. Since the semantic contributions of the various auxiliaries only affect the event term, it is these that are the focus of our attention in what follows. I take a number of different strings which illustrate the various groupings of modal, perfect, progressive and passive, showing the individual contributions of the various verbal elements and the complex event term that results from their combination.

The examples below show how these interpretations are built up starting with a simple combination of futurate *will* with a perfect (9.37), then a future progressive (9.38), and a pluperfect passive (9.39. In each case, I set out the information provided by each TMA expression in the string (after lambda conversion except for the main predicate), then giving resulting formulae and their predicate logic equivalents, without much in the way of discussion, as the results should be self-evident from the formulae themselves.

(9.37) Mary will have sung a song:

a. will $(\mathbf{s}, \mathbf{s}_{\text{now}} < \mathbf{R})$

b. have $(\mathbf{s}, \mathit{State}'(\mathbf{R}))$

c. sung $(\mathbf{s}, \mathit{State}'(\mathbf{R} \wedge \mathbf{s} \bowtie \mathbf{R})$
$\lambda y \lambda x \lambda e[\mathit{Sing}'(e, x, y)]$

This combination of formulae (after formula resolution and partial evaluation of the event term) gives rise to the expanded restrictor

$$a = (\epsilon, \mathbf{s}, \mathbf{s}_{\text{now}} > \mathbf{R} \wedge \mathit{State}'(\mathbf{R}) \wedge \mathbf{s} \bowtie \mathbf{R} \wedge \mathit{Sing}'(\mathbf{s}, \mathit{Mary}', (\epsilon, x, \mathit{Song}'(x))))$$

which operates as the first argument, a, of the formula:

$$\mathit{Sing}'(a, \mathit{Mary}', (\epsilon, x, \mathit{Song}'(x)))$$

and yields an equivalent predicate logic formula after further scope evaluation that asserts that there is some future reference point (unresolved here), consequent on an event of Mary singing a song:

$$\exists \mathbf{s} \exists x[\mathbf{s}_{\text{now}} < \mathbf{s} \wedge \mathit{State}'(\mathbf{R}) \wedge \mathbf{s} \bowtie \mathbf{R} \wedge \mathit{Sing}'(\mathbf{s}, \mathit{Mary}', x) \wedge \mathit{Song}'(x)]$$

The semantic effect of a futurate progressive as in (9.38) on the other hand is to assert the existence of a future reference state at which an activity of singing by Mary holds that could result in the culmination of an event of Mary's singing a song.

(9.38) Mary will be singing a song.

a. will $(\mathbf{s}, \mathbf{s}_{\text{now}} < \mathbf{R})$

b. be $(\mathbf{s}, State'_K(\mathbf{R})$

c. singing $(\mathbf{s}, Activity'(\mathbf{s}) \wedge \mathbf{R} \subseteq \mathbf{s} \wedge \mathbf{State'_K}(\mathbf{R}))$
$\lambda y \lambda x \lambda e[Sing'(e,x) \wedge Possible'(\exists e'[e \subseteq e' \wedge Sing'(e',x,y)])]$

$$Sing'(a, Mary') \wedge Possible'(\exists e'[e \subseteq e' \wedge Sing'(e',x,y)])]$$
$$(\epsilon, x, Song'(x))(Mary')(a)$$

$$a = (\epsilon, \mathbf{s}, \mathbf{s}_{\text{now}} < \mathbf{R} \;\wedge\; State'_K(\mathbf{R}) \;\wedge\; Activity'(\mathbf{s}) \;\wedge \mathbf{R} \subseteq \mathbf{s}$$
$$\wedge\ \lambda y \lambda x[Sing'(\mathbf{s},x) \wedge Possible'(\exists e'[e \subseteq e' \wedge Sing'(e',x,y)])]$$
$$(\epsilon, x, Song'(x)))(Mary'))$$

$$\exists \mathbf{s} \exists x[Sing'(\mathbf{s}, Mary') \wedge \mathbf{s}_{\text{now}} < \mathbf{R} \wedge\ Activity'(\mathbf{s}) \wedge \mathbf{R} \subseteq \mathbf{s} \wedge Song'(x)$$
$$\wedge\ \lambda y \lambda x[Sing'(\mathbf{s},x) \wedge Possible'(\exists e'[e \subseteq e' \wedge Sing'(e',x,y)])](x)(Mary')(\mathbf{s})]$$

The semantics of the third example of a pluperfect (9.39) is that there is a (K-)state prior to the time of utterance that is consequent on some event of some entity's completing the singing of a song.

(9.39) A song had been sung.

a. had $(\mathbf{s}, \mathbf{R} < \mathbf{s}_{\text{now}} \wedge State'_K(\mathbf{R})$

b. been $(\mathbf{s}, State'_K(\mathbf{R} \wedge \mathbf{s} \propto \mathbf{R})$

c. sung $(\mathbf{s}, \mathbf{s} \bowtie \mathbf{R})$
$\lambda y \lambda x \lambda e[Sing'(e, (\epsilon, x, Singer'(x)), y)]$

$$Sing'(a, (\epsilon, x, Singer'(x)), (\epsilon, y, Song'(y)))$$

$$a = (\epsilon, \mathbf{s}, \mathbf{R} < \mathbf{s}_{\text{now}} \wedge State'_K(\mathbf{R}) \wedge \mathbf{s} \bowtie \mathbf{R}$$
$$\wedge Sing'(\mathbf{s}, (\epsilon, x, Singer'(x)), (\epsilon, y, Song'(y))))$$

$$\exists \mathbf{s} \exists x \exists y[Sing'(\mathbf{s},x,y) \wedge Singer'(x) \wedge Song'(y) \wedge \mathbf{R} < \mathbf{s}_{\text{now}}$$
$$\wedge State'_K(\mathbf{R}) \wedge \mathbf{s} \bowtie \mathbf{R}]$$

Collocations of *ing* and *-en* participles may give rise to certain peculiarities in the information expressed by the event term. In particular, the inclusion ($\subseteq$) and consequence ($\bowtie$) relations may give rise to apparent contradictory relations between reference and event points. Consider the following pluperfect progressive sentence and its semantic structure:

(9.40) Mary had been singing a song.

a. had $(\mathbf{s}, \mathit{State}'(\mathbf{R}) \wedge \mathbf{R} < \mathbf{s}_{\text{now}})$
b. been $(\mathbf{s}, \mathit{State}'_K(\mathbf{R}) \wedge \mathbf{s} \propto \mathbf{R})$
c. singing $(\mathbf{s}, \mathit{Activity}'(\mathbf{s}) \wedge \mathit{State}'_K(\mathbf{R}) \wedge \mathbf{R} \subseteq \mathbf{s})$
$\lambda y \lambda x \lambda e[\mathit{Sing}'(e, x, y)]$

Because **s** is an activity the relation $\propto$ introduced by *been* is realized as consequence ($\bowtie$) not overlap, but this construal appears to give rise a contradiction induced by the semantics of the participle *singing*: it entails that the reference state is both contained in ($\mathbf{R} \subseteq \mathbf{s}$), and is consequent on ($\mathbf{s} \bowtie \mathbf{R}$), the event. However, this depends entirely on the notion of consequence. It was noted earlier in section 9.4.2 that the precise interpretation of this relation varies in context and is often hard to specify. For (9.40), for example, it is obvious that there is some reference point prior to now and that the perspective of the activity is from the 'inside' of the event, but the notion of consequence is difficult to determine. In fact, all that seems to be conveyed is that the reference state does not coincide with the initial part of the event: **Mary had been singing a song, but hadn't uttered a note.* So it seems that the consequence relation may be very underspecified as to the relation between its two arguments, merely asserting that some reference state occurs at some time after some part of the event. Recall that I have made no commitment to **s** and **R** actually being times. If we assume that they actually denote eventualities or K-states, and that operators like $\bowtie$ and $\subseteq$ are actually shorthand hand ways of indicating times at which these hold, then they can be given the definitions in (9.41), where *At* is to be read as 'holds at':

(9.41) a. $\mathbf{s} \bowtie \mathbf{R} =_{\text{def}} \exists t \exists t'[\mathit{At}(\mathbf{s}, t) \wedge \neg \mathit{At}(\mathbf{R}, t) \wedge \mathit{At}(\mathbf{R}, t') \wedge t < t']$
b. $\mathbf{R} \subseteq \mathbf{s} =_{\text{def}} \forall x[\mathit{At}(\mathbf{R}, t) \rightarrow \mathit{At}(\mathbf{s}, t)]$

Notice that under these definitions, we do not derive a contradiction from the two relations, and ensure that there is at least an initial part of **s** where **R** does not hold. Of course, this gives a very underspecified means of approaching the relation between the event and its associated reference state, but this is what we need given the variability in interpreting many perfects in English. The point here is that the building up of these complex event terms provides some very underspecified temporal and event structure which need to be enriched in context, just as with the notion of ad hoc concept formation in Relevance Theory, bringing tense and aspect construal closer to that of general argument construal.[31]

[31] One further type of inference also occurs in cases of combinations of *-ing* and

9.6 Conclusion

In this paper, I have shown how an analysis of the complexity of the English auxiliary system can be implemented within Dynamic Syntax and at the same time provide a new perspective on such complex grammatical systems. The introduction of event terms into DS semantic representations allows auxiliaries and verb forms to be seen as intructuions to progressively build up aspectual and tense information as part of an unfolding event term that provides sufficient, but underspecified, semantic structure that leads to different interpretations of tense, progressive and perfect forms. This it does without assuming that the auxiliaries themselves project independent predicate nodes (head their phrases), thus reflecting the grammaticalized nature of the auxiliary verbs (including modals) and the insight that only main verbs project true argument structure. This is further achieved without the need to posit independent and primitive syntactic features like BSE, PRD, AUX and the like. Syntactic differences between different forms and auxiliaries are captured through different actions associated with parsing them that induce different semantic contexts to ensure that unrealized collocational restrictions are not licensed.

Of course, there is much else to be done. The actual semantic structures assigned to the auxiliaries and non-finite verb forms need much better justification than has been possible here and the interaction of pragmatics and semantic underspecification needs considerably more research using data in real linguistic contexts. Additionally, more syntactic phenomena associated with auxiliaries such as negation needs further exploration and elaboration. And, of course, more needs to be done with respect to modal verbs, particularly those like dynamic *can* that imply control structures, and the semi-auxiliaries like *dare* and *need.* Nevertheless, the current analysis shows how an incremental linguistic theory that posits no representational level other than that of semantic content can provide a successful characterization of the syntax and, crucially semantics, of a complex grammatical system and, in doing so, give a much more explanatory account than the setting up of an autonomous and blind syntactic system whose only objective is that of getting the descriptive facts right.

-en participles with respect to accomplishments. In a sentence like *a song was being sung*, the accomplishment is coerced into its activity counterpart and gives no entailment that a song was completed. Since this type of coercion is common in progressives of accomplishments and states, this does not pose any particular problems for the current analysis.

References

The following were cited in this chapter: Asher (1993), Cann (1993, 2000, 2006, 2007), Cann et al. (2005), Cann et al. (2007), Chomsky (1957, 1981), Comrie (1977), Davison (1980), Dowty (1979), Duffley (1992), Falk (2003), Fernando (2006), Gazdar et al. (1982), Gregoromichelaki (2006), Hilbert and Bernays (1939), Huddleston and Pullum (2002), Kamp and Reyle (1993), Kempson et al. (2001), Kim (1969, 1976), van Lambalgen and Hamm (2005), Levin (1993), Levin and Rappaport-Hovav (2005), Maienborn (2003, 2005, 2007), Marten (2000), Michaelis (2006), Mittwoch (1990), Moens and Steedman (1988), Mollá Aliod (1996), Parsons (1989, 1990), Portner (2003), Purver et al. (2006), Reichenbach (1947), Warner (1993, 2000), Wu (2005). See references at end of book for full information.

10

A Dynamic Account of Clitic Climbing: A first sketch

STERGIOS CHATZIKYRIAKIDIS

In this chapter,, I propose an account of Clitic Climbing within the lines of the Dynamic Syntax framework. I argue that once we shift into a dynamic model of syntax, the so-called *restructuring* phenomenon as well as the *functional-lexical* distinction (Cinque, 1999, 2001, 2006; Cardinaletti and Shlonsky, 2004) receive a straightforward explanation. Following, Cann's (this volume) analysis of English auxiliaries (and some of the modals), I assume that restructuring verbs do not project any verbal type value, but only the higher situation nodes. Then, the semantics of restructuring verbs are captured inside the complex situation argument node, by further introducing a world parameter as part of a complex situation formula value containing both a situation and a world parameter. Clitic climbing is then predicted to be possible, in the same sense it is possible with auxiliary verbs (actually it is the only option in this case). Multiple climbing will be shown to be easily captured under the same analysis, assuming that more than one restructuring verbs will not project any verbal type value but will rather project information inside the complex situation argument node. As regards unavailability of negation in restructuring contexts, it will be shown that negating the infinitive in these environments is ungrammatical for

An earlier version of this paper was presented at the 2009 LAGB meeting. I'm grateful to the audience for useful comments. I would also like to thank Ruth Kempson and Ronnie Cann for helpful discussion and insights. The AHRC and the Leventis foundation are gratefully acknowledged for providing partial funding to research related to this paper. Normal disclaimers apply.

The Dynamics of Lexical Interfaces.
Ruth Kempson, Eleni Gregoromichelaki and Christine Howes (eds.).

the same reason negation always precedes lexical and auxiliary verbs in the language examined (Italian).

10.1 Introduction

Clitic Climbing (CC) is one of the phenomena associated with clitics that has received considerable attention within the syntactic literature (Rizzi 1982; Kayne 1989; Miller and Sag 1997; Monachesi 1998, 1999; Cinque 2001, 2006; Cardinaletti and Shlonsky 2004 among others). CC basically refers to a syntactic construction, in which the clitic(s) seems to appear in a domain where no argumental relation with the verb of that domain is established. In effect, the core of the problem can be summarized as a local domain violation, since one basic property of clitics, i.e. the fact that these appear and are interpreted in the local domain of their host, is violated in CC environments. The examples below from Italian and Spanish respectively illustrate the latter point:

(10.1) *Lo voglio comprare*
it want.1SG buy.INF
'Maria wants to buy it.'

(10.2) *Maria lo quiere comprar*
Maria it wants buy.INF
'Maria wants to buy it.'

Example (10.1) and (10.2) are examples of this domain violation. However, the structures in (10.3) and (10.4), where the clitic appears inside its domain of interpretation, are equally grammatical:

(10.3) *Voglio comprarlo*
want.1SG buy.INF-it
'I want to buy it.'

(10.4) *Maria quiere comprarlo*
Maria wants buy.INF-it
'Maria wants to buy it.'

The problem would be easily solvable if clitics had in general the ability to appear in different domains with all types of verbs. However, CC is only possible with a specific number of verbs that have traditionally been called *restructuring verbs* (Rizzi 1982, and practically any analysis within the GB/Minimalism tradition). This latter term refers to modal, aspectual and motion verbs. Clitic Climbing is not possible with any other verbs, as witnessed in the examples from Italian below:

(10.5) **Maria lo prova di comprare*
Maria it tried COMP buy.INF
'Maria wants to buy it.'

(10.6) **Lo detesto vedere in quello stato*
him detest see.INF in that state
'I detest seeing him in that state.'

The earliest approaches within the generative tradition (Rizzi 1982) consider CC as a side-effect of restructuring, a process of structure simplification in which a biclausal structure is turned into a monoclausal one by means of a restructuring rule (formalization is mine):

(10.7) $VP_{Rstr}\ V_{inf} \rightarrow V_{complex}$

The above rule transforms a biclausal structure involving a restructuring verb and an infinitive, into a monoclausal one where the two verbal elements are reanalyzed as a verbal complex.

The newest minimalist approaches, on the other hand (Cardinaletti and Shlonsky 2004; Cinque 2001, 2006), consider CC to occur when the climbing inducing verb appears not as a fully fledged verb heading its own VP but rather as a functional verb, i.e. as the lexical instantiation of an FP within the richly articulated FP clausal structure proposed by Cinque (1999):

- [CP... [FP... [FP V_{restr}[FP... [VP V]]]]] - Climbing case
- [CP... [FP... [FP[VP V_{restr} [CP... [FP... [FP[VP V]]]]]]] - Non-climbing case

Within HPSG, CC has been considered to be an argument-sharing phenomenon (Miller and Sag 1997; Monachesi 1998, 1999 among others). The assumption is that the climbing inducing verb subcategorizes for an infinitive plus its arguments:

(10.8)
$$\begin{bmatrix} \text{HEAD V} \\ \text{VCLASS modal} \vee \text{aspectual} \vee \text{motion} \\ SUBJ\langle NP\rangle \\ \text{COMPS L} \bigoplus \quad \langle\, \text{V} \begin{bmatrix} \text{CLTS}\,\{\} \\ \langle\ \text{NP}\ \rangle \\ \text{COMPS L} \end{bmatrix} \rangle \end{bmatrix}$$

Argument sharing explains why the clitic can climb in CC constructions but does not however have anything to say with respect to restructuring effects found in CC environments like, for example, unavailability of infinitival negation when CC has taken place (example below from Italian):

(10.9) **Lo vuole non vedere*
it.CL-ACC want NEG buy.INF
'I want to not see it.'

(10.10) *Vuole non vederlo*
want NEG buy.INF it.CL-ACC
'I want to not see it.'

Furthermore, it is not clear what subcategorization for an infinitive plus its arguments means and furthermore why non-restructuring verbs are unable to appear with this kind of subcategorization.

It is worth emphasizing, that the common denominator in all these approaches is the implicit or explicit assumption that CC constructions are monoclausal rather than biclausal (see Cinque 2006 for extensive argumentation on the monoclausal hypothesis). I will assume that this assumption is indeed true and using the DS framework, I will try to provide a dynamic analysis where CC directly follows and the functional vs non-functional distinction is captured in dynamic terms.

10.2 Theoretical preliminaries

The version of the DS framework I'm going to use has its basis in the version presented in Cann et al. (2005). I further assume a situation argument being present in the tree structure functioning as the locus where tense and aspect properties are encoded. Building on assumptions by Gregoromichelaki (2006, this volume) and Cann (this volume), this situation argument node is assumed to be of the general type e, but further specified as e_{sit} (with *sit* standing for situation).[1] Furthermore, the situation argument node, in line with the standard analysis of quantificational NPs (Kempson et al. 2001; Cann et al. 2005), is assumed to involve complex structure. All these assumptions are depicted in the tree structure representing the complete parse of the English sentence *Mary sang* adapted from Cann (this volume), as shown in (10.11).

In (10.11), the intransitive verb *sing* is taken to be a two-place predicate, subcategorizing for both a subject and an event/situation argument. In the lowest e_{sit} node, the reference time metavariable $\mathbf{R}$ is introduced. This will combine with the semantic specifications given for the past tense in the lowest functor node ($Fo(\lambda e \lambda e'(e', e' \subseteq e \wedge e < \mathbf{s}_{\mathrm{now}}))$), to return a formula value in which the first lambda bound variable, e, is substituted by $\mathbf{R}$, the reference time, ($Fo(\lambda e'(e', e' \subseteq \mathbf{R} \wedge \mathbf{R} < \mathbf{s}_{\mathrm{now}}))$). This new formula states that the event indicated by the other lambda bound variable e' is contained within or holds at $\mathbf{R}$ ($e' \subseteq \mathbf{R}$) which precedes the utterance time ($\mathbf{R} < \mathbf{s}_{\mathrm{now}}$). In the intermediate e_{sit} node, a situation variable s_i is introduced. This variable will substi-

[1] Under this approach the general type e can have subtypes e_{sit}, e_i for individuals, e_w, for worlds etc. In what follows only *sit* subscripts will appear for simplicity. The same applies to type *cn*.

tute the remaining lambda bound variable (e') to return the formula value $Fo(s_i, s_i \subseteq \mathbf{R} \wedge \mathbf{R} < \mathbf{s}_{\text{now}})$, in effect providing a situation that will satisfy the given tense/aspect specifications:

(10.11) Parsing *Mary sang*

$$Ty(t), Fo(Sing'(Mary')(\epsilon, s_i, s_i \subseteq \mathbf{R} \wedge \mathbf{R} < \mathbf{s}_{\text{now}})), \diamond$$

$$Ty(e_{sit}),\ Fo(\epsilon, s_i, s_i \subseteq \mathbf{R} \wedge \mathbf{R} < \mathbf{s}_{\text{now}}) \qquad Ty(e_{sit} \rightarrow t),\ Fo(Sing'(e)(Mary'))$$

$$Ty(cn_{sit}),\ Fo(s_i, s_i \subseteq \mathbf{R} \wedge \mathbf{R} < \mathbf{s}_{\text{now}}) \qquad Ty(cn_{sit} \rightarrow e_{sit}),\ Fo(\lambda P(\epsilon, P)) \qquad Ty(e),\ Fo(Mary') \qquad Ty(e \rightarrow (e_{sit} \rightarrow t)),\ Fo(Sing'(x)(e))$$

$$Ty(e_{sit}),\ Fo(s_i) \qquad Ty(e_{sit} \rightarrow cn_{sit}),\ Fo(\lambda e'(e', e' \subseteq \mathbf{R} \wedge \mathbf{R} < \mathbf{s}_{\text{now}}))$$

$$Ty(e_{sit}), Fo(\mathbf{R}) \qquad Ty(e_{sit} \rightarrow (e_{sit} \rightarrow cn_{sit})),\ Fo(\lambda e \lambda e'(e', e' \subseteq e \wedge e < \mathbf{s}_{\text{now}}))$$

The last step involves quantifying over the last formula obtained. In the example above, the restrictor specifying a set of situations is combined with, in effect, an existentially quantifying binder, ϵ, to return a formula value which roughly states that such a past situation exists ($Fo(\epsilon, s_i, s_i \subseteq \mathbf{R} \wedge \mathbf{R} < \mathbf{s}_{\text{now}})$). At the end of the parse, the formula value of the complex situation argument node will combine via functional application with the situation functor node of type $Ty(e_{sit} \rightarrow t)$ to return the well-formed type t formula $Fo(Sing'(Mary')(\epsilon, s_i, s_i \subseteq \mathbf{R} \wedge \mathbf{R} < \mathbf{s}_{\text{now}}))$.[2] Lastly, note that the situation argument node along with the containing tense-aspect information is assumed to be directly projected from the verb in this case. In other instances, partial tense and aspect information can be provided by auxiliary verbs, infinitives or even modality and subjunctive markers (see e.g. Chatzikyriakidis forthcoming).

[2]The reference time $\mathbf{R}$, being a metavariable, needs to be substituted by a proper value given standard DS assumptions (Kempson et al. 2001; Cann et al. 2005 among others). The assumption is that the reference time metavariable gets a proper value according to context. As Cann (this volume) argues this reference time metavariable can range not only across times but also events or even worlds, and is always contextually determined. I will not deal with the details of substituting the metavariable $\mathbf{R}$ here. It should however be kept in mind that a complete analysis of tense/aspect will have to take care of this substitution as well.

10.3 A Dynamic account of clitic climbing

10.3.1 Clitics in DS

A number of analyses have been proposed for various clitic properties in DS (Bouzouita 2008a,b; Chatzikyriakidis 2009a, 2009b, forthcoming; Chatzikyriakidis and Kempson 2010; Gregoromichelaki, to appear). In all these analyses, positioning restrictions are defined as restrictions on the current parse state, while the actions projected by the clitic vary according to the level of underspecification involved in each case. For example, 1st/2nd person accusative clitics in Spanish have been analysed as projecting locally unfixed nodes (Cann and Kempson 2008; Chatzikyriakidis and Kempson 2010), a proposal largely motivated by the morphological syncresis of these clitic forms. On the other hand, 3rd person accusative clitics in the same language are treated as projecting fixed structure, in effect building and decorating the direct object node with a type value and a formula metavariable. There are a number of interesting predictions that such a proposal makes, especially with respect to the Person Case Constraint (PCC), but this is something that will not concern us here (see Cann and Kempson (2008) and Chatzikyriakidis and Kempson (2010) for an analysis of the PCC in DS). In this chapter, I will use the Italian 3rd person accusative clitic *lo* as an exemplar and I will not deal with clitic clusters or person case restrictions. The language used will be Italian but the same account is easily extendable to other CC languages as well, e.g., Spanish, Catalan (see also Chatzikyriakidis (forthcoming) for a DS analysis of obligatory climbing in Grecia Salentina Greek). As already stated, positioning restrictions are defined as restrictions on the current parse state. For example, the trigger shown below effectively captures proclisis in Italian:[3]

(10.12) Proclisis trigger:

IF	$?Ty(t)$		
THEN	IF	$[\downarrow^{+}]Tn(a), ?Ty(x)$	
	THEN		...
ELSE	Abort		

The above reads as follows: If the pointer appears at a node with a type t requirement, then, if all fixed nodes (nodes with a Tn address) below that node bear a type requirement, then the clitic can be parsed. This ensures that no verbal element has been parsed yet, since, if it had, we would have at least one fixed node with its type.[4] The next step is

[3]This is a general proclitic trigger and as such will work for languages with similar clitic positioning restrictions (Spanish, Greek, French to name a few).

[4]Note that such an entry will also correctly predict *lo* to be possible after dative clitics in clitic clusters like *me lo*. Assuming that *me* will project an unfixed node

to define the actual actions projected by the clitic. Given a fixed node analysis for 3rd person accusative clitics, *lo* will basically build the direct object node, project a type value and a formula metavariable on that node and return the pointer to the most local type t node above it ($gofirst(?Ty(t))$). Furthermore, an additional trigger is added, specified as a disjunction (OR) in the embedded IF part of the algorithm, positing that the clitic can also be parsed in case an infinitival or an imperative feature is present in the type t requiring node:[5]

(10.13) Lexical entry for the third person accusative clitic *lo*[6]

$$
\begin{array}{lll}
\text{IF} & ?Ty(t) & \\
\text{THEN} & \text{IF} & [\downarrow^{+}]Tn(a), ?Ty(x) \\
 & \text{OR} & \\
 & \text{IF} & (+INF \vee +IMP) \\
 & \text{THEN} & \mathtt{make}(\langle\downarrow_1\rangle); \mathtt{go}(\langle\downarrow_1\rangle); \\
 & & \mathtt{make}(\langle\downarrow_0\rangle); \mathtt{go}(\langle\downarrow_0\rangle) \\
 & & \mathtt{put}(Ty(e), Fo(U_x), ?\exists\mathbf{x}.Fo(\mathbf{x}), \\
 & & gofirst(?Ty(t))) \\
\text{ELSE} & \text{Abort} &
\end{array}
$$

Having sketched the way clitics are treated in DS, it is time to move to the actual analysis of CC in DS.

10.3.2 The analysis

Given the lexical entry for clitics in (10.13) if we assume a biclausal analysis of clitic climbing where the climbing inducing verb subcategorizes for a verbal complement, climbing is predicted to be ungrammatical. This is because parsing of the clitic involves the projection of a type value at the direct object node, a node already containing a type t requirement projected by the climbing inducing verb. In (10.14)[7], the clitic has been parsed first, decorating the direct object with a type e value. However, the existing type t requirement will disallow any well formed parse of the sentence, since in case the type t requirement gets

(following Cann and Kempson 2008; Chatzikyriakidis and Kempson 2010), the clitic *lo* can be parsed.

[5]Note that the features +IMP, +INF are used here as DS diacritics and do not constitute a serious attempt to give an analysis of imperatives and infinitives.

[6]The subscript x in the formula metavariable $\mathbf{U}$ stands for the restrictions on metavariable update that a third person clitic, and in general any third person metavariable, will bear. These will not be specified here but will have to be assumed in a more complete analysis to prevent overgeneration, e.g., avoiding a situation where *lo* is updated by a formula value specified as female. First/second person metavariable restrictions will be denoted as Sp' and Hear', standing for Speaker and Hearer respectively, again pending a more complete analysis.

[7]The higher situation node is not shown here for ease of exposition.

satisfied a type conflict will occur, whereas if it does not, an oustanding requirement will exist in the tree structure.

(10.14) Parsing *vuole* in *lo vuole comprare* 'it-wants to-buy'

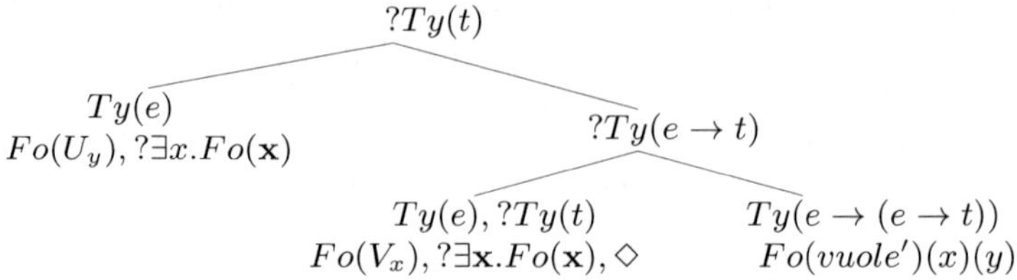

However, as already mentioned, the stance I'm going to take here is that CC involves a monoclausal rather than a biclausal structure, following pretty much everyone in the literature (with the exception possibly being Kayne 1989). Hence, the first thing to look at is how a monoclausal approach to the phenomenon can be pursued. A promising way of approaching the problem is to examine whether other constructions involving monoclausal verbal complexes exhibit climbing. A positive answer comes from perfect constructions in languages like Italian/Spanish (also non-climbing languages, e.g. Greek). In these languages, perfect verbal complexes comprised of an auxiliary verb and the past participle always involve attachment of the clitic to the left of the auxiliary rather than attachment to the past participle:

(10.15) *Gianni l' ho mangiato*
Gianni it$_{\text{CL-ACC}}$ have eaten
'Gianni has eaten it.' [Italian]

(10.16) **Gianni ho (lo) mangiato (lo)*
Gianni have it$_{\text{CL-ACC}}$ eaten it$_{\text{CL-ACC}}$
'Gianni has eaten it.' [Italian]

(10.17) *Juan lo ha comido*
Juan it$_{\text{CL-ACC}}$ have eaten
'Gianni has eaten it.' [Spanish]

(10.18) **Juan ha (lo) comido (lo)*
Juan have it$_{\text{CL-ACC}}$ eaten it$_{\text{CL-ACC}}$
'Gianni has eaten it.' [Spanish]

(10.19) *O Janis to ehi fai*
Gianni it$_{\text{CL-ACC}}$ have eaten
'Gianni has eaten it.' [Greek]

(10.20) **O Janis ehi (to) fai (to)*
Gianni have it$_{\text{CL-ACC}}$ eaten it$_{\text{CL-ACC}}$
'Gianni has eaten it' [Greek]

The main DS assumption behind auxiliaries in English is that these are basically content placeholders (Cann, this volume) projecting their tense and aspect information in the situation argument node. A formula metavariable, $Fo(\mathbf{U})$, is further projected at the predicate node. This will predict that auxiliaries can also appear in VP-ellipsis environments, since update of the predicate formula metavariable can be achieved via substituting a formula value available in the context. The effect of parsing the English auxiliary *have* under Cann's analysis is shown in (10.21), below:[8]

(10.21) Parsing *have*

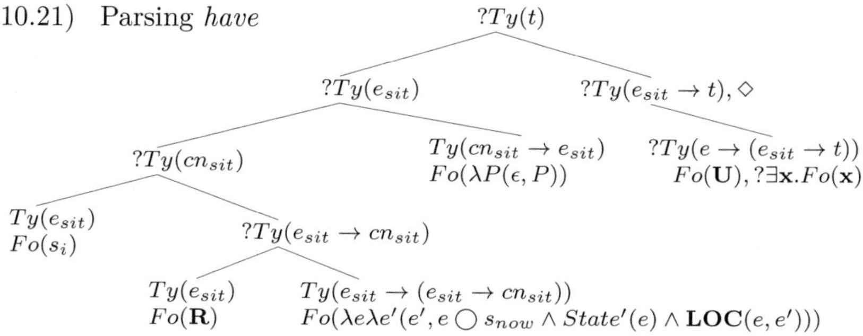

The above analysis can be extended to auxiliaries in Italian with minor modifications. The first modification would involve getting rid of the formula metavariable in the predicate node and possibly getting rid of the whole predicate node. This is because having a formula metavariable in the predicate node predicts that auxiliaries in Italian can appear in VP-ellipsis environments, similarly to English, which is contrary to fact:

(10.22) *Hai* *chiamato* *Gianni?* **Si,* *ho*
have called John yes have-I
'Have you called John? Yes, I have.' [Italian]

The other thing that needs to be taken care of is the subject pro-drop properties associated with Italian. This can be easily accommodated assuming that the auxiliary will also project a type e value and a formula metavariable in the subject node. This is a plausible assumption since all agreement information in Italian is encoded on the auxiliary rather than the past participle. The formula metavariable needs to be updated by a proper formula by the end of the parse. This can be done by the context (covert subject or object) or from the natural language string itself (overt subject or object). In case the verb is comprised of more than one element, one of the two should project the subject information.

[8]See Cann (this volume) for details on the semantic specifications of *have*.

It seems plausible to assume that this information will be contributed by the element that exhibits agreement information, i.e. the auxiliary in our case.[9] Putting these two assumptions together we end up with the following tree, depicting the result of parsing the Italian auxiliary *ho* 'have':

(10.23) The effect of parsing *ho* 'have.1sg' in Italian

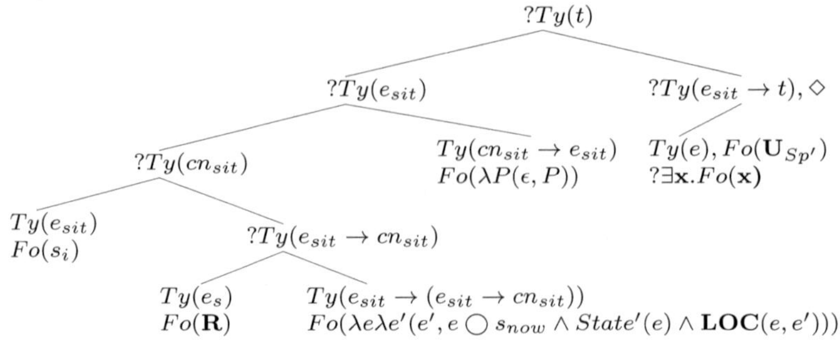

Having processed this lexical entry, the pointer is left at the node that will be annotated with a functor over situation arguments. At this point, the past participle can be parsed. I will not go into the exact details of how the lexical entry for past participles will look, however, following Cann (this volume) I assume that past participles have a $Ty(e_{sit} \to t)$ requirement as their triggering point. This will basically predict climbing to be obligatory with auxiliary constructions in Italian, as is in fact the case. Let us explain. Say we begin with the grammatical auxiliary climbing example shown below:

(10.24) *L' ho comprato*
it have.1SG bought
'I have bought it.'

The clitic is parsed first, giving rise to the structure in (10.25).

[9]There are no consequences for the account given if we assume that the participle and not the auxiliary is projecting the subject information.

(10.25) Parsing *lo* in *L' ho comprato* 'I have bought it'

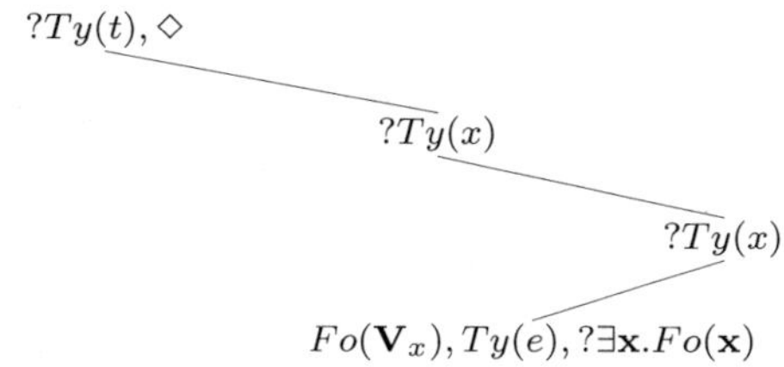

With the pointer at the type t requiring node, the auxiliary can be parsed, projecting the situation argument nodes plus the subject node decorated with a type value and formula metavariable (10.26).

(10.26) The effect of parsing *ho* 'have.1sg' in *L' ho comprato* 'I have bought it'

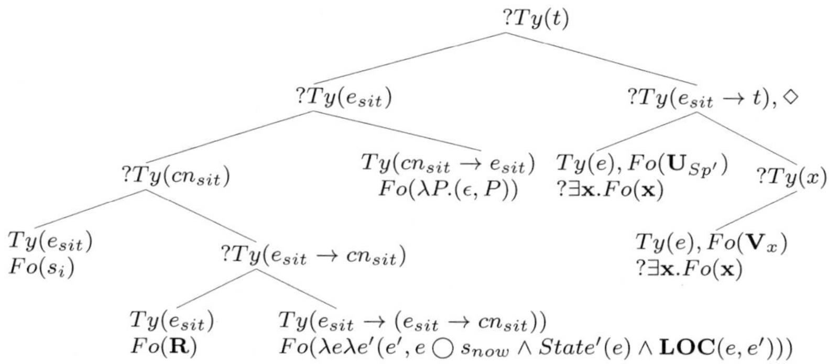

The pointer is at the type $e_{sit} \rightarrow t$ node and thus the past participle can be parsed. Given that the past participle will provide a transitive type and a predicate formula value in the lowest functor node, the parse will turn out to be grammatical, assuming that the metavariables projected by the clitic (in the object node) and the auxiliary (in the subject node) will be updated by proper formula values provided by the context in this case.[10] On the other hand, as a consequence, both (10.27) and (10.28) are predicted to be ungrammatical:

(10.27) **Ho* *lo* *comprato*
have.1SG it bought
'I have bought it.'

(10.28) **Ho* *comprato* *lo*
have.1SG bought it
'I have bought it.'

[10]See Cann (this volume) for a lexical entry of past participles in English.

In the first of the two examples, the auxiliary is parsed, leaving the pointer at the type $e_{sit} \rightarrow t$ requiring node. However, this node does not satisfy the initial trigger of the clitic ($?Ty(t)$), and thus the parsing process stops there.[11] In the case of (10.28), the clitic comes into parse after both the auxiliary and the past participle have been first parsed. What we have not yet shown is the node where the pointer will be left after the past participle is parsed. However, whatever our assumption with respect to the position of the pointer after the past participle has been parsed, parsing of the clitic afterwards will be impossible. Assuming the pointer is left at the type $e_{sit} \rightarrow t$ requiring node, the clitic cannot be parsed for the same reason it cannot be parsed after the auxiliary in (10.27), i.e. because the initial trigger of the clitic ($?Ty(t)$) is not satisfied. Assuming the pointer is left at the type t requiring node, the clitic again cannot be parsed, since there will be at least one node bearing a type value (the predicate type projected by the past participle), and thus the embedded trigger of the clitic will not be satisfied ($[\downarrow^{+}]Tn(a), ?Ty(x)$). Lastly, assuming the pointer is left at the object node (as Cann (this volume) actually assumes for English participles), the initial clitic trigger ($?Ty(t)$) will again not be satisfied, and thus the parse will abort.[12] Thus, the only option in auxiliary constructions is obligatory climbing of the clitic, i.e. attachment of the clitic to the auxiliary and not the past participle.

Given the analysis just sketched for auxiliaries, I would like now to propose that a straightforward account of CC can be put forth in case one assumes that restructuring verbs are parsed as auxiliary-like verbs. Under this proposal, restructuring verbs do not project any verbal type value but only the higher situation nodes plus the subject node. The claim is intriguing but needs to be further refined, since restructuring verbs, unlike auxiliary verbs, are contentful. Treating restructuring verbs in exactly the same way as auxiliaries will give us an incorrect semantic interpretation, since the semantics contributed by these verbs will not be encoded anywhere. So, in pursuing such an analysis, we will have to find a way to capture the semantic properties of these verbs without having to project any verbal predicate type node. Hopefully, there is a straightforward way to do this that will furthermore retain the core of the auxiliary analysis. Following a proposal by Ronnie Cann (p.c.), I will basically assume that the formula value of the intermediate e_{sit} node, introduces a complex formula value comprised of both a situation and a world parameter ($Fo(s_i, w_i)$). Then,

[11] Note that the pointer cannot move up via COMPLETION in this case, since no type or formula requirement has been satisfied at that node.

[12] Again, movement via COMPLETION is impossible.

the $e_{sit} \rightarrow (e_{sit} \rightarrow cn_{sit})$ node, besides carrying tense/aspect specifications, will be further annotated with world information. For example, in the case of *voglio* 'want', the variable which will combine with the world parameter will be specified as belonging to the set of all volitional contexts (W_V), which in turn are a subset of the set of contextually accessible worlds (W). This world specification will then be universally quantified to roughly return the following reading: there is a situation satisfying the given tense and aspect specifications in all volitional contexts that are a subset of the set of contextually accessible possible worlds. Accordingly, the structure we get after parsing *voglio* is shown below (10.29):

(10.29) Parsing *voglio* 'want.1SG'

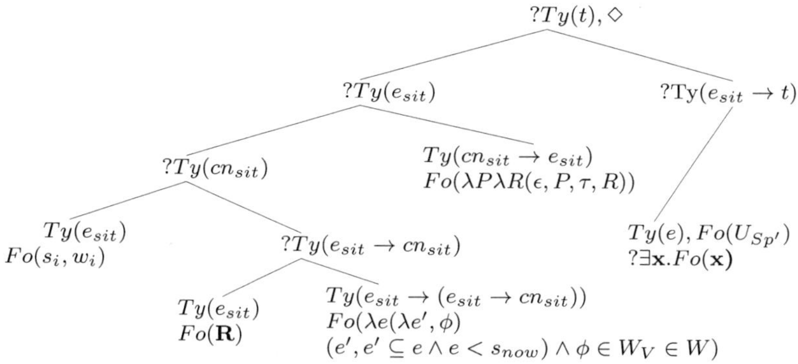

Notice that the pointer is assumed to return to the initial type t requiring node. We have seen that the pointer is left at the situation functor node after an auxiliary has been parsed. However, leaving the pointer at the situation functor node in the case of restructuring verbs will basically predict that infinitives have two distinct parsing triggers, a type t and a type $e_{sit} \rightarrow t$ requiring trigger. The type t requiring trigger is independently needed for constructions where the infinitive functions as the complement of a regular complement taking verb. In that case, and assuming that the complement taking verb will decorate the direct object node with a type t requirement and will leave the pointer there with no other nodes existing below that node, the trigger for the infinitive must be the type t requiring node. In order to avoid redundancy, I posit that the trigger for infinitives is a type t requiring node in all cases.[13] This is actually all we need in order to capture the clitic climbing phenomenon. In fact, these assumptions suffice to

[13] A welcome result of this assumption is that it enables us to distinguish between infinitives and past participles without actually referring to any of their properties. For example, under such an analysis, an infinitive will always be impossible after an

predict both the climbing and the in situ case. Let us see how. Say, we want to parse *lo voglio comprare* 'I want to buy it'. We first parse the clitic (10.30):

(10.30) Parsing *lo* 'it' in *lo voglio comprare* 'I want to buy it'

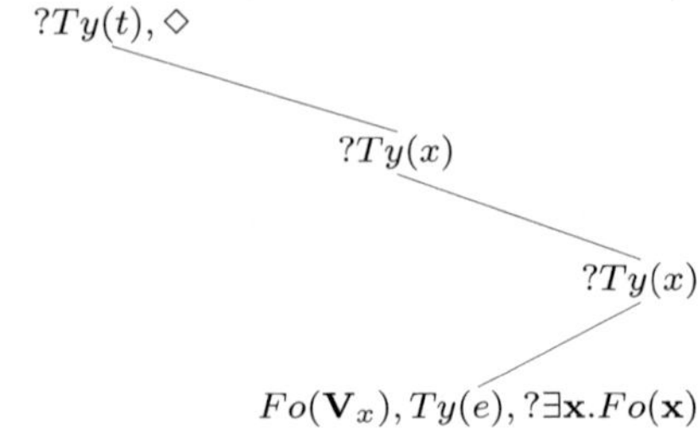

The pointer is then at the type t requiring node. The restructuring verb can now be parsed, projecting the situation nodes plus the subject node (10.31):

(10.31) Parsing *voglio* in *lo voglio comprare*

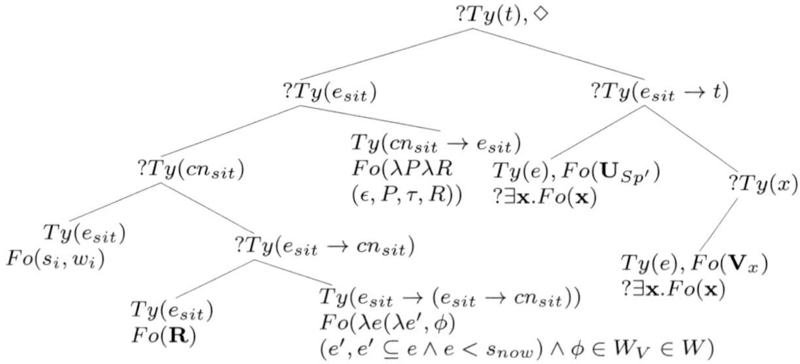

The pointer is again at the type t requiring node. The infinitive comes into parse, projecting the verbal predicate type plus a formula value (10.32):

---

auxiliary has been parsed first, since the pointer in that case will be at the situation functor node.

(10.32) Parsing *comprare* in *lo vuole comprare*

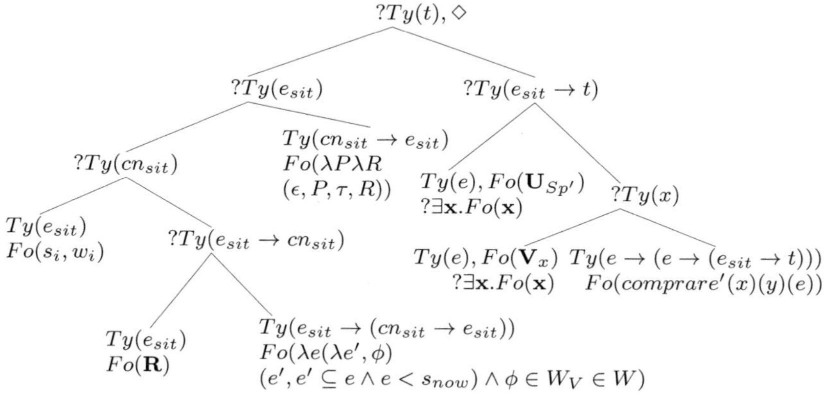

Assuming that the formula metavariables in the object and subject node are substituted by proper values, modus ponens and functional application lead to a well-formed parse:

(10.33) Completing the parse

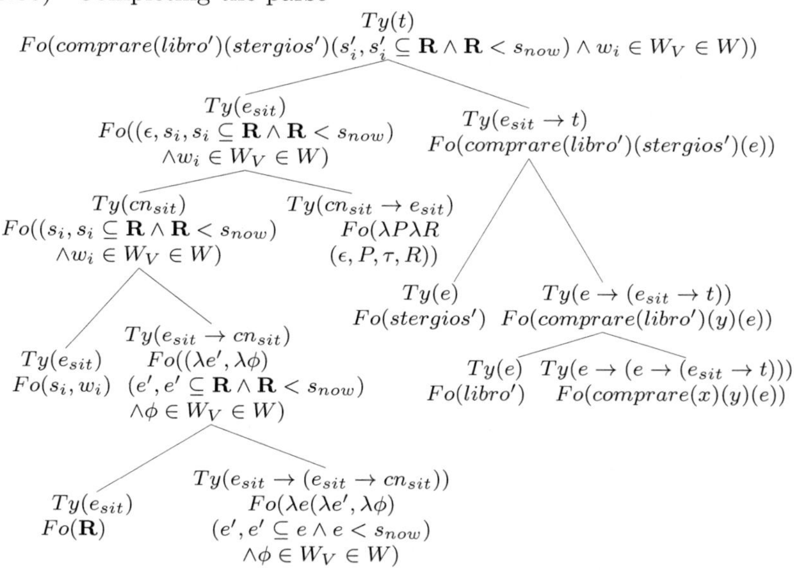

The in situ case (10.3) is also correctly captured in the following way: The restructuring verb plus the infinitive are parsed first. The infinitive annotates the type t node with a +INF specification. The pointer is left at the type t requiring node. The clitic comes into parse and since its second trigger is satisfied $((+INF \vee +IMP))$, parsing of the clitic is possible (10.34):

(10.34) Parsing *voglio comprar(e)* 'I want to buy' in *voglio comprarlo* 'I want to buy it'

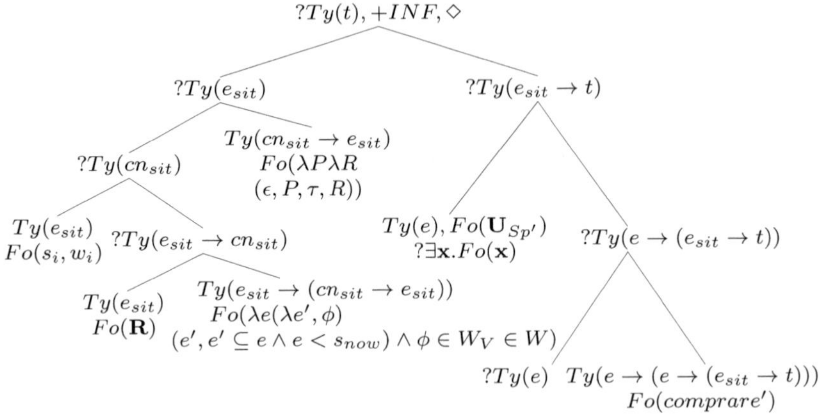

On the other hand, the case where the clitic is parsed in between the restructuring verb and the infinitive is predicted to be ungrammatical. This is because after the restructuring verb is parsed, a fixed node with a type value will exist (the subject node), and thus the clitic's embedded trigger, i.e. $[\downarrow^{+}]Tn(a), ?Ty(x)$, will not be satisfied. One of the consequences of the above account (and any monoclausal account in general) is that restructuring verbs cannot be control verbs anymore. This is because no subject is controlled but rather both the verb and the infinitive share the same subject. This has already been noted in the literature by Cinque (2006: 21) who argues that even apparent control cases like *want*, inherit their subject from the embedded lexical verb and thus are not control phenomena. In our case, no such inheritance is necessary, since both the restructuring verb and the infinitive share the same subject, but the intuition that restructuring does not involve control is common to both accounts.

Multiple verb climbing

Climbing is possible across more than one restructuring verb. Climbing to an intermediate position is also an option:

(10.35) *Lo voglio poter comprare*
it want be-able to-buy
'I want to be able to buy it.'

(10.36) *Voglio poterlo comprare*
want be-able-it to-buy
'I want to be able to buy it.'

(10.37) *Voglio poter comprarlo*
want be-able to-buy-it
'I want to be able to buy it.'

In the above examples, a restructuring infinitive (*poter*) is present along with the restructuring verb *voglio*. I assume that a restructuring infinitive, in the same sense as restructuring verbs, will not project any verbal predicate type but instead its semantics will be captured in the situation argument node. However, no situation or world parameter will be introduced by the restructured infinitive in the intermediate e_{sit} node, since these will have been introduced by the restructuring verb.[14] Its contribution will involve restricting world information associated with the world parameter (modal verbs) or the tense/aspect properties of the situation parameter (e.g. in the case of aspectual verbs). The exact formal details of such a proposal will not be fleshed out here (see Chatzikyriakidis 2009a for a lexical entry of restructuring infinitives), what is crucial here is that multiple climbing uses the exact same mechanisms as single CC. For example, after parsing the clitic in (10.35), the restructuring verb comes into parse providing a complex situation argument involving both a situation and a world parameter. The world parameter specification indicates that the situation must exist in all accessible volitional contexts which are a subset of the set of contextually accessible worlds. Then the restructuring infinitive follows, further restricting the world parameter by positing that the set of volitional contexts must be a subset of the set of ability contexts (W_{AB}) which in turn are a subset of the set of contextually accessible worlds (10.38):

(10.38) Parsing *poter* in *lo voglio poter comprare*

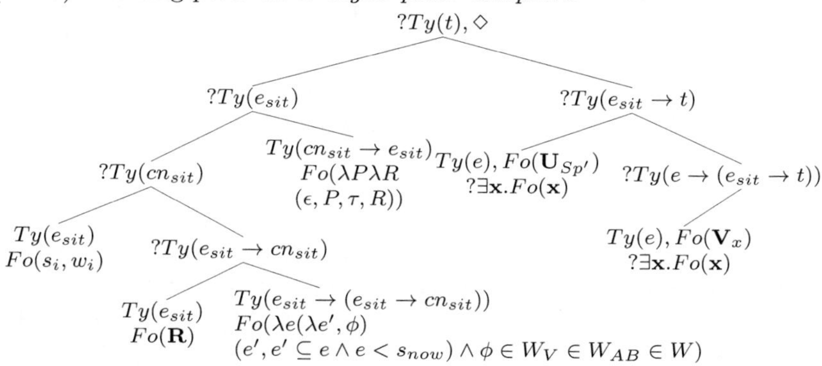

[14]However, there are cases where a restructuring infinitive is the only restructuring verbal element. For these cases see Chatzikyriakidis (2009a) for an analysis.

The rest follows as in single verb climbing. Note that the clitic can be also parsed in the intermediate position, since a +INF feature will exist after the restructured infinitive will be parsed. Thus, multiple climbing is captured in our account using the same mechanisms as in single verb climbing.

Unavailability of negation

One of the phenomena associated with CC is the unavailability of negating an infinitive in case CC has taken place. The relevant data are shown below:[15]

(10.39) **Lo* *vuole* *non* *vedere*
it$_{\text{CL-ACC}}$ want NEG buy$_{\text{INF}}$

(10.40) *Vuole* *non* *vederlo*
want NEG buy$_{\text{INF}}$-it$_{\text{CL-ACC}}$

The account proposed here for CC gives an immediate explanation for the phenomenon just sketched. Unavailability of negating an infinitive in CC contexts will be captured using the same mechanism one must use in order to capture the fact that negation is always preverbal in languages like Italian. Since restructuring verbs are analyzed on a par with auxiliary verbs, the explanation for the preverbal positioning of negation and the unavailability of negating an infinitive in CC environments will boil down to the same explanation: the specification of the negative element, contributing sentential negation, will have to ensure that no verb or auxiliary has already been parsed. Thus, what we really need is a trigger capturing the fact that negation must be preverbal no matter what kind of verb will follow. The following trigger introduces a lexical specification for negation that aborts in case any fixed nodes are present in the tree structure:

(10.41) Lexical entry for sentential negation

IF	$?Ty(t), [\downarrow^{+}]\exists\mathbf{x}.Tn(\mathbf{x})$
THEN	...neg-content...
ELSE	Abort

The above entry will correctly capture preverbal positioning of negation with content and auxiliary verbs alike. Thus, unavailability of negation in CC contexts is also predicted: assuming that a restructuring verb has been parsed, a number of fixed nodes will have been projected. Then,

[15] A counterexample is the case of *sembrare* in Italian, where negation does not seem to block CC in that case. See Cinque (2006) for the relevant data and argumentation.

if negation appears next, its trigger cannot be satisfied, and the parse aborts.

The grammatical example in (10.39) is captured, assuming, in line with Cinque (2001) and Cardinaletti and Shlonsky (2004), that restructuring verbs come in two guises, one functional and one lexical. The latter can only give rise to non-climbing configurations, while the former can give rise to both CC and non-CC constructions.[16] In DS terms, this structural duality is expressed as a disjunction in the entry of restructuring verbs. A lexical entry for a restructuring verb will involve a disjunction in the THEN part of the algorithm that will specify two different sets of actions, one for the functional, auxiliary-like version and one for the lexical version of the restructuring verb. Hence, the entry for the restructuring *voglio* will involve a structure like the one shown below:

(10.42) Lexical entry template for restructuring verbs

IF	?Ty(t)
THEN	**Functional actions**
OR	
THEN	**Lexical actions**
ELSE	Abort

Assuming the above lexical entry template for restructuring verbs, the grammaticality of (10.39) is captured in case the restructuring verb is parsed as a lexical verb. The structure obtained after *vuole* is parsed as a regular lexical verb is shown below (10.43):

(10.43) Parsing *vuole* in *vuole non vederlo*

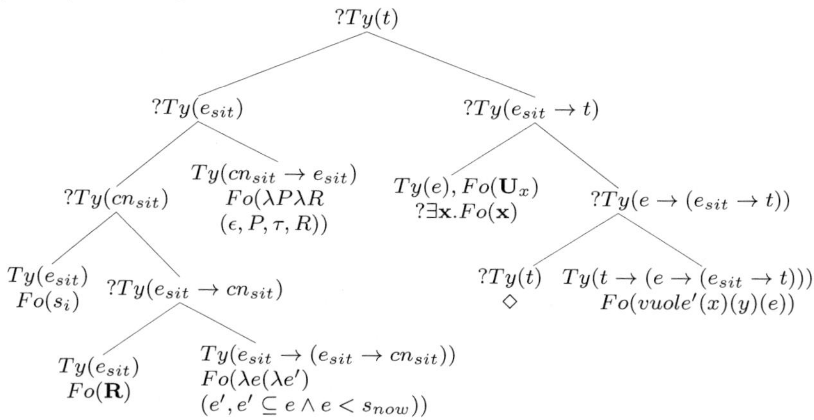

[16]See Cardinaletti and Shlonsky (2004) and Cinque (2006) for the relevant argumentation and examples.

Parsing *vuole* as a lexical verb will result in the projection of a verbal type, specified as $Ty(t \rightarrow (e \rightarrow (e_{sit} \rightarrow t)))$, along with a type t requirement at the object node. Furthermore, only a situation and no world parameter is projected by the actions of lexical *vuole*, since the semantics of the verb are now captured regularly via the formula value in the transitive functor node $(Fo(vuole'(x)(y)(e)))$. The pointer is left at the embedded type t requiring node. It is at this point that sentential negation is processed. As shown in (10.41), its lexical entry specifies that in order to be parsed, all nodes below the current one must be unfixed. The universal statement involved here will be trivially true in the presence of the empty set, i.e. in cases where no nodes are present below the current node. This is indeed the situation we find in the structure (10.43) above, and thus lexical negation can be parsed after *vuole* has been processed as a lexical verb.

10.4 Conclusion

In this chapter, I have presented a first sketch of a DS account of CC. I have argued that the phenomenon of CC can receive a straightforward explanation once one shifts into a dynamic perspective. In particular, I provided an analysis of restructuring verbs in line with auxiliary verbs. Under this analysis, restructuring verbs do not project a verbal type but rather project their semantic contribution inside the complex situation argument node. This last assumption straightforwardly captures the phenomenon of CC. Multiple climbing is then captured using the exact same mechanisms, the difference being that more than one verb project semantic information in the situation argument node. Finally, the unavailability of negating an infinitive is explained as a simple word order phenomenon, and it is captured by the same device used to capture the fact that negation precedes all types of verbs, both content and auxiliary in CC languages like Italian. Since restructuring verbs receive an analysis in line with auxiliary verbs, negation is only possible before the restructuring verb, while the option where negation precedes the infinitive is predicted to be illicit.

References

The following were cited in this chapter: Bouzouita (2008a,b), Cann (this volume), Cann and Kempson (2008), Cann et al. (2005), Chatzikyriakidis (2009a,b, forthcoming), Chatzikyriakidis and Kempson (2010), Cinque (1999, 2001, 2006), Cardinaletti and Shlonsky (2004), Gregoromichelaki (2006, this volume, to appear), Kayne (1989), Kempson et al. (2001), Miller and Sag (1997), Monachesi (1998, 1999), Rizzi (1982). See references at end of book for more information.

11

The *Bei* Construction in Chinese: A Dynamic Approach

RONNIE CANN AND YICHENG WU

11.1 Introduction

The analysis of the *bei* construction in Chinese[1] as a form of passive has long been of great interest and controversy among linguists, and there are a number of different accounts of the construction published in the literature. Nevertheless, a fully unified account of this construction remains to be achieved, and the status of the morpheme *bei* itself remains to be articulated. This controversy is attributable to the fact that the *bei* construction exhibits a somewhat diverse set of properties that are not fully consistent with the interpretation of the passive in languages like English. Consider the data in (11.1) below where (11.1a) represents the canonical agentive pattern, with the pre-*bei* constituent interpreted as the patient and the post-*bei* constituent as the agent. The examples in (11.1b,c) illustrate the "short" passive where the agent is not specified.[2]

(11.1) a. *Zhangsan bei Lisi ma guo.*
Zhangsan BEI Lisi scold EXP
'Zhangsan has been scolded by Lisi.'

[1]As is standard, throughout this chapter, the term *Chinese* when referring to the language should be interpreted as Standard Modern Mandarin Chinese.

[2]The following abbreviations are used throughout the paper: 1, first person; 2, second person; 3, third person; CL, classifier; EXP, experiential; LOC, locative; PFV, perfective; Q, question; PRT, particle.

The Dynamics of Lexical Interfaces.
Ruth Kempson, Eleni Gregoromichelaki and Christine Howes (eds.).

b. *Zhangsan bei ma guo.*
Zhangsan BEI scold EXP
'Zhangsan has been scolded.'

c. *chuanghu bei za le.*
window BEI smash PFV
'The window was smashed.'

The examples above look similar to the English passive in having an apparently fronted object noun phrase with an optional agent and so, despite the fact that Chinese verbs exhibit no passive morphology, could be considered to be analyzable in a similar way. However, there are other patterns which indicate that more is happening in this construction than simple 'promotion of object to subject'. In (11.2a,b), not only is there an apparently fronted object noun phrase before *bei* but also one that appears in the canonical object (post-verbal) position (a 'retained object' within analyses of traditional and generative grammars).

(11.2) a. *Zhangsan bei Lisi daduan le tui.*
Zhangsan BEI Lisi break PFV leg
'Zhangsan's leg was broken by Lisi.'

b. *Zhangsan bei Lisi jian le toufa.*
Zhangsan BEI Lisi cut PFV hair
'Zhangsan's hair was cut by Lisi.'

Furthermore, there are examples like (11.3a,b) which exhibit a pattern which involves another well-known grammatical structure in Chinese, the *ba* construction, where *ba* is itself generally taken to identify the following noun phrase as an object.

(11.3) a. *Zhangsan bei Lisi ba tui daduan le yi-tiao.*
Zhangsan BEI Lisi BA leg break PFV one-CL
'One of Zhangsan's legs was broken by Lisi.'

b. *Zhangsan bei Lisi ba toufa jian le yi-cuo.*
Zhangsan BEI Lisi BA hair cut PFV one-lock
'One lock of Zhangsan's hair was cut by Lisi.'

It is these latter examples that cause most controversy in the analysis of the *bei* construction, as they call into question the standard view of passive as involving some sort of 'promotion' of object to subject (however this notion may be defined in specific theoretical frameworks).

In this paper, we investigate the analysis of the *bei* construction within the framework of Dynamic Syntax (Kempson et al. 2001; Cann et al. 2005) and provide a principled account of the canonical patterns shown in (11.1) and the problematic patterns in (11.2, 11.3). By treating the *bei* construction as a type of hybrid topic/subject construction, we argue that the morpheme *bei* is a grammaticalized particle whose fundamental function is to signal that the **pre-***bei* argument functions as an affected argument of the event expressed by the following clause, giving rise to a pragmatic passive interpretation. Under the dynamic analysis, we show that the various patterns exhibited by the *bei* construction follow without further stipulation.[3]

11.2 *Bei* and its satellites

Wu (this volume) reviews analyses of *bei* as a preposition, a passive particle and as a verb. Although plausible hypotheses in themselves, each gives rise to significant unanswered questions or stipulative solutions to problems for them to be taken as robust explanations for the synchronic analysis of this particle. In this section, we suggest that *bei* is best analyzed in terms of the function it performs in the interpretations of sentences in which it appears. We will conclude that *bei* is a grammaticalized particle with a specific function, as in one part of the dual function hypothesis. However, we argue that this morpheme is not there specifically to mark passive voice or to license the appearance of an agentive nominal but to identify an argument affected by the event expressed by the following clause from which a (pragmatic) passive-like interpretation may be derived. The fact that a non-agent appears before *bei* gives rise to the appearance of left dislocation and so to interpretation of the initial constituent as a kind of topic.

One of the assumptions behind the hypothesis that *bei* is a preposition is that it operates in a similar fashion to the preposition *by* in English: to mark an oblique (adjunct) agent. One corollary of this analysis is that the noun phrase that immediately precedes *bei* is interpreted as the subject of the passive verb. The status of subjects, like much else in Chinese syntax, is a controversial subject, and one that we cannot tackle properly in this paper, for reasons of space, but it is most generally accepted that Chinese is a topic prominent language[4] and what we argue here is that the pre-*bei* noun phrase has both topic and subject properties.

---

[3]These four patterns are the most frequently used of all the constructions involving *bei* (Wang 1959). There are, however, other, more minor, patterns that are not discussed here for reasons of space, although the analysis of the canonical patterns presented in this paper can be readily extended to them.

[4]Li and Thompson (1981), but see Tan (1991) for arguments that this is incorrect.

11.2.1 Topic and passive

The functional similarity of passivization with topicalization has been discussed by a number of linguists like Givón (1979: 186), who defines passivization as 'the process by which a non-agent is promoted into the role of a main topic of the sentence', and Roberts (1998: 112) who claims that 'passivization can be regarded as one way of making a functional topic more prominent syntactically'. The similarity between the *bei* construction and topic constructions in Chinese is noted in Hashimoto (1968), LaPolla (1989), Y. Huang (2000) and many others. Compare the *bei* sentences (11.1a), repeated below as (11.4), with the *bei*-less example in (11.5). In both sets of examples, there is an initial noun phrase associated with an object gap in the following clause. Both topic and passive sentences are truth-conditionally equivalent and to the equivalent sentences without a fronted object (11.6).

(11.4) *Zhangsan bei Lisi ma guo.*
Zhangsan BEI Lisi scold EXP
'Zhangsan has been scolded by Lisi.'

(11.5) *Zhangsan, Lisi ma guo.*
Zhangsan Lisi scold EXP
'Zhangsan, Lisi has scolded.'

(11.6) *Lisi ma guo Zhangsan*
Lisi scold EXP Zhangsan
'Lisi has scolded Zhangsan.'

The *bei* construction shares other properties with the topic construction. For example, topics, rather than subjects, tend to control null anaphors in subsequent sentences (11.7) and they do not require a 'gap' in the main clause (11.8). These properties are also exhibited by the pre-*bei* noun phrase as in (11.9).

(11.7) a. *Zhangsan, zhuren ma guo ta, ye ma guo zhuren.*
Zhangsan head scold EXP 3SG also scold EXP head
'As for Zhangsan$_i$, the head scolded him$_i$ and he$_i$ scolded the head too.'

b. *jiu-ge miyu, Lisi caidui le liu-ge, tai rongyi le.*
nine-CL riddle Lisi resolve PFV six too easy PFV
'Nine riddles, Lisi solved six. They are too easy.'

(11.8) a. *shenghuo, Wangwu xihuan xiao chengshi.*
life Wangwu like small city
'As for life, Wangwu loves towns.'

b. *yuyanxue, Zhangsan pian'ai yuyixue.*
linguistics Zhangsan prefer semantics
'As for Linguistics, Zhangsan prefers semantics.'

(11.9) a. *zhe jiahuo bei baba da guo duo ci,*
this guy BEI dad hit EXP many times
jiushi bu gai.
just not change
'This guy$_i$ had been hit many times by Dad, but he$_i$ just didn't change.'

b. **zhe jiahuo bei da guo duo ci,*
this guy BEI hit EXP many times
baba jiushi bu gai.
Dad just not change
'This guy having been hit many times, Dad just didn't change.'

c. *Zhangsan bei Lisi jian le toufa.*
Zhangsan BEI Lisi cut PFV hair
'Zhangsan's hair was cut by Lisi.'

If the *bei* construction is a form of topic construction, then whatever licenses gapless topics and discourse control in the latter can explain the problematic cases of retained objects in this construction and the discourse control properties of the pre-*bei* noun phrase.

One final property links the *bei* construction with the topic construction and that is that the fronted expression need not be a direct object. In (11.10), for example, a postpositional locative phrase *qiang shang* is fronted in both the *bei* (11.10a) and topicalized variants (11.10b) (cf. Xu and Langendoen 1985).[5]

(11.10) a. *qiang shang bei haizimen wa le yi-ge dong.*
wall on BEI children dig PFV one-CL hole
'A hole was dug on the wall by children.'

b. *qiang shang, haizimen wa le yi-ge dong.*
wall on children dig PFV one-CL hole
'On the wall, children dug a hole.'

[5] An anonymous reviewer points out that in (11.10a) there is a selectional restriction between the verb *wa* and the fronted constituent *qian shang* as the spatial term is required and cannot be omitted without yielding ungrammaticality. Such a selectional restriction is explained on a movement analysis, but not on a topic analysis without a dependency site in the main clause. Our response is that the selectional property is semantic and, given the analysis presented below, it follows that this will need to be satisfied whether the expression is construed as a direct argument of the main verb or not.

c. *haizimen zai qiang shang wa le yi-ge dong.*
children LOC wall on dig PFV one-CL hole
'Children dug a hole on the wall.'

'Peculiar passives' such as (11.11) are known in English (Davison 1980) and there are languages such as Sanskrit (11.12) that can promote adjuncts.

(11.11) a. This bed was slept in by Mary Queen of Scots.
b. ?This plate has been eaten meat off/from.

(11.12) a. *Ratho gramam gacchati.*
cart-nom village-acc go-3sg.pres.act
'The cart is going to the village.'
b. *Rathēna grāmo gamyate*
cart-inst village-nom go-3sg.pres.pass
'The cart is going to the village.'
(Lit. 'The village is being gone to by the cart.')

The phenomenon of promoting non-direct objects in Chinese, however, appears to be more productive, certainly than is the case in English, applying also to non-locative adjuncts, such as (11.13[6]) where the substance from which a garment is made is passivized. The ability to front a range of different categories of expression is more typical of topic constructions, rather than passives of the sort found in Indo-European languages.

(11.13) a. *ta yong na-kuai bu zuo le yi-tiao kuzi.*
3SG with that-CL cloth make PFV one-CL trousers
'He made a pair of trousers with the cloth.'
b. *na-kuai bu bei ta zuo le yi-tiao kuzi.*
that-CL cloth BEI 3SG make PFV one-CL trousers
'The cloth was made into a pair of trousers by him.'

Although there are strong similarities between passivization and topicalization in Chinese, there are nevertheless differences. Syntactically, what is passivized is usually (but not exclusively, see above) the patient argument or something related to the patient in retained object constructions. The pre-*bei* noun phrase can never be associated with the Agent. What is topicalized is not subject to this constraint, as illustrated in (11.14).

(11.14) a. **Lisi bei ma guo Zhangsan.*
Lisi BEI scold EXP Zhangsan
(Intended: 'Lisi scolded Zhangsan.')

[6](11.13b) – L. Li (1980:402).

b. *Lisi ta/zhe jiahuo ma guo Zhangsan.*
Lisi 3SG/this guy scold EXP Zhangsan
'Lisi, he/this guy has scolded Zhangsan.'

Furthermore, while topicalization can involve a long distance dependency, the dependency in the *bei* construction must always be local.

(11.15) a. *?*Zhangsan bei Lisi renwei Wangwu pai jingcha zhua le.*
Zhangsan BEI Lisi think Wangwu send police catch PFV

b. *Zhangsan, Lisi renwei Wangwu pai jingcha zhua le.*
Zhangsan Lisi think Wangwu send police catch PFV
'Zhangsan, Lisi thought that Wangwu had sent the police to catch.'

Although (11.15a) is taken in C.-T. J. Huang (1999) to be grammatical, it is rejected by our native speaker informants who report a clear contrast in acceptability between the dispreferred *bei* example and the ordinary topic construction. Furthermore, as C.-T. J. Huang notes as his reason for adopting an operator movement analysis, the pre-*bei* noun phrase can never have a dependency into an apparently finite clause (however finiteness is to be defined within Chinese). See (11.16) taken from C.-T. J. Huang (1999) example 28.

(11.16) **Zhangsan bei Lisi shuo jingcha zhua-zou le.*
Zhangsan BEI Lisi say police arrest PFV

Additionally, although topic constructions allow a resumptive pronoun to appear in the following clause, these are generally considered to be unacceptable in the *bei* construction (see e.g. Wang 1959, Chao 1968, Lü 1982).[7]

(11.17) a. *Zhangsan, Lisi da guo ta.*
Zhangsan Lisi hit EXP him
'As for Zhangsan, Lisi hit him.'

b. **Zhangsan bei Lisi da guo ta.*
Zhangsan BEI Lisi hit EXP him

Although there are differences between the passive and topic constructions, there are nonetheless significant similarities. In particular, the *bei* construction exhibits a subset of the properties exhibited by the topic construction, such as discourse control of null topics in subsequent sentences and variability in the type of expression that appears in initial position. These properties, we believe, provide sufficient evidence for

[7]We return to this issue in section 11.4.

taking the pre-*bei* noun phrase to be a kind of topic. As we discuss below in relation to our specific analysis, we attribute the topichood of the pre-*bei* constituent to its apparently being left dislocated from the position in which it would normally be expected to occupy. However, the restrictions on the left dislocation of non-agents with dependencies only in local domains and the exclusion of resumptive pronouns are what give rise, we suggest, to the interpretation of this construction as a form of passive.

11.2.2 Agent and topic

If the pre-*bei* noun phrase is a type of topic, as argued above,[8] one question that remains is what its relationship is to any overt post-*bei* noun phrase, typically an agent. As noted above (and in many places in the literature), the distinction between topic and subject is notoriously difficult and controversial, and this is particularly true of Chinese.[9] However, there is one property that subjects in Chinese have incontrovertibly: they function as the controllers in syntactic control structures. Thus, in (11.18a) the subject/agent of the matrix verb *shefa* 'try' also functions as the subject of the second verb *da* 'hit'. This control pattern is not affected if the object is fronted as topic (11.18b). This pattern is maintained in the *bei* construction (11.19).

(11.18) a. *Lisi shefa da Zhangsan.*
Lisi try hit Zhangsan
'Lisi tried to hit Zhangsan.'

b. *Zhangsan, Lisi shefa da (ta).*
Zhangsan Lisi try hit (him)
'As for Zhangsan, Lisi tried to hit him.'
(NOT '*As for Zhangsan$_i$, Lisi tried for him$_i$ to hit (someone).')

(11.19) *Zhangsan bei Lisi shefa da le.*
Zhangsan BEI Lisi try hit PFV
'Lisi tried to hit Zhangsan (and succeeded).'
(NOT 'Zhangsan tried to be hit by Lisi'.)

It would appear from these data that the pre-*bei* noun phrase is not the subject of the sentence that follows and the inference to be derived is that it is the post-*bei* constituent, the subject of the 'active' sentence, remains the subject of the 'passive' clause.

---

[8]Note that we do not claim that the pre-*bei* constituent behaves exactly like all left displaced topics, but merely that it shares *some* properties with them.

[9]See C. Li (1976) and C. Li and Thompson (1981) for a detailed exploration of this debate.

C.-T. J. Huang (1999), however, points out that a property is shared between the pre- and post-*bei* noun phrases is the possibility of binding the anaphor *ziji*. *Ziji* in Chinese is typically analyzed as a subject oriented, possibly long distance, reflexive as illustrated in (11.20).

(11.20) a. *Zhangsan da le ziji.*
Zhangsan hit PFV self
'Zhangsan hit himself.'

b. *Zhangsan shuo Lisi da le ziji.*
Zhangsan say Lisi hit PFV self
'Zhangsan$_i$ said that Lisi$_j$ hit him$_i$/himself$_j$.'

c. *Zhangsan da le ziji xiaohai.*
Zhangsan hit PFV self child
'Zhangsan hit his (own) child.'

In certain circumstances, both satellites of *bei* may bind the anaphor:

(11.21) *Zhangsan bei Lisi guan zai ziji de jiali.*
Zhangsan BEI Lisi lock at self DE home
'Zhangsan was locked by Lisi in his home.' (his = Zhangsan or Lisi) (C.-T. J. Huang 1999: example 15)

However, not all instances of the anaphor can be bound by both constituents. For example, the *bei* counterpart of (11.20c), shown in (11.22), can have only the interpretation that it is Lisi's child that Lisi hit, not Zhangsan's. This has the effect of rendering the example pragmatically unacceptable because of the difficulty of construing Zhangsan as some sort of object of Lisi's beating his own child.

(11.22) **Zhangsan bei Lisi da le ziji xiaohai.*
Zhangsan BEI Lisi hit PFV self child

This again indicates that it is *Lisi* that acts as subject of the clause that follows *bei*, not *Zhangsan*. To indicate that the children being hit by Lisi are Zhangsan's a resumptive pronoun needs to be used:

(11.23) *?Zhangsan bei Lisi da le ta xiaohai.*
Zhangsan BEI Lisi hit PFV he children
'Zhangsan's child was hit by Lisi.'

However, not even a resumptive pronoun replacing *ziji* can make (11.22) completely acceptable (although (11.23) is better than (11.22) according to our informants), partly because the retained object cannot be a definite NP (as indicated by all the examples given in our paper), but an indefinite NP or a kind-denoting NP only.

However, there appear to be examples where *ziji* can be bound by a pre-*bei* noun phrase: when the reflexive appears in the post-*bei* position (at least with prosodic stress on *ziji*).[10]

(11.24) *Zhangsan bei ziji pian le.*
Zhangsan BEI self cheat PFV
'Zhangsan cheated himself.'

Thus, with respect to *ziji*-binding, we have a mixed pattern in the *bei* construction: the pre-*bei* noun phrase is subjectlike in being able to bind the anaphor when it occurs in an adjunct expression (a PP in 11.21) or in embedded subject position, but not when it occurs in object position.

There is one respect in which a pre-*bei* noun phrase behaves fully in a subjectlike manner: it allows the appearance of temporal and locative expressions between it and *bei*. This parallels the appearance of such phrases between subjects and the following verb. Compare the *bei* examples in (11.25) with their possible 'active' counterparts in (11.26).

(11.25) a. *Zhangsan zuotian bei Lisi ma le.*
Zhangsan yesterday BEI Lisi scold PFV
'Zhangsan was scolded by Lisi yesterday.'
(NB. **Zhangsan bei Lisi [zuotian] ma le.*)

b. *Zhangsan zai xuexiao bei Lisi da le.*
Zhangsan in school BEI Lisi hit PFV
'Zhangsan was hit by Lisi in the school.'
(NB **Zhangsan bei Lisi [zai xuexiao] da le.*)

(11.26) a. *Lisi zuotian ma le Zhangsan.*
Lisi yesterday scold PFV Zhangsan
'Lisi scolded Zhangsan yesterday.'

b. *Lisi zai xuexiao da le Zhangsan.*
Lisi in school hit PFV Zhangsan.
'Lisi hit Zhangsan in the school.'

As C.-T. J. Huang (1999) suggests, it thus appears that the pre-*bei* noun phrase does behave as a subject with respect to adverbial placement, and to a certain extent with respect to *ziji*-binding. It does not behave, however, as a subject with respect to control structures where the post-*bei* noun phrase acts as a controller or reflexive binding into argument positions. How then can these mixed properties be accounted for? This question will be answered with respect to the particular theoretical analysis that we provide in section 11.4. Before then, we explore the function of the expression *bei* itself.

[10] We are grateful to an anonymous referee for bringing these data and the significance of reflexive binding to our attention and to Wenshan Li for this particular example (although its acceptability remains controversial amongst our informants).

11.2.3 Locus of affect and the function of *bei*

In the preceding discussion, we argued that the pre-*bei* noun phrase behaves to some extent as both topic and subject, although not fully functioning in all respects as either. Wu (this volume) also argues that *bei* is neither a preposition nor a verb. The implications of these two hypotheses is that *bei* is not directly associated with the noun phrase that immediately follows, as assumed in the preposition hypothesis. Instead, it seems to be the case that the function of *bei* has nothing to do with the agent of the clause or even directly with the verb, but is essentially a device to identify the *preceding* phrase as the topic of the sentence which, while interpreted as a non-subject argument of the clause that follows, nevertheless has subjectlike characteristics. The question is: what are the properties of *bei* that give rise to these characteristics?

One of the interesting things about *bei* in discourse can be seen in (11.27). Here the first speaker pauses after uttering *Zhangsan bei* and the second responds with an event-oriented question about what happened to Zhangsan.

(11.27) A: *Zhangsan bei ...*
B: *Zhangsan bei zenme le?*
Zhangsan bei how PRT
A: *bei (Lisi) da le.*
BEI (Lisi) hit PFV
'He was hit (by Lisi).'

Zenme in the question above can be construed as 'What happened (to Zhangsan)?' or 'How did someone dispose of (Zhangsan)?'. B does not respond with a question about who did something to Zhangsan as would be expected if the function of *bei* were to identify the function of what follows it. Compare (11.27) with a putatively similar exchange in (11.28) where the event oriented question is infelicitous.

(11.28) A: Zhangsan was hit ...
B: By who?
B: # What happened to Zhangsan?

Another way of interpreting *zenme* here is as questioning an event, as indicated by the English translations given above. One way to think of the function of *bei*, therefore, is that it links a topic/subject with an event, the event described by the following clause. But what is that linking relation?

As noted earlier, in the canonical patterns, the pre-*bei* noun phrase is interpreted as the patient argument of the main verb as in (11.1a), repeated below as (11.29).

(11.29) *Zhangsan bei Lisi ma guo.*
Zhangsan BEI Lisi scold EXP
'Zhangsan has been scolded by Lisi.'

But the fronted constituent need not be a patient, but may, for example, be an experiencer (11.30).

(11.30) a. *jingcha kanjian le Zhangsan.*
police see PFV Zhangsan
'The policeman saw Zhangsan.'

b. *Zhangsan bei jingcha kanjian le.*
Zhangsan BEI police see PFV
'Zhangsan was seen by the policeman.'

Although both sentences in (11.30) describe the same event, there is a significant interpretational difference between them. The active sentence (11.30a) simply describes a seeing event involving Zhangsan as the experiencer and the policeman as the agent. In the *bei* version, however, the fronted experiencer is interpreted as being directly affected by the seeing-event. Hence, (11.30b) expresses an unfavourable situation that *Zhangsan* faced as a consequence of the seeing event, e.g. he might be a suspect or on the run, or whatever. We might thus interpret (11.30b) as something like 'there is an event of seeing with the police as agents and Zhangsan as the experiencer and this event affected Zhangsan (adversely)'.

Consider also examples of locative and other phrases that can be fronted in the *bei* construction such as (11.10a) and (11.13b), repeated below as (11.31) and (11.32), respectively.

(11.31) *qiang shang bei haizimen wa le yi-ge dong.*
wall on BEI children dig PFV one-CL hole
'A hole was dug on the wall by children.'
('?On the wall was dug a hole by the children')

(11.32) *na-kuai bu bei ta zuo le yi-tiao kuzi.*
that-CL cloth BEI 3SG make PFV one-CL trousers
'The cloth was made into a pair of trousers by him.'

In (11.31) a locative postpositional phrase appears in pre-*bei* position, while in (11.32) an oblique PP is stripped of its preposition and fronted. In both cases, the fronted expressions are interpreted as strongly (and perhaps adversely)[11] affected by the event denoted by the main verb:

[11]It is worthwhile mentioning the fact that although traditionally *bei* constructions generally have a pejorative implication, yet a certain number of *bei* sentences in Modern Chinese, as discussed in Li and Thompson (1981:496-497), are more or less free of such pragmatic commitments due to the influence of Indo-European lan-

the wall was (badly) affected by the children's hole-digging and the cloth has been, perhaps improperly, affected by the trouser-making. Even in cases where the pre-*bei* noun phrase has not been physically affected, as in (11.33) the entity denoted is nevertheless presented as being strongly affected as no longer being a pleasant or desirable place.

(11.33) *chitang li bei cunmin yang le henduo eyu.*
pond in BEI villagers raise PFV many crocodiles
'A lot of crocodiles were raised in the pond by villagers.'

Example (11.33) shows that this affectedness relation has to be determined inferentially, rather than directly with respect to being an argument of the main verb. This is further illustrated by the way that examples of the *bei* construction with a retained object are interpreted. In these constructions, it is the pre-*bei* noun phrase that is interpreted as being affected by the action described by the verb rather than the retained object. This effect can be seen most clearly in examples like those in (11.34):

(11.34) a. *Zhangsan bei Lisi ma le niang. ta hen qifen.*
Zhangsan BEI Lisi curse PFV mother 3SG very angry
'Zhangsan's mother was cursed by Lisi. He/*She was very angry.'

b. *Zhangsan bei Lisi haisi le die.*
Zhangsan BEI Lisi kill PFV father
'Zhangsan was the victim of father-killing action done by Lisi.'

Niang 'mother' in (11.34a) and *die* 'father' in (11.34b) do not refer to any particular mother or father but to the type of female or male parents. (11.34a) may thus be interpreted as 'Zhangsan was mother-cursed by Lisi' rather than as 'Zhangsan's mother was cursed by Lisi', since it is not Zhangsan's mother but Zhangsan who is affected by the action and no direct cursing of his mother need have taken place at all.[12] Similarly in (11.34b), the focus is on Zhangsan and not on his father. While this sentence strongly implicates that it is Zhangsan's father who was killed (by Lisi), this results rather from inference over father-killing actions and those affected by them (typically the father's children) than a direct encoding of that information. The interpretation of the sentence in (11.2a) above should thus rather be 'Zhangsan was the object of leg-breaking by Lisi' or 'An event of Lisi's breaking a

guages. This indicates that *bei* is undergoing further grammaticalization and may be losing even the remnants of the affected interpretation.

[12]The situation is thus similar to one in which a man might be called a son of a bitch.

leg affected Zhangsan'. The fact that the leg belongs to Zhangsan is inferred from the assumption that Zhangsan is (directly) affected by the action of leg-breaking.

This notion of affectedness is not present in purely topicalized variants without *bei* and therefore must be attributed to the morpheme itself. Since the effect is so marked, it would appear that the notion of affectedness is encoded as a semantic effect of *bei* which we suggest it retains from its original verbal meaning as the ability to 'assign' a participant role to its preceding (originally subject) constituent. We do not, however, claim that *bei* **is** a verb in contemporary (Mandarin) Chinese as it exhibits none of the common grammatical properties expected of full verbs and has no independent semantic contribution to make to the clause beyond that of indicating the affectedness of a nominal that immediately precedes it (or from which it is separated only by a restricted set of adjuncts).

All that remains of *bei*'s origin as a full verb is, as we suggest, the association of its preceding constituent with an affectedness reading. We now go further and suggest that this role is in fact one of an event role of 'locus of affect'. In an analysis of resultative verb constructions in Chinese, Chang (2003) develops ideas put forward in (Croft 1991, 1998) to do with the structure of events and the roles of the participants. Although Chang's concern is with linking roles to argument realization, something that we are not concerned with in this paper, nevertheless his analysis of event roles is pertinent to our analysis of *bei*. Chang (2003), following Croft (1998), suggests that participants are involved at the beginning and endpoints of subevents in some event structure, defining three event roles:

(11.35) a. **Initiator**: an entity that is involved in the initiation or bringing about of an object [or event];
b. **Target of activity**: an entity that undergoes an action;
c. **Locus of affect**: an entity that is involved in the endpoint or resulting state.

(Chang 2003:330, addition ours)

Like Chang, it is the last role that we associate with *bei* since, as we have seen above, the pre-*bei* noun phrase is not necessarily an undergoer argument of the main verb. This is particularly clear in examples involving retained objects where, for example, in (11.2a) it is Zhangsan's leg that is broken (and so is the target of activity in Chang's terms) not Zhangsan. Zhangsan is, however, obviously 'involved in the endpoint' of the leg-breaking event. In examples with locatives and other adjuncts (11.10,11.13), the location or material used is 'involved in the resulting state' whereas the target of activity is the hole dug by the children or the trousers made.

Although in retained object constructions, the target of activity and locus of affect roles are realized by different expressions, in the canonical constructions, this is not the case: the pre-*bei* noun phrase performs both functions, both undergoer and affected argument. Since there is no incompatibility of these two roles, we get a straightforward passive interpretation. For example, in (11.36) the internal argument of *da* 'hit' is a patient necessarily affected by the action and the initial constituent *Zhangsan* is interpreted as locus of affect of the hitting event by reason of *bei*, the most relevant (in the technical sense of Relevance Theory, Sperber and Wilson 1995) and most natural reading is to identify the two, giving rise to an interpretation: 'there is an event of hitting in which Lisi is the agent and Zhangsan the affected patient' without any inferential effect. Since the patient argument is fronted and thereby made syntactically prominent, the analysis of the construction as a passive is straightforward.

(11.36) *Zhangsan bei Lisi da le.*
Zhangsan BEI Lisi hit PFV
'Zhangsan was hit by Lisi'

The information provided about the locus of affect by *bei* also helps explain the interpretation of non-patient pre-*bei* noun phrases such as in (11.30b) repeated below as (11.37).

(11.37) *Zhangsan bei jingcha kanjian le.*
Zhangsan BEI police see PFV
'Zhangsan was seen by the policeman.'

By marking Zhangsan as locus of affect, this construction gives rise to a focus on the endpoint of the seeing, its result state. Since there is no lexically encoded result state of a seeing event, there is an inference that nevertheless some result state does obtain that affects Zhangsan and, because the police are the agents of the seeing, this gives rise to an implication of adversity for Zhangsan.

Chang (2003) is principally concerned with the realization of arguments in different resultative verb constructions. In typical, active constructions he associates the locus of affect with a postverbal position (in fact, the position immediately following the second verb, but the details are not relevant here) and provides a separate linking rule that stipulates that it also may be realized as the pre-*bei* noun phrase ('subject' in his terms). This necessarily excludes his initiators (typically agents) from this position, but by brute force: the account does not explain the constraint. In our account, argument linking has no place (at least in the syntactic process, it may be that such concepts are relevant in the lexicon), and object gaps are construed as anaphoric to the topic. For us, therefore, the problem reduces to excluding the term projected by the pre-*bei* constituent from being interpreted as an agent/initiator argument in the following string.

The concept of affectedness itself does not exclude agents from having an affected reading (Saksena 1980) and so we might expect unaccusatives or verbs of imbibing, etc., to be able to appear with *bei* and interpreted as actor as well as locus of affect, contrary to fact (11.38):[13]

(11.38) **Lisi bei diedao le.*
Lisi BEI fall PFV
(Intended: 'Lisi was affected by falling')

Agents of transitive verbs are also excluded from being identified with the pre-*bei constituent* where there is a gap in object position. Putative examples like that in (11.39) are excluded by binding principle B (or its analogue), since the pronominal would then be bound by the subject.

(11.39) **Lisi*$_i$ *bei* e_i *da le* ta_i/e_i.
Lisi BEI hit PFV him
(Intended: 'Lisi was hit by himself.')

Furthermore, the ungrammaticality of examples like (11.40) with a fronted agent and an overt object follows, we suggest, from a constraint on the construal of a (null or overt) pronominal in the subject position of the clause following *bei* with the pre-*bei* noun phrase. We return to this issue in section 11.4.1.

(11.40) **Lisi*$_i$ *bei* e_i *da le Zhangsan*
Lisi BEI hit PFV Zhangsan

Our overall conclusion, then, is that *bei* identifies the constituent that precedes it as the locus of affect of the event expressed by the following clause. The *bei* construction in Chinese is thus interpreted as a passive construction by virtue of the fact that it encodes action notionally devolving from the standpoint of the locus of affect of a transitive verb.

[13] An anonymous reviewer claims that intransitive verbs may appear with *bei*, citing the following example:

(i) *Ni zenme bei ta pao le*
you how BEI s/he run PFV
'How did you let him run away.'

Our informants reject this example with *bei*, but accept it with *gei*, *jiao* or *rang*. Even if it were acceptable, however, notice that the putative locus of affect *ni* is not identified as the actor of the running *ta* and so does not constitute a counterexample to the current hypothesis.

Thus, the verbs occurring in *bei* sentences, in the words of Lyons (1968: 372), are characterized by "signifying the state of 'being acted upon' or 'suffering the effects of the action"', as can be attested by the fact that they generally take a perfective aspect marker *le* or an experiential aspect marker *guo*. Furthermore, the effect of presenting an initial constituent as having such a role normally associated with syntactic objects gives rise to topic-like discourse properties being associated with that constituent, giving rise to a hybrid topic/subject interpretation of the pre-*bei* noun phrase.

11.3 Towards a Dynamic Syntax of Chinese

Given the above descriptive discussion, we now turn to a formal analysis of these hypotheses within the framework of Dynamic Syntax in which these properties can be made to follow straightforwardly. We will further show how it can provide the basis of a unified account of the various problematic instantiations of the construction.

As is evident from the papers in this volume, *Dynamic Syntax* (Kempson et al. 2001; Cann et al. 2005) models the process of natural language understanding as the monotonic growth of trees representing the semantic content of some string of words uttered in context. The process is goal-driven, beginning with the initial, universal requirement to establish propositional content for some utterance. Such content is represented in terms of binary trees establishing the argument structure of a proposition as it is built up incrementally through the operation of general construction rules, information provided by words, and pragmatic processes of enrichment. The framework articulates a grammar formalism that characterizes the structural properties of language by means of a dynamic parsing process that is strictly incremental. Syntax is thus construed not in terms of static articulated structures defined over strings of words, but in terms of how structures that represent the meaning of a string of words are built up. Intrinsic to this process are concepts of underspecification which are manifested in a number of different ways and whose resolution is driven by the notion of requirements. For immediate purposes, we only introduce some of the machinery of the DS model needed for handling the *bei* construction.

11.3.1 Requirements and tree growth

The logical form corresponding to the interpretation of a string (an expression in the language of thought) is represented as a binary tree which encodes the argument structure of a clause, and the parsing process is the attempt to establish some appropriate tree on the basis of the words provided. Nodes in trees are decorated with values of labels specifying (amongst other things) the type of the node (label Ty[14]), its semantic content shown as a lambda expression (label Fo) and an address specifying where in the tree the node is (label Tn). The structures derived in the output language are thus proof trees of some labelled deductive logic (see Gabbay 1994 inter al.) with each step defined over the types and formulae by modus ponens and functional application. The result of parsing a sentence such as (11.41) is, therefore, the binary structure in (11.42) with each node decorated by an argument or functor expression and associated type.[15]

(11.41) *Lisi ma guo Zhangsan*
Lisi scold EXP Zhangsan
'Lisi scolded Zhangsan.'

(11.42) Output proof tree for *Lisi ma guo Zhangsan*

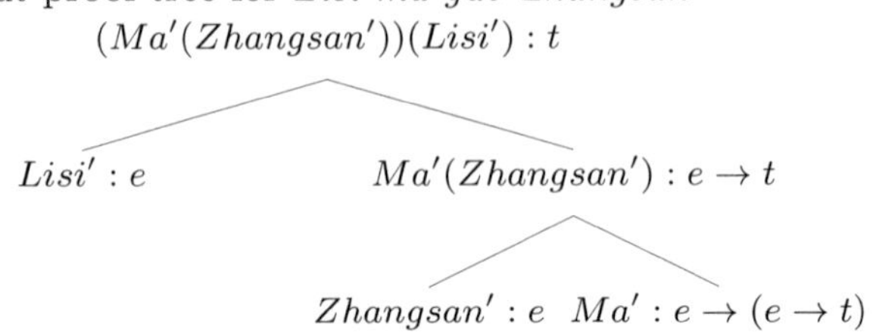

In addition to values of labels, nodes may be decorated by requirements of various sorts which provide the driving force of the parsing process. Requirements may be to specify values for any of the labels that may decorate a node, but the principal drivers of the syntactic process are requirements to establish formula values of certain types, starting from $?t$, an instruction to build a propositional tree decorated with a formula of type t. To satisfy a requirement, a parse relies on information from three sources. First of all, there are general computational rules which are optional, freely available and may be universally or specifically available to a language. Secondly, there are actions associated with a particular word and thirdly from context through pragmatic actions.

The framework is strongly lexicalist and much of the work of the construction of the output logical forms are induced by individual lexical items. However, unlike other lexicalist frameworks such as HPSG (Sag, Wasow and Bender 2003) or LFG (Bresnan 2001), the lexical entries for lexical words are not static feature matrices but procedural

[14]DS uses only a restricted set of types: e the type of a term, t the type of a proposition, cn the type of a common noun, $e \rightarrow t$, the type of a (one-place) predicate and higher arities of predicates, and eventuality sorts of these (see below). The theory eschews the use of type-altering operations.

[15]Here and below, we omit the address of nodes except where relevant.

instructions giving information about how the semantic content of the word is to be construed in the current context. Thus, lexical entries consist of *IF...THEN...ELSE* statements where the *IF* clause states the conditions under which the actions in the *THEN* clause can be run, while the *ELSE* statement gives instructions about the action to be taken if the conditioning context is not met, typically an instruction to abort the parse. In this paper, however, we leave aside all technical details for ease of exposition and rely on the tree displays to show the results of applying syntactic operations.

Wu (this volume) provides a sketch of a DS grammar of Chinese within the framework of Cann et al. (2005). In this paper, we develop the account given there by introducing situation or event terms into the representations (Gregoromichelaki 2006) and pick the hypotheses in Cann (this volume) concerning syntactic subjects as locally unfixed and the behaviour of verbs in projecting full propositional information.

As is common, we take event arguments to be of type e, that of an entity, but sortally distinguished from individual entity-denoting expressions as being of type e_{sit} (where *sit* stands for 'situation'). The result of parsing the simple verb *ma* is shown in (11.43). The diamond, $\diamondsuit$, is the 'pointer' which is used to identify the particular node that is to be developed next, here the event node.[16]

(11.43) Parsing *ma*

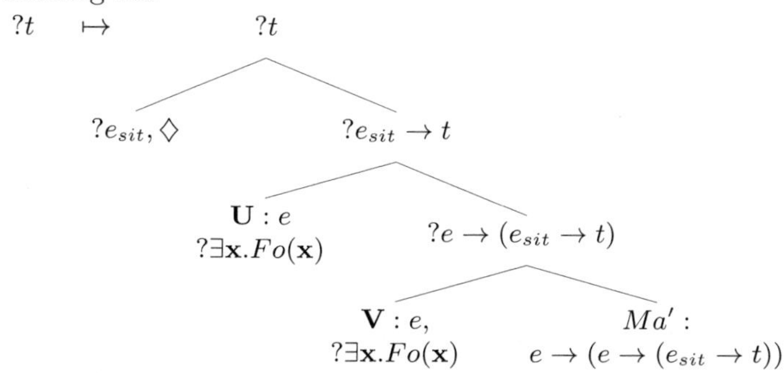

[16]Trees are representations of content with no reflection of linear order. Functor nodes are displayed on the right and argument nodes on the left. In this and subsequent displays, the symbol $\mapsto$ indicates that the tree on the left may be transformed into that on the right. The formal basis of the theory is a description language for partial trees based on the Logic of Finite Trees (LOFT) (Blackburn and Meyer-Viol 1994), a modal logic for describing finite trees. This logic allows reference to any node in a tree from any other node, using two modal operators

$\langle\uparrow\rangle$ the mother relation
$\langle\downarrow\rangle$ the daughter relation

As noted above, the parse of a verb leaves the pointer on the node that requires to be decorated by some event term which, we suggest, is provided by parsing an aspect marker (whether overt or null). It is not possible here to discuss the behaviour and semantics of aspect markers in Chinese, but we assume that they provide information about how the eventuality expressed by the verb is to be interpreted. Specifically, we suggest that the parse of an aspect marker provides an event variable of different sorts, according to the specific marker used. This event variable is then evaluated when the propositional formula expressed by an utterance is computed to give some sort of indexical term that can be updated in various ways (such as relations with other event variables already introduced in the discourse, see Kamp and Reyle 1993) depending on the properties of the aspect marker. We thus envisage the parse of the experiential aspect marker *guo* as providing a fresh event variable annotated to indicate its specific aspect which we represent by boldface **s** superscripted by the gloss used in this paper for the marker and with a subscripted index to differentiate between variables associated with different predicates, e.g. $\mathbf{s_i^{exp}}$. Parsing *ma guo* thus updates the tree in (11.43) to that in (11.44).[17]

(11.44) Parsing *ma guo*

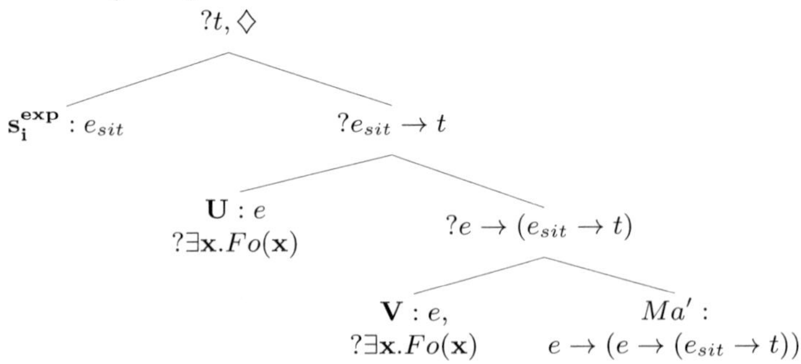

11.3.2 Formula underspecification

In the tree displays in (11.43) and (11.44), the individual argument nodes are annotated with expressions of type e shown as boldface $\mathbf{U}, \mathbf{V}$. These are *metavariables* which act as placeholders for actual formulae and are thus associated a requirement to find *formula values* ($?\exists\mathbf{x}.Fo(\mathbf{x})$) which can only be satisfied if some contentful formula value replaces the metavariable during the course of a parse. Such replacement is associated with a substitution process that is both prag-

[17] In a more elaborated grammar, one might take the aspect marker as constructing an epsilon situation term with an aspectual restrictor, as proposed in Cann (this volume). We leave such a refinement to one side in this paper.

matic and system-external, restricted by pragmatic principles (such as relevance), locality considerations (such as analogues of the Binding Principles, Chomsky 1981, Kempson et al. 2001:97) and, for pronouns, by lexical presuppositions, such as gender, number and person, only the latter being relevant for Chinese in the pronominal system. The effect of parsing verbs in Chinese is thus to have argument nodes decorated with such metavariables as if associated with null pronominals. The reason for adopting this approach is, of course, that Chinese is a radical pro-drop language and speakers freely omit arguments when it is clear what those arguments should be from the context. Thus, all the strings in (11.45) are grammatical in appropriate contexts:[18]

(11.45) a. *Lisi ma guo Zhangsan.*
Lisi scold EXP Zhangsan
'Lisi scolded Zhangsan.'
b. (Who did Lisi scold?)
ma guo Zhangsan.
c. (Who scolded Zhangsan?)
Lisi ma guo.
d. (What did Lisi do to Zhangsan?)
ma guo.

With metavariables projected by verbs in Chinese, there are no presuppositional constraints (because of the lack of morphological agreement) allowing free substitution of some term from context (modulo binding restrictions) which prevent (for example) the substitution of one local argument formula for another. Thus, assuming that *ma guo* is being uttered by Lisi, then the hearer may choose the concept *Lisi′* as the appropriate substituend. By a process called ANTICIPATION in Cann et al. (2005), the pointer may be moved down a tree to some node that contains an open requirement such as the subject node in (11.44), allowing substitution to occur to derive the update in (11.46) where the substitution operation is shown by the double uparrow.

Metavariables may be updated not just through substitution but through the parse of some term-projecting expression. All noun phrases (including quantified ones) are projected as terms of type e in DS, contrary to the higher type associated with the theory of generalized quantifiers (Barwise and Cooper 1981 inter al.), so that a proper name like *Zhangsan* projects a simple individual constant.[19] The parse of a

[18]See Wu 2005 and W. Li fcmg for an alternative approach that allows free metavariable insertion.

[19]Technically, terms in DS are modelled as epsilon terms (Hilbert and Bernays 1939) so that a proper name *Zhangsan* yields an iota term, $\iota, x, Zhangsan'(x)$. We

noun in Chinese may thus be triggered either by a type requirement for a term, $?e$, or by a formula requirement, $?\exists\mathbf{x}.Fo(\mathbf{x})$, on a term node hosting a metavariable. So, after parsing *ma guo* parsing the proper name *Zhangsan* gives the tree in (11.47) from that in (11.46).

(11.46) Identifying the subject argument from context

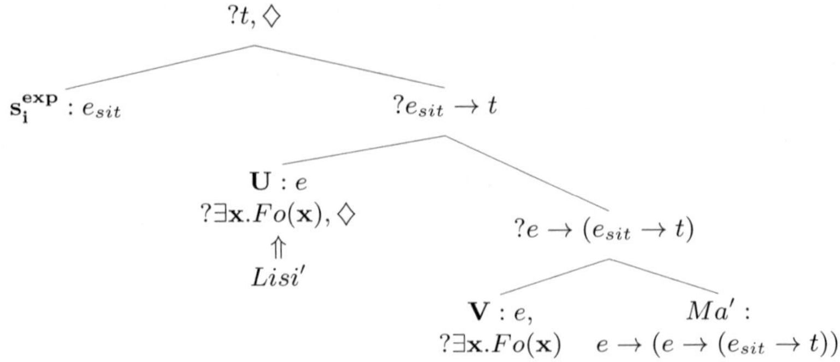

(11.47) Parsing *ma guo Zhangsan*

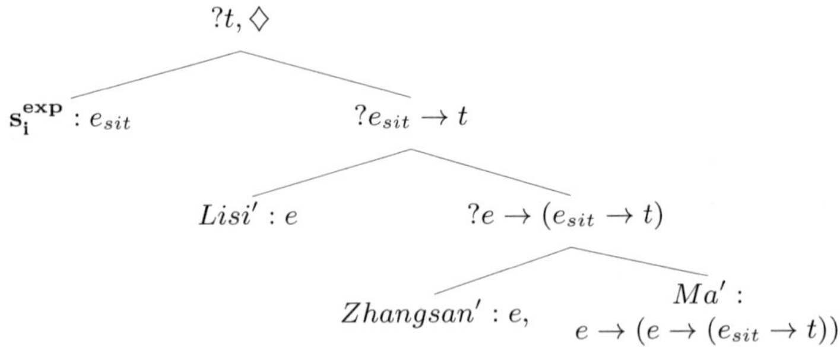

The parsing process is not yet finished, however, as some requirements on the tree remain to be satisfied. Completion of the tree involves functional application of functors over arguments, driven by modus ponens over types. (11.48) shows the completed tree with no outstanding requirements, the root node of which is decorated with a type t formula value, as required.

11.3.3 Left dislocation and syntactic subjects

As already noted, the driving force behind the parsing process in DS is the need to satisfy requirements. Often these requirements need to be satisfied immediately, but some requirements can only be satisfied at some later stage of the parsing process. One of these is used to account for left dislocation. Just as anaphora is analyzed in terms of underspec-

leave this complexity aside, returning to the issue of epsilon terms as they relate to event terms below.

ification of formula, so dislocated dependencies are analyzed in terms of underspecification of final position within an unfolding propositional structure.

(11.48) Completing *ma guo Zhangsan*

$((Ma'(Zhangsan'))(Lisi'))(\mathbf{s_i^{exp}}) : t$

$\mathbf{s_i^{exp}} : e_{sit}$ $\quad$ $(Ma'(Zhangsan'))(Lisi')$ $e_{sit} \rightarrow t$

$Lisi' : e$ $\quad$ $Ma'(Zhangsan') :$ $e \rightarrow (e_{sit} \rightarrow t)$

$Zhangsan' : e$ $\quad$ $Ma' :$ $e \rightarrow (e \rightarrow (e_{sit} \rightarrow t))$

This is achieved using a tree modality that specifies only some undetermined domination relation: $\langle\downarrow_*\rangle\alpha$ from some node β merely indicates that α holds at some node that β dominates (inversely $\langle\uparrow_*\rangle\beta$ from α indicates that β holds at some dominating node).[20] Initial expressions may, by virtue of these operators, be parsed without initially having a fixed position within the tree but being asserted to be only dominated by some node with treenode address n, an address being a string of 0s and 1s with 0 the address of the topnode and argument daughters being assigned an additional 0 while functor daughters are marked with 1. Unfixed nodes also carry a requirement $?\exists\mathbf{x}.Tn(\mathbf{x})$ to identify a fixed address within the current tree.

Certain types of left dislocation are thus analyzed in terms of initially unfixed nodes whose position in the emergent tree structure is fixed at some later stage in the parsing process. For example, analyzing the string *Zhangsan, (ta) ma guo* 'Zhangsan, he/she scolded' in these terms is illustrated in (11.49) with an initially projected unfixed node, licensed by a general computational rule called *ADJUNCTION (read 'star adjunction') allowing the parse of the word *Zhangsan* which bears only a weak dominance relation to the rootnote (with treenode address 0).

From this point, the parse of the string proceeds exactly as in (11.43)–(11.46) to yield the tree in (11.49) where two outstanding requirements remain: a requirement to find a fixed position for the unfixed node and a requirement to find the formula value for the internal

[20] Both relations are defined as the reflexive and transitive closure of the appropriate relation so that $\langle\uparrow_*\rangle\alpha$ states that α holds of the current node or the mother of the current node or of some node dominating the mother of the current node (i.e. $\langle\uparrow_*\rangle\alpha =_{def} \alpha \vee \langle\uparrow\rangle\langle\uparrow_*\rangle\alpha$). See also footnote 16.

argument. In this environment, a process called MERGE[21] can take place which unifies the unfixed treenode with the current node, giving rise to a composite set of decorations which is well-formed just in case there are no contradictory values for labels (shown as the dashed arrow in (11.49)). Ultimately, completion of the tree derives exactly the same tree as in (11.48).

(11.49) Parsing a left dislocated string

$?t, 0 \quad \mapsto \quad ?t, 0 \quad \mapsto \quad ?t, 0, \Diamond$

$?e, \langle\uparrow_*\rangle 0, ?\exists\mathbf{x}.Tn(\mathbf{x}), \Diamond \qquad Zhangsan' : e, \langle\uparrow_*\rangle 0, ?\exists\mathbf{x}.Tn(\mathbf{x})$

Note again that there is no encoding in the output that the string involved left dislocation and thus no encoding of discourse information such as topic or focus in the semantic representations themselves. The effect of focus (or topic) derives from the fact that some expression is presented string initially that might be expected to appear later which initiates in context some inferential effect. This illustrates a significant aspect of the framework: discourse effects are not specifically encoded but are taken to result from (relevance-theoretic) pragmatic reasoning (see Kempson et al. 2006 for some discussion). Notice how this modelling of natural language structure replaces the static configurational approach: concepts such as c-command defined over a fixed structure are replaced by the dynamic concept of left to right processing. That is, with the added dimension of tree growth following a left-right sequence of words, not all explanations need to be provided in the form of hierarchical relationships between fixed elements in a structure. Since such relations are not represented in the proof trees, the notions of topic and focus in DS are treated as pragmatic, discourse constructs whose particular interpretation on any particular occasion of utterance is context dependent. There is no concept that topic and focus are associated with specific truth conditional meaning or particular structural properties (contra Rooth 1992 inter al. but in line with, for example, Wedgwood 2005). Instead, it is assumed that topicalized and focused constituents are introduced by the same syntactic processes, leaving it to the richness of context to determine exactly how such constituents are interpreted on particular occasions of utterance. This seems to be of particular relevance to the analysis of the phenomena in Chinese (and other languages like Korean, see Kiaer 2007). Wu (2005) notes

[21] Not to be confused with the tree-building process of the same name used in Minimalism (Chomsky 1995). A better name for this process would be UNIFICATION which more accurately describes its operation.

briefly that it is often difficult to distinguish topic from focus in Chinese, particularly with respect to clause initial expressions. Compare (11.50) and (11.51):

(11.50) Tomatoes, I like; potatoes, I don't.

(11.51) *xihongshi, wo xihuan; malingshu, wo bu xihuan.*
tomato 1SG like potato 1SG not like
'As for tomatoes, I like (them); As for potatoes, I don't (like them).'
OR 'Tomatoes I like; potatoes I don't.'

While the clause-initial expression *tomatoes* has a focus interpretation in English (Cf. *As for tomatoes I like them*), *xihongshi* could be either interpreted as a focus or topic in Chinese because a pause, which is supposed to use to distinguish them, is not always clearly indicated in discourse. The interpretation of topic or focus within spoken utterances therefore may be determined by context (although syntactic disambiguation can be achieved if a topic particle like *a* is used) after the initial constituent.[22]

Although an unfixed node can be used to analyse true left dislocation, including unbounded dependencies, it does not have to be, as the definition of the modality, $\langle\uparrow_*\rangle n$, merely requires the relevant node to be dominated by node n. Hence, the node can be fixed locally or non-locally and in subject as well as object argument positions. It is thus this device that allows for the appearance of overt subjects in pro-drop languages like Chinese. An initial expression may be parsed as decorating an unfixed node and then once the verb (and any associated aspect marker) is parsed, the unfixed node may be fixed in subject position[23]

11.4 The 'bei' construction

We now have in place all that is necessary to provide a theoretical analysis of the *bei* construction based on the descriptive characterization given in earlier sections. Recall that the particle *bei*, we have argued, marks the pre-*bei* constituent as the locus of affect of the event expressed by the following clause, thus often being interpreted as the internal argument of that verb and giving rise to a passive interpretation.

[22]Notice at this point that this analysis is functionalist in spirit, as in many analyses within DS which provides a formal and explicit framework for exploring such approaches.

[23]In fact, syntactic subjects are typically associated in current versions of DS with a local variant of *ADJUNCTION which requires a node to be fixed within the current predicate-argument array. For the purposes of the current paper, this refinement is not necessary. See Kempson and Cann (2008) for discussion of this process with respect to Medieval Spanish.

Additionally, we argued that this constituent has significant topic-like properties as well as some, but by no means all, the properties associated with subjects in Chinese.

As noted above, a topic effect is achieved within the theory by using *ADJUNCTION to provide an unfixed node to allow the parse of the initial string.[24] The analysis of a canonical *bei* construction like that in (11.1a), repeated below as (11.52), begins as usual with a requirement to construct a propositional structure and the projection of an unfixed node that is decorated by parsing *Zhangsan*, exactly as in (**??**) above.

(11.52) *Zhangsan bei Lisi ma guo.*
Zhangsan BEI Lisi scold EXP
'Zhangsan has been scolded by Lisi.'

At this point, *bei* is parsed and a quite complex set of actions is initiated. As argued above, we take the pre-*bei* noun phrase to be the locus of affect of the event expressed by the following clause. To encode this, bearing in mind that semantic representations are the *only* level of representation in DS, we take *bei* to project a predicate with argument structure, but one that is quite underspecified with respect to content, encoding only that it identifies its individual argument term as the locus of affect of its event argument: $\lambda x[\lambda y[\theta_{LoA}(y, x)]]$ (which we abbreviate to BEI' in the displays). The unfixed node decorated by $Zhangsan'$ is further 'fixed' as the individual argument of the predicate and then a requirement of an event node is constructed above that as illustrated in (11.53)

(11.53) The initial stage of parsing *Zhangsan bei*:

$?t$

$?e_{sit}, \Diamond$ $\quad\quad$ $?e_{sit} \rightarrow t$

$Zhangsan' : e$ $\quad\quad$ $BEI', e \rightarrow (e_{sit} \rightarrow t)$

However, instead of leaving the event node to be annotated by an aspect marker, as with verbs like *ma* above, the construction of a *specific* event term is initiated.

Noun phrases in DS invariably project structures rooted in type *e*, the type of a term (whether an event or an individual); and there is no type-lifting mechanism, unlike in generalized quantifier theory. More specifically, quantifying expressions are analyzed in terms grounded in a proof-theoretic labelled-deduction methodology and are taken to

[24]Note that the use of the same mechanism for subjects helps to explain why, in pro-drop languages, overt subjects often show topic or focus effects in the absence of other expressions *already* identified as playing such roles.

contribute arbitrary names of a sort familiar from natural-deduction predicate logic proofs. These names are defined as denoting the arbitrary witness of their containing assertion. The logic within which these names are defined is the *epsilon calculus*, with the defined names (*epsilon terms*, see also footnote 19) carry a record of the propositional formula within which they occur, based on the following equivalence:

$$\exists x.F(x) \;\equiv\; F(\epsilon x.F(x))$$

The schematic formula on the right hand side of the equivalence sign, an epsilon calculus formula, is an ordinary predicate-argument expression, like e.g. $F(a)$. However, within the argument of this expression, there is a required second token of the predicate F as the *restrictor* for that argument term (ϵ is the variable-binding term operator that is the analogue of the existential quantifier, here binding the variable x). The effect is that the term itself ($\epsilon x.F(x)$) replicates inside it the content of the overall formula that is predicated of it. Further details are not important here (see Hilbert and Bernays 1939, von Heusinger 2002, Kempson et al. 2001, etc.). What is significant is that, although quantified terms are assigned only a low type, they nevertheless have structure, specifically a structure containing a quantifier, a bound variable and a predicate over that variable. So, parsing *bei* induces such a quantificational structure, but with an event *metavariable* in place of the bound variable which provides the event term for the embedded propositional structure, whose value will be provided by any aspect marker appearing with the main verb. Although apparently complex, the structure that results from parsing *Zhangsan bei* which appears in (11.54) provides the right sort of semantic basis for interpreting the *bei* construction.

(11.54) Parsing *Zhangsan bei*

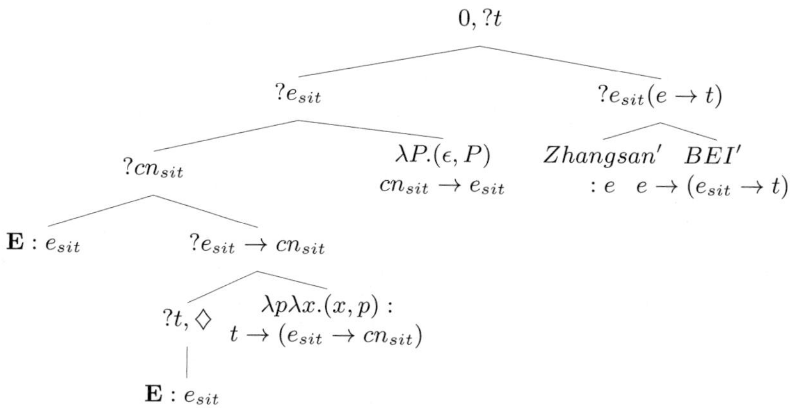

With the pointer at an open propositional node, the parse of the rest of the sentence now proceeds as previously in (11.49)–(**??**). When the last word is parsed, there remains a requirement to identify the content of the internal argument of the main verb (see (**??**), above). To resolve the formula requirement, given that there is no further input, it is necessary to substitute the metavariable with some contentive formula from context. Given that Zhangsan is interpreted as topic by the processes discussed above, this must provide the content of that pronominal as involving least effort and largest inferential effect. (Such an effect is seen also in topic sentences without *bei* which also have a gap in the comment clause, cf. (11.5).) In DS terms, therefore, the formula projected by *Zhangsan* is taken to substitute for the metavariable decorating the undergoer argument node.

The propositional tree may now be completed and compiled to satisfy outstanding requirements, yielding the still incomplete tree in (11.55), with $Zhangsan'$ substituted for $\mathbf{V}$ and the variable projected by the aspect marker $\mathbf{s_i^{exp}}$ substituting for the event metavariable $\mathbf{E}$. (Note that complex types are omitted from the display for ease of reading.) To get the final propositional formula, we continue to go up the tree applying functional application over the nodes. So we apply the node decorated with $t \rightarrow (e_{sit} \rightarrow cn_{sit})$ to yield the following (after lambda reduction):

$$\lambda x.(x, (Ma'(Zhangsan')(Lisi')(\mathbf{s_i^{exp}}))) : e_{sit} \rightarrow cn_{sit}$$

The pointer goes to the event node and substitutes the event variable $\mathbf{S_i^{exp}}$ (necessarily because $\mathbf{E}$ has already been so instantiated) allowing the two nodes to combine to give:

$$(\mathbf{s_i^{exp}}, (Ma'(Zhangsan')(Lisi')(\mathbf{s_i^{exp}}))) : cn_{sit}$$

This then combines with the epsilon operator to yield:

$$(\epsilon, \mathbf{s_i^{exp}}, (Ma'(Zhangsan')(Lisi')(\mathbf{s_i^{exp}}))) : e_{sit}$$

The pointer moves down into the matrix proposition to combine the content of BEI' $(\lambda x[\lambda y[\theta_{LoA}(y, x)]])$ with $Zhangsan'$ and the result then combines with the event term to yield:

$$\theta_{LoA}((\epsilon, \mathbf{s_i^{exp}}, (Ma'(Zhangsan')(Lisi')(\mathbf{s_i^{exp}}))), Zhangsan') : t$$

By the process of term evaluation given in Kempson et al. (2001) (whose details are not relevant here), the epsilon equivalence given above, and unpacking the lexical roles associated with the verb *ma*, we get an equivalent first order logic expression which provides exactly the right set of truth conditions of there being an event of scolding initiated by

Lisi and targeting and affecting Zhangsan, as desired:

$$\exists \mathbf{s_i^{exp}}[Ma'(\mathbf{s_i^{exp}}) \wedge \theta_{Init}(\mathbf{s_i^{exp}}, Lisi')$$
$$\wedge\ \theta_{ToA}(\mathbf{s_i^{exp}}, Zhangsan') \wedge \theta_{LoA}(\mathbf{s_i^{exp}}, Zhangsan')]$$

11.4.1 Some consequences

We have now provided an analysis of the canonical *bei* construction that directly encodes the semantics of the construction we argued for in section 3 without having to assign the expression to any particular syntactic category. In this section, we explore some consequences of the analysis before moving on to our accounts of the agentless and retained object versions of the construction.

As discussed in section 3, the passive reading is derived without assuming that anything specifically encodes passive voice itself. The interpretation of the pre-*bei* noun phrase as the locus of affect role with respect to the event denoted by the main verb, combined with its interpretation as the topic of the sentence means that where there is a gap in the clause it will also be interpreted as the target of affect of the event. the passive reading is thus derived from more general processes of interpretation not from a specific, encoded, passive meaning.

(11.55) Completing *(Zhangsan bei) Lisi ma guo*

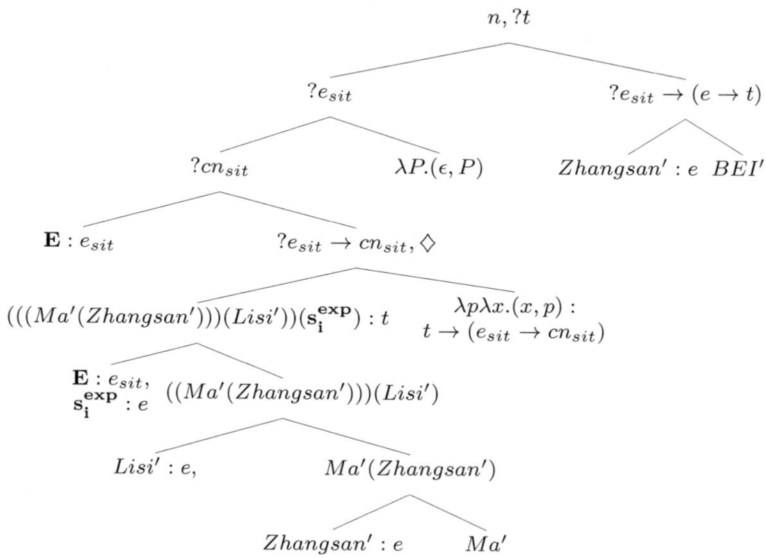

Furthermore, this is achieved without having to assign the morpheme *bei* to any specific syntactic category. The syntax of DS does not use the concept of word class, except as a possible means of structuring the lexicon (as, for example, in the typed lexica associated with HPSG,

Sag 1997). So, although our treatment of *bei* retains some of the lexical actions associated with parsing verbs, such as the construction of argument nodes and the introduction of a predicate, albeit a very weak one, we do not thereby assign it to this particular category. It only makes sense to call *bei* a verb (or adjective, preposition or noun which are other expressions that project argument structure) if some generalizations can be made over the lexical actions it induces that are consistent with other members of such classes. In the absence of such generalizations, such as being able to appear with aspect or negation markers, the expression can be left as an idiosyncratic grammatical morpheme without further categorization. In fact, the specific inability of *bei* to appear with an aspect marker is directly captured by our analysis. Recall that the trigger for parsing aspect markers is a node with a requirement to construct an expression of event type ($?e_{sit}$), a constraint which ensures that a verb has already been parsed. The parse of *bei*, however, leaves the pointer at a proposition-requiring node. This automatically ensures that no aspect marker can appear as the next word in the string and that the next word must either be a subject (introduced by *ADJUNCTION triggered by $?t$) or a verb, again with the same trigger. Thus, we directly account for why *bei* always appears closely associated with a following subject or, in short passives, with a verb.

As noted above, native speakers of Chinese do not, in general, accept long distance dependencies for the pre-*bei* noun phrase, as illustrated in (11.56).

(11.56) a. **Yuehan bei Mali renwei Dawei da guo.*
John BEI Mary think David hit EXP

b. *Yuehan Mali renwei Dawei da guo.*
John Mary think David hit EXP
'John, Mary thinks that David has hit.'

This follows directly from the semantic structure induced by parsing *bei*. The event of which the pre-*bei* noun phrase is construed as the locus of affect is the event expressed by the main predicate of the embedded proposition and not an event associated within any further embedded proposition. The putative output logical structure of (11.56a) would be something like:

$$\theta_{LoA}((\epsilon, \mathbf{s_j}, Renwei'(((Da'(\mathbf{V}))(Dawei')(\mathbf{s_k^{EXP}}))(Mali'))(\mathbf{s_j})), Yuehan')$$

In other words, John is the locus of affect of a state of Mary's *thinking* that David beat someone, but this is semantically incoherent. Therefore, the example is excluded and the effect of locality derives from the association between the pre-*bei* noun phrase and the event described by the main verb of the following clause. For those speakers for whom

C.-T. J.Huang (1999)'s example (24), given in (11.57), is acceptable we would have to say that the combination *pai jingcha zhua-zou* semantically projects a single, complex, event as indicated in Huang's translation for this example.

(11.57) *?Zhangsan bei Lisi pai jingcha zhua-zou le.*
Zhangsan BEI Lisi send police arrest PFV
'Zhangsan was "sent police to arrest" by Lisi.' (Huang's translation)

This would bring such examples on a par with pivotal constructions such as (11.58) in which the conjoined verb *kai-qiang-da-si* 'shoot dead' can be treated as projecting a complex predicate, i.e. defining a single event, where the objects *qiang* 'gun' and *huo* 'fire' are incorporated nouns which cannot be topicalized or passivized.

(11.58) *Zhangsan bei Lisi kai qiang da si le.*
Zhangsan BEI Lisi open gun shoot dead PFV
'Zhangsan was shot dead by Lisi.'

One point needs to be made concerning the possibility of resumption. As noted above resumptive pronouns are generally considered to be unacceptable with the *bei* construction.

(11.59) **Zhangsan bei Lisi da guo ta.*
Zhangsan BEI Lisi hit EXP him

The theory presented here, however, cannot exclude such examples as the link between the topic and the missing argument in the comment clause is anaphoric and so may allow a pronoun to appear in the 'gap' in the string. There have, however, been suggestions that resumption is occasionally acceptable, as in the example in (11.60).

(11.60) *Zhangsan bei wo piping le ta yidun.*
Zhangsan BEI I criticize PFV he once
'Zhangsan was criticized once by me.' (Ting 1998: 322)

Although there is considerable disagreement that this example is really acceptable, the fact that there is controversy is interesting. In a paper on resumptive pronouns in English, Cann et al. (2005b) show, from a database of spoken examples such as those in (11.61), that resumption in English relative clauses is not only possible but fairly common in dialogue.

(11.61) a. She got a couch at Sears that it was on sale.
b. He's a professor that nobody liked him.
c. ... who I was going to have lunch with him....
d. I've had children that they've come on stage.

That paper argues that the apparent unacceptability of these examples when written down or presented without context results from pragmatic infelicity, not ungrammaticality. Since a gap is expected in a relative clause, the use of a pronoun gives rise, by assumptions of Relevance Theory, to additional inferential effects (such as highlighting an agent role associated with what would otherwise be an unemphasizable gap) that cannot be resolved out of context.

Although we do not have evidence for the use of resumptive pronouns with the *bei* construction in spoken Mandarin Chinese, the fact that there is some controversy about whether they are, or are not, acceptable, leads us to conclude that a similar story might be put forward in this case: resumptive pronouns are excluded because, having parsed *bei*, a hearer knows that the pre-*bei* noun phrase is to be construed as locally dependent on the main verb and that it performs the role of locus of affect. Any use of a resumptive pronoun will pragmatically reinforce the association of the topic with some specific, affected, argument role associated with the verb. Since this information is already given by the use of *bei*, there needs to be some strong inferential effect to satisfy the needs of relevance. Without such effects being manifest, speakers (and readers) will judge the examples to be unacceptable.

There is, however, a case of non-resumption which we believe is determined by the grammar. This involves the inability of the pre-*bei* noun phrase to be associated with the subject position of the following clause, as illustrated in examples (11.38, 11.39,11.40) above. We suggest that the identification is excluded because both positions are subjects (highest individual arguments of a predicate) in the same *event domain* where this is the set of all formulae that predicate over the event variable of a proposition. If this is correct, then while a pre-*bei* noun phrase may be construed as an object of the main predicate it will never be construed as its subject, thus excluding the relevant examples.

We do not have space here to explain in detail how the pre-*bei* noun phrase might get the subject-like properties discussed in section 11.2.2 with respect to the placement of adverbials and reflexive binding. But, with respect to the latter, note that the word *Zhangsan* in (11.21) provides the content of *bei*'s sole individual argument, its semantic subject, just as with respect to the predicate projected by *guan*, *Lisi* provides the content of *its* semantic subject. So they share some properties and whatever licenses *ziji* to be bound by *Lisi* in this example may also license binding by *Zhangsan*. Indeed, we can account for all the data displayed in (11.20-11.24) above by adopting two hypotheses. Firstly, as suggested for the Japanese and English reflexive forms in Cann et al. (2005), reflexives, unlike pronouns, do not project metavariables whose content could be identified later in a parse but require formula values to be found in the appropriate domain *immediately* as they are parsed. Secondly, unlike English, we take *ziji* to take a formula value of a (structural) subject in its immediate predicate-argument domain, or, if no such value is available, within its event domain, giving a slightly extended domain of potential antecedents (but not full long distance binding). Given these hypotheses consider the binding of (11.21): *Zhangsan bei Lisi guan zai ziji de jiali* 'Zhangsan was locked by Lisi in his home'. At the point that *ziji* is parsed there are two subjects (highest individual arguments) within the event domain, because the matrix proposition (constructed by parsing *bei*) and the proposition embedded within the event term share the same event variable. Given that the PP is an adjunct and not an argument of the main verb, it is the event domain that is relevant for binding purposes so that the formula the reflexive provides may either be $Zhangsan'$ or $Lisi'$. In (11.22) (**Zhangsan bei Lisi da le ziji xiaohai*), on the other hand, the reflexive occurs within an argument position (even though it is not itself an argument) and so, by the above hypothesis, must take its value from the predicate-argument domain of *da* 'hit'. Hence, it can only take $Lisi'$ as its value, rendering the example incoherent. But now consider (11.24), *Zhangsan bei ziji pian le* 'Zhangsan cheated himself'. At the point where the reflexive is parsed in this example, the pointer is at an unfixed node, exactly as for the parse of a non-reflexive subject, and no local predicate-argument structure has been constructed because no verb has been parsed. The value must therefore be taken from a subject in the current event domain, $Zhangsan'$, yielding a well-formed interpretation that Zhangsan cheated himself. Of course, much more needs to be said about reflexive binding (especially about long distance binding and the bahaviour of *taziji*, Pan 1998), but the sketch given here provides an explanation of why a pre-*bei* noun phrase may behave as a subject in some cases but not in others.

For the placement of adverbials such as *zuotian* and PPs between the initial noun phrase and *bei*, as in (11.25), paralleling the positioning of such expressions between subject and verb in *bei*-less clauses, we do not have space to provide a full account. However the current analysis of *bei* provides a means of accounting for this subject-like property which we now sketch. It is commonplace nowadays to treat certain prepositional phrases and adverbials as predicates over events (Kamp and Reyle 1993 inter al.) rather than as predicates of predicates (Thomason and Stalnaker 1973), so we may treat such expressions when parsed before a verb as constructing an event/situation node, decorating that node with a situation metavariable and providing a predicate over that variable. Technically this can be achieved by the use of a LINK structure. Such structures are independent trees that share some term value with the tree to which they are LINKed, here an event metavariable (see Kempson et al. 2001, Cann at al. 2005 and various papers in this volume for details of the LINK mechanism). Parsing an adverbial like *zuotian* 'yesterday' will be taken to be triggered by an open $?t$ node where no event node has yet been constructed and to involve the actions noted above. Parsing *Zhangsan zuotian* will thus yield a tree like that in (11.62). (Some details are omitted from the tree display.)

(11.62)

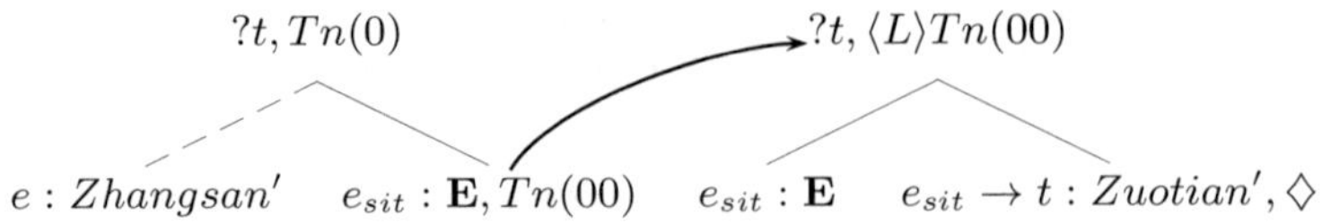

The LINKed tree is compiled to yield a formula value $t : Zuotian'(\mathbf{E})$ and the pointer returns to the open propositional node, at which point either a verb or *bei* may be parsed (or any other word meeting the right contextual conditions). Assuming that *bei* is parsed, the parse will proceed as we have seen above. LINK structures are subject to evaluation rules (see Kempson et al. 2001) and the completed tree will yield a final formula value with *Zuotian′* providing a predicate over the complex event term to yield an expression that identifies Zhangsan as the locus of effect of an event of Lisi's scolding him that happened yesterday:

$$\theta_{LoA}((\epsilon, \mathbf{s_i^{exp}}, (Ma'(Zhangsan')(Lisi')(\mathbf{s_i^{exp}}))), Zhangsan')$$
$$\wedge\ Zuotian'(\epsilon, \mathbf{s_i^{exp}}, (Ma'(Zhangsan')(Lisi')(\mathbf{s_i^{exp}}))$$

To ensure that such adjuncts do not appear after *bei* merely requires an open event node *not* to have been constructed at the point of parsing the adjunct (thus ensuring that it occurs pre-verbally), then it can only appear before *bei* has been parsed. Clearly, much more needs to be said about both these constructions and their analysis, but it appears to us that our analysis of the *bei* construction in principle provides a solid foundation for such accounts.

11.4.2 Agentless 'passives'

The analysis of the canonical *bei* construction provides a template for analyzing the other patterns found, thus providing a unitary characterization of the function of the morpheme *bei*. We begin with the agentless pattern, where we analyse the lack of a subject expression as a simple instance of pro-drop. Thus in *Zhangsan bei ma guo*, after the first two words have been parsed, the pointer is at the propositional node within the constructed event term. This allows either for the parse of a subject (via *ADJUNCTION) or of a verb: both are possible. If the latter option is chosen then the value of the metavariable decorating the higher individual argument node must be derived from context. In parsing a string like *chuanghu bei za le* 'The window was smashed', the post-bei 'gap' may be interpreted either as some salient referent or generically. In favour of this analysis is the fact that after an utterance like (11.63a), an agent-oriented question like (11.63b) is felicitous.

(11.63) a. *chuanghu bei za le.*
window BEI smash PFV
'The window was smashed.'
b. *bei shui za le?*
BEI who smash PFV
'By whom was (the window) smashed?'

Substitution for this metavariable could also be of some arbitrary term standing for 'someone'. However, in spoken discourse, native speakers prefer to use a generic NP like *ren* 'people' in the post-*bei* position instead of a null agent if the agent is unknown to them or unnecessary to specify, as shown in (11.64).[25]

(11.64) a. *Zhangsan bei (ren) da le.*
Zhangsan BEI people hit PFV
'Zhangsan was hit by someone.'
b. *chuanghu bei (ren) za le.*
window BEI people smash PFV
'The window was smashed by someone.'

These data imply that the agentless pattern has obligatory pragmatic effects in the sense that the agent, albeit absent in the syntax, is pragmatically 'present' in the mind of the hearer.[26]

C.-T. J. Huang (1999) argues forcefully against such an approach, preferring to adopt a slightly different analysis for agentless passives from those with expressed agents. His reasons have to do both with historical and synchronic data.[27] Historically, Huang points out that the short passive is older than the long counterpart. Leaving aside notions of derivation of one construction from the other as irrelevant to our

[25]We have queried a group of Chinese-speaking children of ages 6-9 with regard to the interpretation of the agentless *bei* sentences. Interestingly, most of them insist that such sentences are bad because the agent is missing.

[26]Our treatment of the empty node as projecting a metavariable is in spirit compatible with the GB analysis (see Ting 1998) which treats it as a pro-form. Both analyses follow from the fact that Chinese is a pro-drop language.

[27]Huang's argument concerning the inability of agents to delete, we leave to one side as not being relevant for our analysis: no deletion occurs.

analysis, we point out that cross-linguistically short passives are more common than long ones, within linguistic communities short passives are more frequently used and in first language acquisition appear earlier in children's speech (Svartvik 1966; Xiao, McEnery and Qian 2006). Functionally, this is unsurprising, as the passive provides a means of foregrounding, or otherwise highlighting, an undergoer of some sort. This in turn implies a reduction in the discourse prominence of an actor. So, unless the actor needs to be mentioned (for example, the referent is less familiar in the discourse than the passive subject) then it is unlikely to appear. The chronologically earlier appearance of the short *bei* construction thus does not seem to us sufficient to assume it is fundamentally different from the long form.

Secondly, Huang points out that the short form strictly does not allow resumption and that the appearance of gaps in the long form is a recent phenomenon. Again, we believe that this is pragmatically motivated and point to our short discussion of resumption in the previous section. It is notable that the shorter an utterance is, the less likely a resumptive pronoun is likely to be acceptable so that short forms with resumption are likely to be dispreferred than long forms. Additionally, there may be an added factor ruling out such examples. A putative example like **Zhangsan bei ma guo ta* (intended *Zhangsan has been scolded*) might invite an inference that the pronoun is *not* coreferential with the pre-*bei* noun phrase (on standard relevance-theoretic grounds that something extra is more costly to process and so should lead to extra inferential effect to be sufficiently relevant). If this is so, then the addressee is forced to assume that Zhangsan is the scolder, but this is excluded on independent grounds (see discussion in section 11.2.3).

Overall, therefore, we do not think that the evidence provided in C.-T. J. Huang (1999) is sufficient to abandon the idea that the long and short forms of the *bei* construction are essentially different and that the latter are simply (subject) pro-drop variants of the former.

11.4.3 Retained objects

Finally, we come to the two problematic patterns with the *bei* construction noted in section 11.1. In the first place, there are instances of objects appearing in the immediate post-verbal position (the so-called retained object construction) as in (11.65). In the second, there is an object marked by *ba* in pre-verbal position (possibly with a further noun phrase in the post-verbal position) as in (11.66), repeated below.

(11.65) *Zhangsan bei Lisi daduan le tui.*
Zhangsan BEI Lisi break PFV leg
'Zhangsan's leg was broken by Lisi.'

(11.66) *Zhangsan bei Lisi ba tui daduan le yi-tiao.*
Zhangsan BEI Lisi BA leg break PFV one-CL
'One of Zhangsan's legs was broken by Lisi.'

It should be clear at this point that these constructions pose no problem for our analysis and do not require us to postulate significant differences in analysis with the canonical constructions.

As argued in section 11.3, the function of the pre-*bei* noun phrase is not determined at the outset to be that of a direct object of the main verb: there is no direct relation between it and any object gap. Instead, its role is identified by *bei* to be the locus of affect of the event described in the post-*bei* clause. Inferentially, where there is a gap, the pre-*bei* noun phrase may also be interpreted as the target of affect, by virtue of its discourse function as topic. Nothing, however, requires this and its is perfectly possible for the post-verbal position to host an overt noun phrase, which itself is interpreted as the target of affect. Consider the analysis of (11.2a). This proceeds exactly as with our example sentence (*Zhangsan bei Lisi ma guo*) above (although with different concepts decorating the nodes and a differently sorted event variable) up to the point at which the aspect marker has been parsed. With the pointer currently at the internal argument node of the predicate projected by *daduan*, we are in a position to parse a noun (phrase) like *tui* 'leg'. The resulting logical form once compiled yields an expression that identifies Zhangsan as the locus of affect of Lisi's leg-breaking:

$$\theta_{LoA}((\epsilon, \mathbf{s}_{\mathbf{j}}^{\mathbf{pfv}}, ((Daduan'(Tui'))(Lisi'))(\mathbf{s}_{\mathbf{j}}^{\mathbf{pfv}})), Zhangsan'))$$

Cashing this expression out with the lexical semantics of the verb and evaluation yields the truth-conditionally equivalent expression:

$$\exists \mathbf{s}_{\mathbf{j}}^{\mathbf{pfv}}[Daduan'(\mathbf{s}_{\mathbf{j}}^{\mathbf{pfv}}) \wedge \theta_{Init}(\mathbf{s}_{\mathbf{j}}^{\mathbf{pfv}}, Lisi') \\ \wedge\ \theta_{ToA}(\mathbf{s}_{\mathbf{j}}^{\mathbf{pfv}}, Tui') \ \wedge\ \theta_{LoA}(\mathbf{s}_{\mathbf{j}}^{\mathbf{pfv}}, Zhangsan')]$$

It is generally agreed that the relation between the topic and retained object is not random, but confined to possessor-possessee (11.2), kinship (11.34) and part-whole (11.67) relations. On the basis of this observation, Y. A. Li (1990) proposes that the relationship between the two NPs can be schematized as NP_2+de+NP_1, where NP_1 is the retained object and NP_2 the topic. This generalization, however, as Shi (1997) points out, is too restrictive to be accurate. Consider the examples in (11.68,11.69) which cannot be paraphrased in the manner suggested by Y. A. Li.

(11.67) a. *wu-ge li bei Lisi chi le san-ge.*
five-CL pear BEI Lisi eat PFV three-CL
'Three of the five pears were eaten by Lisi.'

b. *jiu-ge miyu bei Lisi cai-dui le liu-ge.*
nine-CL riddle BEI Lisi guess-right PFV six-CL
'Six of the nine riddles were solved by Lisi.'

(11.68) a. *na-kuai bu bei ta zuo le yi-tiao kuzi.*
that-CL cloth BEI 3SG make PFV one-CL trousers
'The cloth was made into a pair of trousers by him.'

b. **na-kuai bu de yi-tiao kuzi bei ta zuo le.*
that-CL cloth DE one-CL trousers BEI 3SG make PFV

(11.69) a. *yifu bei huo shao le yi-ge kulong.*
clothes BEI fire burn PFV one-CL hole
'A hole was burnt into the clothes by fire.' (L.Li 1980: 402)

b. **yifu de yi-ge kulong bei huo shao le.*
clothes DE one-CL hole BEI fire burn PFV

What is happening here is analogous to the construal of the relation between topic and comment in gapless topic constructions such as (11.8) where some 'aboutness' of the comment to the topic is to be inferred. In the retained object construction the relevant relation between topic and retained object is derived from the concept denoted by the complex predicate applied to the term expressed by the fronted locus of affect, mediated by the affectedness presupposition of the latter. For something to be affected by an action applied to something else, there must be some relation that can be established between these two things. Most obviously this may be construed as part-whole or possessive, but it may be the result of the action that supplies the affected interpretation (such as the hole being burnt into the clothes in (11.69)). Consider then the possible interpretation of *Zhangsan bei Lisi daduan le tui* 'Zhangsan's leg was broken by Lisi'. The propositional output of parsing this string is, as noted above, that there is a leg-breaking event by Lisi that affected Zhangsan, from which one can infer that an actual leg was broken (by Lisi):[28]

$$\exists \mathbf{s}_{\mathbf{j}}^{\mathbf{pfv}} \exists x[Daduan'(\mathbf{s}_{\mathbf{j}}^{\mathbf{pfv}}) \wedge Tui'(x) \wedge \theta_{ToA}(\mathbf{s}_{\mathbf{j}}^{\mathbf{pfv}}, x)]$$

Since this event must form part of the event $\mathbf{s}_{\mathbf{j}}^{\mathbf{pfv}}$ which affects Zhangsan, it is straightforward to infer that the leg that was broken was Zhangsan's:

$$\exists \mathbf{s}_{\mathbf{j}}^{\mathbf{pfv}} \exists x[Daduan'(\mathbf{s}_{\mathbf{j}}^{\mathbf{pfv}}) \wedge Tui'(x) \wedge \theta_{ToA}(\mathbf{s}_{\mathbf{j}}^{\mathbf{pfv}}, x) \wedge POSS(Zhangsan', x)]$$

[28]We ignore here the proper construal of non-proper noun phrases in Chinese, although we assume that Chierchia (1989)'s suggestion that they are kind-denoting terms is on the right lines.

We mentioned in section 11.1 the other problematic pattern with the *bei* construction: the co-occurrence of both *bei* and *ba* in the same clause, as in (11.3a). If both are analyzed as object markers, then any explanation for such examples faces the same problems as those faced by the retained object construction. However, under the current assumption that the pre-*bei* noun phrase is only indirectly associated with the object of the content verb in the post-*bei* constituent comment clause, the existence of such examples is expected and unproblematic. The apparent co-occurrence of two objects is merely an artefact of the fact that the topic is necessarily construed as locus of affect of the main verb. Hence, whatever analysis one gives for the *ba* construction (and we leave this to one side), there should be no conflict with the analysis of *bei* presented in this paper.

11.5 Summary and conclusion

In this paper, we have argued from a detailed examination of the data exhibited in the various forms of the *bei* construction in Mandarin Chinese that the function of the particle *bei* is not to encode passive meaning directly, as typically assumed, but indirectly through identifying the constituent that immediately *precedes* it to be the locus of affect of the event denoted by the clause that *follows* it. The morpheme is thus not construed as a specific marker of the passive nor as an agentive preposition governing its immediately following noun phrase. Because the pre-*bei* noun phrase occurs early in the string and is not directly interpreted as an argument of the main verb (although identified indirectly though the event role of locus of affect), it takes on the discourse function of a topic of the remainder of the sentence. By virtue of this function, where there is a (non-agent) gap in the following clause, it appears to bind that gap. From this a passive reading is derived whereby the pre-*bei* noun phrase is interpreted as both locus of affect (because of its association with *bei*) and as target of affect (undergoer), by virtue of its association with an object gap.

We have further provided an analysis of the construction using Dynamic Syntax which eschews structuralist notions of the classification of words and purely syntactic structures defined over these. Instead, output representations are representations of *semantic* content, with syntax itself being construed as the process by which such representations are derived. It is thus not necessary within the framework for *bei* to be assigned to any specific word class, merely that it projects the correct semantic structure to analyse the pre-*bei* noun phrase as the locus of affect of some event given by the interpretation of the rest of the string of words. Thus, we take *bei* to project a semantic relation of affect between whatever it is that is expressed by its immediately preceding constituent and an event constructed as an epsilon term from the semantics of the rest of the sentence. From this, various properties of the *bei* construction are shown to follow directly, such as the apparent locality of the dependency shown by the pre-*bei* noun phrase and any following gap, the requirement that *bei* be immediately followed by a subject or a verb and the exclusion of aspect markers.

Moreover, we have argued that the agentless and retained object patterns within the construction follow without further stipulation. The former we treat as a case of pro-drop with pragmatic explanations provided to explain for apparent differences between 'long' and 'short' passives, cited in C.-T. J. Huang (1999). With respect to the latter, since there is, in the analysis of the canonical constructions, no concept of displacement of the initial expression from some object position, overt objects are not excluded from appearing in the string. The retained object constructions (with or without *ba*) are thus no longer problematic and their interpretation follows straightforwardly from the semantic role provided by *bei* and pragmatic inference over the situation being described and the context in general. The fact that the exact role of the pre-*bei* noun phrase may depend on inference over contextually provided information means that our account identifies the *bei* construction typologically as a form of pragmatic voice (Klaiman 1991).

Of course, there remain significant questions that need to be explored such as the exact differences and interactions of the morphemes *bei* and *ba*, the extension of the analysis to less common patterns of the construction and the formal explanation of the distribution of temporal and other adjuncts in this construction, all obviously major topics in their own right. Nevertheless, our analysis provides a fruitful and new way of viewing this controversial grammatical construction that demonstrates how syntax, semantics and pragmatics go hand in hand in the interpretive process of natural language. This naturally leads us to the conclusion that the dynamics of natural language understanding can, and should, be reflected in grammar formalisms.

References

The following were cited in this chapter: Barwise and Cooper (1981), Blackburn and Meyer-Viol (1994), Bresnan (2001), Cann et al. (2005), Cann (this volume), Chao (1968), Chang (2003), Chierchia (1989), Chomsky (1981), Chomsky (1995), Croft (1991, 1998), C. Li (1976), C. Li and Thompson (1981), Davison (1980), Hashimoto (1968), Kempson et al. (2001), Kempson et al. (2006), Klaiman (1991), LaPolla (1989), Gabbay (1994), Givón (1979), Gregoromichelaki (2006), Hilbert and Bernays (1939), C.-T. J. Huang (1999), Y. Huang (2000), Kamp and Reyle (1993), Kempson and Cann (2008), Kiaer (2007), Y. A. Li (1990), L. Li (1980), W. Li (fcmg), Li and Thompson (1981), Lü (1982), Lyons (1968), Pan (1998), Roberts (1998), Rooth (1992), Sag (1997), Sag, Wasow and Bender 2003), Saksena (1980), Sperber and Wilson (1995), Svartvik (1966), Tan (1991), Thomason and Stalnaker (1973), Ting (1998), von Heusinger (2002), Wang (1959), Wedgwood (2005), Wu (2005), Wu (this volume), Xiao, McEnery and Qian (2006), Xu and Langendoen (1985). See references at the end of the book for full information.

References

Aarts, B. 2007. *Syntactic gradience: The nature of grammatical indeterminacy*. Oxford: Oxford University Press.

Academia de la Llingua Asturiana. 2001. *Gramática de la llingua asturiana*. Academia Llingua Asturiana.

Aho, A. V., S. C. Johnson, and J. D. Ullman. 1973. Deterministic parsing of ambiguous grammars. In *POPL '73: Proceedings of the 1st annual ACM SIGACT-SIGPLAN symposium on principles of programming languages*, pages 1–21. New York: ACM Press.

Alvarez Blanco, M. R., X. L. Regueira, and H. Monteagudo. 1986. *Gramática galega*. Madrid: Galaxia.

Andrews, A. 1985. The major functions of the noun phrase. *Language typology and syntactic description* 1:62–154.

Anipa, K. 2000. A study of the analytic future/conditional in Golden-Age Spanish. *Bulletin of Hispanic Studies* LXXVII(3):317–337.

Anipa, K. 2001. *A critical examination of linguistic variation in Golden-Age Spanish*. New York, NY: Peter Lang.

Aoshima, S., C. Phillips, and A. Weinberg. 2002. Active filler effects and reanalysis: A study of Japanese wh-scrambling constructions. *University of Maryland working papers in linguistics* 12:1–24.

Aoshima, S., C. Phillips, and A. Weinberg. 2004. Processing filler-gap dependencies in a head-final language. *Journal of Memory and Language* 51:23–54.

Aoshima, S., C. Phillips, and M. Yoshida. 2005. The source of the bias for longer filler-gap dependencies in Japanese. In *18th Annual CUNY Conference on Human Sentence Processing*. Tucson: Universityof Arizona.

Arias Alvarez, B. 1995. Colocación de los pronombres átonos en el 'libro de los gatos'. In A. González, L. von der Walde, and C. Company Company,

The Dynamics of Lexical Interfaces.
Ruth Kempson, Eleni Gregoromichelaki and Christine Howes (eds.).

eds., *Palabra e imagen en la Edad Media*, pages 113–125. Mexico City: Universidad Nacional Autónoma de México.

Asher, N. 1993. *Reference to Abstract Objects in English.* Dordrecht, The Netherlands: Kluwer Academic Publishers.

Austin, J. L. 1975. *How to Do Things with Words.* Oxford: Clarendon Press, 2nd edn.

Baker, J. 1979. Trainable grammars for speech recognition. In *Proceedings of the Spring Conference of the Acoustical Society of America.*

Barton, G., R. Berwick, and E. Ristad. 1988. *Computational Complexity and Natural Language.* Cambridge, MA: MIT Press.

Barwise, J. and R. Cooper. 1981. Generalized quantifiers and natural language. *Linguistics and Philosophy* 4:159–219.

Bellman, R. 1957. *Dynamic Programming.* Princeton, NJ: Princeton University Press.

Belnap Jr, N.D. 1970. Conditional assertion and restricted quantification. *Noûs* 4(1):1–12.

Bender, E. 2000. The syntax of Mandarin bă: Reconsidering the verbal analysis. *Journal of East Asian Linguistics* 9(2):105–145.

Bhatt, R. 1996. Universal and existential focus in conditionals. Available at: http://www.ling.upenn.edu/Events/PLC/plc20/abstracts/30/30.html.

Bhatt, R. and R. Pancheva. 2006. Conditionals. In *The Blackwell Companion to Syntax*, vol. I, pages 638–687. Blackwell.

Björnsson, G. and E. Gregoromichelaki. in preparation. A contextualist account of the syntax and semantics of conditionals. Ms., Gothenburg University and King's College London.

Blackburn, P. and L. Meyer-Viol. 1994. Linguistics, logic and finite trees. *Bulletin of the Interest Group of Pure and Applied Logics* 2:2–39.

Blakemore, D. 1987. *Semantic constraints on relevance.* Oxford: Blackwell.

Booth, T. L. 1969. Probabilistic representation of formal languages. In *IEEE Conference Record of the 10th Symposium on Switching and Automata Theory.*

Bouzouita, M. 2002. *Clitic Placement in Old and Modern Spanish.* Master's thesis, Kings College London.

Bouzouita, M. 2007. Processing factors in syntactic variation and change: Clitics in Medieval and Renaissance Spanish. In J. Salmons and D.-S. S., eds., *Historical Linguistics 2005*, pages 51–71. Amsterdam/Philadelphia: John Benjamins.

Bouzouita, M. 2008a. At the syntax-pragmatics interface: clitics in the history of Spanish. In R. Cooper and R. Kempson, eds., *Language in Flux: Dialogue Coordination, Language Variation, Change and Evolution*, pages 221–264. London: College Publications.

Bouzouita, M. 2008b. *Clitic Placement in the History of Spanish.* Ph.D. thesis, King's College London.

Bouzouita, M. 2009. Modelling syntactic variation. *Diálogo de la lengua* 1:1–25.

Bouzouita, M. forthcoming. Los futuros analíticos y sintéticos en la *Fazienda de Ultra Mar*. In *Actas del VIII Congreso Internacional de la Historia de la Lengua Española: Santiago de Compostela, 14-18 de Septiembre, 2009*.

Bouzouita, M. In preparation. Latinising influences in the use of future forms in Medieval Spanish biblical translations. Ms., Universitat de les Illes Balears, Palma.

Bouzouita, M. and S. Chatzikyriakidis. 2009. Clitics as calcified processing strategies. In M. Butt and T. Holloway King, eds., *Proceedings of LFG2009*, pages 188–207. Stanford: CSLI.

Bouzouita, M. and R. Kempson. 2006. Clitic placement in Old and Modern Spanish: a dynamic account. In O. Nedergaard Thomsen, ed., *Competing Models of Linguistic Change*. Amsterdam/Philadelphia: John Benjamins.

Bresnan, J. 2001. *Lexical-functional syntax*. Oxford: Blackwell.

Buell, L. 2006. The Zulu conjoint/disjoint verb alternation: focus or constituency. In L. Downing, L. Marten, and S. Zerbian, eds., *Papers in Bantu Grammar and Description, ZAS Papers in Linguistics*, vol. 43, pages 9–30.

Campos, H. 1989. Clitic position in modern Gallegan. *Lingua* 77(1):13–36.

Cann, R. 1993. *Formal semantics: an introduction*. Cambridge: Cambridge University Press.

Cann, R. 2000. Functional versus lexical: a cognitive dichotomy. *The Nature and Function of Syntactic Categories. Syntax and Semantics* 32:37–78.

Cann, R. 2006. Semantic Underspecification and the interpretation of copular clauses in English. In K. von Heusinger and K. Turner, eds., *Where Semantics Meets Pragmatics*. Oxford: Elsevier.

Cann, R. 2007. Towards a dynamic account of be in English. In I. Comorowski and K. von Heusinger, eds., *Existence: Syntax and Semantics*. Dordrecht, The Netherlands: Kluwer Academic Publishers.

Cann, R., T. Kaplan, and R. Kempson. 2005b. Data at the grammar-pragmatics interface: The case of resumptive pronouns in English. *Lingua* 115(11):1475–1665. Special Issue: On the Nature of Linguistic Data.

Cann, R. and R. Kempson. 2008. Production pressures, syntactic change and the emergence of clitic pronouns. In R. Cooper and R. Kempson, eds., *Language in Flux: Dialogue Coordination, Language Variation, Change and Evolution*, pages 179–220. London: College Publications.

Cann, R., R. Kempson, and L. Marten. 2005. *The Dynamics of Language*. Oxford: Elsevier.

Cann, R., R. Kempson, and L. Marten. forthcoming. Tree growth dynamics. In C. Chesi, ed., *Directions in derivations*. London: Emerald.

Cann, R., R. Kempson, and M. Purver. 2007. Context and well-formedness: The dynamics of ellipsis. *Research on Language and Computation* 5(3):333–358.

Cann, R. and Y. Wu. 2004. The dynamic syntax of Chinese passive constructions. Ms., University of Edinburgh.

Cardinaletti, A. and U. Shlonsky. 2004. Clitic positions and restructuring in Italian. *Linguistic Inquiry* 35(4):519–557.

Carstens, V. 1991. *The Morphology and Syntax of Determiner Phrases in Kiswahili.* Ph.D. thesis, University of California, Los Angeles.

Carston, R. 2002. *Thoughts and Utterances: The Pragmatics of Explicit Communication.*. Oxford: Blackwell.

Castillo Lluch, M. 1996. *La posición del pronombre átono en la prosa hispaníca medieval.* Ph.D. thesis, Universidad Autónoma de Madrid.

Castillo Lluch, M. 2002. Distribución de las formas analíticas y sintéticas de futuro y condicional en español medieval. In M. T. Echenique Elizondo and J. Sánchez Méndez, eds., *Actas del V Congreso Internacional de la Historia de la Lengua Española: Valencia, 31 de enero - 4 de febrero 2000*, vol. 1, pages 541–549.

Chang, J. 2003. Event structure and argument linking in Chinese. *Language and Linguistics* 4(2):317–351.

Chao, Y.R. 1968. *A Grammar of spoken Chinese: Zhong guo hua de wen fa.* Berkeley, CA: University of California Press.

Chappell, H. 1986. Formal and colloquial adversity passives in standard Chinese. *Linguistics* 24(6):1025–1052.

Charniak, E. 1997. Statistical parsing with a context free grammar and word statistics. In *Proceedings of AAAI-97.*

Chatzikyriakidis, S. 2009a. Clitic climbing: A dynamic account. Ms., King's College, London.

Chatzikyriakidis, S. 2009b. Clitics in Grecia Salentina Greek: A dynamic account. *Lingua* 119(12):1939–1968.

Chatzikyriakidis, S. forthcoming. *Clitics in Four Dialects of Modern Greek: A Dynamic Account.* Ph.D. thesis, King's College London.

Chatzikyriakidis, S. and R. Kempson. 2010. The person case constraint as a tree-growth property. Ms., King's College London.

Cheng, L. and L.J. Downing. 2007. The prosody and syntax of Zulu relative clauses. In N. Kula and L. Marten, eds., *Bantu in Bloomsbury: Special Issue on Bantu Linguistics, SOAS Working Papers in Linguistics*, vol. 15, pages 51–63.

Cheng, L. and N. C. Kula. 2006. Syntactic and phonological phrasing in Bemba relatives. In L. Downing, L. Marten, and S. Zerbian, eds., *Papers in Bantu Grammar and Description, ZAS Papers in Linguistics*, vol. 43, pages 31–54.

Chierchia, G. 1989. Structured meanings, thematic roles and control. In G. Chierchia, B. H. Partee, and R. Turner, eds., *Properties, types and meaning, II: Semantic issues.* Dordrecht, The Netherlands: Kluwer Academic Publishers.

Chomsky, N. 1957. *Syntactic structures.* The Hague, The Netherlands: Mouton.

Chomsky, N. 1981. *Lectures on government and binding.* Dordrecht, The Netherlands: Foris Publications.

Chomsky, N. 1986. *Knowledge of language.* New York, NY: Praeger Publishers.

Chomsky, N. 1995. *The minimalist program.* Cambridge, MA: MIT Press.

Chomsky, N. 2000. Minimalist inquiries: The framework. In R. Martin, D. Michaels, and J. Uriagereka, eds., *Step by step: Essays on minimalist syntax in honor of Howard Lasnik*, pages 89–156. Cambridge, MA: MIT Press.

Cinque, G. 1999. *Adverbs and functional heads: a cross-linguistic perspective.* Oxford: Oxford University Press.

Cinque, G. 2001. Restructuring and the order of aspectual and root modal heads. In G. Cinque and G. Salvi, eds., *Current studies in Italian Syntax*, pages 137–155. Oxford: Elsevier.

Cinque, G. 2006. *Restructuring and functional heads.* Oxford: Oxford University Press.

Collins, M. 1999. *Head-Driven Statistical Models of Natural Language Parsing.* Ph.D. thesis, University of Pennsylvania.

Company Company, C. 1985-1986. Los futuros en el español medieval, sus orígenes y su evolución. *Nueva Revista de Filologia Hispánica* 34:48–107.

Company Company, C. 2006. Tiempos de formación romance II. Los futuros y condicionales. In C. Company Company, ed., *Sintaxis histórica de la lengua española: Primera parte, la frase verbal*, vol. 1, pages 349–422. Mexico City: Universidad Nacional Autónoma de México & Fondo de Cultura Económica.

Company Company, C. and A. Medina Urrea. 1999. Sintaxis motivada pragmáticamente: futuros analíticos y futuros sintéticos en el español medieval. *Revista de Filologia Española* 79(1-2):65–100.

Comrie, B. 1976. *Aspect: An introduction to the study of verbal aspect and related problems.* Cambridge: Cambridge University Press.

Comrie, B. 1989. *Language universals and linguistic typology: Syntax and morphology.* Chicago, IL: University of Chicago press.

Contini-Morava, E. 2002. (What) do noun class markers mean? In W. H. Reid, R. Otheguy, and N. Stern, eds., *Signal, meaning, and message: perspectives on sign-based linguistics.* Amsterdam/Philadelphia: John Benjamins.

Costa, F., P. Frasconi, V. Lombardo, P. Sturt, and G. Soda. 2002. Enhancing first-pass attachment prediction. In *Proceedings of the 15th European Conference on Artificial Intelligence*, pages 508–512.

Creissels, D. 1996. Conjunctive and disjunctive verb forms in Setswana. *South African Journal of African Languages* 16(4):109–115.

Croft, W. 1991. *Syntactic categories and grammatical relations: The cognitive organization of information.* Chicago, IL: University of Chicago Press.

Croft, W. 1998. Event structure in argument linking. In M. Butt and W. Geuder, eds., *The projection of arguments: Lexical and compositional factors*, pages 21–63. Stanford, CA: CSLI.

Dancygier, B. and E. Sweetser. 2005. *Mental spaces in grammar: conditional constructions.* Cambridge: Cambridge University Press.

D'Andrés Díaz, R. 1993. *Allugamientu de los pronomes átonos col verbu n'asturianu.* Oviedo: Universidad de Oviedo.

Davison, A. 1980. Peculiar passives. *Language* 56(1):42–66.

Declerck, R. and S. Reed. 2001. *Conditionals: a comprehensive empirical analysis.* Berlin/New York: Mouton de Gruyter.

Delin, J. L. 1990. A multi-level account of cleft constructions in discourse. In *Proceedings of the 13th conference on Computational linguistics (COLING)*, pages 83–88.

Delin, J. L. 1992. Properties of it-cleft presupposition. *Journal of Semantics* 9(4):289.

Dijkstra, E. 1959. A note on two problems in connexion with graphs. *Numerische Mathematik* 1.

Dixon, R. M. W. 1979. Ergativity. *Language* 55(1):59–138.

Dowty, D. R. 1979. *Word meaning and Montague grammar: the semantics of verbs and times in generative semantics and in Montague's PTQ*. Dordrecht, The Netherlands: Kluwer Academic Publishers.

Dowty, D. R. 1991. Thematic proto-roles and argument selection. *Language* 67(3):547–619.

Earley, J. 1970. An efficient context free parsing algorithm. *Communications of the ACM* 13:94–102.

Eberenz, R. 1991. Futuro analítico y futuro sintético en tres obras con rasgos coloquiales: el 'corbacho', 'la celestina' y 'la lozana andaluza'. In K. H. Körner and G. Zimmermann, eds., *Homenaje a Hans Flasche: Festschrift zum 80. Geburtstag am 25. November 1991*, pages 499–507. Stuttgart: Franz Steiner.

Eberenz, R. 2000. *El español en el otoño de la Edad Media. Sobre el artículo y los pronombres.* Madrid: Gredos.

Ebert, C., C. Endriss, and S. Hinterwimmer. 2008. A unified analysis of indicative and biscuit conditionals as topics. In *Proceedings of Sematics and Linguistic Theory (SALT) XVIII.*

Edgington, D. 2003. What if? Questions about conditionals. *Mind & Language* 18(4):380–401.

Elvira, J. 1987. Enclisis pronominal y posición del verbo en español antiguo. *Epos* 3:61–79.

Enrique Arias, A. 2005. When clitics become affixes, where do they come to rest? A case from Spanish. In W. U. Dressler, D. Kastovsky, O. E. Pfeiffer, and F. Rainer, eds., *Morphology and its Demarcations*, pages 67–79. Amsterdam/Philadelphia: John Benjamins.

Erteschik-Shir, N. 1997. *The dynamics of focus structure*. Cambridge: Cambridge University Press.

Falk, Y. N. 2003. The English auxiliary system revisited. In *Proceedings of the LFG03 Conference*.

Farkas, D. 1997. Evaluation indices and scope. In A. Szabolcsi, ed., *Ways of scope taking*, pages 183–215. Dordrecht, The Netherlands: Kluwer Academic Publishers.

Fernando, T. 2006. Representing events and discourse; comments on Hamm, Kamp and van Lambalgen. *Theoretical Linguistics* 32(1):57–64.

Ferrari-Bridgers, F. 2009. A novel semantic and syntactic analysis of the Luganda initial vowel. Ms., Iona College, New Rochelle.

Ferreira, V. 1996. Is it better to give than to donate? Syntactic flexibility in language production. *Journal of Memory and Language* 35:724–755.

Ferreira, V. and G. Dell. 2000. Effect of ambiguity and lexical availability on syntactic and lexical production. *Cognitive Psychology* 40:296–340.

von Fintel, K. 1994. *Restrictions on Quantifier Domains*. Ph.D. thesis, University of Massachusetts-Amherst.

von Fintel, K. to appear. Conditionals. In K. von Heusinger, C. Maienborn, and P. Portner, eds., *Semantics: An international handbook of meaning*, chap. 59. Berlin: Mouton de Gruyter.

Frazier, L. 1987. Sentence processing: a tutorial review. In M. Coltheart, ed., *Attention and performance XII: The psychology of reading*. Hillsdale, NJ: Lawrence Erlbaum.

Gabbay, D. 1996. *Labelled Deductive Systems; principles and applications. Vol 1: Basic Principles*. Oxford: Oxford University Press.

Gargett, A., E. Gregoromichelaki, R. Kempson, M. Purver, and Y. Sato. 2009. Grammar resources for modelling dialogue dynamically. *Cognitive Neurodynamics* 3(4):347–363.

Gazdar, G., G. K. Pullum, and I. A. Sag. 1982. Auxiliaries and related phenomena in a restrictive theory of grammar. *Language* 58(3):591–638.

Geis, M. L. 1985. The syntax of conditional sentences. In M. L. Geis, ed., *Studies in Generalized Phrase Structure Grammar: Working Papers in Linguistics 31*, pages 130–159. Ohio State University.

Gessner, E. 1893. Das spanische Personalpronomen. *Zeitschrift für romanische Philologie (ZrP)* 17(1-4):1–54.

Geurts, B. 2004. On an ambiguity in quantified conditionals. Ms., University of Nijmegen.

Gibson, E. 1998. Linguistic complexity: Locality of syntactic dependencies. *Cognition* 68:1–76.

Gibson, E., G. Hickok, and C. Schütze. 1994. Processing empty categories: a parallel approach. *Journal of Psycholinguistic Research* 23(5):381–405.

Ginzburg, Jonathan and Robin Cooper. 2004. Clarification, ellipsis, and the nature of contextual updates in dialogue. *Linguistics and Philosophy* 27(3):297–365.

Girón Alconchel, J. L. 1997. La doctrina y el uso de los futuros en las gramáticas renacentistas. *Historiographia Linguistica* 24(1/2):15–28.

Girón Alconchel, J. L. 2002. Procesos de gramaticalización del español cláico al moderno. In M. T. Echenique Elizondo and J. Sánchez Méndez, eds., *Actas del V Congreso Internacional de la Historia de la Lengua Española: Valencia, 31 de enero - 4 de febrero 2000*, vol. 1, pages 103–121. Madrid: Gredos.

Girón Alconchel, J. L. 2005. Gramaticalización y gramatización. los futuros analíticos. In L. Santos Río, ed., *Palabras, norma, discurso en memoria de Lázaro Carreter*, pages 581–592. Salamanca: Universidad de Salamanca.

Girón Alconchel, J. L. 2007. De nuevo sobre la gramaticalización del futuro analítico. In I. Delgado Cobos and A. Puigvert Ocal, eds., *Ex admiratione et amicitia. Homenaje a Ramón Santiago*, vol. 1, pages 563–576. Madrid: Ediciones del Orto.

Givón, T. 1969. *Studies in ChiBemba and Bantu grammar*. Ph.D. thesis, University of California, Los Angeles.

Givón, T. 1979. *On Understanding Grammar*. New York, NY: Academic Press.

González i Planas, F. 2007. Sintaxis de los clíticos pronominales en asturleonés. *Ianua. Revista Philologica Romanica* 7:15–35.

Goodall, G. 1992. Spec-head agreement as the motivation for NP-movement. In *23rd Western Conference on Linguistics, Tucson.*

Granberg, R. 1988. *Object Pronoun Position in Medieval and Early Modern Spanish*. Ph.D. thesis, University of California, Los Angeles.

Grecco Ramírez, R. 2001. *Los cambios de colocación del átono pronominal en la Edad Media.*. Master's thesis, Universidad Nacional Autónoma de México.

Gregoromichelaki, E. 2006. *Conditionals: A Dynamic Syntax Account*. Ph.D. thesis, King's College London.

Gregoromichelaki, E. to appear. Clitic Left Dislocation and Clitic Doubling: A Dynamic Perspective on Left-Right Asymmetries in Greek. In *Rightward Movement in a Comparative Perspective*. John Benjamins.

Gregoromichelaki, E., R. Kempson, M. Purver, G. Mills, and R. Cann. submitted. Incrementality and intention-recognition in utterance processing. *Dialogue and Discourse, special issue on Incrementality in Dialogue* .

Gregoromichelaki, E., Y. Sato, R. Kempson, A. Gargett, and C. Howes. 2009. Dialogue modelling and the remit of core grammar. In *Proceedings of IWCS 2009*.

Grewendorf, G. 2001. Multiple wh-fronting. *Linguistic Inquiry* 32(1):87–122.

Grimshaw, J. 1990. *Argument Structure*. Cambridge, MA: MIT Press.

Haegeman, L. 2003. Conditional clauses: External and internal syntax. *Mind & Language* 18(4):317–339.

Haegeman, L. 2006. Conditionals, factives and the left periphery. *Lingua* 116(10):1651–1669.

Haiman, J. 1978. Conditionals are topics. *Language* 54(3):564–589.

Haiman, J. 1993. Conditionals. In J. Jacobs, A. von Stechow, W. Sternefeld, and T. Vennemann, eds., *Syntax, An international handbook of contemporary research*. de Gruyter, Berlin.

Hale, J. 2001. A probabilistic earley parser as a psycholinguistic model. In *Proceedings of NAACL (North American Chapter of ACL) '01*, pages 1–8. Morristown, NJ: Association for Computational Linguistics.

Hale, K. 1973. A note on subject-object inversion in Navajo. In B. B. Kachru, R. B. Lees, Y. Malkiel, A. Pietrangeli, and S. Saporta, eds., *Issues in linguistics: Papers in honor of Henry and Renée Kahane*, pages 300–309. Urbana, IL: University of Illinois Press.

Hashimoto, M. 1969. Observations on the passive construction. *Unicorn* 5:59–71.

Hashimoto, M. 1987. Hanyu beidongshi de lishi quyu fazhan [the historical and geographical development of Chinese passive construction]. *Zhongguo Yuwen [The Chinese Language]* pages 36–49.

Hawkins, J. 2004. *Efficiency and Complexity in Grammars*. Cambridge: Cambridge University Press.

Hedberg, N. 2000. The referential status of clefts. *Language* 76(4):891–920.

Heim, I. 1982. *The Semantics of Definite and Indefinite Noun Phrases*. Ph.D. thesis, University of Massachusetts, Amherst.

von Heusinger, K. 2002. Specificity and definiteness in sentence and discourse structure. *Journal of Semantics* 19(3):245–274. Special Issue on Specificity.

Hickok, G. 1993. Parallel parsing: evidence from reactivation in garden-path sentences. *Journal of Psycholinguistic Research* 22:239Ű250.

Hilbert, D. and P. Bernays. 1939. *Grundlagen der Mathematik II*. Berlin: Julius Springer.

Hofmeister, P., T. F. Jaeger, I. A. Sag, I. Arnon, and N. Snider. 2007. Locality and accessibility in Wh-questions. In S. Featherston and W. Sternefeld, eds., *Roots: Linguistics in search of its evidential base*. Berlin: Walter de Gruyter.

Huang, C.-T. J. 1982. *Logical relation in Chinese and the theory of grammar*. Ph.D. thesis, MIT.

Huang, C.-T. J. 1988. Hanyu zhengfan wenju de mozu yufa [a modular grammar of a-not-a questions in Chinese]. *Zhongguo Yuwen [The Chinese Language]* pages 247–264.

Huang, C.-T. J. 1993. Reconstruction and the structure of VP: Some theoretical consequences. *Linguistic Inquiry* 24(1):103–138.

Huang, C.-T. J. 1999. Chinese passives in comparative perspective. *Tsing Hua Journal of Chinese Studies* 29(4):423–510.

Huang, L. 2008. Advanced dynamic programming in semiring and hypergraph frameworks. In *Computational linguistics (COLING) 2008 Tutorial Notes.*

Huang, Y. 1994. *The syntax and pragmatics of anaphora: a study with special reference to Chinese.* Cambridge: Cambridge University Press.

Huang, Y. 2000. *Anaphora: A cross-linguistic study.* Oxford: Oxford University Press.

Huddleston, R., G. K. Pullum, et al. 2002. *The Cambridge Grammar of English.* Cambridge: Cambridge University Press.

Huitink, J. 2008. *Modals, conditionals and compositionality.* Ph.D. thesis, Radboud University Nijmegen.

Hyman, L. M. and F. X. Katamba. 1993. The augment in Luganda: syntax or pragmatics. In S. A. Mchombo, ed., *Theoretical aspects of Bantu grammar*, pages 209–256. Stanford, CA: CSLI.

Iatridou, S. 1991. *Topics in conditionals.* Ph.D. thesis, MIT.

Inkelas, S. and D. Zec. 1990. *The phonology-syntax connection.* Chicago, IL: University of Chicago Press.

Jackendoff, R. 1983. *Semantics and Cognition.* Cambridge, MA: MIT Press.

Jackendoff, R. 2002. *Foundations of Language: Brain, Meaning, Grammar, Evolution.* Oxford: Oxford University Press.

Jaeggli, O. 1986. Passive. *Linguistic Inquiry* 17:587–622.

Joshi, A. 1985. Tree Adjoining Grammars: How much context-sensitivity is necessary for characterizing structural descriptions. In D. D., L. Karttunen, and A. M. Zwicky, eds., *Natural language parsing: psychological, computational, and theoretical perspectives*, pages 206–250. Cambridge: Cambridge University Press.

Jun, S. 1993. *The Phonetics and Phonology of Korean Prosody.* Ph.D. thesis, The Ohio State University.

Jurafsky, D. 1996. A probabilistic model of lexical and syntactic access and disambiguation. *Cognitive Science* 20:137–194.

Kabatek, J., ed. 2008. *Sintaxis histórica del español y cambio lingüístico: nuevas perspectivas desde las Tradiciones Discursivas..* Madrid: Iberoamericana.

Kamp, H. and U. Reyle. 1993. *From Discourse To Logic.* Dordrecht, The Netherlands: Kluwer Academic Publishers.

Kaplan, R. and A. Zaenen. 1989. Long-distance dependencies, constituent structure, and functional uncertainty. In M. Baltin and A. Kroch, eds., *Alternative Conceptions of Phrase Structure*, pages 17–42. Chicago, IL: University of Chicago Press.

Karamanis, N. 2001. A categorial grammar for Greek. In *Proceedings of the 15th International Symposium on Theoretical and Applied Linguistics. Aristotle University of Thessaloniki.*

Kaye, J. 1989. *Phonology: A cognitive view*. Hillsdale, NJ: Lawrence Erlbaum.

Kayne, Richard S. 1989. Null subjects and clitic climbing. In O. Jaeggli and K. J. Safir, eds., *The Null Subject Parameter*, pages 239–262. Dordrecht, The Netherlands: Kluwer Academic Publishers.

Keenan, E. L. 1976. Towards a universal definition of 'subject'. *Subject and topic* 305:303–333.

Keenan, E. L. 1985. Passive in the world's languages. In T. Shopen, ed., *Language typology and syntactic description: Clause sturucture*. Cambridge: Cambridge University Press.

Kempson, R. and R. Cann. 2007. Dynamic syntax and dialogue modelling preliminaries for a dialogue-driven account of syntactic change. In J. C. Salmons and S. Dubenion-Smith, eds., *Historical Linguistics 2005: Selected Papers from the 17th International Conference on Historical Linguistics, Madison, Wisconsin, 31 July-5 August 2005*, pages 73–102. John Benjamins.

Kempson, R., E. Gregoromichelaki, W. Meyer-Viol, M. Purver, G. White, and R. Cann. to appear. Natural-language syntax as procedures for interpretation: the dynamics of ellipsis construal. In *Proceedings of the PRELUDE Workshop on Games, Dialogues and Interaction*. Lecture Notes in Computer Science, Springer.

Kempson, R., E. Gregoromichelaki, and Y. Sato. 2009a. Incrementality, speaker-hearer switching and the disambiguation challenge. In *Proceedings of SRSL 2009, the 2nd Workshop on Semantic Representation of Spoken Language*, pages 74–81. Athens, Greece: Association for Computational Linguistics.

Kempson, R. and J. Kiaer. 2009. Multiple long-distance scrambling: Syntax as reflections of processing. *Journal of Linguistics* 46(01):127–192.

Kempson, R., J. Kiaer, and R. Cann. 2009b. Periphery effects and the dynamics of tree growth. In *Dislocated Elements in Discourse: Syntactic, Semantic, and Pragmatic Perspectives (Routledge Studies in Germanic Linguistics)*, pages 141–172. New York: Routledge.

Kempson, R. and A. Kurosawa. forthcoming. At the syntax pragmatics interface: Japanese relative clause. In H. Hoshi, ed., *Language, Mind and Brain*. Tokyo: Kuroshio.

Kempson, R. and W. Meyer-Viol. 2004. Indefinites and scope choice. In M. Reimer and A. Bezuidenhout, eds., *Descriptions and Beyond: An Interdisciplinary Collection of Essays on Definite and Indefinite Descriptions*. Oxford: Oxford University Press.

Kempson, R., W. Meyer-Viol, and D. Gabbay. 2001. *Dynamic Syntax: The Flow of Language Understanding*. Oxford: Blackwell.

Keniston, H. 1937. *The syntax of Castilian prose: the sixteenth century*. Chicago, IL: The University of Chicago Press.

Kiaer, J. 2005. Incremental parsing in Korean: At the syntax-phonology interface. Ms., Kings College London.

Kiaer, J. 2007. *Processes and Interfaces in Syntactic Theory: the case of Korean*. Ph.D. thesis, King's College London.

Kiaer, J. forthcoming. Non-accidental word-order variation in Korean and its implication towards grammar. In B. Frellesvig, J. Kiaer, and J. Wrona, eds., *Proceedings of the Nordic Association of Japanese and Korean Linguistics*. Aarhus: Aarhus University Press.

Kim, J. 1969. Events and their descriptions: some considerations. In N. Rescher, ed., *Essays in honor of Carl G. Hempel*, pages 198–215. Dordrecht, The Netherlands: J. Reidel.

Kim, J. 1976. Events as property exemplifications. In M. Brand and D. Walton, eds., *Action theory*, pages 159–177. Dordrecht, The Netherlands: J. Reidel.

Kim, J. H. and J. Yoon. 2006. An empirical study of the long-distance binding of the anaphor caki-casin in Korean. *Harvard Studies in Korean Lingusitics XI* pages 493–505.

Kitagawa, Y. and Y. Hirose. 2006. Anatomy of acceptability judgements. In *The 5th International Workshop on Evolutionary Cognitive Sciences*. Tokyo, Japan.

Klaiman, M. H. 1991. *Grammatical voice*. Cambridge: Cambridge University Press.

Klein, D. and C. Manning. 2003. A* parsing: Fast exact Viterbi parse selection. In *Proceedings of the North American Chapter of the Association for Computational Linguistics*.

Koizumi, M. 2000. String-vacuous overt verb raising. *Journal of East Asian Linguistics* 9:227–85.

König, E. and J. Van der Auwera. 1988. Clause integration in German and Dutch conditionals, concessive conditionals, and concessives. In J. Haiman and S. A. Thompson, eds., *Clause Combining in Grammar and Discourse*, pages 101–133. Amsterdam/Philadelphia: John Benjamins.

Kratzer, A. 1986. Conditionals. In *Chicago Linguistics Society*, vol. 22, pages 1–15.

Kula, N. C. 2002. *The phonology of verbal derivation in Bemba*. Ph.D. thesis, University of Leiden. LOT dissertation series 65.

Kula, N. C. 2007. Effects of phonological phrasing on syntactic structure. *The Linguistic Review* 24(2-3):201–231.

Kula, N. C. 2009. The augment in bemba. Ms., University of Essex.

Kula, N. C. and L. L. S. Cheng. 2007. Phonological and syntactic phrasing in Bemba relatives. *Journal of African languages and linguistics* 28(2):123–148.

van Lambalgen, M. and F. Hamm. 2004. *The proper treatment of events*. Oxford: Blackwell.

Langacker, R. W. and P. Munro. 1975. Passives and their meaning. *Language* 51(4):789–830.

LaPolla, R. J. 1988. Topicalization and the question of lexical passives in Chinese. In *Proceedings of the Third Ohio State Univerisity Conference on Chinese Linguistics (13-14 May 1988)*, pages 170–188.

Lasnik, H. and M. Saito. 1992. *Move α*. Cambridge, MA: MIT Press.

Lema, J. 1994. Los futuros medievales: sincronía y diacronía. *Gramática del español, México, El Colegio de México* pages 139–166.

Lema, J. and M. L. Rivero. 1990. Long head movement: ECP vs. HMC. *Cahiers linguistiques d'Ottawa* 18:61–78.

Lema, J. and M. L. Rivero. 1991. Types of verbal movement in Old Spanish: Modals, futures, and perfects. *Probus* 3(3):237–278.

Lema, J. and M. L. Rivero. 1992. Inverted conjugations and V-second effects in Romance. In C. Laeufer and T. Morgan, eds., *Theoretical Analysis in Romance Linguistics: Selected Papers from XIX Linguistic Symposium on Romance Languages, Ohio State University, April 21-23 1989*, pages 311–328. John Benjamins.

Levin, B. 1993. *English Verb Classes and Alternations*. Chicago, IL: University of Chicago Press.

Levin, B. and M. R. Hovav. 2005. *Argument Realization*. Cambridge: Cambridge University Press.

Li, C. N. 1975. *Word order and word order change*. Austin, TX: University of Texas Press.

Li, C. N. 1976. *Subject and topic*. New York, NY: Academic Press.

Li, C. N. and S. A. Thompson. 1989. *Mandarin Chinese: A functional reference grammar*. Berkeley, CA: University of California Press.

Li, J. X. 1955. *Xinzhu guoyu yufa [New studies in Chinese grammar]*. Beijing: Commercial Press.

Li, L. 1980. Beizi ju [The bei construction]. *Zhongguo Yuwen [Chinese Language]* pages 401–412.

Li, W. forthcoming. *A dynamic analysis of resultative verb constructions in Mandarin Chinese*. Ph.D. thesis, University of Edinburgh.

Li, Y. 1990. On V-V compounds in Chinese. *Natural language & linguistic theory* 8(2):177–207.

Li, Y. A. 1990. *Order and constituency in Mandarin Chinese*. Dordrecht, The Netherlands: Kluwer Academic Publishers.

Liejiong, X. 1986. Free empty category. *Linguistic Inquiry* 17(1):75–93.

Liejiong, X. and D. T. Langendoen. 1985. Topic structures in Chinese. *Language* 61(1):1–27.

Lombardo, V. and P. Sturt. 2002. Incrementality and lexicalism: a treebank study. In S. Stevenson and P. Merlo, eds., *The Lexical Basis of Sentence Processing*, pages 137–156. John Benjamins.

Lü, S. X. 1982. *Zhongguo wenfa yaolue [Essentials of Chinese grammar]*. Beijing: Commercial Press.

Lü, S. X., L. Linding, L. Jian, F. Jiyan, S. Youwei, F. Fanglian, M. Zong, M. Shujun, L. Zhu, C. Jianmin, et al. 1980. *Xiandai Hanyu Babai Ci (Eight Hundred Words in Contemporary Chinese)*. Beijing: Commercial Press.

Lycan, W. G. 2001. *Real conditionals*. Oxford: Oxford University Press.

Lyons, J. 1968. *Introduction to theoretical linguistics*. Cambridge: Cambridge University Press.

Mahajan, A. 1997. Rightward scrambling. In D. Beerman, D. LeBlanc, and H. van Riemsdijk, eds., *Rightward Movement*, pages 185–213. Amsterdam/Philadelphia: John Benjamins.

Maienborn, C. 2003. Against a davidsonian analysis of copula sentences. In *NELS 33 Proceedings*, vol. 33, pages 167–186.

Maienborn, C. 2005. On the limits of the Davidsonian approach: The case of copula sentences. *Theoretical Linguistics* 31(3):275–316.

Maienborn, C. 2007. On Davidsonian and Kimian states. In I. Comorovski and K. von Heusinger, eds., *Existence: Semantics and Syntax*, pages 107–130. Dordrecht, The Netherlands: Springer.

Manning, C. and H. Schütze. 1999. *Foundations of Statistical Natural Language Processing*. Cambridge, MA: MIT Press.

Manzini, R. 1983. *Restructuring and Reanalysis*. Ph.D. thesis, MIT.

Marcus, M.P. 1980. *A theory of syntactic recognition for natural language*. Cambridge, MA: MIT Press.

Marten, L. 2002. *At the Syntax-Pragmatics Interface: Verbal Underspecification and Concept Formation in Dynamic Syntax*. Oxford: Oxford University Press.

Marten, L. 2007. Focus strategies and the incremental development of semantic representations: evidence from Bantu. In E. Aboh, K. Hartmann, and M. Zimmermann, eds., *Focus strategies in African languages: The interaction of focus and grammar in Niger-Congo and Afro-Asiatic*, pages 113–135. Berlin: Mouton de Gruyter.

Marten, L. 2010. The great siSwati locative shift. In A. Breitbarth, C. Lucas, and D. Willis, eds., *Continuity and Change in Grammar*. Amsterdam/Philadelphia: John Benjamins. to appear.

Marten, L. and R. Kempson. 2002. Pronouns, agreement, and the dynamic construction of verb phrase interpretation: A Dynamic Syntax approach to Bantu clause structure. *Linguistic Analysis* 32(3-4):471–504.

Marten, L., R. Kempson, and Bouzouita M. 2008. Concepts of structural underspecification in bantu and romance. In C. de Cat and L. Demuth, eds., *The Romance-Bantu Connection*. Amsterdam/Philadelphia: John Benjamins.

Matute, C. and E. Pato. in press (2010). Morfología y sintaxis. In A. Enrique-Arias, ed., *Biblia romanceada ms. Escorial I.I.6*. Logroño: Centro Internacional de Investigación de la Lengua Española (Cilengua).

Mazuka, R. and K. Itoh. 1995. Can Japanese speakers be led down the garden path. In R. Mazuka and N. Nagai, eds., *Japanese sentence processing*, pages 295–329. Hillsdale, NJ: Lawrence Erlbaum.

Mazuka, R., K. Itoh, and T. Kondo. 2002. Cost of scrambling in Japanese sentence processing. In M. Nakayama, ed., *Sentence processing in East Asian languages*, pages 131–166. Stanford, CA: CSLI.

McConville, M. 2001. *Incremental natural language understanding with combinatory categorial grammar*. Master's thesis, University of Edinburgh.

McCormack, A. 2008. *Subject and object pronominal agreement in Southern Bantu Languages: A Dynamic Syntax perspective*. Ph.D. thesis, SOAS, University of London.

Meeussen, A. E. 1959. *Essai de grammaire rundi*. Museé royal du Congo Belge.

Meier, H. 1965. Futuro y futuridad. *Revista de Filología española* 48(1):60–77.

Menéndez Pidal, R. 1926. Orígenes del español. Estado lingüístico de la Península Ibérica hasta el siglo XI. *Revista de Filología Española* Anejo I.

Michaelis, L. A. 2006. Time and Tense. In B. Aarts and A. MacMahon, eds., *The Handbook of English Linguistics*, pages 220–234. Oxford: Blackwell.

Miller, P. H. and I. A. Sag. 1997. French clitic movement without clitics or movement. *Natural Language and Linguistic Theory* 15(3):573–639.

Miyagawa, S. 2003. A-movement scrambling and options without optionality. In S. Karimi, ed., *Word order and scrambling*, pages 177–200. Oxford: Blackwell.

Miyamoto, E. T. 2002. Case markers as clause boundary inducers in Japanese. *Journal of psycholinguistic research* 31(4):307–347.

Miyamoto, E. T. and S. Takahashi. 2002. The processing of wh-phrases and interrogative complementizers in Japanese. *Japanese/Korean Linguistics* 10:62–75.

Moens, M. and M. Steedman. 1988. Temporal ontology and temporal reference. *Computational linguistics* 14(2):15–28.

Mollá-Aliod, D. 1997. *Aspectual Composition and Sentence Interpretation: a formal approach*. Ph.D. thesis, University of Edinburgh.

Monachesi, P. 1998. Italian restructuring verbs: A lexical analysis. In E. Hinrichs, A. Kathol, and T. Nakazawa, eds., *Complex Predicates in Nonderivational Syntax. Syntax and Semantics 30*, pages 313–368. New York, NY: Academic Press.

Monachesi, P. 1999. The syntactic structure of romanian auxiliary (and modal) verbs. In G. Bouma, E. Hinrichs, G. Kruij, and R. Oehrle, eds., *Constraints and resources in natural language syntax and semantics*. Stanford, CA: CSLI.

Nakayama, M. 1995. Scrambling and probe recognition. In R. Mazuka and N. Nagai, eds., *Japanese sentence processing*, pages 257–273. Hillsdale, NJ: Lawrence Erlbaum.

Newmeyer, F. J. 1998. *Language form and language function.* Cambridge, MA: MIT Press.

Newmeyer, F. J. 2005. *Possible and probable languages: A generative perspective on linguistic typology.* Oxford: Oxford University Press.

Nieuwenhuijsen, D. 1999. *Cambios en la colocación de los pronombres átonos.* Ph.D. thesis, University of Groningen.

Nieuwenhuijsen, D. 2002. Variación de colocación de los pronombres átonos en el español antiguo. *Zeitschrift für romanische Philologie* 118:360–375.

Nieuwenhuijsen, D. 2006. Cambios en la colocación de los pronombres átonos. In C. Company Company, ed., *Sintaxis histórica de la lengua española. Primera parte: la frase verbal*, vol. 2, pages 1337–1404. Mexico City: Universidad Nacional Autónoma de México/ Fondo de Cultura Económica.

Noh, E. J. 1998. A relevance-theoretic account of metarepresentative uses in conditionals. In V. Rouchota and A. H. Jucker, eds., *Current Issues in Relevance Theory*, pages 271–304. Amsterdam/Philadelphia: John Benjamins.

Pan, H. 1998. Closeness, prominence, and binding theory. *Natural Language and Linguistic Theory* 16(4):771–815.

Papafragou, A. 1996. *UCL Working Papers in Linguistics* 8:165–98.

Papafragou, A. 2000. *Modality: Issues in the semantics-pragmatics interface.* Elsevier Oxford. ISBN 008043634X.

Parsons, T. 1989. The progressive in English: Events, states and processes. *Linguistics and Philosophy* 12(2):213–241.

Parsons, T. 1990. Events in the semantics of English: A study in subatomic semantics. In *Current Studies in Linguistics Series no. 19*, page 334. Cambridge, MA: MIT Press.

Peyraube, A. 1989. History of the passive construction in Chinese until the 10th century. *Journal of Chinese Linguistics* 17.

Phillips, C. 1996. *Order and Structure.* Ph.D. thesis, MIT.

Phillips, C. 2003. Linear order and constituency. *Linguistic Inquiry* 34:37–90.

Pickering, M. and S. Garrod. 2004. Toward a mechanistic psychology of dialogue. *Behavioral and Brain Sciences* 27:169–226.

Portner, P. 2003. The (temporal) semantics and (modal) pragmatics of the perfect. *Linguistics and Philosophy* 26(4):459–510.

Prince, E. F. 1978. A comparison of wh-clefts and it-clefts in discourse. *Language* 54(4):883–906.

Purver, M., R. Cann, and R. Kempson. 2006. Grammars as parsers: Meeting the dialogue challenge. *Research on Language and Computation* 4(2-3):289–326.

Purver, M., E. Gregoromichelaki, W. Meyer-Viol, and R. Cann. 2010. Splitting the i's and crossing the you's: Context, speech acts and grammar. In *SemDial 2010 (PozDial), Poznan, Poland.*

Purver, M., C. Howes, E. Gregoromichelaki, and P. G. T. Healey. 2009. Split utterances in dialogue: a corpus study. In *Proceedings of the SIGDIAL 2009 Conference: The 10th Annual Meeting of the Special Interest Group on Discourse and Dialogue*, pages 262–271. Association for Computational Linguistics.

Ramsden, H. 1963. *Weak-pronoun position in the early Romance languages.* Manchester: Manchester University Press.

Recanati, F. 1999. Situations and the Structure of Content. In K. Murasugi and R. Stainton, eds., *Philosophy and Linguistics.* Boulder, CO: Westview.

Riedel, K. 2009. *The Syntax of object marking in Sambaa: a comparative Bantu perspective.* Ph.D. thesis, University of Leiden, Utrecht.

Rivero, M. L. 1991. Clitic and NP climbing in Old Spanish. In H. Campos and F. Martínez-Gil, eds., *Current studies in Spanish linguistics*, pages 241–282. Washington D.C.: Georgetown University Press.

Rivero, M. L. 1997. On two locations for complement clitic pronouns: Serbo-Croatian, Bulgarian, and Old Spanish. In A. van Kemenade and N. Vincent, eds., *Parameters of morphosyntactic change*, pages 170–206. Cambridge: Cambridge University Press.

Rizzi, L. 1982. *Issues in Italian syntax.* Dordrecht, The Netherlands: Foris Publications.

Roark, B. 2001. Probabilistic top-down parsing and language modelling. *Computational Linguistics* 27(2):249–276.

Roberts, C. 1998. Focus, the flow of information, and universal grammar. In P. W. Culicover and L. McNally, eds., *Syntax and semantics, vol. 29: The limits of syntax*, pages 109–160. New York, NY: Academic Press.

Rogers, J. and K. Vijay-Shanker. 1994. Obtaining trees from their descriptions: An application to tree-adjoining grammars. *Computational Intelligence* 10(4):401–421.

Rooth, M. 1992. A theory of focus interpretation. *Natural Language Semantics* 1(1):117–121.

Rooth, M. 1996. Focus. In S. Lappin, ed., *The Handbook of Contemporary Semantic Theory*, pages 271–297. Oxford: Blackwell Publishers.

Ross, J. 1967. *Constraints on variables in syntax.* Ph.D. thesis, MIT.

Rossi, T. M. 1975. Formas de futuro en un romanceamiento bíblico del siglo XIII. *Zeitschrift f*
"ur romanische Philologie (ZrP) 91(3-4):386–402.

Russell, S. and P. Norvig. 2003. *Artificial Intelligence: a modern approach.* Upper Saddle River, NJ: Prentice Hall.

Saco e Arce, J. A. 1868. *Gramática gallega.* Lugo: Soto Freire.

Sag, I. A. 1997. English relative clause constructions. *Journal of linguistics* 33(02):431–483.

Sag, I. A., T. Wasow, and E. M. Bender. 2003. *Syntactic Theory: A Formal Introduction.* Stanford, CA: CSLI.

Saito, M. 1985. *Some asymmetries in Japanese and their theoretical implications*. Ph.D. thesis, MIT.

Saito, M. 1992. Long distance scrambling in Japanese. *Journal of East Asian Linguistics* 1(1):69–118.

Saito, M. 2003. A derivational approach to the interpretation of scrambling chains. *Lingua* 113(4):481–518.

Saksena, A. 1980. The affected agent. *Language* 56(4):812–826.

Sánchez, X. X. and C. Rubiera Tuya. 1985. Enclisis, proclisis y pronomes átonos n'asturianu. *ALLAS, Lletres Asturianes* 18:71–81.

Sanchis Calvo, M. C. 1991. *El lenguaje de la Fazienda de Ultramar*. Madrid: Real Academia España.

Schlenker, P. 2006. Ontological symmetry in language: A brief manifesto. *Mind and Language* 21(4):504.

Schmidely, J. 1998. Ante- y posposición de los pronombres átonos en la 'primera crónica general. In C. García Turza, G. B. F., and M. M. J. J., eds., *Actas del IV Congreso Internacional de Historia de la Lengua Española*, pages 805–818. Madrid: Arco Libros.

Selkirk, Elisabeth O. 1984. *Phonology and syntax : the relation between sound and structure*. Cambridge, MA: MIT Press.

Shaer, B. 2003. An "orphan" analysis of long and short adjunct movement in English. In *Proceedings of the 22nd West Coast Conference on Formal Linguistics*, page 450. Cascadilla Press.

Sharman, J. C. 1956. The tabulation of tenses in a Bantu language (Bemba: Northern Rhodesia). *Africa* 26(1):29–46.

Sharman, J. C. and A. E. Meeussen. 1955. The Representation of Structural Tones, with Special Reference to the Tonal Behaviour of the Verb, in Bemba, Northern Rhodesia. *Africa* 25(4):393–404.

Shi, D. 1997. Issues on Chinese passive. *Journal of Chinese linguistics* 25(1):41–70.

Shi, D. 2000. Topic and topic-comment constructions in Mandarin Chinese. *Language* 76(2):383–408.

Shibatani, M. 1985. Passives and related constructions: A prototype analysis. *Language* 61(4):821–848.

Shibatani, M. 1988. *Passive and voice*. Amsterdam/Philadelphia: John Benjamins.

Silva-Villar, L. 1996. *Enclisis in the Northwestern Iberian Languages: A Diachronic Theory*. Ph.D. thesis, University of California Los Angeles.

Smith, N. and A. Smith. 1988. A relevance-theoretic account of conditionals. In L. M. Hyman and C. Li, eds., *Language, speech, and mind: studies in honour of Victoria A. Fromkin*. London: Routledge.

Sperber, D. and D. Wilson. 1995. *Relevance: Communication and Cognition*. Oxford: Blackwell, 2nd edn.

Staaff, E. 1907. Contribution à la syntaxe du pronom personnel dans le Poème du Cid. *Romanische Forschungen* 23:621–635.

Stainton, R. 2006. *Words and Thoughts: Subsentences, Ellipsis, and the Philosophy of Language.* Oxford: Oxford University Press.

Steedman, M. 2000. *The Syntactic Process.* Cambridge, MA: MIT Press.

Strawson, P. F. 1986. 'if' and '$\supset$'. In R. E. Grandy and R. Warner, eds., *Philosophical Grounds of Rationality*, pages 229–42. Oxford: Oxford University Press.

Sturt, Patrick and Matthew Crocker. 1996. Monotonic syntactic processing: a cross-linguistic study of attachment and reanalysis. *Language and Cognitive Processes* 11:448–494.

Svartvik, J. 1966. *On voice in the English verb.* Berlin: Mouton de Gruyter.

Szendroi, Kriszta. 2001. *Focus and the syntax-phonology interface.* Ph.D. thesis, University College London.

Takano, Y. 2002. Surprising constituents. *Journal of East Asian Linguistics* 11:243–301.

Taljaard, P. C., J. N. Khumalo, and S. E. Bosch. 1991. *Handbook of SiSwati.* Pretoria: JL van Schaik (Pty) Ltd.

Talman, A. 2005. *Computational properties of Dynamic Syntax.* Master's thesis, King's College London.

Tan, F. 1987. The predicate structure of bei. In *Berkeley Linguistic Society*, vol. 13, pages 285–295.

Tan, F. 1991. *The Notion of Subject in Chinese.* Ph.D. thesis, Stanford University.

Taylor, B. 1985. *Modes of Occurrence.* Blackwell. ISBN 0631140263.

Thomason, R. H. and R. C. Stalnaker. 1973. A semantic theory of adverbs. *Linguistic Inquiry* 4(2):195–220.

Ting, J. 1998. Deriving the bei-construction in Mandarin Chinese. *Journal of East Asian Linguistics* 7(4):319–354.

Truckenbrodt, H. 1999. On the relation betwen syntactic phrases and phonological phrases. *Linguistic Inquiry* 30(2):219–255.

Vasishth, S. and R. Lewis. 2006. Argument-head distance and processing complexity: Explaining both locality and anti-locality effects. *Language* 82(4).

Viterbi, A. 1967. Error bounds for convolutional codes and an asymptotically optimum decoding algorithm. *IEEE Transactions on Information Theory* 13(2).

van der Wal, Jennneke. 2009. *Word order and information structure in Makhuwa-Enahara.* Ph.D. thesis, University of Leiden.

Wang, L. 1957. *Zhongguo Xiandai Yufa [A Grammar of modern Chinese].* Beijing: Commercial Press.

Wang, L. 1983. Yingyu he Hanyu de beidongju [Passive voice in English and Chinese]. *Zhongguo Yuwen [The Chinese Language]* pages 409–418.

Wang, L. 1989. *Hanyu Yufa Shi [History of Chinese grammar].* Beijing: Commercial Press.

Warner, A. 2000. English auxiliaries without lexical rules. In R. D. Borsley, ed., *The Nature and Function of Syntactic Categories. Syntax and Semantics vol. 32*, pages 167–220. New York, NY: Academic Press.

Warner, A. R. 1993. *English Auxiliaries: Structure and History*. Cambridge: Cambridge University Press.

Wasow, T. 2002. *Postverbal behavior*. Stanford, CA: CSLI.

Willie, M. A. 2000. The inverse voice and possessive yi-/bi-in Navajo. *International Journal of American Linguistics* 66(3):360–382.

Wilson, D. and R. Carston. 2006. Metaphor, relevance and the Śemergent propertyŠissue. *Mind & Language* 21(3):404–433.

Wu, Y. 2005. *The dynamic syntax of left and right dislocation: with special reference to Chinese*. Ph.D. thesis, University of Edinburgh.

Wu, Y. and R. Cann. 2003. The dynamic syntax of chinese *bei-*. In S. Assimakopoulos, ed., *Proceedings of CamLing*. Cambridge: University of Cambridge Press.

Xiao, R., T. McEnery, and Y. Qian. 2006. Passive constructions in English and Chinese: A corpus-based contrastive study. *Languages in Contrast* 6(1):109–149.

Xove Ferreiro, X. 1986. Sobre a posición do pronome persoal átono en galego: eu o sei e eu seino. In *Actes du XXVIIIe Congrès International de Linguistique et Philologie Romanes*, vol. 2, pages 515–529. Tübingen: Max Niemeyer.

Yamashita, H. 1997. The effects of word-order and case marking information on the processing of Japanese. *Journal of Psycholinguistic Research* 26(2):163–188.

Zeller, J. 2004. Relative clause formation in the Bantu languages of South Africa. *Southern African Linguistics and Applied Language Studies* 22(1):75–93.

Zeller, J. 2006. On the relation between noun prefixes and grammaticalisation in Nguni relative clauses. *Studia Linguistica* 60(2):220–249.

Zhang, B. and Y. S. Hu. 1989. *Hanyu Yufa Yanjiu [Studies in Chinese grammar]*. Beijing: Commercial Press.

Zhang, J. 1987. *Hanyu Yufa Wenti [Issues in Chinese grammar]*. Beijing: Commercial Press.

Ziervogel, D. and E. J. Mabuza. 1976. *A grammar of the Swati language (SiSwati)*. Pretoria: J. L. Van Schaik.

Index